Leuone = equivariance
welch = homogenity violated
Greenacres = collapse levels in a
categorical level

/Solution
ILINK
estimates

MW01013593

SAS® Certification Prep Guide

Studentized/Residuals
Residual
/Standard
error

Statistical Business Analysis Using SAS®9

Joni N. Shreve
Donna Dea Holland

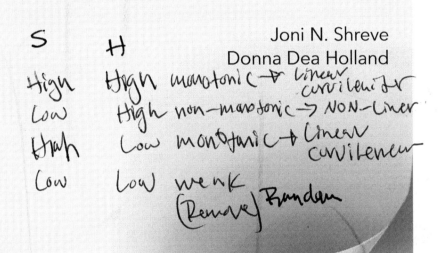

S   H
High   High monotonic → linear
                         curvilinear
Low   High non-monotonic → NON-linear
High   Low monotonic → linear
                        curvilinear
Low   Low weak
        (Remove) Random

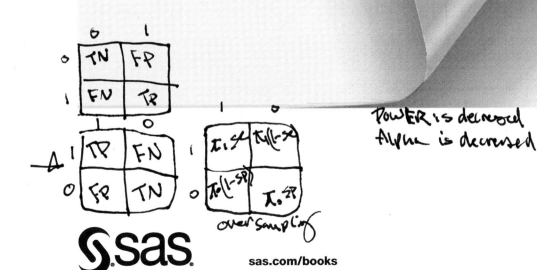

POWER is decreased
Alpha is decreased

over sampling

The correct bibliographic citation for this manual is as follows: Shreve, Joni N. and Donna Dea Holland . 2018. *SAS® Certification Prep Guide: Statistical Business Analysis Using SAS®9*. Cary, NC: SAS Institute Inc.

SAS® Certification Prep Guide: Statistical Business Analysis Using SAS®9

Copyright © 2018, SAS Institute Inc., Cary, NC, USA

978-1-62960-381-0 (Hardcopy)
978-1-63526-352-7 (Web PDF)
978-1-63526-350-3 (epub)
978-1-63526-351-0 (mobi)

SAS Institute Inc., SAS Campus Drive, Cary, NC 27513-2414

December 2018

Contents

About This Book

What Does This Book Cover?

The *SAS® Certification Prep Guide: Statistical Business Analysis Using SAS®9* is written for both new and experienced SAS programmers intending to take the SAS® Certified Statistical Business Analyst Using SAS®9: Regression and Modeling exam. This book covers the main topics tested on the exam which include analysis of variance, linear and logistic regression, preparing inputs for predictive models, and measuring model performance.

The authors assume the reader has some experience creating a SAS program consisting of a DATA step and PROCEDURE step, and running that program using any SAS platform. While knowledge of basic descriptive and inferential statistics is helpful, the authors provide several introductory chapters to lay the foundation for understanding the advanced statistical topics.

Requirements and Details

Exam Objectives

See the current exam objectives at https://www.sas.com/en_us/certification/credentials/advanced-analytics/statistical-business-analyst.html. Exam objectives are subject to change.

Take a Practice Exam

Practice exams are available for purchase through SAS and Pearson VUE. For more information about practice exams, see https://www.sas.com/en_us/certification/resources/sas-practice-exams.html.

Registering for the Exam

To register for the official SAS® Certified Statistical Business Analyst Using SAS®9: Regression and Modeling exam, see the SAS Global Certification website at www.sas.com/certify (https://www.sas.com/en_us/ certification.html).

Syntax Conventions

In this book, SAS syntax looks like this example:

> **DATA** *output-SAS-data-set*
> > (**DROP**=*variables(s)* | **KEEP**=*variables(s)*);
> > **SET** *SAS-data-set* <options>;
> > **BY** *variable(s)*
> > **RUN**;

Here are the conventions used in the example:

- DATA, DROP=, KEEP=, SET, BY, and RUN are in uppercase bold because they must be spelled as shown.
- *output-SAS-data-set*, *variable(s)*, *SAS-data-set*, and *options* are in italics because each represents a value that you supply.
- *<options>* is enclosed in angle brackets because it is optional syntax.
- DROP= and KEEP= are separated by a vertical bar (|) to indicate that they are mutually exclusive.

The example syntax shown in this book includes only what you need to know in order to prepare for the certification exam. For complete syntax, see the appropriate SAS reference guide.

What Should You Know about the Examples?

This book includes tutorials for you to follow to gain hands-on experience with SAS.

Software Used to Develop the Book's Content

To complete examples in this book, you must have access to Base SAS, SAS Enterprise Guide, or SAS Studio.

Example Code and Data

You can access all example code and data sets for this book by linking to the author pages at https://support.sas.com/shreve or https://support.sas.com/dholland. There you will also find directions on how to save the data sets to your computer to ensure that the example code runs successfully. The author pages also include appendices which contain detailed descriptions of the two main data sets used throughout this book: (1) the Diabetic Care Management Case, and (2) the Ames Housing Case.

You can also refer to the section "Getting Started with SAS" in Chapter 1, "Statistics and Making Sense of Our World," for a general description of the two main data sets, a list of all data sets by chapter, and a sample program which illustrates how to access the data within the SAS environment.

SAS University Edition

This book is compatible with SAS University Edition. In order to download SAS University Edition, go to https://www.sas.com/en_us/software/university-edition.html.

Where Are the Exercise Solutions?

Exercise solutions and Appendices referenced in the book are available on the author pages at https://support.sas.com/shreve or https://support.sas.com/dholland.

We Want to Hear from You

 Do you have questions about a SAS Press book that you are reading? Contact us at saspress@sas.com.

 SAS Press books are written *by* SAS Users *for* SAS Users. Please visit sas.com/books to sign up to request information on how to become a SAS Press author.

 We welcome your participation in the development of new books and your feedback on SAS Press books that you are using. Please visit sas.com/books to sign up to review a book

 Learn about new books and exclusive discounts. Sign up for our new books mailing list today at https://support.sas.com/en/books/subscribe-books.html.

 Learn more about these authors by visiting their author pages, where you can download free book excerpts, access example code and data, read the latest reviews, get updates, and more:
https://support.sas.com/shreve
https://support.sas.com/dholland

Chapter 1: Statistics and Making Sense of Our World

Introduction

The goal of this book is to prepare future analysts for the SAS statistical business analysis certification exam.[1] Therefore, the book aims to validate a strong working knowledge of complex statistical analyses, including analysis of variance, linear and logistic regression, and measuring model performance. This chapter covers the basic and fundamental information needed to understand the foundations of those more advanced analyses. We begin by explaining what statistics is and providing definitions of terms needed to get started.

The chapter continues with a birds-eye view of the data analytics process including defining the purpose, data preparation, the analysis, conclusions and interpretation. Special consideration is given to the data preparation phase-- with such topics as sampling, missing data, data exploration, and outlier detection--in an attempt to stress its importance in the validity of statistical conclusions. Where necessary we refer you to additional sources for further readings.

This chapter includes a road map detailing the scope of the statistical analyses covered in this book and how the specific analyses relate to the purpose. Finally, the chapter closes with a description of the data sets to be used throughout the book and provides you the first opportunity to access the data using sample SAS code before proceeding to subsequent chapters.

In this chapter you will learn about:

- statistics' two branches, descriptive statistics and inferential statistics, data mining, and predictive analytics

- variable types and how SAS distinguishes between numeric and character data types

- the data analytics process, including defining the purpose, data preparation, analysis, conclusions and interpretation

- exploratory analysis versus confirmatory analysis

- sampling and how it relates to bias

- selection bias, nonresponse bias, measurement error, confounding variables

- the importance of data cleaning

- the role of data cleaning to identify data inconsistencies, to account for missing data, and to create new variables, dummy codes, and variable transformations

- terms such as missing completely at random (MCAR), missing at random (MAR), and not missing at random (NMAR), and conditions for imputation

- data exploration for uncovering interesting patterns, detecting outliers, and variable reduction

- the roles of variables as either response or predictors

- the analytics road map used for determining the specific statistical modeling approach based upon the business question, the variable types, and the variable roles

- the statistical models to be tested on the certification exam, including two-sample t-tests, analysis of variance (ANOVA), linear regression analysis, and logistic regression analysis
- the use of the training data set and the validation data set to assess model performance
- both the Diabetic Care Management Case and the Ames Housing Case to be used throughout the book, their contents, and the sample SAS code used the read the data and produce an output of contents.

What Is Statistics?

We see and rely on statistics every day. Statistics can help us understand many aspects of our lives, including the price of homes, automobiles, health and life insurance, interest rates, political perceptions, to name a few. Statistics are used across many fields of study in academia, marketing, healthcare, treatment regimes, politics, housing, government, private businesses, national security, sports, law enforcement, and NGOs. The extensive reliance on statistics is growing. Statistics drive decisions to solve social problems, guide and build businesses, and develop communities. With the wealth of information available today, business persons need to know how to use statistics efficiently and effectively for better decision making. So, what is statistics?

Statistics is a science that relies on particular mathematical formulas and software to derive meaningful patterns and extrapolate actionable information from data sets. Statistics involves the use of plots, graphs, tables, and statistical tests to validate hypotheses, but it is more than just these. Statistics is a unique way to use data to make improvements and efficiencies in virtually any business or organization that collects quality data about their customers, services, costs, and practices.

The Two Branches of Statistics

Before defining the two branches of statistics, it is important to distinguish between a population and a sample. The **population** is the universe of all observations for which conclusions are to be made and can consist of people or objects. For example, a population can be made up of customers, patients, products, crimes, or bank transactions. In reality, it is very rare and sometimes impossible to collect data from the entire population. Therefore, it is more practical to take a **sample**--that is, a subset of the population.

There are two branches of statistics, namely descriptive statistics and inferential statistics. **Descriptive statistics** includes the collection, cleaning, and summarization of the data set of interest for the purposes of describing various features of that data. The features can be in the form of numeric summaries such as means, ranges, or proportions, or visual summaries such as histograms, pie charts, or bar graphs. These summaries and many more depend upon the types of variables collected and will be covered in Chapter 2, "Summarizing Your Data with Descriptive Statistics" and Chapter 3, "Data Visualization."

Inferential statistics includes the methods where sample data is used to make predictions or inferences about the characteristics of the population of interest. In particular, a summary measure calculated for the sample, referred to as a **statistic**, is used to estimate a population **parameter**, the unknown characteristic of the population. Inferential methods depend upon both the types of variables and the specific questions to be answered and will be introduced in Chapter 4, "The Normal Distribution and Introduction to Inferential Statistics" and covered in detail in Chapter 5, "Analysis of Categorical Variables" through Chapter 7, "Analysis of Variance."

Another goal of this book is to extend the methods learned in inferential statistics to those methods referred to as predictive modeling. **Predictive modeling**, sometimes referred to as **predictive analytics**, is the use of data, statistical algorithms and machine learning techniques to predict, or identify, the likelihood of a future outcome, based upon historical data. In short, predictive modeling extends conclusions about what has happened to predictions about what will happen in the future. The methods used for predictive modeling will be covered in Chapter 8, "Preparing the Input Variables for Prediction" through Chapter 11, "Measure of Model Performance" and provide a majority of the content for successfully completing the certification exam.

Finally, all content in this book falls under the larger topic, referred to as **data mining**, which is the process of finding anomalies, patterns, and correlations within large data sets to predict outcomes (SAS Institute).

Variable Types and SAS Data Types

All structured data sets are composed of rows and columns, where the rows represent the observations to be studied and the columns represent the variables related to the question or questions of interest. As stated earlier, in order to conduct either descriptive or inferential statistics, it is imperative that the analyst first define the **variable types**. Here we will also distinguish variable types from **data types**.

Variable Types

There are two types of variables, qualitative and quantitative (Anderson, et al., 2014; Fernandez, 2010). A **qualitative variable** is a variable with outcomes that represent a group or a category to which the observation is associated, and is sometimes referred to as a **categorical variable**. A **quantitative variable** is a variable with outcomes that represent a measurable quantity and are numeric in nature. Quantitative variables can be further distinguished as either discrete or continuous. A **discrete variable** is a numeric variable that results from counting; discrete variables can be infinite and do not necessarily have to be whole numbers. A **continuous variable** is a numeric variable that can theoretically take on infinitely many values within an interval and is, therefore, uncountable.

Let's consider an excerpt from a data set collected on patients related to the study of diabetes, as shown in Table 1.1 Data for the Study of Diabetes. It is evident that the variable, GENDER, is categorical, having values M and F, corresponding to males and females, respectively; major adverse event (AE1) is categorical as well. Notice that these variables are made up of textual data.

Table 1.1 Data for the Study of Diabetes

Patient_ID	Gender	Age	Controlled Diabetic	Hemoglobin _A1c	BMI	Syst BP	Diast BP	Cholesterol	NAES	AE1
85348444	F	73	1	4.24	23.12	94.0	69.0	99.57	0	
507587021	F	82	0	11.49	24.82	101.2	75.0	211.66	4	Itching
561197284	F	76	1	0.16	28.70	69.0	45.0	252.33	0	
618214598	M	69	1	0.02	27.95	105.0	89.0	201.21	1	Nausea
1009556938	M	82	0	7.35	29.28	87.0	63.0	275.56	3	Nausea

The clinical data including A1c (Hemoglobin_A1c), BMI, systolic blood pressure (SYST_BP), diastolic blood pressure (DIAST_BP), and cholesterol has quantitative, continuous values. The variable AGE, as measured in years, is a continuous quantitative variable because it measures fraction of a year; although when asked our age, we all report it to the nearest whole number. The number of adverse events (NAES) is quantitative discrete because the values are the result of counting. Note that PATIENT ID is recorded as a number, but really acts as a unique identifier and serves no real analytical purpose.

Finally, it should be noted that a patient's diabetes is controlled if his or her A1c value is less than 7. Otherwise, it is not controlled. For example, patient 1 has an A1c value of 4.24 which is less than 7, indicating that patient 1's diabetes is controlled (CONTROLLED_DIABETIC=1); whereas patient 2 has an A1c value of 11.49 which is greater than or equal to 7, indicating that patient 2's diabetes is not controlled (CONTROLLED_DIABETIC=0). In short, CONTROLLED_DIABETIC is a categorical variable represented by a numeric value.

SAS Data Types

When you are using SAS software, data is distinguished by its data type, either numeric or character. A variable is numeric if its values are recorded as numbers; these values can be positive, negative, whole, integer, rational, irrational, dates, or times. A character variable can contain letters, numbers, and special characters, such as #, %, ^, &, or *.

The three variable types previously discussed overlap with these two data types utilized by SAS. In particular, categorical variables may be character or numeric data types; however, discrete and continuous quantitative variables must be numeric data types. So consider the diabetes data in Table 1.1 Data for the Study of Diabetes. The variable, CONTROLLED_DIABETIC, is categorical with a numeric data type. Although not shown here, the three condition variables, HYPERTENSION, STROKE, and RENAL_DISEASE, also have numeric data type to represent categorical variables. GENDER is a categorical variable with character data type. All quantitative variables discussed previously have numeric data type. While PATIENT_ID is numeric, it makes no sense to perform arithmetic operations, so it is used solely for identifying unique patients, and could have been easily formatted as a character type.

The Data Analytics Process

The process of business analytics is composed of several stages: Defining the Purpose, Data Preparation, Analysis, Conclusions, and Interpretation.

Defining the Purpose

All statistical analyses have a purpose and, as stated previously, the statistical methods depend upon that purpose. Furthermore, the purpose of data analysis can be for either exploratory or confirmatory reasons. In exploratory data analysis, the purpose is strictly to summarize the characteristics of a particular scenario and relies on the use of descriptive statistics. In confirmatory data analysis, there is a specific question to be answered and relies on the use of inferential statistics. Table 1.2 Examples of Analyses by Purpose for Various Industries gives some examples of how statistical analyses are used to answer questions relative to both exploratory and confirmatory analyses in various industries.

Table 1.2 Examples of Analyses by Purpose for Various Industries

INDUSTRY	PURPOSE
Retail	Identify the advertising delivery method most effective in attracting customers
	Describe the best selling products and the customers buying those products
Healthcare	Identify the factors associated with extended length of stay for hospital encounters
	Predict healthcare outcomes based upon patient and system characteristics
Telecommunication	Identify customer characteristics and event triggers associated with customer churn
	Describe revenues collected for various products across various geographic areas
Banking	Identify transactions most likely to be fraudulent
	Predict those customers most likely to default on a personal loan
Education	Describe student enrollment for purposes of budgeting, accreditation, and resource planning
	Identify factors associated with student success
Government	Describe criminal activity in terms of nature, time, location for purposes of resource planning
	Predict tax revenue based upon the values of commercial and residential properties
Travel & Hospitality	Predict room occupancy based upon historical industry occupancy measures
	Describe customer needs and preferences by location and seasonality
Manufacturing	Predict demand for goods based upon price, advertising, merchandising, and seasonality
	Describe brand image and customer sentiment after product launch

Data Preparation

Once the purpose has been confirmed, the analyst must then obtain the data related to the question at hand. Many organizations have either a centralized data warehouse or data marts from which to access data, sometimes requiring the analyst to merge various databases to get the final data set of interest. For example, to study customer behavior, the analyst may need to merge one data set containing the customer's name, address, and other demographic information with a second data set containing purchase history, including products purchased, quantities, costs, and dates of purchases. In other cases, the analysts may have to collect the data themselves. In any event, care must be taken to ensure the quality and the validity of the data used. In order to do this, special consideration should be given to such things as sampling, cleaning the data, and a preliminary exploring of the data to check for outliers and interesting patterns.

Sampling

Sometimes it is either impractical or impossible to collect all data pertinent to the question of interest. That's where sampling comes into play! As soon as the analyst decides to take a sample, extreme care must be given to reduce any sources of bias. **Bias** occurs when the statistics obtained from the sample are not a 'good' representation of the population parameters. Obviously, bias exists when the sample is not representative of the target population, therefore, giving results that are not generalizable to the population. To ensure a representative sample, the analyst must employ some kind of probability sampling scheme. If a probability sample is not taken, the validity of the results should be questioned.

One such example of a probability sample is a **simple random sample** in which all observations in the population have an equal chance of being selected. The statistical methods used in this book assume that a simple random sample is selected. For a more thorough discussion of other probability sampling methods, we suggest reading *Survey Methodology, Second Edition* (Groves, R.M., et al., 2009).

There are other sources of bias and the analyst must pay close attention to the conditions under which the data is collected to reduce the effects on the validity of the results. One source of bias is **selection bias**. Selection bias occurs when subgroups within the population are underrepresented in the sample. For example, suppose the college administration is interested in studying students' opinions on its advising procedures and it uses an 'old' list of students from which to select a random sample. In this case, the sample would include those who have already graduated and not include those who are new to the college. In other words, the sample is not a good representation of the current student population.

Another type of bias is **nonresponse bias**. Nonresponse bias occurs when observations that have data values differ from those that do not have values. For example, suppose a telecommunications company which supplies internet service wants to study how those customers who call and complain differ from those customers who do not complain. If the analyst wants to study the reason for the complaint, there is information only for those who complain; obviously, no reason exists for those who do not call to complain. As a result, an analysis of the complaints cannot be inferred to the entire population of customers. See the section on data cleaning for more details on missing data.

Variable values can also be subjected to **measurement error**. This occurs when the variable collected does not adequately represent the true value of the variable under investigation. Suppose a national retailer provides an opportunity to earn a discount on the next purchase in return for completing an online survey. It could be that the customer is only interested in completing the survey in order to get the discount code and pays no attention to the specifics by answering yes to all of the questions. In this case, the actual responses are not a representation of the customer's true feelings. Therefore, the responses consist of measurement error.

Finally, the analyst should be aware of confounding. A **confounding variable** is a variable external to the analysis that can affect the relationship between the variables under investigation. Suppose a human production manager wants to investigate the effects of background music on employee performance as measured by number of units produced per hour but does not account for the time of day. It could be that the performance of employees is reduced when exposed to background music A as opposed to B. However, background music A is played at the end of the shift. In short, the performance is related to an extraneous variable, time of day, and time of day affects the relationship between performance and type of background music.

Cleaning the Data

Once the analyst has the appropriate data, the cleaning process begins. Data cleaning is one of the most important and often time-consuming aspects of data analysis. The information gleaned from data analysis is only as good as the data employed. Furthermore, it is estimated that data cleaning usually takes about 80% of a project's time and effort. So what is involved in the data cleaning process? Data cleaning involves various tasks, including checking for data errors and inconsistencies, handling missing data, creating new or transforming existing variables, looking for outliers, and reducing the number of potential predictors.

First, the analyst should check for data errors and inconsistencies. For example, certain variables should fall within certain ranges and follow specific business rules--the quantity sold and costs for a product should always be positive, the number of office visits to the doctor should not exceed 31 in a single month, and the delivery date should not fall before the date of purchase.

Then the question is what to do once you find these data inconsistencies. Of course, every effort should be made to find the sources of those errors and correct them; however, what should the analyst do if those errors cannot be fixed? Obviously, values that are in error should not be included in the analysis, so the analyst should replace those values with blanks. In this case, these variables are treated as having missing values. So what are missing values?

A missing value, sometimes referred to as **missing data**, occurs when an observation has no value for a variable. SAS includes for analysis only observations for which there is complete data. If an observation does not have complete data, SAS will eliminate that observation using either listwise or pairwise deletion. In **listwise deletion**, an observation is deleted from the analysis if it is missing data on any one variable used for that analysis. In **pairwise deletion**, all observations are used in analysis; however, only pairs of variables with missing values are removed from analyses. By default, most SAS procedures use listwise deletion, with the exception of the correlation procedure (PROC CORR) which uses pairwise deletion. It is important that the analyst know the sample size for analysis and the deletion method used at all times and to be aware of the effects of eliminating missing data.

So what should the analyst do when there is missing data? Schlomer, Bauman, and Card (2010) cite various suggestions on the percentage of missing observations where the analyst could proceed with little threat to bias; however, they further suggest, instead, looking at the 'pattern of missingness' and why data is missing so that imputation methods may be employed.

Some missing values occur because of a failure to respond or to provide data; others are due to data collection errors or mistakes, as mentioned previously. If the observations are **missing completely at random (MCAR)**, that is, if there are no systematic reasons related to the study for the missing values to exist, then the analysis can proceed using only the complete data without any real threats to bias (Little and Rubin, 2002). In short, it is believed that the observations with missing values make up a random sample themselves and, if deleted, the remaining observations with complete data are representative of the population.

While it is possible for data to be MCAR, that situation is very rare. It is more likely the case that data is **missing at random (MAR)**; MAR occurs if the reason for missing is not related to the outcome variable, but instead, related to another variable in the data set (Rubin, 1976). In either case, MCAR or MAR, there are imputation methods that use the known data to derive the parameter estimates of interest. When these methods are employed, all data will be retained for analyses. See Schlomer et al. (2010) for a description of non-stochastic and stochastic approaches to imputation.

If neither MCAR nor MAR exists, then the data is **not missing at random (NMAR)**. In this case, the reason that data is missing is precisely related to the variable under study. When data is NMAR, imputation methods are not valid. In fact, when observations are NMAR and missing data is omitted from analyses, results will be biased and should not be used for descriptive nor inferential purposes.

While there are various ways to handle missingness in data, we describe one method in particular. In Chapter 8, "Preparing the Input Variables for Prediction", we address this problem by introducing a **dummy variable**, or **missing value indicator**, for each predictor where missing data is of concern. The missing value indicator is coded as '1' for an observation if the variable under investigation is missing for that observation, or '0' otherwise. You are directed to Schwartz and Zeig-Owens (2012) for further discussion, a list of questions to facilitate the understanding of missing data, and the Missing Data SAS Macro as an aid in assessing the patterns of missingness.

In any event, when analyses involving missing data, it is critical to report both (1) the extent and nature of missing data and (2) the procedures used to manage the missing data, including the rationale for using the method selected (Schlomer, Bauman, and Card, 2010).

Another aspect of data cleaning involves creating new variables that are not captured naturally for the proposed analysis purpose. For example, suppose an analyst is investigating those factors associated with hospital encounters lasting more than the standard length of time. One such factor could be whether or not the encounter is considered a readmission. The patient data may not have information specifically indicating if the encounter under investigation is a readmission; however, the hospital admission data could be used to determine that. In other words, the analyst could create a new variable, called READMIT, which has a value of YES if the current encounter has occurred within 30 days of the discharge date of the previous hospital encounter, or NO otherwise.

In another example, suppose a retailer wants to know how many times a customer has made a purchase in the last quarter. Retailers probably don't collect that data at the time of each purchase--in fact, if surveyed, the customer may not correctly recall that number anyway. However, counting algorithms can be applied to transactional data to count the number of purchases for a specific customer ID within a defined period of time.

Many times, the analyst will create **'dummy' variables**, which are coded as '1' if an attribute about the observation exists or '0' if that attribute does not exist. For example, a churn variable could be coded as '1' if the customer has churned or '0' if that customer has been retained.

Next, the analyst may need to transform data. As you will see later in this book, some statistical analyses require that certain assumptions about the data are met. When those assumptions are violated, it may require transforming variables to ensure the validity of results. For example, the analyst may create a new variable representing the natural log of a person's salary as opposed to the salary value itself. Data transformations will be covered in Chapters 8 and 9. In Chapter 8, "Preparing the Input Variables for Prediction", methods to detect non-linearities are discussed in the context of logistic regression. In Chapter 9, "Linear Regression Analysis," we illustrate how to transform predictors for purposes of improving measures of fit in the context of linear regression analysis.

Finally, the analyst should check for **outliers**, that is, observations that are relatively 'far' in distance from the majority of observations; outliers are observations that deviate from what is considered normal. Sometimes outliers are referred to as **influential observations**, because they have undue influence on descriptive or inferential conclusions. Like missing values, the analyst must investigate the source of the outlier. Is it the result of data errors and how can it be fixed? If the observation is a legitimate value, is it influential and how should it be handled? Is there any justification for omitting the outlier or should it be retained? Sometimes outliers are detected during the data cleaning process, but ordinarily outliers are detected when specifically exploring the data, as discussed in the next section.

The data analyst must understand that data cleaning is an iterative process and must be handled with extreme care. For more in-depth information on data cleaning see Cody's *Data Cleaning Techniques Using SAS, Third Edition.*

Exploring the Data

Once the data is cleaned, the analyst should explore the data to become familiar with some basic data attributes--in general, what is the sample size, what products are included in data and which products account for a majority of the purchases, what types of drugs are administered based upon disease type, what geographic areas are represented by your customers, what books are purchased across various age groups.

The analyst should slice the data across groups and provide summary statistics on the variable of interest (such as the mean, median, range, minimum, and maximum or frequencies) or data visualizations (such as the histogram or bar chart) for comparative purposes, to look for various patterns, and to generate ideas for further investigation as it relates to the ultimate purpose. Many of these descriptive tools will be discussed in Chapter 2, "Summarizing Your Data with Descriptive Statistics" and Chapter 3, "Data Visualization." Inferential analyses for confirming relationships between two variables will be discussed in Chapter 5, "Analysis of Categorical Variables," ~~and~~ Chapter 6, "Two-Sample T-Test," and Chapter 7, "Analysis of Variance (ANOVA)."

The analyst can provide scatter diagrams for pairs of variables to establish whether or not linear relationships exist. In situations where there are hundreds of predictors and inevitably correlations among those predictors exist, data reduction methods can be employed so that a few subsets of predictors can be omitted without sacrificing predictive accuracy. In Chapter 8, methods for detecting redundancy will be discussed for purposes of data, or dimension, reduction.

Finally, the analyst should explore the data specifically for detecting outliers. An observation can be an outlier with respect to one variable; methods of detecting these univariate outliers will be covered in both Chapters 2 and 3. Or an observation can be an outlier in a multivariate sense with respect to two or more variables. Specifically, a scatter diagram is a first step in detecting an outlier on a bivariate axis. Methods of detecting multivariate outliers will be covered in Chapter 9, "Linear Regression Analysis."

Analyzing the Data and Roadmap to the Book

Once the data have been prepared, the goal of the analyst is to make sense of the data. The first step is to review the purpose and match that purpose to the analysis approach. If the purpose is explanatory, then the analyst will employ descriptive statistics for purposes of reporting, or describing, a particular scenario.

For example, in Chapter 2, "Summarizing Your Data with Descriptive Statistics," you will learn about ways to describe your numeric data with measures of center (mean, median, mode), variation (range, variance, and standard deviation), and shape (skewness and kurtosis). In Chapter 3," Data Visualization," you will learn how to describe your categorical data using frequencies and proportions. Chapter 3 will illustrate how to employ data visualization techniques to get pie charts and bar graphs for categorical data and histograms, Q-Q plots, and box plots for numeric data. These data visualizations and numeric summaries, when used together, provide a powerful tool for understanding your data and describing what is happening now.

If the purpose of the analysis is confirmatory, then you as analyst will employ inferential statistics for the purposes of using sample data to make conclusions about proposed models in the population. It is when hypotheses about organizational operations--whatever those may be--are confirmed that decision makers are able to predict future outcomes or effect some change for increased operational performance. This book emphasizes the specific statistical models needed to pass the certification exam, as listed in Table 1.3 Summary of Statistical Models for Business Analysis Certification by Variable Role.

Table 1.3 Summary of Statistical Models for Business Analysis Certification by Variable Role

TYPE of Response Variable	TYPE of Predictor Variables	
	CATEGORICAL	CONTINUOUS
CONTINUOUS	t-Tests (Chapter 6) or Analysis of Variance (Chapter 7)	Linear Regression (Chapter 9)
CATEGORICAL	Logistic Regression (Chapter 10)	Logistic Regression (Chapter 10)

As we discuss each model throughout Chapters 5 through 7, 9 and 10, you will begin to associate a specific type of question with a specific type of statistical model; and with each type of model, the variables take on specific roles--either as response or predictor variables. A **response variable** is the variable under investigation and is sometimes referred to as the dependent variable, the outcome variable, or the target variable. A **predictor variable** is a variable that is thought to be related to the response variable and can be used to predict the value of the response variable. A predictor variable is sometimes referred to as the independent variable or the input variable.

So, for example, when the analyst is interested in determining if the categorical response variable--whether or not a customer will churn--is related to the categorical predictor variable—rent or own, the appropriate type of analysis is logistic regression. If the analyst wants to further research churn and includes continuous predictors such as monthly credit card average and mortgage amount, then the appropriate analysis is logistic regression as well. These statistical methods will be covered in Chapter 10, "Logistic Regression Analysis," as illustrated in Table 1.3 Summary of Statistical Models for Business Analysis Certification by Variable Role.

If the analyst is interested in studying how crime rate is related to both poverty rate and median income (where the response variable, crime rate, is continuous and the predictors, poverty rate and median income, are both continuous), then the appropriate analysis in linear regression analysis. This statistical method will be covered in Chapter 9, "Linear Regression Analysis."

Finally, suppose a retailer was interested in testing a promotion type (20% off of any purchase, buy-one-get-one-half-off, or 30% off for one-day-only) and the promotion site (online only purchase or in-store only purchase). If the analyst is interested in studying how sales are related to the promotion type and/or promotion site, then the appropriate method is analysis of variance (ANOVA) where the response variable is continuous and the predictors are categorical. This type of analysis will be covered in Chapter 7, "Analysis of Variance (ANOVA)." Note that when the question about a continuous response variable is restricted to the investigation of one predictor composed of only two groups, then the analyst would use the t-test, as described in Chapter 6, "Two-Sample T-Test."

It is critical to note that if the purpose of data analysis is confirmatory, the analyst must also employ descriptive statistics for exploring the data as a way of becoming familiar with its features. Conducting confirmatory analyses without exploring the data is like driving to your destination without a map.

Finally, when the purpose of the analysis is classification, or predicting a binary categorical outcome using logistic regression analysis, the analyst must incorporate an assessment component to the modeling. In particular, the data is partitioned into two parts, the training data set and the validation data set. The best predictive models are developed and selected using the **training data set**. The performance of those models is tested by applying those methods to the **validation data set**. That model which performs or predicts best when applied to the validation data is the model selected for answering the proposed business question. This and other topics related to measures of model performance will be covered in Chapter 11, "Measure of Model Performance."

Conclusions and Interpretation

As with the other parts of the research process, the conclusion and interpretation are essential. You may have heard that "the numbers speak for themselves." No, they don't! All statistical numbers must be interpreted. Your interpretation should always relate the analytic results back to the research question. If the purpose of the analysis is descriptive, report the findings and use those findings to describe the current state of affairs.

If the purpose of the analysis is confirmatory, or inferential, in nature, state the analytical conclusions and provide interpretations in terms of how an organization can be proactive to effect some improvement in operations. Always consider whether there is an alternative way to interpret the results. When two or more possible interpretations of the results exist, it is the analyst's job to follow each possible explanation and provide detailed reasons for interpreting one outcome in a one particular way or another way. Reliance on the subject matter expert is imperative to ensure proper interpretation.

Getting Started with SAS

Throughout the book, we introduce various business questions to illustrate which statistical analyses are used to generate the corresponding answers. Specifically, we define the problem relative to the chapter content, construct-the necessary SAS code-for generating output, and provide an interpretation of the results for purposes of answering the question.

In order to provide a context for questions, we use various data sets that accompany the book. The two main data sets, and variants of those data sets, are (1) the Diabetic Care Management Case, and (2) the Ames Housing Case. Those two data sets are described in this section.

Diabetic Care Management Case

The data file provided with this book, DIABETICS, contains demographic, clinical, and geo-location data for patients who have been diagnosed with diabetes. The observation under investigation is the patient, each having variables that fall into the following categories:

1. Demographic information, such as patient ID, gender, age, and age range.
2. Date of the last doctor's visit and the general state of the patient, including height, weight, BMI, systolic and diastolic blood pressure, type of diabetes, if the diabetes is controlled, medical risk, if the patient has hypertension, hyperlipidemia, peripheral vascular disease (PVD), renal disease, and if the patient has suffered a stroke.
3. The results of 57 laboratory tests, including those tests from the comprehensive metabolic panel (CMP) which are used to evaluate the how the organs function and to detect various chronic diseases.
4. Information related to prescription medicine, including type of medication, dosage form, and the number and nature of adverse events with duration dates.
5. Geo-location data including the City and State where the patient resides, along with longitude and latitude.

In some cases, a random sample of 200 patients, in a file called DIAB200, is used for analysis. A complete data dictionary of the full data set with detailed descriptions is found in the Appendix B.

Ames Housing Case

The second major data set used for this book is the Ames Housing data, created by Dean deCock as an alternative to the Boston housing data (deCock, 2011). The original data was collected from the Ames Assessor's Office and contains 2,920 properties sold in Ames, IA, from 2006 through 2010. The data includes 82 variables on each of the houses.

The observation under investigation is the house, each having data on the following types of variables:

1. Quantitative measures of area for various parts of the house (above ground living area, basement, lot area, garage, deck, porch, pool, etc.).
2. Counts of various amenities (number of bedrooms, kitchens, full baths above ground and in basement, half baths above ground and in basement, fireplaces, number of cars the garage will hold).
3. Ratings--from excellent to very poor--for various house characteristics (overall quality, overall condition, along with the quality and condition of the exterior, basement, kitchen, heating, fireplace, garage, fence, etc.).
4. Descriptive characteristics, including year built, type of road access to property, lot shape and contour, lot configuration, land slope, neighborhood, roof style, roof material, type of exterior, type of foundation, basement exposure, type of heating and air, type of electrical system, garage type, whether or not driveway is paved, etc. Go to http://ww2.amstat.org/publications/jse/v19n3/Decock/DataDocumentation.txt to see the original documentation.

For this book, we consider a specific group of properties; in particular, the population of interest is defined as all single-family detached, residential-only houses, with sale conditions equal to 'family' or 'normal.' The sale condition allows for excluding houses that were sold as a result of a foreclosure, short sale, or other conditions that may bias the sale price.

As a result, the data set used in this book, called AMESHOUSING, contains 1,984 houses. After extensive exploration and purposes related to topics in this book, we created additional variables, resulting in a total of 103 variables, as defined in Appendix A. For the chapters covering topics related to predictive modeling, twenty-nine (29) total numeric and binary input variables are considered in the modeling process. The book does reference variations of the Ames housing data, along with other data sets, as listed in Table 1.4 List of Data Sets Used in the Book by Chapter.

Table 1.4 List of Data Sets Used in the Book by Chapter

Chapter	Data Set Name	Chapter	Data Set Name
1	ameshousing, diabetics	7	cas
2	all, diab200	8	ames300miss, ames70
3	diabetics, diab200, sunglasses	9	amesreg300, revenue
4	diabetics, diab25f	10	ames300, ames70, amesnew
5	ames300	11	ameshousing, ames70, ames30
6	ames300, alt40		

Accessing the Data in the SAS Environment

As stated earlier, we are assuming that you have a basic understanding of the SAS environment and the components of the SAS program, namely the DATA step and the procedure or PROC step. Recall that in order to access a SAS data set using the DATA step, the analyst must first use a LIBNAME statement pointing to where the data set is located. In this book, all SAS code references data sets located in the SASBA folder on the C drive.

Each data set is saved in its own subfolder within the SASBA parent folder. So, for example, the Ames housing data set is saved in the AMES subfolder, and the LIBNAME statement used to point to the data location has the form:

```
libname SASBA 'c:\sasba\ames';
```

The diabetes data used in the Diabetic Care Management Case is saved in the HC subfolder and is accessed using the following LIBNAME statement:

```
libname SASBA 'c:\sasba\hc';
```

In order to ensure that all readers are able to run the code found in subsequent chapters, we start with a very simple SAS program so that you can both access the data for the Diabetes Care Management Case and run a basic CONTENTS procedure for purposes of reviewing the specific details of the data set. Consider the Program 1.1 PROC CONTENTS of the Diabetes Care Management Case Data Set.

Program 1.1 PROC CONTENTS of the Diabetes Care Management Case Data Set

```
libname SASBA 'c:\sasba\hc';
data patient;
   set sasba.diabetics;
run;

proc contents data=patient;
run;
```

First, you can see from Program 1.1 that the LIBNAME statement defines a library called SASBA which points to the C:\SASBA\HC directory for accessing data. The permanent data set, DIABETICS located in the SASBA library, is placed into the temporary data set, PATIENT, and PROC CONTENTS is then applied to the data set, PATIENT. When the SAS code is run, the analyst should get the SAS LOG 1.1 PROC CONTENTS of the Diabetes Care Management Case Data Set.

SAS Log 1.1 PROC CONTENTS of the Diabetes Care Management Case Data Set

```
1   libname SASBA 'c:\sasba\hc';
NOTE: Libref SASBA was successfully assigned as follows:
      Engine:        V9
      Physical Name: c:\sasba\hc
2  data patient;
3     set sasba.diabetics;
```

```
NOTE: There were 200 observations read from the data set SASBA.DIABETICS.
NOTE: The data set WORK.PATIENT has 200 observations and 125 variables.
NOTE: DATA statement used (Total process time):
      real time              0.01 seconds
      cpu time               0.01 seconds


4   proc contents data=patient;
5   run;

NOTE: PROCEDURE CONTENTS used (Total process time):
      real time              0.07 seconds
      cpu time               0.06 seconds
```

Remember that the LOG file documents everything you do when running a SAS session. The lines in the LOG beginning with numbers are the original SAS statements in your program. The remaining lines begin with a SAS message--either NOTE, INFO, WARNING, ERROR, or an error number--and provide the analyst with valuable information as to the accuracy of the output.

From the LOG file, you can see that the library reference was successfully assigned. You can then see that 63,108 observations were read from the permanent SAS data set, DIABETICS, and then read into the temporary data set, PATIENT, having 125 variables, followed by the CONTENTS procedure. Included in the LOG is total process time as well.

It should be noted that it is very important to review the LOG file after every program execution for errors and warnings. Keep in mind that executing a SAS program and getting output does not necessarily mean that the results are correct. While there may be no run-time errors, there may be logical errors, many of which can be detected by checking the LOG file for what the analyst thinks is reasonable given the task at hand.

Once the analyst has checked the LOG file and has reasonable certainty that the program has run successfully, he or she can review the output as illustrated in Output 1.1 PROC CONTENTS of the Diabetes Care Management Case Data Set.

Output 1.1 PROC CONTENTS of the Diabetes Care Management Case Data Set

Data Set Name	WORK.PATIENT	Observations	63108
Member Type	DATA	Variables	125
Engine	V9	Indexes	0
Created	2018/09/03 11:25:37	Observation Length	1056
Last Modified	2018/09/03 11:25:37	Deleted Observations	0
Protection		Compressed	NO
Data Set Type		Sorted	NO

Alphabetic List of Variables and Attributes					
#	Variable	Type	Len	Format	Informat
105	ABDOMINAL_PAIN	Num	8	BEST12.	BEST12.
37	AE1	Char	14	$CHAR14.	$CHAR14.
38	AE2	Char	14	$CHAR14.	$CHAR14.
39	AE3	Char	14	$CHAR14.	$CHAR14.
14	AE_DURATION	Num	8	BEST12.	BEST12.
12	AE_STARTDT	Num	8	DATE9.	DATE9.
13	AE_STOPDT	Num	8	DATE9.	DATE9.
3	AGE	Num	8	BEST12.	BEST12.
4	AGE_RANGE	Char	12	$CHAR12.	$CHAR12.
40	Acetoacetate	Num	8	F12.2	BEST12.

Alphabetic List of Variables and Attributes					
#	Variable	Type	Len	Format	Informat
...	...	...	...	...	...
90	White_Blood_Cell_Count	Num	8	F12.2	BEST12.
91	Zinc_B_Zn	Num	8	F12.2	BEST12.

From the output, you can see that the first table summarizes information about the data set. Specifically, you can see that the temporary data set, PATIENT, has 63,108 observations with 125 variables, along with the creation data. The second table, representing an excerpt of the output, summarizes information about each individual variable; namely, the number (#) indicating the column location in the data set, the variable name, the variable type (numeric or character), the storage size in bytes (Len), the format for printing purposes, and the informat for input. If the variables had labels, those were included as well.

Key Terms

bias	nonresponse bias
categorical variable	not missing at random (NMAR)
character variable	numeric variable
confirmatory data analysis	outliers
confounding variable	pairwise deletion
continuous variable	parameter
data mining	population
data types	predictor variable
descriptive statistics	predictive modeling
discrete variable	qualitative variable
dummy variables	quantitative variable
exploratory data analysis	response variable
inferential statistics	sample
influential observations	selection bias
listwise deletion	simple random sample
measurement error	statistic
missing at random (MAR)	statistics
missing completely at random (MCAR)	training data set
missing data	validation data set
missing value indicator	variable types

---

[1] Officially, the name is the SAS Statistical Business Analysis Using SAS®9 Regression and Modeling exam.

Chapter 2: Summarizing Your Data with Descriptive Statistics

Introduction

In this chapter, we will focus on measures of center, spread, and shape for summarizing numeric data and how to produce these measures across various groups of interest. These types of data descriptions are critical for understanding data and provide the foundations for both data visualization (Chapter 3, "Data Visualization") and inferential statistics (Chapters 4 through 11).

As stated in Chapter 1, "Statistics and Making Sense of Our World," defining the variable type must precede all data analyses. There are two types of variables and each variable type warrants a specific path for analysis. Recall that a categorical variable is one which has outcomes in the form of a name or a label and helps to distinguish between various characteristics in the data (for example, gender or academic classification). A numeric variable measures a quantity and can be either discrete or continuous. A discrete numeric variable is one which takes on a finite, countable number of values. An example would be the number of smart devices a person owns having outcomes, say, 1, 2, 3, 4, or 5. A numeric continuous variable is one which has an uncountable number of outcomes and is usually in the form of a decimal. An example is the amount of money spent on online purchases.

This chapter will focus on describing summary measures for numeric data, and therefore, these fall under the category of descriptive statistics. For example, when describing the amount a customer spends on a single visit to an online retail site, the sales manager may report the mean, which is a single number that represents the typical amount purchased on any one visit. Or, suppose you manage a local supermarket and observe the variability in the customer traffic at various times of the day to determine the number of workers needed to maintain excellent customer service. Yet another example includes summarizing sales data across different departments and geographic locations. In any of these situations, there exist mounds of data of which to make sense, and summary information is critical.

In this chapter, you will learn about:

- the measures of center – mean, median, and mode
- the measures of variation – range, variance, and standard deviation
- the measures of shape – skewness and kurtosis

- other descriptive measures, including percentiles, the five-number summary, and the interquartile range
- the MEANS procedure for generating specified descriptive statistics and how to customize output
- ways to generate statistics for comparing groups using the CLASS and BY statements
- customizing output across multiple classes using the WAYS and TYPES statements
- saving the results of the MEANS procedure using the OUTPUT statement
- how missing data is handled in the MEANS procedure

Measures of Center

Suppose you teach an introductory statistics class and walk into the classroom on the first day; suppose also that a student asks you about how students performed last semester. Would you answer the question by reciting a list of the final course grades earned by each student from last semester? Probably not! However, you may answer by reporting the average, that is, a single number that represents the class-wide performance. Or you may even report the mode, the grade that occurred most often. In short, the typical response is to report a summary number without including the agonizing details. Frankly, students would have a hard time interpreting a list of grades. However, they have an innate understanding of, say, the mean or the mode. So, in order to describe the typical, or representative, value, the business analyst will report what's called **measures of center**. The measures of center are the mean, the median, and the mode.

Mean

The mean is calculated by adding all values and dividing by the total number of observations in the data set. If our data makes up the entire population of observations in which we are interested, then we would represent the **population mean** with the Greek symbol, μ, which is calculated using the formula:

$$\mu = \frac{\sum_{i=1}^{N} X_i}{N}$$

where X_i represents the ith observation in the data set and N represents the population size. If the data is made up of a sample of observations selected from a population, then we would represent the **sample mean** with the symbol, $\bar{X}$, and calculate it using the formula:

$$\bar{X} = \frac{\sum_{i=1}^{n} X_i}{n}$$

where n represents the sample size. Let's illustrate the calculation of the mean through an example. Suppose you are the warehouse manager for an online retail site and recognize that the key to fast delivery to your customer is in the processing of the order; that is, your goal is to fill the order and have it available for delivery pickup as quickly as possible. You take a random sample of orders and record the time taken to process each order and have it ready for delivery. The process times (in hours) are listed in the Figure 2.1 Time to Process Online Orders (in Hours):

Figure 2.1 Time to Process Online Orders (in Hours)

5	6	6	6	7	7	7	8	9	9

Because the data represents the sample, we would calculate the sample mean as follows:

$$\bar{X} = \frac{\sum_{i=1}^{10} X_i}{10} \quad \frac{5+6+6+6+7+7+7+8+9+9}{10} = 7$$

In conclusion, the average process time for our sample is 7 hours. As we will see in Chapter 4, "The Normal Distribution and Introduction to Inferential Statistics," when we do statistical inference, we will use the sample mean to estimate the population mean. For example, we could say that, based upon our sample, we have evidence and, therefore, expect the average processing time of all orders to be 7 hours. Note that had we collected the processing times for *all* orders, we would have used the Greek symbol, μ, to denote the population mean.

While the mean is commonly used as a measure of center, the business analyst must exercise caution in its use when the data includes **outliers**, that is, very large or very small values. When outliers exist, the mean is 'pulled' in one direction or the other. Consider the current example dealing with order processing time and suppose the tenth order had been mishandled and had, instead, taken 36 hours to process. The sample mean process time would now be 9 hours. In this case, the mean of 9 is now greater than 8 of the 10 observations in the data set and may not be the best measure of 'center.' In the case of outliers, the median may be a better measure of center.

Median

Consider a set of numeric data in the form of an **ordered array**, that is, an ordered series of numbers. The **median** is defined as the midpoint of the ordered array. Basically, the median 'cuts' the data in half such that half of the values are above the median and half of the values are below. Therefore, the median is defined to be the 50th percentile as well. In the case where the data set size is even, where there is no midpoint, the median is typically defined as the average of the two middle values, but other definitions do exist.   2 3 4 5 ~3.5

Consider, again, the process times (in hours) for a random sample of online orders, found in Figure 2.1 Time to Process Online Orders (in Hours). With 10 observations, there is no middle value; specifically, there are 5 observations in the first half and 5 observations in the last half. So, the median is the average of the two middle values, 7 and 7, which is 7. In other words, 7 hours is the process time where half of the observations fall below and half fall above. Keep in mind that if the data set size is odd, the median is the single middle value, found in the (n+1)/2 position of the ordered array.

Note also that if the last order had taken 36 hours to process instead of the 9 hours, the median would still be 7. In short, the median is not influenced by the extreme value of 36 hours. It should also be noted that the mean is calculated using *all* observations in the data set, so, it is influenced by a change in any one observation; however, the median is determined by the middle value or two middle values only, so it is not necessarily influenced when observation values change.

Mode

The **mode** of a data set is the observation value that occurs most often. So, in our random sample of online orders, note that the two processing times, 6 hours and 7 hours, each occur three times, while 9 occurs twice, and 5 and 8 occur only once. Because both 6 and 7 occur the most number of times, the mode is 6 and 7. In this case, our data is called bimodal. In some situations, a data set has one mode (called unimodal) or even multiple modes (called multimodal); in data sets where each observation value occurs only once, the data set has no mode.

The mode is also insensitive to either very large or very small numbers. Finally, unlike the mean and the median, the mode can be used to describe categorical data. For example, according to the National Center for Health Statistics (2016), there were approximately 2.6 million deaths in the United States in 2014. You can see from Table 2.1 Number of Deaths for Top Ten Causes – 2014 United States, that the leading cause of death is heart disease because it had the highest number of deaths at 614,348. In other words, the mode for the primary cause of death is disease of the heart.

Table 2.1 Number of Deaths for Top Ten Causes – 2014 United States

All Causes	**2,626,418**
Diseases of heart	614,348
Cancer	591,699
Chronic lower respiratory diseases	147,101
Unintentional injuries	136,053
Cerebrovascular diseases	133,103
Alzheimer's disease	93,541
Diabetes mellitus	76,488
Influenza and pneumonia	55,227
Nephritis, nephrotic syndrome, and nephrosis	48,146
Suicide	42,773
Total Top 10 Causes	1,938,479

Measures of Variation

When describing numeric data, it is not enough to know only the measures of center. In many situations, it is equally important to describe how observations differ from each other. Numeric summaries that describe these differences are called **measures of variation** and include the **range**, **variance**, and **standard deviation**.

Range

The most basic measure of variation is the **range** and measures the distance between the smallest value and the largest value in a data set. The range is defined as follows:

Range = Maximum Value – Minimum Value

Let's consider the following example. Suppose you want to compare the performance of two online retailers in terms of the numeric variable, the time it takes to process an order and get ready for delivery. Consider the first online retailer, discussed in the previous section, and a second online retailer, where data is collected on 10 randomly selected orders for each retailer, as found in Table 2.2 Time to Process Orders (in Hours) by Retailer.

Table 2.2 Time to Process Orders (in Hours) by Retailer

Online Retailer 1		Online Retailer 2	
5	7	1	8
6	7	5	8
6	8	6	8
6	9	7	9
7	9	7	11

Consider the histogram for each data set in Figure 2.2 Time to Process Orders (in Hours) which illustrates that the time to process an order is more variable for online retailer 2 when compared to online retailer 1. In particular, the histogram is wider for online retailer 2, indicating more variation, with a minimum of 1, a maximum of 11, and range of 10; whereas the histogram for online retailer 1 is more narrow, with a minimum of 5, a maximum of 9, and a range of 4. In short, the range simply tells us the width of the data or histogram.

Figure 2.2 Time to Process Orders (in Hours)

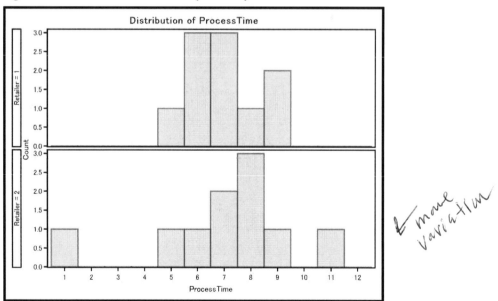

From the retail example, it is evident that the range is influenced by outliers. In fact, the value of the range is a function of both the minimum and maximum values and, by its very nature, is very vulnerable to both very small and very large values. The range depends only upon two values from the data set and ignores all other values and their variation or concentration.

Variance

All of us have a very good, intuitive understanding of the range; however, many struggle to understand the meaning of both variance and standard deviation. Suffice it to say that all three of these measures of variation have the same basic interpretation, but are measured on different scales. It will help to recognize, at first glance, that if a data set has all observations with equal values, then there is no variation; that is, the range, variance, and standard deviation are all equal to zero. If values in a data set are highly varied and relatively far apart, then all measures of variation (range, variance, and standard deviation) are relatively large to reflect a larger spread. If values are very similar and relatively close, then all measures of variation are relatively small to reflect a smaller spread.

Before getting into the details of variance and standard deviation, let's consider the descriptive statistics on time to process orders for online retailers 1 and 2, as provided in Table 2.3 Descriptive Statistics for Time to Process Orders. While we have not yet discussed variance nor standard deviation, you can see that those measures of variation, like the range, are ways to represent the width of the histograms. Specifically, notice that the variance for retailer 2 is 7.111, whereas the variance for retailer 1 is 1.778, indicating that the data for retailer 2 is more dispersed than that for retailer 1 because the variance for retailer 2 is larger. Notice also that the standard deviation of time for retailer 2 is 2.667, whereas the standard deviation for retailer 1 is 1.333, similarly indicating that the data for retailer 2 is more dispersed than that for retailer 1.

Table 2.3 Descriptive Statistics for Time to Process Orders

Time (in Hours)	Online Retailer 1	Online Retailer 2
Mean	7	7
Variance	1.778	7.111
Standard Deviation	1.333	2.667
Range	4	10
Minimum	5	1
Maximum	9	11

So how is variance derived? As mentioned previously, the range depends upon only two values from the data set and ignores all other values. So, we would like to consider a measure of variation that utilizes *all* observations in the data set. One such measure is the **variance** which is an index that reflects how each value in a data set deviates from the mean. If the data represents the population, the variance is denoted with the symbol σ^2; if the data represents a sample taken from the population, the variance is denoted with the symbol s^2. The formulae for variance are as follows:

$$\sigma^2 = \frac{\sum_{i=1}^{N}(X_i - \mu)^2}{N} \qquad\qquad s^2 = \frac{\sum_{i=1}^{n}(X_i - \bar{X})^2}{n-1}$$

Let's assume, for the moment, that the time to process an order for online retailer 1 represents the population of orders, where the average time to process an order is 7 as illustrated in Table 2.4 Calculations for Variance as Average Squared Deviations. Note, the information in column II measures how each observation deviates from the mean. So for example, observation 1 has a value of 5 hours which is 2 hours below the mean of 7, so the deviation is -2; while for observation 10, with a value of 9 hours, the deviation is +2. Finally, note that the average of the deviations from the mean is equal to zero. In fact, this is true for all data sets, regardless of the variation in values, because the positives and negatives always cancel out. In short, the average deviation would be useless as a measure of variation.

Table 2.4 Calculations for Variance as Average Squared Deviations

Observation	I TIME (X)	II (X-MEAN)	III (X-MEAN)^2
1	5	-2	4
2	6	-1	1
3	6	-1	1
4	6	-1	1
5	7	0	0
6	7	0	0
7	7	0	0
8	8	1	1
9	9	2	4
10	9	2	4
Average	7	0	1.6

In order to eliminate the negatives, a common practice is to square the deviations as shown in column III. So, while the unit of measure is now squared hours, the values are still reflective of the distance from the mean. So a squared deviation of 4 (for observations 1, 9, and 10) means that the observation's value is farther from the mean than, say, observation 4 with a squared deviation of 1. By definition, the population variance is the average of the squared deviations, that is, the average of the values in column III, as follows:

$$\sigma^2 = \frac{\sum_{i=1}^{10}(X_i-7)^2}{10} = \frac{4+1+1+1+0+0+0+1+4+4}{10} = 1.6$$

In reality, the data for retailer 1 is a sample, so the sample variance, as shown in Table 2.3 Descriptive Statistics for Time to Process Orders, is

$$s^2 = \frac{\sum_{i=1}^{10}(X_i-7)^2}{10-1} = \frac{4+1+1+1+0+0+0+1+4+4}{9} = 1.778$$

Now, why does the formula for sample variance contain (n-1) in the denominator, whereas the population variance has simply (N) in the denominator? Remember, that when we take a sample and calculate the variance of that sample, we ultimately want to use that sample variance as an estimate of the population variance. In fact, in the long run, if we took repeated random samples from the population, and calculated the sample variances, we would want the average, or the expected value, of those sample variances to equal the population variance. This is true for the sample variance only when dividing by (n-1); therefore, we refer to s^2 as **unbiased estimate** of σ^2.

Standard Deviation

The variance is calculated using squared deviations and is, therefore, measured in squared units. In order to describe variation using the original unit of measure, we must simply use the square root of the variance. By definition, the **standard deviation** is the square root of the variance. When we are describing the population, we use the symbol σ; when we are describing the sample, we use the letter, s. The formulae are as follows:

$$\sigma = \sqrt{\sigma^2} \qquad s = \sqrt{s^2}$$

So, let's go back to the comparison of process times for both online retailer 1 and online retailer 2. The sample standard deviation of the process times for retailer 1 is $\sqrt{s^2} = \sqrt{1.778}$, or 1.333 hours; and the sample standard deviation for retailer 2 is $\sqrt{7.111}$, or 2.667 hours. As we will see in Chapter 4, "The Normal Distribution and Introduction to Inferential Statistics" and beyond, the standard deviation has many properties that are very useful in both descriptive and inferential statistics.

Before continuing with other data descriptions, consider so far the summary information on process times for both retailers 1 and 2, from Table 2.3 Descriptive Statistics for Time to Process Orders. It is evident that, if the customer could obtain the same products from either online retailer, that the customer would choose retailer 1. So, while the average process times for both retailers is 7 hours, the variation is smaller for retailer 1 as reflected in the lower range, variance, and standard deviation, indicating that retailer 1 is somewhat more consistent in its process time. While this is a simple example of how statistics are used to describe and compare across different groups, it is a great illustration of the power of data descriptions for making decisions. The remaining part of this chapter provides more tools for making those decisions.

Measures of Shape

In addition to measures of center and shape, distributions can be described and differentiated in terms of their shapes. Specifically, the shape of data can be characterized by measures of skewness and kurtosis.

Skewness

Skewness is the tendency of observations to deviate from the mean in one direction or the other (SAS Institute Inc., 2011). In other words, skewness gives an indication of whether more data is concentrated at lower values or higher values. This imbalance in the spread of the observations around the mean is referred to as asymmetry. If the observations are spread evenly on each side of the mean, the data is considered symmetric and the skewness measure is zero. An example would be the heights of adult males which are represented by a bell-shaped curve; here the shape of the curve above the mean is identical to that of the curve below the mean, as illustrated in the middle panel of Figure 2.3 Examples of Symmetric and Asymmetric Distributions. Note also that a distribution does not necessarily have to be bell-shaped to be symmetric; the bell-shaped histogram is a special example of symmetry.

If observations with high values tend to be farther from the mean, then the data is considered positively or right-skewed, as illustrated in the left panel of Figure 2.3; if observations with low values tend to be farther from the mean, then the data is negatively or left-skewed, as illustrated by the right panel of Figure 2.3. An example of right-skewed data would be the incomes of American adults; in particular, there are more American workers making below the mean than above the mean. In fact, in 2015, the top 5% of individuals had incomes exceeding $100,000, (U.S. Census Bureau, Current Population Survey. 2007) which means 95% of Americans made $100,000 or less.

Figure 2.3 Examples of Symmetric and Asymmetric Distributions

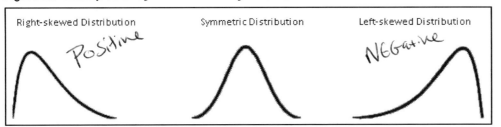

The formula for skewness is:

$$skewness = \frac{n}{(n-1)(n-2)} \sum_{i=1}^{n} \left(\frac{X_i - \bar{X}}{s} \right)^3 = \frac{n}{(n-1)(n-2)} \sum_{i=1}^{n} Z^3$$

Consider, for example, the time to process orders (X) for online retailer 1 as provided in Table 2.5 Sum of Z^3 Values for Calculating Skewness. First, note column II which measures, for each observation, the distance between X and the sample mean $\bar{X}$ in standard deviation units. For example, the first order, observation 1, took 5 hours to be processed, and is 1.50 standard deviations below the mean, whereas observation 10 which took 9 hours to be processed is 1.50 standard deviations above the mean. These values are referred to as standardized Z-scores and will be covered in more detail in Chapter 4, "The Normal Distribution and Introduction to Inferential Statistics."

Table 2.5 Sum of Z^3 Values for Calculating Skewness

	I	II	III
Observation	TIME (*X*)	Z = (*X*-Mean)/*S*	Z^3
1	5	-1.50	-3.37500
2	6	-0.75	-0.42188
3	6	-0.75	-0.42188
4	6	-0.75	-0.42188
5	7	0	0
6	7	0	0
7	7	0	0
8	8	0.75	0.42188
9	9	1.50	3.37500
10	9	1.50	3.37500
Sum		0.00	2.53125

In order to measure overall spread from the mean for all observations simultaneously and also take into account direction, the measure of skewness utilizes Z^3 so that the signs (+ or -) are retained. Specifically, skewness is obtained by taking the sum of the Z^3 values found in column III and multiplying that number by a sample size correction factor.

Based upon the formula, we can see that if the number of observations falling relatively far below the mean exceeds the number of observations falling relatively far above the mean, then the skewness is negative; however, if the number of observations falling relatively far above the mean exceeds those below, then the skewness is positive. If the sum of the Z^3 values is zero, resulting in a skewness value equal to zero, there is an indication that the data is symmetric where the observations values both above and below the mean balance out. It should be noted that skewness values range from -3 to +3.

For our example, skewness is

$$skewness = \frac{10}{(10-1)(10-2)}(2.53125) = +0.3516$$

indicating that (X) the time to process online orders for retailer 1 is slightly positively skewed. In fact, from Table 2.5 Sum of Z^3 Values for Calculating Skewness, we can see that the two relatively large values above the mean (observations 9 and 10) outweigh the one relatively small value (observation 1) below the mean. Skewness will be revisited in Chapter 3, "Data Visualization" when visualizing data in the form of graphs and charts.

Kurtosis

Kurtosis measures the heaviness of the tails of a data distribution (SAS Institute Inc.b 2011.) In essence, this index determines whether a distribution is flat or peaked as compared to a bell-shaped, or normal, distribution. So, for example, when reviewing Figure 2.4 Examples of Kurtosis as Compared to the Normal Distribution, you can see the flattest distribution has fewer observations concentrated around the mean as compared to the normal distribution, and instead has more observations concentrated in the tails. Therefore, resulting in heavier tails. The more peaked distribution has more observations concentrated around the mean as compared to the normal distribution, resulting is relatively flat tails. The formula for kurtosis is:

$$kurtosis \ \frac{n(n+1)}{(n-1)(n-2)(n-3)}\sum_{i=1}^{n} Z^4 - \frac{3(n-1)^2}{(n-2)(n-3)}$$

Data that has a bell-shaped curve will have a kurtosis value of zero. If a distribution has heavy tails, the kurtosis is positive; if a distribution has relatively flat tails, the kurtosis is negative.

Figure 2.4 Examples of Kurtosis as Compared to the Normal Distribution

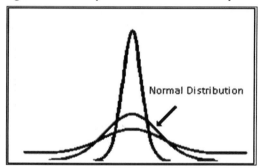

Again, consider the time to process orders (X) for online retailer 1 as provided in Table 2.6 Sum of Z^4 Values for Calculating Kurtosis, where column III illustrates the values of Z^4. For our example, kurtosis is

$$kurtosis = \frac{10(11)}{(9)(8)(7)}(16.45313) - \frac{3(9)^2}{(8)(7)} = 3.59096 - 4.33929 = -0.74833$$

indicating that (X), the time to process online orders for retailer 1, has relatively flat tails.

While the average time to process is 7 hours for both online retailers 1 and 2, the kurtosis for retailer 2 is +2.51, indicating heavier tails than that for retailer 1; in other words, for online retailer 2, there are more observations which have relatively large deviations from the mean. A review of Figure 2.2 Time to Process Orders (in Hours) illustrates exactly that fact, where online retailer 2 has extreme values in both tails.

Table 2.6 Sum of Z^4 Values for Calculating Kurtosis

	I	II	III
Observation	TIME (X)	Z=(X-Mean)/S	Z^4
1	5	-1.50	5.06250
2	6	-0.75	0.31641
3	6	-0.75	0.31641
4	6	-0.75	0.31641
5	7	0	0.00000
6	7	0	0.00000

	I	II	III
7	7	0	0.00000
8	8	0.75	0.31641
6	9	1.50	5.06250
10	9	1.50	5.06250
Sum		0.00	16.45313

Other Descriptive Measures

When exploring numeric data, there are additional measures which can provide more granular descriptions of the data and can aid in comparing numeric variables across various groups. These measures are sometimes referred to as **order statistics**, that is, numbers that imply the location of an observation in an order array.

Percentiles, the Five-Number-Summary, and the Interquartile Range (IQR)

Specifically, this section will describe various order statistics, including **percentiles** and the **five-number-summary and the Interquartile Range (IQR)**.

Percentiles

In the early section on measures of center, we discussed the median, which is the value where half the values are below and half of the values are above. By definition, the median is defined as the 50th percentile. In general, the ith **percentile** is the value where i percent of the observations are at or below.

When finding the ith percentile, the analyst basically wants to cut the data set into two parts. The lower part consists of those values less than or equal to the ith percentile, and the upper part consists of those values greater than or equal to the ith percentile. To find the ith percentile, the analyst must first start with an ordered array, and then find the *position* of the percentile in that order array. The SAS procedure illustrated in this chapter allows the analyst to employ various ways for finding the position of the percentile; here we will illustrate the default method (SAS Institute, n.d.), referred to as definition 5, using the following formula:

$$Position_i = (n)\left(\frac{i}{100}\right) = j + g$$

where j = the integer part of the position and g = the decimal part of the position. If the decimal value of the position is non-zero ($g>0$), then the percentile is in the $(j+1)^{th}$ position. If the decimal value of the position is zero ($g=0$), then the percentile is the average of the two observations in the jth and $(j+1)^{th}$ position, respectively.

Consider the example of finding the 25th percentile of process time for online retailer 2. The position in the ordered array is calculated as:

$$Position_{25} = (10)\left(\frac{25}{100}\right) = (10)(.25) = 2.5$$

Because the position value is 2.50, with j=2 and g=.5 (g>0), the 25th percentile is in the j+1=2+1, or 3rd position. Consequently, the 25th percentile is 6; that is, 25 percent of the process times is less than or equal to 6 hours. Consider now the 75th percentile. The position is as follows:

$$Position_{75} = (10)\left(\frac{75}{100}\right) = (10)(.75) = 7.5$$

The position value is 7.5, with j=7 and g=.5 (g>0), so the 75th percentile is in the j+1=7+1, or 8th position. In short, the 75th percentile is 8, meaning that 75 percent of the process times is less than or equal to 8 hours.

Finally, let's consider both the 10th and 90th percentiles, using the following formula:

$$Position_{10} = (10)\left(\frac{10}{100}\right) = (10)(.10) = 1.0$$

$$Position_{90} = (10)\left(\frac{90}{100}\right) = (10)(90) = 9.0$$

Because the decimal values are zero, the 10th percentile is the average of the 1st and 2nd observations (1 hour and 5 hours), which is 3 hours. The 90th percentile is the average of the 9th and 10th observations (9 hours and 11 hours), which is 10 hours. In conclusion, 10 percent of the data is at or below 3 hours, and 90 percent of the data is at or below 10 hours.

The Five-Number-Summary and the Interquartile Range (IQR)

The **five-number-summary** for a data set is defined to be the **minimum, the first quartile (Q_1), the median (Q_2), the third quartile (Q_3), and the maximum**. Note that the 25th percentile is equivalent to the 1st quartile (Q_1), the median is the second quartile (Q_2), and the 75th percentile is the 3rd quartile (Q_3).

This summary helps to describe various characteristics of the data; in particular, the median measures the center, while the range (maximum – minimum) measures the spread or variation. In addition, the **interquartile range (IQR)** is defined as the difference between the third and first quartile ($Q_3 - Q_1$) and is used to measure the variation in the middle 50 percent of the data. Finally, it may be noted that the five-number-summary cuts the data set into four parts.

Consider online retailer 2 and the time to process order. The five-number summary is 1, 6, 7.5, 8, and 11, and represents four parts of the data, as illustrated in Figure 2.5 Time to Process Online Orders (in Hours) for Retailer 2. In particular, the first quarter of the data starts at the minimum of 1 hour and continues to 6 hours; the second quarter starts at 6 hours and continues to 7.5 hours; the third quarter starts at 7.5 hours and continues to 8 hours; and finally, the last quarter starts at 8 hours and continues to the maximum of 11 hours. The interquartile range (IQR) is 2 hours, indicating that the middle 50 percent of the data differs by no more than 2 hours; whereas the range is 10 hours.

Figure 2.5 Time to Process Online Orders (in Hours) for Retailer 2

1	5	6	7	7	8	8	8	9	11

Outliers

In general, an observation is considered an **outlier** if it is 'far' in distance from other observations. Depending on the situation, there are various ways to define that distance. When exploring a single variable, an observation is considered an outlier if its distance from the middle 50 percent of the observations is more than 1.5 times the interquartile range (IQR). Specifically, an observation is considered an outlier if its value falls outside of the lower and upper limits defined as follows:

$$\text{Upper Limit} = Q_3 + 1.5\text{IQR}$$

$$\text{Lower Limit} = Q_1 - 1.5\text{IQR}$$

Consider once again online retailer 2. In order to check for outliers, we must calculate the upper and lower limits as follows:

$$\text{Upper Limit} = Q_3 + 1.5\text{IQR} = 8 + 1.5(8\text{-}6) = 8 + 3 = 11$$

$$\text{Lower Limit} = Q_1 - 1.5\text{IQR} = 6 - 1.5(8\text{-}6) = 6 - 3 = 3$$

When reviewing the process times for the 10 observations, we see that observation 1 is the only observation with a value outside of 3 hours and 11 hours, with a value of 1 hour. As a result, observation 1 is considered an outlier. For a visual representation of the five-number-summary and detecting outliers, go to Chapter 3, "Data Visualization" for a discussion of the **box-and-whisker plot**.

The MEANS Procedure

The MEANS procedure is employed for reporting summary measures, or descriptive statistics, for numeric data. In particular, the means procedure produces measures of center, variation, and shape, in addition to quantiles and confidence limits for the mean. The procedure can also be used for identifying extreme values and performing t-tests. The procedure allows for separating the analyses on various grouping variables for comparison purposes. Finally, the means procedure also provides the option to save the descriptive statistics to a separate SAS data set for future reference.

Procedure Syntax for PROC MEANS

PROC MEANS has the general form:

PROC MEANS DATA=*SAS-data-set* <*options*><statistic-keyword(s)>;
BY <**DESCENDING**> *variable-1* ... <**DESCENDING**>...*variable-n*;
VAR *variables*;
CLASS *variable(s)* </*option(s)*>;
OUTPUT <**OUT**=*SAS-data-set*><output-statistic-specification(s)> </ *option(s)*> ;
TYPES *request(s)*;
WAYS *list*;
 RUN;

To illustrate the MEANS procedure, consider the process time example for our online retailer. Of course, this is a small data set, but suppose we want to provide a very detailed description of how the online retailer performs in terms of the numeric variable, time (in hours) to process an order (X), including the amount spent on each order. To generate the descriptive statistics, the analyst would use Program 2.1 PROC MEANS of Process Time and Amount Spent for Retailer 1.

Program 2.1 PROC MEANS of Process Time and Amount Spent for Retailer 1

```
data retailer1;
input time amount @@;
datalines;
5 50.97
6 54.17
6 51.31
6 57.56
7 69.01
7 60.17
7 54.12
8 58.50
9 53.58
9 55.85
;
run;

proc means data=retailer1;
   TITLE 'Description Of Process Time and Amount Spent';
run;
```

First, you can see from Program 2.1 PROC MEANS of Process Time and Amount Spent for Retailer1 that the temporary data set, RETAILER1, is created and the data for both variables, TIME and AMOUNT, is read into that data set using the INPUT statement. PROC MEANS is then applied to the data set using the DATA= option, and the output is generated as seen in Output 2.1 PROC MEANS of Process Time and Amount Spent for Retailer 1.

Output 2.1 PROC MEANS of Process Time and Amount Spent for Retailer 1

Description Of Process Time and Amount Spent

The MEANS Procedure

Variable	N	Mean	Std Dev	Minimum	Maximum
time	10	7.0000000	1.3333333	5.0000000	9.0000000
amount	10	56.5240000	5.2982811	50.9700000	69.0100000

Note that, in the absence of any other statements, descriptive statistics are provided for all variables in the data set, namely, TIME and AMOUNT. Also note that when no options are given, by default, five statistics are reported; namely, the sample size, mean, standard deviation, minimum and maximum values. So for 10 online orders for online retailer 1, the average time to process an order is 7.0 minutes, with a standard deviation of 1.3333333 minutes, minimum of 5 minutes and maximum of 9 minutes. Those same 10 orders averaged $56.52, with a standard deviation of $5.2982811, minimum of $50.97, and maximum of $69.01.

Customizing Output with the VAR statement and Statistics Keywords

Suppose you want to concentrate on describing only one variable and include additional statistics for a more thorough description. In order to customize your output, you would use the VAR statement and may want to include a list of keywords for the desired statistics. In particular, the analyst could use Program 2.2 PROC MEANS with Additional Descriptive Statistics of Process Time for Retailer 1.

Program 2.2 PROC MEANS with Additional Descriptive Statistics of Process Time for Retailer 1

```
data retailer1;
input time amount @@;
datalines;
5 50.97
6 54.17
6 51.31
6 57.56
7 69.01
7 60.17
7 54.12
8 58.50
9 53.58
9 55.85
;
run;

proc means data=retailer1
   n mean max min range q1 mode median q3 qrange
   std n nmiss skew kurtosis clm t maxdec=2;
   var time;
   TITLE 'Description Of Process Time';
run;
```

[handwritten annotation: Var trumps input if "input time amount" and "var time", only time will have descriptive statistics]

As described previously, the variables TIME and AMOUNT are read and saved in the temporary data file, RETAILER1. The VAR statement is now added to the MEANS procedure to indicate that descriptive statistics are to be generated only for the variable, TIME. With the inclusion of various keywords in the MEANS procedure, additional statistics will be provided as well, as seen in Output 2.2 PROC MEANS with Additional Descriptive Statistics of Process Time for Retailer 1.

Output 2.2 PROC MEANS with Additional Descriptive Statistics of Process Time for Retailer 1

Description Of Process Time

The MEANS Procedure

						Analysis Variable : time			
N	Mean	Maximum	Minimum	Range	Lower Quartile	Mode *[25%]*	Median *[50%]*	Upper Quartile *[75%]*	Quartile Range
10	7.00	9.00	5.00	4.00	6.00	6.00	7.00	8.00	2.00

			Analysis Variable : time			
Std Dev	N Miss	Skewness	Kurtosis	Lower 95% CL for Mean	Upper 95% CL for Mean	t Value
1.33	0	0.35	-0.75	6.05	7.95	16.60

First, note that using the MAXDEC= option requests that statistics be reported to two decimals and provides a little more clarity when reviewing the output. Note also that including the keywords provides additional statistics not reported when the default is used. In particular, you now can see that the median is 7 hours, indicating that that half the orders took less than or equal to 7 hours and half took more than or equal to 7 hours. You can also see that 25% of the orders took less than or equal to 6 hours, whereas 75% of the orders took less than or equal to 8 hours; these differ by 2 hours which is represented by the inter-quartile range (IQR). As seen in the previous example, we can see the minimum and maximum times to process an order, but as requested here, we can now see that the range in processing times is 4 hours (maximum − minimum). Finally, we can see that the data is slightly positively skewed (skew = +0.35) and tails are slightly flat as measured by the negative kurtosis (kurtosis = -0.75). Finally, you can see that the output provides the upper and lower class limits for the 95% confidence interval for the mean and the t-value used for hypothesis testing, all of which will be covered in detail in Chapter 4, "The Normal Distribution and Introduction to Inferential Statistics." Finally, the order in which the statistics are reported is determined by the order in which the keywords appear in the MEANS procedure.

Key Words for Generating Desired Statistics

When you are customizing your output, note that the statistics available for reporting fall into three categories, (1) descriptive statistics, (2) quantile statistics, and (3) statistics for hypothesis testing (SAS Institute, n.d.) as listed in Table 2.7 Keywords for Requesting Statistics in the MEANS Procedure. Most of these statistics have been described in detail in this chapter. However, see Chapter 4, "The Normal Distribution and Introduction to Inferential Statistics" for additional coverage of the remaining statistics.

Table 2.7 Keywords for Requesting Statistics in the MEANS Procedure

Descriptive Statistics	Keywords	Statistics	Keywords	Statistics
	CLM	Confidence Limit for the Mean	NMISS	Number of Missing Observations
	CSS	Corrected Sums of Squares	RANGE	Range
	CV	Coefficient of Variation	SKEW	Skewness
	KURT	Kurtosis	STD	Standard Deviation
	LCLM	Lower Class Limit for Mean	STDERR	Standard Error
	MAX	Maximum	SUM	Sum
	MEAN	Mean	SUMWGT	Sum of the Weights
	MIN	Minimum	UCLM	Upper Class Limit for Mean
	MODE	Mode	USS	Uncorrected Sums of Squares
	N	Sample Size	VAR	Variance
Quantile Statistics	Median | P50	Median, 50th Percentile	Q3| P75	Third Quartile, 75th Percentile
	P1	First Percentile	P90	90th Percentile
	P5	Fifth Percentile	P95	95th Percentile
	P10	Tenth Percentile	P99	99th Percentile
	Q1 | P25	First Quartile, 25th Percentile	QRANGE	Interquartile Range
Hypothesis Testing	PROBT | PRT	P-Value for the T-Test Statistic	T	T-Test Statistic

Comparing Groups Using the CLASS Statement or the BY Statement

Many times, in practice, there are situations where you want to compare various groups on a particular numeric variable of interest. For example, you may want to compare the grades of students who take an online class versus a traditional classroom environment; or consider investigating the average sales of a chain of women's clothes when advertising using email versus direct-mail advertising. In these cases, you basically want to ask SAS to separate your data into the distinct groups and produce statistics for the groups separately for comparative purposes. This can be done by including either the CLASS statement or the BY statement.

PROC MEANS Using the CLASS Statement

Consider our example, where data is collected on the numeric variable, (X), time to process an order for both online retailers 1 and 2. In order to compare the two retailers on their process time, the analyst would use Program 2.3 PROC MEANS of Process Time for Retailers 1 and 2 Using the CLASS Statement.

Program 2.3 PROC MEANS of Process Time for Retailers 1 and 2 Using the CLASS Statement

```
libname sasba 'c:\sasba\data';
data all;
   set sasba.all;
   run;

proc means data=all
   n mean max min range q1 mode median q3 qrange
   std nmiss skew kurtosis maxdec=2;
   var time;
   class retailer;
   title 'Description Of Process Time By Retailer';
run;
```

The variables RETAILER, TIME, and AMOUNT are read and saved in the temporary data file, ALL. As in the previous example, the VAR statement indicates that the MEANS procedure will be applied to the variable TIME, and the keywords define the specific statistics to be produced. Finally, the CLASS statement indicates that the statistics will be calculated separately for each of the two levels of the variable RETAILER, namely retailers 1 and 2, as seen in Output 2.3 PROC MEANS of Process Time for Retailers 1 and 2 Using the CLASS Statement.

Output 2.3 PROC MEANS of Process Time for Retailers 1 and 2 Using the CLASS Statement

Description Of Process Time By Retailer

The MEANS Procedure

Analysis Variable : TIME									
RETAILER	N Obs	N	Mean	Maximum	Minimum	Range	Lower Quartile	Mode	Median
1	10	10	7.00	9.00	5.00	4.00	6.00	6.00	7.00
2	10	10	7.00	11.00	1.00	10.00	6.00	8.00	7.50

Analysis Variable : TIME							
Upper Quartile	Quartile Range	Std Dev	N Miss	RETAILER	N Obs	Skewness	Kurtosis
8.00	2.00	1.33	0	1	10	0.35	−0.75
8.00	2.00	2.67	0	2	10	-1.10	2.51

From the output, you can see that both retailers have 10 observations, and average 7 hours of processing times, with very similar medians and 7.00 and 7.50 hours, respectively. Both retailers also have similar characteristics in the middle 50% of the distribution; in particular, each has the middle 50% of the data ranging from 6 hours to 8 hours with an interquartile range of 2 hours.

There are some clear differences as well. You can see that retailer 2 has a wider variation in processing time as measured by the range of 10 hours with a minimum of 1 hour and a maximum of 11 hours, and a standard deviation of 2.67 hours; whereas retailer 1 has a range of 4 hours, with a minimum of 5 hours and a maximum of 9 hours, and a standard deviation of 1.33 hours. Furthermore, retailer 1 takes 6 hours most of the time as measured by the mode, whereas retailer 2 takes 8 hours. Finally, as mentioned earlier, the processing time for retailer 2 is negatively skewed with heavy tails, as measured by skewness and kurtosis, respectively; whereas the processing time for retailer 1 is close to symmetric with relatively flat tails.

So given this information, if both retailers had the same products available for you to purchase, the consumer would more than likely purchase from retailer 1 as opposed to retailer 2. While the average processing times are the same at 7 hours, the measures of variation, skewness, and kurtosis indicate that the processing time for retailer 1 is much more reliable and consistent.

It should be noted that NOBS (the number of observations) is automatically included in the output, by default, when the CLASS statement is used; therefore, it is not necessary to include the keyword, *N*, which gives the same information.

PROC MEANS Using the BY Statement

The previous example illustrated how the analyst could produce summary information for a numeric variable across multiple groups using the CLASS statement. When using the MEANS procedure, the analyst could instead use the BY statement to define the unique groups on which to analyze the numeric variable. Suppose again that we wanted to compare the two online retailers on the numeric variable, (X), time to process an order. The analyst would use Program 2.4 PROC MEANS of Process Time for Retailers 1 and 2 Using the BY Statement.

Program 2.4 PROC MEANS of Process Time for Retailers 1 and 2 Using the BY Statement

```
libname sasba 'c:\sasba\data';
data all;
   set sasba.all;
   run;
```

```
proc sort data=all;
   by retailer;
    run;

proc means data=all
   n mean max min range q1 mode median q3 qrange
   std n nmiss skew kurtosis maxdec=2;
   var time ;
   by retailer;
   title 'Description Of Process Time By Retailer';
run;
```

The variables RETAILER, TIME, and AMOUNT are read and saved in the temporary data file, ALL. As in the previous example, the VAR statement indicates that the MEANS procedure will be applied to the variable TIME, and the keywords define the specific statistics to be produced. Finally, the BY statement indicates that the statistics will be calculated separately for each of the two levels of the variable RETAILER, namely retailers 1 and 2, as seen in Output 2.4 PROC MEANS of Process Time for Retailers 1 and 2 Using the BY Statement. Note that before using the BY statement with any procedure (in this case, the MEANS procedure), the analyst must first include a SORT procedure with a BY statement corresponding to the categorical grouping variable. In other words, if the analyst is running a MEANS procedure BY RETAILER, then it must follow a SORT procedure BY RETAILER as well.

Output 2.4 PROC MEANS of Process Time for Retailers 1 and 2 Using the BY Statement

Description Of Process Time By Retailer

"by" + "sort"
but no
"nobs" by defu[l]

The MEANS Procedure

RETAILER=1

			Analysis Variable : TIME				
N	Mean	Maximum	Minimum	Range	Lower Quartile	Mode	Median
10	7.00	9.00	5.00	4.00	6.00	6.00	7.00

	Analysis Variable : TIME				
Upper Quartile	Quartile Range	Std Dev	N Miss	Skewness	Kurtosis
8.00	2.00	1.33	0	0.35	-0.75

RETAILER=2

			Analysis Variable : TIME				
N	Mean	Maximum	Minimum	Range	Lower Quartile	Mode	Median
10	7.00	11.00	1.00	10.00	6.00	8.00	7.50

	Analysis Variable : TIME				
Upper Quartile	Quartile Range	Std Dev	N Miss	Skewness	Kurtosis
8.00	2.00	2.67	0	-1.10	2.51

From Output 2.4 PROC MEANS of Process Time for Retailers 1 and 2 Using the BY Statement, you can see that the same information is provided as that obtained using the CLASS statement by RETAILER; however, the format of the output is slightly different. Here you can see that the information is provided in two separate tables, labeled as Retailer 1 and Retailer 2, respectively. Also notice that the NOBS is not included because it is the default for the CLASS statement, but not for the BY statement. Again, this information can be used to decide which online retailer performed best and more consistently.

The analyst can further customize the output if the order of the class is important by including the DESCENDING option in the BY statement, as seen in the partial program, Program 2.5 Analysis of Process Time for Retailers 1 and 2 Using BY DESCENDING.

Program 2.5 Analysis of Process Time for Retailers 1 and 2 Using BY DESCENDING

```
by descending retailer;
```

In this case, the summary statistics are printed by retailer, starting with the largest value, descending in order until all classes are printed, as illustrated in Output 2.5 Analysis of Process Time for Retailers 1 and 2 Using BY DESCENDING.

Output 2.5 Analysis of Process Time For Retailers 1 and 2 Using BY DESCENDING

Description Of Process Time By Retailer

The MEANS Procedure

RETAILER=2

Analysis Variable : TIME							
N	Mean	Maximum	Minimum	Range	Lower Quartile	Mode	Median
10	7.00	11.00	1.00	10.00	6.00	8.00	7.50

Analysis Variable : TIME					
Upper Quartile	Quartile Range	Std Dev	N Miss	Skewness	Kurtosis
8.00	2.00	2.67	0	-1.10	2.51

RETAILER=1

Analysis Variable : TIME							
N	Mean	Maximum	Minimum	Range	Lower Quartile	Mode	Median
10	7.00	9.00	5.00	4.00	6.00	6.00	7.00

Analysis Variable : TIME					
Upper Quartile	Quartile Range	Std Dev	N Miss	Skewness	Kurtosis
8.00	2.00	1.33	0	0.35	-0.75

Multiple Classes and Customizing Output Using the WAYS and TYPES Statements

There may be times when the analyst wants to investigate a numeric variable across more than one group and subsequent subgroups. For example, you may want to compare the appraised home values across cities or whether home values differ between new construction and existing dwellings, or a combination of the two groups or classes; for example, you may be interested in how values of new homes in one city compare to values of existing homes in another city. In fact, there may be certain combinations of groups, sometimes referred to as interactions, that are of more interest and the analyst may want to restrict reports to include only that pertinent information. This section will cover ways to investigate differences in means across various combinations, or interactions, of groups.

Using Multiple Classes in the CLASS Statement

To illustrate, consider the Diabetic Care Management Case introduced in Chapter 1, "Statistics and Making Sense of Our World," and specifically the numeric variable KETONES. Ordinarily the body gets energy from carbohydrates; however, when the body is unable to use glucose properly, it must instead burn fat for energy and in the process produces ketones as well. So elevated ketones may be associated with diabetes, especially when a person's diabetes is uncontrolled, and is, in fact, more common for those with Type I diabetes. Suppose the analyst is interested in seeing how ketones differ when comparing those patients with controlled diabetes to those with uncontrolled diabetes (CONTROLLED_DIABETIC), by gender (GENDER), and by whether or not the patient has renal disease (RENAL_DISEASE), or any interaction to see what factors may be associated with elevated ketones. The analyst would use Program 2.6 Three-Way Analysis of Ketones by Diabetes Status, Renal Disease, and Gender.

Program 2.6 Three-Way Analysis of Ketones by Diabetes Status, Renal Disease, and Gender

```
libname sasba 'c:\sasba\hc';
data patient;
   set sasba.diab200;
   run;

proc format;
   value yesno 0=No 1=Yes;
   run;

proc means data=patient
   mean std max min median nmiss maxdec=2;
   var ketones;
   class controlled_diabetic renal_disease gender;
   format renal_disease controlled_diabetic yesno.;
   title 'Ketones By Gender, Renal Disease, and Diabetes Status';
run;
```

The code provided here is identical to previous examples with the exception of having multiple variables referenced in the CLASS statement so that the numeric variable, KETONES, can be analyzed across multiple groups. Data is read from the permanent data set, DIAB200 and placed in the temporary data set, PATIENT. The MEANS procedure with the VAR statement and options requests specific statistics on the numeric variable, KETONES.

By default, all variables in the CLASS statement are used for subgrouping the data, so with three class variables, we have what is referred to as a 3-way analysis. In our example, with 2 levels of each variable, there are 8 possible groups on which to compare ketones (2 CONTROLLED_DIABETIC groups crossed with 2 RENAL_DISEASE groups crossed with 2 GENDERs). Notice that the order of the class variables determines the order of the columns in the output, namely, CONTROLLED_DIABETIC first followed by RENAL_DISEASE and GENDER.

From the output in Output 2.6 Three-Way Analysis of Ketones by Diabetes Status, Renal Disease, and Gender, you can see that the 200 patients have been placed into seven subgroups, defined by membership based upon the interaction of the three class variables. Remember that with three class variables, we expected eight groups; however, we only see seven because there were no female (GENDER=F) patients with controlled diabetes (CONTROLLED_DIABETIC=YES) and renal disease (RENAL_DISEASE=YES).

$2 \times 2 \times 2 = 8$

Output 2.6 Three-Way Analysis of Ketones by Diabetes Status, Renal Disease, and Gender

Ketones By Gender, Renal Disease, and Diabetes Status

The MEANS Procedure

Analysis Variable : Ketones									
CONTROLLED_DIABETIC	RENAL_DISEASE	GENDER	N Obs	Mean	Std Dev	Maximum	Minimum	Median	N Miss
No	No	F	52	15.19	9.24	49.65	0.01	13.59	0
		M	66	15.34	11.96	61.64	0.02	14.49	0
	Yes	F	9	22.83	14.36	48.36	8.73	18.63	0
		M	9	11.19	4.97	17.94	0.04	11.88	0
Yes	No	F	30	5.01	8.27	26.37	0.01	0.25	0
		M	32	6.45	10.73	35.36	0.00	0.22	0
	Yes	M	2	12.35	17.38	24.64	0.06	12.35	0

From Output 2.6 Three-Way Analysis of Ketones by Diabetes Status, Renal Disease, and Gender, generally speaking, those with uncontrolled diabetes (found in the first four lines of the output) have higher ketones, with the exception of those nine males with renal disease, having a mean ketone value of 11.19 than those with controlled diabetes (the last three lines of output). Most of the patients have uncontrolled diabetes and no renal disease (the first two lines of output) and are almost equally represented by both males and females. The largest mean value for ketones is 22.83 and represents the subgroup of nine female patients with uncontrolled diabetes and renal disease; whereas the lowest mean ketone value of 5.01 is for the 30 female patients with controlled diabetes and no renal disease. In fact, because males with controlled diabetes, no renal disease, and a mean ketone value of 6.45 are very similar to those same females, it may be useful to ignore gender for that subgroup. However, gender is important when comparing ketones of all who have uncontrolled diabetes and renal disease, where females have a mean ketone value of 22.83, twice that of males with a mean ketone value of 11.19.

The WAYS Statement for Multiple Classes

Now suppose that the analyst in interested in differences in ketones using only 2-way interactions, or analyses. In other words, you would like to create subgroups by crossing just two class variables. In order to do that, the analysts would use the WAYS statement within the MEANS procedures to define the n-way analyses. For example, Program 2.7 Two-Way Analysis of Ketones by Diabetes Status, Renal Disease, and Gender simply adds the WAYS statement to the previous code to restrict the number of subgroups.

Program 2.7 Two-Way Analysis of Ketones by Diabetes Status, Renal Disease, and Gender

```
libname sasba 'c:\sasba\hc';
data patient;
   set sasba.diab200;
   run;

proc format;
   value yesno 0=No 1=Yes;
   run;

proc means data=patient
   mean std max min median nmiss maxdec=2;
   var ketones;
   class controlled_diabetic renal_disease gender;
   ways 2;
   format renal_disease controlled_diabetic yesno.;
   title 'Ketones For 2-Way Combinations Of Groups';
run;
```

In general, the WAYS statement includes a list of numbers which refer to the requested 'ways' in which the groups are to be crossed. So Program 2.7 Two-Way Analysis of Ketones by Diabetes Status, Renal Disease, and Gender above requests that the numeric variable, KETONES, be analyzed using all possible unique 2-way interactions of the variables referenced in the CLASS statement.

Output 2.7 Two-Way Analysis of Ketones by Diabetes Status, Renal Disease, and Gender

Ketones For 2-Way Combinations Of Groups

The MEANS Procedure

Analysis Variable : Ketones								
RENAL_DISEASE	GENDER	N Obs	Mean	Std Dev	Maximum	Minimum	Median	N Miss
No	F	82	11.47	10.13	49.65	0.01	11.10	0
	M	98	12.44	12.26	61.64	0.00	12.44	0
Yes	F	9	22.83	14.36	48.36	8.73	18.63	0
	M	11	11.40	7.09	24.64	0.04	11.88	0

Analysis Variable : Ketones								
CONTROLLED_DIABETIC	GENDER	N Obs	Mean	Std Dev	Maximum	Minimum	Median	N Miss
No	F	61	16.32	10.37	49.65	0.01	14.20	0
	M	75	14.85	11.41	61.64	0.02	13.95	0
Yes	F	30	5.01	8.27	26.37	0.01	0.25	0
	M	34	6.80	10.92	35.36	0.00	0.22	0

Analysis Variable : Ketones								
CONTROLLED_DIABETIC	RENAL_DISEASE	N Obs	Mean	Std Dev	Maximum	Minimum	Median	N Miss
No	No	118	15.28	10.80	61.64	0.01	14.21	0
	Yes	18	17.01	12.03	48.36	0.04	13.22	0
Yes	No	62	5.76	9.57	35.36	0.00	0.24	0
	Yes	2	12.35	17.38	24.64	0.06	12.35	0

In Output 2.7 Two-Way Analysis of Ketones by Diabetes Status, Renal Disease, and Gender, notice that the first two-way interaction to be provided in the output is RENAL DISEASE by GENDER, which is specifically determined by the order in which the CLASS variables are listed, namely the second-to-last CLASS variable and the right-most CLASS variable. The next set of interactions is determined by the third-to-last CLASS variable, CONTROLLED_DIABETIC, and the right-most class variable, GENDER. Finally, the last set of interactions is determined by two left-most CLASS variables, namely, CONTROLLED_DIABETIC and RENAL_DISEASE.

In terms of the order of the tables, for the general CLASS statement, with the following WAYS statement, we have

```
class a b c;
ways 2;
```

The order in which the tables are printed will be B*C, A*C, and A*B.

Finally, the WAYS statement may have a list of numbers as follows:

```
proc means data=patient
   mean std max min median nmiss maxdec=2;
   var ketones;
   class controlled_diabetic renal_disease gender;
   ways 2 3;
```

In this case, the output would include all two-way interactions and the one three-way interaction as well. This single WAYS statement would give the analyst the output found in both Output 2.6 Three-Way Analysis of Ketones by Diabetes Status, Renal Disease, and Gender and Output 2.7 Two-Way Analysis of Ketones by Diabetes Status, Renal Disease, and Gender (the two previous outputs) combined.

The TYPES Statement for Multiple Classes

When using a MEANS procedure and defining *n* classes, the default limits the output to the largest n-way analysis, as seen in Output 2.6 Three-Way Analysis of Ketones by Diabetes Status, Renal Disease, and Gender. Recall also that the WAYS statement provides a way to define all desired n-way analyses. It may be, however, that the analyst prefers one or more specific types. In order to do that, the TYPES statement can be used, as seen in Program 2.8 One- and Two-Way Analyses of Ketones by Diabetes Status, Renal Disease, and Gender.

Program 2.8 One- and Two-Way Analyses of Ketones by Diabetes Status, Renal Disease, and Gender

```
libname sasba 'c:\sasba\hc';
data patient;
   set sasba.diab200;
   run;

proc format;
   value yesno 0=No 1=Yes;
   run;

proc means data=patient
   mean std max min median nmiss maxdec=2;
   var ketones;
   class gender renal_disease controlled_diabetic;
   types controlled_diabetic controlled_diabetic*(gender renal_disease);
   format renal_disease controlled_diabetic yesno.;
   title 'Ketones For Diabetes Status And With Gender Or Renal Disease';
run;
```

From the TYPES statement, the analyst is requesting that summary statistics be supplied for the numeric variable, KETONES, first by CONTROLLED_DIABETIC, because it appears in the statement first. The asterisk (*) and parentheses both indicate that summary statistics will be provided for CONTROLLED_DIABETIC by RENAL_DISEASE, and then CONTROLLED_DIABETIC by GENDER, as illustrated in Output 2.8 One- and Two-Way Analyses of Ketones by Diabetes Status, Renal Disease, and Gender.

Output 2.8 One- and Two-Way Analyses of Ketones by Diabetes Status, Renal Disease, and Gender

Ketones For Diabetes Status And With Gender Or Renal Disease

The MEANS Procedure

Analysis Variable : Ketones							
CONTROLLED_DIABETIC	N Obs	Mean	Std Dev	Maximum	Minimum	Median	N Miss
No	136	15.51	10.94	61.64	0.01	14.07	0
Yes	64	5.96	9.74	35.36	0.00	0.24	0

Analysis Variable : Ketones								
RENAL_DISEASE	CONTROLLED_DIABETIC	N Obs	Mean	Std Dev	Maximum	Minimum	Median	N Miss
No	No	118	15.28	10.80	61.64	0.01	14.21	0
	Yes	62	5.76	9.57	35.36	0.00	0.24	0
Yes	No	18	17.01	12.03	48.36	0.04	13.22	0
	Yes	2	12.35	17.38	24.64	0.06	12.35	0

		N						N
	Analysis Variable : Ketones							
GENDER	**CONTROLLED_DIABETIC**	**Obs**	**Mean**	**Std Dev**	**Maximum**	**Minimum**	**Median**	**Miss**
F	No	61	16.32	10.37	49.65	0.01	14.20	0
	Yes	30	5.01	8.27	26.37	0.01	0.25	0
M	No	75	14.85	11.41	61.64	0.02	13.95	0
	Yes	34	6.80	10.92	35.36	0.00	0.22	0

Saving Your Results Using the OUTPUT Statement

So far, the results of the MEANS procedure have been displayed in the output window by default. However, there are some situations where the analyst may want to save the results of the analyses to a new temporary or permanent data set for future use. In this case, the analyst would add the OUTPUT statement to the MEANS procedure. Let's consider the simplest example where the analyst is interested in the descriptive statistics on the variable, KETONES, for all 200 patients in the Diabetic Care Management Case, Program 2.9 Ketones for the Diabetic Care Management Case.

Program 2.9 Ketones for the Diabetic Care Management Case

```
libname sasba 'c:\sasba\hc';
data patient;
   set sasba.diab200;
   run;

proc means data=patient noprint;
   var ketones;
   output out=sasba.ketonesummary mean=average_ketone std=std_ketone
            min=min_ketone max=max_ketone;
   run;

proc print data=sasba.ketonesummary;
   title 'Average Ketones For The Diabetic Care Management Case';
run;
```

First, it should be noted that, as in previous examples, the code requests that SAS summarize the variable, KETONES. In order to save the results, the OUTPUT OUT= statement is included, along with keywords which define the specific statistics to be saved, namely, MEAN, STD, MIN, and MAX. Also note that the statistics are saved in the permanent SAS data set called KETONESUMMARY in the directory, C:\SASBA\HC. Finally, the analyst may want to see the contents of the final data set by using the accompanying PRINT procedure, and accordingly, the NOPRINT option is included in the MEANS procedure so that the output is not duplicated, as illustrated in Output 2.9 Ketones for the Diabetic Care Management Case.

Output 2.9 Ketones for the Diabetic Care Management Case

Average Ketones For The Diabetic Care Management Case

Obs	_TYPE_	_FREQ_	average_ketone	std_ketone	min_ketone	max_ketone
1	0	200	12.45	11.45	0.00	61.64

From the output, we can see that the 200 patients have an average ketone value of 12.45, with a standard deviation of 11.45, a minimum of 0.00, and a maximum of 61.64. It should be noted that SAS creates two new variables, _TYPE_ and _FREQ_. The _TYPE_ variable has a value of '0' when the statistics provided are for the entire data set; the FREQ variable indicates the sample size associated with the output as well.

The CLASS Statement and the _TYPE_ and _FREQ_ Variables

As stated previously, the analyst will more than likely be interested in describing how a numeric variable varies across various groups, or classes. When the results of this analysis are saved to an external data set, whether temporary or permanent, it is imperative that the analyst understand the meaning of both the TYPE_and FREQ_variables when interpreting the results. Let's consider an analysis of KETONES across the class, CONTROLLED_DIABETIC. The following code is identical to the previous code with the exception of the CLASS statement and the syntax for creating a FORMAT for the class variable:

Program 2.10 Ketones by the Class Controlled_Diabetic

```
libname sasba 'c:\sasba\hc';
data patient;
   set sasba.diab200;
run;

proc format;
   value yesno 0=No 1=Yes;
run;

proc means data=patient noprint;
   var ketones;
   class controlled_diabetic;
   output out=sasba.ketonesummary mean=average_ketone std=std_ketone
            min=min_ketone max=max_ketone;
run;

proc print data=sasba.ketonesummary;
   format controlled_diabetic yesno.;
   title 'Ketones By Diabetes Status';
run;
```

From Output 2.10 Ketones by the Class Controlled_Diabetic, you can see that the MEANS procedure produces two summaries, namely, an analysis of all observations as indicated by _TYPE_=0 and an analysis of the observations by class as indicated by _TYPE_=1. As indicated earlier, the line associated with TYPE=0 is associated with statistics for all 200 patients; the two lines with _TYPE_=1 provided summary statistics for the two levels of the class variable CONTROLLED_DIABETIC. In particular, there are 136 patients with uncontrolled diabetes, as defined by FREQ, having a mean ketone value of 15.51, with a standard deviation of 10.94, a minimum of 0.01, and a maximum of 61.64, as compared to 64 patients with controlled diabetes having a mean ketone value of 5.96, with a standard deviation of 9.74, a minimum of 0.00, and a maximum of 36.36. Finally, it should be noted that the _FREQ_ values for fixed _TYPE_ should always add up to the total size. For example, for _TYPE_=1, the two frequencies, 136 and 64, add up to a total of 200, representing the total sample size.

Output 2.10 Ketones by the Class Controlled_Diabetic

Ketones By Diabetes Status

Obs	CONTROLLED_DIABETIC	_TYPE_	_FREQ_	average_ketone	std_ketone
1	.	0	200	12.45	11.45
2	No	1	136	15.51	10.94
3	Yes	1	64	5.96	9.74

Obs	CONTROLLED_DIABETIC	min_ketone	max_ketone
1	.	0.00	61.64
2	No	0.01	61.64
3	Yes	0.00	35.36

Now suppose we want to explore ketones across a combination of two classes by adding a second class, RENAL_DISEASE. The analyst would simply add the variable, RENAL_DISEASE, to variable list of the CLASS statement to the previous code to get the following:

Program 2.11 Ketones by the Classes Controlled_Diabetic and Renal_Disease

```
libname sasba 'c:\sasba\hc';
data patient;
   set sasba.diab200;
run;
```

```
proc format;
   value yesno 0=No 1=Yes;
run;

proc means data=patient noprint;
   var ketones;
   class controlled_diabetic renal_disease;
   output out=sasba.ketonesummary mean=average_ketone std=std_ketone
            min=min_ketone max=max_ketone;
run;

proc print data=sasba.ketonesummary;
   format controlled_diabetic renal_disease yesno.;
   title 'Ketones By Diabetes Status And Renal Disease';
run;
```

In Output 2.11 Ketones by the Classes Controlled_Diabetic and Renal_Disease, you can see that the MEANS procedure now produces four summaries, namely, an analysis of all observations as indicated by _TYPE_=0, an analysis of the observations by the second class (RENAL_DISEASE) as indicated by TYPE_=1, an analysis of the observations by the first class (CONTROLLED_DIABETIC) as indicated by _TYPE_=2, and the interaction of both classes as indicated by _TYPE_=3. Again, note that the _FREQ_ values for a fixed _TYPE_ should add up to the total sample size; for example, for _TYPE_ = 3, the frequencies (118, 19, 62, and 2) add up to 200, the total number of patients in the data set.

Output 2.11 Ketones by the Classes Controlled_Diabetic and Renal_Disease

Ketones By Diabetes Status And Renal Disease

Obs	CONTROLLED_DIABETIC	RENAL_DISEASE	_TYPE_	_FREQ_	average_ketone
1	.	.	0	200	12.45
2	.	No	1	180	12.00
3	.	Yes	1	20	16.54
4	No	.	2	136	15.51
5	Yes	.	2	64	5.96
6	No	No	3	118	15.28
7	No	Yes	3	18	17.01
8	Yes	No	3	62	5.76
9	Yes	Yes	3	2	12.35

Obs	std_ketone	min_ketone	max_ketone
1	11.45	0.00	61.64
2	11.32	0.00	61.64
3	12.14	0.04	48.36
4	10.94	0.01	61.64
5	9.74	0.00	35.36
6	10.80	0.01	61.64
7	12.03	0.04	48.36
8	9.57	0.00	35.36
9	17.38	0.06	24.64

In fact, when two classes, A and B, are used in the CLASS statement, the number of observations created in the permanent data set, SASBA.KETONESUMMARY, is equal to

$$1+a+b+a*b$$

where a = the number of levels of class A and b = the number of levels of class B. So for example, where CONTROLLED_DIABETIC has 2 levels (a=2) and RENAL_DISEASE has 2 levels (b=2), then the number of observations is equal to $1 + 2 + 2 + 2*2 = 9$, as indicated in the log file found in SAS Log 2.1 Ketone Analysis by Two Classes.

SAS Log 2.1 Ketone Analysis by Two Classes

```
NOTE: SAS initialization used:
      real time            1.81 seconds
      cpu time             1.54 seconds

1     libname sasba 'c:\sasba\hc';
NOTE: Libref SASBA was successfully assigned as follows:
      Engine:        V9
      Physical Name: c:\sasba\hc
2     data patient;
3         set sasba.diab200;
4     run;

NOTE: There were 200 observations read from the data set SASBA.DIAB200.
NOTE: The data set WORK.PATIENT has 200 observations and 125 variables.
NOTE: DATA statement used (Total process time):
      real time            0.02 seconds
      cpu time             0.00 seconds

5
6     proc format;
7         value yesno 0=No 1=Yes;
NOTE: Format YESNO has been output.
8     run;

NOTE: PROCEDURE FORMAT used (Total process time):
      real time            0.02 seconds
      cpu time             0.01 seconds

9
10    proc means data=patient noprint;
11        var ketones;
12        class controlled_diabetic renal_disease;
13        output out=sasba.ketonesummary mean=average_ketone std=std_ketone
14                  min=min_ketone max=max_ketone;
15    run;

NOTE: There were 200 observations read from the data set WORK.PATIENT.
NOTE: The data set SASBA.KETONESUMMARY has 9 observations and 8 variables.
NOTE: PROCEDURE MEANS used (Total process time):
      real time            0.03 seconds
      cpu time             0.04 seconds

16
17    proc print data=sasba.ketonesummary;
NOTE: Writing HTML Body file: sashtml.htm
18        format controlled_diabetic renal_disease yesno.;
19        title 'Ketones By Diabetes Status And Renal Disease';
20    run;

NOTE: There were 9 observations read from the data set SASBA.KETONESUMMARY.
NOTE: PROCEDURE PRINT used (Total process time):
      real time            0.44 seconds
      cpu time             0.31 seconds
```

Finally, let's assume the analyst is interested in describing the numeric variable, KETONES, across three classes, CONTROLLED DIABETIC, RENAL_DISEASE, and GENDER, by adding the third class variable, GENDER, to the previous code to get Program 2.12 Ketones by the Classes Controlled_Diabetic, Renal_Disease, and Gender.

Program 2.12 Ketones by the Classes Controlled_Diabetic, Renal_Disease, and Gender

```
libname sasba 'c:\sasba\hc';
data patient;
   set sasba.diab200;
run;

proc format;
   value yesno 0=No 1=Yes;
run;

proc means data=patient noprint;
   var ketones;
   class controlled_diabetic renal_disease gender;
   output out=sasba.ketonesummary mean= std= min= max= / autoname;
run;

proc print data=sasba.ketonesummary;
   format controlled_diabetic renal_disease yesno.;
   title 'Ketones By Diabetes Status, Renal Disease, And Gender';
run;
```

Further inspection of the code illustrates an alternative to defining the statistics of interest. In particular the statistics keywords are included with the AUTONAME option. As seen in Output 2.12 Ketones by the Classes Controlled_Diabetic, Renal_Disease, and Gender, each of the desired statistics names are defined using 'Ketones_' as the prefix.

Output 2.12 Ketones by the Classes Controlled_Diabetic, Renal_Disease, and Gender

Ketones By Diabetes Status, Renal Disease, And Gender

Obs	CONTROLLED_DIABETIC	RENAL_DISEASE	GENDER	_TYPE_	_FREQ_	Ketones_Mean
1	.	.	.	0	200	12.45
2	.	.	F	1	91	12.59
3	.	.	M	1	109	12.34
4	.	No		2	180	12.00
5	.	Yes		2	20	16.54
6	.	No	F	3	82	11.47
7	.	No	M	3	98	12.44
8	.	Yes	F	3	9	22.83
9	.	Yes	M	3	11	11.40
10	No	.		4	136	15.51
11	Yes	.		4	64	5.96
12	No	.	F	5	61	16.32
13	No	.	M	5	75	14.85
14	Yes	.	F	5	30	5.01
15	Yes	.	M	5	34	6.80
16	No	No		6	118	15.28
17	No	Yes		6	18	17.01
18	Yes	No		6	62	5.76

Obs	CONTROLLED_DIABETIC	RENAL_DISEASE	GENDER	_TYPE_	_FREQ_	Ketones_Mean
19	Yes	Yes		6	2	12.35
20	No	No	F	7	52	15.19
21	No	No	M	7	66	15.34
22	No	Yes	F	7	9	22.83
23	No	Yes	M	7	9	11.19
24	Yes	No	F	7	30	5.01
25	Yes	No	M	7	32	6.45
26	Yes	Yes	M	7	2	12.35

Obs	Ketones_StdDev	Ketones_Min	Ketones_Max
1	11.45	0.00	61.64
2	11.06	0.01	49.65
3	11.82	0.00	61.64
4	11.32	0.00	61.64
5	12.14	0.04	48.36
6	10.13	0.01	49.65
7	12.26	0.00	61.64
8	14.36	8.73	48.36
9	7.09	0.04	24.64
10	10.94	0.01	61.64
11	9.74	0.00	35.36
12	10.37	0.01	49.65
13	11.41	0.02	61.64
14	8.27	0.01	26.37
15	10.92	0.00	35.36
16	10.80	0.01	61.64
17	12.03	0.04	48.36
18	9.57	0.00	35.36
19	17.38	0.06	24.64
20	9.24	0.01	49.65
21	11.96	0.02	61.64
22	14.36	8.73	48.36
23	4.97	0.04	17.94
24	8.27	0.01	26.37
25	10.73	0.00	35.36
26	17.38	0.06	24.64

From the output, you can also see that the MEANS procedure now produces eight summaries, as described in Table 2.8 TYPE Values and the Subgroups Produced by Three-Way Analyses.

Table 2.8 TYPE Values and the Subgroups Produced by Three-Way Analyses

TYPE	Patients are Summarized by:
0	across all groups
1	GENDER
2	RENAL_DISEASE
3	RENAL_DISEASE and GENDER
4	CONTROLLED_DIABETIC
5	CONTROLLED_DIABETIC and GENDER
6	CONTROLLED_DIABETIC and RENAL_DISEASE
7	CONTROLLED_DIABETIC, RENAL_DISEASE, and GENDER

In general, when 'c' class variables are used in the CLASS statement, 2^c different summaries are generated by the MEANS procedure. Recall when no CLASS statement is used, there is $2^0 = 1$ summary as found in Output 2.9 Ketones for the Diabetic Care Management Case; when one class variable, CONTROLLED_DIABETIC, is used, $2^1 = 2$ summaries are provided as found in Output 2.10 Ketones by the Class Controlled_Diabetic; when two class variables, CONTROLLED_DIABETIC and RENAL_DISEASE, are used, $2^2 = 4$ summaries are provided as found in Output 2.11 Ketones by the Classes Controlled_Diabetic and Renal_Disease; when three class variables are used, $2^3 = 8$ summaries are provided as found in Output 2.12 Ketones by the Classes Controlled_Diabetic, Renal_Disease, and Gender. Consequently, if the analyst had used four class variables, $2^4 = 16$ summaries would have been generated.

Finally, it should be noted that _TYPE_ $= 2^c$ represents all one-way analysis results; in other words, for c = 0, 1, and 2, the respective TYPES 1, 2, and 4, provide summary statistics for the one-way analyses, GENDER, RENAL_DISEASE, and CONTROLLED_DIABETIC, respectively.

Now, when three classes, A, B, and C are used in the CLASS statement, the number of observations created in the permanent data set, SASBA.KETONESUMMARY, is equal to

$$1 + a + b + a*b + c + a*c + b*c + a*b*c$$

where a = the number of levels of class A, and b = the number of levels of class B. So for example, where CONTROLLED_DIABETIC has 2 levels (a=2), RENAL_DISEASE has 2 levels (b=2), and GENDER has 2 levels (c=2) then the number of observations is equal to $1 + 2 + 2 + 2*2 + 2 + 2*2 + 2*2 + 2*2*2 = 27$. However, both Output 2.12 Ketones by the Classes Controlled_Diabetic, Renal_Disease, and Gender and SAS Log 2.2 Ketone Analysis by the Classes Controlled_Diabetic, Renal_Disease, and Gender indicate instead that there are only 26 observations; remember for our data set there are no observations that fall into the three-way analysis (females, having controlled diabetes and having renal disease).

SAS Log 2.2 Ketone Analysis by the Classes Controlled_Diabetic, Renal_Disease, and Gender

```
NOTE: SAS initialization used:
      real time             1.98 seconds
      cpu time              1.79 seconds

1     libname sasba 'c:\sasba\hc';
NOTE: Libref SASBA was successfully assigned as follows:
      Engine:         V9
      Physical Name: c:\sasba\hc
2     data patient;
3         set sasba.diab200;
4     run;

NOTE: There were 200 observations read from the data set SASBA.DIAB200.
NOTE: The data set WORK.PATIENT has 200 observations and 125 variables.
NOTE: DATA statement used (Total process time):
      real time             0.02 seconds
      cpu time              0.01 seconds

5
6     proc format;
7         value yesno 0=No 1=Yes;
NOTE: Format YESNO has been output.
8     run;

NOTE: PROCEDURE FORMAT used (Total process time):
      real time             0.02 seconds
      cpu time              0.00 seconds
```

```
9
10    proc means data=patient noprint;
11       var ketones;
12       class controlled_diabetic renal_disease gender;
13       output out=sasba.ketonesummary mean= std= min= max= / autoname;
14    run;

NOTE: There were 200 observations read from the data set WORK.PATIENT.
NOTE: The data set SASBA.KETONESUMMARY has 26 observations and 9 variables.
NOTE: PROCEDURE MEANS used (Total process time):
      real time            0.03 seconds
      cpu time             0.01 seconds

15
16    proc print data=sasba.ketonesummary;
NOTE: Writing HTML Body file: sashtml.htm
17       format controlled_diabetic renal_disease yesno.;
18       title 'Ketones By Diabetes Status, Renal Disease, And Gender';
19    run;

NOTE: There were 26 observations read from the data set SASBA.KETONESUMMARY.
NOTE: PROCEDURE PRINT used (Total process time):
      real time            0.48 seconds
      cpu time             0.34 seconds
```

Table 2.9 TYPE, WAYS, Subgroups, and Number of Observations for One-, Two-, and Three-Way Analyses (SAS Institute Inc., 2011) illustrates the values of the WAY and TYPE variables when the MEANS procedure is applied to an analysis variable using three CLASS variables, A, B, and C. The figure also includes a description of the subgroups generated for n-way analysis, along with the number of observations by _TYPE_, _WAY_, and in the overall analysis.

Table 2.9 TYPE, WAYS, Subgroups, and Number of Observations for One-, Two-, and Three-Way Analyses

C	B	A	_WAY_	_TYPE_	Subgroup defined by	Number of observations of this _TYPE_ and _WAY_ in the data set	Total number of observations in the data set
0	0	0	0	0	Total	1	1+a
0	0	1	1	1	A	a	
0	1	0	1	2	B	b	1+a+b+a*b
0	1	1	2	3	A*B	a*b	
1	0	0	1	4	C	c	
1	0	1	2	5	A*C	a*c	1+a+b+a*b+c+a*c+b*c+a*b*c
1	1	0	2	6	B*C	b*c	
1	1	1	3	7	A*B*C	a*b*c	
Character binary equivalent of _TYPE_ (CHARTYPE option)					A, B, C=CLASS variables	a, b, c=number of levels of A, B, C, respectively	

The CLASS Statement and Filtering the Output Data Set

Suppose now that the analyst was interested in looking at KETONES across four class variables but wanted to see summary results for the one-way analyses only. The analyst would include the CLASS statement below which defines the four classes, TYPE_2, CONTROLLED_DIABETIC, RENAL DISEASE, and GENDER. This would create $2^4 = 16$ possible types, where the one-way analyses are represented by _TYPES_ = 2^c, for c = 0, 1, 2, and 3, or _TYPES_ equal to 1, 2, 4, and 8. So, while the MEANS procedure in Program 2.13 Ketone Analysis by Four Classes creates a new data set, KETONESUMMARY, containing 76 observations, or rows of summary statistics as indicated in SAS Log 2.3 Ketone Analysis by Four Classes, the PRINT procedure only prints the one-way analyses, shown in Output 2.13 Filter of Output File for Only One-Way Analyses (_TYPE_ = 1, 2, 4, 8), by using the WHERE statement in Program 2.13 Ketone Analysis by Four Classes.

Program 2.13 Ketone Analysis by Four Classes

```
libname sasba 'c:\sasba\hc';
data patient;
   set sasba.diab200;
run;

proc format;
   value yesno 0=No 1=Yes;
run;

proc means data=patient noprint;
   var ketones;
   class type_2 controlled_diabetic renal_disease gender;
   output out=sasba.ketonesummary mean= std= min= max= / autoname;
run;

proc print data=sasba.ketonesummary;
   where _type_ in (1,2,4,8);
   format type_2 controlled_diabetic renal_disease yesno.;
   title 'Ketones By Diabetes Type, Diabetes Status, Renal Disease,And Gender';
run;
```

SAS Log 2.3 Ketone Analysis by Four Classes

```
NOTE: SAS initialization used:
      real time           1.93 seconds
      cpu time            1.71 seconds

1     libname sasba 'c:\sasba\hc';
NOTE: Libref SASBA was successfully assigned as follows:
      Engine:        V9
      Physical Name: c:\sasba\hc
2     data patient;
3        set sasba.diab200;
4     run;

NOTE: There were 200 observations read from the data set SASBA.DIAB200.
NOTE: The data set WORK.PATIENT has 200 observations and 125 variables.
NOTE: DATA statement used (Total process time):
      real time           0.03 seconds
      cpu time            0.03 seconds

5
6     proc format;
7        value yesno 0=No 1=Yes;
NOTE: Format YESNO has been output.
8     run;

NOTE: PROCEDURE FORMAT used (Total process time):
      real time           0.03 seconds
      cpu time            0.01 seconds

9
10    proc means data=patient noprint;
11       var ketones;
12       class type_2 controlled_diabetic renal_disease gender;
13       output out=sasba.ketonesummary mean= std= min= max= / autoname;
14    run;

NOTE: There were 200 observations read from the data set WORK.PATIENT.
NOTE: The data set SASBA.KETONESUMMARY has 76 observations and 10 variables.
NOTE: PROCEDURE MEANS used (Total process time):
      real time           0.04 seconds
      cpu time            0.01 seconds

15
16    proc print data=sasba.ketonesummary;
NOTE: Writing HTML Body file: sashtml.htm
17       where _type_ in (1,2,4,8);
18       format type_2 controlled_diabetic renal_disease yesno.;
```

```
19        title 'Ketones By Diabetes Type, Diabetes Status, Renal Disease,And Gender';
20   run;

NOTE: There were 8 observations read from the data set SASBA.KETONESUMMARY.
      WHERE _type_ in (1, 2, 4, 8);
NOTE: PROCEDURE PRINT used (Total process time):
      real time            0.52 seconds
      cpu time             0.35 seconds
```

From Output 2.13 Filter of Output File for Only One-Way Analyses (_TYPE_ = 1, 2, 4, 8), we can now see that those 132 patients with Type 2 diabetes differ tremendously on ketones, when compared to those 68 patients that do not have Type 2 diabetes. In particular, those with Type 2 diabetes have an average ketone value of 18.33 with a standard deviation of 9.25, a minimum of 8.67, and a maximum of 61.64; whereas those without Type 2 diabetes have an average ketone value just a fraction of that for those with Type 2 diabetes. The standard deviation and maximum ketone values for those without Type 2 diabetes are approximately half those for those who do – very clear differences.

Output 2.13 Filter of Output File for Only One-Way Analyses (_TYPE_ = 1, 2, 4, 8)

Ketones By Diabetes Type, Diabetes Status, Renal Disease, And Gender

Obs	Type_2	CONTROLLED_DIABETIC	RENAL_DISEASE	GENDER	_TYPE_	_FREQ_
2	.	.	.	F	1	91
3	.	.	.	M	1	109
4	.	.	No		2	180
5	.	.	Yes		2	20
10	.	No	.		4	136
11	.	Yes	.		4	64
27	No	.	.		8	68
28	Yes	.	.		8	132

Obs	Ketones_Mean	Ketones_StdDev	Ketones_Min	Ketones_Max
2	12.59	11.06	0.01	49.65
3	12.34	11.82	0.00	61.64
4	12.00	11.32	0.00	61.64
5	16.54	12.14	0.04	48.36
10	15.51	10.94	0.01	61.64
11	5.96	9.74	0.00	35.36
27	1.04	4.65	0.00	35.36
28	18.33	9.25	8.67	61.64

Finally, it should be noted that the same output found in Output 2.13 Filter of Output File for Only One-Way Analyses (_TYPE_ = 1, 2, 4, 8) could be generated by replacing the WHERE statement with the WAYS statement, specifically WAYS 1, thereby producing only one-way analysis results.

The NWAY Option and Comparisons to the WAYS and TYPES Statements

When considering multiple classes, be aware that the NWAY option will restrict the results of the MEANS procedure to include only those statistics for the largest n-way combination. So if two variables are included in the CLASS statement, the results are generated only for the two-way interactions; if the CLASS statement contains three class variables, then statistics are generated only for the three-way interactions. In other words, including the NWAY option limits the output statistics to those observations with the highest value of _TYPE_.

Consider Program 2.14 Three-Way Analysis of Ketones Using the NWAY Option where the analyst is interested in the differences in ketones across three possible classes, or groups. However, note that the NWAY option is now included in the MEANS procedure.

Program 2.14 Three-Way Analysis of Ketones Using the NWAY Option

```
libname sasba 'c:\sasba\hc';
data patient;
   set sasba.diab200;
   run;
proc format;
   value yesno 0=No 1=Yes;
   run;

proc means data=patient noprint nway;
   var ketones;
   class controlled_diabetic renal_disease gender;
   output out=sasba.ketonesummary mean= std= min= max= / autoname;
   run;

proc print data=sasba.ketonesummary;
   format controlled_diabetic renal_disease yesno.;
   title 'Ketones By Diabetes Status, Renal Disease, And Gender';
run;
```

Note that the largest value of _TYPE_ is 7 for all three-way interactions, so that only those statistics are provided as illustrated in Output 2.14 Three-Way Analysis of Ketones Using the NWAY Option. Note also that in general there are eight three-way interactions for classes having two levels; again, remember that one of the three-way interactions has no observations, so in the log file, the analyst would see that only seven observations are saved in the permanent data set, KETONESUMMARY.

Output 2.14 Three-Way Analysis of Ketones Using the NWAY Option

Ketones By Diabetes Status, Renal Disease, And Gender

Obs	CONTROLLED_DIABETIC	RENAL_DISEASE	GENDER	_TYPE_	_FREQ_	Ketones_Mean
1	No	No	F	7	52	15.19
2	No	No	M	7	66	15.34
3	No	Yes	F	7	9	22.83
4	No	Yes	M	7	9	11.19
5	Yes	No	F	7	30	5.01
6	Yes	No	M	7	32	6.45
7	Yes	Yes	M	7	2	12.35

Obs	Ketones_StdDev	Ketones_Min	Ketones_Max
1	9.24	0.01	49.65
2	11.96	0.02	61.64
3	14.36	8.73	48.36
4	4.97	0.04	17.94
5	8.27	0.01	26.37
6	10.73	0.00	35.36
7	17.38	0.06	24.64

Based upon the information covered in previous sections, the analyst should recognize that there are several ways to get the same output as just obtained using NWAY and illustrated in Output 2.14 Three-Way Analysis of Ketones Using the NWAY Option. Consider Program 2.15 Alternative 1 for Three-Way Analysis of Ketones Using the NWAY Option.

Program 2.15 Alternative 1 for Three-Way Analysis of Ketones Using the NWAY Option

```
libname sasba 'c:\sasba\hc';
data patient;
   set sasba.diab200;
run;

proc format;
   value yesno 0=No 1=Yes;
run;

proc means data=patient noprint;
   var ketones;
   class controlled_diabetic renal_disease gender;
   ways 3;
   output out=sasba.ketonesummary mean= std= min= max= / autoname;
run;

proc print data=sasba.ketonesummary;
   format controlled_diabetic renal_disease yesno.;
   title 'Ketones By Diabetes Status, Renal Disease, And Gender';
run;
```

The analyst is requesting that KETONES is summarized using the three class variables, CONTROLLED_DIABETIC, RENAL_DISEASE, and GENDER, but provides only three-way interactions as defined by the WAYS 3 statement. In short, this approach also gives the results as illustrated in Output 2.14 Three-Way Analysis of Ketones Using the NWAY Option.

Finally, the last two sets of programming code that both generate results for only three-way interactions are identical in results to Program 2.16 Three Class Variables Connected by the Asterisk (*) in the TYPES Statement.

Program 2.16 Three Class Variables Connected by the Asterisk (*) in the TYPES Statement

```
libname sasba 'c:\sasba\hc';
data patient;
   set sasba.diab200;
run;

proc format;
   value yesno 0=No 1=Yes;
run;

proc means data=patient noprint;
   var ketones;
   class controlled_diabetic renal_disease gender;
   types controlled_diabetic*renal_disease*gender;
   output out=sasba.ketonesummary mean= std= min= max= / autoname;
run;

proc print data=sasba.ketonesummary;
   format controlled_diabetic renal_disease yesno.;
   title 'Ketones By Diabetes Status, Renal Disease, And Gender';
run;
```

The BY Statement and the _TYPE_ and _FREQ_ Variables

When using the BY statement within the MEANS procedure, it is important the analyst understand how the variables _TYPE_ and _FREQ_ are defined, especially if used in conjunction with the CLASS statement.

For example, suppose the analyst is interested in generating statistics for the variable, KETONES, in terms of the patients CONTROLLED_DIABETIC status; however, instead of using a CLASS statement, the analyst uses a BY statement, as illustrated in Program 2.17 Ketones by Controlled_Diabetic.

Program 2.17 Ketones by Controlled_Diabetic

```
libname sasba 'c:\sasba\hc';
data patient;
   set sasba.diab200;
run;

proc format;
   value yesno 0=no 1=yes;
run;

proc sort;
   by controlled_diabetic;
run;

proc means data=patient noprint;
   by controlled_diabetic;
   var ketones;
   output out=sasba.ketonesummary mean= std= min= max= / autoname;
run;

proc print data=sasba.ketonesummary;
   format controlled_diabetic yesno.;
   title 'Ketones By Diabetes Status';
run;
```

In essence, the analyst is requesting that the data set PATIENT be separated into two different data sets, one containing those patients with controlled diabetes and the other containing those patients with uncontrolled diabetes. In doing so, it is required that the analyst first use the SORT procedure, in order to sort the data by CONTROLLED_DIABETIC as defined by the BY statement. In fact, it is required that a BY statement within the SORT procedure be used first before including a BY statement within any other procedure.

As a result, the MEANS procedure is applied to each set of data separately and the overall statistics are generated for each group so that the _TYPE_ variable for each is 0, as illustrated in Output 2.15 Ketones by Controlled_Diabetic. Note also that the _FREQ_ variable pertains to each group, such that there are 136 in the NO group and 64 in the YES group. After careful inspection, the analyst can see that the information provided in Output 2.15 Ketones by Controlled_Diabetic is identical to that in Output 2.10 Ketones by the Class Controlled_Diabetic, with the exception of the _TYPE_ variable values.

Output 2.15 Ketones by Controlled_Diabetic

Ketones By Diabetes Status

Obs	CONTROLLED_DIABETIC	_TYPE_	_FREQ_	Ketones_Mean	Ketones_StdDev	Ketones_Min	Ketones_Max
1	No	0	136	15.51	10.94	0.01	61.64
2	Yes	0	64	5.96	9.74	0.00	35.36

To further illustrate the difference between the BY statement and the CLASS statement when used within the MEANS procedure, consider Program 2.18 Ketones by Controlled_Diabetic for Two Classes.

Program 2.18 Ketones by Controlled_Diabetic for Two Classes

```
libname sasba 'c:\sasba\hc';
data patient;
   set sasba.diab200;
run;

proc format;
   value yesno 0=no 1=yes;
run;

proc sort;
   by controlled_diabetic;
run;
```

```
proc means data=patient noprint;
   by controlled_diabetic;
   var ketones;
   class renal_disease gender;
   output out=sasba.ketonesummary mean= std= min= max= / autoname;
run;

proc print data=sasba.ketonesummary;
   format controlled_diabetic renal_disease yesno.;
   title 'Ketones By Diabetes Status, Renal Disease, And Gender';
run
```

Note that the MEANS procedure is requesting an analysis of the KETONES variable, as defined in the VAR statement, in terms of the CLASS variables RENAL_DISEASE and GENDER. Note also that the analysis is requested for each level of CONTROLLED_DIABETIC as defined by the BY statement; therefore, the data must first be sorted by CONTROLLED_DIABETIC using the SORT procedure.

Again the data set is separated into two parts, namely, one containing those patients with controlled diabetes and the other containing those patients with uncontrolled diabetes. Each is analyzed using the two class variables as illustrated in Output 2.16 Ketones by Controlled_Diabetic for Two Classes.

Output 2.16 Ketones by Controlled_Diabetic for Two Classes

Ketones By Diabetes Status, Renal Disease, And Gender

Obs	CONTROLLED_DIABETIC	RENAL_DISEASE	GENDER	_TYPE_	_FREQ_	Ketones_Mean
1	No	.		0	136	15.51
2	No	.	F	1	61	16.32
3	No	.	M	1	75	14.85
4	No	No		2	118	15.28
5	No	Yes		2	18	17.01
6	No	No	F	3	52	15.19
7	No	No	M	3	66	15.34
8	No	Yes	F	3	9	22.83
9	No	Yes	M	3	9	11.19
10	Yes	.		0	64	5.96
11	Yes	.	F	1	30	5.01
12	Yes	.	M	1	34	6.80
13	Yes	No		2	62	5.76
14	Yes	Yes		2	2	12.35
15	Yes	No	F	3	30	5.01
16	Yes	No	M	3	32	6.45
17	Yes	Yes	M	3	2	12.35

Obs	Ketones_StdDev	Ketones_Min	Ketones_Max
1	10.94	0.01	61.64
2	10.37	0.01	49.65
3	11.41	0.02	61.64
4	10.80	0.01	61.64
5	12.03	0.04	48.36
6	9.24	0.01	49.65
7	11.96	0.02	61.64
8	14.36	8.73	48.36
9	4.97	0.04	17.94
10	9.74	0.00	35.36
11	8.27	0.01	26.37
12	10.92	0.00	35.36
13	9.57	0.00	35.36
14	17.38	0.06	24.64
15	8.27	0.01	26.37
16	10.73	0.00	35.36
17	17.38	0.06	24.64

From the output, you can see that the data set is sorted by CONTROLLED_DIABETIC, where observations 1 through 9 represent those patients with uncontrolled diabetes and observations 10 through 17 represent those patients with controlled diabetes.

For those with uncontrolled diabetes, the analysis of ketones is performed using the two classes, RENAL_DISEASE and GENDER. Therefore the _TYPE_ variable has values 0 through 3, as is always the case for two classes. The same values of the _TYPE_ variable apply also to the patients with controlled diabetes. In fact, the statistics in Output 2.16 Ketones by Controlled_Diabetic for Two Classes are the reduced set of statistics found in lines 10 to 26 in Output 2.12 Ketones by the Classes Controlled_Diabetic, Renal_Disease, and Gender, and with different _TYPE_ values.

Handling Missing Data with the MISSING Option

The examples so far have included data sets with no missing values on the variables used, but, in reality, missing data is very probable. As a result, the analyst must take missing data into account when conducting analyses.

If patients in the previous examples had missing values on ketones, those observations would have been excluded from the statistics calculations. In fact, if those patients had missing data on any of the class variables under consideration, those patients would have been excluded as well. Because all analyses accounted for all 200 patients, we can assume that no observations had missing data.

To illustrate how to handle missing data, consider again the Diabetic Care Management Case. Depending upon diabetes type, patients are given drugs to treat the effects of diabetes, and obviously these drugs have some adverse events, like abdominal pain, dizziness, headaches, and vomiting, to name a few. Data included in the data set is the number of days that a patient experiences the adverse event, represented by the variable, AE_DURATION. Sometimes patients have no adverse events. Therefore, the duration would be missing in the data set.

Suppose the analyst would like to see the average glucose levels as related to the duration of adverse events. In this case, the analyst would use Program 2.19 The MEANS Procedure of Glucose by AE_DURATION Including Missing Values.

Program 2.19 The MEANS Procedure of Glucose by AE_DURATION Including Missing Values

```
libname sasba 'c:\sasba\hc';
data patient;
   set sasba.diab200;
   run;
```

```
proc means data=patient maxdec=2 missing;
   var glucose;
   class ae_duration;
   title 'Glucose By Duration Of Adverse Event Duration';
   output out=sasba.glucosesummary mean= std= min= max= / autoname;
   run;

proc print data=sasba.glucosesummary;
   title 'Glucose By Duration Of Adverse Event Duration';
run;
```

The MEANS procedure is requesting an analysis of the variable, GLUCOSE, as defined by the VAR statement, by the CLASS variable AE_DURATION. Note also that the MEANS procedure includes the MISSING option as well, which requests that observations with missing values on the CLASS variable be included in its separate group as indicated in Output 2.17a The MEANS Procedure of Glucose by AE_DURATION Including Missing Values. From the output, we can see that 29 observations had no value for AE_DURATION, possibly indicating that the patient had no adverse events, and may not have had any drug treatment at all. In fact, it is interesting to note that those with missing AE_DURATION had the smallest average glucose possible indicating the group with the best glucose values.

Output 2.17a The MEANS Procedure of Glucose by AE_DURATION Including Missing Values

Glucose By Duration Of Adverse Event Duration

AE_DURATION	N Obs	N	Mean	Std Dev	Minimum	Maximum
.	29	29	137.85	90.57	3.84	352.40
1	14	14	201.61	93.62	28.94	375.17
2	18	18	189.32	118.24	12.88	448.89
3	20	20	169.77	90.94	0.87	351.35
4	19	19	166.25	92.44	16.34	332.95
5	13	13	172.00	70.24	34.19	265.86
6	16	16	163.15	123.10	30.18	410.91
7	17	17	161.93	88.94	30.11	357.44
8	15	15	191.26	92.71	13.64	375.49
9	22	22	163.48	75.05	9.45	341.81
10	17	17	169.67	72.73	68.69	329.78

Analysis Variable : Glucose

The code also requests that the results be saved in the permanent data set, GLUCOSESUMMARY, and printed as illustrated in Output 2.17b Glucose by AE_DURATION Including Missing Values. Note that the line pertaining to _TYPE_=0 refers to all patients having an average glucose value of 168.66, with a standard deviation of 92.12, minimum of 0.87, and maximum of 448.89. Note that the remaining lines pertaining to _TYPE_=1 contain statistics for each of the levels as defined by the CLASS variable, AE_DURATION, and can be compared to the overall mean (_TYPE_=0) for interpretation purposes. Note that had the missing option been omitted, any output having AE_DURATION = missing would have been omitted from the output.

Output 2.17b Glucose by AE_DURATION Including Missing Values

Glucose By Duration Of Adverse Event Duration

Obs	AE_DURATION	_TYPE_	_FREQ_	Glucose_Mean	Glucose_StdDev	Glucose_Min	Glucose_Max
1	.	0	200	168.66	92.12	0.87	448.89
2	.	1	29	137.85	90.57	3.84	352.40
3	1	1	14	201.61	93.62	28.94	375.17
4	2	1	18	189.32	118.24	12.88	448.89
5	3	1	20	169.77	90.94	0.87	351.35
6	4	1	19	166.25	92.44	16.34	332.95
7	5	1	13	172.00	70.24	34.19	265.86
8	6	1	16	163.15	123.10	30.18	410.91
9	7	1	17	161.93	88.94	30.11	357.44
10	8	1	15	191.26	92.71	13.64	375.49
11	9	1	22	163.48	75.05	9.45	341.81
12	10	1	17	169.67	72.73	68.69	329.78

Every analysis which provides summary statistics should also be accompanied by a picture of the data as well. Please refer to Chapter 3, "Data Visualization" which provides a visual description of data. Specifically, it covers the UNIVARIATE procedure for numeric data which provides histograms and box plots, and the FREQ procedure which provides bar charts for character data.

As stated in the beginning of this chapter, the focus here has been on producing statistical measures for describing numeric data through the use of the MEANS procedure. These data descriptions include measures of center, variation, shape, and relative location, which can also be summarized across various groups and subgroups. There are other procedures which provide summary measures for numeric data, including the SUMMARY, UNIVARIATE, and TABULATE procedures, as well as the FREQ procedure for character data.

Key Terms

box-and-whisker plot
deviation
first quartile (Q1)
five-number-summary
five-number-summary.
interquartile range (IQR)
Kurtosis
maximum
median
minimum
mode

order statistics
ordered array
outlier
percentiles
population mean
range
sample mean
Skewness
third quartile (Q3)
variance

Chapter Quiz

Select the best answer for each of the following questions:

1. Suppose you take a random sample of students from a statistics class and their grades on the final exam are 63, 75, 77, 77, 81, 85, 85, and 91. Which of the following statements is true?
   a. the average is 79.0
   b. the median is 79.0
   c. the mode is 97.0
   d. none of the above
   e. all of the above

2. 2. Suppose you take a random sample of students from a statistics class and their grades on the final exam are 63, 75, 77, 77, 81, 85, 85, and 91. Which of the following statements is true?
   a. the data is symmetric
   b. the 25th percentile is 77
   c. the interquartile range (IQR) is 9
   d. a grade of 63 is considered an outlier
   e. all of the above

3. Suppose you take a random sample of students from a statistics class and their grades on the final exam are 63, 75, 77, 77, 81, 85, 85, and 91. What is the standard deviation?
   a. 8.45
   b. 7.90
   c. 71.36
   d. 62.44
   e. none of the above

4. Which of the following descriptive measures is influenced by extreme values?
   a. mean
   b. range
   c. standard deviation
   d. all of the above
   e. only a and c

5. Which of the following can be used for investigating skewness?
   a. histogram
   b. box plot
   c. descriptive statistics
   d. all of the above
   e. none of the above

6. The default statistics when using the MEANS procedure include the following:
   a. mean, median, mode, standard deviation, and range
   b. sample size, mean, standard deviation, minimum and maximum values
   c. sample size, mean, median, mode, and range
   d. mean, median, standard deviation, minimum and maximum values

Chapter 2: Summarizing Your Data with Descriptive Statistics **51**

7. Which PROC MEANS generates the following output:

The MEANS Procedure

		Analysis Variable : Ketones					
CONTROLLED_DIABETIC	N Obs	Mean	Std Dev	Maximum	Minimum	Median	N Miss
NO	136	15.51	10.94	61.64	0.01	14.07	0
YES	64	5.96	9.74	35.36	0.00	0.24	0

a. proc means data=patient
mean std max min median nmiss maxdec=2;
var ketones;
class controlled_diabetic;
run;

b. proc means data=patient
mean std max min median nmiss maxdec=2;
var ketones;
by controlled_diabetic;
run;

c. proc means data=patient
var ketones;
class controlled_diabetic;
run;

d. proc means data=patient
stat=mean std max min median nmiss maxdec=2;
var ketones;
class controlled_diabetic;
run;

8. Which PROC MEANS generates the following output:

Analysis Variable : Glucose									
CONTROLLED_DIABETIC	RENAL_DISEASE	GENDER	N Obs	Mean	Std Dev	Maximum	Minimum	Median	N Miss
No	No	F	52	210.33	82.25	448.89	34.19	198.00	0
		M	66	171.21	78.31	357.44	9.45	154.96	0
	Yes	F	9	184.29	98.80	410.91	109.15	144.18	0
		M	9	187.70	105.50	404.96	70.39	142.07	0
Yes	No	F	30	104.80	85.26	329.78	0.87	95.26	0
		M	32	143.55	101.56	375.49	13.64	148.53	0
	Yes	M	2	204.17	78.75	259.85	148.48	204.17	0

a. proc means data=patient
   mean std max min median nmiss maxdec=2;
   var glucose;
   class controlled_diabetic*renal_disease*gender;
   run;

b. proc means data=patient
   mean std max min median nmiss maxdec=2;
   var glucose;
   class controlled_diabetic renal_disease gender;
   type 3;
   run;

 c. proc means data=patient
   mean std max min median nmiss maxdec=2;
   var glucose;
   class controlled_diabetic renal_disease gender;
   run;

d. All of the above

9. How many sets of means are generated from the following PROC MEANS?
```
proc means data=patient
  mean std max min median nmiss maxdec=2;
  var ketones;
  class controlled_diabetic renal_disease gender;
  ways 1 2 3;
run;
```

a. 3
b. 6
 c. 7
d. 8

10. What is the value of _TYPE_ for the main effects of RENAL_DISEASE when printing the KETONESUMMARY data set?
```
proc means data=patient noprint;
  var ketones;
  class controlled_diabetic renal_ disease;
  output out=sasba.ketonesummary
  mean=average_ketone std=std_ketone min=min_ketone
    max=max_ketone;
proc print data=sasba.ketonesummary;
run;
```

a. 8
b. 7
c. 3
 d. 1

Chapter 3: Data Visualization

Introduction

Have you ever wondered where the term 'bit' originated? Very few know that the term, along with many other statistical terms, was first conceived in the late 1940s by the renowned statistician, John W. Tukey, while at Bell Labs developing many of the statistical methods we apply today. For many statisticians, Tukey (1977) is best known for his seminal introduction of Exploratory Data Analysis (EDA). Exploratory data analysis is a philosophy that emphasizes the use of tools for summarizing data through both numeric and visual representations. In his 1977 book, Tukey emphasized that exploring your data is just as important as confirming your hypotheses and that, 'The greatest value of a picture is when it forces us to notice what we never expected to see.' In fact, Church (1979), in his review of Tukey's book, quite eloquently reiterates that 'it is necessary to discover facts before they can be confirmed.'

In this era of Big Data, where data sources comprise millions of rows and hundreds - or even thousands - of columns, it is impossible to visualize or make any summary statements about the data. Therefore, the data analyst must employ exploratory data analyses as a way of reducing mounds of data into manageable numeric summaries and pictures which are much more easily interpreted. Tukey's emphasis was on the visual aspects of data summaries, topics which are the center of discussion in this chapter.

Remember, defining the variable type must precede all data analyses. There are two types of variables and each variable type warrants a specific path for analysis. Recall that a categorical variable is one which has outcomes in the form of a name or a label and helps to distinguish between various characteristics in the data, for example, gender or academic classification. A numeric variable measures a quantity and can be either discrete or continuous. A discrete numeric variable is one which takes on a finite, countable number of values. An example would be the number of smart devices a person owns having outcomes of, say, 1, 2, 3, 4, or 5. A numeric continuous variable is one which has an uncountable number of outcomes and is usually in the form of a decimal. An example would be the amount of money spent on online purchases.

So, if the variable to be analyzed is categorical, the analyst will summarize the data by way of a summary table, crosstab, bar chart, pie chart, all accompanied by descriptive statistics such as frequency counts and proportions. If the variable is a numeric, the analyst will create summaries by way of a frequency table, histogram (sometimes bar charts), box-and-whisker plot, and Q-Q plots, accompanied by the mean, median, mode, range, variance, standard deviation, and skewness, to name a few. Also, there are methods to display relationships between two variables, whether the relationship is between two categorical variables, a numeric variable and a categorical variable, or two numeric variables; in particular, the relationship between two numeric variables can be displayed using a bivariate scatter plot.

In this chapter, you will learn about:

- the procedures used to visualize numeric continuous and categorical data

- the FREQ procedure and the TABLES statement and how to produce and interpret frequency tables and crosstabulation tables

- the use of the crosstabulations to explain the association between two categorical variables

- the PLOTS option within the TABLES statement for producing bar charts

- the MISSING option within the TABLES statement for detecting the number of missing observations

- the UNIVARIATE procedure and how to produce descriptive statistics for numeric variables

- the HISTOGRAM statement within the UNIVARIATE procedure and how to define the class limits of a histogram, the scale of the vertical axis, overlay the histogram with a normal curve

- the QQPLOT statement within the UNIVARIATE procedure for producing Q-Q plots for exploring normality

- the PLOTS option of the UNIVARIATE procedure for producing a box plot, and how to calculate and interpret the five-number summary

- the criteria for detecting outliers and how to identify outliers using the box plot

- the CLASS statement within the UNIVARIATE procedure for exploring the differences on a numeric variable across groups

- exploring bivariate relationships between numeric continuous variables using the SCATTER and REG statements within the SGPLOT procedure

- fitting regression line and quadratic (curve) using the DEGREE option within the REG statement

- the DATALABEL option within the SCATTER statement to label points by group

- the GROUP= option within the REG statement to fit a separate line for each group

- the VBAR statement, along with various options, within the SGPLOT procedure for producing vertical bar charts for categorical data

View and Interpret Categorical Data

When analyzing a variable, consider that the variable values are found in a single column within the data set where each row corresponds to an observation. Unless the sample size is very small, it is virtually impossible for the analyst to peruse the data and get a sense of the data without summarizing or condensing that variable into a form more easily interpreted. The problem is compounded when looking at relationships across two or more categorical variables. In this section, we will cover approaches for summarizing categorical data and, later, representing it visually in order to describe the sample or population of interest.

Frequency and Crosstabulation Tables Using the FREQ Procedure

Recall that categorical variables are those variables where the values are used to determine group membership, including those measured at the nominal or ordinal level. A natural question to ask is: 'How many observations make up each of the unique groups?' Or the analyst may want to know: 'What unique groups exist in my data when looking at a variable of interest?' and 'Which group is largest?' Those questions are aimed at analyzing a single categorical variable and can be summarized using a **Frequency Table**, or **Frequency Distribution**. The analyst can also ask questions dealing with bivariate relationships between two categorical variables by representing the frequencies in a **Crosstabulation Table**; in particular, the analyst may wonder if an observation's membership in one group on one variable is associated with being in a particular group on a second variable. For example, the analyst may wonder if more females (one group of gender) have controlled diabetes (one group of a variable representing diabetes status) as opposed to having uncontrolled diabetes when compared to males. In order to answer these types of univariate and bivariate questions, the analyst can employ the FREQ procedure.

Procedure Syntax for PROC FREQ

PROC FREQ is a procedure used to create one-way and n-way tabular summaries and has the general form:

PROC FREQ DATA=*SAS-data-set*;
TABLES *variable(s) </options>*;
RUN;

To illustrate the FREQ procedure, consider the Diabetic Care Management Case introduced in Chapter 1, "Statistics and Making Sense of Our World." Note, in the excerpt of data shown in Figure 3.1 Diabetic Care Management Case Data that the categorical variable, GENDER, has 200 rows with outcomes defined as *M* or *F*, representing *Males* and *Females*, respectively. Even with two possible outcomes, it is impossible to get a sense of the gender breakdown for this sample under investigation. This is especially true for the original data set consisting of all 63,108 observations. In short, here we want to reduce the 200 rows to just a few rows for purposes of interpretation.

Figure 3.1 Diabetic Care Management Case Data

Obs	Patient_ID	GENDER	AGE	WEIGHT	BMI	Hemoglobin_A1c	CONTROLLED_DIABETIC
1	1390961026	M	67	70.42	28.28	11.03	0
2	8908127888	F	66	55.21	23.74	7.76	0
3	25897154892	F	82	53.07	23.49	10.56	0
4	12999229817	M	66	82.75	36.46	11.58	0
5	3330961567	F	76	68.70	31.67	9.56	0
...	...	...	...	...	...	...	...
196	20286015512	M	74	60.04	22.97	6.74	1
197	23386238487	M	73	74.04	31.66	0.91	1
198	2950079397	F	79	54.16	23.40	6.52	1
199	15845973157	F	74	60.82	27.79	3.57	1
200	14837662381	F	70	66.31	31.01	1.03	1

In essence, when the FREQ procedure is run, SAS identifies each unique outcome, M and F, counts the number of times each of those outcomes occurs in the data set, and provides the summary in a tabular format. To generate the frequency table for GENDER, the analyst would use Program 3.1 Frequency Tables of GENDER, AGE_RANGE, and CONTROLLED_DIABETIC.

Program 3.1 Frequency Tables of GENDER, AGE_RANGE, and CONTROLLED_DIABETIC

```
libname sasba 'c:\sasba\hc';
data patient;
   set sasba.diab200;
   run;

proc freq data=patient;
tables gender age_range controlled_diabetic;
run;
```

First, you can see from the program that the permanent data set, DIAB200, is placed into the temporary data set, PATIENT, and PROC FREQ is applied to the data set, PATIENT. The TABLES statement requests a one-way frequency table for each of the variables listed, namely, GENDER, AGE_RANGE and CONTROLLED_DIABETIC, respectively, as displayed in Output 3.1 Frequency Tables of GENDER, AGE_RANGE, and CONTROLLED_DIABETIC. Notice that PROC FREQ has reduced a data matrix with 200 rows to a frequency table with 2 rows representing the numbers of males and females, respectively. This allows for extreme ease in interpretation.

In particular, you can see that of the 200 patients in the data set, 91 (45.50%) are females (F), and 109 (54.50%) are males (M); specifically, there are approximately 9% more males than females. You can also see that those patients with controlled diabetes make up 32.00% of the data, or 64 patients, as compared to 68.00% accounting for those with uncontrolled diabetes; basically, the group with uncontrolled diabetes is approximately twice as large as that with controlled diabetes.

The FREQ procedure also provides cumulative information. Specifically, note that 38 patients are listed in the row '65-70' meaning that 38 patients are in that category and all previous categories; in other words, 38 patients are 70 years of age or younger, 94 patients are 75 years of age or younger, 129 patients are 80 years of age or younger, etc. Similar cumulative information is provided for percent; using this information, you can conclude, for example, that almost half, 47%, of the patients are 75 years of age or younger; or very few (16%) patients are older than 85 years of age.

Output 3.1 Frequency Tables of GENDER, AGE_RANGE, and CONTROLLED_DIABETIC

The FREQ Procedure

GENDER	Frequency	Percent	Cumulative Frequency	Cumulative Percent
F	91	45.50	91	45.50
M	109	54.50	200	100.00

AGE_RANGE	Frequency	Percent	Cumulative Frequency	Cumulative Percent
64 and under	5	2.50	5	2.50
65-70	33	16.50	38	19.00
71-75	56	28.00	94	47.00
76-80	35	17.50	129	64.50
81-85	39	19.50	168	84.00
86-90	21	10.50	189	94.50
over 90	11	5.50	200	100.00

CONTROLLED_DIABETIC	Frequency	Percent	Cumulative Frequency	Cumulative Percent
0	136	68.00	136	68.00
1	64	32.00	200	100.00

PLOTS Options within the TABLES Statement

There are various options that can be used within the TABLES statement for tailoring the output of the FREQ procedure. One option, in particular, is the PLOTS option which provides a visual representation of the frequency table. For one-way frequency tables when summarizing a single variable alone, there are only three possible requests, one of which--FREQPLOT--will be illustrated here. For example, if the analyst would like an accompanying **bar chart** for visualizing GENDER, the PLOTS option with the FREQPLOT request would be applied as in Program 3.2 Frequency Table and Bar Chart of GENDER.

Program 3.2 Frequency Table and Bar Chart of GENDER

```
libname sasba 'c:\sasba\hc';
data patient;
    set sasba.diab200;
run;

proc freq data=patient;
tables gender
    /plots=freqplot(scale=percent);
    title 'Exploration of Gender for Diabetic Care Management Study';
run;
```

Output 3.2 Frequency Table and Bar Chart of GENDER now includes a bar chart where the heights of the bars represent the percentages for each of the respective groups, as requested by the PLOT option (SCALE=PERCENT). The picture of the data, in terms of GENDER, easily illustrates the idea that, while there are more males in the data set than females, the group sizes are not widely disparate. Note that if the analyst prefers the Y-axis to represent the actual frequencies, then the (SCALE=FREQ) option would be used instead. Finally, note that the bars representing the categories do not touch indicating that the values on the X-axis are distinct, non-overlapping groups having no scale; this representation is always warranted when summarizing categorical variables.

Output 3.2 Frequency Table and Bar Chart of GENDER

Exploration of Gender for Diabetic Care Management Study

The FREQ Procedure

GENDER	Frequency	Percent	Cumulative Frequency	Cumulative Percent
F	91	45.50	91	45.50
M	109	54.50	200	100.00

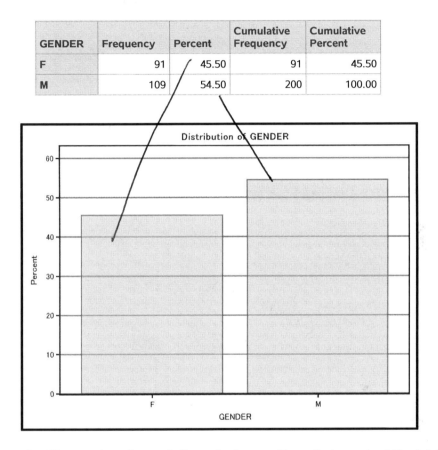

Crosstabulations for Illustrating Associations between Two Categorical Variables

Now let us consider an investigation into whether or not there is an association between two categorical variables. Consider, first, the two variables, GENDER and CONTROLLED_DIABETIC, and Program 3.3 Crosstabulation of Gender by Diabetes Status used to generate crosstabulations.

Program 3.3 Crosstabulation of Gender by Diabetes Status

```
libname sasba 'c:\sasba\hc';
data patient;
    set sasba.diab200;
run;

proc format;
    value yesno 0=No 1=Yes;
    value  $gender "M"="Males" "F" ="Females";
run;

proc freq data=patient;
    tables gender*controlled_diabetic
    /plots=freqplot(scale=percent);
    format controlled_diabetic yesno. gender $gender.;
    title 'Exploration of Gender by Diabetes Status';
run;
```

In the code provided above, the FREQ procedure is identical to the code used to generate three separate one-way tables in Output 3.1 Frequency Tables of GENDER, AGE_RANGE, and CONTROLLED_DIABETIC--with one exception.

Note that the two categorical variables, GENDER and CONTROLLED_DIABETIC, are now joined by an asterisk (*). This notation is used to generate a two-way table, or crosstabulation, as seen in Output 3.3a Crosstabulation of Gender by Diabetes Status.

Of course, we have enhanced the SAS output by including a FORMAT procedure with a FORMAT statement to define how the values of the GENDER and CONTROLLED_DIABETIC are printed. In Output 3.3a Crosstabulation of Gender by Diabetes Status, for example, notice that gender is now displayed as 'Males' or 'Females' as opposed to using the letters, M or F, respectively; and diabetes status is now displayed as either 'YES' or 'NO' as opposed to 1 or 0, respectively. In addition, the TITLE statement has been added to identify the context of the output.

Output 3.3a Crosstabulation of Gender by Diabetes Status

Exploration of Gender by Diabetes Status

The FREQ Procedure

Table of GENDER by CONTROLLED_DIABETIC			
GENDER	**CONTROLLED_DIABETIC**		
Frequency Percent Row Pct Col Pct	**No**	**Yes**	**Total**
Females	61 30.50 67.03 44.85	30 15.00 32.97 46.88	91 45.50
Males	75 37.50 68.81 55.15	34 17.00 31.19 53.13	109 54.50
Total	136 68.00	64 32.00	200 100.00

Let's consider the entries in each cell of the table, namely, **frequency**, **percent**, **row percent**, and **column percent**, respectively, as indicated in the top left corner of the crosstabulation.

1. The top numbers in each cell represent the **frequency** of observations in that particular cell as defined by the intersection of the row and column. For example, there are 61 females with uncontrolled diabetes and 30 females with controlled diabetes, for a row total of 91 females in the data; there are 75 males with uncontrolled diabetes and 34 males with controlled diabetes, for a row total of 109 males. You can also add the frequencies of females and males in each column to get the column totals of 136 with uncontrolled diabetes versus 64 with controlled diabetes. Notice that the column totals add up to 200, as do the row totals.

2. The **percent** for each of the four cells, 30.50, 15.00, 37.50, and 17.00, accounts for 100 percent of the data. Specifically note that, of all 200 patients, 30.50% (or 61 patients) are females with uncontrolled diabetes. Notice that the row percents, 30.50 and 15.00, add up to 45.50 percent of the data representing females; the row percents, 37.50 and 17.00, add up to 54.50 percent of the data representing males. The same operation can be done to get the column percents.

3. Consider now the **row percent**, blocked off in Output 3.3a Crosstabulation of Gender by Diabetes Status. When looking at females, 67.03 percent of the data consists of patients with uncontrolled diabetes and 32.97 percent of the data consists of patients with controlled diabetes. These row percents are also known as **conditional percents**; in other words, these are percents given, or conditioned on the fact, that we are looking only at females. The breakdown of the conditional percents is very similar for males, where 68.81 percent of males consist of patients with uncontrolled diabetes and 31.19 percent of the data consists of males with controlled diabetes. Overall, 68.00 percent of the data consists of patients with uncontrolled diabetes and 32.00 percent of the data consists of those with controlled diabetes, for a total of 100 percent.

4. An inspection of **column percent** shows that, when looking at those with uncontrolled diabetes, 44.85 percent are females and 55.15 percent are males; while for those with controlled diabetes, 46.88 percent are females and

53.13 percent are males. Those are fairly consistent with the row percents which show that, overall, females make up 45.50 percent of the data, while males make up 54.50 percent of the data. Column percents are also referred to as conditional percents; in other words, these are percents of females and males, respectively, conditioned on selecting either patients with or without controlled diabetes.

Now that we understand the information provided by the FREQ procedure, how do we use this information to describe the **association**, or the relationship, between the two categorical variables, GENDER and CONTROLLED_DIABETIC? First, let's consider this fact: two categorical variables have **no association** with each other if the row percents are similar across all rows, in other words, if the distribution of diabetic status is the same across both genders. When looking at Output 3.3 Crosstabulation of Gender by Diabetes Status, we can see that the row percents blocked off for both males and females are similar; therefore, we can say that the two variables GENDER and CONTROLLED_DIABETIC status are not associated with each other. As a result, we can say, in general, that the percentage of controlled versus uncontrolled is the same for regardless of gender and can, therefore, describe the CONTROLLED_DIABETIC status while ignoring gender. In short, we can use the total percents of each column, blocked off as well, to describe the diabetes status and that statements about diabetes status would apply to any gender.

Practically speaking, this seems to indicate that when trying to identify a patient's diabetic status, gender would not be helpful. Notice also that this conclusion is further illustrated through visualization, as shown in Output 3.3b Crosstabulation of Gender by Diabetes Status: Frequency Pots of Gender by Diabetes Status, where the shape of the bars for females is *similar* to the shape of the bars for males, indicating that the trend in diabetes status is the same regardless of gender.

Output 3.3b Crosstabulation of Gender by Diabetes Status: Frequency Pots of Gender by Diabetes Status

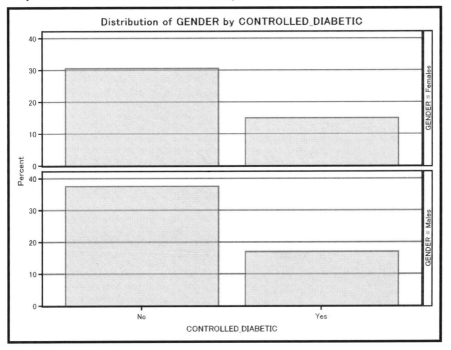

Let's now consider, for the same data, the possible relationship between diabetes status and renal disease. Program 3.4 Cross Tabs and Frequency Plots of Diabetes Status and Renal Disease is used to generate the crosstabulations found in Output 3.4 Cross Tabs and Frequency Plots of Diabetes Status and Renal Disease.

Program 3.4 Cross Tabs and Frequency Plots of Diabetes Status and Renal Disease

```
libname sasba 'c:\sasba\hc';
data patient;
   set sasba.diab200;
run;


proc format;
    value yesno 0=No 1=Yes;
run;
```

```
proc freq; tables controlled_diabetic*renal_disease
  /plots=freqplot(scale=percent);
format controlled_diabetic yesno. renal_disease yesno.;
title 'Exploration of Diabetes Status and Renal Disease';
run;
```

We can see that overall, 90 percent of patients do not have renal disease compared to 10 percent who do. However, notice that there is a shift when we take into account a second variable, a patient's diabetes status, as indicated by the row percents. Specifically, we see that for those patients whose diabetes is not controlled, 13.24 percent have renal disease. For those patients whose diabetes is controlled, 3.13 percent have renal disease – less than a quarter of those with uncontrolled diabetes. The row percents for RENAL_DISEASE are not the same across the two levels of CONTROLLED_DIABETIC, therefore indicating an association between RENAL_DISEASE and CONTROLLED_DIABETIC.

As a result, the analyst cannot use the percents, for renal disease (90 percent do not have renal disease versus 10 percent have renal disease), ignoring diabetes status, to describe the nature of the data. The analyst must take into account whether or not the patient has controlled his or her diabetes. In other words, a patient's renal disease status is associated with diabetes status. In particular, if your diabetes is controlled, you have a 3.13 percent chance of having renal disease; on the other hand, if your diabetes is not controlled, you have a 13.24 percent chance of having renal disease. (Note: In Chapter 5, "Analysis of Categorical Variables," we will discuss using sample data to test associations between two categorical variables in the population.)

Output 3.4 Cross Tabs and Frequency Plots of Diabetes Status and Renal Disease

Exploration of Diabetes Status and Renal Disease

The FREQ Procedure

Table of CONTROLLED_DIABETIC by RENAL_DISEASE			
CONTROLLED_DIABETIC	RENAL_DISEASE		
Frequency Percent Row Pct Col Pct	No	Yes	Total
No	118 59.00 86.76 65.56	18 9.00 13.24 90.00	136 68.00
Yes	62 31.00 96.88 34.44	2 1.00 3.13 10.00	64 32.00
Total	180 90.00	20 10.00	200 100.00

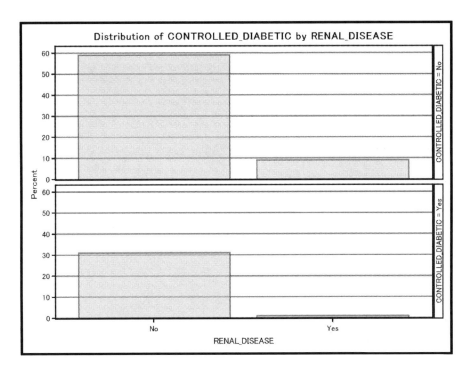

MISSING Option within the TABLES Statement

If an observation is missing a value on any variable that is included in the TABLES statement, that observation is excluded from the table analysis. This can be misleading, so the analyst may want to include all observations in the analysis by using the MISSING option in the TABLES statement.

Consider the population of patients in Diabetic Care Management Case. Suppose we are interested in seeing the relationships between two categorical variables, namely CONTROLLED_DIABETIC (diabetes status) and PRIMARY_MED (primary medication). Program 3.5 Crosstabulation of Diabetes Status and Primary Medication with Missing Obs Excluded produces the output found in Output 3.5 Crosstabulation of Diabetes Status and Primary Medication with Missing Obs Excluded.

Program 3.5 Crosstabulation of Diabetes Status and Primary Medication with Missing Obs Excluded

```
libname sasba 'c:\sasba\hc';
data patient;
   set sasba.diabetics;
run;

proc format;
     value yesno 0=No 1=Yes;
run;

proc freq; tables controlled_diabetic*primary_med;
   format controlled_diabetic yesno.;
   title 'Exploration of Diabetes Type and Medicine';
run;
```

Notice that 20,592 (32.6%) of 63,108 diabetic patients have missing values on either variables CONTROLLED_DIABETIC, PRIMARY_MED, or both. Also all percentages are based upon a data set size of 42,516, so that distribution of the bivariate responses is not representative of the entire population.

Output 3.5 Crosstabulation of Diabetes Status and Primary Medication with Missing Obs Excluded

Exploration of Diabetes Type and Medicine

The FREQ Procedure

Table of CONTROLLED_DIABETIC by PRIMARY_MED						
CONTROLLED_DIABETIC	**PRIMARY_MED**					
Frequency Percent Row Pct Col Pct	**AG Inhibitor**	**Amylin Mimetic**	**Biguanide**	**DPP-4 Inhibitor**	**Incretin Mimetic**	**Meglitinide**
No	6048 14.23 16.68 85.65	117 0.28 0.32 46.61	6202 14.59 17.10 86.16	5834 13.72 16.09 86.14	94 0.22 0.26 47.00	6079 14.30 16.76 85.62
Yes	1013 2.38 16.20 14.35	134 0.32 2.14 53.39	996 2.34 15.92 13.84	939 2.21 15.01 13.86	106 0.25 1.69 53.00	1021 2.40 16.32 14.38
Total	7061 16.61	251 0.59	7198 16.93	6773 15.93	200 0.47	7100 16.70
Frequency Missing = 20592						

Table of CONTROLLED_DIABETIC by PRIMARY_MED			
CONTROLLED_DIABETIC	**PRIMARY_MED**		
Frequency Percent Row Pct Col Pct	**Sulfonylurea**	**Thiazolidinedione**	**Total**
No	6210 14.61 17.13 85.54	5677 13.35 15.66 85.07	36261 85.29
Yes	1050 2.47 16.79 14.46	996 2.34 15.92 14.93	6255 14.71
Total	7260 17.08	6673 15.70	42516 100.00
Frequency Missing = 20592			

In order to include all observations, the analyst can include the MISSING option as follows:

Program 3.6 Crosstabulation of Diabetes Status and Primary Medication with Missing Obs Included

```
libname sasba 'c:\sasba\hc';
data patient;
   set sasba.diabetics;
run;

proc format;
   value yesno 0=No 1=Yes;
run;

proc freq; tables controlled_diabetic*primary_med/missing;
   format controlled_diabetic yesno.;
   title 'Exploration of Diabetes Type and Medicine';
run;
```

Notice, in Output 3.6 Crosstabulation of Diabetes Status and Primary Medication with Missing Obs Included, that all 63,108 observations are included in the table analysis. In fact, including the missing observations gives the analyst additional information. For example, you can see that all observations with missing values (20,592) are missing only values on the primary medication. Furthermore, you can see that of those missing values on PRIMARY_MED, 14,012 (68.05%) have their diabetes controlled, whereas 6580 (31.95%) do not as illustrated in Output 3.6 Crosstabulation of Diabetes Status and Primary Medication with Missing Obs Included. This is in contrast to those not missing on PRIMARY_MED, where 14.17% have their diabetes controlled and 85.29% do not. In addition, note that the values of the percents change now that all observations are included in the analysis.

Finally, for those whose diabetes is controlled, 69.14% have missing primary medications; however, for those whose diabetes is not controlled, only 15.36% have missing primary medications. Consequently, missingness on PRIMARY_MED is predictive of controlled diabetes.

Output 3.6 Crosstabulation of Diabetes Status and Primary Medication with Missing Obs Included

Exploration of Diabetes Type and Medicine

The FREQ Procedure

Table of CONTROLLED_DIABETIC by PRIMARY_MED							
CONTROLLED_DIABETIC	**PRIMARY_MED**						
Frequency Percent Row Pct Col Pct		**AG Inhibitor**	**Amylin Mimetic**	**Biguanide**	**DPP-4 Inhibitor**	**Incretin Mimetic**	**Meglitinide**
No	6580 10.43 15.36 31.95	6048 9.58 14.12 85.65	117 0.19 0.27 46.61	6202 9.83 14.48 86.16	5834 9.24 13.62 86.14	94 0.15 0.22 47.00	6079 9.63 14.19 85.62
Yes	14012 22.20 69.14 68.05	1013 1.61 5.00 14.35	134 0.21 0.66 53.39	996 1.58 4.91 13.84	939 1.49 4.63 13.86	106 0.17 0.52 53.00	1021 1.62 5.04 14.38
Total	20592 32.63	7061 11.19	251 0.40	7198 11.41	6773 10.73	200 0.32	7100 11.25

including the missing values provided more information (handwritten annotation)

Table of CONTROLLED_DIABETIC by PRIMARY_MED			
CONTROLLED_DIABETIC	**PRIMARY_MED**		
Frequency Percent Row Pct Col Pct	**Sulfonylurea**	**Thiazolidinedione**	**Total**
No	6210 9.84 14.50 85.54	5677 9.00 13.25 85.07	42841 67.89
Yes	1050 1.66 5.18 14.46	996 1.58 4.91 14.93	20267 32.11
Total	7260 11.50	6673 10.57	63108 100.00

View and Interpret Numeric Data

In the previous section, we discussed procedures for visualizing categorical data. We now turn our attention to continuous numeric data. Recall that numeric variables are those whose values represent quantities. When analyzing numeric data, the analyst will want a picture of the data in order to answer questions such as, 'Where are the observations clustered?' or 'What is the shape of the data--symmetric or skewed?' The analyst will also be interested in how wide the data is, do outliers--or errors--exist in the data, and may even want to compare these numeric variables across different groups. Here, we will discuss three kinds of plots commonly used to describe the distribution of numeric variables, namely, the histogram, normal probability plot, and box-and-whisker plot. These plots, along with the measures of center, variation, and shape, discussed in Chapter 2, "Summarizing Your Data with Descriptive Statistics" allow for a broader understanding of the data.

Histograms Using the UNIVARIATE Procedure

A **histogram** is a graphical display of numeric data where the x-axis represents the values of the numeric variable and the y-axis represents the frequencies or proportion of observations within the various classes along the X-axis, as illustrated in Figure 3.2 Histogram for Numeric Data.

Figure 3.2 Histogram for Numeric Data

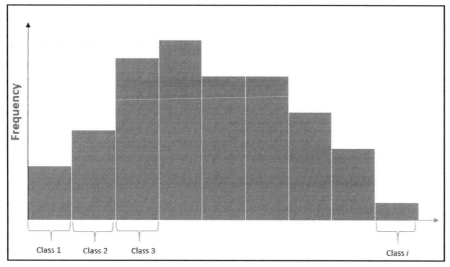

Note that each **class** is made up of a range of values, all having the same width. Furthermore, the bars of a histogram must touch; in other words, where one class ends, the next must begin. This criterion takes into account the continuous nature of numeric data where all values along the x-axis are possible. This is certainly to be distinguished from the fact that the bars of a bar chart do not touch, where the values of categorical variables are distinct, having no overlap nor ordering. In order to generate the histogram and other visual displays, the analyst can employ the UNIVARIATE procedure.

Procedure Syntax for PROC UNIVARIATE

PROC UNIVARIATE is a procedure used to create histograms, normal probability plots, and box-and-whisker plots and has the general form:

PROC UNIVARIATE DATA=*SAS-data-set* <*options*>;
CLASS *variable-1 variable-2*;
VAR *variable(s)*;
HISTOGRAM *variable(s)* <*/options*>;
QQPLOT *variable(s)* <*/options*>;
INSET *keyword(s)* <*/options*>;
RUN;

To illustrate the UNIVARIATE procedure, let's revisit the Diabetic Care Management Case and consider the numeric continuous variable BMI, the Body Mass Index. The BMI is calculated by taking a person's weight (in kilograms) and dividing by his or her height squared (meters^2); the BMI is used for purposes of grouping a person into weight categories associated with certain health risks. Before illustrating the visual displays, let's start with the most basic output, consisting of only descriptive statistics for BMI, using Program 3.7 Univariate Statistics on BMI for 200 Diabetic Patients.

Program 3.7 Univariate Statistics on BMI for 200 Diabetic Patients

```
libname sasba 'c:\sasba\hc';
data patient;
   set sasba.diab200;
run;

proc univariate data=patient;
   var bmi;
run;
```

As seen previously, the permanent data set, DIAB200, is placed into the temporary data set, PATIENT, and PROC UNIVARIATE is applied to the data set, PATIENT. The VAR statement requests that univariate statistics are provided for the variable BMI. If the VAR statement is omitted, SAS will conduct univariate procedures on all numeric variables in the data set.

The UNIVARIATE procedure produces five tables of summary information, as seen in Output 3.7 Univariate Statistics on BMI for 200 Diabetic Patients, four of which are for descriptive purposes and will be discussed here. Each of the tables provides for the following:

1. The first three tables provide various descriptive summaries described in Chapter 2, "Summarizing Your Data with Descriptive Statistics." Specifically, those tables include measures of center (mean, median, and mode), dispersion (range, variance, and standard deviation), and shape (skewness and kurtosis). The interquartile range represents the range of the middle 50 percent of the data.

2. The fourth table tests for location, provides for inferential tests, and will be discussed in Chapter 4, "The Normal Distribution and Introduction to Inferential Statistics."

3. The fifth table, referred to as Quantiles (Definition 5), lists the numeric values that represent the location along the x-axis (minimum, maximum, percentile, and quartiles). It should be noted that the **interquartile range** is the difference between Q_1 and Q_3. For example, the 75th percentile (Q_3) is 32.7516, indicating that 75%, or three-quarters, of the patients have BMI less than 32.7516.

4. The last table provides a list of the extreme values, specifically, the five smallest values and the five largest values. The default number of high and low values provided is five and can be changed to *n* by adding the NEXTROBS= option to the procedure as follows:

```
proc univariate data=patient nextrobs=n;
```

Note that a more in depth description of this output will be provided after more coverage of the UNIVARIATE procedure.

Output 3.7 Univariate Statistics on BMI for 200 Diabetic Patients

Moments			
N	200	Sum Weights	200
Mean	30.072601	Sum Observations	6014.5202
Std Deviation	5.60985177	Variance	31.4704368
Skewness	1.0693403	Kurtosis	1.9520074
Uncorrected SS	187134.883	Corrected SS	6262.61693
Coeff Variation	18.6543617	Std Error Mean	0.39667642

Basic Statistical Measures			
Location		Variability	
Mean	30.07260	Std Deviation	5.60985
Median	29.46455	Variance	31.47044
Mode	.	Range	32.45714
		Interquartile Range	7.17870

Tests for Location: Mu0=0				
Test		Statistic	p Value	
Student's t	t	75.81142	Pr > |t|	<.0001
Sign	M	100	Pr >= |M|	<.0001
Signed Rank	S	10050	Pr >= |S|	<.0001

Quantiles (Definition 5)	
Level	Quantile
100% Max	52.4590
99%	49.1948
95%	38.8705
90%	37.2570
75% Q3	32.7516
50% Median	29.4646
25% Q1	25.5729
10%	23.7092
5%	22.7304
1%	20.8097
0% Min	20.0018

Extreme Observations			
Lowest		Highest	
Value	Obs	Value	Obs
20.0018	189	46.5296	17
20.7570	116	46.5842	135
20.8624	131	47.2062	32
21.4191	92	51.1834	188

Extreme Observations			
Lowest		Highest	
Value	Obs	Value	Obs
21.7975	147	52.4590	83

Now let's elaborate on this output and provide the histogram for visualizing the summary measures just discussed. To do that, the analyst could simply add the HISTOGRAM statement. If the HISTOGRAM statement is used with no accompanying options, then SAS will decide how many classes the histogram should have and the width for the classes. As an analyst, you may prefer to use what you know about the data to customize the histogram. In order to do that consider the following steps:

1. Decide on the number of classes, or bars, in your histogram.
2. Determine the width of each class.
3. Define the lower-class limits and upper-class limits for each bar.
4. Define the midpoint as the average of the lower-class and upper-class limits.

Solution:

Step 1: Let's say, for example, the analyst wants to first consider using 10 classes.

Step 2: To determine the width of each class, consider that you are taking the x-axis, starting at the minimum BMI of 20.0018 and ending at the maximum of 52.4590, and cutting it into ten equal parts, using the formula:

$$Width = \frac{Range}{Number\ of\ Classes} = \frac{52.4590 - 20.0018}{10} = 3.25$$

While the calculated width is 3.25 BMI units, you should always select a width that simplifies the interpretation. As a result, let's round up to a width of 5.0.

Step 3: When constructing the limits for the first class, the analyst must consider that the class must contain the first observation which is the minimum value of 20.0018. So while the analyst may be justified in using 20.0018 as the lower-class limit, for ease of interpretation, he or she may prefer to start the class at a value of 20.0 instead. Because the width is 5, the upper-class limit of the first class would be a BMI of 25, excluding 25. The next class would start at 25, including 25, and then end at 30, excluding 30, and so on. As a result, the classes would be defined as seen in Table 3.1 Summary Data for the Variable BMI.

Step 4: To calculate the midpoints of each class, simply take the average of the lower-class and upper-class limits of the associated class. Note that the values of the midpoints will be used to tailor the SAS output.

Table 3.1 Summary Data for the Variable BMI

BMI Class	BMI Midpoint ▼	Frequency	Percent	Cumulative Frequency	Cumulative Percent
20 up to 25	22.5	35	17.5	35	17.5
25 up to 30	27.5	71	35.5	106	53.0
30 up to 35	32.5	60	30.0	166	83.0
35 up to 40	37.5	26	13.0	192	96.0
40 up to 45	42.5	3	1.5	195	97.5
45 up to 50	47.5	3	1.5	198	99.0
50 up to 55	52.5	2	1.0	200	100.0

In order to generate the histogram, the analyst would add the HISTOGRAM statement with the MIDPOINTS option. The default scale for the Y-axis is percent, so in order to change the scale to counts, the VSCALE= option was included. Finally, the analyst would include the NORMAL option so that the normal curve having the mean and standard deviation as the original data would overlay the histogram, as seen in Program 3.8 Histogram of the Variable BMI.

Program 3.8 Histogram of the Variable BMI

```
libname sasba 'c:\sasba\hc';
data patient;
    set sasba.diab200;
run;

proc univariate data=patient;
    var bmi;
    histogram /midpoints = 22.5 to 52.5 by 5
                vscale=count
                normal kernel;
    run;
```

The histogram provided in Output 3.8 Histogram of the Variable BMI, along with the descriptive information from Figure 5.10, gives the analyst the information needed to describe Body-Mass-Index, BMI, for the 200 diabetic patients. In particular, we can say that:

1. BMI has a range of 32.5, with a minimum of 20.0 and a maximum of 52.5. The five smallest values range from 20.0 to 21.8 and the five largest values range from 46.5 to 52.5. The extreme values are represented in this histogram by both a long right tail and values bunched on the left side. Also note that the five largest BMI values are represented by the 3 rightmost bars, whereas the five smallest values are represented by the one leftmost bar.

2. With respect to measures of center, the mean BMI is 30.0, which is the typical value or the balance point of the histogram. The median BMI is 29.5 which is the midpoint; that tells us that half of the patients have BMI less than 29.5 and half of the patients have BMI more than 29.5. Because no BMI value appears more than once, there is no mode; however, you can tell from the histogram that the largest number of patients, 71, has BMI around 27.5, say, between 25 and 30, as indicated by the highest bar.

3. The BMI values are right, or positively, skewed (skewness = +1.07). This pattern is especially obvious by the long right tail. Four percent of the patients have BMI at or larger than 40. Eight-three percent of patients have BMI under 35. Note also that the histogram deviates from the normal curve, indicating that the data is not normal.

4. Sixty-five percent of the patients have BMI between 25 and 35 which is approximately one standard deviation from the mean.

Output 3.8 Histogram of the Variable BMI

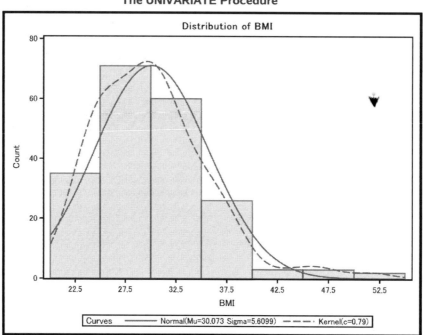

Some concluding remarks are in order. First, notice that we initially set the number of bars to ten but the number of bars produced was seven. This sometimes happens when rounding the width and/or selecting the lower-class limit of the first class so as to enhance the simplicity in interpretation. Suffice it to say that creating a histogram is just as much art as science and any two people will arrive at two different versions of the representation; however, the general conclusions should be the same. Keep in mind, however, that the analyst should use anywhere from, say, 5 to 20 classes; where a relative small number of classes is best for small data sets, and as the data set gets larger, the analyst should consider more classes. Furthermore, the KERNEL option requests a curve that fits more closely to the histogram, which supports the conclusion that the data is not normal.

Q-Q Plots Using the UNIVARIATE Procedure

When you are exploring your data, there are many tools available to investigate the nature of numeric data. One such tool is the **quantile-quantile plot**. The quantile-quantile plot, also referred to as the **Q-Q plot**, is a tool used by the analyst as a visual approach to inspecting whether or not a numeric variable originates from a theoretical distribution, for example, the normal distribution. The Q-Q plot is more effective and useful in certain circumstances than the histogram in that it is more sensitive to subtle deviations from normality.

The Q-Q plot is created from a set of n ordered pairs, (Z_i, X_i), where Z_i represents the expected Z-score for observation i under the assumption that the observation originates from a normal population, and X_i is the actual value of the variable for observation i.

To illustrate, let's consider a small data set consisting of eight teenagers and the number of texts each received in an hour, having ranks 1 through 7:

10   12   14   16   18   20   22

Simulation studies have shown that, for repeated random samples selected from normal populations, the ith observation in an ordered array has a standardized Z-score such that $i/(n+1)$ proportion of the area under the normal curve is below that Z-score. So, to get the expected Z-scores for each of the n observations, we would divide the standard normal distribution into $(n+1)$ equal parts, each with $1/(n+1)$ area under the curve.

For our example, with a sample size of 7, we would divide the standard normal distribution into 8 equal parts, each making up 1/8, 0.125, of the entire area. So, for example, using the cumulative Z-table found in Appendix C Z Table, you will find a Z-score of -1.15 associated with 0.125 area under the curve. In short, you would expect 7 observations randomly selected from a normal population to have the Z-scores, as illustrated in Table 3.2 Expected Z-Scores for Number of Texts,

Table 3.2 Expected Z-Scores for Number of Texts

X=Number of Texts	Observation Number	Cumulative Area Below the Z-Score	Z-Score
10	1	1/(7+1)=0.125	-1.15
12	2	2/(7+1)=0.250	-0.67
14	3	3/(7+1)=0.375	-0.32
16	4	4/(7+1)=0.500	0.00
18	5	5/(7+1)=0.625	0.32
20	6	6/(7+1)=0.750	0.67
22	7	7/(7+1)=0.875	1.15

The Z-scores paired with the original X values give the following Q-Q plot, as illustrated in Figure 3.3 Q-Q Plot for Number of Texts.

Figure 3.3 Q-Q Plot for Number of Texts

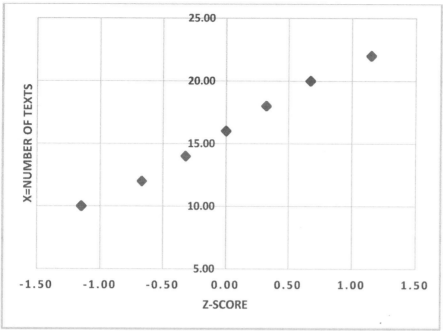

Interpreting the Q-Q Plots

In general, if the points on the Q-Q plot fall on or near a straight line, then the data under investigation is considered approximately normal. Specifically, if the data under investigation has a mean of 0 and a standard deviation of 1, then the points should fall on or near the straight line defined by $y = x$. If the data under investigation differs in its mean and standard deviation from the theoretical distribution, then the points should fall on or near the straight line defined by $y = mx + b$, where b is the estimated mean and m is the estimated standard deviation of the theoretical distribution. The interpretation of the Q-Q plots requires some judgment. So, the closer the points fall around a line, the stronger the evidence that the data is normally distributed.

In order to generate the Q-Q plot, the analyst can employ the UNIVARIATE procedure as in Program 3.9 Q-Q Plot for the Variable BMI.

Program 3.9 Q-Q Plot for the Variable BMI

```
libname sasba 'c:\sasba\hc';
data patient;
   set sasba.diab200;
run;

proc univariate data=patient;
   var bmi;
   histogram /midpoints = 22.5 to 52.5 by 5
              vscale=count;
   qqplot/normal (mu=est sigma=est);
run;
```

As stated previously, Program 3.9 Q-Q Plot for the Variable BMI provides descriptive statistics and the histogram. With the addition of the QQPLOT statement, the output now provides the Q-Q plot. The NORMAL option indicates that the theoretical distribution for comparing to the data is the normal distribution. Other theoretical distributions can be tested, including exponential, gamma, and Weibull, to name a few. The NORMAL options, MU= and SIGMA=, request a distribution reference line with the specified population mean and standard deviation, respectively, and EST requests that the sample mean and sample standard deviation be used as estimates of the population mean and standard deviation, respectively.

Output 3.9 Q-Q Plot for the Variable BMI

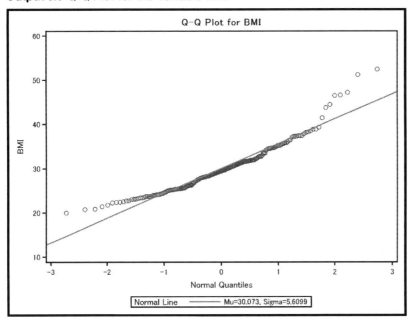

From the Q-Q plot provided in Output 3.9 Q-Q Plot for the Variable BMI, there is an indication that the data is right skewed. So how does the analyst interpret the Q-Q plot for describing the characteristics of the data? In general, the following rules of thumb can be used for interpretation purposes:

1. When the Q-Q plot is concave up, the data distribution is right skewed.
2. When the Q-Q plot is concave down, the data distribution is left skewed.
3. When the Q-Q plot has points below the line on the left side and above the line on the right side, the data distribution has long tails.
4. When the Q-Q plot has points above the line on the left side and below the line on the right side, the data distribution has short tails.
5. When a few points deviate from the line, there may be outliers.

Box-and-Whisker Plot Using the UNIVARIATE Procedure

The **box-and-whisker plot**, often referred to as the box plot, is a graphical way of representing various characteristics of the data, and is especially useful when comparing numeric variables across multiple groups. First introduced by John W. Tukey in the 1970s, the box plot is constructed using a **five-number summary**, consisting (in order) of the minimum, the quartiles (Q_1, Median, Q_3), and the maximum values of the data. These values aid in describing the shape of the distribution, the middle half of the data, and extreme values, including outliers.

Calculating Quartiles for Five-Number Summary

Before describing the box plot, let's discuss the calculation of the **quartiles**. To illustrate, let's consider the small data set consisting of eight teenagers and the number of texts each received in an hour, having ranks 1 through 7:

10   12   14   16   18   20   22

The quartiles split the data set into quarters. The first quartile is the value where 25% of the observations are at or below, the second quartile is the value where 50% of the observations are at or below and is equivalent to the median, and the third quartile is the value where 75% of the observations are at or below.

In order to determine the quartiles, the data set must be placed into an **ordered array** that ranks the observations from smallest to largest. For n observations in an ordered array, the positions of the first quartile (Q_1) and the third quartile (Q_3) are found using the following formula:

$$Position\ of\ Q_1 = \frac{(n+1)}{4} \qquad\qquad Position\ of\ Q_3 = \frac{3(n+1)}{4}$$

So for our sample data set, the position of Q_1 is calculated using:

$$Position\ of\ Q_1 = \frac{(n+1)}{4} = \frac{(7+1)}{4} = 2$$

Therefore, Q_1 is located in the second position of the ordered array, $Q_1 = 12$, meaning that one-quarter, or 25%, of the data is at or below 12 texts. The position of the Q_3 is calculated using:

$$Position\ of\ Q_3 = \frac{3(n+1)}{4} = \frac{3(7+1)}{4} = 6$$

Therefore, Q3 is located in the sixth position of the ordered array, Q3 = 20, meaning that three-quarters, or 75%, of the data is at or below 20 texts.

Notice that for our sample size of 7, the positions of the quartiles are integers, but this may not always be the case. If the position number is composed of a half, for example, 3.5, then the quartile is halfway between the third and the fourth observation and is the average of the numbers in the third and the fourth positions, respectively. If the position number is any other decimal value, round that position number to the nearest integer and select the data value in that corresponding position.

Now that we have the quartiles, we can identify the minimum and maximum values, along with the median to get the five-number summary (10, 12, 16, 20, 22). The box plot is constructed along the y-axis by placing a horizontal line at each point on the y-axis corresponding to the five numbers, connecting the quartiles to form the box, and then connecting the extreme values to the box to form the whiskers, as seen in Figure 3.4 Box Plot for Number of Texts.

Figure 3.4 Box Plot for Number of Texts

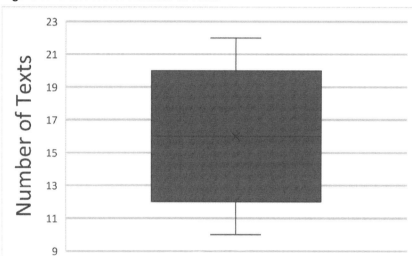

Notice that the box plot for our texts data is symmetric. The median cuts the box in half and the whiskers are the same length. In fact, for symmetric data, the mean and median are equal; in our example, the mean and median number of texts is 16. These facts are all an indication that our data is symmetric.

Interpreting the Box Plot

When you are inspecting the box plot, there are some general guidelines for determining the characteristics of the data:

1. The data is symmetric when the median cuts the box in half and the lengths of the whiskers are equal. As you may recall from Chapter 2, "Summarizing Your Data with Descriptive Statistics" when data is symmetric, the mean and median are equal.
2. The data is right skewed (positively skewed) if the median is below the center of the box and the upper whisker is longer than the lower whisker. Note that if the median is below the center of the box, there is a bunching of the data at the lower end of the y-axis and fewer observations at the upper end. Also keep in mind that when the upper whisker is longer, the upper 25% of the data has a larger range.
3. The data is left skewed (negatively skewed) if the median is above the center of the box and the lower whisker is longer than the upper whisker. Note that if the median is above the center of the box, there is a bunching of

the data at the upper end of the y-axis and fewer observations at the lower left end. Also keep in mind that when the lower whisker is longer, the lower 25% of the data has a larger range.

4. The **interquartile range (IQR)** is the range of the middle half of the data and is defined as Q_3-Q_1. If any observation is more than 1.5 x IQR from the box, that observation is considered an **outlier**. An outlier is designated by an asterisk (*) on the box plot.

In order to generate the box plot, the analyst can employ the UNIVARIATE procedure as follows:

Program 3.10 Distribution and Probability Plot for BMI

```
libname sasba 'c:\sasba\hc';
data patient;
   set sasba.diab200;
run;

proc univariate data=patient plots;
   var bmi;
   histogram / midpoints = 22.5 to 52.5 by 5
               vscale=count;
run;
```

Notice that the PLOTS option is added to the PROC UNIVARIATE statement and, as a result, the output provided in Output 3.10 Distribution and Probability Plot for BMI includes both the box plot and Q-Q plot. The QQPLOT statement was not included here so as to prevent duplication.

Output 3.10 Distribution and Probability Plot for BMI

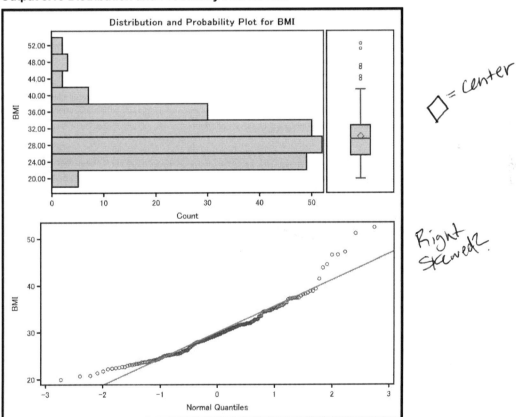

At first glance, we have three graphics supporting the notion that BMI values are right skewed, namely, the histogram, Q-Q plot, and the box plot. Consider now the box plot, created from the five-number summary, 20.00, 25.57, 29.46, 32.75, 52.46. Notice that the median cuts the box in half; however, the upper whisker is longer, indicating a right skewed distribution.

Note also the outliers at the upper end of the distribution as indicated by the circles in the box plot-- those are observations whose values are more than 1.5xIQR units from either of the quartiles, Q_1 or Q_3. Those limits are defined by:

$$\text{Upper Limit} = Q_3 + 1.5\text{IQR} = 32.75 + 1.5(7.18) = 43.52$$

$$\text{Lower Limit} = Q_1 - 1.5\text{IQR} = 25.57 - 1.5(7.18) = 14.8$$

In other words, any observations outside of BMI values 14.8 and 43.52 are outliers. There are no BMI values below 14.8. Therefore, there are no outliers on the lower end of the distribution. However, an inspection of the data values indicates that seven BMI values exceed 43.52, as shown by the outliers on the box plot. Notice also that the outliers (extremely large numbers) pull the mean to the right as indicated by the diamond to the right of the median. In short, the box plot is a very effective tool for detecting unusual observations.

UNIVARIATE Procedures Using the INSET Statement

As described in previous sections, the UNIVARIATE procedure provides the analyst with a wealth of information through visual plots and accompanying descriptive statistics which help to make sense of the plots. The INSET statement can be included so that the pertinent statistics are directly printed on the graph as illustrated in Program 3.11 Histogram with Descriptive Statistics of BMI.

Program 3.11 Histogram with Descriptive Statistics of BMI

```
libname sasba 'c:\sasba\hc';
data patient;
   set sasba.diab200;
run;

proc univariate data=patient plots;
   var bmi;
   histogram / midpoints = 22.5 to 52.5 by 5
               vscale=count
               normal;
   inset mean median q1 q3 std min max nobs nmiss skewness / pos = ne;
run;
```

Notice that the INSET statement has been added with various statistics keywords requesting that the mean, median, first quartile, third quartile, standard deviation, minimum, maximum, number of observations, number of missing observations, and skewness, to name a few. Notice also that the INSET statement has the POS= option which allows the analyst to define where the inset should be included in relation to the graph; in particular, NE requests that the statistics be included in the 'northeast' quadrant of the graph, as illustrated in Output 3.11 Histogram with Descriptive Statistics of BMI. In short, many of the conclusions we made previously about BMI from many pages of output can be reduced to one plot.

Output 3.11 Histogram with Descriptive Statistics of BMI

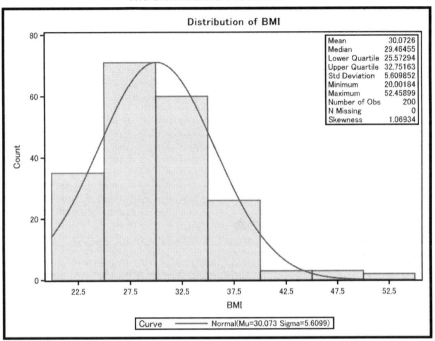

UNIVARIATE Procedures Using the CLASS Statement

In many situations, a numeric variable may differ naturally across various groups, and consequently, the variable should be analyzed separately for each group. For example, males and females differ significantly on weight. Consequently, we should investigate the bivariate relationship between the numeric variable, weight, and the categorical variable, gender. If the analyst produces numeric and graphical summaries of an entire data set, ignoring gender, there would be a distorted view of weight for the observations under investigation.

For the diabetic care management case, the average weight of all 200 patients is 154.1 pounds with a standard deviation of 28.9 pounds. Obviously the average weight for females is less than 154.1 pounds and the average weight of males is more. Furthermore, because there are group differences in weights across males and females, the standard deviation for the entire 200 observations is larger than that for each of the respective groups which are more similar in their weights and have relatively smaller standard deviations.

So how would the analyst go about describing each group separately? Each SAS procedure can incorporate a BY statement to obtain separate analyses. The analyst could also use the CLASS in order to conduct univariate analyses on WEIGHT by the class, GENDER. The difference between using the BY statement and the CLASS statement is that, not only do you not need to sort using a CLASS statement, but you get a single table and single panel plot for all CLASS groups with the CLASS statement, allowing you to easily compare measures or plots. With a BY statement, the output for each BY group is displayed separately. In Program 3.12 Histogram of Pounds with Descriptive Statistics by Gender, we use the CLASS statement.

Program 3.12 Histogram of Pounds with Descriptive Statistics by Gender

```
libname sasba 'c:\sasba\hc';
data patient;
   set sasba.diab200;
   pounds = weight*2.20462;
run;

proc univariate data=patient plots;
   class gender;
   var pounds;
   histogram /midpoints = 100 to 270 by 10
            vscale=count;
   inset mean median q1 q3 std min max range nobs nmiss skewness / pos = ne;
run;
```

An inspection of the output shows many pages of information that distinguishes the weights between males and females. However, Program 3.12 Histogram of Pounds with Descriptive Statistics by Gender uses the INSET statement, along with the CLASS statement, allowing us to focus on a summary of those statistics with the accompanying histograms, for each males and females, as shown in Output 3.12 Histogram of Pounds with Descriptive Statistics by Gender.

Output 3.12 Histogram of Pounds with Descriptive Statistics by Gender

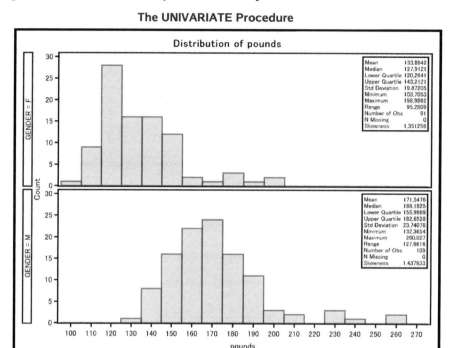

In a single picture we can see that the weights differ between males and females in terms of their position on the X-axis, as measured by the mean, median, quartiles, minimum and maximum values; in general males weigh more than females. In particular, females average 133.9 pounds, with a median of 133.9 pounds, a minimum of 103.7 pounds, a maximum of 199.0 pounds, first quartile of 120.2 pounds, and third quartile of 143.2 pounds; whereas males average 171.5 pounds, with a median of 169.2 pounds, a minimum of 132.4 pounds, a maximum of 260.0 pounds, first quartile of 156.0 pounds, and third quartile of 182.7 pounds

Males and females differ in terms of their spread and shape. Females have less dispersion in weights with a range of 95.3 pounds and a standard deviation of 19.9 pounds, than do males with a range of 127.7 pounds and a standard deviation of 23.7. Note that the mean, range, and standard deviation for males weight may be influenced by the outlying male weights in the 230 to 260 range; these outliers may also account for a slightly longer right tail for males, as measured by the skewness of 1.44.

In short, this data supports the idea that WEIGHT is associated with, or depends upon, GENDER. In fact, in Chapter 6, "Two-Sample T-Test," you will see how hypothesis testing is used to determine if means differences exist across two populations, based upon sample data. Specifically, we will discuss methods for using sample data to detect differences in weight, for example, when comparing males and female populations.

Visual Analyses Using the SGPLOT Procedure

SAS software was initially developed as code-based software where the emphasis was placed on statistical analysis. Recognizing that data visualization is the first step in any statistical analysis, a new suite of Statistical Graphics, or SG, procedures were introduced in SAS 9.2, including SGPLOT, SGPANEL, SGSCATTER, and SGRENDER. The purpose of these procedures is to provide data visualizations as a complement to the graphics generated by ordinary statistical procedures. This section will specifically describe selected features of the SGPLOT procedure which is designed to produce one or more plots overlaid on a single set of axes. Note, the SGPLOT procedure is being used to introduce some concepts seen in scatter plots. The exam does not test on SGPLOT.

Procedure Syntax for PROC SGPLOT

PROC SGPLOT is a procedure used to create various types of plots, or data visualizations, and includes (Heath, 2007):

1. Basic Plots--scatter, series, step, band, and needle
2. Fits and Confidence--loess, regression, penalized B-spline, and ellipse
3. Distributions--horizontal and vertical box plots, histogram, normal curve, and kernel density estimate
4. Categorizations--dot plot, horizontal and vertical bar charts, horizontal and vertical line charts

The SGPLOT procedure has the general form:

PROC SGPLOT DATA = *SAS-data-set<option(s)>*;
REG X= *numeric-variable* Y= *numeric-variable </option(s)>*;
SCATTER X= *variable* Y= *variable </option(s)>*;
HBAR *category-variable < /option(s) >*;
HBOX *response-variable </option(s)>*;
HISTOGRAM *response-variable < /option(s)>*;
DENSITY *response-variable </option(s)>*;
VBAR *category-variable < /option(s)>*;
VBOX *response-variable </option(s)>*;
RUN;

Exploring Bivariate Relationships with Basic Plots, Fits, and Confidence

In previous sections of this chapter, we investigated bivariate relationships. In particular, we reviewed the FREQ procedure and crosstabulations as a means of establishing a relationship between two categorical variables, specifically Diabetes Controlled Status and Renal Disease. We then utilized the UNIVARIATE procedure in conjunction with the BY statement to investigate the relationship between one continuous numeric variable and one categorical variable; in this case, we observed how weight differed across gender. Finally, we used the CHART procedure to further investigate relationships between two or more variables, using the GROUP= and SUBGROUP= options. Here we will specifically explore the relationship between two numeric continuous variables using the SGPLOT procedure and will provide alternatives to exploring bivariate relationships among categorical and/or numeric variables. Keep in mind here that we will discuss selected options for various statements as a way to illustrate the features of the SGPLOT procedure; however, you should refer to the online SAS reference guides to investigate the entire suite of possibilities for tailoring your output.

The SCATTER and REG Statements

To illustrate the SGPLOT procedure, let's revisit the Diabetic Care Management Case and consider the two numeric continuous variables, namely systolic blood pressure (SYST_BP) and diastolic blood pressure (DIAST_BP). In reality, there is a positive relationship between systolic blood pressure and diastolic blood pressure; however, let's explore that question by using Program 3.13 Scatter Plot of Systolic and Diastolic Blood Pressure.

The SGPLOT in conjunction with the SCATTER statement requests SAS to create a bivariate **scatter plot** on the data set PATIENT as indicated with the DATA= statement using the X and Y coordinates as defined by the two numeric continuous variables, SYST_BP and DIAST_BP, respectively. Note also that the marker attributes option, MARKERATTRS, is illustrated as a means of defining the plot symbol and color, and is an example of the many options that can be used with the SCATTER statement.

Program 3.13 Scatter Plot of Systolic and Diastolic Blood Pressure

```
ods html style = journal;
libname sasba 'c:\sasba\hc';
data patient;
   set sasba.diab200;
run;

proc sgplot data=patient;
   scatter x=syst_bp y=diast_bp
      / markerattrs=(symbol=diamondfilled color=black);
   title 'Diabetic Patients Systolic vs Diastolic Blood Pressure';
run;
```

So, as illustrated in Output 3.13 Scatter Plot of Systolic and Diastolic Blood Pressure, we see that the observations are represented by black diamonds as opposed to the default black open circles. We can see also that the scatter plot confirms our thought that systolic blood pressure and diastolic blood pressure are positively related.

Output 3.13 Scatter Plot of Systolic and Diastolic Blood Pressure

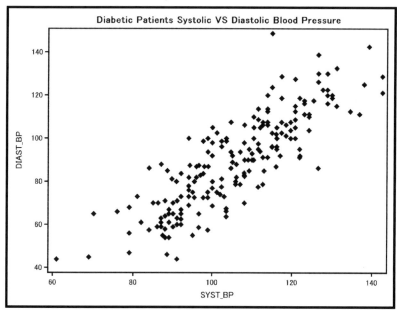

We can enhance the relationship visually by including a **regression line** or **confidence limits** as illustrated in the partial Program 3.14 Regression Line and Confidence Limits on Bivariate Scatter Plot. The SGPLOT in conjunction with the REG statement requests SAS to create a bivariate scatter plot using the X and Y coordinates as defined by the two numeric continuous variables, SYST_BP and DIAST_BP, respectively, and overlays the regression plot. DEGREE=n requests that SAS fit a polynomial of degree *n*. The default DEGREE is 1 requesting that SAS fit a straight line to the scatter plot, as depicted in Program 3.14 Regression Line and Confidence Limits on Bivariate Scatter Plot.

Program 3.14 Regression Line and Confidence Limits on Bivariate Scatter Plot

```
proc sgplot data=patient;
   reg x=syst_bp y=diast_bp / degree=1 clm cli alpha=.10;
   title 'Diabetic Patients Systolic VS Diastolic Blood Pressure';
```

Notice also that the options CLM and CLI request confidence intervals of the predicted MEAN and the INDIVIDUAL predicted values, respectively. The default confidence level for the confidence limits is 95%; however, the ALPHA option provides for setting an alternative level at (1-ALPHA)% level of confidence. In our example, we define ALPHA=.10, therefore requesting 90% confidence limits. As result, the 90% confidence limits for the predicted mean are illustrated by the gray shaded area around the estimated prediction line, and the 90% prediction limits for an individual Y are illustrated by the dotted lines, as shown in Output 3.14 Regression Line and Confidence Limits on Bivariate Scatter Plot.

Output 3.14 Regression Line and Confidence Limits on Bivariate Scatter Plot

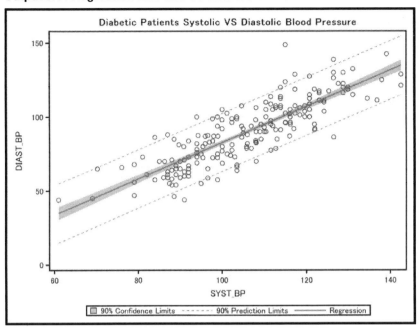

In some situations, we expect the relationship between X and Y to be curvilinear. A typical example is that of demand as a function of price. We all know that as the price of an item increases, the demand as measured by the quantity sold will decrease. However, as the price exceeds a particular amount, the decrease in demand may not be as pronounced. In other words, the change in demand is not constant for a fixed per unit change in price, and may even decrease for each change in price.

Let's consider the case of a brand of sunglasses that is sold at randomly selected stores in a chain where the price (PRICE_X) is set to different values and the manager records the quantity sold (QTY_SOLD_Y) over a certain period of time. In order to explore the relationship between price and quantity sold, we would execute Program 3.15 Scatter Plot of Price by Quantity Sold.

Notice that the first REG statement has DEGREE=2 for fitting a quadratic function to the data, whereas the second REG statement has DEGREE=1 for fitting a straight line. The **LOESS (locally weighted smoothing) curve** is also provided and is constructed to fit the data without imposing a functional form of the relationship as does a linear or quadratic function.

Because SGPLOT implies that all executed statements are overlayed onto the same coordinate plane, the output not only has the data points plotted onto the coordinate plane, but it also has the quadratic, linear, and LOESS plots superimposed onto that same coordinate plane, as illustrated in Output 3.15 Scatter Plot of Price by Quantity Sold. In order to distinguish one line from the other, the LEGENDLABEL= option is included so that the plot generated by DEGREE=2 is labeled as 'Quadratic' and the plot generated by DEGREE=1 is labeled as 'Linear;' otherwise by default each plot would be labeled as 'Regression.' By default, the label for the loess curve is provided.

Program 3.15 Scatter Plot of Price by Quantity Sold

```
ods html style = journal;
libname sasba 'c:\sasba\data';
data sunglasses;
   set sasba.sunglasses;
run;

proc sgplot data=sunglasses;
   reg x=price_x y=qty_sold_y / degree=2 legendlabel="quadratic";
   reg x=price_x y=qty_sold_y / degree=1 legendlabel="linear";
   loess x=price_x y=qty_sold_y;
   title 'Quantity of Sunglasses Sold Based upon Price';
run;
```

Upon inspection of Output 3.15 Scatter Plot of Price by Quantity Sold, it seems that the relationship between price and quantity sold is curvilinear.

Output 3.15 Scatter Plot of Price by Quantity Sold

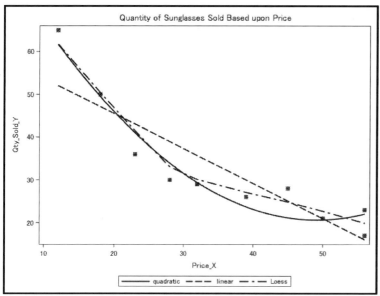

Finally, in some situations, we expect the relationship between X and Y to differ across different groups. In those cases, it is necessary to fit a different regression line for each of the respective groups. Consider the case of weight and blood pressure. In general, there is evidence that blood pressure is related to weight; in particular, as weight increases, we expect blood pressure to increase, and vice versa. In addition, we know from personal experience that males and females differ on weight, not to mention that this is also illustrated with our diabetic care data. There is evidence that males and females differ in systolic blood pressure, and subsequently, it may be then that the relationship between weight and blood pressure differs when considering gender.

So in our Diabetic Care Management Case, let's consider the relationship between the two numeric continuous variables, WEIGHT and Systolic Blood Pressure (SYST_BP) and how the relationship may differ when considering GENDER. Consider the partial Program 3.16 Scatter Plot of Weight and Blood Pressure by Gender.

The SCATTER statement requests that all 200 observations are plotted on the XY-coordinate plane and the DATALABEL= option requests that all male observations be represented by the value of GENDER, in particular 'M,' and all females observations be represented by an 'F'. The REG statement requests that a single regression line be fit to the data, ignoring GENDER, as illustrated in Output 3.16a Scatter Plot of Weight and Blood Pressure by Gender.

Program 3.16 Scatter Plot of Weight and Blood Pressure by Gender
```
ods html style = journal;
libname sasba 'c:\sasba\hc';
data patient;
    set; sasba.diab200;
    run;

proc sgplot data=patient;
    reg x=weight y=syst_bp;
    scatter x=weight y=syst_bp / datalabel=gender;
    title 'Diabetic Patients Weight and Blood Pressure by Gender';
run;
```

Output 3.16a Scatter Plot of Weight and Blood Pressure by Gender

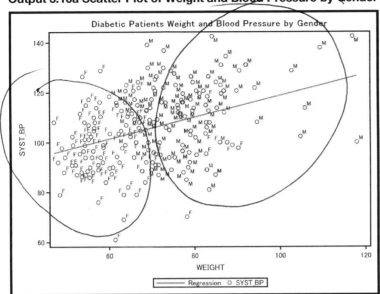

The scatter plot seems to indicate that there is a positive relationship between weight and systolic blood pressure as indicated by the regression line having a positive slope. However, on closer inspection, it seems that males as indicated by 'M' are found in greater number on the upper right hand side of the scatter plot. Specifically, it seems that the males have a different pattern than females. In order to investigate further, let's provide for separate regression lines for males and females by adding the GROUP= option to the REG statement and defining the variable, GENDER, to be the grouping variable as follows:

```
reg x=weight y=syst_bp / group=gender;
```

The pattern found in Output 3.16b Scatter Plot of Weight by Systolic Blood Pressure by Gender seems to point to the idea that the relationship between weight and systolic blood pressure differs when comparing males and females, warranting two different regression lines. In particular, our data, as illustrated by the solid line placed higher than the dotted line, shows that systolic blood pressure, on average, is greater for males than females, across the range of weight. Also note that the solid male line extends further to the right than the dotted female line indicating that there are several male weights exceeding the maximum female weight. Furthermore, it seems that there is a slightly positive slope for males, indicating a positive relationship, whereas the slope for females seems relatively flat, possibly supporting the idea that systolic blood pressure is not related to weight for females. When interpreting the output, keep in mind that our sample comes from a population of diabetic patients which have different health profiles from the general population. Therefore, patterns may deviate from what we expect when looking at other populations.

Output 3.16b Scatter Plot of Weight by Systolic Blood Pressure by Gender

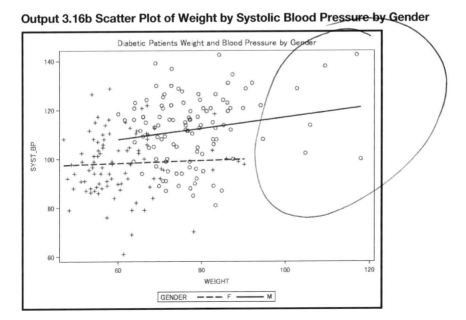

Exploring Other Relationships Using SGPLOT

Categorical data can also be summarized using the HBAR and VBAR statements within the SGPLOT procedure. Let's consider the DIABETIC_CONTROLLED variable in the Diabetic Care Management Case, where the variable outcome is 1 if the patient's diabetes is controlled or 0 otherwise. Program 3.17 Vertical Bar Charts for Diabetes Status produces the appropriate bar graph with the SGPLOT procedure.

The VBAR statement requests that SAS create a vertical bar graph for the variable CONTROLLED_DIABETIC where the FORMAT statement defines the 0 outcomes to be labeled as 'No' and the 1 outcomes to be labeled as 'Yes.' Note also that the DATALABEL option requests that the frequencies be provided for each bar produced as illustrated in Output 3.17 Vertical Bar Charts for Diabetes Status.

Program 3.17 Vertical Bar Charts for Diabetes Status

```
ods html style = journal;
libname sasba 'c:\sasba\hc';
data patient; set sasba.diab200;
run;

proc format;
   value yesno 0=No 1=Yes;
run;

proc sgplot data=patient;
  format controlled_diabetic yesno.;
  vbar controlled_diabetic / datalabel;
  title "Diabetic Care Management Case";
run;
```

Output 3.17 Vertical Bar Charts for Diabetes Status

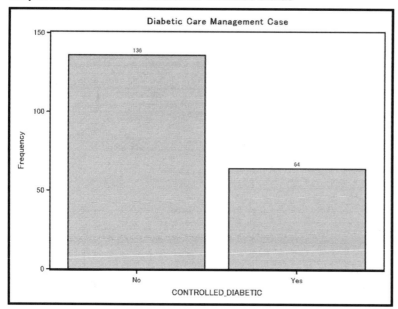

SGPLOT allows for additional capabilities. In order to take advantage of the overlay capabilities, we can use an additional VBAR statement within the SGPLOT procedure to include the number of patients with renal disease for each level of CONTROLLED_DIABETIC status using Program 3.18 Bar Chart of Diabetes Status by Renal Disease.

Program 3.18 Bar Chart of Diabetes Status by Renal Disease

```
ods html style = journal;
libname sasba 'c:\sasba\hc';
data patient; set sasba.diab200;
run;

proc format;
   value yesno 0=No 1=Yes;
run;
```

```
proc sgplot data=patient;
  format controlled_diabetic yesno.;
  vbar controlled_diabetic / datalabel;
  vbar controlled_diabetic / datalabel response=renal_disease stat=sum
     barwidth = 0.5 transparency = 0.2;
  title "Diabetic Care Management Case";
run;
```

As seen in the previous code, the first VBAR statement produces a bar chart of the variable CONTROLLED_DIABETIC. The second VBAR statement requests that, for each level of CONTROLLED_DIABETIC, the response variable RENAL_DISEASE, which must have a numeric value, must also be summarized and displayed on the vertical axis. The STAT=SUM variable requests that the values of RENAL_DISEASE be added for each level of CONTROLLED_DIABETIC. Because RENAL_DISEASE is coded 1 for YES and 0 for NO, the STAT=SUM is essentially requesting that the number of patients with renal disease should be displayed as illustrated in Output 3.18 Bar Chart of diabetes Status by Renal Disease.

You can see from the bar graphs that of the 200 patients, 136 do not have their diabetes controlled, whereas 64 patients do have their diabetes controlled. Furthermore, of the 136 patients who have uncontrolled diabetes, 18 (13.24%) have renal disease, and of the 64 patients with controlled diabetes, 2 (3.13%) have renal disease. Note that Output 3.18a Bar Chart of Diabetes Status by Renal Disease is an overlay of the two bar charts generated with the FREQ procedure in Output 3.4 Cross Tabs and Frequency Plots of Diabetes Status and Renal Disease.

Output 3.18a Bar Chart of Diabetes Status by Renal Disease

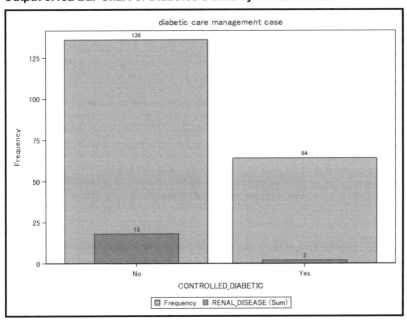

For aesthetic purposes, you can include a BARWIDTH option which defines the width of the bars as a ratio of the maximum width, where the maximum width is the distance between the centers of adjacent bars. In particular, if you set the width equal to 1, there is no distance between the bars; however, if you set the width equal to 0.5, then the width of the bars is identical to the space between the bars. You can also define the transparency of the bars, where a value of 0 requests that the bars are completely opaque and a value of 1 requests that the bars are completely transparent.

Note that in the previous example, if we had included only the second VBAR statement as indicated below, SAS would have generated the output as found in Output 3.18b Numbers with Renal Diseases by Diabetes Status.

```
Vbar controlled_diabetic / datalabel response=renal_disease stat=sum
barwidth = 0.5 transparency = 0.2;
```

Output 3.18b Numbers with Renal Diseases by Diabetes Status

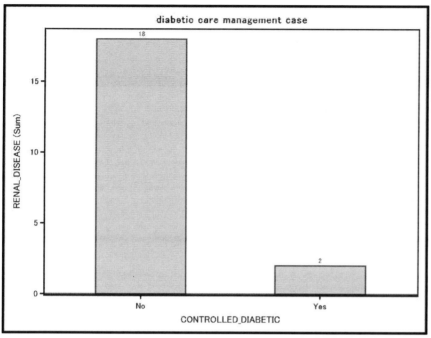

In some cases, we may want to visualize summaries of numeric variables across various categorical groups. Suppose, for example, we want to compare both the average systolic and diastolic blood pressures across the two groups, controlled and uncontrolled diabetes. We can define the categorical variable, CONTROLLED_DIABETIC, using the VBAR statement and the numeric outcomes of interest using the RESPONSE option in Program 3.19 Bar Charts for Diastolic and Systolic BP by Diabetes Status.

Program 3.19 Bar Charts for Diastolic and Systolic BP by Diabetes Status

```
ods html style = journal;
libname sasba 'c:\sasba\hc';
data patient; set sasba.diab200;
run;

proc format;
   value yesno 0=No 1=Yes;
run;

proc sort data=patient;
   by controlled_diabetic;
run;

proc means data=patient;
   var syst_bp diast_bp;
   by controlled_diabetic;
   format controlled_diabetic yesno.;
run;

proc sgplot data=patient;
   format controlled_diabetic yesno.;
   vbar controlled_diabetic / response = diast_bp stat=mean
      datalabel datalabelattrs=(size=9 weight=bold);
   vbar controlled_diabetic / response = syst_bp stat=mean
      datalabel datalabelattrs=(size=9 weight=bold)
      barwidth = 0.5 transparency = 0.4;
   title "Diabetic Care Management Case";
run;
```

The code requests that vertical bars are created for each of the groups, as represented by CONTROLLED_DIABETIC. One set of vertical bars will represent diastolic blood pressure as defined by the RESPONSE= option, and the other set of vertical bars will represent systolic blood pressure as defined by the RESPONSE= option. For each set of vertical bars, the mean of the response variable will be plotted, as defined by the STAT=MEAN option. Note also that the results of the MEANS procedure were also generated as a complement to the chart in Output 3.19 Bar Charts for Diastolic and Systolic BP by Diabetes Status.

Output 3.19 Bar Charts for Diastolic and Systolic BP by Diabetes Status

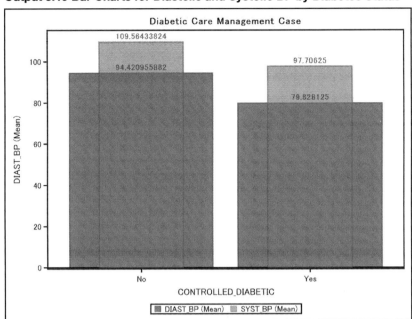

From the output, the analyst can see that both the systolic and diastolic blood pressures are higher for those with uncontrolled diabetes when compared to those with controlled diabetes. In particular, if a patient's diabetes is uncontrolled, the average systolic blood pressure is 109.6 as compared to those with controlled diabetes with an average 97.7. If a patient's diabetes is uncontrolled, the average diastolic blood pressure is 94.4 as compared to those with controlled diabetes with an average diastolic blood pressure of 79.8.

This chapter has covered many ways of visualizing and getting to know the details. When reporting the details of your data, visual representations must accompany any numeric summaries. In the following chapters, you will learn many methods aimed at inferential statistics, that is, making inferences about a population based upon sample information. It is equally imperative to use visual analysis when conducting inferential statistics as well.

Key Terms

association	histogram
bar chart	interquartile range (IQR)
box-and-whisker plot	loess curve
column percent	ordered array
conditional percent	outlier
confidence limits	outlierscatter plot
crosstabulation table	percent
five-number summary	quantile-quantile (Q-Q) plot
frequency	quartile
frequency distribution	regression line
frequency table	row percent

Chapter Quiz

Select the best answer for each of the following questions:

1. Which of the following procedures can be used to visualize both numeric and categorical data?
    a. FREQ
    b. UNIVARIATE
    c. SGPLOT
    d. All of the above.
    e. Only a and b.

2. Suppose you had data for students attending a local community college (data name = CC_STUDENT) and you were to analyze employment status (variable name = WORK_STATUS) with the four possible values (full-time, part-time, unemployed, unknown). Which of the following would produce both a frequency table and bar chart?
    a. data student; set cc_student;
        proc univariate data=student;
        tables work_status / plots=freqplot; run;
    b. data student; set cc_student;
        proc freq data=student;
        tables work_status / plots=freqplot; run;
    c. data student; set cc_student;
        proc freq data=student;
        plots=work_status; run;
    d. data student; set cc_student;
        proc univariate data=student;
        plots=work_status; run;

3. Suppose you randomly selected 200 community college students and asked if they used Facebook. Using the frequency table below, which of the following is true?
    a. When looking at males, the probability of using Facebook is 0.3750.
    b. When looking at females, the probability of using Facebook is 0.50.
    c. Facebook usage is associated with gender.
    d. The probability that you randomly select a female student that does not use Facebook is 0.375.

Table of FACEBOOK_USE by GENDER			
FACEBOOK_USE	**GENDER**		
Frequency Percent Row Pct Col Pct	Female	Male	Total
No	75 37.50 50.00 75.00	75 37.50 50.00 75.00	150 75.00
Yes	25 12.50 50.00 25.00	25 12.50 50.00 25.00	50 25.00
Total	100 50.00	100 50.00	200 100.00

(handwritten notes)
75 females do not use Facebook
7.5% are females who don't use Facebook
% of the data contains females that do not use Facebook
5% are females

Suppose you had data for students attending a local community college (data name = CC_STUDENT) and you were to analyze the number of credit hours completed as of the previous semester (variable name = CREDIT_HRS). Use this information to answer questions 4 – 6:

4. If the minimum value is 0 and the maximum value is 135, which of the following would produce a histogram consisting of 9 bars?

   a. data student; set cc_student;
      proc univariate data=student; var credit_hrs;
      histogram /midpoints = 7.5 to 133.5 by 15; run;

   b. data student; set cc_student;
      proc univariate data=student; var credit_hrs;
      histogram /midpoints = 0 to 135 by 9; run;

   c. data student; set cc_student;
      proc sgplot data=student; var credit_hrs;
      histogram /midpoints = 7.5 to 133.5 by 15; run;

   d. data student; set cc_student;
      proc sgplot data=student; var credit_hrs;
      histogram /number=9; run;

5. When creating a histogram, which of the following statements would be used with the PROC to both fit a normal curve over the histogram and provide an inset containing the mean, median, mode, and standard deviation?

   a. data student; set cc_student;
      proc xxxxxxxx data=student; var credit_hrs;
      histogram=normal / inset mean median mode std; run;

   b. data student; set cc_student;
      proc xxxxxxxx data=student; var credit_hrs;
      histogram / normal;
      inset mean median mode std; run;

   c. data student; set cc_student;
      proc xxxxxxxx data=student; var credit_hrs;
      histogram / normal inset = mean median mode std; run;

   d. data student; set cc_student;
      proc xxxxxxxx data=student; var credit_hrs;
      normal / histogram = inset (mean median mode std); run;

6. If the analyst wants to explore credit hours by gender, which of the following statements must be added to the procedure?

   a. group gender;
   b. class=gender;
   c. class gender;
   d. group=gender;

7. When exploring the shape of numeric data, which of the following can be used?

   a. histogram, box plot, Q-Q plot
   b. bar chart, box plot, Q-Q plot
   c. histogram, crosstabulations, box plot
   d. All of the above.
   e. Only *a* and *b*

8. Suppose you had data for students attending a local community college (data name = CC_STUDENT) and you were to analyze the number of credit hours completed as of the previous semester (variable name = CREDIT_HRS). If the five-number summary is 0, 30, 39, 58, 135, which of the following statements is true?
   a. The IQR is 27.
   b. There is at least one outlier.
   c. The data is right skewed.
   d. All of the above statements are true.
   e. Only *a* and *c* are true.

9. Consider a random sample of college graduates. Which of the following statements in the SGPLOT procedure will produce a scatter plot of GPA by HRS_STUDY (average number of hours spent studying per week)?
   a. scatter x=gpa y=hrs_study;
   b. reg x=gpa y=hrs_study;
   c. plot x=gpa y=hrs_study;
   d. All of the above.
   e. Only *a* and *b*.

10. Consider a random sample of college graduates. Which of the following statements in the SGPLOT procedure will produce a bar graph of GENDER?
    a. bar gender;
    b. hbox gender;
    c. vbar gender;
    d. plot gender;

Chapter 4: The Normal Distribution and Introduction to Inferential Statistics

Introduction

In Chapter 2, "Summarizing Your Data with Descriptive Statistics," we described the analysis procedures for exploring and describing quantitative data. In particular, we provided instruction on how to generate visual representations of our data using histograms, bar charts, pie charts, and scatter diagrams, to name a few. We further described the numeric measures used for summarizing the characteristics of those visual displays in terms of center, spread, shape, and extreme values. All of these procedures give us context and useful information about our sample data and, in turn, this descriptive information can be used to make sense of the population. In this chapter, we will explore, in detail, the foundation of **inferential statistics** which requires first a strong understanding of a particular class of quantitative variables, namely, **normal continuous random variables**. These are variables having 'bell-shaped' histograms, or distributions. Once you are familiar with the characteristics of normal distributions, we will introduce the **empirical rule** and use it to assess the percentage of observations within a particular distance from the mean and expand that topic to the use of the **standard normal distribution** for answering probability questions about normal random variables. We will then introduce the concept of **sampling distributions** and apply **the central limit theorem** to answer questions about the probability of selecting a sample mean value when we know the population characteristics. Finally, we will introduce terminology and use the sampling distribution to develop the rationale for inferential statistics by using sample data to confirm or not our belief about the population. Specifically, we will describe the formal procedures for testing our belief about the population in a process referred to as **hypothesis testing**.

In this chapter, you will learn how to:

- describe the characteristics of a normal distribution
- apply the empirical rule to normal random variables
- describe the characteristics of a standard normal distribution
- use the standard normal z-table to calculate the probability that a z-score has values within a defined range
- convert any normal random variable to a standard normal distribution and understand that a z-score represents the number of standard deviations from the mean

- use the standard normal z-table to calculate the probability that the value of a normal random variable has values within a defined range
- construct a sampling distribution and understand that the mean of the sampling distribution is equal to the mean of the population and the standard error is the standard deviation of the sampling distribution
- describe the standard error as a function of sample size; and understand that as the sample size increases, the standard error decreases; and as the sample size decreases, the standard error increases
- apply the central limit theorem to define the shape of the sampling distribution; and understand that if the population is normal, then the sampling distribution is normal; and if the shape of the population is non-normal or unknown and the sample size is large (n ≥ 30), the shape of the sampling distribution is normal
- use the characteristics of the sampling distribution and the standard normal z-table to calculate the probability that the sample mean has values within a defined range
- set up the null and alternative hypotheses based upon the inferential statement to be tested; and know when to use a one-tailed or two-tailed test
- use sample data and the z-test (when σ is known) to test hypotheses to make conclusions about the population based upon the level of significance
- use the p-value of the z-test to test hypotheses to make conclusions about the population
- use sample data and the t-test (when σ is unknown) to test hypotheses to make conclusions about the population
- calculate the confidence interval of the sample mean; and know that the calculation requires a z-value when σ is known or a t-value when σ is unknown
- use the confidence interval to estimate the population mean and make conclusions about the hypothesis test
- use both the sample size or level of confidence to change the width of the confidence interval

Continuous Random Variables

There are two types of numeric random variables, namely, **discrete** and **continuous**. This chapter will concentrate its discussion on continuous random variables, that is, variables whose outcomes have an infinite number of possible of outcomes. There are many types of numeric continuous random variables, each having unique characteristics. The most important variable type has a bell-shaped curve, or a normal probability distribution. Because of its wide application, that type of variable will be discussed here in detail.

Normal Random Variables

Many continuous random variables are naturally described by a **normal distribution**. For example, weight, height, IQ, lifetime of automobile tires, fuel efficiency of mid-size automobiles, contents of cereal boxes, number of hours of sleep per night among Americans adults, and daily consumption of coffee, to name a few, all have bell-shaped distributions. Secondly, the normal probability distribution provides the theoretical framework for many statistical analyses through the application of the central limit theorem. In order to understand the application of normal probability distributions, the analyst must first recognize the characteristics of all normal random variables.

First, there is an entire family of normal distributions specifically defined by the mean (μ) and the standard deviation (σ). The probability distribution function, which provides the bell-shaped graph of the histogram, is defined as

$$f(x) = \frac{1}{\sigma\sqrt{2\pi}} \exp\left(\frac{-(x-\mu)^2}{2\sigma^2}\right)$$

The mean defines the center, or the balance point, of the data and the standard deviation defines the spread around the center. Histograms that are wider and flatter have relatively large standard deviations, while histograms that are thinner and more peaked have relatively small standard deviations.

To illustrate, consider the distribution of weights for three populations as depicted in Figure 4.1 Distributions of Adult Weights for Three Populations. The first normal curve represents the weight of adult women in the United States, whereas the second curve represents the weight of men. Notice that women are further to the left on the horizontal axis indicating that women typically weigh less than men. Note also that those two histograms have the same standard deviation indicating that the weights have the same variation or spread around their respective means. Let's now suppose the third normal curve represents the weight of defensive linemen who play professional football--not only do they weigh more than the average man and woman, but their weights are similar and have very little variation around the mean as indicated by a relatively small standard deviation (a narrower histogram).

Figure 4.1 Distributions of Adult Weights for Three Populations

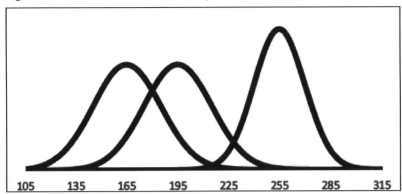

Second, normal distributions are symmetric around the mean; in other words, if you were to fold the histogram in half at the mean, the left side would be a mirror image of the right side. The mean provides the axis of symmetry which cuts the histogram in half, so by definition, that point coincides with the median. Finally, the axis of symmetry also occurs at the point where the histogram is highest and represents an area of higher concentration. For the case of women in the United States, the weights are concentrated around the mean weight of 165 pounds where half of women weigh less than 165, half weigh more than 165.

Finally, normal distributions are asymptotic, meaning that the normal curve approaches the X-axis but never crosses it. Consequently, values of a normal random variable can range from -∞ to +∞. It should also be noted that the total area under a normal curve is 1.0 and that area is associated with the probability that the value of a normal random variable occurs.

The Empirical Rule

Once we know that a numeric variable follows a normal distribution, we can make some general conclusions about the percentage of observations falling within a certain distance of the mean. The **empirical rule** is illustrated in Figure 4.2 Visualization of the Empirical Rule and stated as follows:

- 68% of observations are within 1 standard deviation of the mean.
- 95% of observations are within 2 standard deviations of the mean.
- 99.7% of observations are within 3 standard deviations of the mean.

Figure 4.2 Visualization of the Empirical Rule

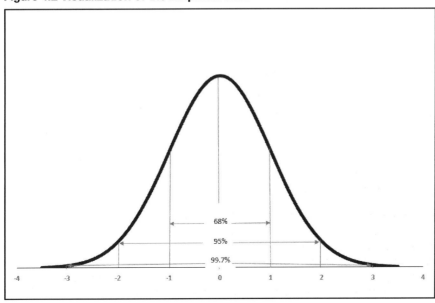

Example: Consider the complete data that makes up the Diabetic Care Management Case described in Chapter 1, "Statistics and Making Sense of Our World." In particular, let's review the height (in inches) of male diabetics with the following visual generated from the UNIVARIATE procedure, as illustrated in Figure 4.3 Empirical Rule Applied to Height of Diabetic Males.

Figure 4.3 Empirical Rule Applied to Height of Diabetic Males

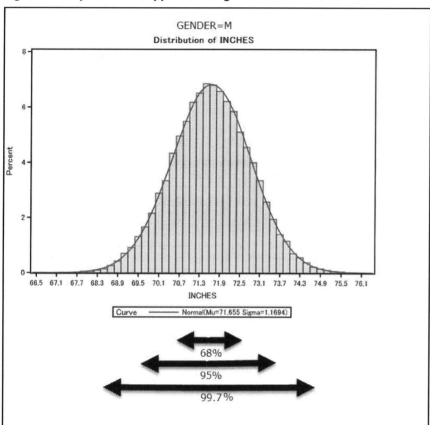

Applying the empirical rule for μ equal to 71.66 and σ equal to 1.17, we have the following:

- $\mu \pm 1\sigma = 71.66 \pm 1(1.17) = (70.49, 72.83)$
- $\mu \pm 2\sigma = 71.66 \pm 2(1.17) = (69.32, 74.00)$
- $\mu \pm 3\sigma = 71.66 \pm 3(1.17) = (68.15, 75.17)$

In other words, knowing that male heights in the Diabetic Care Management Case are normally distributed, with a mean of 71.66 inches and a standard deviation of 1.17 inches, we can approximate that:

- 68% of males have heights between 70.49 and 72.38 inches (5'10'' and 6'0'')
- 95% of males have heights between 69.32 and 74.00 inches (5'9'' and 6'2'')
- 99.7% of males have heights between 68.15 and 75.17 inches (5'8" and 6'3")

When running Program 4.1 Actual Percentage of Males Having Heights within 1, 2, and 3 Standard Deviations from the Mean and generating the accompanying output, Output 4.1 Actual Percentage of Males Having Heights within 1, 2, and 3 Standard Deviations from the Mean, you can see that the actual percentages of heights within 1, 2, and 3 standard deviations from the mean, respectively, match almost exactly the percentages as defined in the empirical rule. In short, we would have been just as accurate in our assessments of those percentages by applying the empirical rule to the data, without the need to 'count' the observations within those ranges.

Program 4.1 Actual Percentage of Males Having Heights within 1, 2, and 3 Standard Deviations from the Mean

```
libname sasba 'c:\sasba\hc';
data males;
   set sasba.diabetics;
```

```
    if gender='M';
    ul68 = 71.66+1.17;   ll68 = 71.66-1.17;
    ul95 = 71.66+2.34;   ll95 = 71.66-2.34;
    ul100 = 71.66+3.51;  ll100 = 71.66-3.51;
    within1sd=0; within2sd=0; within3sd=0;
    if inches ge ll68 and inches le ul68 then within1sd=1;
    if inches ge ll95 and inches le ul95 then within2sd=1;
    if inches ge ll100 and inches le ul100 then within3sd=1;
run;

    proc format;
    value yesno 0=No 1=Yes;
run;

proc freq;
    tables within1sd within2sd within3sd;
    format within1sd within2sd within3sd yesno.;
run;
```

Output 4.1 Actual Percentage of Males Having Heights within 1, 2, and 3 Standard Deviations from the Mean

within1sd	Frequency	Percent	Cumulative Frequency	Cumulative Percent
No	11114	32.00	11114	32.00
Yes	23619	68.00	34733	100.00

within2sd	Frequency	Percent	Cumulative Frequency	Cumulative Percent
No	1563	4.50	1563	4.50
Yes	33170	95.50	34733	100.00

within3sd	Frequency	Percent	Cumulative Frequency	Cumulative Percent
No	92	0.26	92	0.26
Yes	34641	99.74	34733	100.00

The Standard Normal Distribution

Consider the following scenario: Suppose you take a test in your statistics class and make an 80--would you be happy with that score? At face value, probably not, assuming that you would certainly prefer a higher grade. However, you don't have enough information to make a fair assessment. If the test scores of the class were approximately normally distributed with mean of 70 and standard deviation of 10, you might be somewhat satisfied in the fact that you were one standard deviation above the mean. Now, if instead, the average of the test scores was 70 with a standard deviation of 5, you may be very happy to know that you scored two standard deviations above the mean. In short, your performance depends upon, not only the mean, but also on the variation of the scores around the mean.

In order to standardize the scores, taking into account the variation in the data and allowing for comparisons, the analyst would convert each exam score (X) to a standardized Z-score using the following formula:

$$Z = \frac{(X - \mu)}{\sigma}$$

In fact, consider every student taking the statistics test, for example. If you standardized all of the test scores for each student, the new data set--made up of Z-scores--would have a mean of 0 and a standard deviation of 1. Also, the histogram of the Z-scores would be normally distributed, representing the **standard normal distribution.**

Each Z-score basically answers the question 'How many standard deviations is the X-value from the average X-value?' So for example, if your friend made a 64 on the statistics exam where the standard deviation was 5, his or her Z-score would be -1.20 indicating that the test score is 1.20 standard deviations below the mean.

Finally, we can use z-scores to restate the empirical rule. When a numeric random variable is normally distributed, we can say that

- 68% of observations have Z-scores between ±1
- 95% of observation have Z-scores between ±2
- 99.7% of observations have Z-scores between ±3

Suppose, now, that we wanted to extend what we know to answer more precise statements about the percentage, or proportion, of observations with various distances from the mean, other than the distances as defined by the empirical rule. Consider the following example:

Example 1: Given a standard normal Z-distribution, what proportion of observations have Z-values falling below -1.15? This is identical to asking the question, what is the probability that Z is less than -1.15, P(Z<-1.15), and is represented by the distribution in Figure 4.4 Proportion of Z-Values Less Than -1.15, P(Z<-1.15).

Figure 4.4 Proportion of Z-values Less Than -1.15, P(Z < -1.15)

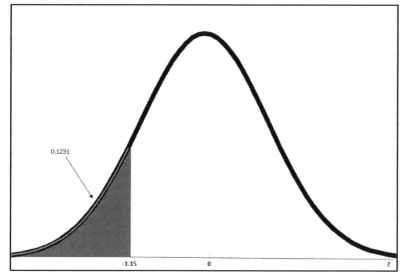

Solution: In order to find the proportion, we would utilize the standard normal **Z-table** (from Appendix C Z-Table), referenced in Table 4.1 Excerpt from Standard Normal Cumulative Area (for Z ≤ 0). Notice that a Z-value of -1.15 is represented as -1.1 when truncated to one decimal place, thereby pointing to the row where the appropriate proportion will be found. Note also that a Z of -1.15 has a 5 in the second decimal place, represented as 0.05, and is an indicator of the column where the appropriate proportion will be found. Specifically, when you see the intersection of the appropriate row and column as indicated by the overlap of the boxes, you can see that the desired proportion is 0.1251.

So, this means that 12.51% of Z-scores are below -1.15; in other words, 12.51% of any population represented by a normal probability distribution will have values more than 1.15 standard deviations below the mean. In the case of male diabetics, this translates into the statement, 12.5% of males have heights less than 1.15 standard deviations (1.15x1.17) below the mean of 71.66 inches, or 12.5% are less than 70.31 inches tall.

Table 4.1 Excerpt from Standard Normal Cumulative Area (for Z ≤ 0)

Z	0.00	0.01	0.02	0.03	0.04	0.05	0.06	0.07	0.08	0.09
0.0	0.5000	0.4960	0.4920	0.4880	0.4840	0.4801	0.4761	0.4721	0.4681	0.4641
-0.1	0.4602	0.4562	0.4522	0.4483	0.4443	0.4404	0.4364	0.4325	0.4286	0.4247
-0.2	0.4207	0.4168	0.4129	0.4090	0.4052	0.4013	0.3974	0.3936	0.3897	0.3859
-0.3	0.3821	0.3783	0.3745	0.3707	0.3669	0.3632	0.3594	0.3557	0.3520	0.3483
-0.4	0.3446	0.3409	0.3372	0.3336	0.3300	0.3264	0.3228	0.3192	0.3156	0.3121
-0.5	0.3085	0.3050	0.3015	0.2981	0.2946	0.2912	0.2877	0.2843	0.2810	0.2776
-0.6	0.2743	0.2709	0.2676	0.2643	0.2611	0.2578	0.2546	0.2514	0.2483	0.2451
-0.7	0.2420	0.2389	0.2358	0.2327	0.2296	0.2266	0.2236	0.2206	0.2177	0.2148
-0.8	0.2119	0.2090	0.2061	0.2033	0.2005	0.1977	0.1949	0.1922	0.1894	0.1867
-0.9	0.1841	0.1814	0.1788	0.1762	0.1736	0.1711	0.1685	0.1660	0.1635	0.1611
-1.0	0.1587	0.1562	0.1539	0.1515	0.1492	0.1469	0.1446	0.1423	0.1401	0.1379
-1.1	0.1357	0.1335	0.1314	0.1292	0.1271	0.1251	0.1230	0.1210	0.1190	0.1170
-1.2	0.1151	0.1131	0.1112	0.1093	0.1075	0.1056	0.1038	0.1020	0.1003	0.0985
-1.3	0.0968	0.0951	0.0934	0.0918	0.0901	0.0885	0.0869	0.0853	0.0838	0.0823
-1.4	0.0808	0.0793	0.0778	0.0764	0.0749	0.0735	0.0721	0.0708	0.0694	0.0681
-1.5	0.0668	0.0655	0.0643	0.0630	0.0618	0.0606	0.0594	0.0582	0.0571	0.0559

Example 2: Given a standard normal Z-distribution, what proportion of observations have Z-values falling below +1.15? This is identical to asking the question, what is the probability that Z is less than +1.15, P(Z<+1.15), and is represented by the distribution in Figure 4.5 Proportion of Z-Values Less Than 1.15, P(Z<+1.15).

Figure 4.5 Proportion of Z-values Less Than 1.15, P(Z < +1.15)

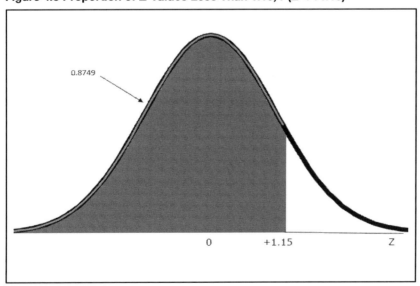

Solution: Referring to Table 4.2 Excerpt from Standard Normal Cumulative Area (for Z ≥ 0) and utilizing the Z-table in the same way as previously described, we would look at the intersection of the 1.1 row and the 0.05 column to get the answer, 0.8749. So, this means that 87.49% of Z-scores are below +1.15. In the case of male diabetics, this translates into the statement, 87.49% of males have heights less than 1.15 standard deviations (1.15x1.17) below the mean of 71.66 inches, or 87.49% of male diabetics are less than 73.01 inches tall.

Table 4.2 Excerpt from Standard Normal Cumulative Area (for Z ≥ 0)

Z	0.00	0.01	0.02	0.03	0.04	0.05	0.06	0.07	0.08	0.09
0.0	0.5000	0.5040	0.5080	0.5120	0.5160	0.5199	0.5239	0.5279	0.5319	0.5359
0.1	0.5398	0.5438	0.5478	0.5517	0.5557	0.5596	0.5636	0.5675	0.5714	0.5753
0.2	0.5793	0.5832	0.5871	0.5910	0.5948	0.5987	0.6026	0.6064	0.6103	0.6141
0.3	0.6179	0.6217	0.6255	0.6293	0.6331	0.6368	0.6406	0.6443	0.6480	0.6517
0.4	0.6554	0.6591	0.6628	0.6664	0.6700	0.6736	0.6772	0.6808	0.6844	0.6879
0.5	0.6915	0.6950	0.6985	0.7019	0.7054	0.7088	0.7123	0.7157	0.7190	0.7224
0.6	0.7257	0.7291	0.7324	0.7357	0.7389	0.7422	0.7454	0.7486	0.7517	0.7549
0.7	0.7580	0.7611	0.7642	0.7673	0.7704	0.7734	0.7764	0.7794	0.7823	0.7852
0.8	0.7881	0.7910	0.7939	0.7967	0.7995	0.8023	0.8051	0.8078	0.8106	0.8133
0.9	0.8159	0.8186	0.8212	0.8238	0.8264	0.8289	0.8315	0.8340	0.8365	0.8389
1.0	0.8413	0.8438	0.8461	0.8485	0.8508	0.8531	0.8554	0.8577	0.8599	0.8621
1.1	0.8643	0.8665	0.8686	0.8708	0.8729	0.8749	0.8770	0.8790	0.8810	0.8830
1.2	0.8849	0.8869	0.8888	0.8907	0.8925	0.8944	0.8962	0.8980	0.8997	0.9015
1.3	0.9032	0.9049	0.9066	0.9082	0.9099	0.9115	0.9131	0.9147	0.9162	0.9177
1.4	0.9192	0.9207	0.9222	0.9236	0.9251	0.9265	0.9279	0.9292	0.9306	0.9319
1.5	0.9332	0.9345	0.9357	0.9370	0.9382	0.9394	0.9406	0.9418	0.9429	0.9441

From Example 1 and Example 2, and referring to the standard normal Z-table in Appendix C Z Table, it should be noted that the standard normal Z-table is made up of two pages, namely page 1 which provides proportions for negative Z-values and page 2 proportions for positive Z-values. Note also that the table gives only the area under the curve 'below' a particular Z-value. Consequently, we can use the standard normal Z-table to arrive at proportions under the curve 'above' a particular Z-value, as illustrated in Example 3.

Example 3: Given a standard normal Z-distribution, what proportion of observations have Z-values falling above +1.15? This is identical to asking the question, what is the probability that Z is more than +1.15, P(Z>+1.15), and is represented by the distribution in Figure 4.6 Proportion of Z-Values Greater Than 1.15, P(Z > +1.15).

Figure 4.6 Proportion of Z-Values Greater Than 1.15, P(Z > +1.15)

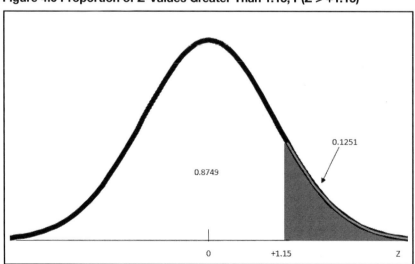

Solution: From Example 2, we know that 0.8749 of Z-values are below +1.15, so using the fact that the total area under a normal curve is equal to 1.0, we know that the area under the curve *above* +1.15 is 0.1251, or 1.0 – 0.8749. So anytime you use the Z-table to find the area under the curve *below* a Z-value, you can subtract that proportion from 1.0 to arrive at the area under the curve above that Z-value.

We can also use the property of symmetry to answer the question posed in Example 3. In other words, if the P(Z < -1.15) = 0.1251, as seen in Example 1, then the P(Z > +1.15) = 0.1251, as well. In other words, the tail area below a Z-value of -1.15 is identical to the tail area above a Z-value of +1.15.

Example 4: Given a standard normal Z-distribution, what proportion of observations have Z-values falling between -1.00 and +1.00? This is identical to asking the question, what is the probability that Z is more than -1.00 and less than +1.00, P(-1.00<Z<+1.00), and is represented by the distribution in Figure 4.7 Proportion of Z-Values between -1.00 and +1.00, P(-1.00 < Z < +1.00).

Figure 4.7 Proportion of Z-Values between -1.00 and +1.00, P(-1.00 < Z < +1.00)

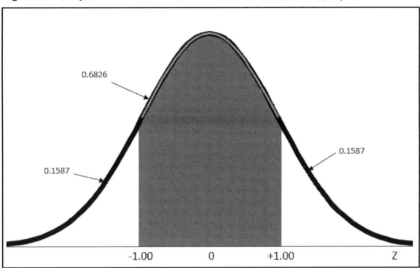

Solution: Referring to the first page of the Z-table in Appendix C Z Table, you will find that the area under the curve below a Z-value of -1.00 is 0.1587. Because of symmetry, the area under the curve above a Z-value of +1.00 is also 0.1587. Consequently, finding the area between -1.00 and +1.00 requires lopping off the tails; that is, the area under the curve between -1.00 and +1.00 is 1.00 – 2(0.1587), or 0.6826. In conclusion, 68.26% of observations from a normal distribution fall within 1 standard deviation of the mean. Note that this is a more precise statement of the empirical rule. In fact, try using the standard normal Z-table to verify that 95.44% of observations are within 2 standard deviations of the mean, and that 99.73% of observations are within 3 standard deviations of the mean.

Example 5: Given a standard normal Z-distribution, what proportion of observations have Z-values falling between -1.96 and +1.96? This is identical to asking the question, what is the probability that Z is more than -1.96 and less than +1.96, P(-1.96<Z<+1.96), and is represented by the distribution in Figure 4.8 Proportion of Z-Values between -1.96 and +1.96, P(-1.96<Z+1.96).

above = 1 - .8749

tails = 1 - 2(.1587)

Figure 4.8 Proportion of Z-Values between -1.96 and +1.96, P(-1.96 < Z < +1.96)

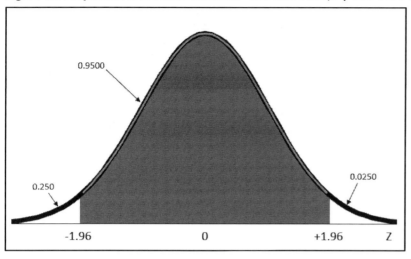

Solution: Referring to the first page of the Z-table in Appendix C Z Table, you will find the area under the curve below a Z-value of -1.96 is 0.0250. Because of symmetry, the area under the curve above a Z-value of +1.96 is also 0.0250. Therefore, the area under the curve between -1.96 and +1.96 is 1.00 – 2(0.0250), or 0.9500. In conclusion, 95% of observations from a normal distribution fall within 1.96 standard deviations of the mean.

Applying the Standard Normal Distribution to Answer Probability Questions

As mentioned earlier in this chapter, there are infinitely many values for any numeric continuous random variable, so the probability that you randomly select a specific numeric continuous value, c, is 0, that is, P(X=c) = 0. However, we can ask the question, 'What proportion of observations fall within a certain range?' For example, you may want to know the proportion of students graduating from a local university who have earned starting salaries between $45,000 and $50,000. Currently, we have already considered two approaches: first, you could count the number of students who have starting salaries between $45,000 and $50,000, and then divide by the total number of graduates to get the proportion, or probability. Or, if the numeric variable of interest is normally distributed, you could apply the empirical rule to get approximations based upon the relative distance from the mean. A third, and computationally extensive, approach would involve using integral calculus to find the area under the curve between $45,000 and $50,000. The first requires you to have the actual data; the second provides for an approximation only relative to 1, 2, and 3 standard deviations from the mean; and the third is nearly impossible!

A better, commonly used approach can be used if both the distribution is normal and the mean and standard deviation are known. Simply convert the data to a standard normal distribution and use a standard normal Z-table to answer probability questions. Let's describe this approach through an example.

Example 6: In the United States, the daily consumption of sugar is epidemic averaging 126 grams (Ferdman, 2015), two-and-a-half times larger than the amount recommended by the World Health organization (WHO, 2014). According to WHO, the total recommended daily sugar consumption for an adult having a normal BMI (Body Mass Index) is less than 50 grams (less than 10% of the total daily energy intake). So the question is: 'What proportion of Americans exceed the recommended daily sugar consumption?' In other words, 'Given that the daily consumption of sugar among Americans averages 126 grams, what proportion of Americans exceed 50 grams per day?'

Assume the daily sugar consumption among all Americans is normal with a mean of 126 grams and standard deviation of 45 grams.

Solution: The normal distribution found at the left in Figure 4.9 Proportion of Americans Exceeding Recommended Daily Sugar Consumption illustrates the proportion of Americans exceeding 50 grams of sugar per day when the average daily consumption is 126 grams. In order to find that proportion, we must first determine how many standard deviations 50 is from the mean of 126, using the formula:

$$Z=\frac{(X-\mu)}{\sigma}=\frac{50-126}{45}=-1.69$$

Our question then becomes, what proportion of Americans have sugar consumption more than 1.69 standard deviations below the mean? When referring to the standard normal Z-table, you see that the area below a Z of -1.69 is 0.0455; therefore, the area above Z is 0.9545, as illustrated at the right of Figure 4.9 Proportion of Americans Exceeding Recommended Daily Sugar Consumption. In conclusion, knowing that the daily consumption of sugar is normally distributed, with a mean of 126 grams and a standard deviation of 45 grams, we can conclude that 95.45% have daily sugar consumption greater than 50 grams. In other words, 95.45% of Americans exceed the recommended daily sugar consumption.

Figure 4.9 Proportion of Americans Exceeding Recommended Daily Sugar Consumption

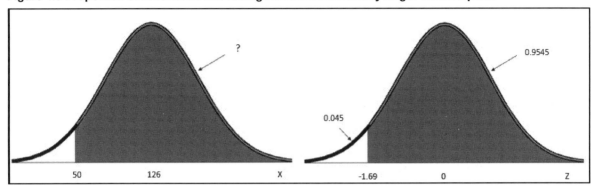

Example 7: College students spend an average of 11.4 hours per day using their 6 digital devices. Let's assume that (X), the time college students spend using digital devices, is normally distributed with a mean of 11.4 hours and a standard deviation of 1.2 hours. What proportion of college students use digital devices more than 14 hours per day? In other words, what is the probability that a randomly selected college student spends more than 14 hours per day using a digital device, P(X>14.0), as illustrated in Figure 4.10 Proportion of College Students Spending More Than 14 Hours Using Digital Devices?

Solution: The normal distribution found at the left in Figure 4.10 Proportion of College Students Spending More Than 14 Hours Using Digital Devices illustrates the proportion of college students using digital devices more than 14 hours per day. Again, we must convert 14 hours to a Z, using the formula:

$$Z = \frac{(X-\mu)}{\sigma} = \frac{14 - 11.4}{1.2} = +2.17$$

$$\frac{140-120}{9} \pm 2.22$$

Referring to the standard normal Z-table, you see that the area below a Z of +2.17 is 0.9850; therefore, the area above Z is 0.0150, as illustrated at the right of Figure 4.10 Proportion of College Students Spending More Than 14 Hours Using Digital Devices. In conclusion, based upon the fact that the population of digital device usage among college students is normally distributed with a mean of 14 hours and standard deviation of 1.2 hours, the proportion of students who have usage exceeding 14 hours is 0.0150, or 1.5%--a relatively small percentage.

Figure 4.10 Proportion of College Students Spending More Than 14 Hours Using Digital Devices

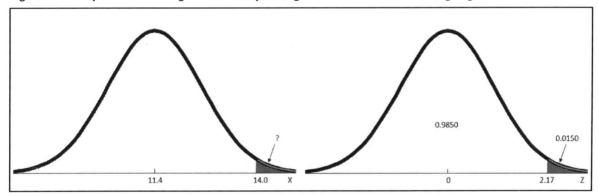

The Sampling Distribution of the Mean

In Chapter 3, "Data Visualization," you learned how to use numeric indices to describe your data, namely measures of center, dispersion, and shape, and how to produce those measures using the UNIVARIATE procedure. Because we rarely have the population, the natural tendency is to make statements about the population based upon on descriptions of the sample. For example, based upon the 2015 American Time Use Survey (ATUS), the Bureau of Labor Statistics (2015) estimates that young Americans 15-19 years of age sleep an average of 9.7 hours every night. Intuitively we know it is improbable that the sample mean will be identical to the true population mean; however, we trust that it will reasonably close within some margin of error.

The sample average is the best guess for what exists in the population, but how can we assess the accuracy of our statement? First, consider this: suppose various researchers take their own, respective, random samples from the population of young Americans aged 15 – 19 years of age, in an attempt to estimate the average number of hours of sleep. Obviously, each researcher will select different samples; therefore, each of those sample means will be different and it's very unlikely that any one of those sample means will be exactly identical to the actual population mean. A very small proportion of sample means will be relatively 'far' from the population mean, but generally speaking, you would expect the sample means to be close to the population mean. The accuracy of the sample mean as an estimate for the population mean depends upon the variability of the sample mean. If the sample means are relatively close to each other, then any one sample mean would be relatively 'close' to the population mean. If the sample means are widely dispersed, then the sample means are relatively 'far' from the population mean. So, even though in practice we use only one sample mean for making inferences about the population mean, we must investigate how all possible sample means behave or vary.

In this section, we will describe the characteristics of the set of all possible sample means when we know the population mean (μ) and population standard deviation (σ). The set of all possible sample means is referred to as the **sampling distribution of the sample mean** and will provide the foundation for making inferences about an unknown population mean based upon a single sample mean.

Characteristics of the Sampling Distribution of the Mean

In order to understand the basis of inferential statistics, the analyst must understand how a sampling distribution is constructed and its characteristics. First, the sampling distribution of the sample mean ($\bar{X}$) is defined as the set of all possible sample means obtained by taking all possible random samples of size n from the population. This set of sample means basically make up a set of numbers and, like all numbers, this data can be summarized by the mean, standard deviation, and shape.

In order to build a hypothetical sampling distribution, let's first consider the numeric random variable (X), the time it takes for customers to be seated at a casual-dining restaurant. Suppose all wait-times for a casual-dining restaurant are exponentially distributed (right skewed) with a mean and standard deviation of 20 minutes, as illustrated in Figure 4.11 Distribution of Wait-Times at a Casual-Dining Restaurant.

Figure 4.11 Distribution of Wait-Times at a Casual-Dining Restaurant

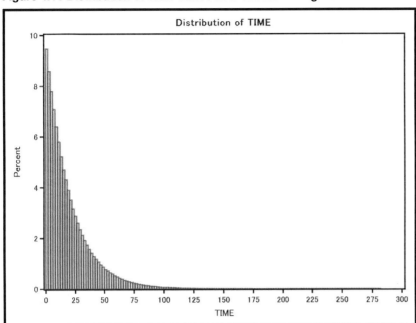

Theoretically, to create a sampling distribution, the analyst would select the first random sample of a fixed sample size from the population of wait-times, record the mean wait-time ($\bar{X}_1$), then 'throw' that sample back into the population, take a second random sample of the same size, record the mean wait-time ($\bar{X}_2$), and again 'throw' that sample back into the population. This process would be repeated until all possible j random samples of a fixed sample size are selected from the population, (i.e., through ($\bar{X}_j$)). In the end, the analyst would have a 'new' data set with all possible sample means.

Program 4.2 Description of the Sampling Distribution of Mean Wait-Times is a simulation of what the analyst would have to do to create a sampling distribution of 100,000 sample means by taking 100,000 random samples of size 100 customers from an exponential population having a mean of 20 minutes.

Program 4.2 Description of the Sampling Distribution of Mean Wait-Times

```
data restaurant;

call streaminit(1); *set random seed;
do j = 1 to 100000;
   do i = 1 to 100;
      time = rand("exponential",20);
      output;
      end;
   end;
run;

proc sort data=restaurant; by j;
run;

proc means noprint;
   var time;    *calculate sample mean time for 100,000 samples;
   output out=samplingdistr mean=meantime;
   by j;
run;

proc univariate data=samplingdistr
   histogram meantime;
   var meantime;
run;
```

In Program 4.2 Description of the Sampling Distribution of Mean Wait-Times, data is generated and saved in a temporary SAS data set called RESTAURANT. Within the DO LOOP (I = 1 to 100), the value of an exponential numeric random variable with a mean of 20 minutes is generated for each of the i observations to make up a sample of size 100. The DO LOOP (J = 1 to 100000) indicates that random samples of size 100 are created 100,000 times. The PROC SORT and PROC MEANS steps both provide for sorting the observations by the sample number j, calculating the sample mean for each sample j, and then saving those 100,000 means, each named MEANTIME, to a temporary SAS data set called SAMPLINGDISTR. Note that because the data set, SAMPLINGDISTR, theoretically, contains all possible samples, this data set represents the population of sample means. Finally, the last step employs the UNIVARIATE procedure for describing the sampling distribution in terms of mean, standard error, and shape, as illustrated in Output 4.2 Description of the Sampling Distribution of Mean Wait-Times. It should also be noted that, in order to reproduce the same set of random values each time the program is run, CALL STREAMINIT is required before invoking the RAND function; the specific number in parentheses determines the specific set of random numbers generated via the RAND function.

Output 4.2 Description of the Sampling Distribution of Mean Wait-Times

Basic Statistical Measures			
Location		Variability	
Mean	20.00721	Std Deviation	2.00143
Median	19.95005	Variance	4.00572
Mode	.	Range	17.20544
		Interquartile Range	2.69622

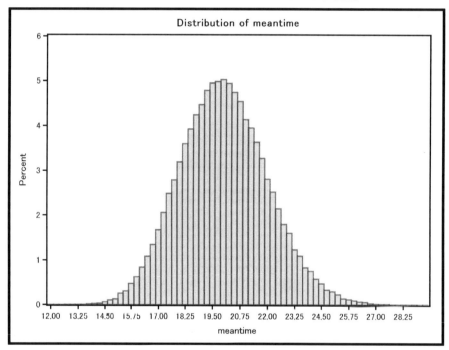

In summary, we observe the following characteristics from the univariate analysis:

1. The population mean of the sample means is 20.0 minutes ($\mu_{\bar{x}} = 20.0$). Notice that the mean of the sampling distribution is represented by the Greek symbol μ because the data is considered a population and the subscript indicates that 20.0 minutes is the population mean of the *sample means*.

2. The population standard deviation of the sample means is 2.0 minutes ($\sigma_{\bar{x}} = 2.0$) and is referred to as the **standard error** of the mean.

3. An inspection of the histogram illustrates that the sampling distribution of the mean is normal, even though the population is not normal. We will see shortly that the shape of the sampling distribution will always be normal under specific situations.

The Central Limit Theorem

As illustrated through our simulation example, generating a sampling distribution of all infinitely many sample means to investigate its properties involves an incredible amount of work and is, therefore, impractical; in most cases, it is impossible. However, there are some basic conclusions that are always true and, consequently, can always be made in lieu of creating the sampling distribution. These conclusions are related directly to the mean, standard deviation, and shape of the sampling distribution and are as follows:

- $\mu_{\bar{X}} = \mu$

- $\sigma_{\bar{X}} = \dfrac{\sigma}{\sqrt{n}}$

- The shape of the sampling distribution is normal under either of these conditions:

  (1) The shape of the sampling distribution is normal if the population is normal. (2) When the shape of the population is not normal or unknown, the shape of the sampling distribution is approximately normal when the sample size is sufficiently large, where large is considered 30 or more. This statement is known as the **central limit theorem**.

The first item indicates that the mean of the sampling distribution is equal to the mean of the population. In other words, we expect the sample mean to be equal to the population mean. Secondly, the standard error of the mean, $\sigma_{\bar{X}}$ gives the analyst an idea of how the sample means, $(\bar{X}_j)$, varies from sample to sample. In fact, when the standard error is relatively small, we expect relatively little variation in the sample means around the population mean; when the standard error is relatively large, we expect relatively large variation in the sample means around the population mean. Finally, item 3 gives conditions where the sampling distribution is normal and, as mentioned earlier, will provide the foundation for conducting inferential statistics.

So, let's revisit our exponential wait-time example. Instead of actually creating a sampling distribution of means and analyzing that to get basic descriptions, we can now apply the three statements above to get those descriptions. In other words, knowing only that we are to take a random sample of size 100 from a non-normal population of wait-times with both a mean and standard deviation of 20 minutes, we would have concluded that:

- The mean of the sampling distribution is 20 minutes ($\mu_{\bar{X}} = \mu = 20$).

- The standard error is 2.0 minutes ($\sigma_{\bar{X}} = \dfrac{\sigma}{\sqrt{n}} = \dfrac{20}{\sqrt{100}} = 2.0$), where n=100.

  The shape of the sampling distribution is approximately normal because the sample size of 100 is large (i.e., greater than 30), even though the population is non-normal.

There are a few comments in order now that we have described the characteristics of the sampling distribution. First, when the population is not normal and the sample size is small, we cannot say that the sampling distribution is normal; however, the first two statements pertaining to the mean and standard error are always true. In fact, you can rerun the SAS code used to generate the sampling distribution for sample sizes less than 30 (for example, for a sample size of 10, use DO I = 1 to 10;) and you will see that the sampling distribution is no longer normal. However, $\mu_{\bar{X}} = 20$ minutes and $\sigma_{\bar{X}} = 20/\sqrt{10} = 6.325$ minutes. On your own, you can also run the simulation program to show that for a normal population, the sampling distribution is normal for small sample sizes.

Finally, notice in our example, for a sample of size 100, the standard error $(\sigma_{\bar{X}})$ is 2, while for a sample size of 10, the standard error $(\sigma_{\bar{X}})$ is 6.325. In other words, we have less variability in the sample means when the sample size is larger.

It should make good intuitive sense that the standard error depends upon the sample size; basically, as the sample size increases and approaches the population size, the sample 'looks' more like the population and the sample means $(\bar{X}_j)$ will approach the population mean (μ). Consider the difference in the two sampling distributions for sample sizes 30 and 100, respectively, in Figure 4.12 Sampling Distribution of Average Wait-Times by Sample Size. In short, for a sample of size 30, the variation in means is larger than for a sample size of 100.

Figure 4.12 Sampling Distribution of Average Wait-Times by Sample Size

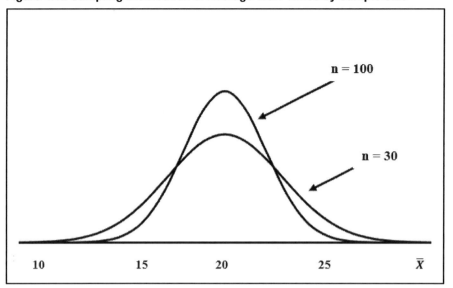

Application of the Sampling Distribution of the Mean

Now let's use the characteristics of the sampling distribution to help us assess that chances that the sample mean takes on a value within a specific *range*. Let's revisit our restaurant wait-time example. Suppose we know that, for a casual-dining restaurant, the wait-time (X) is exponentially distributed (right skewed) with a mean and standard deviation of 20 minutes.

Suppose you take a random sample of 50 customers during lunch. Based upon your sample of 50 customers, if the population of wait-times is non-normal with a mean of 20 minutes and standard deviation of 20 minutes, what is the probability that the average wait-time will be more than 25.0 minutes, $P(\bar{X} > 25.0)$?

In order to answer any questions about sample means, we must first look at how we expect the sample means to behave by applying our rules for the sampling distribution of the mean. Doing so gives us the following:

- The mean of the sampling distribution is 20 minutes ($\mu_{\bar{X}} = 20$).

- The standard error is 2.8284 minutes ($\sigma_{\bar{X}} = \dfrac{20}{\sqrt{50}} = 2.8284$).

- The shape of the sampling distribution is approximately normal because the sample size of 50 is considered large (i.e., n>30), even though the population is non-normal.

So, the question we are asking can be translated into the following sampling distribution as illustrated in Figure 4.13 Sample Distribution of the Mean Based upon a Sample Size of 50.

Figure 4.13 Sample Distribution of the Mean Based upon a Sample Size of 50

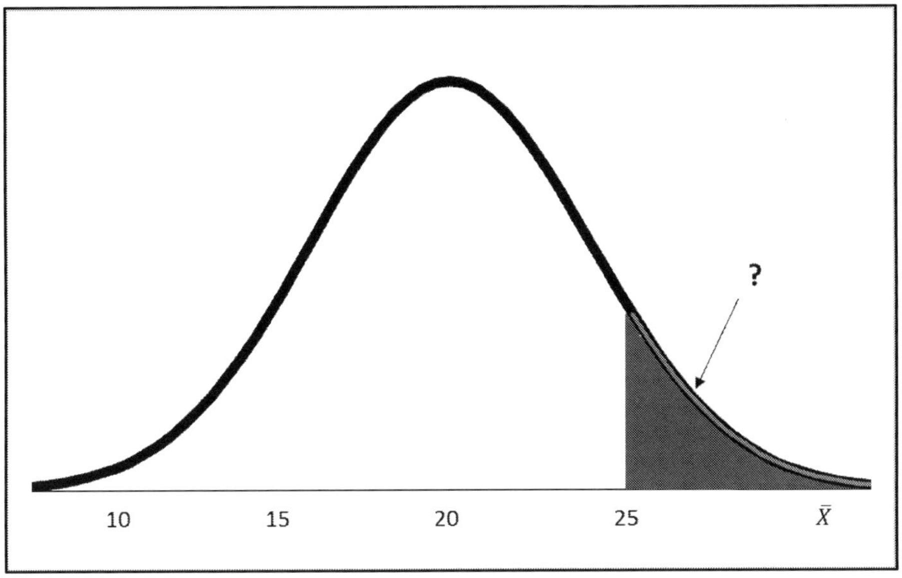

Secondly, we are now looking at the probability that the sample mean falls within a particular range where all possible sample means (i.e., the sampling distribution) have a shape that is normal. So how do we calculate a probability? By now, you may recognize that anytime you ask a probability question about a normal distribution, you must convert a numeric value to a Z-score and use your standard normal Z-table.

So how do you standardize? In the beginning of this chapter, you saw that when asking a probability question about X falling within a certain range within a normal distribution, you subtracted the mean from X, and then divided by the standard deviation of X. Now, you are interested in finding the probability with respect to a sample mean, so you must standardize the sampling distribution of the sample mean by subtracting the mean of the sampling distribution and dividing by the standard deviation of the sample mean, or the standard error. In short, to convert $\bar{X}$ to a Z-score, you must use the following formula:

$$Z = \frac{\bar{X} - \mu}{\sigma_{\bar{X}}} = \frac{\bar{X} - \mu}{\sigma/\sqrt{n}}$$

So our sample mean of 25 minutes is converted to a standardized Z score as follows:

$$Z = \frac{25.0 - 20}{20/\sqrt{50}} = +1.77$$

The Z-score of +1.77 indicates that the sample mean of 25 is 1.77 standard errors above the population mean of 20. In order to find the probability, you must locate 1.77 in the Z-table to find the area under the curve; that is, 0.9616. So the area under the curve above Z is 0.0384, as shown in Figure 4.14 Probability That Z > +1.77. In conclusion, when the average time to seat customers at a casual-dining restaurant is non-normal with a mean of 20 minutes and a standard deviation of 20 minutes, the probability of selecting a sample of size 50 having an average wait-time more than 25 minutes is 0.0384, or 3.84%--in other words, somewhat unlikely.

Figure 4.14 Probability That Z > +1.77

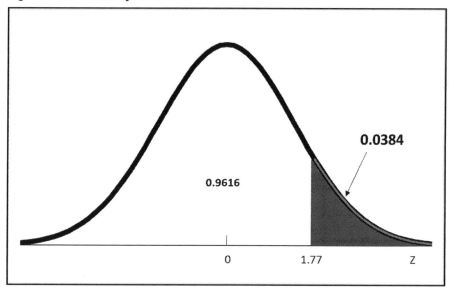

Effects of Sample Size on the Sampling Distribution

As stated previously, sample size affects the variation of the sample means and that variation is specifically defined by the standard error. Remember that as sample size increases, the standard error decreases and, vice versa: as the sample size decreases, the standard error increases. Well, how does that affect our probability questions about the sample mean? In order to illustrate its effects, let's revisit the previous problem with a different sample size.

Example 8: Consider the population of wait-times at a casual-dining restaurant which is non-normal, having a mean of 20 minutes and standard deviation of 20 minutes. Suppose you now take a random sample of 100 customers and ask the question, what is the probability that the average wait-time will be more than 25.0 minutes, $P(\bar{X} > 25.0)$? Notice that the appropriate sampling distribution is more peaked as illustrated in Figure 4.15 Sampling Distribution of the Mean for Two Sample Sizes.

Solution: Note that the process of answering the question remains the same. However, the standard error changes because it is a function of sample size, and consequently, the value of Z-score changes as follows:

$$Z = \frac{25.0 - 20}{20 / \sqrt{100}} = +2.50$$

The question now becomes, what is the probability that Z is greater than +2.50, that is P(Z>2.50)? Using your Z-table, you should arrive at the answer 0.0062. In other words, if you take a random sample of size 100 from a population that is non-normal with a mean and standard deviation of 20, you have a 0.62% chance of selecting a mean of 25 or more. From a practical perspective, you should see that the probability of getting a sample mean in the tail (i.e., relatively far from the mean) is less likely for the sample size of 100 (0.0062) when compared to a sample of size 50 (.0384) as further shown in Figure 4.15 Sampling Distribution of the Mean for Two Sample Sizes. It should make intuitive sense that, as the sample size increases, you expect the sample mean to be 'closer' to the population mean as opposed falling in the tails.

$$Z = \frac{140 - 120}{9 / \sqrt{5}}$$

Figure 4.15 Sampling Distribution of the Mean for Two Sample Sizes

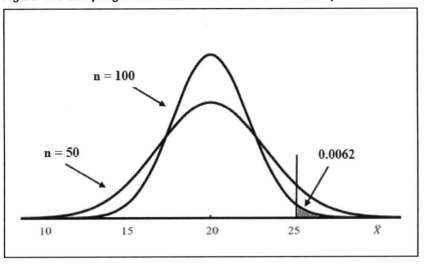

Introduction to Hypothesis Testing

In Chapter 2, "Summarizing Your Data with Descriptive Statistics" and Chapter 3, "Data Visualization," we used procedures to summarize the data we select from a single sample in terms of both numeric descriptions and visual descriptions. These procedures are referred to as **descriptive statistics**. We now turn out attention to the topic of **inferential statistics** where we use sample data to infer some conclusion about the population.

In the previous section, we introduced the sampling distribution which gives us a way to assess some expectation about our sample means when we know the true population mean. We will now consider only those situations where we do not know the value of the population mean. Specifically, we will make an assumption about the population mean and, along with this assumption, we have some 'expectation' about the values of the sample mean, based upon what we know about the sampling distribution.

So when we select a random sample, and consider our single 'observed' mean, we must ask ourselves the following question: Is the observed mean relatively far from what we 'expect' when our assumption is true? If the answer to that question is 'Yes,' that is, our data differs from what we expect, then we must question our initial assumption. If our answer is 'No,' then we have no reason to question our initial assumption and assume it is still intact.

We all, at some time or another, make observations and consequently make generalizations based upon those observations. Let's consider an example to which most of us can relate--traffic and how long it takes us to drive to work each day. After working a job for a period of time, you begin to make a generalization about the time it takes to get to work and, therefore, leave at the same time each morning to ensure you get to work on time. Suppose, for example, your commute time is 20 minutes. As long as nothing changes for your morning commute--barring the typical traffic accident or bad weather--you expect to get to work on time each day if you allow 20 minutes for commuting. If you follow your normal routine and continue to get to work on time, you can assume that the average commute time for all mornings (in the population) remains unchanged at 20 minutes.

Suppose now that on random days you are late for work, along with, say, friends and co-workers who drive the same distance, and find that the average commute time is now 30 minutes. You may then change your routine to allow more time because you have reason to believe that the commute time, in general, has now increased. Now, would you necessarily change your routine if you had, for example, experienced an average commute time of 22? In other words, would the difference in what you observe (22 minutes) and what you expect (20 minutes) be large enough to consider a change in your normal routine? Maybe not!

In this section, we will introduce a systematic approach for testing our initial assumption about the population based upon a single sample in a process called **hypothesis testing**. In particular, we will make an initial assumption about the population parameter, take a random sample from that population and calculate the sample statistic, and then provide a decision rule for how far our observed statistic must deviate from our expected population parameter before we are willing to abandon our initial assumption.

Defining the Null and Alternative Hypotheses

In order to carry out a hypothesis test, the analyst must first make a formal statement about the population parameter of interest--in our case, the population mean. The statement consists of two parts: the null hypothesis and the alternative hypothesis. The **null hypothesis (H_o)** is the initial statement about the population and ordinarily represents a commonly accepted state of affairs, or the status quo. The null hypothesis is tentatively assumed to be true unless overwhelmingly contradicted by data. The **alternative hypothesis (H_1)** is the opposite of the null hypothesis and is ordinarily a statement of what the analyst wishes to prove.

Let's revisit our restaurant wait-time example. Suppose you are the manager of a casual-dining restaurant and your restaurant's practices ensure that your customers are seated in an average of 20 minutes after they walk in the door. Suppose you are considering some creative ways to reduce your customer wait-time and have decided to implement a new video-monitoring system to identify choke points in your restaurant. If the new system is successful, then the wait-time should be reduced. As with any technology, the new system could cause some unexpected inefficiencies and result in an increase in wait-time. In short, you are interested in detecting a change in either direction. In order to detect either the reduction or increase in the wait-time, you must first define your hypotheses. In essence, you take a random sample of customers to test the new technology and want to show that the newly implemented technology is effective in *changing* the wait-time. Remember --what you want to show is associated with the alternative hypothesis. The null hypothesis is the opposite: that is, the technology has no effect and that the wait-time has remained the same. Therefore, the hypotheses of interest are:

$$H_o: \mu = 20 \quad \text{versus } H_1: \mu \neq 20.$$

This specific hypothesis set is referred to as **directional hypotheses** as the analyst is interested in detecting a change in either direction, a reduction or an increase in wait-time.

Before testing the hypotheses, the analyst must also describe the appropriate sampling distribution so that he or she has an idea of what to expect if the null hypothesis is true. Remember, if the original population is normal or if the sample size is sufficiently large (central limit theorem), then the sampling distribution is normal, with mean (μ_0) and standard error ($\sigma_{\bar{x}}$), where μ_0 is the hypothesized population mean, as indicated in Figure 4.16 Rejection Region for a Two-Tailed Test.

Figure 4.16 Rejection Region for a Two-Tailed Test

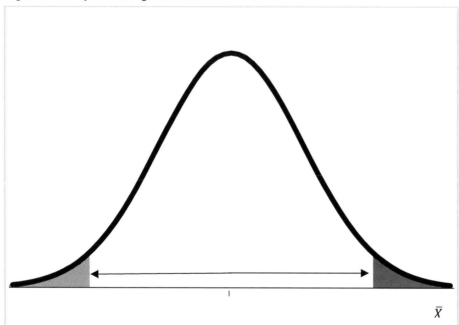

$\bar{X}$

So, when we take our single sample of customers and obtain our sample mean wait-time, if that sample mean is relatively 'far' from what we expect (μ_0), then we must reject the null hypothesis. In other words, we will reject the null if the sample mean is either significantly less than μ_o or significantly more than μ_o. The **rejection region**, as shaded in Figure 4.16 Rejection Region for a Two-Tailed Test, indicates those sample means that are not expected if the null hypothesis is true. Note that this test is also referred to as a **two-tailed** test, as the rejection region resides in both tails.

Suppose, instead, that the manager is interested only in detecting a reduction in wait-time. Then the appropriate hypothesis set would be:

$$H_o: \mu \geq 20 \quad \text{versus} \quad H_1: \mu < 20$$

Notice that what the manager wants to show is a decrease in wait-time as illustrated in the alternative hypothesis. Here, if the sample mean is significantly less than the hypothesized mean μ_o, we will reject the null hypothesis in favor of the alternative. This specific hypothesis set is a **directional test** and is also known as a one-tailed, lower-tailed test as shown in Figure 4.17 Rejection Region for a Lower-Tailed Test.

Figure 4.17 Rejection Region for a Lower-Tailed Test

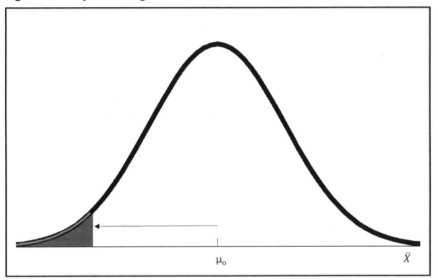

On the other hand, suppose the manager is interested in determining only if the restaurant's performance has diminished (i.e., that the wait-time has increased). Then the appropriate hypothesis set would be:

$$H_o: \mu \leq 20 \quad \text{versus} \quad H_1: \mu > 20$$

In this case, if the sample mean is significantly more than the hypothesized mean μ_o, we will reject the null hypothesis. This specific hypothesis set is a **directional test** and is also known as a one-tailed, upper-tailed test as shown in Figure 4.18 Rejection Region for an Upper-Tailed Test.

Figure 4.18 Rejection Region for an Upper-Tailed Test

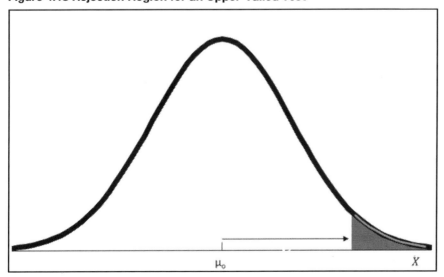

Defining and Controlling Errors in Hypothesis Testing

Remember, when doing an inferential study, we are making an assumption about some unknown population parameter--in this chapter that is the population mean. So when we take a sample and use that information to make a decision about the null hypothesis, we can never be assured that we are making the right decision. Therefore, our goal is to develop a decision rule that ensures we are minimizing the chance of making an error. In order to do that, we must first define the two types of errors.

A **Type I error** occurs if we reject a true null hypothesis and can be viewed as a 'false alarm.' A **Type II error** occurs if we accept a false null hypothesis and can be viewed as a 'missed opportunity.' We will define α as the probability of making a Type I error and β as the probability of making a Type II error. Of course, we really count on making a correct decision, where we either accept a true null hypothesis or reject a false null hypothesis.

To illustrate the implications of each type of error, let's consider our restaurant wait-time example, where the industry-standard wait-time is 20 minutes and the manager wants to show a decrease (improvement) in wait-time after implementing the new technology:

$$H_o: \mu \geq 20 \text{ versus } H_1: \mu < 20$$

Consider, first, the Type I error--Suppose that the manager implements the new technology and, in reality, the null hypothesis is true. That is, the technology is ineffective and, accordingly, all customers have an average wait-time of at least 20 minutes. Suppose also that the manager takes a random sample of customers, records the wait-times, observes that the sample mean is 'significantly' less than the expected mean of 20 minutes, and, consequently, rejects the null hypothesis. In this case, the manager has committed a Type I error. In other words, there is a false alarm where the manager concludes that the newly implemented technology is effective when in reality it's a dud! In this case, the manager claims that his investment in the new technology was effective, when in reality the technology was implemented with no true improvement in wait-time.

Consider, now, the Type II error. Suppose, in reality, the null hypothesis is false and all customers have an average wait-time less than 20 minutes. Suppose, in this case, the manager takes a random sample of customers, notes a sample mean relatively close to or greater than 20 minutes, and, consequently, accepts the null hypothesis. In this case, the manager has committed a Type II error. In short, there is a missed opportunity where the manager concludes that the newly implemented technology is not effective when in reality it's a success! Here, the manager may opt to remove the technology and, thus, will miss an opportunity to increase revenue through reduced wait-times and increased customer satisfaction.

When conducting a hypothesis test, the analyst is interested in minimizing the chance of committing an error. The only way to minimize both types of errors is to increase the sample size. Ordinarily, we are dealing with limited resources and increasing the sample size may be infeasible or even impossible. In the case of a fixed sample size, the analyst cannot minimize or control both types of errors at the same time. So why is this? Remember that you can commit a Type I error only when a true null is rejected. So the analyst could avoid a Type I error by accepting the null; however, as soon as the decision is made to accept the null, by definition, it is now possible to make a Type II error. As a result, the analyst must decide which type of error is to be controlled--Type

In reality, the analyst should consider the relative costs of
hypothesis testing, it is a commonly accepted practice to d
words, the analyst will define a decision rule that prohibits
unless the observed sample statistic is relatively far from t
defines a distance $|\bar{X} - \mu_0|$ where he or she is relatively co

Ultimately, the question becomes: What distance is consid
significance (α), the maximum allowable Type I error rate   1, 0.05,
or 0.10. So if you really want to play it safe, you would set   were to
set a distance criterion for rejecting the null and applied tha   mistake
by rejecting only 1 out of 100 times. If however, we wante   our
level of significance to 0.10, indicating that we are willing
Hopefully, you can see that setting the significance level at   that the
distance criterion is larger than that for 0.10 or even 0.05. I   ce
suggests that our intention is to reject the null only in cases   lecision.
Shortly, we will see why this is true when we use the level   the
null.

Hypothesis Testing for the Population Mean (σ Known)

In this section, we lay out a five-step process for testing hypotheses about the population mean (μ) when σ is known. We illustrate both the two-tailed and one-tailed approach, followed by an explanation and illustration of the p-value approach.

Two-Tailed Tests for the Population Mean (μ)

Consider, again, our restaurant wait-time example. As you may recall, it is common in casual-dining restaurants to wait an average of 20.0 minutes before being seated. Suppose you are an analyst hired by the manager and your task is to determine how a new video-monitoring system performs when used to identify choke points. Because you are not sure of the effects, you are interested in testing the system for both possible influences--either the system is successful in identifying bottlenecks and helps to reduce wait-times or the system is unsuccessful because it causes unexpected inefficiencies resulting in an increased wait-time. Therefore, the hypotheses you are interested in testing are:

$$H_o\text{: } \mu = 20 \quad \text{versus } H_1\text{: } \mu \neq 20.$$

After implementing the video-monitoring system, suppose you randomly select 60 customers and find that the average time to seat customers is 15.5 minutes. Obviously, your sample mean of 15.5 is not equal to your hypothesized population mean of 20; however, keep in mind that the real question is asking: 'Is 15.5 minutes far enough from my hypothesized mean time of 20.0 minutes to conclude that, if I had the entire population, the true population mean wait-time is now different than 20 minutes?

Assume that the distribution of the wait-times is exponentially distributed with a population standard deviation $\sigma = 20.0$ minutes. You decide to set your level of significance (α) at 0.05 for determining the rejection rule. The process of hypothesis testing can be summarized in five steps.

Step 1: So that the analyst knows what to expect if the null hypothesis is true, the analyst must first identify and describe the appropriate sampling distribution. In other words, if the null hypothesis is true, you can make some assumptions about how the set of all possible sample means behaves by applying the central limit theorem. So while the original population is non-normal, because the sample size 60 is considered sufficiently large, the sampling distribution is normal with mean (μ_0) and standard error ($\sigma_{\bar{X}}$). So for our hypothesis test, we can describe the three following characteristics of the sampling distribution:

1. The sampling distribution of the mean is normal because the sample size is large (n=60 > 30), even though the shape of the population is not normal.
2. The mean of the sampling distribution ($\mu_{\bar{X}}$) is equal to the mean of the hypothesized population (μ_0). That is, $\mu_{\bar{X}} = 20$.
3. The standard error of the mean which measures the variation in the sample means is equal to
   $\sigma / \sqrt{n} = 20 / \sqrt{60} = 2.5820$

Step 2: Once the analyst knows the characteristics of the sampling distribution, he or she must define the decision rule for rejecting the null hypothesis based upon the set level of significance (α). In other words, we want to define the **critical region** so that if the sample mean exceeds a certain distance from the hypothesized mean, our chance of making a Type I error will be lower than that allowed by the α-level. To set up the scenario, consider the sampling distribution for our example in Figure 4.19 Rejection Region for a Two-Tailed Test at $\alpha = 0.05$.

Figure 4.19 Rejection Region for a Two-Tailed Test at α = 0.05

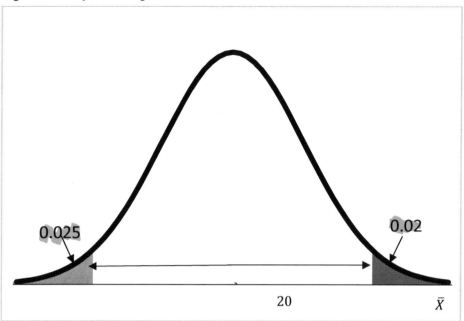

Let's define the rejection region to be the shaded area. This shaded area corresponds to all sample means considered relatively far where the analyst is justified in rejecting the null hypothesis even though the null is true. This represents the proportion of sample means where we would erroneously reject the null hypothesis and commit a Type I error. So we want a distance from the hypothesize mean of 20, where we will reject incorrectly and, thereby, commit a Type I error only 5% of the time (for α=0.05). Because we are considering a two-tailed test, that distance corresponds to 0.025 of the area in each tail. In essence, the shaded area represents the .05 proportion of times that a sample mean will be that far from μ_o when μ_o is actually true.

When an analyst conducts a hypothesis test, it is common to measure the distance between μ_o and $\overline{X}$ in terms of the number of standard errors, in other words, using the Z-score. So our question becomes, how many Z-scores does the sample mean have to be from the hypothesized mean in order to reject and stay below the .05 level of significance? This Z-score is referred to as the **critical value.** This is equivalent to asking the question, what is the Z-value where .025 proportion of the Z-values is in each of the tails. Because we have established that the sampling distribution is normal, we can use our Z-table to find the Z-value resulting in .025 proportion in each tail.

When looking in the Z-table, as illustrated in Table 4.3 Finding Z-Value Associated with 0.025 Area in the Lower Tail, you are working backwards, so you must look in the body of the table to find the appropriate proportion, .0250, and the entry defines the row and column needed to identify the Z-value. So 0.025 of the Z-values are below the Z-value of - 1.96, and by symmetry, 0.025 of the Z-values are above the Z-value of +1.96. In conclusion, our critical values are ± 1.96.

Table 4.3 Finding Z-Value Associated with 0.025 Area in the Lower Tail

Z	0.00	0.01	0.02	0.03	0.04	0.05	0.06	0.07	0.08	0.09
0.0	0.5000	0.4960	0.4920	0.4880	0.4840	0.4801	0.4761	0.4721	0.4681	0.4641
-0.1	0.4602	0.4562	0.4522	0.4483	0.4443	0.4404	0.4364	0.4325	0.4286	0.4247
-0.2	0.4207	0.4168	0.4129	0.4090	0.4052	0.4013	0.3974	0.3936	0.3897	0.3859
-0.3	0.3821	0.3783	0.3745	0.3707	0.3669	0.3632	0.3594	0.3557	0.3520	0.3483
-0.4	0.3446	0.3409	0.3372	0.3336	0.3300	0.3264	0.3228	0.3192	0.3156	0.3121
-0.5	0.3085	0.3050	0.3015	0.2981	0.2946	0.2912	0.2877	0.2843	0.2810	0.2776
-0.6	0.2743	0.2709	0.2676	0.2643	0.2611	0.2578	0.2546	0.2514	0.2483	0.2451
-0.7	0.2420	0.2389	0.2358	0.2327	0.2296	0.2266	0.2236	0.2206	0.2177	0.2148
-0.8	0.2119	0.2090	0.2061	0.2033	0.2005	0.1977	0.1949	0.1922	0.1894	0.1867
-0.9	0.1841	0.1814	0.1788	0.1762	0.1736	0.1711	0.1685	0.1660	0.1635	0.1611
-1.0	0.1587	0.1562	0.1539	0.1515	0.1492	0.1469	0.1446	0.1423	0.1401	0.1379
-1.1	0.1357	0.1335	0.1314	0.1292	0.1271	0.1251	0.1230	0.1210	0.1190	0.1170
-1.2	0.1151	0.1131	0.1112	0.1093	0.1075	0.1056	0.1038	0.1020	0.1003	0.0985
-1.3	0.0968	0.0951	0.0934	0.0918	0.0901	0.0885	0.0869	0.0853	0.0838	0.0823
-1.4	0.0808	0.0793	0.0778	0.0764	0.0749	0.0735	0.0721	0.0708	0.0694	0.0681
-1.5	0.0668	0.0655	0.0643	0.0630	0.0618	0.0606	0.0594	0.0582	0.0571	0.0559
-1.6	0.0548	0.0537	0.0526	0.0516	0.0505	0.0495	0.0485	0.0475	0.0465	0.0455
-1.7	0.0446	0.0436	0.0427	0.0418	0.0409	0.0401	0.0392	0.0384	0.0375	0.0367
-1.8	0.0359	0.0351	0.0344	0.0336	0.0329	0.0322	0.0314	0.0307	0.0301	0.0294
-1.9							0.0250	0.0244	0.0239	0.0233
-2.0	0.0228	0.0222	0.0217	0.0212	0.0207	0.0202	0.0197	0.0192	0.0188	0.0183

These values are used to establish our *rejection rule*: We will reject the null hypothesis if the sample mean has a Z-value more than +1.96 or less than -1.96. In other words, we will reject the null hypothesis if our sample mean is more than 1.96 standard errors from our hypothesized mean, as illustrated in Figure 4.20 Critical Values for a Two-Tailed Test at α = 0.05.

Figure 4.20 Critical Values for a Two-Tailed Test at α = 0.05

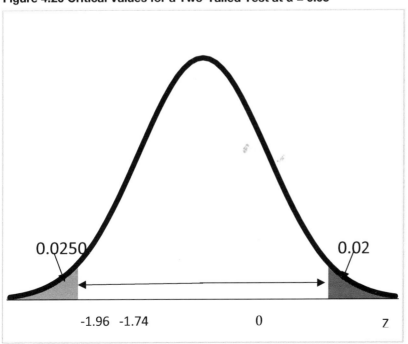

Step 3: The form of the rejection rule requires that we convert our sample mean to a Z-score. In other words, we are asking the question: How many standard errors is my sample mean from my hypothesized mean. We can answer that question using the following formula:

$$Z = \frac{(\bar{X}-\mu)}{\sigma/\sqrt{n}} = \frac{15.5 - 20}{20/\sqrt{60}} = -1.74$$

This Z-value is referred to as the **test statistic** and tells the analyst that the sample mean of 15.5 is 1.74 standard errors *below* the hypothesized mean of 20.

Step 4: Now that we know our test statistic, we can make our final decision about the null hypothesis; that is, because our test statistic, -1.74, is between our critical values (±1.96), we do not reject the null. In short, as illustrated in Figure 4.20 Critical Values for a Two-Tailed Test at α = 0.05, our sample mean is not far enough to reject the null and maintain a Type I error rate less than 0.05.

Step 5: Once we make our final decision, we must interpret that decision in terms of the alternative hypothesis. Because we do not reject the null hypothesis, we conclude that there is not enough evidence to say that the alternative hypothesis is true, that the average wait-time in the population has changed from 20 minutes. In other words, there is not enough evidence, based upon our sample of 60 customers, to say that the newly installed video-monitoring system had any effects on the average wait-time of all casual-dining customers.

The methodology just introduced for conducting the hypothesis test for a population mean is called the **Z-test for means** because the sampling distribution of the means is normal and allows us to use the Z-table for finding critical values. This approach is sometimes referred to as the **Critical Value Approach**.

One-Tailed Tests for the Population Mean (μ)

The specific nature of the business question always determines the direction of the test. Suppose, in the case of our wait-time example, the restaurant manager is interested only in detecting a decrease in the wait-time instead. This question would warrant using a one-tailed, lower-tailed test where the appropriate hypotheses would be:

$$H_o: \mu \geq 20 \quad \text{versus} \quad H_1: \mu < 20$$

For wait-times, assume that the distribution of the wait-times is exponentially distributed with a population standard deviation σ = 20.0 minutes. Suppose, again, that the manager randomly selects 60 customers and finds that the average time to seat customers is 15.5 minutes, and tests the hypothesis at a 0.05 level of significance.

Consider each of the steps needed to conduct the hypothesis test:

Step 1: The sampling distribution of the means is normal because the sample size is large (n=60 > 30) where the mean of the sampling distribution ($\mu_{\bar{x}}$) is 20 and the standard error of the mean is equal to $\sigma/\sqrt{n} = 20/\sqrt{60} = 2.5820$. Notice that this is identical to our two-tailed test example because our data conditions have not changed.

Step 2: Based upon the level of significance, we must now find the critical value and state our rejection rule. Because the alternative hypothesis represents 'less than,' we will conduct a one-tailed, lower-tailed test. The critical value is that Z-value where .05 (or 5%) of the Z-values are below, as indicated in Figure 4.21 Critical Value for a One-Tailed Test at α = 0.05.

Figure 4.21 Critical Value for a One-Tailed Test at α = 0.05

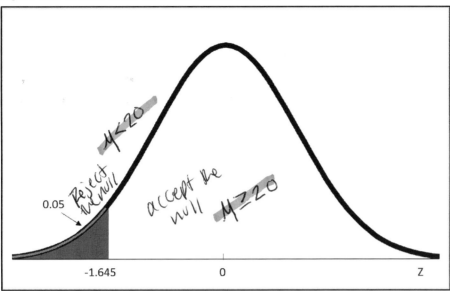

To find the Z-value, you will look in the body of the Z-table in Appendix C Z-Table where you will look for 0.0500. While you will not locate 0.0500 exactly, you will find both areas 0.0495 and 0.0505, associated with critical values -1.64 and -1.65, respectively. Using linear interpolation, we will use -1.645 as the critical value for a lower-tailed test at .05 level of significance.

This value is used to establish our *rejection rule*: We will reject the null hypothesis if our test statistic is less than -1.645.

Step 3: Based upon the sample data, calculate the test statistic, as follows:

$$Z = \frac{(\bar{X} - \mu)}{\sigma/\sqrt{n}} = \frac{15.5 - 20}{20/\sqrt{60}} = -1.74$$

Step 4: Our test statistic -1.74 is less than the critical value of -1.645, so we will reject the null hypothesis, as illustrated in Figure 4.22 Test Statistic Compared to the Critical Value.

Figure 4.22 Test Statistic Compared to the Critical Value

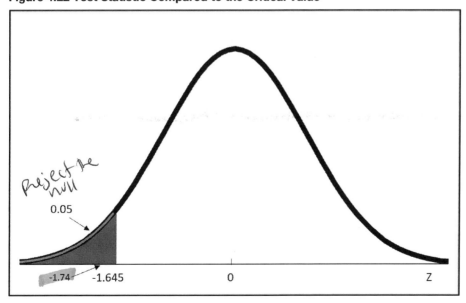

Step 5: Based upon our sample of 60 customers, we have reason to believe that the average wait-time for the casual-dining restaurant has declined since installing the new video-monitoring system.

Now that you have conducted your first hypothesis test, there are a few comments to be noted. First, when conducting more sophisticated tests of hypotheses (in this book and in other references), the same five basic steps will be employed to arrive at a decision to reject the null hypothesis or not.

Secondly, notice that, in our wait-time example, when we conducted the two-tailed versus the lower-tailed test, our decisions differed. For a fixed α-level (in our case, $\alpha = 0.05$), when we conducted the two-tailed test, we did not reject the null hypothesis; however, when we conducted the lower-tailed test we rejected. In fact, changing the level of significance (α) or whether the test is one- or two-tailed will affect what you use for critical values as seen in Table 4.4 Critical Values Based upon α-Level and One-Tailed versus Two-Tailed Tests. Notice also because of symmetry, the magnitudes of the critical values are identical when comparing one- and two-tailed tests. So had the manager, for some reason, wanted to detect only an increase in wait-time, then at .05 level of significance, the critical value would have been +1.645.

Table 4.4 Critical Values Based upon α-Level and One-Tailed versus Two-Tailed Tests

α-Level	Two-Tailed	Upper-Tailed	One-Tailed (Lower)
0.01	±2.575	+2.33	-2.33
0.05	±1.96	+1.645	-1.645
0.10	±1.645	+1.28	-1.28

Next, when conducting any hypothesis test, it should be noted that there are only two decisions and each has a specific interpretation. In short,

- If you ***reject*** the null hypothesis, there ***is evidence*** that the alternative hypothesis is true.
- If you ***do not reject*** the null hypothesis, there ***no is evidence*** that the alternative hypothesis is true.

The analyst must keep these interpretations clear in order to make subsequent decisions.

Finally, consider how sample size can affect the results of a hypothesis test. Holding all other values constant, what would happen to the test statistic if the sample size had been larger, say, 100? You can do the math, but consider that if the sample size increases, then the standard error decreases; if the standard error decreases, then the z-test statistic increases and is more likely to exceed the critical value. So for a fixed level of significance (i.e.: fixed critical value), you are more likely to reject the null when you increase your sample size. This has to do with the **power of the test**--that is, the probability of rejecting the null when the null is actually false, denoted by $(1-\beta)$. This, in essence, is the probability of *not* committing a Type II error.

Hypothesis Testing Using the P-Value Approach

In the previous section, hypothesis testing required finding the critical value(s) based upon the level of significance (α), and this criterion was used to make your decision. Remember the level of significance is the maximum allowable chance of making a Type I error. In this section, we will use the p-value approach to make our decision. Both the critical value approach and the p-value approach are different ways of coming up with the same decision. So in practice, you would use one approach or the other, not both. You will see, however, in practice, that all statistical packages supply a p-value in the output, so the use of the p-value allows for making decisions in an instant and also provides the magnitude of the evidence to reject or not.

So what is a p-value? The **p-value** is the *actual* chance of making a Type I error using your sample data. How do you calculate the p-value? Basically, the p-value is the probability of getting your sample mean or some value farther in the tail when, in reality, the null is true. In order to visualize what the p-value is telling us, let's consider our one-tailed test where the manager was interested in detecting a reduction in the wait-time for customers at a casual-dining restaurant after implementing a new video-monitoring system.

$$H_o: \mu \geq 20 \quad \text{versus} \quad H_1: \mu < 20$$

Remember, the manager tests 60 randomly selected customers and finds that the average time to seat customers is 15.5 minutes after implementing the video-monitoring system. Assuming that the distribution of the wait-times is exponentially distributed with a population standard deviation $\sigma = 20.0$ minutes, suppose you want to test the hypothesis at a 0.05 level of significance.

When looking at Figure 4.23 p-Value for a One-Tailed Test, by definition the p-value is the shaded area. The shaded area is the probability of getting a mean of 15.5 or less when the null is true--that is, when the sampling distribution is centered at 20 minutes.

Figure 4.23 p-Value for a One-Tailed Test

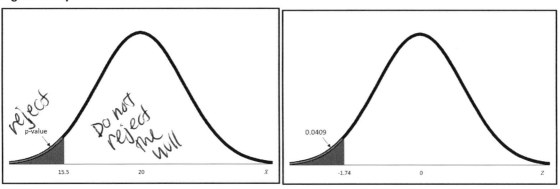

Notice that we are asking a probability question about a normal distribution, so you should immediately think: Convert the sample mean to a Z-value and use your Z-table. Remember the sample mean of 15.5 minutes has a Z-value of -1.74, so when looking up that value in your Z-table, you will find a p-value of 0.0409, as shown in Figure 4.23 p-Value for a One-Tailed Test.

The p-value corresponds to the proportion of times you would reject the null, with a mean of 15.5 minutes or less, when, in reality, the null hypothesis is actually true. Because the chance of making a Type I error is less than the maximum allowable as set by the α-level (0.05), you can reject the null hypothesis.

In conclusion, the *rejection rule* when using the p-value is:

- If p-value $< \alpha$, then reject the null hypothesis.
- If p-value $\geq \alpha$, then do not reject the null hypothesis.

Now that you have conducted your first hypothesis test using the p-value approach, there are some points to make. First, note that the same decision was made using the p-value approach for the one-tailed test as was made when using the critical value approach. In both cases, you used the same sample data and, therefore, you must obviously come up with the same results. This is true always--remember that these are different ways of answering the same question.

Second, for comparative purposes, suppose you had observed an average wait-time of 16.75 minutes for the 60 randomly selected customers. The Z-value for that sample mean is -1.26 with a p-value of 0.1038. In that situation, your chance of making a Type I error exceeds 0.05 level of significance, so you would not reject the null hypothesis.

Notice also, when comparing the results for the sample mean of 15.5 minutes versus the sample mean of 16.75 that the sample mean of 15.5 is farther from the hypothesized mean of 20 minutes, which obviously provides stronger evidence for rejecting the null than for the sample mean of 16.75. In fact, the sample mean of 15.5 is farther in the tail which is associated with a smaller tail area than that associated with the sample mean of 16.75.

The P-Value for the Two-Tailed Hypothesis Test

In the last section, the p-value approach was developed using a one-tailed test. When using this approach for the two-tailed test, the analyst must take into account that a Type I error could be committed if the sample mean falls in either tail, and the analyst erroneously rejects the null hypothesis. So how do you take that into account when calculating the p-value?

Going back to the two-tailed test of restaurant wait-times, consider a random sample of 60 customers resulting in a sample mean wait-time of 15.5 minutes used to test the hypotheses (assume $\sigma = 20$ minutes):

$$H_o: \mu = 20 \quad \text{versus } H_1: \mu \neq 20.$$

Remember, by definition, the p-value represents the chance of making a Type I error if you reject with a mean at 15.5 minutes or something more extreme where you would reject incorrectly. But you must also take into account that you could have made a mistake by rejecting in the other direction. Therefore, in order to arrive at the correct p-value, you must add the area for both tails, as indicated in Figure 4.24 p-Value for a Two-Tailed Test, to get a p-value of 2(0.0409), or 0.0818. Because your p-value of 0.0818 exceeded the 0.05 level of significance, you do not reject the null hypothesis. In conclusion, there is no evidence that the average wait-time for the casual-dining restaurant has changed after implementing the new video-monitoring system. Again, note that this conclusion is identical to that using the critical value approach.

Figure 4.24 p-Value for a Two-Tailed Test

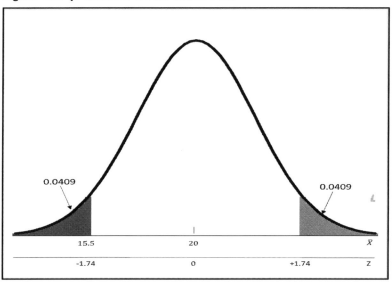

Hypothesis Testing for the Population Mean (σ Unknown)

As you know, inferential statistics is a way of making conclusions about unknown population parameters based upon sample information. In many cases, when the analyst is conducting hypothesis tests about the population mean, not only is μ unknown, but so too is the population standard deviation (σ). In this section, we will discuss how to conduct hypothesis tests when σ is unknown.

One-Tailed Tests for the Population Mean (μ)

The best estimate we have for the unknown population standard deviation is the sample standard deviation(s). So, in hypothesis testing of the population mean, we will take a random sample, calculate the sample mean, and then compute a test statistic using the following equation:

$$t = \frac{(\bar{X}-\mu)}{s/\sqrt{n}}$$

This new random variable is called a t-test statistic because it has the shape of a t-distribution which is symmetric with a mean of zero but has 'heavier' tails than that of a normal distribution. In fact, there is a family of t-distributions specifically defined by degrees of freedom (n-1) which is a function of sample size. As the sample size decreases, the tails become heavier, and as the sample size increases, the tails become flatter.

In order to use the t-distribution, you must assume that the sampling distribution of the mean is normal. In other words, the central limit theorem must apply; that is, the population must be normal or the sample size must be large ($n \geq 30$). It should be noted that as the sample size increases, the t-distribution approaches normality, as illustrated in Figure 4.25 The t-Distribution for Various Sample Sizes.

Figure 4.25 The t-Distribution for Various Sample Sizes

So when σ is unknown, the appropriate reference distribution is the t-distribution and the appropriate hypothesis test is referred to as a **t-test for means**. It should be noted that to carry out a hypothesis test, the steps are identical to the steps illustrated for the Z-test, with one exception. Because we are now converting our sample mean to a t-test statistic, we must obtain our critical value from a **t-table**, as found in Appendix D t-Table. We can also use the SAS TTEST procedure to generate the p-value in order to make our conclusion as well. Let's consider the following example where the t-test would be appropriate.

Example: According to the National Center for Health Statistics (2009), obesity rates have doubled among children and adults since the 1970s. In fact, more than one-third of American adults are obese (Centers for Disease Control and Prevention, 2018). Body-Mass-Index (BMI) is a commonly used index for categorizing a person's weight as either underweight, normal, overweight, or obese. According to the Centers for Disease Control and Prevention (CDC), a person with normal weight has a BMI score from 18.5 up to 25.0; a BMI score of 25.0 through 29.9 is considered overweight. The ranges apply to both males and females.

Consider the Diabetic Care Management Case introduced in Chapter 1, "Statistics and Making Sense of Our World." Suppose we take a random sample of 25 females to show the population of diabetic female patients that are not overweight, that is, that have a BMI less than 30. Our hypothesis set is as follows:

$$H_o: \mu \geq 30 \quad \text{versus } H_1: < 30$$

Using 0.10 level of significance, carry out the five steps for hypothesis testing:

Step 1: The analyst must first identify and describe the appropriate sampling distribution. Because σ is unknown, we must conduct a t-test of means. So for our hypothesis test, we can describe the three following characteristics of the sampling distribution using the descriptive statistics from Table 4.5 Descriptive Statistics of BMI for 25 Female Diabetic Patients.

- The sampling distribution of the mean is shaped like a t-distribution when the population is assumed to be normal, even though the sample size is small (n=25 > 30).
- The mean of the sampling distribution ($\mu_{\bar{x}}$) is equal to the mean of the hypothesized population (μ_0). That is, $\mu_{\bar{x}} = 30$.
- The estimated standard error of the mean is $s/\sqrt{n} = 5.2635/\sqrt{25} = 1.0527$.

Table 4.5 Descriptive Statistics of BMI for 25 Female Diabetic Patients

N	Mean	Std. Dev	Minimum	Maximum
25	27.412549	5.2634631	21.7975294	44.5076468

Step 2: Because the appropriate sampling distribution is the t-distribution, you must find the critical t-value based upon the level of significance (α) and the degrees of freedom (n-1). When looking in the t-table, as illustrated in Table

4.6 Excerpt from the t-Table, you must use alpha to define the column (0.10) and degrees of freedom (25-1, or 24) to define the column. In conclusion, our critical value is -1.318 since we are conducting a lower-tailed test. So our rejection rule is: We will reject the null hypothesis if the sample mean has a t-value less than -1.318. In other words, we will reject the null hypothesis if our sample mean is more than 1.318 standard errors below our hypothesized mean, as illustrated in Figure 4.26 t-Test Statistic Compared to the Critical Value.

Table 4.6 Excerpt from the t-Table

		Upper-Tail Area			
df	**0.10**	**0.05**	**0.025**	**0.01**	**0.01**
1	3.078	6.314	12.706	31.821	63.657
2	1.886	2.920	4.303	6.965	9.925
3	1.638	2.353	3.182	4.541	5.841
...	...	...	...	...	...
23	1.319	1.714	2.069	2.500	2.807
24	1.318	1.711	2.064	2.492	2.797
25	1.316	1.708	2.060	2.485	2.787

It should be noted that had the analysis been a two-tailed test, the analyst would have used a one-tail area (namely 0.05) and used that column to find the critical values ±1.711.

Figure 4.26 t-Test Statistic Compared to the Critical Value

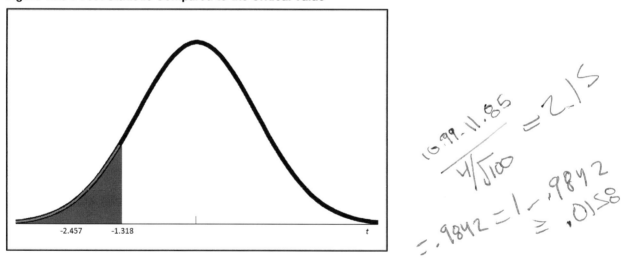

-2.457   -1.318   t

(handwritten: $\frac{16.99 - 11.85}{4/\sqrt{100}} = 2.15$ $= .9842 = 1 - .9842 \geq .0158$)

Step 3: We must now convert our sample mean to a t-test statistic using the following formula:

$$t = \frac{(\bar{X} - \mu)}{s/\sqrt{n}} = \frac{27.413 - 30}{5.2635/\sqrt{25}} = -2.457$$

This t-value tells the analyst that the sample mean of 27.413 is 2.457 standard errors below the hypothesized mean of 30.

Step 4: Our test statistic -2.457 is less than the critical value of -1.318, so we will reject the null hypothesis, as illustrated in Output 4.3 t-Test of BMI for Female Diabetics.

Step 5: Based upon our sample of 25 female diabetic patients, we have reason to believe that the average BMI is less than the BMI associated with being overweight. In other words, we have evidence that our target population is not overweight.

Let's now consider how to generate the output for conducting a t-test using the TTEST procedure. Here we will see that the output gives us the appropriate p-value for making our decision.

Procedure Syntax for PROC TTEST

PROC TTEST is a procedure used to conduct hypothesis tests for the mean when the population standard deviation is unknown and has the general form:

PROC TTEST DATA=*SAS-data-set<options>*;
VAR *variable(s)* </options>;
RUN;

Program 4.3 t-Test of BMI for Female Diabetics is used to test our hypothesis about BMI for female diabetics.

In Program 4.3 t-Test of BMI for Female Diabetics, you see that the permanent data set, DIAB25F, is placed into a temporary data set called PATIENT using the SET statement. The PROC TTEST requests SAS to conduct a one-sample t-test on the data set PATIENT as indicated with the DATA= statement option. The VAR statement defines the numeric variable, BMI, under investigation in our hypothesis test. Note also that the program uses the analysis options ALPHA=.10 and H0=30 which requests that SAS conduct the test at 0.10 level of significance and defines the hypothesized mean (μ_o) BMI to be 30. The results are found in Output 4.3 t-Test of BMI for Female Diabetics.

Program 4.3 t-Test of BMI for Female Diabetics

```
ods graphics on;
libname sasba 'c:\sasba\hc';
data patient;   Temporary
  set sasba.diab25f;  Permanent
run;

proc ttest data=patient
  alpha=.10 h0=30;
  var bmi;
  title 't-test of BMI for Female Diabetics';
run;
```

Notice that the output includes descriptive statistics so that we can see our sample size, sample mean, sample standard deviation, standard error, minimum and maximum values. You can also see the test statistic of -2.46 with 24 degrees of freedom (25 females minus 1) and a p-value of 0.0216 for a two-tailed test as indicated by Pr > |t|. In order to get the appropriate p-value for a one-tailed test, we must divide the p-value in half to get 0.0108.

So, using the p-value approach, our p-value (0.0108) is less than 0.10 level of significance; therefore, we reject the null hypothesis, concluding that there is evidence that the female diabetics have a BMI less than 30.

Output 4.3 t-Test of BMI for Female Diabetics

N	Mean	Std Dev	Std Err	Minimum	Maximum
25	27.4125	5.2635	1.0527	21.7975	44.5076

Mean	90% CL Mean		Std Dev	90% CL Std Dev	
27.4125	25.6115	29.2136	5.2635	4.2730	6.9291

DF	t Value	Pr > |t|
24	-2.46	0.0216

two tailed Pr>|t|

Confidence Intervals for Estimating the Population Mean

As you may recall, hypothesis testing falls under the category of inferential statistics, that is, the branch of statistics where the analyst makes conclusions about the population based upon a single sample. In this section, we will cover another inferential analysis approach--estimation.

Consider the Diabetic Care Management Case previously used to illustrate the t-test conducted on body mass index (BMI). For the sample of 91 female diabetics, the sample average BMI is 27.3. This sample mean is an estimate of the BMI for the population of all female diabetics and is referred to as a point estimate. In reality and very often, we all use the sample mean as a single number to represent an unknown population mean. Now, consider the fact that, for all random samples of female diabetics, the sample means vary and, more than likely, will never exactly equal the true population mean. Therefore, to estimate the population mean, we may prefer to construct instead an interval estimate. Specifically, in this section, we will discuss the **confidence interval**, which provides a range of values that we believe contains the true population mean based upon a certain level of confidence.

Confidence Interval for the Population Mean (σ Known)

The calculation of the confidence interval depends upon two factors: (1) the standard error of the mean and (2) the level of confidence. First, the confidence interval takes into account how the sample means vary around the population mean. If the standard error is small, in other words, if we expect the sample means to have relatively little variation around the population mean, then we expect the confidence interval to be small compared to the confidence interval where the standard error is large. Secondly, we must consider the levels of confidence, with commonly used levels of 90%, 95%, and 99%. In the case of 99% level of confidence, we would arrive at a formula that ensures the confidence interval will contain the true population mean 99 times when taking 100 random samples, whereas a level set at 95% ensures that the confidence interval will contain the true population mean 95 times out of the 100 random samples. In this case, you can deduce that the 99% confidence interval would be wider than the 95% confidence interval; the 90% confidence interval would be narrower than both the 95% and 99% confidence interval, respectively.

So how do we arrive at the calculation of the confidence interval? Let's first consider a 95% confidence interval. As indicated in Figure 4.27 Confidence Intervals as Related to the Sampling Distribution, we can see that 95% of Z-values are within 1.96 Z-scores of the mean. Given that the sampling distribution of the mean is normal, this can be translated to sample means; that is, we can say that 95% of sample means ($\bar{X}$'s) fall with 1.96 standard errors of the population mean, as illustrated in Figure 4.27 Confidence Intervals as Related to the Sampling Distribution.

Figure 4.27 Confidence Intervals as Related to the Sampling Distribution

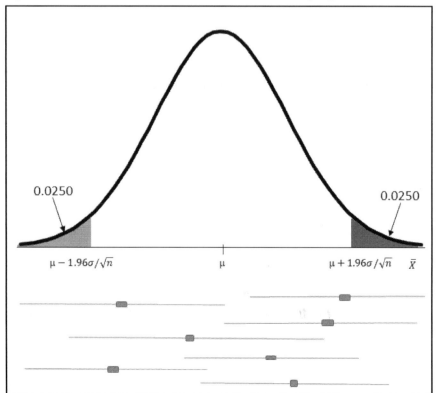

In fact, consider the intervals in Figure 4.26 Confidence Intervals as Related to the Sampling Distribution where the midpoints correspond to sample means with endpoints at $\bar{X} \pm 1.96\sigma/\sqrt{n}$. Notice that interval 1 does not contain the true population mean (μ), while interval 2 has its upper limit exactly at μ, and interval 3 has lower limit exactly at μ. Intervals 4, 5, and 7 contain μ, while interval 6 does not. Note specifically that any means that fall in the shaded areas have intervals that do not contain μ, while any means that fall in the unshaded areas have intervals that do contain μ. In other words, 95% of intervals contain μ, whereas 5% of the intervals do not contain μ. In short, using $\pm 1.96\sigma/\sqrt{n}$ to construct the interval ensures that 95% of the time we have intervals that contain mean. So to calculate confidence intervals, we would use the formula:

$$CI_{100(1-\alpha)} = \bar{X} \pm Z_{\alpha/2}\left(\sigma/\sqrt{n}\right)$$

In general, a confidence interval has the form: Point Estimate $\pm$ Margin of Error. It should also be noted that the use of the formula is only justified if the sampling distribution of the mean is normal; in other words, the central limit theorem must hold.

Example 9: Consider, again, our restaurant wait-time example. After implementing the video-monitoring system, suppose you randomly select 60 customers and find that the average time to seat customers is 15.5 minutes. What is the 95% confidence interval for estimating the true population mean wait-time? Assume that the distribution of the wait-times is exponentially distributed with a population standard deviation $\sigma = 20.0$ minutes.

Solution: First, the sampling distribution of the mean is normal because the sample size is large; therefore, it is appropriate to use the formula for the confidence interval. At .05 level of significance, the formula has the form:

$$CI_{95} = CI_{100(1-.05)} = \bar{X} \pm Z_{.05/2}\left(\sigma/\sqrt{n}\right)$$

Note that for the 95% level of confidence, we are essentially using the Z-value for a two-tailed test at .05 level of significance, namely, 1.96. So the confidence interval becomes:

$$CI_{95} = 15.5 \pm 1.96\left(20/\sqrt{60}\right) = 15.5 \pm 5.06 = (10.44, 20.56)$$

So when estimating, we have evidence that the population mean wait-time is somewhere between 10.44 and 20.56 minutes with 95% level of confidence.

In terms of interpreting the meaning of the confidence interval, consider a 95% confidence interval. A 95% confidence interval implies that we've calculated a margin of error such that had we taken 100 randomly selected samples and used that margin of error, then 95 out of 100 confidence intervals would contain the true population mean, and 5% would not. Many interpret confidence level as the probability that the interval contains the true population mean, when in reality, the confidence interval basically says that of all possible confidence intervals, the probability that any confidence interval contains the true population mean is 95%.

Effects of Level of Confidence and Sample Size on Confidence Intervals

How would the confidence interval above change if we changed the level of significance to 0.01 or 0.10? The level of confidence determines the Z-value used for computing the margin of error. Specifically, the Z-values for 90% and 99% level of confidence, respectively, are 1.645 and 2.575. Therefore, for our restaurant wait-time example, the confidence intervals would be as follows:

$$CI_{90} = 15.5 \pm 1.645\left(20/\sqrt{60}\right) = 15.5 \pm 4.25 = (11.25, 19.75)$$

$$CI_{99} = 15.5 \pm 2.575\left(20/\sqrt{60}\right) = 15.5 \pm 6.65 = (8.85, 22.15)$$

Notice that the 99% level of confidence with a 6.65 margin of error is wider than both the 90% and 95% confidence interval with 4.25 and 5.06 margins of error, respectively. This makes intuitive sense as well; in particular, you expect the 99% confidence interval to be wider because you are more confident that it contains the true population mean than for the 90% and 95% confidence interval. In general, as the level of confidence increases, the margin of error increases, and the interval is wider; as the level of confidence decreases, the margin of error decreases, and the interval is narrower.

Now--how would the confidence interval change if we changed the sample size? Consider again the wait- time example where the analyst estimates the population mean using a 95% confidence interval. Suppose now that the sample size is 100. The confidence interval is

$$CI_{95} = 15.5 \pm 1.96(20/\sqrt{100}) = 15.5 \pm 3.92 = (11.58, 19.42)$$

Notice that the margin of error (3.92) is less than that for a sample of size 60. In general, as the sample size increases, the margin of error decreases and the width of the confidence interval decreases; as the sample size decreases, the margin of error increases and the width of the confidence interval increases.

Confidence Interval for the Population Mean (σ Unknown)

As you may recall, when the population standard deviation (σ) is unknown, the analyst can use the sample standard deviation(s) to estimate the standard error of the mean, and consequently the reference distribution would be the t-distribution. So when estimating the population mean (μ), the formula for the confidence interval is as follows:

$$CI_{100(1-\alpha)} = \overline{X} \pm t_{\alpha/2}(s/\sqrt{n}) \text{ with (n-1) degrees of freedom}$$

Example 10: Consider the Diabetic Care Management Case where we are interested in determining if the population of diabetic female patients is not, as a whole, overweight, as measured by BMI. Consider our random sample of 25 females with a sample mean BMI of 27.4125 and sample standard deviation of 5.2635. Let's compute the 90% confidence interval for the population mean BMI.

Solution: First, because the sample size of 25 is considered small, we must assume the population of BMI values is normally distributed so that the sampling distribution of the mean is normal. Remember the central limit theorem must apply in order to use the formula for the confidence interval. For a 90% confidence level, the formula has the form:

$$CI_{90} = CI_{100(1-.10)} = \overline{X} \pm t_{.10/2}(s/\sqrt{n})$$

Second, in order to find the appropriate t-value, the analyst must identify the degrees of freedom and the tail area (α/2). Because the tail area is 0.10/2, or 0.05, and the degrees of freedom are (25-1), or 24, the appropriate t-value can be found in the .05 column and 24th row of the t-table, found in Appendix D T-Table. Therefore, the t-value is 1.711.

$$CI_{90} = 27.4125 \pm 1.711\left(\frac{5.2635}{\sqrt{25}}\right) = 27.4125 \pm 1.8012 = (25.61, 29.21)$$

So when estimating, we have evidence that the population mean BMI of female diabetics is somewhere between 25.61 and 29.21 units with 90% level of confidence.

It should be noted that in the case where σ is unknown, the width of the confidence interval is still influenced by sample size and level of confidence.

Key Terms

alternative hypothesis (H1)	p-value
central limit theorem	rejection region
confidence interval	sampling distribution
continuous	sampling distribution of the sample mean
critical value	standard normal distribution
descriptive statistics	standard normal distribution.
directional hypotheses	t-table
discrete	t-test for means
empirical rule	two-tailed directional test
inferential statistics	Type I error
inferential statistics	Type II errorp-value
normal continuous random variables	Z-table
normal distribution	Z-test for means
null hypothesis (Ho)	

Chapter Quiz

Select the best answer for each of the following questions:

1. Which of the following characteristics is true for *any* normal probability distribution?
    a.   The mean, median, and mode are equal to zero.
    b.   A relatively small standard deviation means that the observations are relatively close to the mean.
    c.   Approximately 95.44% of the observations fall within 2 standard deviation of the mean.
    d.   All of the above statements are true.
    e.   None of the above statements are true.

2. $P(-1.20 \leq Z \leq +1.50) =$ do the tails seperate
    a.   0.0483
    b.   0.4332
    c.   0.8181
    d.   0.3849

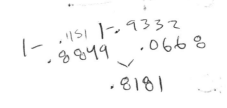

3. Suppose a popular sports car takes 36 hours to produce with a standard deviation of 2.5 hours. If the production time is normally distributed, what is the probability that a sports car will be produced in less than 32 hours?
    a.   0.1096
    b.   0.0548
    c.   0.9452
    d.   0.8904

4. Suppose a local company takes an average of 120 days to complete a small commercial building project. Assume that completion times are normally distributed with a standard deviation of 9 days. Consider also that projects taking more than 140 days are assessed a penalty. What proportion of projects are assessed a penalty for not being completed within 140 days?
    a.   0.0166
    b.   0.0132
    c.   0.9452
    d.   0.0150

5. Suppose the grades on an exam are left skewed with a mean of 45 minutes and a standard deviation of 5 minutes. If you randomly select 25 students, which of the following statements is true?
    a.   The mean of the sampling distribution is 45 minutes.
    b.   The standard error of the sampling distribution is 5 minutes.
    c.   The shape of the sampling distribution is normally distributed.
    d.   As the sample size increases the standard error increases.

6. Suppose the price per gallon of unleaded gasoline in the southeast region of the United States is normally distributed with a mean of \$2.75 and standard deviation of \$0.40. Suppose you take a random sample of 50 gas stations in that area. What is the probability that the average price per gallon is between \$2.60 and \$2.90?
    a.   0.0112
    b.   0.0056
    c.   0.0080
    d.   0.0040

In general, the time customers spend online purchasing sporting goods is normal with an average of 11.85 minutes with a population standard deviation of 4.0 minutes. Suppose that the web designer updates the site and you want to show that the average purchase time has now decreased. You take a random sample of 100 purchases and find that the average time spent online purchasing products is 10.99 minutes. Answer questions 7 – 9 in order to test the following hypothesis at 0.10 level of significance:

$$H_0: \mu \geq 11.85 \quad \text{versus} \quad H_1: \mu < 11.85$$

Avg 11.85

$\sigma = 4$

$n = 100$

$4/\sqrt{100} = .4$

$\dfrac{11.85 - 4}{4/\sqrt{100}} = \dfrac{7.85}{.4} = 19.625$

$= -.2$

7. What is the test statistic?
   a. 1.96
   b. 2.85
   c. 2.15
   d. 1.75

8. What is the critical value?
   a. ± 1.645
   b. -1.28
   c. ± 1.96
   d. -2.33

9. The p-value for the hypothesis test is _____.
   a. 0.0158
   b. 0.0316
   c. 0.0401
   d. 0.0802

10. Suppose you monitor quality assurance for a local hospital and want to estimate the average length of stay (LOS) at your hospital. You take a random sample of 30 patients and find that the average LOS is 3.8 days with a sample standard deviation of 1.2 days. What is the 90% confidence interval for the population average length of stay?
    a. (3.51 ,4.09)
    b. (3.20, 4.40)
    c. (3.35, 4.25)
    d. (3.43, 4.17)

Chapter 5: Analysis of Categorical Variables

Introduction

Every day we come across statements of association: students living on campus are more likely to graduate from college, obesity is associated with sleep apnea, females are more likely to wear seat belts, employees who telecommute are more likely to be loyal to their employers, to name a few. Specifically, in Chapter 2, "Summarizing Your Data with Descriptive Statistics," we looked at descriptive statistics and data visualization as ways to show that those in our study with uncontrolled diabetes were more likely to have renal disease. In this chapter, we will use hypothesis testing procedures, in conjunction with descriptive statistics and data visualization, as a way to establish evidence that associations among categorical variables exist in the population.

In this chapter, you will learn how to:

- interpret a contingency table for two categorical variables

- use the chi-square test of independence for two categorical variables

- generate the output for the chi-square test of independence using the CHISQ option within the TABLES statement of the FREQ procedure

- interpret Cramer's V, the phi coefficient, and odds ratios as measures of strength of association

- check the assumptions for conducting a chi-square test of independence and the use of Fisher's exact test for small samples

- use the chi-square test as a preliminary test before conducting predictive analytics

Testing the Independence of Two Categorical Variables

In Chapter 3, "Data Visualization," we discussed the use of crosstabulations for describing and visualizing the association between two categorical variables. For the Diabetic Care Management Case, the crosstabulation in Output 3.4 Crosstabs and Frequency Plots of Diabetes Status and Renal Disease indicated that there was a relationship between the two categorical variables, diabetes status and renal disease. Recall that, for those patients whose diabetes is not controlled, 13.24 percent have renal disease, whereas for those patients whose diabetes is controlled, 3.13 percent have renal disease.

If the data had, instead, indicated that 10% of those with controlled diabetes have renal disease and 10% of those with uncontrolled diabetes have renal disease, then we could say, in general, that 10% of all patients have renal disease regardless of their diabetes status. In this case, renal disease is not associated with diabetes status; in other words, we would say diabetes status is independent of renal disease. In this section, we will use tools from hypothesis testing to see if there is enough evidence from our sample to conclude an association in the population between two categorical variables.

Hypothesis Testing and the Chi-Square Test

As discussed in Chapter 4, "The Normal Distribution and Introduction to Inferential Statistics," hypothesis testing is a way to make inferences about the population by providing a standardized measure of the difference between what you observe from your sample and what you expect in the population if your initial claim (H_o) is true. So we must first state the null and alternative hypotheses as follows:

H_o: Two categorical variables are independent (variables are not related).

H_1: Two categorical variables are not independent (variables are related).

Consider the following example along with the rationale for constructing the hypothesis test - Suppose an analyst wants to investigate the relationship between two categorical variables, gender and shopping preference (online versus not online). The hypotheses to be tested are:

H_o: Shopping Preference and Gender are independent   *not related*

H_1: Shopping Preference and Gender are not independent *Related*

A random sample of 100 male and 100 female shoppers is selected, and the shoppers are asked about their shopping preference. Suppose that 40 (20%) of the 200 people prefer online shopping whereas 160 (80%) do not, as recorded in a **contingency table** in Table 5.1 Expected Frequency Count of Online Shopping by Gender.

Table 5.1 Expected Frequency Count of Online Shopping by Gender

	Male	Female	Total
Online	(20)	(20)	40
Not Online (In-Store)	(80)	(80)	160
Total	100	100	200

If shopping preference has nothing to do with gender (i.e., if the null hypothesis is true), then the analyst would expect the percentage of those who prefer online shopping to be the same regardless of their gender. In short, if the null is true, the analyst would expect 20% of all males and 20% of all females to prefer online shopping; that is equivalent to 20% of all shoppers preferring online shopping, regardless of gender. As a result, you would get the expected frequencies as indicated in parentheses.

Now that the analyst knows what to expect, he or she must compare those expected frequencies to the actual or 'observed' frequencies. If the observed frequencies are relatively far from the expected frequencies, then the analyst must reject the null hypothesis; here the analyst has evidence to support the alternative that shopping preference and gender are not independent. If the observed frequencies do not deviate significantly from the expected frequencies, then the analyst has no evidence to reject the null. In this case, the analyst must maintain the status quo.

The **chi-square (χ^2) test of independence** (introduced by Karl Pearson in 1900) is a statistical test to determine if there is an association between two categorical variables. The chi-square test statistic measures how much the observed frequencies deviate from the expected frequencies if the null hypothesis is true and is calculated as follows:

$$\chi^2 = \sum_{i=1}^{r} \sum_{j=1}^{c} \left[\frac{(O_{ij}-E_{ij})^2}{E_{ij}} \right]$$

where O_{ij} = the **observed frequency** in row i, column j and the **expected frequency** in row i, column j is calculated using

$$E_{ij} = \frac{(\text{Row i Total})(\text{Column j Total})}{n}$$

where n = the total sample size, r = the number of rows, c = the number of columns, and the degrees of freedom are (r-1)(c-1).

Now suppose we have the observed frequencies as found in Table 5.2 Observed and Expected Frequencies Count of Online Shopping by Gender. Note that for the sample data, 32% of males prefer online shopping whereas 8% of females prefer online shopping. The question then is: Did these differences in percentages happen by chance or do these reflect true differences in the population? To answer that question, the analyst calculates the χ^2-test statistic as follows:

$$\chi^2 = \frac{(32-20)^2}{20} + \frac{(8-20)^2}{20} + \frac{(68-80)^2}{80} + \frac{(92-80)^2}{80} = 7.2 + 7.2 + 1.8 + 1.8 = 18$$

Table 5.2 Observed and Expected Frequencies Count of Online Shopping by Gender

	Male	Female	Total
Online	32 (20)	8 (20)	40
Not Online (In-Store)	68 (80)	92 (80)	160
Total	100	100	200

With (2-1)(2-1) = 1 degree of freedom and 0.05 level of significance, the critical value is 3.841 (see Chi-Square in Appendix E Chi-Square). In conclusion, the test statistic is greater than the critical value (18 > 3.841); therefore, the analyst has evidence to reject the null hypothesis. In short, we have sufficient evidence, based upon data, to conclude that shopping preference and gender are dependent in the population.

From the bivariate bar graph in Figure 5.1 Bivariate Bar Charts of Gender and Online Shopping, we can see that, in our sample, males are more likely to shop online than females.

Figure 5.1 Bivariate Bar Charts of Gender and Online Shopping

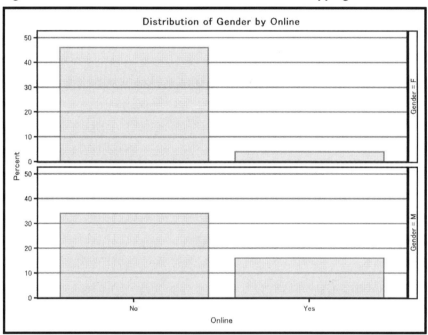

The Chi-Square Test Using the FREQ Procedure

As mentioned previously, the FREQ procedure was covered in detail in Chapter 3, "Data Visualization" as a means of providing both crosstabulations for two categorical variables and bivariate bar charts to visualize that relationship. The FREQ procedure can also be used to conduct a chi-square test of independence by adding options in the TABLE statement as follows:

Procedure Syntax for PROC FREQ

PROC FREQ is a procedure used to create one-way and n-way tabular summaries and has the general form:

> **PROC FREQ DATA**=*SAS-data-set*;
> **TABLES** *variable(s)* </*options*>;
> **RUN;**

where *options* include CHISQ, RELRISK, EXPECTED, and PLOTS=, to name a few.

To illustrate the FREQ procedure for tests of independence, consider the Ames Housing Case introduced in Chapter 1, "Statistics and Making Sense of Our World." Architects agree that the kitchen and baths are the most expensive areas of the house with respect to construction costs, not to mention those are the rooms where people spend the most time. So in our example, let's see if the quality of the kitchen is related to whether or not an agent received a bonus. Remember that Bonus=1 if the agent earned a bonus by selling the house at a price greater than $175,000. The appropriate hypotheses are:

H_0: Bonus and Kitchen Quality are independent
H_1: Bonus and Kitchen Quality are not independent

To conduct a chi-square test of independence, the analyst would use the CHISQ and other options in the TABLES statement in Program 5.1 Testing Association between Bonus and Kitchen Quality.

Program 5.1 Testing Association between Bonus and Kitchen Quality

```
libname sasba 'c:\sasba\ames';
data ames;
   set sasba.ames300;
run;

proc format;
   value Quality 0=No 1=Yes;
   value YesNo 0=No 1=Yes;
run;

proc freq data=ames;
   tables Bonus*High_Kitchen_Quality
   /chisq relrisk expected plots=freqplot(scale=percent);
   format Bonus YesNo. High_Kitchen_Quality Quality.;
   title 'Test of Independence for Bonus and Kitchen Quality';
run;
```

Note first that the FREQ procedure is applied to the Ames data set. The TABLES statement then specifically defines the two categorical variables to be tested, namely BONUS and HIGH_KITCHEN_QUALITY, where the first variable listed will be displayed as the rows and the second variable will be displayed as the columns, as illustrated in Output 5.1 Testing Association between Bonus and Kitchen Quality. The CHISQ option requests that SAS provide the results of the chi-square test. The RELRISK and EXPECTED options are included to provide for odd-ratios and the expected frequencies, respectively. For a visual representation of the relationship, the PLOTS= option with SCALE=PERCENT requests that SAS provide the bivariate bar charts with percent on the y-axis. Finally, the program includes the FORMAT procedure and the FORMAT statement for representing the bivariate outcome values.

From the 2x2 frequency table in Output 5.1a Testing Association between Bonus and Kitchen Quality, you can see that there are 300 homes in the study, where 121 (40.33%) received bonuses (BONUS =1) and 179 (59.67%) did not. Furthermore, 122 (40.67%) were homes with high kitchen quality, whereas 178 (59.33%) had kitchens not considered high kitchen quality, as indicated in the marginal totals.

Output 5.1a Testing Association between Bonus and Kitchen Quality

Test of Independence for Bonus and Kitchen Quality

The FREQ Procedure

Table of Bonus by High_Kitchen_Quality			
Bonus	**High_Kitchen_Quality**		
Frequency Expected Percent Row Pct Col Pct	**No**	**Yes**	**Total**
No	148 106.21 49.33 82.68 83.15	31 72.793 10.33 17.32 25.41	179 59.67
Yes	30 71.793 10.00 24.79 16.85	91 49.207 30.33 75.21 74.59	121 40.33

Table of Bonus by High_Kitchen_Quality			
Bonus	**High_Kitchen_Quality**		
Frequency Expected Percent Row Pct Col Pct	**No**	**Yes**	**Total**
Total	178 59.33	122 40.67	300 100.00

Statistics for Table of Bonus by High_Kitchen_Quality

Statistic	DF	Value	Prob
Chi-Square	1	100.2674	<.0001
Likelihood Ratio Chi-Square	1	104.8383	<.0001
Continuity Adj. Chi-Square	1	97.8826	<.0001
Mantel-Haenszel Chi-Square	1	99.9331	<.0001
Phi Coefficient		0.5781	
Contingency Coefficient		0.5005	
Cramer's V		0.5781	

Fisher's Exact Test	
Cell (1,1) Frequency (F)	148
Left-sided Pr <= F	1.0000
Right-sided Pr >= F	<.0001
Table Probability (P)	<.0001
Two-sided Pr <= P	<.0001

Odds Ratio and Relative Risks			
Statistic	Value	95% Confidence Limits	
Odds Ratio	14.4817	8.2242	25.5004
Relative Risk (Column 1)	3.3348	2.4277	4.5809
Relative Risk (Column 2)	0.2303	0.1646	0.3223

For each cell, the output provides the observed frequency, expected frequency, cell percent of the total, row percent, and column percent. When reviewing the upper left cell, for example, you can see that 148 (49.33%) of the 300 total homes did not received a bonus (BONUS=0) and had kitchens that were not rated as high quality. You can also see that, of the 179 homes that did not receive a bonus, 148 (82.68%) had kitchens that were not high quality; of the 178 homes with kitchens not rated as high quality, 148 (83.15%) did not receive a bonus.

Finally, let's consider what the frequency table tells us about the relationship between BONUS and HIGH_KITHCEN_QUALITY. Remember that, overall, 40.33% of the homes received a bonus, whereas 59.67% did not. Now consider only those 122 homes having high quality kitchens; 74.59% (91) received a bonus, whereas 25.41% (31) did not. For those 178 homes with kitchens not rated as high quality, 16.95% (30) received a bonus, whereas 83.15% (148) did not. It certainly seems to indicate that the bonus status depends upon kitchen quality, and is further illustrated by the bivariate bar chart, as illustrated in Output 5.1b Testing Association between Bonus and Kitchen Quality: Bivariate Bar Charts of Bonus and Kitchen Quality.

Output 5.1b Testing Association between Bonus and Kitchen Quality: Bivariate Bar Charts of Bonus and Kitchen Quality

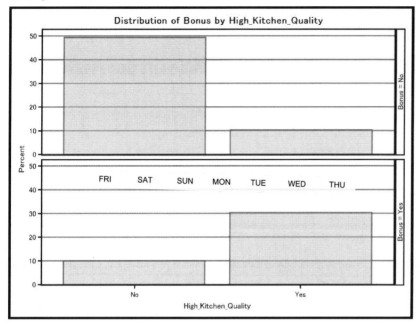

Now consider our statistical test of independence for inferring to the population. From the output in Output 5.1 Testing Association between Bonus and Kitchen Quality, you can see the chi-square test statistic (100.2674) with p-value < .0001 and, therefore, the analyst will reject the null hypothesis. In short, based upon the data, there is evidence that bonus and kitchen quality are dependent in the population. Specifically, if the kitchen is rated as high quality, 74.6% receive a bonus; however, if the kitchen quality is not rated as high quality, only 16.9% receive a bonus.

Assumptions

As with all statistical tests, assumptions must be met to ensure their validity. For the χ^2 test of independence, the analyst must make sure that the sample size is large enough such that all expected frequencies are at least five. When referring to Output 5.1 Testing Association between Bonus and Kitchen Quality, it should be noted that all expected frequencies (106.21, 72.793, 71.793, and 49.207, respectively) are greater than 5. Therefore, the chi-square test is appropriate. If this condition is not met, then **Fisher's exact test** should be used instead (Agresti, 1992). Of course, if this assumption is violated, the analyst could combine two or more columns (or rows) so that the newly created categories have expected frequencies meeting the size requirement.

Measuring the Strength of Association between Two Categorical Variables

In the previous section, we found evidence that bonus is associated with kitchen quality; however, the test gives no indication of the **strength of association**. **Effect size** gives an indication of the practical association, in contrast to the statistical association as measured by the p-value, and it allows for comparisons across studies. In this section, we discuss two measures of association, Cramer's V and the odds ratio.

Cramer's V

A common measure of association, or effect size, for a contingency table with r rows and c columns (for $r, c \geq 2$) is **Cramer's V** (Sarma, 2013) and is given by the formula:

$$V = \sqrt{\frac{\chi^2}{n(k-1)}}$$

where n is the total sample size and k is the minimum of the number of rows and columns. Cramer's V ranges from 0 to 1, where a value of 0 indicates no association between the categorical variables, and 1 indicates a perfect association. Cohen (1988) provided general guidelines for determining the magnitude of the effect size; namely, 0.1 is considered a small effect size, 0.3 is considered medium, and 0.5 is considered large.

It should be noted that the coefficient is appropriate for variables measured at the nominal level and will have the same value regardless of which variable is defined as the row or column. Finally, when the analysis is conducted for a 2x2 table, Cramer's V is equivalent to the **Phi Coefficient** and is defined as:

$$V = \phi = \frac{O_{11}O_{22} - O_{12}O_{21}}{\sqrt{O_{1.}O_{2.}O_{.1}O_{.2}}}$$

where O_{ij} = the observed frequency in row i, column j, $O_{i.}$ is the observed row total, and $O_{.j}$ is the observed column total. For the 2x2 case, Cramer's V ranges from -1 to +1. So, for our Ames Housing Case, as illustrated in Output 5.1a Testing Association between Bonus and Kitchen Quality:

$$V = \frac{(91)(148)-(31)(30)}{\sqrt{(179)(121)(178)(122)}} = 0.5781$$

From this, we can say that, based upon our sample, there is a relatively large association between bonus and kitchen quality.

The Odds Ratio

The **odds ratio** is also a measure of the strength of association between two categorical variables. In order to discuss odds ratio, we must first define the **odds** of an event. Consider the general form of a 2x2 contingency table as provided in Table 5.3 General Form of the 2x2 Contingency Table.

Table 5.3 General Form of the 2x2 Contingency Table

EVENT OF INTEREST	GROUP		
	1	2	Total
Yes	a	b	a + b
No	c	d	c + d
Total	a + c	b + d	n

Note that *a* is the number of observations in event *Yes* and Group 1, *b* is the number of observations in event *Yes* and Group 2, *c* is the number of observations in event *No* and Group 1, and *d* is the number of observations in event *No* and in Group 2.

We define odds as the probability that an outcome occurs divided by the probability that an outcome does not occur. Suppose we define our event of interest to be *Yes*; we can, therefore, calculate the odds of *Yes* for each of the two groups, as follows:

The odds of Yes for Group 1 = Probability(a)/Probability(c) = [a/(a+c)]/[c/(a+c)] = a/c

The odds of Yes for Group 2 = Probability(b)/Probability(d) = [b/(b+d)]/[d/(b+d)] = b/d

The **odds ratio** for an event is defined as the odds of the event for Group 1 divided by the odds of the event for Group 2, and specifies how much more likely the event occurs in Group 1 when compared to Group 2. So for the event of interest, *Yes*, the odds ratio of Group 1 to Group 2 is defined as:

$$\text{Odds Ratio(Yes)} = \frac{\left[\frac{a}{c}\right]}{\left[\frac{b}{d}\right]} = \left[\frac{ad}{bc}\right]$$

Note that if the probability of *Yes* for Group 1 is $a = 0.50$, then the odds of *Yes* for Group 1 = 0.50/0.50 = 1.0, indicating that both outcomes are equally likely. As the probability of *a* increases, the odds increase as well. This also applies for the odds of *Yes* for Group 2. Note also that we can represent the odds ratio of *No* when comparing Group 1 to Group 2 as (bc/ad) and is simply the inverse of the odds ratio of *Yes*.

Example 1: Consider the results summarized in Table 5.1 Expected Frequency Count of Online Shopping by Gender.

The odds ratio for Online when comparing males to females is (20*80)/(20*80) = 1, and specifies that males and females have the same odds of shopping online. In other words, there is no difference in males and females shopping preference, and is equivalent to a χ^2-test statistic and Cramer's V both equal to zero.

Example 2: Consider the results summarized in Table 5.2 Observed and Expected Frequencies Count of Online Shopping by Gender.

The odds ratio for Online when comparing males to females is $(32*92)/(8*68) = 5.41$, and specifies that the odds a male shops online is 5.41 times the odds a female shops online, with $\chi^2 = 18$ and Cramer's V = 0.30.

Example 3: Consider the Ames Housing analysis testing the association between Bonus and Kitchen Quality, as illustrated in Output 5.1a Testing Association between Bonus and Kitchen Quality. The odds ratio of BONUS when comparing HIGH_KITCHEN_QUALITY (*Yes* versus *No*) is as follows:

odds of Bonus (1=*Yes*) for Kitchens rated as High Quality/odds of Bonus (1=*Yes*) for Kitchens rated as Not High Quality =

$$= (91/31)/(30/148) = (91*148)/(31*30) = 14.4817$$

The odds ratio indicates that the odds of earning a bonus when the kitchen quality is rated as high is 14.5 times the odds of earning a bonus when the kitchen quality is not rated as high. Note also that the output includes the 95% confidence interval for the odds ratio, namely, 8.22 to 25.50. In short, with 95% level of confidence, we estimate that the true odds ratio for all homes in Ames, Iowa, is between 8.22 and 25.50.

To generate the odds ratio, the analyst would add RELRISK to the TABLES option in the FREQ procedure as follows:

```
proc freq data=ames;
    tables Bonus*High_Kitchen_Quality
    /chisq relrisk expected plots=freqplot(scale=percent);
```

In conclusion, it should be noted that an odds ratio of 1.0 indicates that the odds of being in the group of interest (for one categorical variable) are equal when considering the outcomes of the second categorical variable; in other words, there is no association between the two categorical variables. In fact, the test of independence is equivalent to testing that the population odds ratio = 1.0. If the odds ratio is greater than 1.0, then group 1 is more likely to have the outcome of interest when compared to group 2. If the odds ratio is less than 1.0, then group 2 is more likely to have the outcome of interest.

Using Chi-Square Tests for Exploration Prior to Predictive Analytics

As seen in the previous section, the chi-square test is used to determine whether or not two categorical variables are related. If it is found that there is a relationship, it is reasonable to use one variable as a predictor of the other. So in our Ames Housing Case, it seems reasonable that because bonus and kitchen quality are dependent, the analyst could use kitchen quality as a predictor of bonus.

In predictive modeling, the potential list of predictor variables is sometimes voluminous and the analyst must consider strategies for assessing variable importance and eventually reducing the initial set of predictors. When both the outcome variable and the predictors are categorical, the chi-square test of independence can be used to assess variable importance (Sarma, 2013).

Let's revisit our Ames Housing Case where the analyst may consider other variables possibly related to bonus. Many real estate agents argue that homes located on a corner lot can command a higher sales price for reasons related to curb appeal, fewer neighbors (one on the side and behind), increased lot size. Others may argue the contrary due to lack of privacy or traffic on two sides. The hypothesis of interest is:

H₀: Bonus and Corner Lot are independent
H₁: Bonus and Corner Lot are not independent

The SAS code is identical to the code provided previously; however now the TABLES statement includes the variables, BONUS and CORNER. Note also, that there is no specific variable for corner lot, so the code includes a step for creating that variable based upon the lot configuration, as follows:

Program 5.2 Testing Association between Bonus and Corner Lot

```
libname sasba 'c:\sasba\ames';
data ames;
    set sasba.ames300;
```

```
        Corner=0;
          if Lot_Config='' then Corner=.;
          if Lot_Config='Corner' then Corner=1;
run;

proc format;
    value Quality 0=No 1=Yes;
    value YesNo 0=No 1=Yes;
run;

proc freq data=ames;
    tables Bonus*Corner
    /chisq relrisk expected plots=freqplot(scale=percent);
    format Bonus Corner YesNo.;
    title 'Test of Independence for Bonus and Corner Lot';
run;
```

From the output in Output 5.2a Testing Association between Bonus and Corner Lot, we can see (using a p-value of 0.1537) that we do not reject the null; there is no evidence that bonus is associated with the home being on a corner lot. The strength of association, 0.0824, indicates that the association can be attributed only to chance. Furthermore, the odds ratio of 1.5407 has a 95% confidence interval ranging from 0.8486 to 2.7974; the confidence interval contains 1.0 which means there is no evidence that the odd-ratio differs from 1.0. In short, the chance of getting a bonus is equal when comparing homes on a corner and homes not on a corner, as illustrated in Output 5.2b Testing Association between Bonus and Corner Lot: Bivariate Bar Charts of Bonus and Corner Lot.

Output 5.2a Testing Association between Bonus and Corner Lot

Table of Bonus by Corner			
Bonus	**Corner**		
Frequency Expected Percent Row Pct Col Pct	No	Yes	Total
No	152 147.38 50.67 84.92 61.54	27 31.623 9.00 15.08 50.94	179 59.67
Yes	95 99.623 31.67 78.51 38.46	26 21.377 8.67 21.49 49.06	121 40.33
Total	247 82.33	53 17.67	300 100.00

Statistic	DF	Value	Prob
Chi-Square	1	2.0355	0.1537
Likelihood Ratio Chi-Square	1	2.0078	0.1565
Continuity Adj. Chi-Square	1	1.6190	0.2032
Mantel-Haenszel Chi-Square	1	2.0287	0.1544
Phi Coefficient		0.0824	
Contingency Coefficient		0.0821	
Cramer's V		0.0824	

Odds Ratio and Relative Risks			
Statistic	Value	95% Confidence Limits	
Odds Ratio	1.5407	0.8486	2.7974
Relative Risk (Column 1)	1.0816	0.9672	1.2095
Relative Risk (Column 2)	0.7020	0.4315	1.1420

contains 1 (handwritten annotation)

Test of Independence for Bonus and Corner Lot

The FREQ Procedure

Table of Bonus by Corner			
Bonus	**Corner**		
Frequency Expected Percent Row Pct Col Pct	**No**	**Yes**	**Total**
No	152 147.38 50.67 84.92 61.54	27 31.623 9.00 15.08 50.94	179 59.67
Yes	95 99.623 31.67 78.51 38.46	26 21.377 8.67 21.49 49.06	121 40.33
Total	247 82.33	53 17.67	300 100.00

Statistics for Table of Bonus by Corner

Statistic	DF	Value	Prob
Chi-Square	1	2.0355	0.1537
Likelihood Ratio Chi-Square	1	2.0078	0.1565
Continuity Adj. Chi-Square	1	1.6190	0.2032
Mantel-Haenszel Chi-Square	1	2.0287	0.1544
Phi Coefficient		0.0824	
Contingency Coefficient		0.0821	
Cramer's V		0.0824	

Fisher's Exact Test	
Cell (1,1) Frequency (F)	152
Left-sided Pr <= F	0.9423
Right-sided Pr >= F	0.1021
Table Probability (P)	0.0444
Two-sided Pr <= P	0.1670

Odds Ratio and Relative Risks			
Statistic	Value	95% Confidence Limits	
Odds Ratio	1.5407	0.8486	2.7974
Relative Risk (Column 1)	1.0816	0.9672	1.2095
Relative Risk (Column 2)	0.7020	0.4315	1.1420

Output 5.2b Testing Association between Bonus and Corner Lot: Bivariate Bar Charts of Bonus and

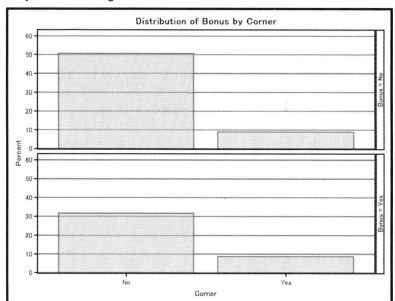

In summary, the first chi-square test indicates that when trying to predict whether or not an agent receives a bonus for the sale of a home, there is evidence that kitchen quality is related to bonus (p<.0001, Cramer's V=0.5781); however, the second chi-square test indicates that corner lot is not related to bonus (p=.1537, Cramer's V=0.0824).

It should be noted, however, that these are univariate tests and do not take into account the other variables. It is possible that a predictor found to be non-significant in a univariate situation can very well be significant when considered within a multivariate model. Therefore, we use the results of the chi-square test for ordering the predictor variables by importance using the **variable worth** (Sarma, 2013):

$$Worth = -2\log(p)$$

where p is the p-value for the chi-square test of independence. For kitchen quality, the worth is 45.75, whereas for corner lot, the worth is 1.63. Here we can see that kitchen quality is more importance than corner lot when looking at the association with bonus.

Strategies for reducing the initial set of predictors will be covered in detail in Chapter 8, "Preparing the Input Variables for Prediction." In Chapter 10, "Logistic Regression," we will cover topics related to predicting a categorical outcome; there, specific attention will be given to selecting the 'best' set of variables within the context of the problem using both statistically based strategies as well as practical experience and common sense. Knowing the variable worth provides additional information to the variable selection process.

Key Terms

chi-square (χ2) test of independence	observed frequency
concordant	odds
confounding	odds ratio
contingency table	paired-samples test.
Cramer's V	phi coefficient
discordant	repeated measures test.
effect size	strength of association
expected frequency	variable worth
Fisher's exact test	

Chapter Quiz

Select the best answer for each of the following questions:

1. A chi-square test of independence is used to test the relationship between_____ and _____.
   a. one categorical variable, one numeric continuous variable
   b. one categorical variable, more than one continuous numeric variable
   c. one categorical variable, one categorical variable
   d. one categorical variable, more than one categorical variable

2. Suppose you are trying to determine if Gender (GENDER) and Political Party Affiliation (PARTY) are dependent. Which of the following options would be used in the TABLE statement?
   a. tables
   b. chisq
   c. exact mcnem
   d. cmh

3. Which of the following is an assumption of the chi-square test of independence?
   a. The sample size must be greater than 30 per cell.
   b. The odds of an event must be at least 0.50.
   c. All expected cell frequencies must be greater than 5.
   d. All of the above statements are true.
   e. None of the above statements are true.

Suppose you wanted to determine if bonus (BONUS) depends upon whether or not a house has two or more full bathrooms (FULLBATH_2PLUS). Use the output provided below to answer questions 4 through 6:

Test of Independence for Bonus and 2 or More Full Bathrooms

The FREQ Procedure

Table of Bonus by fullbath_2plus			
Bonus	**fullbath_2plus**		
Frequency Expected Percent Row Pct Col Pct	No	Yes	Total
No	138 85.92 46.00 77.09 95.83	41 93.08 13.67 22.91 26.28	179 59.67
Yes	6 58.08 2.00 4.96 4.17	115 62.92 38.33 95.04 73.72	121 40.33
Total	144 48.00	156 52.00	300 100.00

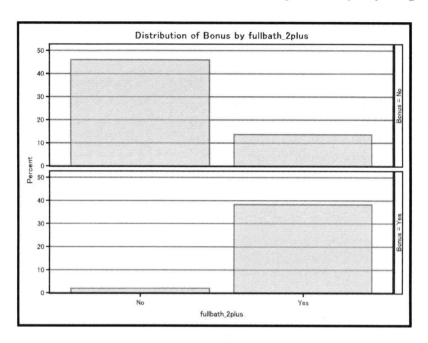

Statistics for Table of Bonus by fullbath_2plus

Statistic	DF	Value	Prob
Chi-Square	1	150.5152	<.0001
Likelihood Ratio Chi-Square	1	175.0132	<.0001
Continuity Adj. Chi-Square	1	147.6390	<.0001
Mantel-Haenszel Chi-Square	1	150.0134	<.0001
Phi Coefficient		0.7083	
Contingency Coefficient		0.5780	
Cramer's V		0.7083	

Dependent

Fisher's Exact Test	
Cell (1,1) Frequency (F)	138
Left-sided Pr <= F	1.0000
Right-sided Pr >= F	<.0001
Table Probability (P)	<.0001
Two-sided Pr <= P	<.0001

Odds Ratio and Relative Risks			
Statistic	Value	95% Confidence Limits	
Odds Ratio	64.5122	26.4466	157.3672
Relative Risk (Column 1)	15.5475	7.0976	34.0570
Relative Risk (Column 2)	0.2410	0.1836	0.3163

Sample Size = 300

4. Which of the following statements is true?
   a. The assumption for the chi-square test is violated since one cell has less than 10 observations and Cramer's V is 0.3703 indicating a median effect size.
   b. Houses with less than two full bathrooms and houses with two or more full bathrooms are equally likely of having a bonus.
   c. The odds ratio of getting a bonus for homes with two or more full bathrooms when compared to homes that have less than two full bathrooms that are not of above average quality is 64.5.
   d. None of the above statements is true.

5. Which of the following statements is true?
   a. 52.00% of the houses in the sample have at least two full bathrooms.
   b. 73.72% of houses where the agent earned a bonus have at least two full bathrooms.
   c. 4.17% of houses that have fewer than two full bathrooms have agents that earn a bonus.
   d. All of the above are correct.
   e. only *a* and *c* are correct

6. In assessing variable importance as it related to the variable, BONUS, the value of Worth for the variable, FULLBATH_2PLUS, is:
   a. 67.75
   b. 45.13
   c. 78.42
   d. 23.33

   $-2\log(P)$
   $-2\log(.153)$

7. How many chi-squared tests of independence are conducted using the following PROC FREQ statement?
   ```
   proc freq data=ames300;
       tables (bonus overall_quality)*(high_kitchen_quality lot_shape)
       \chisq relrisk expected;
       run;
   ```
   a. 6
   b. 4
   c. 3
   d. 2

8. When running a chi-square test of independence, which of the following TABLES options is required in order to generate a bivariate bar chart?
   a. plots=
   b. barchart
   c. trend=
   d. test
   e. contents=

9. True or False? A categorical predictor with the smallest value of worth is not related to the outcome variable.

10. Which of the following statements is true?
    a. An odds ratio of 1.0 means that there is a perfect relationship between the two categorical variables under investigation.
    b. If the confidence interval for the odds ratio does not contain 1.0, there is no relationship between the two categorical variables under investigation.
    c. The range of the odds ratio is -∞ to +∞.
    d. All of the above statements are true.
    e. None of the above statements is true.

Chapter 6: Two-Sample *t*-Test

Introduction

In Chapter 5, "Analysis of Categorical Variables," you were introduced to analysis wherein both the independent variable and the dependent variable were categorical. This type of analysis was useful to determine relationships between only these specific types of variables, such as if shopping preference varied by gender, and if the quality of the kitchen is related to whether or not an agent received a bonus. There are many times when we wonder how one variable is related to another. This chapter will describe the *t*-test, which is used to assess the bivariate relationship between a categorical independent variable and a numeric continuous dependent variable. There are two types of *t*-tests: independent samples *t*-test and dependent samples *t*-test. This chapter will cover the specific situations that warrant each of these tests, respectively, and will illustrate how these tests are carried out using the TTEST procedure.

In this chapter, you will learn about:

- the TTEST procedure for assessing the bivariate relationship between numeric continuous and categorical data
- the steps for conducting the independent samples *t*-test to test differences in the means when the two populations under investigation are independent
- the assumptions for ensuring the validity of the independent samples *t*-test
- how to determine the appropriateness of the pooled variance *t*-test and the Satterthwaite *t*-test for unequal variances using the folded F-test
- the use of histograms, box plots, and Q-Q plots to visualize and assess the normality of the numeric continuous variable for each of the two groups under investigation
- the UNIVARIATE procedure and the Kolmogorov-Smirnov test to test the normality of the numeric continuous variable for each of the two groups under investigation
- the sample size requirement when there is evidence that one or more populations are not normal
- the steps for conducting the paired samples *t*-test to test differences in the means when the two populations under investigation are dependent
- the assumptions for ensuring the validity of the paired samples *t*-test
- the use of histograms, box plots, and Q-Q plots to visualize and assess the normality of the difference score when comparing paired groups
- the UNIVARIATE procedure and the Kolmogorov-Smirnov test to test the normality of the difference score when comparing paired groups
- the interpretation of results based upon the context of the problem

Independent Samples

As illustrated in Chapter 3, "Data Visualization," there are many situations where a numeric variable may differ naturally across various groups, therefore warranting an analysis of that variable separately by group. In particular, using the Diabetic Care Management Case, we applied data visualization procedures to investigate the characteristics of weight for both males and females, separately. While it is obvious that males and females differ in weight, it is not so obvious in many other situations; therefore, statistical hypothesis testing can be applied to test such differences.

To investigate the differences in means when two populations of interest are independent, the analyst must rely on the **independent samples *t*-test**. Two samples are independent when the measures from one population have no effect on the measures selected from a different population. Consider the Ames Housing Case. Suppose we have this question, "Is earning a bonus on the sale of a house related to the square footage of the above ground living area?" Or, to put it another way, "Does earning a bonus on the sale of a house depend upon the square footage of the above ground living area?" Here, we are looking at two populations, homes where agents earn a bonus and homes where agents do not earn a bonus, and specifically asking the question "Do these populations differ on their above ground living area?" This form of the question can be answered through the following hypothesis test:

$$H_0: \mu_0 = \mu_1 \quad \text{versus} \quad H_1: \mu_0 \neq \mu_1$$

where 0=No Bonus for the real estate agent and 1=real estate agent received a Bonus. If you do not reject the null hypothesis, then there is no evidence of a mean difference; consequently, the answer to your question is no--earning a bonus is not related to square footage for the population of all homes in Ames County. However, if you reject the null hypothesis and the answer to that question is yes, then the sample results provide some evidence that the bonus status is related to the square footage of the above ground living area; in other words, square footage does matter when trying to earn a bonus.

The Pooled Variance *t*-Test

When conducting a test of hypotheses for the difference in unknown population means, it makes sense to take a random sample from each of the populations under investigation in order to assess the extent to which the sample means differ; therefore, it is necessary to refer to the sampling distribution of the difference of the means, $(\bar{X}_1 - \bar{X}_2)$. For statistical inference, if the sampling distribution is normal, we can use a z-test to test our hypothesis, and the appropriate z-test statistic has the form:

$$z = \frac{(\bar{X}_1 - \bar{X}_2) - (\mu_1 - \mu_2)}{\sqrt{\left(\frac{\theta_1^2}{n_1} + \frac{\theta_2^2}{n_2}\right)}}$$

where $\bar{X}_1$ and $\bar{X}_2$ are the sample means, μ_1 and μ_2 are the hypothesized population means, θ_1^2 and θ_2^2 are population variances, and n_1 and n_2 are the sample sizes, for populations 1 and 2, respectively.

Ordinarily, when conducting hypotheses for two unknown populations' means, the population variances are unknown as well, so the common approach is to conduct a two-sample *t*-test using estimates of the two populations' variances, namely, S_1^2 and S_2^2. When it is assumed that the two populations' variances are equal, the appropriate analysis would be the **pooled variance *t*-test**. The *t*-test statistic is then defined as follows:

$$t = \frac{(\bar{X}_1 - \bar{X}_2) - (\mu_1 - \mu_2)}{\sqrt{S_p^2 \left(\frac{1}{n_1} + \frac{1}{n_2}\right)}}$$

where the pool variance is defined as:

$$S_p^2 = \frac{(n_1 - 1)S_1^2 + (n_2 - 1)S_2^2}{(n_1 - 1) + (n_2 - 1)}$$

and degrees of freedom are $(n_1 + n_2 - 2)$. Note that the two populations' variances are assumed to be equal, so that a single estimate of variance is used, namely, the pooled variance, S_p^2.

Assumptions

Every statistical test has a set of assumptions that underlie the test statistic. When the assumptions are violated, the test results may be invalid, rendering improper conclusions from faulty analyses. The assumptions are as follows:

1. The observations are randomly selected from each of the two independent populations. Remember, all inferential tests rely on random selection.

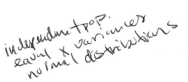

2. The variances of the dependent variable, X, for each population are equal. This allows for calculation of the pool variance.

3. The distributions of the dependent variable, X, are normal for each of the populations.

   Because the sampling distribution of the mean differences, $(\bar{X}_1 - \bar{X}_2)$, is derived from a linear combination of two variables, $\bar{X}_1$ and $\bar{X}_2$, then $\bar{X}_1$ and $\bar{X}_2$ must originate from respective populations that are normal.

There are a few exceptions where the assumptions may be violated. One such case is the assumption that the data is normally distributed. This assumption of the *t*-test can be violated when each sample has at least 30 observations. This violation is possible because the sampling distribution of the differences in means is shaped approximately like a *t*-distribution. The pooled variance *t*-test is robust and can tolerate deviations from normal when sample sizes are larger than 30 and the variances are equal. When these conditions are not met, you must either use another statistical procedure, or transform the data in such a way as to create data that is normally distributed.

Procedure Syntax of PROC TTEST Procedure

The TTEST procedure is employed for testing differences in population means and has the general form:

PROC TTEST DATA=*SAS-data-set* *<options>*;
CLASS *variable*;
PAIRED *variables*;
VAR *variables*;
RUN;

To illustrate the pooled variance *t*-test, consider again the Ames Housing Case to answer the question "Is earning a bonus on the sale of a house related to the square footage of the above ground living area?" First, we define the dependent variable to be living area square footage, GR_LIV_AREA, and the independent, or grouping, variable to be whether or not the real estate agent received a bonus, BONUS. The appropriate hypothesis is:

$$H_o: \mu_0 = \mu_1 \text{ versus } H_1: \mu_0 \neq \mu_1$$

where real estate agents who received a bonus are represented by 1 and real estate agents who did not receive a bonus are represented by 0. To conduct the *t*-test , the analyst would use PROC TTEST as in Program 6.1 Independent Samples *t*-Test for Mean Differences in Above Ground Living Area.

Program 6.1 Independent Samples *t*-Test for Mean Differences in Above Ground Living Area

```
libname sasba 'c:\sasba\ames';
data ames;
   set sasba.ames300;
run;

proc format;
   value yesno 0=No 1=Yes;
run;

proc ttest data =ames plots (only)=qq alpha=.05 h0=0;
class bonus;
var gr_liv_area;
format bonus yesno.;
   title 'Independent Samples t-test for Mean Differences with Q-Q Plots';
run;
```

From the program, you can see that the PROC TTEST requests SAS to conduct an independent two-sample *t*-test on the AMES data set as indicated in the DATA =AMES statement. The CLASS statement tells SAS that the variable BONUS defines the categories of the populations of interest, and the VAR statement tells SAS which continuous variable to use to compute the means for each category of the population. We included the PLOTS(ONLY)=QQ in order to generate the Q-Q plots for visually assessing the normality assumptions. We set the significance level at 0.05 by including the ALPHA=.05 option and we specify that the hypothesized mean difference (μ_1-μ_2) is zero. The defaults settings for PROC TTEST provide for including **histograms**, **box plots**, and **Q-Q plots** for each independent populations of interest. If you omit the (ONLY) designation, SAS will provide the default plots for alternative ways to assess normality.

The output provides, as illustrated in Output 6.1a Independent Samples *t*-Test for Ames Housing, Above Ground Living Area by Bonus, basic statistics for describing each of the two samples with respect to above ground living area. First, you can see that 179 realtors did not receive a bonus when selling the home and that those homes typically averaged

1248.6 square feet, whereas the 121 realtors who received a bonus did so for homes averaging 1927.2 square feet. Other statistics included the standard deviation, minimums and maximum square footages for each of the two groups, respectively. Notice specifically, the fact that the two standard deviations do seem to differ, giving an indication that the equal variance assumption is suspect (we will address that question shortly).

Finally, the actual mean difference is reported as -678.7, which indicates that the average square footage for the first group (BONUS=No) is 678.7 less than the second group (BONUS=Yes). It is this difference that we are interested in testing. We want to know if this difference is large enough, statistically, to conclude that one population differs from the other in terms of average square footage.

Output 6.1a Independent Samples *t*-Test for Ames Housing, Above Ground Living Area by Bonus

The TTEST Procedure

Variable: Gr_Liv_Area

Bonus	N	Mean	Std Dev	Std Err	Minimum	Maximum
No	179	1248.6	340.2	25.4247	520.0	2654.0
Yes	121	1927.2	399.5	36.3197	1152.0	3279.0
Diff (1-2)		-678.7	365.2	42.9833		

Bonus	Method	Mean	95% CL Mean		Std Dev	95% CL Std Dev	
No		1248.6	1198.4	1298.7	340.2	308.2	379.6
Yes		1927.2	1855.3	1999.1	399.5	354.7	457.3
Diff (1-2)	Pooled	-678.7	-763.3	-594.1	365.2	338.1	397.1
Diff (1-2)	Satterthwaite	-678.7	-766.0	-591.3			

Method	Variances	DF	t Value	Pr > |t|
Pooled	Equal	298	-15.79	<.0001
Satterthwaite	Unequal	229.3	-15.31	<.0001

Equality of Variances				
Method	Num DF	Den DF	F Value	Pr > F
Folded F	120	178	1.38	0.0512

Testing the Equal Variance Assumption Using the Folded F-Test

Before conducting the *t*-test, however, we must first test the validity of using the pool variance *t*-test by testing the equal variance assumption. In order to do that, we must test the following hypotheses:

$$H_o: \sigma_0^2 = \sigma_1^2 \quad \text{versus} \quad H_1: \sigma_0^2 \neq \sigma_1^2$$

where we want to determine if the variance of the dependent variable for BONUS=0 is different from the variance of the dependent variable for BONUS=1. The **folded F-statistic** is suitable to test our hypothesis. The folded F-statistic is

$$F = \frac{\text{larger sample variance}}{\text{smaller sample variance}}$$

where the degrees of freedom is calculated by the (sample size of the larger group – 1) and the (sample size of the smaller group – 1). We first calculate the maximum variance by squaring the standard deviation (399.5) for BONUS=1, and the minimum variance by squaring the standard deviation (340.2) for BONUS=0 to calculate the folded F-test statistic:

$$F = \frac{(399.5)^2}{(340.2)^2} = 1.38$$

As indicated in Output 6.1a Independent Samples *t*-Test for Ames Housing, Above Ground Living Area by Bonus, the p-value for the test 0.0512. At .05 level of significance, we do not reject the null hypothesis and conclude that there is no significant differences in variances when comparing both groups. In short, we are correct in using the pooled variance *t*-test .

The third table in Output 6.1a Independent Samples *t*-Test for Ames Housing, Above Ground Living Area by Bonus contains information for carrying out the *t*-test. Because we are justified in using the pooled variance *t*-test , our attention is directed to the row where the method is labeled as 'Pooled', the variances are determined to be 'Equal' and the p-value for the two-tailed test is displayed. Specifically, the *t*-test statistic is -15.79 with 298 degrees of freedom and a p-value of $< .0001$. Because the p-value is less than our cut-off of .0.05, we can reject the null, and conclude that the average above ground living area does differ across the two groups. In other words, BONUS is related to GR_LIV_AREA.

In addition to conducting a *t*-test for the mean differences, the analyst could have used the confidence interval approach as described in Chapter 4, "The Normal Distribution and Introduction to Inferential Statistics." The TTEST option, alpha=.05, determines the level of confidence, so in the second table of Output 6.1a Independent Samples *t*-Test for Ames Housing, Above Ground Living Area by Bonus, the 95% confidence interval around the mean difference is reported to be -763.3, -594.1. In other words, while the point estimate of the mean difference is -678.7, we estimate with a 95% level of confidence that the average above ground living area when comparing the two groups differs anywhere from 595.1 to 763.3 square feet. This interval does not contain zero, which allows us to reject the null hypothesis as well.

Note that the sign of *t*-test statistic or the mean difference (positive or negative) is irrelevant to the interpretation of the significant difference. The sign is simply related to the order in which the groups are listed alphanumerically. Note further, that had the p-value been greater than our 0.05 cut-off, we would not have rejected the null hypothesis, concluding that there is no evidence to relate above ground living area square footage to bonus status.

Verifying the Assumptions of a Two-Sample *t-Test*

The previous conclusions rest on the assumptions of the *t*-test. Anytime the assumptions of a test are violated, the analyst runs the risk of making errors when making conclusions about the population. In order to test the normality assumption, the PROC TTEST option, PLOT (ONLY) = QQ, is used to request that SAS provide Q-Q plots for each of the two groups defined in the CLASS statement. Data that is normally distributed will follow a line at the 45-degree angle. Non-normal data will not have a linear trend along the 45-degree angle. Remember, as mentioned in Chapter 3, "Data Visualization," the interpretation of the Q-Q plots requires some judgment, so the closer the points fall around a line, the stronger the evidence that the data is normally distributed.

The Q-Q Plots of GR_LIV_AREA for each of the two groups are provided in Output 6.1b Normal Probability Plots for Above Ground Living Area by Bonus. The left plot represents the data for BONUS=0, as indicated by the '0' in the upper left of the graphic, and the right plot represents data for BONUS=1, as indicated by the '1' in the upper left the graphic. Our data seems to deviate slightly from the 45-degree trend. Therefore, our assumption of normality is questionable.

Output 6.1b Normal Probability Plots for Above Ground Living Area by Bonus

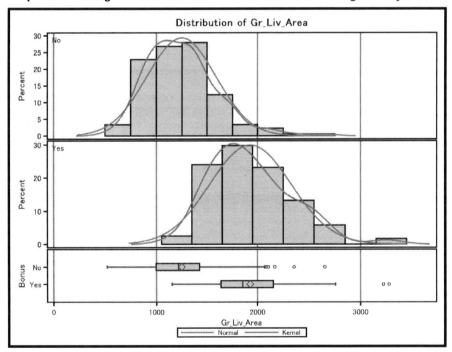

Supplemental Plots for Data Visualization

When running PROC TTEST, we illustrated how to get specific plots using the PLOTS (ONLY) = QQ option, namely the Q-Q plot. If the analyst had omitted the PLOTS option, SAS would have provided the histograms and box plots for the variable defined in the VAR statement for each level of the CLASS variable. In our example, PROC TTEST would have generated those plots for the dependent variable, GR_LIV_AREA, by both groups of the independent variable, BONUS=0 and BONUS=1, respectively, as illustrated in Output 6.1c Histograms and Box Plots for Above Ground Living Area by Bonus.

Output 6.1c Histograms and Box Plots for Above Ground Living Area by Bonus

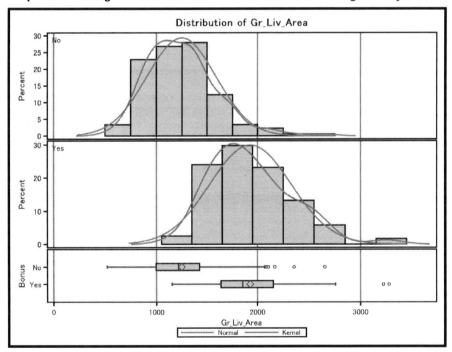

The first panel provides a histogram of the above ground living area for those homes where a bonus is not received (BONUS=0). The solid line represents the normal curve having the mean and standard deviation of the actual data; the dashed line represents the kernel density curve. The second panel provides the same information for those homes where the agent received a bonus (BONUS=1). Finally, the last panel provides the box-and-whisker plot for both groups.

From the top two panels, it seems that the distributions deviate slightly from the normal curve and there are a few outliers in the right tails, as shown in the box-and-whisker plots. In fact, additional information can be gleaned from the box-and-whisker plots. First, for BONUS=0, the whiskers are approximately equal in length and notice that the boxes are approximately in the middle of the distribution. However, the mean, represented by the diamond, is slightly to the right of the median indicating that it may be influenced by the outliers. Secondly, for BONUS=1, the area of the box to the right of the median is slightly larger than the area to the left of the median, indicating lack of symmetry; the mean is greater than the median again, indicating some influence of outliers. All of these patterns support the notion that the data is slightly non-normal. Further investigation of outliers may be warranted.

Testing the Normality Assumption Using the Kolmogorov-Smirnov Test

While visual plots are helpful in describing the shape of the data, the analyst can use the **Kolmogorov-Smirnov (K-S) test** to test the normality assumption. Specifically, the UNIVARIATE procedure generates the output containing the K-S test which can be used to test the following hypotheses:

H_0: Data originates from a population that is normal. *Normal*

H_1: Data does originate from a population that is normal. *Non-Normal*

In order to test the normality of GR_LIV_AREA for each group (BONUS=0 and BONUS=1), consider Program 6.2 Kolmogorov-Smirnov Test of Normality for Above Ground Living Area by Bonus.

Program 6.2 Kolmogorov-Smirnov Test of Normality for Above Ground Living Area by Bonus

```
libname sasba 'c:\sasba\ames';
data ames;
   set sasba.ames300;
run;

proc format;
   value yesno 0=No 1=Yes;
run;

proc univariate data = ames normal;
   class bonus;
   var gr_liv_area;
   format bonus yesno.;
    title 'Kolmogorov-Smirnov Test of Normality Assumption for Gr_Liv_Area by Bonus';
run;
```

In Program 6.2 Kolmogorov-Smirnov Test of Normality for Above Ground Living Area by Bonus, the UNIVARIATE procedure is applied to the AMES300 data set and the NORMAL option is included to test the normality of the GR_LIV_AREA by BONUS, as defined by the VAR and CLASS statements, respectively. The output can be found in Output 6.2 Kolmogorov-Smirnov Test of Normality for Above Ground Living Area by Bonus.

Output 6.2 Kolmogorov-Smirnov Test of Normality for Above Ground Living Area by Bonus

Bonus = No

Tests for Normality				
Test	Statistic		p Value	
Shapiro-Wilk	W	0.95815	Pr < W	<0.0001
Kolmogorov-Smirnov	D	0.073052	Pr > D	0.0201
Cramer-von Mises	W-Sq	0.22885	Pr > W-Sq	<0.0050
Anderson-Darling	A-Sq	1.525645	Pr > A-Sq	<0.0050

Bonus = Yes

Tests for Normality				
Test		Statistic		p Value
Shapiro-Wilk	W	0.959722	Pr < W	0.0011
Kolmogorov-Smirnov	D	0.087217	Pr > D	0.0231
Cramer-von Mises	W-Sq	0.206855	Pr > W-Sq	<0.0050
Anderson-Darling	A-Sq	1.242709	Pr > A-Sq	<0.0050

Because the p-values for the K-S test for each of the two groups are 0.0201 and 0.0231, respectively, and are less than 0.05, we reject the null for both groups. In short, there is evidence that GR_LIV_AREA is non-normal for both groups.

Keep in mind also that the two group sample sizes are considered relatively large, at 179 and 121, respectively; so although we violated the normality assumption, the sampling distribution of the mean differences still has the shape of a t-distribution. In other words, the central limit theorem holds and, as a result, the *t*-test is appropriate for testing mean differences.

Finally, it should be noted also that the validity of the folded F-test is questionable when the populations are not normal. If that is the case, the equal variance hypotheses should be tested using Levene's test, as covered in Chapter 7, "Analysis of Variance (ANOVA)."

Satterthwaite *t*-Test for Unequal Variances

There are times when the population variances are not equal. In short, the analyst may reject the equal variance assumption using the folded F-test. In these instances, the pooled variance *t*-test is inadequate for drawing conclusions, and the analyst must, instead, use **Satterthwaite's separate-variance *t*-test** (Satterthwaite, 1946). The Satterthwaite *t*-test statistic is calculated using the following equation:

$$t = \frac{(\bar{X}_1 - \bar{X}_2) - (\mu_1 - \mu_2)}{\sqrt{\left(\frac{S_1^2}{n_1} + \frac{S_2^2}{n_2}\right)}}$$

and the degrees of freedom are calculated using the two sample variances and the two sample sizes.

Consider the Ames Housing Case where the analyst is interested in answering the question, "Is receiving a bonus related to the total square footage of the basement of the home?" In this case, the analyst would define the dependent variable as TOTAL_BSMT_SF and the independent variable as BONUS and the hypothesis test would be:

$$H_o: \mu_0 = \mu_1 \text{ versus } H_1: \mu_0 \neq \mu_1$$

The program would be identical to that previously discussed, with the exception that TOTAL_BSMT_SF is used in the VAR statement, as illustrated in Program 6.3 Independent Samples *t*-Test for Mean Differences in Total Basement Area.

Program 6.3 Independent Samples *t*-Test for Mean Differences in Total Basement Area

```
libname sasba 'c:\sasba\ames';
data ames;
   set sasba.ames300;
run;

proc format;
   value yesno 0=No 1=Yes;
run;

proc ttest data =ames alpha=.05 h0=0;
class bonus;
var total_bsmt_sf;
format bonus yesno.;
   title 'Independent Samples t-Test for Mean Differences with Q-Q Plots';
run;
```

The output for this analysis is found in Output 6.3 Independent Sample *t*-Test for Ames Housing, Total Basement Area by Bonus. Recall that, first, the analyst must check to see if the equal variance assumption is tenable. From the first table, it is evident that the standard deviation of basement area for those homes earning a bonus (519.6) is about two times larger than that for homes not earning a bonus (275.8), giving the analyst some descriptive evidence that the equal variance assumption is not reasonable. From the folded F-test, found in the fourth table, we can see that the largest variance is 3.55 times larger than the smallest variance, with a p-value < .0001. Therefore, there is evidence that the population variances of TOTAL_BSMT_SF are not equal across the two groups. As a result, the analyst must test the hypothesis using Satterthwaite's *t*-Test.

In table 1 of Output 6.3 Independent Sample *t*-Test for Ames Housing, Total Basement Area by Bonus, note that the average basement area of homes where the agent receives a bonus is 1237.0 square feet, whereas the average basement area for those homes where the agent does not receive a bonus is 888.9 square feet, differing by 348.1 square feet. The *t*-test statistic for that difference is -6.76 (df=166.02) and has a p-value <.0001, which is less than our 0.05 cut-off. Therefore, we reject the null hypothesis and conclude that there is sufficient evidence that the average total basement area differs when comparing the two groups. In other words, receiving a bonus is related to the square footage of the basement of the home. Note also that the 95% confidence interval indicates the difference may lie somewhere between 246.4 and 449.9 square feet, as provided on the row labeled Satterthwaite method.

Finally, it should be notes from the histograms that some homes where a bonus was not earned had zero basement area, meaning that those homes had no basements. This very fact could play into the idea that buyers are more willing to pay higher values simply because the home has a basement; further investigation would be needed to determine the details.

Output 6.3 Independent Sample *t*-Test for Ames Housing, Total Basement Area by Bonus

Bonus	N	Mean	Std Dev	Std Err	Minimum	Maximum
No	179	888.9	275.8	20.6158	0	1740.0
Yes	121	1237.0	519.6	47.2328	384.0	3206.0
Diff (1-2)		-348.1	392.6	46.2067		

Bonus	Method	Mean	95% CL Mean		Std Dev	95% CL Std Dev	
No		888.9	848.2	929.6	275.8	249.9	307.8
Yes		1237.0	1143.5	1330.6	519.6	461.3	594.8
Diff (1-2)	Pooled	-348.1	-439.1	-257.2	392.6	363.5	426.9
Diff (1-2)	Satterthwaite	-348.1	-449.9	-246.4			

Method	Variances	DF	t Value	Pr > |t|
Pooled	Equal	298	-7.53	<.0001
Satterthwaite	Unequal	166.02	-6.76	<.0001

Equality of Variances				
Method	Num DF	Den DF	F Value	Pr > F
Folded F	120	178	3.55	<.0001

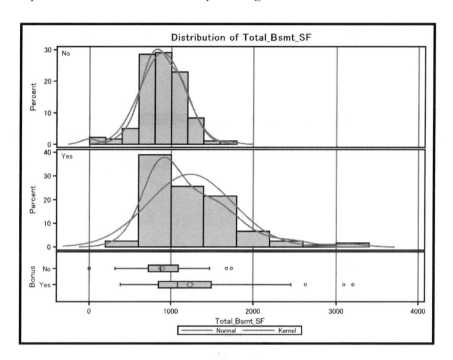

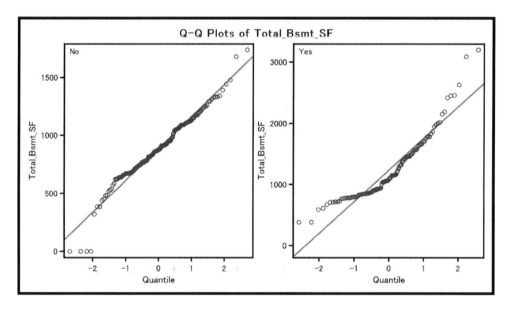

Finally, we must examine the distribution of the dependent variable to evaluate the normality assumption for each group. The normality assumption appears to be met when BONUS=0 because the values on the plot tend to follow the 45-degree trend line, the whiskers on the box-and-whiskers plot are approximately equal, and the measures of central tendency are approximately in the middle of the box. However, the normality assumption is disputable for BONUS=1. The overlay of the normal curve on the values shows that the distribution of values is skewed. Furthermore, the box-and-whiskers plot shows that one whisker is longer than the other, and the measures of central tendency are located to one side of the middle of the box. These patterns demonstrate that the normality assumption is questionable. In this case, because we have a larger sample size, we may proceed with Satterthwaite's test. In short, the *t*-test is robust enough to provide meaningful results.

Summary of Steps for the *t*-Test of Two Independent Populations

From the discussion of the TTEST procedure, you can see that the following steps are required for conducting a *t*-test of two independent populations:

1. Define the dependent and independent variables, state the hypotheses, and run the TTEST procedure.
2. Assess the normality of the dependent variable for each level of the independent variable, using histograms, Q-Q plots, box plots, and the Kolmogorov-Smirnov test. Use sample size requirements to support the tenability; otherwise, consider transforming the variables for further analysis. Pay close attention to outliers.
3. Once the normality assumption is deemed tenable, use the folded F-test to assess the equal variance assumption.
4. If the folded F-test is not rejected, use all output relative to the pooled variance *t*-test for testing your initial hypothesis and making conclusions about group differences. If the folded F-test is rejected, use instead all output relative to Satterthwaite's *t*-test.

Notice that, based upon the design of the studies discussed, we have assumed that the measures on the dependent variable from one group are independent of and not connected to the measures on the dependent variable from the second group. If there is reason to believe that two populations are related on the dependent variable, the analyst must conduct a **paired samples *t*-test**, as described in the next section.

Paired Samples

When the analyst is investigating paired samples, the data across the pairs is considered dependent. There are two primary situations where we encounter paired data. The first is where we have just one sample with repeated measures on the same dependent variable. With repeated measures, the statistic of interest is the difference between the time 1 and time 2 measures on the dependent variable. Here, the statistical analysis is conducted on the differences, as illustrated in the one-sample *t*-test covered in Chapter 4, "The Normal Distribution and Introduction to Inferential Statistics," and not on the specific measures collected from each group. We have a treatment between time 1 and time 2. The data represents the same cases across time, where those cases have undergone a treatment.

For example, with housing data, the analyst may be interested in the home values before and after remodeling (adding a room or a new garage, for example). The paired *t*-test would assess the statistical difference between the home value before and after the home improvement. The impact of the remodeling on home value is determined by testing the difference in those measures. Thus, you may find that these tests are referred to as paired-samples, repeated-measures, or pre-test and post tests.

Using data matched on similar characteristics from different populations requires looking at the differences in two samples. This second situation is referred to as a **paired-samples *t*-test**. For a sample of n-pairs, you are testing the differences, where d_1= the difference between X_1 and X_2 for the first pair, d_2 = the difference between X_1 and X_2 for the second pair, …, and d_n = the difference between X_1 and X_2 for the nth pair. So the *t*-test statistic is:

$$t=\frac{\bar{d}-\mu_0}{S_d}$$

with (n-1) degrees of freedom, where $\bar{d}$ = the average of the sample differences, S_d = the sample standard deviation of the differences, and μ_0 is the hypothesized mean difference.

Assumptions

When conducting a paired-sample *t*-test, the assumption is that the difference scores are normally distributed. There are visual tests of normality as discussed in the previous sections, including histograms, Q-Q plots, and box plots. In addition, statistical tests can be applied to difference scores using PROC UNIVARIATE to obtain results of the Kolmogorov-Smirnov test for normality.

The Paired-Sample *t*-Test Using the PAIRED Statement in the TTEST Procedure

To illustrate the paired sample *t*-test, suppose we are interested in determining if the assessed property tax value is significantly different from the 2012 payment year when compared to the 2016 payment year. Consider a randomly selected sample of data from the Whitley County, Indiana, property tax assessed values for the 2012 and 2016 payment years, with an excerpt provided in Table 6.1 Whitley County, Indiana, 2012 and 2016 Tax Assessed Property Values Sample Data. Notice that the data set contains 4 variables where OBS is the observation number,

TOTAL_BASE_VALUE_2012 is the 2012 property tax assessed value, TOTAL_BASE_VALUE is the 2016 property tax assessed value, and the DIFFERENCE is the amount of change from the 2012 and 2016 property tax assessed values.

Table 6.1 Whitley County, Indiana, 2012 and 2016 Tax Assessed Property Values Sample Data

Obs	TOTAL_BASE_VALUE_2012	TOTAL_BASE_VALUE	difference
1	82200	99230	17030
2	139900	167560	27660
3	93000	114120	21120
4	337300	359200	21900
5	73800	90440	16640

You might believe that the tax assessed property values would increase in a period of 4 years, leading us to test our hypotheses:

$$H_0: \mu_1 = \mu_2 \text{ versus } H_1: \mu_1 \neq \mu_2$$

where group 1 represents the tax assessed property values in 2012 and group 2 represents the tax assessed property values of the same houses in 2016. The appropriate SAS code is in Program 6.4 Kolmogorov-Smirnov Test of Normality Assumption on the Difference Score Using the UNIVARIATE Procedure.

Program 6.4 Kolmogorov-Smirnov Test of Normality Assumption on the Difference Score Using the UNIVARIATE Procedure

```
libname sasba 'c:\sasba\ames';
data alt40;
   set sasba.alt40;
   difference=total_base_value_2012-total_base_value;
run;

proc univariate data=alt40 normal;
   qqplot / normal;
   var difference;
   title 'Kolmogorov-Smirnov Test Of Normality Assumption On The Difference Score Using The
Univariate Procedure';
run;

proc ttest data=sasba.alt40
   plots=qq alpha=.05 h0=0;
   paired total_base_value_2012*total_base_value;
   title 'Paired t-test';
run;
```

First, Program 6.4 Kolmogorov-Smirnov Test of Normality Assumption on the Difference Score Using the UNIVARIATE Procedure reads the ALT40 SAS data set and saves that data in the temporary SAS data set, ALT40. In order to use the UNIVARIATE procedure for testing the normality of the differences and generating the Q-Q plot, the analysis is conducted on the variable, DIFFERENCE. The results of the PROC UNIVARIATE are found in Output 6.4a Kolmogorov-Smirnov Test of Normality Assumption on the Difference Score Using the UNIVARIATE Procedure. The Kolmogorov-Smirnov test is used to test the following hypotheses:

H_0: Data originates from a population that is normal.
H_1: Data does not originate from a population that is normal.

Because the p-value for the test, >0.1500, is greater than the 0.05 level of significance, we do not reject the null hypothesis. In short, there is no evidence that the differences are not normal. A visual inspection using the Q-Q plot seems to support that conclusion as well.

Output 6.4a Kolmogorov-Smirnov Test of Normality Assumption on the Difference Score Using the UNIVARIATE Procedure

Tests for Normality				
Test	Statistic		p Value	
Shapiro-Wilk	W	0.91966	Pr < W	0.0075
Kolmogorov-Smirnov	D	0.102085	Pr > D	>0.1500
Cramer-von Mises	W-Sq	0.072363	Pr > W-Sq	>0.2500
Anderson-Darling	A-Sq	0.621684	Pr > A-Sq	0.0987

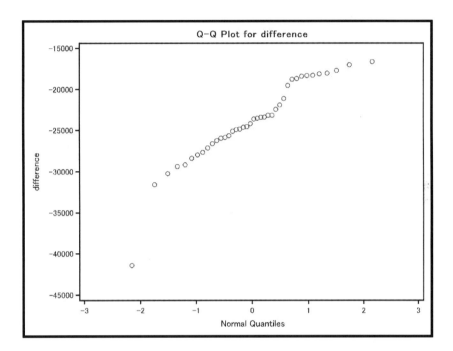

Referring back to Program 6.4 Kolmogorov-Smirnov Test of Normality Assumption on the Difference Score Using the UNIVARIATE Procedure, for the paired-sample *t*-test, the TTEST procedure must include a PAIRED statement naming the two variables representing the paired values, connected by an '*.' Notice that the PLOTS option is included which directs SAS to provide a Q-Q plot of the differences. Partial results are found in Output 6.4b Paired *t*-Test Results for Differences in Tax Assessed Property Values.

Output 6.4b Paired *t*-Test Results for Differences in Tax Assessed Property Values

N	Mean	Std Dev	Std Err	Minimum	Maximum
40	-23907.8	4905.0	775.5	-41400.0	-16640.0

Mean	95% CL Mean		Std Dev	95% CL Std Dev	
-23907.8	-25476.4	-22339.1	4905.0	4018.0	6298.2

DF	t Value	Pr > |t|
39	-30.83	<.0001

The output first gives the descriptive statistics for the differences between the tax assessed property values. There are 40 homes, where the average difference between the 2012 and 2016 values is -23907.8, meaning that the assessed values in 2012 were, on average, $23,097.80 less than those reported in 2016. The standard deviation of the differences is 4905.0, with a minimum difference of -41400.0 and a maximum difference of -16640.0. The second table then reports the 95%

confidence interval for the mean difference, so while the point estimate of the difference is $23,907.80, it is estimated that the difference may be somewhere between $22,339.10 and $25,476.40.00. Finally, the *t*-test statistic is calculated as follows:

$$t=\frac{\bar{d}-\mu_0}{S_d}=\frac{-23907.8-0}{775.5}=-30.83$$

Notice that the *p*-value is always reported for the two-tailed test only. Therefore, we conclude that there is evidence that the tax assessed property values are significantly different in 2012 than in 2016.

Finally, the PLOT option is included in the TTEST procedure as an alternative to testing the assumptions. The following plots, as illustrated in Output 6.4c Accompanying Plots for the Paired-Sample *t*-Test, accompany the test for a paired sample.

Output 6.4c Accompanying Plots for the Paired-Sample *t*-Test

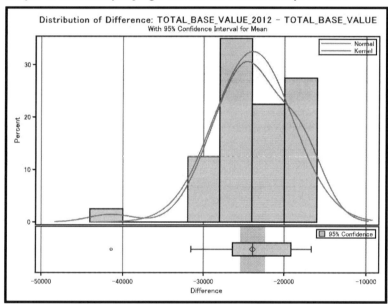

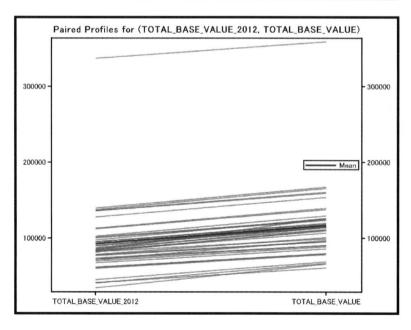

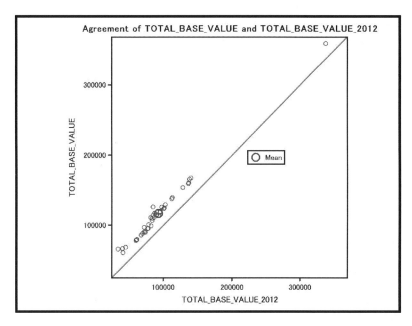

The first plot displays the distribution of difference, along with the normal distribution overlay. By examining this distribution, it is tricky to determine if the normal distribution of the differences assumption is met. This is common when using a small data set. In situations like this, where you cannot clearly determine if the distribution is normal, you must do as we did previously: run PROC UNIVARIATE and examine the appropriate normality test results. The Shapiro-Wilk and Kolmogorov-Smirnov tests are not significant, nor are any of the other normality tests, as found in Output 6.4a Kolmogorov-Smirnov Test of Normality Assumption on the Difference Score Using the UNIVARIATE Procedure, all supporting the notion that the distribution is normal.

The second visual display is the paired profiles. Each line connects the case values for the 2012 and 2016 tax assessed property values. The lines show an overall increase from one tax year to the other for each home, as the lines rise from left to right. The distinct thicker line is the mean values from 2012 to 2016, showing that, overall, the values increase.

Finally, the last visual display is the agreement plot. Each smaller circle represents the ordered pair (value for year 2012, value for year 2016). The clear pattern on this plot indicates that all data points fall above the 45-degree angle line which is the point where no change would be represented. As all data points are above this line, all data points represent an increase in tax assessed property values between 2012 and 2016. If data points fell on the line, they would indicate no change in tax assessed property values from 2012 to 2016. Also, if the data points were below the line, those points would represent a decrease in tax assessed property values from 2012 to 2016. The larger circle represents the mean of the 2012 and 2016 tax assessed property values.

It should be noted that the PLOTS=QQ option in the TTEST procedure would have generated the same Q-Q plot as that in the UNIVARIATE procedure and will not be repeated here. It was included in the SAS code for illustrative purposes only.

Key Terms

independent samples *t*-test
pooled variance *t*-test
histograms
box plots
Q-Q plots
folded f-statistic
Satterthwaite's separate-variance *t*-test
paired-samples *t*-test
Kolmogorov-Smirnov

Chapter Quiz

1. Suppose you want to see if the amount owed on a bill is related to whether or not the bill is paid. Which one of the following would you use to do an independent samples *t*-test?

   a. proc ttest;
      class *paid_bill*;
      paired;
      var *amount_owed paid_bill*;
      run;

   b. proc ttest;
      class *paid_bill*;
      var *amount_owed*;
      run;

   c. proc ttest;
      class *amount_owed*;
      var *paid_bill*;
      run;

   d. proc ttest;
      class *yes*;
      paired *yes*;
      var *amount_owed*;
      run;

2. Suppose you want to see if the average amount owed on a bill differs when comparing those who paid their bill versus those who have not. Given this SAS output, which of the statements is accurate? (use 0.05 level of significance)

Variable	DebtAmt	N	Mean	Lower CL Mean	Upper CL Mean	Std Dev	Lower CL Std Dev	Upper CL Std Dev	Std Err
paid	0	91	47.975	50.121	52.267	8.9947	10.305	12.066	1.0803
paid	1	109	53.447	54.991	56.535	7.1786	8.1337	9.3843	0.7791
paid	Diff (1-2)		-7.442	-4.87	-2.298	8.3622	9.1846	10.188	1.3042

t-Tests

Variable	Method	Variances	DF	t Value	Pr > |t|
paid	Pooled	Equal	198	-3.73	0.0002
paid	Satterthwaite	Unequal	170	-3.66	0.0003

Equality of Variances

Variable	Method	Num DF	Den DF	F Value	Pr > F
paid	Folded F	90	108	1.61	0.0187

   a. The significant folded f indicates that the variances for the two groups are different.
   b. The significant folded f indicates that the variances for the two groups are not different.
   c. The appropriate test statistic is $t = -3.73$ (p.0002).
   d. None of the above.

3. Using the output listed in #2, what conclusion is appropriate?
   a. There is evidence that the amount owed is different when comparing those who paid their bill (paid=1) and those who did not (paid=0).
   b. People who did not pay (paid=0) have significantly more debt.
   c. Amount owed is not related to whether or not people paid.
   d. None of the above.

4. Scenario: The *t*-test statistic for the difference is -10.34 (df=85) and has a p-value <.01, which is less than our 0.05 cut-off. Given this scenario, what do you conclude?
   a. Accept the null hypothesis and conclude that there is sufficient evidence that the variable of interest differs when comparing the two groups.
   b. Accept the null hypothesis and conclude that there is insufficient evidence that the variable of interest differs when comparing the two groups.
   c. Reject the null hypothesis and conclude that there is insufficient evidence that the variable of interest differs when comparing the two groups.
   d. Reject the null hypothesis and conclude that there is sufficient evidence that the variable of interest differs when comparing the two groups.

5. When using the folded F-test at 0.05 level of significance, a p-value less than 0.05 indicates that
   a. the pooled variance *t*-test should be used.
   b. Satterthwaite's *t*-test should be used.
   c. there is a relationship between the independent and dependent variables.
   d. none of the above.

6. When you want to compare the means scores for the same group on two different occasions, you should use the:
   a. F-test.
   b. Levine's test.
   c. independent samples *t*-test.
   d. paired samples *t*-test.

7. Suppose you want to test to see if a weight loss program is effective by taking the weight before and after to see if there was a significant decrease in weight after six weeks. Which one of the following would you use to conduct the test?
   a. proc ttest;
      class groups;
      paired weight_before*weight_after;
      var weight_before weight_after;
      run;
   b. proc ttest;
      var weight_before weight_after;
      run;
   c. proc ttest;
      class *weight*;
      var before after;
      run;
   d. proc ttest;
      paired weight_before*weight_after;
      run;

8. Which of the following is true given a significant paired-samples *t*-test result from Time 1 (mean=43.97, SD=6.12) to Time 2 (mean=39.46, SD=4.95), with *t*(30)=6.01 p<.01?
   a. There was no difference in scores between Time 1 and Time 2.
   b. There was a mean increase in scores from Time 1 and Time 2.
   c. There was a mean decrease in scores from Time 1 and Time 2.
   d. None of the above.

9. When *t*=-6.43 and p<.001 in an independent samples *t*-test you may conclude that
    a. there is a relationship between the independent and dependent variables.
    b. the folded F-test should be used.
    c. you must use Satterthwaite's *t*-test.
    d. there is no significant difference between groups.

10. For the research question: is there a significant change in home values following $20,000 or more in home improvements?
    a. An independent *t*-test will tell you whether there is a statistically significant difference between groups.
    b. An F-test will tell you whether there is a statistically significant difference between Time 1 and Time 2.
    c. A paired-samples *t*-test will tell you whether there is a statistically significant difference in mean scores for Time 1 and Time 2.
    d. None of the above.

Chapter 7: Analysis of Variance (ANOVA)

Introduction

In Chapter 6, "Two Sample *t*-Test, we introduced the pooled-variance *t*-test for testing the relationship between a categorical variable with two levels and a numeric continuous variable. In particular, we analyzed the relationship between the variable, bonus, namely, whether or not an agent earned a bonus when selling a house, and ground living area. In many situations, the categorical variable has more than two levels. For example, you may want to see if there is a relationship between the overall quality of a house (having three levels--good, average, and poor) and the average sale price.

When the outcome variable is continuous and the distribution of errors is assumed to be normal, the **General Linear Model** can be used to represent the relationship between the predictor variables and the outcome variable. Specifically, when the analyst is interested in assessing the differences in a continuous numeric outcome across two or more populations, the appropriate statistical analysis is an **Analysis of Variance** (ANOVA).

When looking at the effects of one predictor, or one factor, on the outcome of interest, the analysis is referred to a **one-way analysis of variance**. However, in many situations, there may be other factors that affect the outcome of interest and we can extend the general linear model to include these additional effects. Specifically, in this chapter, we will illustrate the one-way analysis of variance, followed by both the **randomized block design** and the **two-way analysis of variance** for investigating multiple effects on the outcome of interest.

In this chapter, you will learn how to:

- describe the linear model for the one-factor analysis of variance (ANOVA), the randomized block design, and the two-factor analysis of variance (ANOVA)

- explore the data in order to describe the characteristics of data across the populations under investigation

- use the GLM procedure to perform ANOVA, including the CLASS and MODEL statements

- interpret the statistical output of the GLM procedure, including the ANOVA table, F-test statistic, p-value, and r-square

- evaluate the null hypothesis using the GLM output

- assess the equal variance assumption using the MEANS statement with the HOVTEST option within the GLM procedure to generate Levene's test

- verify the assumptions of ANOVA using diagnostic fit plots generated by the PLOTS=DIAGNOSTICS option of the GLM procedure
- interpret graphical output of the GLM procedure
- generate predicted values and the residuals using the OUTPUT statement
- perform post hoc tests to evaluate treatment effects
- use the LSMEANS statement in the GLM procedure to perform pairwise comparisons
- use the PDIFF option of the LSMEANS statement to generate p-values for each pairwise comparison
- use the ADJUST= option in the LSMEANS statement to define the adjustment method used for the multiple comparison procedure
- interpret the results of the ADJUST option for both Tukey and Dunnett approaches to pairwise comparisons
- interpret diffograms to evaluate pairwise comparisons
- interpret control plots to evaluate pairwise comparisons
- use blocking to reduce error variance and how to test the usefulness of blocking
- use the MODEL statement within GLM procedure to produce output that will help determine the significance of the interaction between factors
- interpret the results of a two-factor ANOVA to identify interaction effects or main effects
- understand when Type III sums-of-squares should be used versus Type I sums-of-squares
- use the LSMEANS statement with the SLICE= option to interpret interaction effects

One-Factor Analysis of Variance

When the analyst is investigating differences in a continuous outcome across two or more populations, the appropriate statistical test is the one-way, or one-factor, analysis of variance. Specifically, the statistical model of interest represents a linear relationship between the outcome variable and a single categorical variable, where the categorical variable represents various populations, or groups.

The One-Factor ANOVA Model

The one-factor ANOVA model is represented by

$$Y_{ik} = \mu + \tau_i + \varepsilon_{ik}$$

where Y_{ik} is the value of the outcome variable for observation k in group i, μ is the overall mean for the outcome variable, τ_i is the treatment effect for each observation in group i, and ε_{ik} is the error in prediction for observation k in group i. In essence this equation means that we expect the value of Y to differ from the mean, μ, as a function of its group membership, i, and some random error. If the treatment effect of being in group i is zero, then Y is simply a function of the overall mean and random error.

The general form of the hypotheses for testing differences in g population means (for i = 1 to g) is:

$$H_0: \mu_1 = \mu_2 = \ldots = \mu_g \quad \text{versus} \quad H_1: \text{not all } \mu_i\text{'s are equal}$$

which is equivalent to testing whether or not treatment effects exist:

$$H_0: \tau_1 = \tau_2 = \ldots = \tau_g = 0 \quad \text{versus} \quad H_1: \text{not all } \tau_i\text{'s equal zero}$$

Constructing the Test Statistic: Estimating Variance among Groups and Variance within Groups

While our main focus is on detecting differences in means, the construction of the test statistic relies on the estimation of two variances; the first variance measures the variation *among* the group means and the second variance measures the variation of the observations *within* each group. Consider the six observations belonging to each of two groups, respectively, listed in Table 7.1 Deviations within and across Groups. Note that the mean of all six observations, referred to as the overall mean $\overline{\overline{Y}}$, has a value of 7 while the means for groups 1 and 2, respectively, are 4 and 10.

Now let's specifically review differences with respect to observation 1. The difference between its Y and the overall mean, $Y - \bar{\bar{Y}}$, is -4 as indicated in column I. That difference can be partitioned into two components: the difference due to being in group 1, namely, $Y - \bar{Y}_i$, which has a value of -1 (column II) and the difference in the group mean and the overall mean, $\bar{Y}_i - \bar{\bar{Y}}$, which has a value of -3 (column III). It is important to note that the largest difference, in absolute value, is -3, meaning that the difference between Y and $\bar{\bar{Y}}$ is attributed to the fact that observation 1 belongs to group 1 (i.e., group 1 mean differs from the overall mean).

Table 7.1 Deviations within and across Groups SST

Group	Y_i	$\bar{Y}_i$	$\bar{\bar{Y}}$	I $Y - \bar{\bar{Y}}$	II $Y - \bar{Y}_i$	III $\bar{Y}_i - \bar{\bar{Y}}$
1	3	4	7	-4	-1	-3
1	4	4	7	-3	0	-3
1	5	4	7	-2	1	-3
2	9	10	7	2	-1	3
2	10	10	7	3	0	3
2	11	10	7	4	1	3
			SUM	0	0	0

In fact, an inspection of column I across all observations gives you an idea of the overall differences between the Y values and $\bar{\bar{Y}}$. This overall variation can be attributed, largely, to the differences between the group means and the overall mean (column III), whereas very little variation exists between the individual observations and the mean of the group to which they belong (column II). Consequently, the variation between the Y values and $\bar{\bar{Y}}$ in column I seems to be driven by the difference in group means, column 3. In other words, group membership matters when explaining the outcome Y; that is, the independent variable as defined by the grouping variable explains the variability in the outcome Y. In terms of prediction, you could also say that there is less error in predicting the Y values if you used the group average, $\bar{Y}_g$, as opposed to the overall mean, $\bar{\bar{Y}}$.

The goal of ANOVA is to determine if these differences occur by chance or if those differences are significantly large enough to allow us to infer differences in population means. In order to test that, we must first develop measures-- representing the three sources of variation found in columns I, II, and III, respectively, as shown in Table 7.2 Squared Deviations within and across Groups--which take into account the entire sample.

Consider the variation between the values of Y and $\bar{\bar{Y}}$. Note that adding the deviations in Table 7.1 Deviations within and across Groups is useless because the positives and negatives cancel out, giving a total deviation of zero in all situations, even those where the data is widely dispersed. To eliminate this problem, it is common to add the squared deviations, as seen in Table 7.2 Squared Deviations within and across Groups to get to the **Total-Sums-of-Squares, SST**,

$$SST = \sum_{i=1}^{g} \sum_{k=1}^{n_g} (Y_{ik} - \bar{\bar{Y}})^2$$

where Y_{ik} is the outcome of the kth observation in the ith group, $\bar{\bar{Y}}$ is the overall mean, g is the number of groups, and n_g is the number of observations in group g.

The total-sums-of-squares, SST, is a single number that represents the overall variability in our outcome variable. (Note that SST is the numerator in the formula for variance referenced in Chapter 2, "Summarizing Your Data with Descriptive Statistics.") For our data, as seen in Table 7.2 Squared Deviations within and across Groups, SST = $(3-7)^2 + (4-7)^2 + (5-7)^2 + (9-7)^2 + (10-7)^2 + (11-7)^2 = 58$. Note that this is the sums of squares value in column I.

Table 7.2 Squared Deviations within and across Groups

					I	II	III
Group	Y	Y^2	$\bar{Y}_i$	$\bar{\bar{Y}}$	$(Y - \bar{\bar{Y}})^2$	$(Y - \bar{Y}_i)^2$	$(\bar{Y}_i - \bar{\bar{Y}})^2$
1	3	9	4	7	16	1	9
1	4	16	4	7	9	0	9
1	5	25	4	7	4	1	9
2	9	81	10	7	4	1	9
2	10	100	10	7	9	0	9
2	11	121	10	7	16	1	9
SUM	42	352	42	42	58	4	54

The computational formula for **SST** is:

$$SST = \sum_{i=1}^{g}\sum_{k=1}^{n_g} Y_{ik}^2 - \left[\sum_{i=1}^{g}\sum_{k=1}^{n_g} Y_{ik}\right]^2 / n_T$$

Applying that formula to our example, we see that SST = 352 – (42)²/6 = 58.

The second source of variation measures how the observations vary within each group. This is the random error within each group g, that is, the difference between Y and $\bar{Y}_i$, and is measured by the **Sums-of-Squares-Error, SSE,**

$$SSE = \sum_{i=1}^{g}\sum_{k=1}^{n_g}(Y_{ik} - \bar{Y}_i)^2$$

where Y_{ik} is the outcome of the kth observation in the ith group, $\bar{Y}_i$ is the mean of group i, g is the number of groups, and n_g is the number of observations in group g.

The sums-of squares-error is a single number that represents how the observations vary within each of their respective groups. For our example, SSE = (3-4)² + (4-4)² + (5-4)² + (9-10)² + (10-10)² + (11-10)² = 4. Note that this is the sums of squares value in column II.

The computational formula for SSE utilizes the variances and can be used instead:

$$SSE = \sum_{i=1}^{g}(n_i - 1)\, S_i^2$$

where n_i and S_i^2 represent the sample size and variances for each of the i groups, respectively. For our example, the sample size for each group is 3, the variance of group 1 values (3, 4, and 5) is 1, and the variance for group 2 values (9, 10, and 11) is 1. So, SSE = (3-1)(1) + (3-1)(1) = 4

Finally, the third source of variation measures how the group means vary from the overall mean and is represented by the **Sums-of-Squares Among-Groups, SSA.** It is defined as follows:

$$SSA = \sum_{i=1}^{g}\sum_{k=1}^{n_g}(\bar{Y}_i - \bar{\bar{Y}})^2$$

where $\bar{Y}_i$ is the mean of group i, $\bar{\bar{Y}}$ is the overall mean, g is the number of groups, and n_g is the number of observations in group g.

The sums-of squares-among-groups is a single number that represents how the group means vary from the overall mean. For our example, SSA = (4-7)² + (4-7)² + (4-7)² + (10-7)² + (10-7)² + (10-7)² = 54. Note that this is the sums of squares value in column III.

The computational formula for

$$SSA = \sum_{i=1}^{g} n_i \left(\overline{Y}_i - \overline{\overline{Y}} \right)^2$$

where n_i is the sample size for group *i*. For our example, $SSA = 3(4\text{-}7)^2 + 3(10\text{-}7)^2 = 54$.

Note that if all of the group means, $\overline{Y}_i$, are equal, then they are also equal to the overall mean and SSA=0, meaning that there is no variation in the group means. On the other hand, as the group means become more dispersed, the SSA increases. In our example, the overall variation in Y is 58, where 54 of that is derived or explained by group mean differences and 4 is a result of random error within each group. Here, it seems that the group means vary to the extent that 93.1% (100% x 54/58) of the overall variation is attributed to the variation in the group means. Following we will discuss how large the variation in means must be before making inferences to the population.

Let's now consider these values in terms of variances. Recall in Chapter 2, "Summarizing Your Data with Descriptive Statistics," that the variance of Y is described as an average squared deviation, or the sum-of-squared-deviations divided by (n-1). The average squared deviation is equivalent to a mean square; in fact, to calculate any mean square, you can take sum-of-squares and divide by degrees of freedom. Therefore, we define the **variance across group means (MSA)** and the **variance within groups (MSE)** as follows:

$$MSA = \frac{SSA}{g\text{-}1} \quad \text{and} \quad MSE = \frac{SSE}{n_T\text{-}g}$$

where g = the number of groups and the variance within each group and n_T = the total number of observations in the study. Generally, you expect observations in one group to have similar values, thus having relatively small variance (i.e., relatively small MSE); however, you expect observations in different groups to be dissimilar and exhibit relatively large variance (i.e., relatively large MSA.) Therefore, the statistic of interest in measuring group differences is the ratio of the variance across groups to the variance within groups, which is MSA/MSE. If there are no group differences, we expect the MSA to reflect only random variations around the overall means; consequently, MSA and MSE are equal so that the ratio is approximately equal to 1.0. For relatively large variations in group means, we expect the ratio to be greater than 1.0.

For our hypothesis test for mean differences, we will reject the null when the test statistic (MSA/MSE) is significantly greater than 1.0 (i.e., significantly large). Our benchmark for deciding how large the test statistic must be, while minimizing the chance of making a Type I error, relies on the sampling distribution, as introduced in Chapter 4, "The Normal Distribution and Introduction to Inferential Statistics."

When taking repeated random samples from g normal populations, the ratio of MSA/MSE is calculated for each sample and, in total, these ratios make up a sampling distribution. This sampling distribution is referred to as the **F-distribution** with numerator degrees of freedom (g-1) and denominator degrees of freedom ($n_T - g$), and is displayed in Figure 7.1 The F-Distribution.

Figure 7.1 The F-Distribution

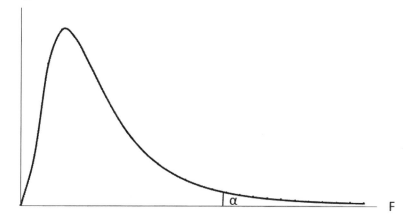

The upper-tail area of the F-distribution is determined by the level of significance and represents the proportion of times the analyst would make a Type I error by rejecting when, in actuality, the null hypothesis is true. Consequently, the critical F-value that determines the critical region can be found using an F-table, as found in Appendix F F-Table.

The analyst would, therefore, conduct an analysis of variance using the following steps:

1. Determine the Critical F-value based on α and $(g-1)$ and $(n_T - g)$ degrees of freedom.
2. Using sample data, calculate the F-test statistic.
3. Make the decision: If the F-test statistic > Critical Value, then reject H_o; otherwise, if the F-test statistic < Critical Value, then do not reject H_o (or using the p-value: if the p-value associated with the F-test statistic is less than α, then reject H_o).
4. Interpret the results.

When conducting an analysis of variance procedure, the results are displayed in an ANOVA table as illustrated in Table 7.3 General Form of the Analysis of Variance Table.

Table 7.3 General Form of the Analysis of Variance Table

Source of Variation	Sums of Squares	Degrees of Freedom	Mean Square (Variance)	F-Test Statistic
Among Groups	SSA	g-1	MSA	MSA/MSE
Within Groups	SSE	$n_T - g$	MSE	
Total	SST	$n_T - 1$		

When conducting an ANOVA, there are certain assumptions that must hold to ensure the validity of the results. If any of these assumptions are violated, the analyst is susceptible to errors when making inferences about the population. The following are assumptions of analysis of variance:

* The observations must be randomly selected from independent populations.

* For each population, the residuals are normally distributed.

* The variances of the outcome variable for all populations are equal.

The GLM Procedure for Investigating Mean Differences

The GLM procedure has the general form:

PROC GLM DATA= *SAS-data-set* **PLOTS**=options;
CLASS *variables*;
MODEL *dependents=independents* </options>;
MEANS *effects* </options>;
LSMEANS *effects* </options>;
OUTPUT OUT=*SASdataset* <keyword=variable...>;
RUN;

Consider the following application of the analysis of variance (ANOVA) procedure. Suppose an analyst in the college of business for a fictitious university wants to identify incoming freshman comfortable with information technology for purposes of career counseling. In short, the analyst wants to show that computer anxiety differs across various groups of incoming freshmen.

First, in order to quantify computer anxiety, suppose the analyst develops an 8-statement 5-point Likert survey where the student is asked to select one of the following five responses for each statement: 'Strongly Disagree,' 'Disagree,' 'Neutral,' 'Agree,' or 'Strongly Agree,' having values of 1 to 5, respectively. Examples of statements include 'I feel very uncomfortable when installing software on my laptop,' or 'I feel very uncomfortable troubleshooting problems on my laptop.' Consequently, if a student answers 'strongly agree' to all eight statements, each statement assigned a value of 5, then that student would have a total computer anxiety score of 40, indicating very high anxiety. A student who answers 'strongly disagree' to all eight statements, each statement assigned a value of 1, would have a total computer anxiety score of 8, indicating very low anxiety.

Suppose, in particular, the analyst wants to show that the computer anxiety score (CAS) is associated with the freshman's declared academic major--Management, Information Systems, and Economics; therefore, the hypothesis to be tested is:

$$H_0: \mu_1 = \mu_2 = \mu_3 \quad \text{versus} \quad H_1: \text{not all } \mu_i\text{'s are equal}$$

where 1=Management (MGT), 2=Information Systems (IS), and 3=Economics (ECON).

The analyst randomly selects students from each of the three academic majors, administers the computer anxiety survey and records the scores. As illustrated in both Chapter 2 "Summarizing Your Data with Descriptive Statistics" and Chapter 3 , "Data Visualization," the analyst first explores the data to get an overall description of the data, including a preliminary view of group mean differences and visuals of the normality and equal variance assumptions, as well as outliers. Program 7.1 Descriptive Statistics for Computer Anxiety by Academic Major provides an example of how to generate the descriptive statistics:

Program 7.1 Descriptive Statistics for Computer Anxiety by Academic Major

```
libname cas 'c:\sasba\data';
data one;
   set cas.cas;
run;

proc format;
   value major
   1=MGT 2=IS 3=ECON;
proc sort data=one; by major;
run;

proc means data=one maxdec=4;
   format major.;
   var cas;
   class major;
   title 'Descriptive statistics for computer anxiety by academic major';
run;

proc sgplot data=one;
   vbox cas / category=major;
   format major.;
   title 'Box and whisker plots for computer anxiety by academic major';
run;
```

The descriptive statistics are displayed in Output 7.1 Exploration of Computer Anxiety by Academic Major:

Output 7.1 Exploration of Computer Anxiety by Academic Major

			Analysis Variable : CAS			
MAJOR	N Obs	N	Mean	Std Dev	Minimum	Maximum
MGT	105	105	30.0095	6.1088	16.0000	40.0000
IS	60	60	22.7500	6.6067	8.0000	36.0000
ECON	75	75	24.4800	5.8963	11.0000	37.0000

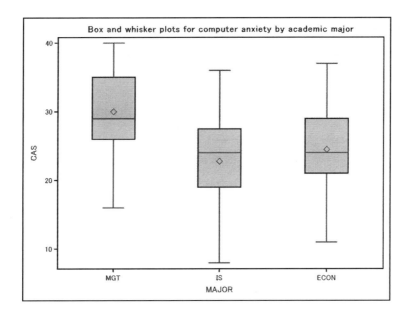

From the output, the analyst can see that management students make up the largest group having the highest level of computer anxiety, with a sample size of 105, an average computer anxiety score of 30.01, a minimum score of 16, and a maximum score of 40. The group of 60 students intending to major in information systems has a lower anxiety score with an average score of 22.75, a minimum score of 8 and a maximum score of 36. Those students declaring economics as a major seem to have similar anxiety levels as information systems students, having an average computer anxiety score of 24.48, minimum score of 11, and maximum score of 37.

From the box plot, the analyst can see that there are no outliers; and while the spreads seem to be similar across the three groups, the distributions seem to be slightly skewed. Visually, it seems that IS and ECON students have very similar levels of anxiety and somewhat lower than the anxiety scores of MGT students. In order to infer to differences in the population, the analyst must test the stated hypothesis using Program 7.2 One-Way ANOVA for Testing Differences in Computer Anxiety.

Program 7.2 One-Way ANOVA for Testing Differences in Computer Anxiety

```
libname cas 'c:\sasba\data';
data one;
   set cas.cas;
run;

proc format;
   value major
   1=MGT 2=IS 3=ECON;
run;

proc glm data=one;
   format major.;
   class major;
   model cas=major;
   title 'One Way ANOVA for testing differences in computer anxiety across academic majors';
run;
```

In Program 7.2 One-Way ANOVA for Testing Differences in Computer Anxiety, the permanent SAS data set, called CAS, is referenced using the LIBNAME statement and saved in the temporary data set called ONE. The FORMAT procedure is used to provide labels for each of the three academic majors. The GLM procedure is applied to data set, ONE, to test mean differences across groups, where the CLASS statement defines the categorical grouping variable, MAJOR, and the MODEL statement defines the numeric variable, CAS, to be tested as a function of MAJOR. The results are displayed in Output 7.2 One-Way ANOVA for Testing Differences in Computer Anxiety:

Output 7.2 One-Way ANOVA for Testing Differences in Computer Anxiety

Class Level Information		
Class	Levels	Values
MAJOR	3	ECON IS MGT

Number of Observations Read	240
Number of Observations Used	240

The GLM Procedure

Dependent Variable: CAS

Source	DF	Sum of Squares	Mean Square	F Value	Pr > F
Model	2	2442.77286	1221.38643	32.06	<.0001
Error	237	9028.96048	38.09688		
Corrected Total	239	11471.73333			

R-Square	Coeff Var	Root MSE	CAS Mean
0.212938	23.32091	6.172267	26.46667

Source	DF	Type I SS	Mean Square	F Value	Pr > F
MAJOR	2	2442.772857	1221.386429	32.06	<.0001

Source	DF	Type III SS	Mean Square	F Value	Pr > F
MAJOR	2	2442.772857	1221.386429	32.06	<.0001

The output first includes the class level information indicating that there are three levels, or groups, of the class variable, MAJOR, having values ECON, IS, and MGT, respectively. The output also provides both the number of observations read and used, namely 240. Note that when the observations read equals the number of observations used, there are no missing values on any of the variables included in the analysis.

Next the output displays the results of the analysis in the form of the ANOVA table. The analyst can see that the degrees of freedom for the model are equal to 2, or g-1 for g=3 groups; the degrees of freedom for the error are 237, or $n_T - g =$ 240 – 3, for a total sample size of 240. Each mean square is obtained by taking the sums-of-squares and dividing by their respective degrees of freedom.

Finally, the F-test statistic of 32.06 is calculated by dividing the mean square model (MSA) by the mean square error (MSE); and the F-test statistic has a p-value < .0001. Suppose the analyst uses 0.05 level of significance. Because the p-value, 0.0001, is less than the alpha of 0.05, the null hypothesis is rejected. In conclusion, based upon our data, there is evidence in the population that computer anxiety (CAS) differs across the academic majors.

Predicted Values and Residuals Using the OUTPUT Statement

As mentioned earlier, analysis of variance is a way to determine whether or not there is a relationship between a categorical predictor variable and a continuous numeric outcome variable. If it is determined that there is a significant relationship, the categorical variable is significant in predicting the numeric outcome. As a result, you can obtain the predicted values and residuals for each observation. The residuals are the errors in prediction; that is, the difference between the actual Y and the predicted Y. For each observation k, the **residual** is calculated using the following equation:

$$e = Y - \hat{Y}$$

The **predicted values** and the residuals for each observation can be obtained using Program 7.3 Predicted Values and Residuals for Computer Anxiety Scores.

Program 7.3 Predicted Values and Residuals for Computer Anxiety Scores

```
libname cas 'c:\sasba\data';
data one;
   set cas.cas;
run;

proc format;
   value major
   1=MGT 2=IS 3=ECON;
run;

proc glm data=one;
   format major.;
   class major;
   model cas=major;
   output out=pred predicted=pred_cas
          residual=res_cas;
run;

proc print data=pred;
   var student_id major cas pred_cas res_cas;
   title 'Predicted Values and Residuals for Computer Anxiety Scores';
run;
```

Note that the OUTPUT statement is added to the GLM procedure to create a file (called PRED) which contains all of the original data in addition to the predicted values of the computer anxiety score (PRED_CAS) and the residuals (RES_CAS). The PRINT procedure is used to display the contents of PRED and an excerpt is displayed in Output 7.3 Predicted Values and Residuals for Computer Anxiety Scores:

Output 7.3 Predicted Values and Residuals for Computer Anxiety Scores

Obs	STUDENT_ID	MAJOR	CAS	pred_cas	res_cas
1	1001	MGT	16	30.0095	-14.0095
2	1002	MGT	16	30.0095	-14.0095
3	1003	MGT	17	30.0095	-13.0095
4	1004	MGT	19	30.0095	-11.0095
	...	...	...	...	...
106	1106	IS	8	22.7500	-14.7500
107	1107	IS	9	22.7500	-13.7500
	...	...	...	...	...
239	1239	ECON	37	24.4800	12.5200
240	1240	ECON	37	24.4800	12.5200

Note that the predicted value for each observation is the mean of the group in which that observation belongs. For example, observation 1 represents a student who has declared management as a major with an actual computer anxiety score of 16; the predicted computer anxiety score is the mean anxiety score for all management majors, namely, 30.0095; therefore, the residual is 16 minus 30.0095, or -14.0095.

Measures of Fit

When conducting an analysis of variance, the primary goal is to determine whether or not the variation in the data can be attributed to the factor under investigation. Once it has been determined that a factor is significant, the next logical question to ask is how well does that model perform in terms of explaining the total variation.

A common metric for assessing performance is the **Coefficient of Determination (R^2)** and is defined as follows:

$$R^2 = \frac{SSA}{SST} = \frac{SSA}{SSA + SSE}$$

R^2 is an index that measures the proportion of the total variability in the data that can be explained by the factor of interest. When there is no error in the model, that is, when knowing an observation's group membership allows you to predict the outcome variable perfectly (i.e., SSE=0), you are explaining all of the variation in the data as a function of the factor. Consequently, SSA=SST, and R^2=1. However, when you are explaining no variation in the data by using the factor, SSA=0, and as a result R^2=0. In short, the larger the value of R^2, the more variation you are explaining using that factor in the model.

In our example, from Output 7.2 One-Way ANOVA for Testing Differences in Computer Anxiety, note that SSA=2442.77286 and SST=11471.73333, resulting in an R^2 value equal to approximately 0.2129. Subsequently, we are explaining 21.3% of the variation in computer anxiety (CAS) by using academic major in our model.

While 0.2129 may not seem large, in some areas of research, relatively small values of R^2 are acceptable in the absence of any other viable factors. So the performance of a model most certainly depends upon the specific situation in which the research is being conducted. In fact, because academic major is significant in explaining CAS, R^2 is considered statistically large. Keep in mind also that R^2 provides a mechanism for comparing various models in terms of performance and will be illustrated in the following sections.

Another measure of fit is the standard error of the prediction, which measures the average distance between the actual response value (Y) and the predicted values ($\hat{Y}$), or the average error. The **standard error of the prediction** is defined as

$$RMSE = \sqrt{\frac{SSE}{n_T - g}}$$

In Output 7.2 One-Way ANOVA for Testing Differences in Computer Anxiety, the standard error is referred to as the root mean square error (Root MSE) as the term under the radical is the mean-square-error (MSE). In this example,

$$RMSE = \sqrt{\frac{9028.96048}{240-3}} = \sqrt{38.09688} = 6.172267$$

In other words, when we predict computer anxiety scores using academic major, on average, the predicted score will be 6.2 units from the actual score.

Note that as our predictor improves, our error in prediction will decrease, and consequently our standard error will decrease. In fact, if our predictor is perfect, our predicted values will be identical to our actual values, and the standard error will be zero. As our prediction worsens, the standard error increases.

Now, like R-squared, it is a judgment as to whether the standard error is small enough. If there are significant differences in our group means, then our standard error is considered significantly small. Furthermore, the standard error can be used to compare the performance of linear models as we will soon see when we introduce additional factors, or predictors.

The Normality Assumption and the PLOTS Option

As stated previously, certain assumptions must hold in order for the results of the ANOVA to be valid. The assumptions are that the observations are randomly selected from independent populations where the residuals are normally distributed and the variances of the outcome variable are equal across those populations.

The first assumption dealing with the random selection of observations has more to do with how the study was designed. The analyst can easily assess whether or not some type of randomization process has been incorporated into the study. In terms of independence, the analyst must be confident that the occurrence of numeric values for one population does not affect the probability of occurrence for numeric values in the other populations.

Consider now the normality assumption. In order to assess the normality of the errors, the analyst can produce diagnostic plots by adding the PLOTS option to the GLM procedure as follows:

```
proc glm data=one plots=diagnostics;
```

In the diagnostics panel, as displayed in Output 7.4 Fit Diagnostics for the One-Way Analysis of Variance, there are two plots of interest; the normal quantile plot and the histogram of residuals. If data originates from a population that is normal, the points for each observation would fall directly on the reference line. A visual inspection of the normal quantile plot illustrates that the points are relatively close to the reference line, so the assumption of normality is reasonable. Further inspection of the histogram illustrates that the errors are normally distributed. The analyst could also conduct a **Kolmogorov-Smirnov test**, as illustrated in Chapter 6, "Two-Sample *t*-Test," in order to obtain a p-value for testing the normality of the residuals.

Output 7.4 Fit Diagnostics for the One-Way Analysis of Variance

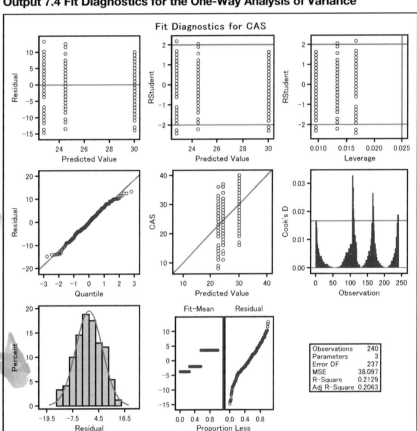

Levene's Test for Equal Variances and the MEANS Statement

The last assumption of ANOVA requires that the variances of the outcome variable must be equal for all populations. For *g* groups, the hypothesis of interest has the general form:

$$H_0: \sigma_1 = \sigma_2 = \ldots = \sigma_g \qquad \text{versus} \qquad H_1: \text{not all } \sigma_i\text{'s are equal}$$

and can be tested using **Levene's test for equal variances** (Levene, 1960). Before conducting the test, the analyst must determine the median of the outcome variable for each of the *g* groups and compute the difference between the outcome variable and the group median for each observation. The ANOVA procedure is then conducted using the absolute value of the differences.

Suppose for the computer anxiety example, using 0.05 level of significance, the analyst wants to test the hypothesis that the variances of the anxiety scores are equal for all three academic majors:

$$H_0: \sigma_1 = \sigma_2 = \sigma_3 \qquad \text{versus} \qquad H_1: \text{not all } \sigma_i\text{'s are equal}$$

The analyst would include the MEANS statement and the HOVTEST=LEVENE option within the GLM procedure as illustrated in Program 7.4 The MEANS Statement for Additional Tests of Computer Anxiety Scores.

Program 7.4 The MEANS Statement for Additional Tests of Computer Anxiety Scores

```
libname cas 'c:\sasba\data';
data one;
   set cas.cas;
run;

proc format;
   value major
   1=MGT 2=IS 3=ECON;
run;

proc glm data=one;
   format major major.;
   class major;
   model cas=major;
   means major/tukey hovtest=levene;
   title 'One Way ANOVA for testing differences in computer anxiety across academic majors';
run;
```

The partial output is displayed in Output 7.5 Levene's Homogeneity of Variance Test for Computer Anxiety Scores. Note that the p-value of 0.5454 is greater than 0.05; therefore, the null hypothesis is not rejected. In conclusion, there is no evidence that the equal variance assumption is violated. Consequently, the ANOVA results can be used to test mean differences in computer anxiety scores.

$$H_0 = \left[\mu = \mu\right] \quad H_i = \left[\mu \neq \mu\right]$$

Output 7.5 Levene's Homogeneity of Variance Test for Computer Anxiety Scores

Levene's Test for Homogeneity of CAS Variance ANOVA of Squared Deviations from Group Means					
Source	DF	Sum of Squares	Mean Square	F Value	Pr > F
MAJOR	2	2556.6	1278.3	0.61	0.5454
Error	237	498396	2102.9		

It should be noted that the HOVTEST option is available only when there is one grouping variable (i.e., MAJOR). When there is more than one grouping variable, as discussed later in this chapter, the analyst can use the plot of the residuals by the predicted values to inspect the variance across the groups. That plot can be found in the upper left corner of Output 7.4 Fit Diagnostics for the One-Way Analysis of Variance; here it seems that the spread of the residuals is constant across the three groups, supporting the equal variance assumption.

When the sample sizes for the groups are all equal, the effects of violating the equal variance assumption are minimal and the analyst can use the ANOVA results to making conclusions about the means. However, when the equal variance assumption is violated and the group sample sizes are unequal, the ANOVA results are not valid. In this case, the analyst can transform the data and use the transformed data to carry out the ANOVA procedures. Finally, if data transformation does not remedy the problem, the analyst can instead use nonparametric procedures (Conover, 2000).

Post Hoc Tests: The Tukey-Kramer Procedure and the MEANS Statement

When an ANOVA is conducted and the null hypothesis is rejected, the analyst has evidence only of mean differences; however, there is no information about *which* pairs of means are not equal. Consequently, **post hoc tests** must be conducted to determine where the differences exist.

When the analyst conducts a single hypothesis test, he or she sets a level of significance (α) that represents the maximum risk he or she is willing to take when rejecting the null hypothesis. This error rate is referred to as a **comparison-wise error rate**. As the number of comparisons increases, as is the case with comparing pairwise means, the chance of rejecting the null for at least one of the comparisons increases, even if no real differences exist. In fact, for C comparisons which make up an entire system of hypothesis tests, the probability of making a Type I error is $\alpha_e = 1 - C(1-\alpha)$ and is referred to as the **experiment-wise error rate**. Hence, for the computer anxiety example, if we were to compare all pairwise means as three single tests with an alpha of 0.05, that experiment-wise error rate would be $1 - 3(1-0.05) = 0.1426$, clearly more than the desired 0.05 level.

To ensure that the error rate for the entire system of tests remains at a constant level of significance (α), the analyst must use approaches that control the experiment-wise error rate. There are many options available in SAS for conducting multiple comparisons which control for this error rate. Here we will illustrate the **Tukey-Kramer procedure**, also referred to as Tukey's Honest Significant Difference (HSD), followed by a review of the SAS output. The set of hypotheses to be tested has the form:

$$H_0: \mu_i = \mu_{i'} \quad \text{for i=1,2,...g for i≠i'}$$

$$H_1: \mu_i \neq \mu_{i'}$$

When investigating g groups, there are g(g-1)/2 possible pairwise comparisons; therefore, for the computer anxiety example with three academic majors, there are 3(3-1)/2 = 3 pairwise comparisons. The three pairs of means to be compared can be tested using the following hypotheses:

$$H_0: \mu_1 = \mu_2 \quad \text{versus} \quad H_1: \mu_1 \neq \mu_2 \quad \text{(MGT vs IS)}$$

$$H_0: \mu_1 = \mu_3 \quad \text{versus} \quad H_1: \mu_1 \neq \mu_3 \quad \text{(MGT vs ECON)}$$

$$H_0: \mu_2 = \mu_3 \quad \text{versus} \quad H_1: \mu_2 \neq \mu_3 \quad \text{(IS vs ECON)}$$

In order to test differences among pairs of population means, the analyst must first compute the differences in the sample means. These are the observed, or actual, mean differences. For each hypothesis set, observed mean differences have the general form:

$$|\bar{X}_i - \bar{X}_{i'}| \quad \text{for i = 1, 2, ..., g and i ≠ i'}$$

For the computer anxiety example, having three sets of hypotheses requires computing three observed mean differences:

$$|\bar{X}_1 - \bar{X}_2| = |30.0095 - 22.7500| = 7.2595$$

$$|\bar{X}_1 - \bar{X}_3| = |30.0095 - 24.4800| = 5.5295$$

$$|\bar{X}_2 - \bar{X}_3| = |22.7500 - 24.4800| = 1.7300$$

where 1 = MGT, 2 = IS, and 3 = ECON. When comparing IS majors to ECON majors, the average computer anxiety scores differ by 1.73, whereas the differences in computer anxiety scores are relatively large when comparing MGT majors to IS majors (7.2595) and MGT majors to ECON majors (5.5295).

In order to make inferences to the population, the analyst must determine if the actual mean differences are sufficiently large; therefore the next step is to calculate a critical mean difference. This critical mean difference, referred to as the **critical range,** is calculated using:

$$CR = Q \sqrt{\left(\frac{MSE}{2}\right)\left(\frac{1}{n_i} + \frac{1}{n_{i'}}\right)}$$

where Q = upper tail critical value from a studentized distribution with g and n_T - g degrees of freedom for level of significance equal to α. MSE is the mean-square-error within the groups from the analysis of variance table, with n_i and $n_{i'}$ representing the sample sizes associated with the pair of means being compared from groups i and i', respectively. The Q-value is provided in the SAS output or can be found using any standard Q-table.

To test the hypotheses, the rejection rule is: If the observed mean difference is greater than the critical range, then reject H_0. In short,

$$\text{if } |\bar{X}_i - \bar{X}_{i'}| > CR, \text{ then reject } H_0 \text{ for i=1,2,...g and i ≠ i'}$$

When determining the critical range, note that there are two numbers that remain the same for each comparison. The first is the Mean-Square-Error from the ANOVA table in Output 7.2 One-Way ANOVA for Testing Differences in Computer Anxiety; that value is 38.09688. The second is the value of Q with 3 and 237 degrees of freedom. At 0.05 level of significance, the Q value is 3.34 as found in Output 7.6 Tukey-Kramer for Testing Pairwise Differences in Computer Anxiety.

Using the value of MSE and Q, the critical ranges are calculated for each hypothesis as follows:

For comparing computer anxiety scores for 1=MGT majors and 2=IS majors, with $n_1 = 105$ and $n_2 = 60$, the hypothesis to be tested is $H_0: \mu_1 = \mu_2$ versus $H_1: \mu_1 \neq \mu_2$. The critical range is

$$CR = 3.34 \sqrt{\left(\frac{38.09688}{2}\right)\left(\frac{1}{105} + \frac{1}{60}\right)} = 2.359$$

For comparing computer anxiety scores for 1=MGT majors and 3=ECON majors, with $n_1 = 105$ and $n_3 = 75$, the hypothesis to be tested is $H_0: \mu_1 = \mu_3$ versus $H_1: \mu_1 \neq \mu_3$. The critical range is

$$CR = 3.34 \sqrt{\left(\frac{38.09688}{2}\right)\left(\frac{1}{105} + \frac{1}{75}\right)} = 2.204$$

For comparing computer anxiety scores for 2=IS major and 3=ECON majors, with $n_2 = 60$ and $n_3 = 75$, the hypothesis to be tested is $H_0: \mu_2 = \mu_3$ versus $H_1: \mu_2 \neq \mu_3$. The critical range is

$$CR = 3.34 \sqrt{\left(\frac{38.09688}{2}\right)\left(\frac{1}{60} + \frac{1}{75}\right)} = 2.525$$

The critical range for comparing MGT and IS majors, for example, indicates that the observed mean difference in anxiety must be larger than 2.359 points in order to reject the null and control for 0.05 level of significance.

- For comparing computer anxiety scores for 1=MGT and 2=IS majors, $H_0: \mu_1 = \mu_2$ versus $H_1: \mu_1 \neq \mu_2$, the observed mean difference of 7.2595 > CR=2.359; therefore the null hypothesis is rejected.

- For comparing computer anxiety scores for 1=MGT and 3=ECON majors, $H_0: \mu_1 = \mu_3$ versus $H_1: \mu_1 \neq \mu_3$, the observed mean difference of 5.5295 > CR=2.204; therefore the null hypothesis is rejected.

- For comparing computer anxiety scores for 2=IS and 3=ECON majors, $H_0: \mu_2 = \mu_3$ versus $H_1: \mu_2 \neq \mu_3$, the observed mean difference of 1.7300 < CR=2.525; therefore the null hypothesis is not rejected.

In conclusion, the overall ANOVA test indicates evidence of mean differences. Using the Tukey-Kramer procedure, there is sufficient evidence to support specifically that the computer anxiety scores differ when comparing MGT and IS majors and MGT and ECON majors, respectively. There is no evidence to support a difference in computer anxiety between IS and ECON majors.

When calculating critical range, note that the formula allows for comparing groups with differing sample sizes, resulting in different critical ranges for different pairwise comparisons. Note also that when the group sample sizes are all equal, there is only one critical range for the entire set of comparisons.

To generate output for the Tukey-Kramer procedure, consider Program 7.4 The MEANS Statement for Additional Tests of Computer Anxiety Scores. Note specifically that the MEANS statement includes the TUKEY option. The partial output is displayed in Output 7.6 Tukey-Kramer for Testing Pairwise Differences in Computer Anxiety:

Output 7.6 Tukey-Kramer for Testing Pairwise Differences in Computer Anxiety

Note: This test controls the Type I experiment wise error rate.

Alpha	0.05
Error Degrees of Freedom	237
Error Mean Square	38.09688
Critical Value of Studentized Range	3.33547

Comparisons significant at the 0.05 level are indicated by ***.				
MAJOR Comparison	Difference Between Means	Simultaneous 95% Confidence Limits		
MGT - ECON	5.5295	3.3286	7.7304	***
MGT - IS	7.2595	4.9036	9.6154	***
ECON - MGT	-5.5295	-7.7304	-3.3286	***
ECON - IS	1.7300	-0.7914	4.2514	
IS - MGT	-7.2595	-9.6154	-4.9036	***
IS - ECON	-1.7300	-4.2514	0.7914	

In the output, note the **studentized Q** value 3.33547 for 0.05 level of significance, along with the Mean-Square-Error of 38.09688, used to calculate the critical range. If the sample sizes had been the same for all academic majors, the output would also have included the value of the critical range.

Note also that the output provides duplicate information for the three multiple comparisons twice (taking into account the reversal in the order of comparison). For example, the difference in average computer anxiety scores for MGT and ECON majors is +5.5295 indicating that MGT has the higher computer anxiety score; on the other hand, the difference in average computer anxiety scores for ECON and MGT majors is -5.5295 indicating that ECON has the lower computer anxiety score.

To detect differences in average computer anxiety scores, the three asterisks (***) indicate those differences that are significant at the stated level of significance (0.05). For example, MGT and ECON, along with MGT and IS, have significant mean differences as indicated by ***. For the IS and ECON comparison, there are no asterisks indicating that there are no mean differences when comparing those two groups of majors. These results are identical to the conclusions made using the calculations previously illustrated.

Other Post Hoc Procedures, the LSMEANS Statement, and the Diffogram

The analysis discussed in the previous section concentrates on the actual mean differences and the threshold difference, or critical range, needed in order to reject the null hypothesis. The analyst can request other types of output in order to address multiple comparisons by including options after a slash (/) in the LSMEANS statement within the GLM procedure.

For example, the PDIFF= option requests p-values for each of the paired comparisons. The ADJUST= option defines the adjustment method used for the multiple comparison procedure. In order to generate all p-values using Tukey's method of adjustment, you would include the following LSMEANS statement in place of the MEANS statement within PROC GLM, resulting in Output 7.7 LSMEANS Statement for Testing Pairwise Differences in Computer Anxiety.

```
lsmeans major/pdiff=all adjust=tukey;
```

Output 7.7 LSMEANS Statement for Testing Pairwise Differences in Computer Anxiety

MAJOR	CAS LSMEAN	LSMEAN Number
ECON	24.4800000	1
IS	22.7500000	2
MGT	30.0095238	3

	Least Squares Means for effect MAJOR Pr > |t| for H0: LSMean(i)=LSMean(j) Dependent Variable: CAS		
i/j	1	2	3
1		0.2399	<.0001
2	0.2399		<.0001
3	<.0001	<.0001	

[Handwritten annotations: "ECON IS MGT", "ECON IS MGT"]

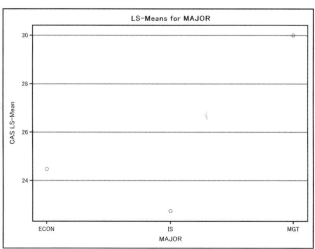

[Handwritten annotations: "MGT vs ECON", "MGT vs IS", "Significant", "IS vs ECON", "NOT Significant"]

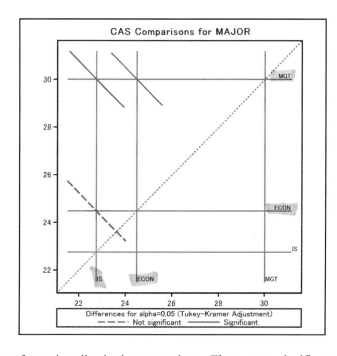

[Handwritten annotation: "Diffog"]

First note the table of p-values for testing all pairwise comparisons. There are no significant differences when comparing ECON and IS majors (having LSMEAN number equal to 1 and 2, respectively) as indicated by a p-value of 0.2399. However, there are significant differences when comparing groups having LSMEAN number 1 and 3 (ECON vs MGT) and groups having LSMEAN number 2 and 3 (IS vs MGT), both with p-values <.0001. These differences are displayed in the LSMEAN plot.

The **diffogram** provides a graphical approach to conducting pairwise comparisons. Each downward sloping segment represents each pairwise comparison, where the midpoint is the ordered pair for the sample means of the two groups being compared, and the length of the segment represents the confidence interval of the mean differences. For example, the segment in the lower-left quadrant has coordinates (22.75, 24.48) representing the group means for IS and ECON majors, respectively.

The dotted diagonal line increases at a 45-degree angle, indicating the points where the X and Y coordinates are equal, that is, where the pairs of sample means are equal. In short, the diagonal line represents the conditions where there are no mean differences. If the segment for a paired difference crosses the dotted line, this indicates that the confidence interval includes zero, and, as a result, the mean differences are statistically nonsignificant. On the other hand, when the segment does not cross the dotted line, you can conclude that there are significant mean differences.

In our example, the segment illustrating the comparison IS and ECON majors crosses the dotted line; therefore, we conclude that there are no significant differences when comparing those two groups. The two remaining segments do not cross the dotted line; therefore, we conclude that there are significant differences when comparing both ECON and MGT majors and IS and MGT majors, respectively.

If the ADJUST= option is not specified, the Tukey method will be used by default, whereas the ADJUST=T option requests that no adjustments be made. Other methods include the Bonferroni (ADJUST=BON), Nelson (ADJUST=NELSON), Scheffe (ADJUST=SCHEFFE), and Sidak (ADJUST=SIDAK) adjustments, to name a few.

If the analyst is interested in comparing experimental groups to a control group, then the **Dunnett's method of adjustment** is recommended and the LSMEANS statement would have the following general form:

```
lsmeans / pdiff=control('control level') adjust=dunnett;
```

To illustrate this type of comparison, let's consider our computer anxiety example and assume that the MGT major is defined as the control group. We would use the following LSMEANS statement within PROC GLM:

```
lsmeans major/pdiff=control('MGT') adjust=dunnett;
```

to get the following partial Output 7.8 Dunnett Adjustment for Testing Pairwise Differences in Computer Anxiety.

Output 7.8 Dunnett Adjustment for Testing Pairwise Differences in Computer Anxiety

MAJOR	CAS LSMEAN	H0:LSMean=Control Pr > |t|
ECON	24.4800000	<.0001
IS	22.7500000	<.0001
MGT	30.0095238	

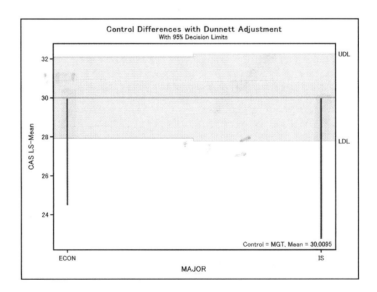

When reviewing the output for the Dunnett adjustment, note first that the control group is that group which has no reported p-value, namely the MGT major. Next, inspect the p-values using 0.05 level of significance. Note that the p-value for testing differences in mean computer anxiety score between both ECON and MGT majors and IS and MGT majors is < .0001. That value is less than 0.05. Therefore, we reject the null.

The LSMEANS statement also provides a visual analysis of the means. When reviewing the chart, note that the horizontal line corresponds to the mean computer anxiety score for the control group, 30.01 for MGT majors, along with the shaded confidence limits. Each bold vertical line represents the difference between the control group and each of the remaining groups, namely ECON and IS, respectively. Because the segments for both ECON and IS extend beyond the confidence limit, there is evidence of mean differences when comparing each of the groups to the control group, MGT majors.

In this section, we discussed many issues that must be considered in conducting a one-factor analysis of variance. When you aggregate all SAS procedures, statements, and options discussed, the entire code is in Program 7.5 Complete Analysis of Difference in Computer Anxiety Scores Across Academic Majors.

Program 7.5 Complete Analysis of Difference in Computer Anxiety Scores Across Academic Majors

```
libname cas 'c:\sasba\data';
data one;
   set cas.cas;
run;

proc format;
   value major
   1=MGT 2=IS 3=ECON;
run;

proc glm data=one plots=diagnostics;
   format major major.;
   class major;
   model cas=major;
   output out=pred predicted=pred_cas
          residual=res_cas;
   means major/tukey hovtest=levene;
   lsmeans major/pdiff=all adjust=tukey;
   lsmeans major/pdiff=control('MGT') adjust=dunnett;
   title 'One Way ANOVA for testing differences in computer anxiety across academic majors';
run;

proc print data=pred;
   var student_id major cas pred_cas res_cas;
   title 'Predicted Values and Residuals for Computer Anxiety Scores';
run;
```

The Randomized Block Design

As you may well know, when considering variations in any measure, there are potentially many factors, or predictors, involved. While a one-factor analysis of variance may indicate that differences exist as a function of the factor under investigation, other sources of variation are unaccounted for and are erroneously considered random variation. For example, you would expect, as we saw in the one-factor ANOVA example, that the computer anxiety scores differ when comparing academic majors; but there are other factors or variables that should be taken into account as well.

Consider a general measure of college preparedness in the area of mathematics, namely the ACT quantitative score. It makes sense that those who score relative high on the ACT test have had relatively more exposure to the mathematical sciences, thus exhibiting less anxiety towards computers, regardless of academic major. In fact, those declaring economics as a major may have lower anxiety strictly because they have had more math classes and not necessarily because they have chosen to major in the economics field. In this case, the relationship between computer anxiety scores and academic major may be interfered with or confounded by ACT quantitative scores; that is, ACT quantitative scores may be related to both computer anxiety and academic major so that the relationship between computer anxiety and academic major is not clear.

While you may not be particularly interested in the differences in computer anxiety as a function of math preparedness, you certainly want to take into account the possibility that the variation does exist. Factors that affect the dependent variable but are not of interest to the researcher are called nuisance factors.

When a researcher wants to take into account variations attributed to nuisance, or confounding, factors, the analyst may utilize a research design, referred to as a **Randomized Block Design**. The idea is to arrange the observations into homogenous groups, or blocks, where there is little or no variation in the nuisance factor but where the factor under investigation is allowed to vary. In this type of design, once the blocks are created, the observations are randomly assigned to the treatment groups under investigation.

The ANOVA Model for the Randomized Block Design

The Randomized Block Design is represented by the linear model

$$Y_{ijk} = \mu + \tau_i + \beta_j + \varepsilon_{ijk}$$

where Y_{ijk} is the value of the outcome variable for observation k in group i and block j , μ is the overall mean for the outcome variable, τ_i is the treatment effect for each observation in group i, β_j is the effect of belonging to block j, and ε_{ijk} is the error in prediction for observation k in group i and block j.

In essence, the variability in the outcome variable as a function of the blocking variable is estimated and, therefore, is partitioned from the random error. Consequently, this produces better estimates of the treatment effects. Note also that if the block effect is zero, then the model reduces to a one-factor analysis of variance.

The general form of the GLM procedure is:

PROC GLM DATA= *SAS-data-set* **PLOTS**=options;
CLASS *variables*;
MODEL *dependents=independents </options>*;
MEANS *effects </options>*;
LSMEANS *effects </options>*;
OUTPUT OUT=*SASdataset* <keyword=variable...>;
RUN;

Note that the general syntax for conducting a randomized block design is the same as that for the one-factor analysis of variance. However, it is repeated here to illustrate that the blocking variable should be listed in the CLASS statement as a variable and in the MODEL statement as an independent effect.

Example and Interpretation of the Randomized Block Design

In our example, we created blocks of students that are similar on mathematics college preparedness but vary on declared academic major. Specifically, we created groups based upon ACT quantitative scores consistent with rules that determine college placement into either algebra, pre-calculus, and calculus courses, respectively. Those students scoring less than 20 were assigned to block 0, corresponding to algebra placement; those scoring from 20 to 24 were assigned to block 1, corresponding to pre-calculus placement; those scoring more than 24 were assigned to block 2, corresponding to calculus placement.

In our study, we are interested in answering two questions: First, should we be blocking in the first place? In other words, are we correct in assuming that the computer anxiety score (CAS) differs across the three blocks as defined by ACT scores? Second, if our decision to block is correct and we are able to separate the effects of ACT and MAJOR on CAS, does CAS differ across academic majors? In other words, when we take into account ACT scores, or blocks, can we still attribute differences in computer anxiety scores to a student's declared academic major?

Before addressing those questions, the analyst must conduct exploratory analyses using Program 7.6 Exploration of Computer Anxiety by Academic Major and Block.

Program 7.6 Exploration of Computer Anxiety by Academic Major and Block

```
libname cas 'c:\sasba\data';
data one;
   set cas.cas;
run;

proc format;
   value major
   1=MGT 2=IS 3=ECON;
   value act
   0=Algebra Placement 1=Precalculus Placement 2=Calculus Placement;
run;

proc means data=one mean var std nway;
   format major major. block act.;
   class major block;
```

```
    var cas;
    title 'Descriptive Statistics for computer anxiety across academic majors and ACT
blocks';
run;

proc sgplot data=one;
    vline major /group=block stat=mean response=cas markers;
format major major. block act.;
run;
```

Notice that in the PROC MEANS statement, the statistics of interest are the mean, variance, and standard deviation. Notice also that the NWAY option is included which specifies that the statistics should be reported for the combinations of groups defined in the CLASS statement, namely MAJOR and BLOCK. The VAR statement indicates that the statistics will be generated for the variable CAS, Computer Anxiety Score.

These statements, in essence, request that SAS produce the mean, standard deviation, and variance for the variable CAS for the combinations of nine groups (each of the three academic majors crossed with each of the three blocks as defined by the quantitative ACT scores). Upon inspection of Output 7.9 Exploration of Computer Anxiety by Academic Major and Block, note, for example, that there are 28 students who have declared MGT as their major placed in algebra, averaging 32.39 on CAS with variance 45.51 and standard deviation 6.75.

Initially, the numbers in the table are quite cumbersome, and interpretation, while possible, takes some in-depth review. In this case, a visual plot of cell means is very helpful to facilitate inspection. In PROC SGPLOT, the VLINE statement basically requests the plot on the vertical axis of the response variable (RESPONSE=CAS) across all BLOCKS, as defined on the horizontal axis, for each of the GROUPS, as defined by the variable MAJOR. The MARKER option includes 'circles' on the plotted lines which correspond to the group means.

When inspecting the mean plots, it seems that the trend of computer anxiety scores is similar for each of the block levels. In particular, when we ignore the blocks (levels of math placement), we can make a general statement that computer anxiety is highest for MGT majors, followed by a significant decrease in IS majors and then a slight leveling off for ECON majors. Further inspection seems to indicate that computer anxiety is highest for those who place into algebra, followed by pre-calculus and then calculus, and that the relative differences are similar when viewing across each of the declared academic majors.

Output 7.9 Exploration of Computer Anxiety by Academic Major and Block

Analysis Variable : CAS					
MAJOR	BLOCK	N Obs	Mean	Variance	Std Dev
MGT	Algebra Placement	28	32.3928571	45.5066138	6.7458590
	Precalculus Placement	47	31.2978723	25.8658649	5.0858495
	Calculus Placement	30	25.7666667	23.6333333	4.8614127
IS	Algebra Placement	16	26.4375000	19.8625000	4.4567365
	Precalculus Placement	22	24.2727273	32.3982684	5.6919477
	Calculus Placement	22	18.5454545	44.7359307	6.6884924
ECON	Algebra Placement	22	27.1818182	39.1082251	6.2536569
	Precalculus Placement	38	24.1842105	25.4516358	5.0449614
	Calculus Placement	15	21.2666667	35.0666667	5.9217115

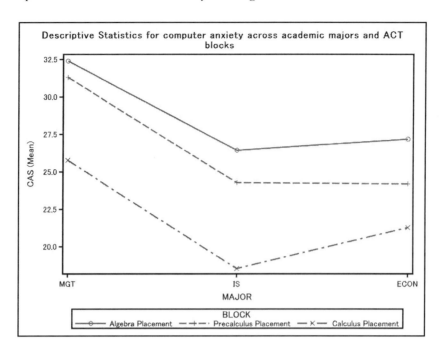

The analyst will use the randomized block design to answer two questions: First, is blocking effective in explaining the variation in computer anxiety? In other words, should we use blocking (controlling for differences in math placement) when investigating differences in computer anxiety (CAS)?

And second, if we are correct in our decision to block and control for differences in math placement, is there evidence of differences in computer anxiety when comparing academic major?

To answer these two questions, consider the general form of the ANOVA table as seen in Table 7.4 The ANOVA Table for the Randomized Block Design.

Table 7.4 The ANOVA Table for the Randomized Block Design

Source of Variation	Sums of Squares	Degrees of Freedom	Mean Square (Variance)	F-Test Statistic
Among Groups	SSA	$g-1$	MSA	MSA/MSE
Blocks	SSB	$b-1$	MSB	MSB/MSE
Error	SSE	$n_T - g - b + 1$	MSE	
Total	SST	$n_T - 1$		

Specifically, to test for significant differences in block means, the appropriate hypothesis set is

$$H_0: \beta_1 = \beta_2 = \ldots = \beta_b$$

$$H_1: \text{not all } \beta_j\text{'s are equal} \qquad \text{for } j = 1 \text{ to } b \text{ blocks}$$

and the F-test statistic of interest is F = MSB/MSE with $(b-1)$ and $(n_T-g-b+1)$ degrees of freedom. To test for significant differences among treatment means, the appropriate hypothesis set is

$$H_0: \mu_1 = \mu_2 = \ldots = \mu_i$$

$$H_1: \text{not all } \mu_i\text{'s are equal} \qquad \text{for } i = 1 \text{ to } g \text{ groups}$$

And the F-test statistic of interest is F = MSA/MSE with $(g-1)$ and $(n_T-g-b+1)$ degrees of freedom.

Program 7.7 Randomized Block Design for Testing Differences in Computer Anxiety will produce the output necessary in answering the two questions associated with the two sets of hypotheses.

Program 7.7 Randomized Block Design for Testing Differences in Computer Anxiety

```
libname cas 'c:\sasba\data';
data one;
   set cas.cas;
run;

proc format;
   value major
   1=MGT 2=IS 3=ECON;
   value act
   0=Algebra Placement 1=Precalculus Placement 2=Calculus Placement;
run;

proc glm data=one plots=diagnostics;
   format major major. block act.;
   class major block;
   model cas=major block;
    title 'Testing differences in computer anxiety scores across academic majors using a
   block design';
run;
```

Note that the only difference between this code and the code for the one-factor analysis of variance is the addition of the blocking variable, BLOCK, in both the CLASS and MODEL statements. The results are displayed in Output 7.10 Randomized Block Design for Testing Differences in Computer Anxiety.

Output 7.10 Randomized Block Design for Testing Differences in Computer Anxiety

Class Level Information		
Class	Levels	Values
MAJOR	3	ECON IS MGT
BLOCK	3	Algebra Placement Calculus Placement Precalculus Placement

Number of Observations Read	240
Number of Observations Used	240

Dependent Variable: CAS

Source	DF	Sum of Squares	Mean Square	F Value	Pr > F
Model	4	4123.29691	1030.82423	32.97	<.0001
Error	235	7348.43642	31.26994		
Corrected Total	239	11471.73333			

R-Square	Coeff Var	Root MSE	CAS Mean
0.359431	21.12829	5.591953	26.46667

Source	DF	Type I SS	Mean Square	F Value	Pr > F
MAJOR	2	2442.772857	1221.386429	39.06	<.0001
BLOCK	2	1680.524057	840.262029	26.87	<.0001

Source	DF	Type III SS	Mean Square	F Value	Pr > F
MAJOR	2	2432.055734	1216.027867	38.89	<.0001
BLOCK	2	1680.524057	840.262029	26.87	<.0001

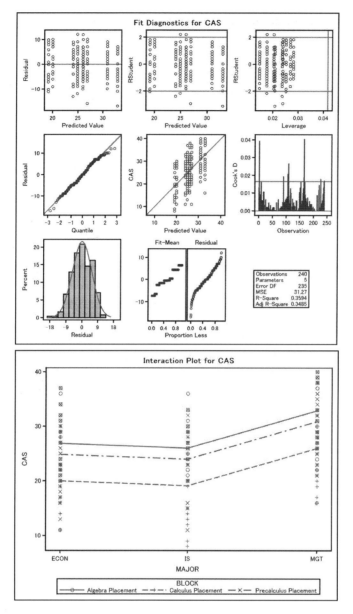

The first page of the output lists the two classes (MAJOR for the grouping variable and BLOCK for the blocking variable) and the number and description of the levels in each class, in addition to the number of observations read for analysis purposes.

The second page of the output provides the analysis of variance results and various fit statistics. The first effect to be tested is that of the blocking variable; this is to ensure that we are correct in using a blocking variable in our analysis design. Remember, blocking is to explain or eliminate effects on computer anxiety that are not attributed to our factor of interest, namely declared major. If there is no evidence of differences in the blocks (math placement), then our initial assumption that blocking matters is erroneous and we should eliminate that blocking variable from our design.

The hypothesis of interest is as follows:

$$H_0: \beta_1 = \beta_2 = \beta_3$$

$$H_1: \text{not all } \beta_j\text{'s are } =$$

From the output, note that the F-test statistic for the effects of blocking is 26.87 with a p-value < 0.0001; therefore, we reject the null and conclude that, based upon our sample data, there is evidence that the population computer anxiety scores (CAS) differ by math placement. In other words, we are correct in blocking by math placement.

Consequently, we are able to partition out the effects of math placement and subsequently test for differences in CAS a function of academic major as follows:

$$H_0: \mu_1 = \mu_2 = \mu_3$$

$$H_1: \text{not all } \mu_i\text{'s are} =$$

In Output 7.10 Randomized Block Design for Testing Differences in Computer Anxiety, note that the test statistic for testing differences by academic major is 38.89 with a p-value < 0.0001; therefore, we reject the null and conclude that there are significant differences in computer anxiety across the three academic majors. (Note: when an analysis is unbalanced--that is, the sample sizes are different for each of the cells under investigation--the appropriate test statistic is based upon Type III Sum-of-Squares. This will be discussed at the end of this section on Randomized Block Design.)

Finally, recall that in the one-factor ANOVA, the analyst determined that computer anxiety is related to academic major with R^2 equal to 0.212938. For the block design, there was an improvement in fit as measured by an R^2 equal to 0.359431. In fact, the standard error of the prediction for the block design is 5.6, which means when we predict computer anxiety scores using academic major and blocking on mathematics placement, on average, the predicted score will be 5.6 units from the actual score, compared to 6.2 for the one-factor ANOVA.

Post Hoc Tests Using the LSMEANS Statement

As seen in the one-factor analysis of variance, once you find evidence of differences in academic major in the presence of blocking, you must follow up with statistical tests that investigate differences in pair-wise means controlling for experiment-wise error level.

In order to conduct the Tukey-Kramer procedure, the analyst can include the LSMEANS statement within the GLM procedure as follows:

```
lsmeans major/pdiff=all adjust=tukey;
```

An excerpt of the results is displayed in Output 7.11 LSMEANS Statement for Testing Pairwise Differences in Computer Anxiety When Blocking.

Output 7.11 LSMEANS Statement for Testing Pairwise Differences in Computer Anxiety When Blocking

MAJOR	CAS LSMEAN	LSMEAN Number
ECON	23.9090415	1
IS	23.0465985	2
MGT	29.9107311	3

Least Squares Means for effect MAJOR Pr > |t| for H0: LSMean(i)=LSMean(j)			
Dependent Variable: CAS			
i/j	1	2	3
1		0.6526	<.0001
2	0.6526		<.0001
3	<.0001	<.0001	

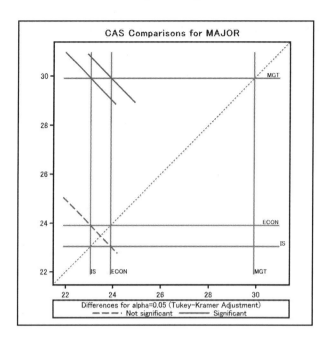

Notice that the comparisons involve the unweighted means which take into account the unbalanced nature of the study. Furthermore, using 0.05 level of significance, when we control for math placement, there is evidence that computer anxiety scores differ when comparing both IS and MGT and ECON and MGT, with p-values less than 0.0001. However, when comparing ECON and IS, with p-value = 0.6526, there is no evidence that ECON and IS majors differ on computer anxiety scores. These results are also supported when interpreting the diffogram.

Assessing the Assumptions of a Randomized Block Design Using the PLOTS Option

There are assumptions when conducting a Randomized Block Design; namely, (1) the random errors ε_{ijk} are independent and normally distributed, (2) the effects of each level of the blocks are normally distributed with equal variances, (3) the differences across the levels of factor A are the same for all block levels; in other words, there are no interactions effects of Factor A and blocks.

As stated previously when addressing the validity of the analyses, the first assumption has more to do with how the study was designed in terms of ensuring a randomization process. Similarly, in terms of independence, the analyst must be confident that the occurrence of numeric values for one population does not affect the probability of occurrence for numeric values in the other populations.

In assessing the normality of the errors, note that the SAS code for the randomized block design includes the PLOTS= option within PROC GLM for producing diagnostic plots:

```
proc glm data=one plots=diagnostics;
```

A visual inspection of the normal quantile plot in Output 7.10 Randomized Block Design for Testing Differences in Computer Anxiety illustrates that the points are relatively close to the reference line, so the assumption of normality is reasonable. Further inspection of the histogram illustrates that the errors are normally distributed. To test statistically, we could conduct a Kolmogorov-Smirnov test on the residuals in order to obtain a p-value for testing the normality. In addition, the residual by predicted value plot indicates that the variances are similar across the groups under investigation.

Unbalanced Designs, the LSMEANS Statement, and Type III Sums of Squares

When conducting a one-factor analysis of variance, you may have noticed that the statistical tests using either Type I or Type III sums of squares are identical. However, once an additional source of variation is introduced into the model, as is the case with the addition of a blocking variable, the results of the statistical tests differ when comparing Type I versus Type III sums of squares. This occurs when the analysis involves an **unbalanced design**, that is, a design where the sample sizes differ across all of the treatment-block combinations.

Consider a randomized block design as applied to the totally fabricated data illustrated in Table 7.5 Cell Means and Sample Sizes for Computer Anxiety Scores.

Table 7.5 Cell Means and Sample Sizes for Computer Anxiety Scores

	Block				
Major	Algebra	Pre-Calculus	Calculus	Weighted Mean	Unweighted Mean
MGT	32 (8)	30 (1)	25 (1)	31.1	29
IS	27 (1)	24 (1)	18 (8)	19.5	23
ECON	28 (1)	25 (8)	22 (1)	25.0	25

A review of the table illustrates that there are nine factor-block combinations (Major by Math Placement) where, in the first cell, there are eight students majoring in MGT and placed into algebra, averaging 32 points on the computer anxiety scale (CAS), and in the ninth cell, there is one student majoring in ECON and placed into calculus, averaging 22 points on the computer anxiety scale (CAS).

Now, consider the two types of mean anxiety scores for the three academic majors, namely, the weighted and unweighted means. The **weighted mean** anxiety score for MGT majors is obtained by taking each of the ten scores, adding them together, and then dividing by the ten students in that group. The weighted means are also calculated for IS and ECON as follows:

$$\bar{W}_{MGT} = [32(8) + 30(1) + 25(1)]/10 = 31.1$$

$$\bar{W}_{IS} = [27(1) + 24(1) + 18(8)]/10 = 19.5$$

$$\bar{W}_{ECON} = [28(1) + 25(8) + 22(1)]/10 = 25.0$$

The **unweighted mean** anxiety score is simply the mean of the cell means across the three blocks:

$$\bar{U}_{MGT} = (32 + 30 + 25)/3 = 29$$

$$\bar{U}_{IS} = (27 + 24 + 18)/3 = 23$$

$$\bar{U}_{ECON} = (28 + 25 + 22)/3 = 25$$

Notice that the weighted means ignore the effects of math placement (blocks). In fact, notice that for the weighted mean anxiety score of MGT majors, the mean is derived from eight (of 10 total) students placed into algebra who exhibit a relatively high anxiety score; as a result, the mean may be artificially high because it's made up of students who place lowest out of the three possible math placements. Notice also that the weighted mean anxiety score for IS majors is derived from eight (of 10 total) students placed into calculus who exhibit a relatively low anxiety score; as a result, the mean may be artificially low because it's made up of students who place highest out of the three possible math placements.

The unweighted mean anxiety scores, on the other hand, control for the effects of the block by eliminating the effects of the differing sample sizes by giving each cell mean an equal weighting. Consider the difference in anxiety when comparing MGT and IS majors using weighted means. The difference is 11.6 (31.1 minus 19.5) and ignores the fact that most MGT majors have relatively low math placement and most IS majors have relatively high math placement. However, when considering the difference in their unweighted means, IS majors average 6 points lower than MGT majors--almost half the difference when using weighted means.

In conclusion, for unbalanced designs, you must test for mean differences using the unweighted (marginal) means. In order to obtain the appropriate output, you must use the statistical tests associated with Type III sums of squares and use the LSMEANS statement in PROC GLM to conduct pairwise tests of the unweighted means. If the design is balanced, then Type I and Type III sums of squares will be identical.

Two-Factor Analysis of Variance

In the case of one-factor analysis of variance, we investigated the relationship between two variables, namely one numeric continuous outcome variable and one categorical predictor variable having two or more levels. In our coverage of a randomized block design, we extended our investigation of the effects of a single factor by controlling the effects of other nuisance factors using a blocking variable.

In this section, we will consider the effects of two or more unknown sources of variation on our outcome variable of interest. In fact, we would expect that the numeric continuous outcome of interest can be explained by two or more categorical predictor variables. In this case, the analyst would conduct an *n*-way analysis of variance to investigate the simultaneous effects of the *n*-factors.

The Two-Factor ANOVA Model

Here, we will consider the specific case of two predictors, as investigated by a **Two-Way Analysis of Variance (ANOVA) with interaction.** The Two-Way ANOVA Model is represented by

$$Y_{ijk} = \mu + \alpha_i + \beta_j + (\alpha\beta)_{ij} + \varepsilon_{ijk}$$

where Y_{ijk} is the value of the outcome variable for observation k in group i of factor A and group j of factor B, μ is the overall mean for the outcome variable, α_i is the effect of belonging to group i of Factor A, β_j is the effect of belonging to group j of Factor B, $\alpha\beta_{ij}$ is the interaction effect of factors A and B, and ε_{ijk} is the error in prediction.

We will illustrate how to conduct a two-way analysis of variance to answer three questions. The first two questions have to do with testing **main effects**, that is, the unique effect of each Factor A and Factor B on the outcome variable; the third question addresses unique **interaction** effects.

First, is Factor A significant in explaining the differences, or variation, in the outcome variable, in the presence of factor B and interaction effects? Second, is Factor B significant in explaining the variation in the outcome variable, in the presence of Factor A and interaction effects? Third, is the interaction of Factors A and B significant in explaining the variation of the outcome variable, in the presence of Factors A and B?

To answer these three questions, consider Table 7.6 General Form of the Two-Factor ANOVA Table.

Table 7.6 General Form of the Two-Factor ANOVA Table

Source of Variation	Sums of Squares	Degrees of Freedom	Mean Square (Variance)	F-Test Statistic
Factor A	SSA	a - 1	MSA	MSA/MSE
Factor B	SSB	b - 1	MSB	MSB/MSE
Interaction	SSAB	(a-1)(b-1)	MSAB	MSAB/MSE
Error	SSE	n_T - ab	MSE	
Total	SST	n_T - 1		

where a = the number of levels of Factor A, b = the number of levels of Factor B, and n_T = the total number of observations in the study.

To test for significant differences in means as a function of Factor A, the appropriate hypothesis set is

$$H_0: \mu_{1.} = \mu_{2.} = \ldots = \mu_{i.}$$

$$H_1: \text{not all } \mu_{i.}\text{'s are equal} \qquad \text{for } i = 1 \text{ to } a$$

and the F-test statistic of interest is F_A = MSA/MSE with (a-1) and (n_T – ab) degrees of freedom. To test for significant differences in means as a function of Factor B, the appropriate hypothesis set is

$$H_0: \mu_{.1} = \mu_{.2} = \ldots = \mu_{.j}$$

$$H_1: \text{not all } \mu_{.j}\text{'s are equal} \qquad \text{for } j = 1 \text{ to } b$$

and the F-test statistic of interest is F_B = MSB/MSE with (b-1) and (n_T - ab) degrees of freedom. Finally to test for significant differences in means as a function of the interaction of both Factor A and Factor B, the appropriate hypothesis set is

$$H_0: \mu_{11} = \mu_{12} = \mu_{21} = \mu_{22} \ldots = \mu_{ij}$$

$$H_1: \text{not all } \mu_{ij}\text{'s are equal} \qquad \text{for } i = 1 \text{ to } a; \ j = 1 \text{ to } b$$

and the F-test statistic of interest is F_{AB} = MSAB/MSE with (a-1)(b-1) and (n_T - ab) degrees of freedom.

The general form of the GLM procedure is:

PROC GLM DATA= *SAS-data-set* **PLOTS**=options;
CLASS *variables*;
MODEL *dependents=independents* </options>;
MEANS *effects* </options>;
LSMEANS *effects* </options>;
OUTPUT OUT=*SASdataset* <keyword=variable...>;
RUN;

Note again that the general syntax for conducting a two-factor analysis of variance is the same as that for both the one-factor analysis of variance and the randomized block design. However, it is important to note that the two factor variables should be listed in the CLASS statement corresponding to Factor A and Factor B. Three terms should be listed in the MODEL statement as independent effects, namely Factor A, Factor B, and the interaction term.

Example and Interpretation of the Two-Factor ANOVA

Let's revisit the one-factor analysis of variance example where we found evidence that computer anxiety scores (CAS) differed across declared academic major. While this model may be deemed adequate, in reality, the analyst is interested in improving the model by incorporating other factors that may affect anxiety--for example, gender.

Consider now the effects of two factors on computer anxiety; namely, declared academic major and gender. As always, the analyst explores the data in order to get a preliminary view, as illustrated in Program 7.8 Exploration of Computer Anxiety by Academic Major and Gender.

Program 7.8 Exploration of Computer Anxiety by Academic Major and Gender

```
libname cas 'c:\sasba\data';
data one;
   set cas.cas;
run;

proc format;
   value major
   1=MGT 2=IS 3=ECON;
   value gender
   0=Females 1=Males;
run;

proc means data=one mean var std nway;
   format major major. gender gender.;
   class major gender;
   var cas;
   title 'Descriptive statistics for computer anxiety across academic majors and gender';
run;
```

```
proc sgplot data=one;
   vline major /group=gender stat=mean response=cas markers;
    format major major. gender gender.;
run;
```

The results are displayed in Output 7.12 Descriptive Statistics for Computer Anxiety by Academic Major and Gender.

Output 7.12 Descriptive Statistics for Computer Anxiety by Academic Major and Gender

Analysis Variable : CAS					
MAJOR	GENDER	N Obs	Mean	Variance	Std Dev
MGT	Females	54	32.4074074	30.5478686	5.5270126
	Males	51	27.4705882	32.4541176	5.6968516
IS	Females	40	22.9250000	48.8916667	6.9922576
	Males	20	22.4000000	34.9894737	5.9151901
ECON	Females	43	23.8372093	32.9966777	5.7442735
	Males	32	25.3437500	36.9425403	6.0780375

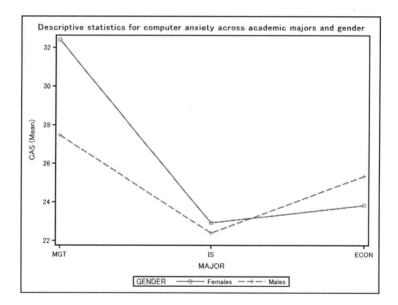

Notice that there are 54 females majoring in MGT, having a mean anxiety score of 32.41, a variance of 30.55, and a standard deviation of 5.53; ending with 32 males majoring in ECON, having a mean anxiety score of 25.34, a variance of 36.94, and a standard deviation of 6.08. The mean plot provides an additional mechanism for description. For example, the biggest difference in anxiety when comparing males and females exists for MGT majors with females exhibiting a higher level of anxiety than males. The smallest difference between males and females is among IS majors (although possibly an insignificant difference). Note also that for ECON majors, males now have a slightly higher level of anxiety than females, but this difference may be insignificant as well.

Finally, when differences across one factor (say Gender here) are not the same for all levels of the second factor, (Major), we may suspect that an interaction between the two factors exists--which seems to be the case here, but we must test statistically. In short, remember that a visual inspection alone is not sufficient for determining statistically significant differences.

Before conducting our statistical tests, let's look more deeply at two hypothetical examples to get a better idea of what interaction means: (1) a two-way analysis of variance without interaction and (2) a two-way analysis of variance with interaction. Consider the same two factors, Gender and Academic Major, and the outcome variable computer anxiety as illustrated in Figure 7.2 Mean Computer Anxiety Scores by Academic Major and Gender

Figure 7.2 Mean Computer Anxiety Scores by Academic Major and Gender

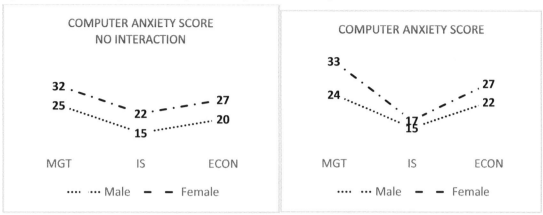

Notice in the first figure, that females have an average anxiety score 7 more than males for each of the three majors: MGT, IS, and ECON. Because these differences are uniform across all three majors, we could make a single statement that, on average, females score 7 more than males, regardless of major. In fact, we can ignore major altogether. When you can make a conclusion about differences using one factor (Gender) while ignoring the second factor (Major), you can say that interaction between the two factors does not exist.

Notice in the second figure, when interpreting differences, you must take into account BOTH factors. For example, when looking at MGT majors, males and females' average anxiety scores differ by 9, while the difference in gender is 2 when looking at IS majors and 5 for ECON majors. In other words, the difference between the genders depends upon major; that is, the interpretation must take into account both factors, gender and major. Consequently, there is interaction between gender and major. When interaction exists, we cannot make conclusions about mean differences when looking at a single factor alone. By definition, when interaction effects exist, we cannot look at the single effects of one factor or another. However, if statistical tests indicate that interaction effects do not exist, then we are free to move forward and test for main effects.

In general, parallel lines indicate that no interaction exists among the two factors, whereas a significant deviation from parallel lines indicates that interaction does exist. Note that these effects can be tested statistically in order to make inferences to the population.

In order to determine what factors affect computer anxiety, at .05 level of significance, consider the two-way analysis of variance in Program 7.9 Two-Factor ANOVA for Testing Differences in Computer Anxiety.

Program 7.9 Two-Factor ANOVA for Testing Differences in Computer Anxiety
```
libname cas 'c:\sasba\data';
data one;
   set cas.cas;
run;

proc format;
   value major
   1=MGT 2=IS 3=ECON;
   value gender
   0=Females 1=Males;
run;

proc glm data=one plots=diagnostics;
   format major major. gender gender.;
   class major gender;
   model cas=major gender major*gender;
   lsmeans major*gender / diff slice=major  slice=gender;
   title 'Testing differences in computer anxiety across academic major and gender with
interaction';
run;
```

The form of PROC GLM is identical to that when conducting a one-factor analysis of variance and a randomized block design in terms of the CLASS and MODEL statements. Note, however, in the MODEL statement, an interaction term is included (MAJOR*GENDER). The LSMEANS statement provides output for testing each of the mean pairs, and the DIFF and SLICE options for each factor provide a visual output of the mean differences.

The results are displayed in Output 7.13a Two-Factor ANOVA for Testing Differences in Computer Anxiety through Output 7.13d Analysis of Simple Effects in the Presence of Interaction.

Output 7.13a Two-Factor ANOVA for Testing Differences in Computer Anxiety

Class Level Information		
Class	Levels	Values
MAJOR	3	ECON IS MGT
GENDER	2	Females Males

Number of Observations Read	240
Number of Observations Used	240

The GLM Procedure

Dependent Variable: CAS

Source	DF	Sum of Squares	Mean Square	F Value	Pr > F
Model	5	3127.33620	625.46724	17.54	<.0001
Error	234	8344.39713	35.65982		
Corrected Total	239	11471.73333			

R-Square	Coeff Var	Root MSE	CAS Mean
0.272612	22.56266	5.971584	26.46667

Source	DF	Type I SS	Mean Square	F Value	Pr > F
MAJOR	2	2442.772857	1221.386429	34.25	<.0001
GENDER	1	204.587840	204.587840	5.74	0.0174
MAJOR*GENDER	2	479.975502	239.987751	6.73	0.0014

Source	DF	Type III SS	Mean Square	F Value	Pr > F
MAJOR	2	2292.681008	1146.340504	32.15	<.0001
GENDER	1	93.324732	93.324732	2.62	0.1071
MAJOR*GENDER	2	479.975502	239.987751	6.73	0.0014

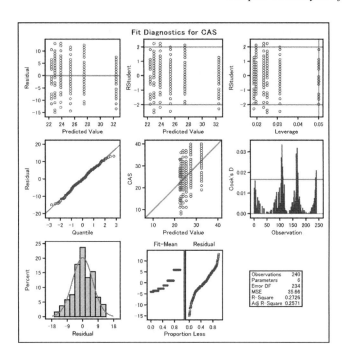

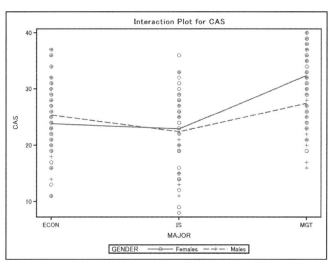

The first page of the output provides the two classes, Major and Gender, with the numbers of levels for each and their corresponding labels. The first page also provides the number of observations read, namely 240. The second page provides the analysis of variance tables with the various fit statistics; the third and fourth pages provide the diagnostics panel and the interaction plot, respectively.

When reviewing the second page of the output for inference purposes, you should always survey the output for significant interactions effects first. Remember, if there are significant interaction effects, you should not test for the main effects because the unique effects of one factor are not constant across levels of the second factor. The test statistic for interaction (using Type III sums of squares) is 6.73, with a p-value of 0.0014. The p-value is less than α of 0.05; therefore, the null hypothesis is rejected. In conclusion, there is evidence, based upon our data, that mean computer anxiety scores are affected by the interaction of both academic major (Factor A) and gender (Factor B). This is further supported by the interaction plot of the mean computer anxiety scores (CAS).

Note that for the two-factor ANOVA, there was an improvement in fit as measured by an R^2 equal to 0.272612, compared to 0.212938 for the one-factor ANOVA. Furthermore, the standard error of the prediction for the two-factor ANOVA is 5.97, compared to 6.17 for the one-factor ANOVA.

Because it is inappropriate to test for main effects, the analyst must, instead, interpret the interaction effects of both academic major and gender as displayed in Output 7.13b Least Squares Means for Major by Gender Interaction Effects.

Output 7.13b Least Squares Means for Major by Gender Interaction Effects

MAJOR	GENDER	CAS LSMEAN	LSMEAN Number
ECON	Females	23.8372093	1
ECON	Males	25.3437500	2
IS	Females	22.9250000	3
IS	Males	22.4000000	4
MGT	Females	32.4074074	5
MGT	Males	27.4705882	6

Least Squares Means for effect MAJOR*GENDER Pr > |t| for H0: LSMean(i)=LSMean(j) Dependent Variable: CAS						
i/j	1	2	3	4	5	6
1		0.2810	0.4875	0.3748	<.0001	0.0036
2	0.2810		0.0890	0.0851	<.0001	0.1156
3	0.4875	0.0890		0.7485	<.0001	0.0004
4	0.3748	0.0851	0.7485		<.0001	0.0015
5	<.0001	<.0001	<.0001	<.0001		<.0001
6	0.0036	0.1156	0.0004	0.0015	<.0001	

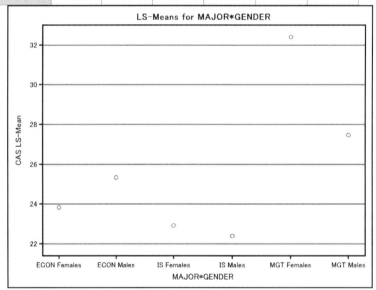

Output 7.13b Least Squares Means for Major by Gender Interaction Effects provides a list of ls-means for each of the six combinations of effects (two genders crossed with three majors). For example, it is evident that male IS majors with ls-mean number of 4, exhibit the lowest average anxiety (22.40), whereas female MGT majors with ls-means number of 5, exhibit the highest average anxiety (32.41). A visual inspection of the plot of ls-means for MAJOR*GENDER illustrates the magnitude of the differences between all six mean computer anxiety scores (CAS).

Remember the total number of paired comparisons is g(g-1)/2 where g = number of groups being compared. In this example, there are 6(6-1)/2 = 15 paired comparisons. To test for significant differences in the means across the combinations of major and gender, note the table of p-values for comparing all possible pairs of means, for the ls-means numbered 1 through 6.

For example, the p-value in column I and row 2 (0.2810) is used to test female ECON majors to male ECON majors. Because the p-value is greater than 0.05 level of significance, we can conclude that there is no evidence that mean anxiety scores differ when comparing the two groups. In all, we can see that there is no evidence of differences for seven of the fifteen comparisons; namely 1 versus 2, 3, and 4 (female ECON majors do not differ from male ECON, female IS, and male IS majors) with means 23.84, 25.34, 22.93, and 22.40, respectively; 2 versus 3, 4, and 6 (male ECON majors do not differ from IS females, IS males, and MGT males), with means 25.34, 22.93, 22.40, and 27.47, respectively; and 3 versus 4 (female IS majors do not differ from male IS majors) with means 22.93 and 22.40, respectively.

Again the analyst can rely on the interaction plot of LSMEANS for MAJOR*GENDER which illustrates the insignificant differences in those seven pairs of mean computer anxiety scores (CAS). These nonsignificant differences are also evident in the Output 7.13c Diffogram of MAJOR by GENDER Means. Note that seven of the confidence intervals (or segments) cross the 45-degree dotted diagonal line, where the X and Y coordinates are equal, indicating that the pairs of sample means are equal.

With respect to the eight significant interactions, notice that the largest difference is between 4 and 5 (IS males and MGT females, with means 22.40 and 32.41, respectively) and is also depicted in both the interaction plot and the diffogram. Specifically note that, in the diffogram, the segment representing IS males and MGT females is at the top rightmost corner indicating that the midpoint of the segment is farthest from the 45-degree line. In short, that segment represents the largest mean difference. In fact, the upper-most five segments show that MGT females have computer anxiety scores significantly different from the other five groups, respectively; this is further illustrated in the interaction plot.

Output 7.13c Diffogram of MAJOR by GENDER Means

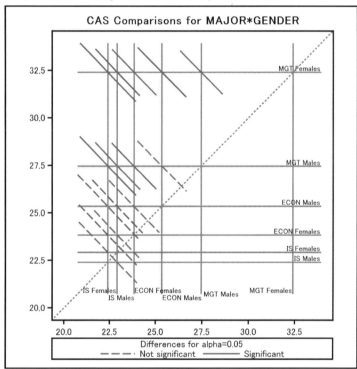

Analyzing Simple Effects When Interaction Exists Using the LSMEANS Statement with the SLICE Option

When the analyst wants to provide additional information for interpreting interaction effects, the LSMEANS statement with the SLICE option can be used. This option provides tests of simple effects. In other words, when interaction exists, you can test the effect of Factor A within each level of Factor B. Note that in Program 7.9 Two-Factor ANOVA for Testing Differences in Computer Anxiety, the following LSMEANS statement is included within PROC GLM:

```
lsmeans major*gender / diff slice=major diff slice=gender;
```

The first table, MAJOR*GENDER sliced by MAJOR, displayed in Output 7.13d Analysis of Simple Effects in the Presence of Interaction, provides a test for differences in GENDER when looking across MAJORS. Because the p-value for MGT is less than .05 level of significance, we can conclude that differences in mean computer anxiety scores exist between males and females when looking at MGT majors. We can also see this in the interaction plot, where the points (or means) for each gender are close for IS and ECON majors but deviate significantly for MGT majors. A similar interpretation can be made when slicing by gender.

put 7.13d Analysis of Simple Effects in the Presence of Interaction

MAJOR*GENDER Effect Sliced by MAJOR for CAS					
MAJOR	DF	Sum of Squares	Mean Square	F Value	Pr > F
ECON	1	41.640785	41.640785	1.17	0.2810
IS	1	3.675000	3.675000	0.10	0.7485
MGT	1	639.247557	639.247557	17.93	<.0001

MAJOR*GENDER Effect Sliced by GENDER for CAS					
GENDER	DF	Sum of Squares	Mean Square	F Value	Pr > F
Females	2	2672.969834	1336.484917	37.48	<.0001
Males	2	380.129737	190.064868	5.33	0.0055

Assessing the Assumptions of a Two-Factor Analysis of Variance

So far, much attention has been paid to interpreting the results of two-factor analysis of variance. Remember, the analyst must always check the assumptions to ensure the results of the analysis are valid; otherwise, there is the risk of making a mistake when attempting to make conclusions about the population of interest. The assumptions of two-way analysis of variance are identical to those of the one-factor analysis. These assumptions are as follows:

- The observations must be randomly selected from independent populations.
- The residuals are normally distributed for each of the populations under investigation.
- The variances of the residuals are equal across all populations under investigation.

As stated previously, the first assumption has more to do with how the study was designed in terms of ensuring a randomization process. In terms of independence, the analyst must be confident that the occurrence of numeric values for one population does not affect the probability of occurrence for numeric values in the other populations.

In assessing the normality of the errors, note that Program 7.9 Two-Factor ANOVA for Testing Differences in Computer Anxiety included the PLOTS= option within PROC GLM for producing diagnostic plots:

```
proc glm data=one plots=diagnostics;
```

A visual inspection of the normal quantile plot on the diagnostics panel of Output 7.13a Two-Factor ANOVA for Testing Differences in Computer Anxiety illustrates that the points are relatively close to the reference line, so the assumption of normality is reasonable. Further inspection of the histogram illustrates that the errors are normally distributed. To test statistically, we could conduct a Kolmogorov-Smirnov test on the residuals in order to obtain a p-value for testing the normality as well. Also the residual by predicted value plot indicates that the variances are similar across all six treatment combinations.

Key Terms

analysis of variance (ANOVA)
coefficient of determination (R^2)
comparison-wise error rate
critical range
diffogram
Dunnett's method of adjustment
experiment-wise error rate
F-distribution
general linear model
interaction
Kolmogorov-Smirnov test
Levene's test for equal variances
main effects
one-way analysis of variance
post hoc tests

predicted values
randomized block design
residual
standard error of the prediction
studentized Q
sums-of-squares among-groups (SSA)
sums-of-squares-error (SSE)
total-sums-of-squares (SST)
Tukey-Kramer procedure
two-way analysis of variance
unbalanced design
unweighted mean
variance across group means (MSA)
variance within groups (MSE)
weighted mean

Chapter Quiz

1. Which of the following statements is an assumption of one-factor analysis of variance?
   a. The outcome variable is categorical.
   b. The sample size is greater than 30.
   c. The variances of predictor for each level of the outcome are independent.
   d. The error terms are normally distributed.

2. For a one-factor ANOVA, if all of the treatment means are equal, which of the following statements is true?
   a. $R^2 = 0$
   b. SSA = 0
   c. F = 0
   d. All of the above statements are true.
   e. None of the above statements are true.

3. When testing differences in job performance (variable name = JOBPERF) across three training programs (variable name = TRAINING), the appropriate SAS code is:
   a. proc glm; class jobperf; model training=jobperf;
   b. proc glm; class training; model jobperf=training;
   c. proc glm; class jobperf; model jobperf=training;
   d. proc glm; class training; model training=jobperf;

4. When assessing the equal variance assumption when testing differences in job performance (variable name = JOBPERF) across three training programs (variable name = TRAINING), the appropriate SAS code is:
   a. proc glm;
      class training;
      model jobperf=training;
      means training / hovtest=levene;
   b. proc glm hovtest=levene;
      class jobperf;
      model training=jobperf;
   c. proc glm;
      class jobperf;
      model jobperf=training / hovtest=levene;
   d. proc glm;
      class training /hovtest=levene;
      model training=jobperf;

5. You are testing differences in job performance (variable name = JOBPERF) across three training programs (variable name = TRAINING). Suppose you find mean differences. Then, the appropriate SAS code for conducting a Tukey-Kramer post hoc analysis is:
   a. proc glm; diff=jobperf/tukey;
   b. proc glm; means jobperf/tukey;
   c. proc glm; means training/tukey;
   d. proc glm; diff=training/tukey;

6. When testing differences in job performance (variable name = JOBPERF) across three training programs (variable name = TRAINING, with values PRG1, PRG2, and PRG3), the following pairwise comparisons are provided. Based upon the output, there is evidence that:
   a. Performance differs between program 1 and 2.
   b. Performance differs between program 1 and 3.
   c. Performance differs between program 2 and 3.
   d. All programs differ in performance.

Comparisons significant at the 0.05 level are indicated by ***.				
TRAINING Comparison	**Difference Between Means**	**Simultaneous 95% Confidence Limits**		
PRG1 - PRG2	1.5295	-0.7304	4.3286	
PRG1 – PRG3	7.2595	4.9036	9.6154	***
PRG2 – PRG1	-1.5295	-4.3286	0.7304	
PRG2 – PRG3	1.7300	-0.7914	4.2514	
PRG3 - PRG1	-7.2595	-9.6154	-4.9036	***
PRG3 - PRG2	-1.7300	-4.2514	0.7914	

7. Suppose you are testing differences in job performance (variable name = JOBPERF) across three training programs (variable name = TRAINING), and blocking on IQ (defined as high, average, or low). The appropriate SAS code is:
   a. proc glm;
       class training iq;
       model jobperf = training iq;
   b. proc glm;
       class training iq;
       model jobperf = training iq training*iq;
   c. proc glm;
       class training;
       model jobperf = training iq;
   d. proc glm;
       class training;
       model jobperf = training iq training*iq;

8. Suppose you conduct a two-factor analysis of variance and find significant interaction effects. What should you do to aid in further explanation of mean differences?
   a. Conduct tests for main effects.
   b. Use the SLICE option to review simple effects.
   c. Use PLOTS=DIAGNOSTICS to generate p-values for post hoc tests.
   d. Rerun with the analysis without the interaction term.

9. In a two-factor ANOVA with 3 levels of factor A and 4 levels of factor B, conducted on as sample of size 200, the degrees of freedom for interaction are:
   a. 6
   b. 188
   c. 2
   d. 3

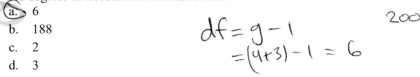

200

$$df = g - 1$$
$$= (4 + 3) - 1 = 6$$

10. Suppose a real estate agent wants to determine if the saleprice of a home is related to the overall condition (good, average, or poor) or high kitchen quality (yes or no) or a combination of the two. She randomly selects 300 houses and collects data to generate the results of the ANOVA. Using the output below, which of the following statements is true?
    a. The error degrees of freedom are 295.
    b. There is a significant interaction effect on saleprice.
    c. There are no main effects due to overall condition.
    d. There are no main effects due to high kitchen quality.

Source	DF	Type I SS	Mean Square	F Value	Pr > F
Overall_Condition	2	56201600134	28100800067	35.06	<.0001
High_Kitchen_Quality	1	61479010913	61479010913	76.70	<.0001
Overall_Condition*High_Kitchen_Quality	2	11339760599	5669880299	7.07	0.0010

Source	DF	Type III SS	Mean Square	F Value	Pr > F
Overall_Condition	2	36012410379	18006205190	22.46	<.0001
High_Kitchen_Quality	1	1692878754	1692878754	2.11	0.1472
Overall_Condition*High_Kitchen_Quality	2	11339760599	5669880299	7.07	0.0010

Chapter 8: Preparing the Input Variables for Prediction

Introduction

Predictive modeling consists of various statistical and machine learning techniques aimed at establishing the relationship between an outcome variable and various predictor variables for purposes of predicting and/or explaining a future outcome. Two of these techniques, linear regression and logistic regression, will be covered in detail in Chapter 9, "Linear Regression Analysis" and Chapter 10, "Logistic Regression Analysis."

Very rarely is the data in a usable form--ready for predictive modeling. Therefore, the analyst must first take great care in exploring, understanding, and preparing or 'cleaning' the data. As stated in Chapter 1, "Statistics and Making Sense of Our World," the information gleaned from predictive modeling is only as good as the data employed and, accordingly, the **data preparation** phase ordinarily takes about 80% of a project's time and effort. Furthermore, this process should also incorporate the aid of a subject matter expert to make sure that any changes to the data are done in the context of the specific business environment and with a clear business understanding.

Before preparing the input variables for predictive modeling, the analyst must first take measures to prevent **overfitting** of the predictive model. When a predictive model is constructed and its performance is then assessed using the same data on which the classifier was constructed, there is an inherent overestimate in its performance; consequently, it is unlikely that the model will perform as well when applied to the population of interest.

To avoid overfitting, the analyst must split the data into two data sets--the **training data set** and the **validation data set** (or hold out data set). This topic is described in detail in Chapter 11, "Measure of Model Performance," but it must be addressed before preparing the input data for modeling in order to avoid **information leakage**.

Information leakage occurs when any information from a holdout data set 'leaks' into the training data set (Wujek, Hall, and Günes, 2016). Therefore, the entire process of preparing input variables, as discussed in this chapter, should be carried out on the training data only. Once the input variables are prepared using the training data, those same preparation steps should be applied to the validation data set.

Keep in mind that if the target of interest is considered a **rare event**, the analyst must consider oversampling to account for the rarity. This has implications for the training and validation data sets, so oversampling, as well, should be done before the input variables are prepared for modeling. Oversampling of rare events is also discussed in detail in Chapter 11, "Measure of Model Performance."

Once the data preparation stage begins, there are many challenges to consider. For example, as mentioned in Chapter 1, "Statistics and Making Sense of Our World," **outliers** can have very negative effects on parameter estimates and inferential conclusions. For a relatively small data set, a very large value for a single observation will greatly inflate the mean and variance and have serious consequences on any conclusions. However, when data sets are relatively large, say 100,000+, it is very unlikely that outliers will affect parameter estimates and conclusions.

In the data preparation stage, univariate statistics and data visualization techniques can be used to identify outliers for purposes of finding errors in data coding. While the analyst should be cognizant of outliers at every phase of predictive modeling, we will investigate their influence when discussing diagnostic procedures in the following chapters on predictive modeling.

In this chapter, we will discuss the major challenges in a specific order and suggest remedies for those challenges in an attempt to present a process for creating a final data set ready for the modeling stage. First, we will discuss missing data and how to impute missing values, including a rationale and method for creating new missing value indicator variables aimed at addressing the missing value problem.

Once variables have been imputed and new missing value indicator variables are created, those variables, along with all other input variables to be considered in the modeling stage, will be reviewed for redundancy. Redundant variables are those variables whose inclusion adds no information to the predictive modeling problem. Therefore, we will discuss how to screen variables for inclusion and drop those variables that are redundant, thereby creating a reduced set of input variables.

Next, using the reduced set of input variables, we will illustrate screening methods to determine which input variables are relevant to the target variable--the variable we want to predict. Any variables that are deemed irrelevant will be dropped from all subsequent analyses; the remaining variables will make up the final set of input variables for modeling.

Last, once the final set of input variables is determined, we will screen those variables for non-linearity using the empirical logit plot and provide suggestions for addressing violations to the linearity assumption.

In this chapter, you will learn how to:

- describe a process for preparing input variables for predictive modeling
- understand complete case analysis and its limitations
- identify problems in predictive modeling due to missing values
- use arrays, DO loops, and output statements when creating missing value indicators
- do median value imputation for missing values
- score new observations which have missing values
- explain problems caused when categorical variables have numerous levels
- explain quasi-complete separation and recognize its consequences to predictive modeling
- explain Greenacre's methods for combining levels of a categorical variable
- use the CLUSTER procedure to carry out Greenacre's method, including the METHOD=WARD option, the FREQ, VAR, and ID statements, and ODS OUTPUT to create an output data set
- interpret the results of Greenacre's method
- based upon the results from Greenacre's method, create dummy variables to represent the reduced levels of the categorical variable
- use the VARCLUS procedure and interpret the results in order to identify redundant input variables
- use the $1-R^2$ ratio to identify the variable that best represents a cluster
- explain the Spearman's correlation coefficient and Hoeffding's D statistic and how they are used to detect irrelevant variables and non-linear associations
- use the CORR procedure, including the VAR and WITH statements, to create the Spearman's correlation and Hoeffding's D statistic
- create and interpret a scatter plot of the ranks of the Spearman's correlation and Hoeffding's D statistic in order to screen for irrelevant variables and non-linear associations
- bin an input variable, calculate the empirical logit for each bin, and produce an empirical logit plot to assess the relationship between the input variable and the target

Missing Values

A **missing data** value occurs when an observation has no value for a variable. Missing information can arise from various situations. When data is collected by way of a survey, respondents can refuse to answer a question or they may not have the information at hand. In many data collection situations, a variable may be blank simply because the scenario does not apply to that customer, business transaction, or hospital encounter, for example. In the Ames Housing Case, the variable, Lot_Frontage, defined as the linear feet of street connected to the property, has missing data, possibly because the home is on a property that has no connection to a street. In any event, analysis with complete data is rare, so handling missing data is imperative!

Suffice it to say that most statistical procedures assume that the data source is complete, that is, all information is known for all observations in the data set. So, what should the analyst do when that is not the case? There are two strategies, **complete-case analysis** and **imputation**, both of which will be discussed in this section.

Complete-Case Analysis

Most SAS procedures, by default, utilize **listwise deletion**. Here an observation is deleted from the analysis if it is missing data on any one variable used in that analysis, thereby resulting in a complete-case analysis. A complete-case analysis is acceptable if the percentage of missing values is small and occurs for very few variables.

However, there are some situations where complete-case analysis is unacceptable. First, when the analysis involves a large number of k predictors, or **high dimensionality**, the analyst should expect missing data to be an even bigger problem. Specifically, the expected proportion of complete cases is $(1-\alpha)^k$, where α is the proportion of missing observations for each predictor. For example, if a data set has 5% missing on each of 50 variables, a complete-case analysis would be conducted on only 7.7% of the original sample.

Also, in cases where the percentage of missing observations on a single input variable is relatively large, a complete-case analysis is obviously not acceptable. An alternative approach would be to utilize a subject matter expert to verify that either the variable is not important to the business case or that there are proxy variables with complete data which can be used in the analysis instead.

Using Imputation with a Missing Value Indicator

An alternative to the complete-case approach is imputation. Imputation methods employ statistical strategies for replacing the missing values with representative non-missing values. As a result, all observations have complete (or imputed) values and are retained for analyses.

In order to consider imputation approaches, the analyst must first consider the 'pattern of missingness' as mentioned in Chapter 1, "Statistics and Making Sense of Our World." If observations are either (1) **missing completely at random (MCAR)**, which is rarely the case, or (2) **missing at random (MAR)**, where the reason for missing is not related to the outcome variable, it is an acceptable practice to use imputation methods. Remember, when observations are **not missing at random (NMAR)** and are omitted from analyses, the results will be biased and should not be used for descriptive nor inferential purposes (see Chapter 1 , "Statistics and Making Sense of Our World," for more information on missing data).

When conducting predictive modeling, a big concern exists when the pattern of missingness is related to the **target variable**, the variable to be predicted. One solution to this problem is to consider both imputation and a **missing value indicator variable**. For example, if the variable having missing values is numeric continuous, the analyst would create a missing value indicator variable associated with that variable, where the indicator variable would be assigned a value of 1 if the observation has a missing value on the variable of interest, or 0 otherwise. At the same time, the analyst would then replace the value of the missing variable with a representative value, say the median.

If the variable having missing values is a binary categorical variable, coded 0 for 'No' and 1 for 'Yes,' the analyst would still use the median for imputation, which is equivalent to assigning the value that occurs most often in place of the missing value. A missing value indicator variable would be created as well.

Consider the Ames Housing data and the 29 potential numeric and binary inputs variables considered for modeling in this book. Only one of the 29 input variables (EXCELLENT_HEAT_QC) has missing values and for only one of the 1389 houses. As a result, we have created a version of AMES300 SAS data set (called AMES300MISS) for illustrative purposes, where missing values were randomly assigned on these numeric variables: above ground living area (GR_LIV_AREA) and total basement area (TOTAL_BSMT_SF) and the binary-coded kitchen quality variable (HIGH_KITCEN_QUALITY).

Program 8.1 Ames Housing Data with Missing Values reads the AMES300MISS SAS data set and saves it in the temporary data set called AMESMISS. The PRINT procedure is applied to the AMESMISS data set and provides a listing of the first 24 values as seen in Output 8.1 Ames Housing Data with Missing Values.

Program 8.1 Ames Housing Data with Missing Values

```
libname sasba 'c:\sasba\ames';
data amesmiss;
   set sasba.ames300miss;
run;

proc print data=amesmiss(obs=24);
   var Total_Bsmt_SF Gr_Liv_Area High_Kitchen_Quality;
   title 'Ames Housing with Missing Data';
run;
```

From Output 8.1 Ames Housing Data with Missing Values, you can see that there is missing data on the variables, TOTAL_BSMT_SF for observations 7 and 21, GR_LIV_AREA for observations 14, 17, and 19, and HIGH_KITCHEN_QUALITY for observations 13, 21, and 24.

Output 8.1 Ames Housing Data with Missing Values

Obs	Total_Bsmt_SF	Gr_Liv_Area	High_Kitchen_Quality
1	864	864	0
2	1829	1829	0
3	1328	1328	0
4	1056	1063	0
5	1947	2207	0
6	972	972	0
7	.	912	0
8	1978	1978	1
9	1501	1801	0
10	2002	2018	1
11	882	882	0
12	1090	1370	0
13	1064	1350	.
14	3094	.	1
15	1566	1600	1
16	2020	2020	1
17	3206	.	1
18	2452	2452	1
19	2458	.	1
20	1114	1114	1
21	.	864	.
22	1740	1740	1
23	1048	1728	0
24	1313	1313	.

Program 8.2 Ames Housing with Imputed Data creates a dummy variable for each of the three variables having missing values and then replaces those missing values on each of the variables with the median.

Program 8.2 Ames Housing with Imputed Data

```
data amesmi;
   set amesmiss;
   array mi{*} MI_Total_Bsmt_SF MI_Gr_Liv_Area MI_High_Kitchen_Quality;
   array x_impute{*} Total_Bsmt_SF Gr_Liv_Area High_Kitchen_Quality;
```

```
  do i=1 to dim(mi);
    mi{i}=(x_impute{i}=.);
  end;
run;

proc stdize data=amesmi
           reponly
           method=median
           out=med_impute;
       var Total_Bsmt_SF Gr_Liv_Area High_Kitchen_Quality;
run;

proc print data=med_impute(obs=24);
   var Total_Bsmt_SF MI_Total_Bsmt_SF
       Gr_Liv_Area MI_Gr_Liv_Area
       High_Kitchen_Quality MI_High_Kitchen_Quality;
       title 'Ames Housing with Imputed Data';
run;
```

From Program 8.2 Ames Housing with Imputed Data, we can see that a new temporary data set, called AMESMI, is created which will contain all missing indicator information. Within that new data set, two data arrays are created. The first array statement creates an array called MI which groups the three new missing value indicator variables, MI_TOTAL_BSMT_SF, MI_GR_LIV_AREA , and MI_HIGH_KITCHEN_QUALITY. The second array statement creates an array called X_IMPUTE which groups the original variables, TOTAL_BSMT_SF, GR_LIV_AREA, and HIGH_KITCHEN_QUALITY. Note that because each array has three elements, the dimension of each array is three.

Next, the DO loop populates each of the three the missing value indicator variables, as i is incremented from 1 to DIM(MI), where DIM(MI)=3. So, for example, when $i = 1$, MI(1), which represents MI_TOTAL_BSMT_SF, is set to 1 if X_IMPUTE(1) is missing, in other words, where the first element of the array, TOTAL_BSMT_SF, is missing; otherwise MI_TOTAL_BSMT_SF is set to 0. This process is done for all observations, and then i is incremented to 2. Here, MI(2), which represents MI_GR_LIV_AREA, is set to 1 if X_IMPUTE(2) is missing, or 0 otherwise. Finally, the same process is carried out when $i = 3$, for MI_HIGH_KITCHEN_QUALITY.

The STDIZE procedure is ordinarily used to standardize values on variables named in the VAR statement. Here, we use the REPONLY option which requests that the only operation to be invoked is the replacement of missing values; data is not standardized. The METHOD=MEDIAN requests that missing values on a variable are replaced by the median value of that variable. The results of the procedure are saved in the temporary SAS data set, called MED_IMPUTE. Finally, the PRINT procedure is used to illustrate the values of the newly created variables, as displayed in Output 8.2 Ames Housing with Imputed Data.

Output 8.2 Ames Housing with Imputed Data

Obs	Total_Bsmt_SF	MI_Total_B smt_SF	Gr_Liv_Area	MI_Gr_Liv_ Area	High_Kitchen_ Quality	MI_High_Kitchen_ Quality
1	864	0	864	0	0	0
2	1829	0	1829	0	0	0
3	1328	0	1328	0	0	0
4	1056	0	1063	0	0	0
5	1947	0	2207	0	0	0
6	972	0	972	0	0	0
7	915	1	912	0	0	0
8	1978	0	1978	0	1	0
9	1501	0	1801	0	0	0
10	2002	0	2018	0	1	0
11	882	0	882	0	0	0
12	1090	0	1370	0	0	0
13	1064	0	1350	0	0	1
14	3094	0	1434	1	1	0
15	1566	0	1600	0	1	0
16	2020	0	2020	0	1	0
17	3206	0	1434	1	1	0
18	2452	0	2452	0	1	0
19	2458	0	1434	1	1	0
20	1114	0	1114	0	1	0
21	915	1	864	0	0	1
22	1740	0	1740	0	1	0
23	1048	0	1728	0	0	0
24	1313	0	1313	0	0	1

From Output 8.2 Ames Housing with Imputed Data, first note observations 7 and 21, which originally had missing values on the numeric continuous variable TOTAL_BSMT_SF, now have their missing values set to 915, the median; the missing value indicator variable, MI_TOTAL_BSMT_SF, is assigned a value of 1, indicating that TOTAL_BSMT_SF has been assigned the median value for that observation. All other observations, where the values on TOTAL_BSMT_SF are non-missing, are assigned a value of 0 for the missing value indicator.

Similarly, median value imputation is applied to the numeric continuous variable, GR_LIV_AREA, where the median of 1434 is assigned for observations 14, 17, and 19. The missing value indicator, MI_GR_LIV_AREA is set to 1 for those observations as well.

Finally, for the categorical dummy variable, HIGH_KITCHEN_QUALITY, the median value is equal to 0, indicating that at least 50% of the houses were coded as '0' for high kitchen quality; therefore, all houses with missing values on this variable are assigned as value of 0; again, the missing value indicator, MI_HIGH_KITCHEN_QUALITY is set to 1, as seen for observations 13, 21, and 24.

All six variables, the three imputed variables and the three indicator variables, can be used in subsequent predictive modeling; however, there are some considerations before doing so:

First, if a variable has a very large proportion of missing values (say, more than 0.50), then the imputed values are based upon a reduced sample size, and therefore, may be inaccurate. Also, in that case, a large number of missing values are assigned the imputed value, resulting in a reduced (and biased) variance for that variable and making the imputed variable worthless; in this case, the missing value indicator can still be considered.

Second, if a variable has a very small proportion of missing, say less than 0.01, then the missing indicator variable has little value in predictive modeling; however, the imputed variable will have little, if any, bias.

Finally, it is imperative that the analyst know the sample size for analysis and the deletion method used by the software in order to adequately assess the effects of missing data and apply these techniques where appropriate.

While the approach described here is relatively simple, there are some advantages. As stated earlier, imputation allows the analyst to utilize all observations under investigation. Furthermore, it allows for scoring future cases which may also have missing data. In this case, the analyst can simply code the missing value indicator as 1 and, at the same time, substitute the missing value with the median of the data used to build the predictive model (note that scoring will be covered in detail in Chapter 11, "Measure of Model Performance").

Categorical Input Variables

In predictive modeling, the analyst can use both numeric and categorical input variables. Each type of variable poses different kinds of problems. In this section, we consider only categorical variables, paying specific attention to sparse events and quasi-complete separation. We discuss Greenacre's method as a possible remedy.

Sparse Events and Quasi-Complete Separation

While there are many problems that can arise when using categorical input variables for predictive modeling, the analyst should pay close attention to the most common issues. Those occur when: (1) there are numerous outcomes, or levels, of the categorical input variable, (2) a categorical input variable has a level that rarely occurs, or (3) a categorical input variable has a level that almost always occurs.

Consider, first, the problem of having numerous levels for a categorical input. Ordinarily, when using a categorical input, the analyst will create a dummy variable. For example, when using gender as an input for predictive modeling, the analyst would create the dummy variable, GENDER, which is coded as '1' for Males and '0' for Females. Specifically, there are $k=2$ levels (male and female), thereby warranting one dummy variable. As the number of levels, k, increases, the number of dummy variables ($k-1$) increases. Here the analyst must then be concerned with the **curse of dimensionality** (Bellman, 1957), where more data is needed to ensure that a sufficient number of observations exist for the combinations of variables under investigation.

Consider the Ames Housing Case where the analyst interested in predicting BONUS possibly using the categorical input variable, NEIGHBORHOOD, with twenty possible levels, as shown in Table 8.1 Contingency Table of Bonus by Neighborhood. This categorical variable would then warrant creating 19 dummy variables. With the large number of categories, note that the dummy variables representing the four smallest neighborhoods (SWISU, Somerset, Stone Brooke and Veenker) account for less than 4.5% of the entire data set.

Furthermore, when considering the frequency of bonus by neighborhood, there are four levels, or neighborhoods (North Ridge, North Ridge Heights, Sommerset, and Stone Brooke) where 100% of the houses have BONUS=1 (and no houses have BONUS=0). This scenario is referred to as **quasi-complete separation**, where the target (BONUS) occurs either always or never for a specific level of the categorical input variable. When there is little or no variation in an input variable, as is the case for rare and frequent events, that input variable serves as a poor discriminator. In fact, as will be seen in Chapter 10, "Logistic Regression Analysis," when there is quasi-complete separation exists, the odds-ratios for the target will be infinity and prevent interpretation.

Note that having many levels for a categorical variable is directly related to the problems of rare or frequent events. In fact, as the number of levels for a variable increases, the chance of sparse cells increases. Furthermore, it is entirely possible that if the analyst considers a third variable in combination with bonus and neighborhood, many more cells would be **sparse**. In any of these situations, there is not enough information to model that combination of events.

In the case where the number of levels is relatively small, however, there is still the possibility that rare (or frequent) events occur. Consider, again, the Ames Housing Case. One variable, UTILITIES, describes whether or not the home had direct access to electricity, gas, water, or sewerage. All homes except one (99.95%) had the value of 'AllPub' while a single home had access to all but sewerage, coded as 'NoSewr.' In this case, UTILITIES would not be used in predictive modeling.

To remedy the problem, the analyst may attempt to collect more data to fill in the empty cells, but that can sometimes be impossible or impractical. An alternative solution is to collapse levels of the categorical variable.

The next section will describe Greenacre's method, which is a way to collapse levels of a categorical input variable measured at the nominal level.

Greenacre's Method Using the CLUSTER Procedure

In the absence of a subject matter expert, the analyst may want to use a more autonomous remedy for the quasi-complete separation problem. **Greenacre's method** (1988) is a data-driven approach for collapsing the levels of the categorical input variable such that the reduction in the chi-square value for measuring its relationship with the target variable is minimized.

For example, in the Ames Housing Case, the chi-square test statistic for measuring the relationship between, or independence of, BONUS and NEIGHBORHOOD is 657.78. As you will soon see, it is possible to collapse the neighborhoods into five groups so that the chi-square statistic is reduced only to 649.65. In this case, very little information about the relationship is lost by collapsing the number of levels of the input variable from twenty to five.

The basic idea is to collapse categories that have the same proportions of the levels in the target variable. For example, as displayed in Table 8.1 Contingency Table of Bonus by Neighborhood, the proportions of BONUS=1 versus BONUS=0 for the neighborhood College Creek (CollgCr) are about a 72% and 28%, respectively; those same proportions are 70% and 30% for the neighborhood Gilbert. Because the breakdown of bonus to no-bonus is relatively the same for both neighborhoods, those two neighborhoods could be combined with little impact to their relationship to the target (BONUS).

Table 8.1 Contingency Table of Bonus by Neighborhood

Bonus	\multicolumn{11}{c}{Neighborhood}

Table of Bonus by Neighborhood

Fre Percent Row Pct Col Pct	Brk Side	Clear Cr	Collg Cr	Crawf or	Edwards	Gilbert	IDOTRR	Mitchel	N Ames	NW Ames	No Ridge
0	67	6	43	25	76	26	30	37	226	33	0
	4.82	0.43	3.10	1.80	5.47	1.87	2.16	2.66	16.27	2.38	0.00
	8.11	0.73	5.21	3.03	9.20	3.15	3.63	4.48	27.36	4.00	0.00
	91.78	20.69	28.29	39.06	87.36	29.55	93.75	67.27	88.28	40.24	0.00
1	6	23	109	39	11	62	2	18	30	49	48
	0.43	1.66	7.85	2.81	0.79	4.46	0.14	1.30	2.16	3.53	3.46
	1.07	4.09	19.36	6.93	1.95	11.01	0.36	3.20	5.33	8.70	8.53
	8.22	79.31	71.71	60.94	12.64	70.45	6.25	32.73	11.72	59.76	100.00
Total	73	29	152	64	87	88	32	55	256	82	48
	5.26	2.09	10.94	4.61	6.26	6.34	2.30	3.96	18.43	5.90	3.46

Bonus	Neighborhood									
Freq Percent Row Pct Col Pct	Nridg Ht	Old Town	SWISU	Sawyer	Sawyer W	Somerst	Stone Br	Timber	Veenker	Total
0	0	116	23	89	22	0	0	5	2	826
	0.00	8.35	1.66	6.41	1.58	0.00	0.00	0.36	0.14	59.47
	0.00	14.04	2.78	10.77	2.66	0.00	0.00	0.61	0.24	
	0.00	93.55	88.46	97.80	37.93	0.00	0.00	12.82	15.38	
1	49	8	3	2	36	17	6	34	11	563
	3.53	0.58	0.22	0.14	2.59	1.22	0.43	2.45	0.79	40.53
	8.70	1.42	0.53	0.36	6.39	3.02	1.07	6.04	1.95	
	100.00	6.45	11.54	2.20	62.07	100.00	100.00	87.18	84.62	
Total	49	124	26	91	58	17	6	39	13	1389
	3.53	8.93	1.87	6.55	4.18	1.22	0.43	2.81	0.94	100.00

Table of Bonus by Neighborhood

In fact, the analyst could collapse various neighborhoods with relative ease and check for an insignificant reduction in the chi-squared test statistic using the newly created neighborhood variable with now only 19 levels; however, the process would prove to be tedious. Therefore, we will describe, by parts, Program 8.3 Combining Neighborhoods from Ames Housing Data Using Greenacre's Method (SAS Institute, 2012):

Program 8.3 Combining Neighborhoods from Ames Data Housing Using Greenacre's Method

```
libname sasba 'c:\sasba\ames';
data ames70;
   set sasba.ames70;
run;

********Part A which produces Output8.3a******;
proc freq data=ames70 noprint;
   tables bonus*neighborhood/chisq;
   output out=chi (keep=_pchi_) chisq;
run;

proc print data=chi;
   title 'Chi-square for Bonus by Neighborhood';
run;

********Part B which produces Output8.3b******;
proc means data=ames70 noprint nway;
   class neighborhood;
   var bonus;
   output out=propbonus mean=prop;
run;

proc print data=propbonus;
   title 'Proportion of Houses with Bonus by Neighborhood';
run;


********Part C which produces Output8.3c and Output8.3d******;
proc cluster data=propbonus method=ward outtree=treeinfo
        plots=(dendrogram(vertical height=rsq));
   freq _freq_;
   var prop;
   id neighborhood;
run;

title 'Results of Cluster Analysis on Ames Neighborhoods';
ods output clusterhistory=cluster;
run;
```

```
********Part D which produces Output8.3e******;
proc print data=cluster;
title 'Contents of the Cluster History';
run;


********Part E which produces Output8.3f******;
data cutoff;
    if _n_=1 then set chi;
    set cluster;
    chisquare=_pchi_*rsquared;
    degfree=numberofclusters-1;
    logpvalue=logsdf('CHISQ',chisquare,degfree);
run;

proc print data=cutoff;
    var numberofclusters Semipartialrsq rsquared chisquare degfree
        logpvalue;
    title 'Log P-Value Information and the Cluster History';
run;

********Part F which produces Output8.3g******;
proc sgplot data=cutoff;
    scatter y=logpvalue x=numberofclusters
            / markerattrs=(color=blue symbol=circlefilled);
    xaxis label="Number of Clusters";
    yaxis label="Log of P-Value" min=-350 max=-250;
    title "Plot of Log P-Value by Number of Clusters";
run;


********Part G which produces Output8.3h******;
proc sql;
    select numberofclusters into :ncl
    from cutoff
    having logpvalue=min(logpvalue);
quit;
run;

proc tree data=treeinfo nclusters=&ncl out=clus_solution;
    id neighborhood;
run;

proc sort data=clus_solution;
    by clusname;
run;

proc print data=clus_solution;
    by clusname;
    id clusname;
    title 'List of Neighborhoods by Cluster';
run;
```

For Greenacre's method, the value of the chi-squared statistic for BONUS by NEIGHBORHOOD is needed. Therefore, as described in Part A of Program 8.3 Combining Neighborhoods from Ames Data Housing Using Greenacre's Method, the FREQ procedure with the CHISQ option is used on the AMES70 data set. The NOPRINT option suppresses the contingency table, although we provide it in Table 8.1 Contingency Table of Bonus by Neighborhood. The OUTPUT statement is used to save the chi-square test statistic in a temporary SAS file called CHI, as displayed in Output 8.3a Chi-square for Bonus by Neighborhood.

Output 8.3a Chi-square for Bonus by Neighborhood

Obs	_PCHI_
1	657.781

The next step in the process requires saving both the numbers and proportions of houses where a bonus is earned (BONUS=1) for each of the 20 neighborhoods. Note that the mean of a binary (0-1) variable is simply the proportion of 1s. Therefore, Part B of Program 8.3 uses the MEANS procedure on the variable BONUS. The NWAY option requests the mean for each of the neighborhoods as defined by the CLASS statement. The OUTPUT statement requests that the results of the MEANS procedure be saved in the temporary SAS data set called PROPBONUS and renames the variable MEAN to PROP. The PRINT procedure provides for a listing of the data set PROPBONUS, as displayed in Output 8.3b Proportion of Houses with Bonus by Neighborhood.

Output 8.3b Proportion of Houses with Bonus by Neighborhood

Obs	Neighborhood	_TYPE_	_FREQ_	Prop
1	BrkSide	1	73	0.08219
2	ClearCr	1	29	0.79310
3	CollgCr	1	152	0.71711
4	Crawfor	1	64	0.60938
5	Edwards	1	87	0.12644
6	Gilbert	1	88	0.70455
7	IDOTRR	1	32	0.06250
8	Mitchel	1	55	0.32727
9	NAmes	1	256	0.11719
10	NWAmes	1	82	0.59756
11	NoRidge	1	48	1.00000
12	NridgHt	1	49	1.00000
13	OldTown	1	124	0.06452
14	SWISU	1	26	0.11538
15	Sawyer	1	91	0.02198
16	SawyerW	1	58	0.62069
17	Somerst	1	17	1.00000
18	StoneBr	1	6	1.00000
19	Timber	1	39	0.87179
20	Veenker	1	13	0.84615

3 Next, a cluster analysis is conducted using the SAS data set PROPBONUS, as illustrated in the Part C of Program 8.3. The CLUSTER procedure with the METHOD=WARD option and the FREQ statement will provide clustering of groups with similar proportions identical to that of Greenacre's method (SAS Institute, 2012).

4 The PLOTS=DENDROGRAM option with the VERTICAL and HEIGHT options requests that a vertical **dendrogram** be provided with height based upon the RSQ value. Information on the final clusters is saved in the temporary SAS data set, TREEINFO, using the OUTTREE= option and the ID statement requests that observations are identified by their neighborhood in the TREEINFO data set when the cluster history is printed.

5 Finally, the results of the CLUSTER procedure are saved in a temporary SAS data set, called CLUSTER, using the ODS OUTPUT statement. The results of the CLUSTER procedure and the dendrogram are displayed in Output 8.3c Results of Cluster Analysis on Ames Neighborhoods and Output 8.3d Dendrogram of Cluster Analysis Results by Neighborhoods, respectively.

Output 8.3c Results of Cluster Analysis on Ames Neighborhoods

Cluster History						
Number of Clusters	Clusters Joined		Freq	Semipartial R-Square	R-Square	Tie
19	NoRidge	NridgHt	97	0.0000	1.00	T
18	CL19	Somerst	114	0.0000	1.00	T
17	CL18	StoneBr	120	0.0000	1.00	
16	NAmes	SWISU	282	0.0000	1.00	
15	IDOTRR	OldTown	156	0.0000	1.00	
14	Crawfor	SawyerW	122	0.0000	1.00	
13	Edwards	CL16	369	0.0000	1.00	
12	Timber	Veenker	52	0.0000	1.00	
11	CollgCr	Gilbert	240	0.0001	1.00	
10	CL14	NWAmes	204	0.0001	1.00	
9	BrkSide	CL15	229	0.0001	1.00	
8	ClearCr	CL12	81	0.0006	.999	
7	CL9	Sawyer	320	0.0009	.998	
6	CL7	CL13	689	0.0043	.994	
5	CL8	CL11	321	0.0062	.988	
4	CL5	CL10	525	0.0147	.973	
3	CL6	Mitchel	744	0.0181	.955	
2	CL4	CL17	645	0.0587	.896	
1	CL3	CL2	1389	0.8962	.000	

From Output 8.3c Results of Cluster Analysis on Ames Neighborhoods, note in the first row that the neighborhoods, NoRidge and NridgHt, are combined first, to form cluster 19 (CL19) resulting in 97 total neighborhoods. The R-square value represents the proportion of the chi-square in the original 20x2 contingency table ($\chi2 = 657.781$) remaining after those two neighborhoods are combined; the semipartial R-square represents the change in the chi-square. So in the first step, when the two neighborhoods are combined there is no change in the chi-square value to the fourth significant digit; in other words essentially 100% of the original chi-square value is retained after collapsing to 19 clusters.

In the second row, note that cluster 19 (CL19 already made up of NoRidge and NridgHt) and the neighborhood Somerset are combined to form a new cluster 18 (CL18) containing 114 neighborhoods. The reduction from 19 to 18 clusters results in no significant reduction in the chi-square, as represented by both the R-square and semipartial R-square values.

The third row shows that the neighborhood StoneBr is combined with CL18 to form cluster 17 (CL17), made up now of four neighborhoods, as illustrated by the rightmost branch of the dendrogram in Output 8.3d Dendrogram of Cluster Analysis Results by Neighborhoods. In fact, the dendrogram gives a great visual on how the R-square changes with every collapse of two clusters, and specifically illustrates where the collapsing may end.

Finally, this process continues so that each subsequent cluster results in a minimal reduction in the original chi-square until all neighborhoods are combined into one cluster; this is represented in the last line when clusters 2 and 3 are combined resulting in a total reduction in the original chi-square.

Note that the first two observations each have a variable, Tie, with a value of 'T.' This is an indication that the clustering at that level is not unique. If a tie occurs early in the cluster history, ordinarily there is little effect on the later stages; however, if a tie occurs midway or later in the process, the analyst should investigate further.

Output 8.3d Dendrogram of Cluster Analysis Results by Neighborhoods

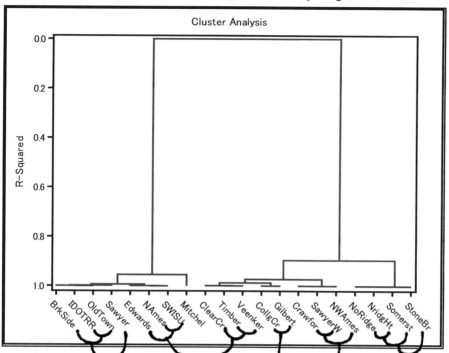

A PRINT procedure is included in Part D of Program 8.3 Combining Neighborhoods from Ames Data Housing Using Greenacre's Method to illustrate the contents of the CLUSTER data set as displayed in Output 8.3e Contents of Cluster History, along with the names of variables needed for subsequent analysis.

Output 8.3e Contents of the Cluster History

Obs	NumberOfClusters	Idj1	Idj2	FreqOfNewCluster	SemipartialRSq	RSquared	Tie
1	19	NoRidge	NridgHt	97	0.0000	1.00	T
2	18	CL19	Somerst	114	0.0000	1.00	T
3	17	CL18	StoneBr	120	0.0000	1.00	
4	16	Names	SWISU	282	0.0000	1.00	
5	15	IDOTRR	OldTown	156	0.0000	1.00	
6	14	Crawfor	SawyerW	122	0.0000	1.00	
7	13	Edwards	CL16	369	0.0000	1.00	
8	12	Timber	Veenker	52	0.0000	1.00	
9	11	CollgCr	Gilbert	240	0.0001	1.00	
10	10	CL14	NWAmes	204	0.0001	1.00	
11	9	BrkSide	CL15	229	0.0001	1.00	
12	8	ClearCr	CL12	81	0.0006	.999	
13	7	CL9	Sawyer	320	0.0009	.998	
14	6	CL7	CL13	689	0.0043	.994	
15	5	CL8	CL11	321	0.0062	.988	
16	4	CL5	CL10	525	0.0147	.973	
17	3	CL6	Mitchel	744	0.0181	.955	
18	2	CL4	CL17	645	0.0587	.896	
19	1	CL3	CL2	1389	0.8962	.000	

Upon review of the cluster results, the question becomes--out of the nineteen steps in the cluster analysis, where in this process does the analyst stop when there is no subject matter expertise? In other words, how can the process be automated so that the analyst selects the best number of clusters?

The ultimate answer can be found using the p-value of the chi-square value at each step of the clustering. In other words, the analyst can define a stopping criterion as that iteration where the p-value of the chi-square test statistic between the target variable and the collapsed input variable is minimized. For ease of data visualization, the log of the p-values at each step is calculated and plotted using Part E of Program 8.3 Combining Neighborhoods from Ames Data Housing Using Greenacre's Method.

In the first step, the chi-square statistic (_PCHI_ = 657.781) from the original contingency table of BONUS by the 20 levels of NEIGHBORHOOD must be merged with each of the 19 rows of the cluster history data. An inspection of Part E of Program 8.3 Combining Neighborhoods from Ames Data Housing Using Greenacre's Method shows that a new data set, called CUTOFF, is created using both a SET and a conditional SET statement. In general, a conditional SET statement serves as a RETAIN statement for all variables in the data set, CHI, namely, the _PCHI_ variable; where the value of _CHI_ is retained for each observation in the CLUSTER data as it is placed in the CUTOFF data set (Warren, 2007).

Using the original chi-square statistic and the R-square, the chi-square value for each iteration is calculated, along with its degrees of freedom and log p-value. The details of that data are displayed in Output 8.3f Log P-Value Information and Cluster History. A visual display is provided using the SGPLOT procedure, as shown in Output 8.3g Plot of Log P-Value by Number of Clusters. A visual inspection of the plot further illustrates that the number of clusters which results in the minimum reduction of the original chi-square statistic is five.

Output 8.3f Log P-Value Information and the Cluster History

Obs	NumberOfClusters	SemipartialRSq	RSquared	chisquare	degfree	Logpvalue
1	19	0.0000	1.00	657.781	18	-293.105
2	18	0.0000	1.00	657.781	17	-294.949
3	17	0.0000	1.00	657.781	16	-296.824
4	16	0.0000	1.00	657.781	15	-298.733
5	15	0.0000	1.00	657.780	14	-300.677
6	14	0.0000	1.00	657.764	13	-302.651
7	13	0.0000	1.00	657.740	12	-304.664
8	12	0.0000	1.00	657.713	11	-306.720
9	11	0.0001	1.00	657.677	10	-308.822
10	10	0.0001	1.00	657.616	9	-310.967
11	9	0.0001	1.00	657.549	8	-313.171
12	8	0.0006	.999	657.145	7	-315.279
13	7	0.0009	.998	656.526	6	-317.362
14	6	0.0043	.994	653.704	5	-318.448
15	5	0.0062	.988	649.652	4	-319.039
16	4	0.0147	.973	639.981	3	-316.984
17	3	0.0181	.955	628.083	2	-314.041
18	2	0.0587	.896	589.499	1	-298.167
19	1	0.8962	.000	0.000	0	.

Output 8.3g Plot of Log P-Value by Number of Clusters

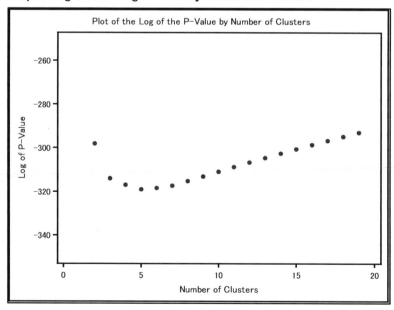

The analyst can review the cluster history in Output 8.3e Contents of the Cluster History to determine which neighborhoods belong to which cluster. Or the analyst can implement an automatic approach by using the information saved from the OUTTREE option, namely the TREEINFO SAS data set, along with Part G of Program 8.3 Combining Neighborhoods from Ames Data Housing Using Greenacre's Method.

First, the SQL procedure is used to both scan the CUTOFF data and select only that record associated with the 5-cluster solution, as indicated by the minimum log p-value. The number of clusters from that record, which has a value of 5, is saved in the value of NCL.

Next, the TREE procedure is used to create a temporary data set, called CLUS_SOLUTION, containing a variable to indicate the disjoint clusters at a specified level in the tree. The NCLUSTERS= option with &NCL=5, as defined in PROC SQL, requests that information be saved only for the 5-cluster solution. The ID statement identifies the leaves of the tree, or the neighborhoods; when it is included, the ID is copied to the output data set. As a result, CLUS_SOLUTION will contain the neighborhoods. Finally, the PRINT procedure provides a line listing of the data set, which includes the neighborhoods as assigned to the five clusters, and is displayed in Output 8.3h List of Neighborhoods by Cluster.

Output 8.3h List of Neighborhoods by Cluster

CLUSNAME	Neighborhood	CLUSTER
CL10	Crawfor	3
	SawyerW	3
	NWAmes	3

CLUSNAME	Neighborhood	CLUSTER
CL17	NoRidge	1
	NridgHt	1
	Somerst	1
	StoneBr	1

CLUSNAME	Neighborhood	CLUSTER
CL5	Timber	4
	Veenker	4
	CollgCr	4
	Gilbert	4
	ClearCr	4

CLUSNAME	Neighborhood	CLUSTER
CL6	NAmes	2
	SWISU	2
	IDOTRR	2
	OldTown	2
	Edwards	2
	BrkSide	2
	Sawyer	2

CLUSNAME	Neighborhood	CLUSTER
Mitchel	Mitchel	5

It should be noted that when a new variable, NBR_CLUS, is created to represent the five newly collapsed neighborhood clusters, the resulting chi-square statistic for the 5x2 contingency table is 649.652, a slight reduction from 657.781 for the original 20 neighborhoods. In conclusion, the Greenacre method provides an automatic solution for collapsing 20 neighborhoods to 5 neighborhoods.

Note that once the analyst collapses the levels of the categorical variable, an inspection of the target variable by the newly collapsed levels is warranted. Specific to our Ames Housing data, we see from Table 8.2 Contingency Table of Bonus by Clustered Neighborhoods that there is still a problem with quasi-complete separation, where 100% of the houses in NBR_CLUS=1 have agents who earned a bonus. As a result, the analyst would get a warning of model validity for the LOGISTIC procedure when using NBR_CLUS as a predictor of bonus, not to mention an infinite (>999.999) odds-ratio.

Table 8.2 Contingency Table of Bonus by Clustered Neighborhoods

Table of Bonus by nbr_clus						
Bonus	**nbr_clus**					
Frequency Percent Row Pct Col Pct	**1**	**2**	**3**	**4**	**5**	**Total**
0	0 0.00 0.00 0.00	627 45.14 75.91 91.00	80 5.76 9.69 39.22	82 5.90 9.93 25.55	37 2.66 4.48 67.27	826 59.47
1	120 8.64 21.31 100.00	62 4.46 11.01 9.00	124 8.93 22.02 60.78	239 17.21 42.45 74.45	18 1.30 3.20 32.73	563 40.53
Total	120 8.64	689 49.60	204 14.69	321 23.11	55 3.96	1389 100.00

To remedy the problem and for purposes of considering the variable, NBR_CLUS, in our list of candidate predictors, we will combine the new clusters, 1 and 4, because of their relatively similar proportions of bonus. Finally, in order to use the categorical variable, NBR_CLUS, three dummy variables (NBR_CLUS1, NBR_CLUS2, and NBR_CLUS3) will be used in all subsequent analyses using the following SAS code:

```
nbr_clus1=0; nbr_clus2=0; nbr_clus3=0;
if neighborhood='NoRidge' or neighborhood='NridgHt' or
   neighborhood='Somerst' or neighborhood='StoneBr' or
   neighborhood='Timber' or neighborhood='Veenker' or
   neighborhood='CollgCr' or neighborhood='Gilbert' or
   neighborhood='ClearCr' then nbr_clus1=1;
if neighborhood='NAmes' or neighborhood='SWISU' or neighborhood='IDOTRR'
   or neighborhood='OldTown' or neighborhood='Edwards'
   or neighborhood='BrkSide' or neighborhood='Sawyer' then nbr_clus2=1;
if neighborhood='Mitchel' then nbr_clus3=1;
```

From the SAS code, note that the neighborhoods not assigned to a dummy variable (Crawfor, SawyerW, and NWAmes) will serve as the reference group. Specifically, when a house has a value of 0 for all three dummy variables, meaning that the house does not belong to any of those neighborhoods, that house is assumed to be in the reference group.

Variable Clustering

In many situations, the analyst is faced with hundreds, even thousands, of input variables. Obviously using all input variables is not desired and is even detrimental to the validity of the results. First, larger sample sizes are needed when using a relatively large number of input variables to ensure the stability of parameter estimates. Furthermore, with a large number of input variables, it is almost certain that some of them are highly correlated; in this case, analysis results can be ambiguous and interpretation is impossible. In short, when there are numerous input variables, the initial set should be reduced to manageable size using statistical methodology and, of course, the help of a subject matter expert.

When reducing the initial set of inputs, the analyst should take into account both relevancy and redundancy. In predictive modeling, an input variable is **irrelevant** if it is not related to the target, or dependent, variable. Redundancy, on the other hand, does not take into account the dependent variable, but instead must be assessed in terms of the input variables. An input variable is **redundant** if its inclusion provides no additional information to the set of input variables --in other words, there is no loss of information in the set of inputs when the irrelevant variable is excluded.

A common strategy among analysts is to first tackle the issue of redundancy, that is, reduce the initial set of variable inputs to a manageable, smaller set of inputs to be used in the modeling process. This section will address input redundancy using the VARCLUS procedure. Subsequent sections will address the issue of variable relevancy.

The VARCLUS Procedure for Variable Reduction

When redundant variables exist, the goal of the analyst is to place those variables with similar information into various groups, or clusters, such that each variable within a cluster is highly correlated with its own cluster while uncorrelated with other clusters. Ultimately, the analyst will select the variable that best represents the cluster, and use that variable to represent the cluster, thus eliminating the remaining variables in that cluster from subsequent analyses.

Consider the following example. Suppose we randomly selected 200 business students and asked them to rate the following statements on a scale of 1 to 10, where 1 is strongly disagree and 10 is strongly agree.

Q1: I think that the major in information technology (IT) is more difficult than any other major.

Q2: I think that the major in IT is more demanding than any other major.

Q3: Most IT jobs require heavy programming skills.

Q4: Most IT jobs require extensive technical training.

Q5: I feel confident working on a laptop computer.

Q6: I feel confident using a variety of software programs.

Q7: I feel confident getting software up and running.

Suppose further we correlate their responses to get the correlation matrix in Table 8.3 Correlation Matrix for Variables Q1 through Q6.

Table 8.3 Correlation Matrix for Variables Q1 through Q6

	Q1	Q2	Q3	Q4	Q5	Q6
Q2	0.77					
Q3	0.13	0.15				
Q4	0.09	0.13	0.62			
Q5	-0.10	-0.06	-0.11	-0.01		
Q6	-0.06	-0.03	-0.14	-0.04	0.70	
Q7	-0.05	-0.02	-0.15	-0.05	0.63	0.79

From the correlation coefficients, we can see that responses for questions 1 and 2 are highly correlated, along with questions 3 and 4, and questions 5, 6, and 7, respectively. In this case, we would group the initial 7 questions into 3 clusters of similar variables. In fact, using correlations and possibly subject matter expertise, we could use, say, Q1, Q3, and Q5 as representative of the original set of variables because those variables seem to represent the redundant information in questions 2, 4, 6, and 7.

In order to do this type of clustering, the analyst can apply the variable cluster (VARCLUS) procedure, which is related to **principal component analysis.** A brief description of principal component analysis is as follows: When considering p input variables, there is a fixed amount of variance in that set of variables and is defined as the sum of the variance of the p predictors. This variability is necessary when building predictive models--remember an input variable having no variability also has no predictive power. So, the goal of the analyst is to reduce the set of p inputs to size q (for q < p) so as to retain as much variation in the inputs as possible. One such data reduction approach is principal component analysis.

Principal component analysis produces a set of p principal components which are weighted linear combinations of the original variables, having the form:

$$PRIN_1 = a_{11}X_1 + a_{12}X_2 + ... + a_{1p}X_p$$
$$PRIN_2 = a_{21}X_1 + a_{22}X_2 + ... + a_{2p}X_p$$
$$PRIN_3 = a_{31}X_1 + a_{32}X_2 + ... + a_{3p}X_p$$
$$...$$
$$PRIN_q = a_{q1}X_1 + a_{q2}X_2 + ... + a_{qp}X_p$$
$$...$$
$$PRIN_p = a_{p1}X_1 + a_{p2}X_2 + ... + a_{pp}X_p$$

The weights of the first principal component (a_{11} through a_{1p}) are calculated so that $PRIN_1$ accounts for the greatest variation in the original set of inputs. It should be noted that this could be achieved by setting the weights very large; so the weights are determined under the additional constraint that the square of the weights must add to 1.0. This constraint also ensures a unique solution.

Next, the second principal component, PRIN$_2$, is determined so that it accounts for the second highest variation, while at the same time having zero correlation with the first principal component. This process continues until there are p principal components, where the sum of the variances of PRIN$_1$ through PRIN$_p$ is equal to the total variation of the original set of input variables. The new set of principal component variables is optimal such that no other combination of variables explains more variance in the original set of inputs. Furthermore, each principal component has zero correlation with all other principal components.

The principal components are ordinarily calculated using the covariance matrix; however, to account for the differing scales of the input variables, the variables should be standardized. As an equivalent alternative, principal component analysis can be conducted using the correlation matrix; here the variance of each standardized input variable is 1 and the total variance of the standardized inputs is the sum of the diagonals which equals p.

There are various criteria for selecting the number of principal components (q where q < p); one such criterion is to select those principal components whose variance is greater than one, that is, where the **eigenvalue** is greater than 1.0. The reduced set of q principal components accounts for a sufficient amount of variance in the original set of variables and can be used for subsequent analyses. **Variable clustering** is a variation of principal component analysis and is used to create a set of clusters containing unique variables based upon a similarity measure, such as the correlation coefficient.

When conducting a variable clustering procedure, first, all variables begin in a single cluster. The principal component algorithm is applied to that cluster and if the variance of the first two principal components is greater than 1 (eigenvalue > 1.0), then those two principal components are rotated, where the principal component coefficients are mathematically transformed and used for cluster assignment (Harris and Kaiser, 1964). So those variables having relatively large coefficients on the first principal component are assigned the first cluster and those variables having relatively large coefficients on the second principal component are assigned to the second cluster.

In short, the variables with relatively high coefficients on a principal component are highly correlated. At the same time, the principal component algorithm ensures that the clusters have a little correlation among themselves.

Next, one of the two newly created clusters is split, namely the cluster with the largest second eigenvalue, to create two new principal components; each variable within that parent cluster is assigned to one of the two new clusters based upon its rotated coefficients on the two new principal components. Additionally, when that split occurs, all other variables are reviewed and possibly reassigned to a different cluster if it has a higher correlation with the different cluster.

Next, the one cluster having the largest second eigenvalue is split; again, the variables within that cluster are assigned to two new clusters, while all other variables are reviewed for reassignment to a different cluster. This process continues until the second eigenvalue is less than 1, or less than the value defined by MAXEIGEN.

It should be noted that in ordinary principal component analysis, all principal components are computed using the same full set of inputs, such that none of the principal components are correlated. In the VARCLUS procedure, each cluster component is computed from a different subset of variables, and those components may have some correlation.

Procedure Syntax for PROC VARCLUS

PROC VARCLUS is a procedure used to create variable clustering and has the general form:

PROC VARCLUS DATA=*SAS-data-set <options>*;
VAR *variable(s)*;
RUN;

where *options* include MAXEIGEN=n, SHORT, and HI, to name a few. MAXEIGEN=n specifies the largest value of the second eigenvalue permitted in each cluster and is used as a stopping rule; the SHORT option omits from the output the cluster structure, scoring coefficients, and the intercluster correlation matrices; the HI (or HIERARCHY) option prevents variables from being transferred to different clusters when a split is made, thereby maintaining a hierarchical structure--in other words, a variable will remain in a cluster once it is assigned to that cluster.

To illustrate the VARCLUS procedure, consider the Ames Housing data set including the initial set of 29 input variables, in addition to the three neighborhood cluster/dummy variables created after applying the Greenacre method (Note that had we had missing value indicator variables and imputed variables, those would have been included in our initial set of inputs as well).

In our example, it is conceivable that the various characteristics (variables) of the house are correlated; obviously, a house with a large number of rooms is expected to have more square footage than one with a small number of rooms; a multi-story home is expected to have more square footage than a one-story home; a large house is more likely to be built on a larger lot than a smaller house, etc.

In using these characteristics to predict value (as measured here by BONUS), it is obvious that many of those variables have inherent redundant information and lend themselves well to the idea of variable reduction. As a result, the analyst would perform a variable clustering procedure using Program 8.4 The VARCLUS Procedure for Reducing Ames Housing Inputs.

Program 8.4 The VARCLUS Procedure for Reducing Ames Housing Inputs

```
libname sasba 'c:\sasba\ames';
data ames70;
    set sasba.ames70;
    AboveAverage_Quality=0; BelowAverage_Quality=0;
    AboveAverage_Condition=0; BelowAverage_Condition=0;
    if Overall_Quality=3 then AboveAverage_Quality=1;
    if Overall_Quality=1 then BelowAverage_Quality=1;
    if Overall_Condition=3 then AboveAverage_Condition=1;
    if Overall_Condition=1 then BelowAverage_Condition=1;
    if Heating_QC="Ex" then Excellent_Heat_QC=1;
        if Heating_QC="Gd" or Heating_QC="Fa" or Heating_QC="TA"
        then Excellent_Heat_QC=0;
    if Lot_Shape="IRR" then Irreq_Lot_Shape=1;
        if Lot_Shape="Reg" then Irreq_Lot_Shape=0;
    if Central_Air="Y" then C_Air=1;
        if Central_Air="N" then C_Air=0;
    nbr_clus1=0; nbr_clus2=0; nbr_clus3=0;
    if neighborhood="NoRidge" or neighborhood="NridgHt" or
        neighborhood="Somerst" or neighborhood="StoneBr" or
        neighborhood="Timber" or neighborhood="Veenker" or
        neighborhood="CollgCr" or neighborhood="Gilbert" or
        neighborhood="ClearCr" then nbr_clus1=1;
    if neighborhood="NAmes" or neighborhood="SWISU" or
        neighborhood="IDOTRR" or neighborhood="OldTown" or
        neighborhood="Edwards" or neighborhood="BrkSide" or
        neighborhood="Sawyer" then nbr_clus2=1;
    if neighborhood="Mitchel" then nbr_clus3=1;
***define full set with 32 inputs*** 4th neighborhood is reference group;
%let fullset=Gr_Liv_Area Total_Bsmt_SF Bsmt_Fin_SF Bsmt_Unf_SF Lot_Area
    Age_At_Sale Bedroom_AbvGr High_Kitchen_Quality Fullbath_2Plus
    Fireplace_1Plus TwoPlusCar_Garage High_Exterior_Cond
    High_Exterior_Qual One_Floor Vinyl_Siding CuldeSac Has_Fence
    Land_Level Poured_Concrete Paved_Driveway Total_Functionality
    Normal_Prox_Cond AboveAverage_Quality BelowAverage_Quality
    AboveAverage_Condition BelowAverage_Condition Excellent_Heat_QC
    Irreq_Lot_Shape C_Air nbr_clus1 nbr_clus2 nbr_clus3;
run;

proc varclus data=ames70 maxeigen=.60 hi short plots=dendrogram;
    var &fullset;
run;
```

In Program 8.4 The VARCLUS Procedure for Reducing Ames Housing Inputs, the permanent data set AMES70 is read and new input variables are created, including the neighborhood clusters created in the previous section. Note that we created additional variables to be included among the possible inputs. The %LET statement creates a macro variable called FULLSET which is a character string, or list of input variables to be referenced later.

The VARCLUS procedure is applied to AMES70 and clusters are split as long as the second eigenvalue exceeds 0.60, as defined by MAXEIGEN. The HI option ensures that once a variable is placed in a cluster it stays in that cluster and the SHORT option reduces the volume of output. The results of the variable clustering procedure will be explained by partial outputs as follows:

First, the output displays the number of observations, the number of variables to be clustered, and the criterion for the maximum eigenvalue, as illustrated in Output 8.4a Summary Information for VARCLUS Procedure for Ames Housing Input Data. Note that one observation is deleted because it has one missing value on one input variable.

Output 8.4a Summary Information for VARCLUS Procedure for Ames Housing Input Data

Oblique Principal Component Cluster Analysis

Observations	1388	Proportion	0
Variables	32	Maxeigen	0.6

Clustering algorithm converged.

Cluster Summary for 1 Cluster					
Cluster	Members	Cluster Variation	Variation Explained	Proportion Explained	Second Eigenvalue
1	32	32	7.665278	0.2395	2.2732

Total variation explained = 7.665278 Proportion = 0.2395

Cluster 1 will be split because it has the largest second eigenvalue, 2.273223, which is greater than the MAXEIGEN=0.6 value.

Note that the cluster variation is equal to 32, which is always identical to the number of variables; the total variation explained by the first principal component is 7.665278, which accounts for 23.95% of the total variation of the input variables (7.665278 divided by 32). The second eigenvalue (2.273223) of cluster 1 is larger than the 0.60 as determined by the MAXEIGEN option; therefore, cluster 1 will be split, as illustrated in Output 8.4b Cluster Summary for 2 Clusters for Ames Housing Input Data.

Output 8.4b Cluster Summary for 2 Clusters for Ames Housing Input Data

Cluster Summary for 2 Clusters					
Cluster	Members	Cluster Variation	Variation Explained	Proportion Explained	Second Eigenvalue
1	19	19	6.713918	0.3534	1.8615
2	13	13	2.604492	0.2003	1.5801

Total variation explained = 9.31841 Proportion = 0.2912

2 Clusters		R-squared with		
Cluster	Variable	Own Cluster	Next Closest	1-R**2 Ratio
Cluster 1	Gr_Liv_Area	0.4147	0.1844	0.7176
	Bsmt_Unf_SF	0.0928	0.0022	0.9092
	Age_at_Sale	0.6109	0.3430	0.5922
	Bedroom_AbvGr	0.0922	0.0227	0.9288
	High_Kitchen_Quality	0.4601	0.0991	0.5993
	Fullbath_2plus	0.6099	0.1482	0.4580
	TwoPlusCar_Garage	0.4036	0.1746	0.7226
	High_Exterior_Cond	0.0206	0.0039	0.9832
	High_Exterior_Qual	0.5740	0.1237	0.4861
	One_Floor	0.0399	0.0129	0.9726
	Vinyl_Siding	0.4265	0.0281	0.5901
	Has_Fence	0.0981	0.0036	0.9052
	Poured_Concrete	0.6122	0.0872	0.4248
	Normal_Prox_Cond	0.0229	0.0097	0.9867
	AboveAverage_Quality	0.4351	0.1800	0.6890
	AboveAverage_Condition	0.2957	0.0271	0.7239
	Excellent_Heat_QC	0.3138	0.0617	0.7314
	nbr_clus1	0.5942	0.1607	0.4835
	nbr_clus2	0.5969	0.2262	0.5209
Cluster 2	Total_Bsmt_SF	0.4758	0.2226	0.6744
	Bsmt_Fin_SF	0.4278	0.0212	0.5846
	Lot_Area	0.1457	0.0225	0.8740
	Fireplace_1plus	0.2453	0.1239	0.8615
	CuldeSac	0.0814	0.0145	0.9321
	Land_Level	0.0085	0.0006	0.9921
	Paved_Driveway	0.3161	0.0704	0.7357
	Total_Functionality	0.0392	0.0175	0.9779
	BelowAverage_Quality	0.2471	0.0749	0.8139
	BelowAverage_Condition	0.1027	0.0179	0.9136
	Irreq_Lot_Shape	0.2313	0.0940	0.8484
	C_Air	0.2781	0.0491	0.7592
	nbr_clus3	0.0055	0.0001	0.9946

Cluster 1 will be split because it has the largest second eigenvalue, 1.861523, which is greater than the MAXEIGEN=0.6 value.

Note that of the two clusters created, the largest second eigenvalue occurs for cluster 1 (1.8615), while at the same time exceeding the maximum eigenvalue criterion of 0.60, so cluster 1 is split in the next step.

The splitting continues with the creation of 22 clusters where the largest second eigenvalue (occurring for cluster 1 is 0.603022) is larger than the maximum criterion of 0.60, warranting another split. When 23 clusters are created, the largest second eigenvalue for cluster 13 (0.5962) does not exceed the maximum required level of 0.60, as illustrated in Output 8.4c Cluster Summary for 23 Clusters for Ames Housing Input Data, and the splitting process ends.

The variation explained corresponds to the contribution of the variables in that cluster and not to all of the original variables, as is the case in factor analysis. Finally, note that the sum of the Variation Explained is 28.07205, which means that 23 clusters account for 87.73% (28.07205/32) of the total variance in the original 32 input variables.

Output 8.4c Cluster Summary for 23 Clusters for Ames Housing Input Data

Cluster Summary for 23 Clusters					
Cluster	Members	Cluster Variation	Variation Explained	Proportion Explained	Second Eigenvalue
1	4	4	2.916174	0.7290	0.4423
2	2	2	1.55347	0.7767	0.4465
3	2	2	1.540439	0.7702	0.4596
4	1	1	1	1.0000	
5	1	1	1	1.0000	
6	1	1	1	1.0000	
7	1	1	1	1.0000	
8	3	3	2.033304	0.6778	0.5347
9	1	1	1	1.0000	
10	1	1	1	1.0000	
11	1	1	1	1.0000	
12	1	1	1	1.0000	
13	3	3	2.028662	0.6762	0.5962
14	1	1	1	1.0000	
15	1	1	1	1.0000	
16	1	1	1	1.0000	
17	1	1	1	1.0000	
18	1	1	1	1.0000	
19	1	1	1	1.0000	
20	1	1	1	1.0000	
21	1	1	1	1.0000	
22	1	1	1	1.0000	
23	1	1	1	1.0000	

Total variation explained = 28.07205 Proportion = 0.8773

The cluster summary is then followed by a detailed listing of the final 23 cluster components and the variable assignments within each cluster, along with various statistics, as illustrated in Output 8.4d R-Squared with Own Cluster and Next Closest Cluster for Ames Housing Input Data.

For each variable, the output provides its squared correlation with both its own cluster and the next closest cluster, respectively. For example, AGE_AT_SALE and Cluster 1 have an r-square of 0.7614, while AGE_AT_SALE and its closest cluster have an r-square of 0.3570. The r-square with its own cluster should be larger than that for the nearest cluster. Small r-squared values with the next closest cluster represent relatively well separated clusters. That output is followed by a message indicating that 'no cluster meets the criterion for splitting.'

Output 8.4d R-Squared with Own Cluster and Next Closest Cluster for Ames Housing Input Data

23 Clusters		R-squared with		
Cluster	Variable	Own Cluster	Next Closest	1-R**2 Ratio
Cluster 1	Age_at_Sale	0.7614	0.3570	0.3711
	Poured_Concrete	0.6777	0.3900	0.5285
	nbr_clus1	0.7434	0.3083	0.3710
	nbr_clus2	0.7337	0.4049	0.4474
Cluster 2	Total_Bsmt_SF	0.7767	0.1863	0.2744
	Bsmt_Fin_SF	0.7767	0.3213	0.3289
Cluster 3	Gr_Liv_Area	0.7702	0.4010	0.3836
	Bedroom_AbvGr	0.7702	0.1480	0.2697
Cluster 4	Paved_Driveway	1.0000	0.1239	0.0000
Cluster 5	Bsmt_Unf_SF	1.0000	0.0548	0.0000
Cluster 6	Irreq_Lot_Shape	1.0000	0.1141	0.0000
Cluster 7	Lot_Area	1.0000	0.0692	0.0000
Cluster 8	Fullbath_2plus	0.7205	0.4003	0.4661
	TwoPlusCar_Garage	0.6485	0.2859	0.4922
	AboveAverage_Quality	0.6643	0.2536	0.4498
Cluster 9	Total_Functionality	1.0000	0.0736	0.0000
Cluster 10	Normal_Prox_Cond	1.0000	0.0240	0.0000
Cluster 11	nbr_clus3	1.0000	0.0056	0.0000
Cluster 12	AboveAverage_Condition	1.0000	0.2718	0.0000
Cluster 13	High_Kitchen_Quality	0.7197	0.2899	0.3947
	High_Exterior_Qual	0.7362	0.3951	0.4361
	Excellent_Heat_QC	0.5727	0.2110	0.5415
Cluster 14	Has_Fence	1.0000	0.0600	0.0000
Cluster 15	Fireplace_1plus	1.0000	0.1707	0.0000
Cluster 16	Land_Level	1.0000	0.0370	0.0000
Cluster 17	BelowAverage_Quality	1.0000	0.1026	0.0000
Cluster 18	BelowAverage_Condition	1.0000	0.0736	0.0000
Cluster 19	High_Exterior_Cond	1.0000	0.0780	0.0000
Cluster 20	CuldeSac	1.0000	0.1141	0.0000
Cluster 21	C_Air	1.0000	0.1239	0.0000
Cluster 22	One_Floor	1.0000	0.2159	0.0000
Cluster 23	Vinyl_Siding	1.0000	0.3742	0.0000

No cluster meets the criterion for splitting.

The last table created by the VARCLUS procedure is displayed in Output 8.4e Summary of Cluster Splitting by Stage. It gives a summary of key indices for each stage of the splitting process, starting with cluster 1 and ending with cluster 23, specifically the proportion of variance explained at each point and the maximum second eigenvalue among the clusters. So, while the algorithm provides for 23 clusters, the additional statistics, complemented by the dendrogram in Output 8.4f Dendrogram Illustration of Cluster Splits for Ames Housing Input Data, and subject-matter expertise can be used to force fewer clusters or allow more clusters.

To do this, the analyst can try various values for the maximum eigenvalue. If the eigenvalue threshold for splitting is reduced, the number of clusters will obviously increase; consequently, if the threshold is increased, the number of clusters will decrease. Note that the common practice is to use a value of 1.0; however, a value of 0.70 is suggested to account for sampling variability (Jackson, 1991).

Notice that in our example, we used MAXEIGEN=0.60 because it provided for four additional clusters. As a result, we selected the variables that best represent those additional clusters, because univariate chi-square tests indicated a relationship with our target variable, BONUS.

Output 8.4e Summary of Cluster Splitting by Stage

Number of Clusters	Total Variation Explained by Clusters	Proportion of Variation Explained by Clusters	Minimum Proportion Explained by a Cluster	Maximum Second Eigenvalue in a Cluster	Minimum R-squared for a Variable	Maximum 1-R**2 Ratio for a Variable
1	7.665278	0.2395	0.2395	2.273223	0.0000	
2	9.318410	0.2912	0.2003	1.861523	0.0055	0.9946
3	10.782647	0.3370	0.2003	1.580090	0.0055	0.9990
4	12.144808	0.3795	0.2667	1.277230	0.0076	0.9970
5	13.201264	0.4125	0.2667	1.199255	0.0076	0.9970
6	14.336373	0.4480	0.3097	1.037528	0.0237	0.9807
7	15.334638	0.4792	0.3667	1.030320	0.0268	0.9792
8	16.188235	0.5059	0.3667	1.013512	0.0348	0.9712
9	17.171782	0.5366	0.3767	0.995020	0.0348	0.9712
10	18.144308	0.5670	0.3767	0.984173	0.0893	0.9149
11	19.127675	0.5977	0.3767	0.963315	0.2945	0.8158
12	20.055136	0.6267	0.5152	0.851749	0.3235	0.8158
13	20.846620	0.6515	0.5152	0.845288	0.3235	0.8158
14	21.691908	0.6779	0.5152	0.839398	0.3235	0.8158
15	22.525565	0.7039	0.5152	0.807658	0.4048	0.6632
16	23.333223	0.7292	0.5152	0.806703	0.4048	0.6632
17	24.139607	0.7544	0.6357	0.728683	0.5484	0.6346
18	24.868290	0.7771	0.6358	0.720631	0.5484	0.6346
19	25.588921	0.7997	0.6358	0.662151	0.5484	0.6346
20	26.251072	0.8203	0.6358	0.647995	0.5484	0.6346
21	26.899067	0.8406	0.6358	0.637553	0.5484	0.6346
22	27.532155	0.8604	0.6753	0.603022	0.5484	0.6346
23	28.072048	0.8773	0.6762	0.596157	0.5727	0.5415

Output 8.4f Dendrogram Illustration of Cluster Splits for Ames Housing Input Data

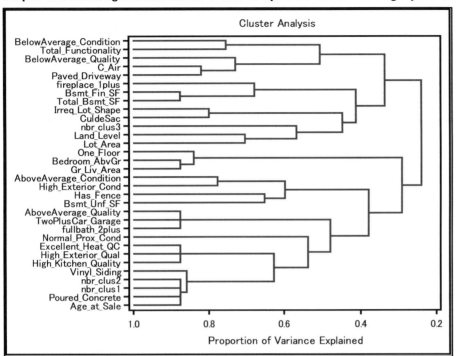

Cluster Representative and Best Variable Selection

While the analyst could use the 23 principal component scores as the 'new' inputs, a common practice is to select a single variable from each cluster that best represents that cluster, therefore ending with a reduced set of 23 inputs. In order to select the representative variable, the analyst can use the 1-R² ratio, which is defined as:

$$1 - R^2 ratio = \frac{1 - R^2_{own\ cluster}}{1 - R^2_{next\ closest}}$$

As a general rule, when looking at a particular cluster, the best variable representation is that one having the smallest 1-R² ratio. The occurs when its relationship with its own cluster is highest, as measured by $R^2_{own\ cluster}$, and its relationship with the nearest cluster is lowest, as measured by $R^2_{next\ closest}$ --in other words, when the numerator is closest to zero and its denominator is closest to 1.0.

So, consider cluster 2 for example. The variable with the smallest 1-R² ratio (0.2744) is the variable total area of basement space (TOTAL_BSMT_SF) as shown in Output 8.4d R-Squared with Own Cluster and Next Closest Cluster for Ames Housing Input Data; therefore, the analyst would select that variable for subsequent analyses and omit the variable BSMT_FIN_SF, total area of finished basement space. It makes good common sense that those two variables are related, further supported by the relatively large R² of 0.7767 and, as such, eliminating one-variable results in a relatively small loss of information.

Now consider cluster 3, made up of the two variables, GR_LIV_AREA and BEDROOM_ABVGR. While BEDROOM_ABVGR has the smallest 1-R² ratio (0.2697), it is common knowledge that an industry standard is to price homes according to square footage; therefore, we will select GR_LIV_AREA to represent cluster 3 and eliminate BEDROOM_ABVGR from subsequent analyses.

Finally, for cluster 8, we selected the variable, FULLBATH2_PLUS, which indicates whether or not the house had two or more full bathrooms, as opposed to the binary variable, ABOVEAVERAGE_QUALITY. While quality is certainly important, we thought that the number of full bathrooms is easy to measure and probably pretty accurate, whereas, quality ratings may be more subjective.

After reviewing the 1-R² ratio and considering variables that made more sense, we will proceed with the following set of potential input variables, as listed in Table 8.4 Reduced Set of Inputs After Deleting Redundant Variables for Ames Housing.

Table 8.4 Reduced Set of Inputs After Deleting Redundant Variables for Ames Housing

From Cluster	Selected Input	R-squared with Own Cluster	R-squared with Next Closest	1-R**2 Ratio
Cluster 1	Age_at_Sale	0.7614	0.357	0.3711
Cluster 2	Total_Bsmt_SF	0.7767	0.1863	0.2744
Cluster 3	Gr_Liv_Area	0.7702	0.4010	0.3836
Cluster 4	Paved_Driveway	1.0000	0.1239	0.0000
Cluster 5	Bsmt_Unf_SF	1.0000	0.0548	0.0000
Cluster 6	Irreq_Lot_Shape	1.0000	0.1141	0.0000
Cluster 7	Lot_Area	1.0000	0.0692	0.0000
Cluster 8	Fullbath_2plus	0.7205	0.4003	0.4661
Cluster 9	Total_Functionality	1.0000	0.0736	0.0000
Cluster 10	Normal_Prox_Cond	1.0000	0.0240	0.0000
Cluster 11	nbr_clus3	1.0000	0.0056	0.0000
Cluster 12	AboveAverage_Condition	1.0000	0.2718	0.0000
Cluster 13	High_Kitchen_Quality	0.7191	0.2899	0.3947
Cluster 14	Has_Fence	1.0000	0.0600	0.0000
Cluster 15	Fireplace_1plus	1.0000	0.1707	0.0000
Cluster 16	Land_Level	1.0000	0.0370	0.0000
Cluster 17	BelowAverage_Quality	1.0000	0.1026	0.0000
Cluster 18	BelowAverage_Condition	1.0000	0.0736	0.0000
Cluster 19	High_Exterior_Cond	1.0000	0.0780	0.0000
Cluster 20	CuldeSac	1.0000	0.1141	0.0000
Cluster 21	C_Air	1.0000	0.1239	0.0000
Cluster 22	One_Floor	1.0000	0.2159	0.0000
Cluster 23	Vinyl_Siding	1.0000	0.3742	0.0000

Variable Screening

As mentioned earlier, the analyst should take into account both relevancy and redundancy. Using the VARCLUS procedure and some subject-matter expertise in the previous section, we have arrived at a reduced set of 23 potential inputs in an attempt to address the redundancy problem.

Now, we will review methods for detecting irrelevance. A simple approach for detecting relevance, or the association between two variables, is the Pearson correlation coefficient, as described in Chapter 9, "Linear Regression Analysis." However, this coefficient measures only linear relationships, requires variables to be measured at either interval or ratio levels, and is influenced by outliers. Therefore, in this section, we will discuss the use of alternative indices for measuring associations which take into account the form of the data at hand. These indices are Spearman's correlation and Hoeffding's D statistic for measuring association, or relevancy, with the target.

Once the final input variables are determined, they should also be analyzed to determine if there are any non-linear associations.

The CORR Procedure for Detecting Associations

The **Spearman's rank-order correlation coefficient** ranges from -1.0 to +1.0 and is a measure of the strength and direction of the monotonic relationship between two ranked variables; **monotonic** refers to the fact that the direction of the relationship never changes and is either always positive, always negative, or always constant.

In order to obtain the Spearman's correlation coefficient between two variables, X and Y, the observations must be ranked by X and ranked by Y, respectively; then the ranks are correlated. So, if observations have similar ranks on X and Y, the coefficient is positive. If their ranks are dissimilar, then the coefficient is negative. Correlating ranks results in an index that is less sensitive to both non-linear relationships and outliers.

Hoeffding's D statistic (Hoeffding, 1948) is also a rank-based approach to measuring associations, whether linear, monotonic, or non-monotonic. Note that a linear trend is monotonic, but a monotonic trend is not always linear. So, for example, exponential and logarithmic functions are monotonic; a parabolic function across the domain of real numbers is non-monotonic.

Hoeffding's D ranges from -0.50 to +1.0, and while the sign has no meaning, larger values indicate the strength of the relationship. An advantage of using Hoeffding's D is that it will detect non-monotonic relationships that can go undetected using Spearman's coefficient.

So, consider a target variable (Y) and a potential predictor (X). If both the Spearman's correlation coefficient and Hoeffding's D are relatively small (or statistically zero as measured by their respective large p-values), then there is evidence that X has no association with Y. In short, a relatively large p-value for Spearman's correlation coefficient indicates that there is no monotonic relationship; and a relatively large p-value for Hoeffding's D indicates that there is no relationship--monotonic, non-monotonic, nor linear.

A visualization tool which utilizes both indices for detecting associations, or irrelevance, is a scatterplot of the rank of Spearman's coefficient by the rank of the Hoeffding's D. To illustrate, consider the Ames Housing Case and Program 8.5 Description of Input Variables Screened for Relevance for Ames Housing Data described in parts.

Program 8.5 Description of Input Variables Screened for Relevance for Ames Housing Data

```
********Part A which produces Output8.5a and Output8.5b******;
libname sasba 'c:\sasba\ames';
data ames70;
   set sasba.ames70;
   AboveAverage_Quality=0; BelowAverage_Quality=0;
   AboveAverage_Condition=0; BelowAverage_Condition=0;
   if Overall_Quality=3 then AboveAverage_Quality=1;
   if Overall_Quality=1 then BelowAverage_Quality=1;
   if Overall_Condition=3 then AboveAverage_Condition=1;
   if Overall_Condition=1 then BelowAverage_Condition=1;
   if Heating_QC="Ex" then Excellent_Heat_QC=1;
      if Heating_QC="Gd" or Heating_QC="Fa" or Heating_QC="TA"
      then Excellent_Heat_QC=0;
   if Lot_Shape="IRR" then Irreq_Lot_Shape=1;
      if Lot_Shape="Reg" then Irreq_Lot_Shape=0;
   if Central_Air="Y" then C_Air=1;
      if Central_Air="N" then C_Air=0;
   nbr_clus1=0; nbr_clus2=0; nbr_clus3=0;
   if neighborhood="NoRidge" or neighborhood="NridgHt" or
      neighborhood="Somerst" or neighborhood="StoneBr" or
      neighborhood="Timber" or neighborhood="Veenker" or
      neighborhood="CollgCr" or neighborhood="Gilbert" or
      neighborhood="ClearCr" then nbr_clus1=1;
   if neighborhood="NAmes" or neighborhood="SWISU" or
      neighborhood="IDOTRR" or neighborhood="OldTown" or
      neighborhood="Edwards" or neighborhood="BrkSide" or
      neighborhood="Sawyer" then nbr_clus2=1;
   if neighborhood="Mitchel" then nbr_clus3=1;
**********define reduced set with 23 inputs*********;
%let reducedset=Age_at_Sale Total_Bsmt_SF Gr_Liv_Area Paved_Driveway
   Bsmt_Unf_SF Irreq_Lot_Shape Lot_Area Fullbath_2plus
   Total_Functionality Normal_Prox_Cond nbr_clus3 AboveAverage_Condition
```

```
      High_Kitchen_Quality Has_Fence Fireplace_1plus Land_Level
      BelowAverage_Quality BelowAverage_Condition High_Exterior_Cond
      CuldeSac C_Air One_Floor Vinyl_Siding;
ods output spearmancorr=spearman
          hoeffdingcorr=hoeffding;
run;

proc corr data=ames70 spearman hoeffding rank;
   var &reducedset;
   with bonus;
   title 'Spearman and Hoeffding Correlation Coefficients';
run;

proc print data=spearman;
   title 'ODS Output of Spearman Data';
run;

********Part B which produces Output8.5c******;


data spearmanrank (keep=variable scorr spvalue ranksp);
   length variable $25;
   set spearman;
   array best(*) best1 -- best23;
   array r(*) r1 -- r23;
   array p(*) p1 -- p23;
   do i = 1 to 23;
     variable=best(i);
      scorr=r(i);
      spvalue=p(i);
      ranksp=i;
      output;
      end;
run;

data hoeffdingrank (keep=variable hcorr hpvalue rankhoeff);
   length variable $25;
   set hoeffding;
   array best(*) best1 -- best23;
   array r(*) r1 -- r23;
   array p(*) p1 -- p23;
   do i = 1 to 23;
      variable=best(i);
      hcorr=r(i);
      hpvalue=p(i);
      rankhoeff=i;
      output;
      end;
run;

proc sort data=spearmanrank; by variable;
proc sort data=hoeffdingrank; by variable;
run;

data final;
  merge spearmanrank hoeffdingrank;
  by variable;
proc sort data=final;
  by ranksp;
run;

proc print data=final;
   var variable ranksp rankhoeff scorr spvalue hcorr hpvalue;
   title 'Spearman and Hoeffding D Correlation Data Sorted by Spearman Rank';
run;

********Part C which produces Output8.5d******;
proc sgplot data=final;
   refline 23 / axis=y;
   refline 16 / axis=x;
   scatter y=ranksp x=rankhoeff / datalabel=variable;
```

```
   yaxis label = "Rank of Spearman Correlation";
   xaxis label = "Rank of Hoeffding Correlation";
   title 'Ranks of Spearman Correlations by Ranks of Hoeffding Correlations';
run;
```

In Part A of Program 8.5 Description of Input Variables Screened for Relevance for Ames Housing Data, the AMES70 data set is read, new variables are created, the reduced set of 23 input variables is defined using the %LET REDUCEDSET=, and the CORR procedure is applied to that reduced set. Specifically note that both correlation coefficients are computed by including the SPEARMAN and HOEFFDING options; those measure the relationship between the reduced set of input variables and the target variable, BONUS, as requested by the WITH statement.

The output includes a summary of the variables included in the analysis as displayed in Output 8.5a Summary of Input Variables Screened for Relevance for Ames Housing Data, and a list of all requested correlation coefficients, which will not be included here. That information is needed, however, for subsequent analyses, so the output generated from the CORR procedure is saved in the two files, SPEARMAN and HOEFFDING, each containing the respective correlation coefficients, as defined in the ODS OUTPUT statement. The PRINT procedure is used here to illustrate the structure of the data set which is displayed in Output 8.5b ODS Output of Spearman Data.

Output 8.5a Summary of Input Variables Screened for Relevance for Ames Housing Data

1 With Variables:	Bonus			
23 Variables:	Age_at_Sale	Total_Bsmt_SF	Gr_Liv_Area	Paved_Driveway
	Bsmt_Unf_SF	Irreq_Lot_Shape	Lot_Area	Fullbath_2plus
	Total_Functionality	Normal_Prox_Cond	nbr_clus3	
	AboveAverage_Condition	High_Kitchen_Quality	Has_Fence	
	Fireplace_1plus	Land_Level	BelowAverage_Quality	
	BelowAverage_Condition	High_Exterior_Cond	CuldeSac	
	One_Floor	Vinyl_Siding	C_Air	

In Output 8.5b ODS Output of Spearman Data, the target variable, Bonus, is listed under the column heading, Variable, and the input variables are assigned to variables names, Best1 to Best23, indicating the order of magnitude of the Spearman's correlation coefficient. The coefficients and associated p-values are assigned to the variable names R1 to R23 and P1 to P23, respectively. This data is contained in one row as one observation.

Note that the input variable, FULLBATH_2PLUS, which has the largest correlation with the target variable, BONUS, is assigned to the variable, Best1, with a Spearman correlation coefficient of R1 = 0.69311, and smallest p-value represented by P1 < .0001; whereas the input variable with the weakest correlation is NBR_CLUS3, assigned to the variable Best23, with correlation coefficient R23 = -0.03228 and p-value P23 = 0.2292. Keep in mind that the data set, HOEFFDING, created using ODS OUTPUT has the same one-row structure.

Output 8.5b ODS Output of Spearman Data

Obs	Variable	Best1	Best2	Best3	Best4
1	Bonus	Fullbath_2plus	Gr_Liv_Area	Age_at_Sale	High_Kitchen_Quality

Obs	Best5	Best6	Best7	Best8	Best9
1	Total_Bsmt_SF	Vinyl_Siding	Lot_Area	fireplace_1plus	AboveAverage_Condition

Obs	Best10	Best11	Best12	Best13	Best14
1	Irreq_Lot_Shape	BelowAverage_Quality	Has_Fence	Paved_Driveway	C_Air

Obs	Best15	Best16	Best17	Best18	Best19
1	BelowAverage_Condition	CuldeSac	One_Floor	Bsmt_Unf_SF	Normal_Prox_Cond

Obs	Best20	Best21	Best22	Best23	R1	R2
1	Total_Functionality	High_Exterior_Cond	Land_Level	nbr_clus3	0.69311	0.68632

Obs	R3	R4	R5	R6	R7	R8	R9	R10
1	-0.60139	0.57537	0.44553	0.42397	0.42184	0.41753	-0.32587	0.31056

Obs	R11	R12	R13	R14	R15	R16	R17	R18
1	-0.23791	-0.21988	0.20885	0.16156	-0.13948	0.13861	-0.13734	0.13506

Obs	R19	R20	R21	R22	R23	P1	P2	P3	P4
1	0.12976	0.08453	-0.07683	-0.05089	-0.03228	<.0001	<.0001	<.0001	<.0001

Obs	P5	P6	P7	P8	P9	P10	P11	P12	P13	P14
1	<.0001	<.0001	<.0001	<.0001	<.0001	<.0001	<.0001	<.0001	<.0001	<.0001

Obs	P15	P16	P17	P18	P19	P20	P21	P22	P23
1	<.0001	<.0001	<.0001	<.0001	<.0001	0.0016	0.0042	0.0579	0.2292

Part B of Program 8.5 Description of Input Variables Screened for Relevance for Ames Housing Data is used to convert the Spearman and Hoeffding data to columns and merge them to create one final data set. First, the Spearman's data is saved to a temporary SAS data set, called SPEARMANRANK, and then three arrays, each with a dimension of 23, are created for assigning each of the 23 variable names, correlation coefficients, and p-values, respectively.

The DO loop assigns each of the variables, Best1 through Best23, to the variable, called VARIABLE. The Spearman's correlation coefficients, R1 though R23, are assigned to the variable, SCORR, and the p-values are assigned to the variable SPVALUE. Because the variables are in order from best to worse, the index *i* is identical to the rank and is saved as the variable, RANKSP. For each value of *i* from 1 to 23, variables are assigned and then output to the SPEARMANRANK data set; therefore, at the end of the loop, the data set has 23 observations, one for each of the four variables.

The data set, HOEFFDINGRANK, is created in the same way using a DO loop, and will result in the variables, VARIABLE, HCORR, HPVALUE, RANKHOEFF, corresponding to the variables names, correlation coefficients, p-values, and ranks. It contains 23 observations.

Next, both data sets are sorted by VARIABLE, and then merged by VARIABLE into the final data set, called FINAL. The data set is then sorted and printed by the rank of the Spearman's correlation coefficient, RANKSP, as displayed in Output 8.5c Spearman's and Hoeffding's D Correlation Data Sorted by Spearman's Rank.

Upon inspection of the correlation data in Output 8.5c Spearman's and Hoeffding's D Correlation Data Sorted by Spearman's Rank, it is evident that the top ten variables are related to the target, BONUS, basically having p-values of zero. In fact, if a variable has relatively high correlations with the target using both Spearman's and Hoeffding's D coefficients--corresponding to low values on RANKSP and RANKHOEFF, respectively--that variable is deemed monotonically related, or relevant, to the target and retained for subsequent analyses. If a variable has relatively low correlations with the target, corresponding to high values on both RANKSP and RANKHOEFF, that variable is considered irrelevant and excluded from subsequent analyses.

Output 8.5c Spearman's and Hoeffding's D Correlation Data Sorted by Spearman's Rank

Obs	Variable	ranks p	rankhoeff	scorr	spvalue	hcorr	hpvalue
1	Fullbath_2plus	1	3	0.69311	0.00000	0.053415	0.00001
2	Gr_Liv_Area	2	1	0.68632	0.00000	0.087528	0.00001
3	Age_at_Sale	3	2	-0.60139	0.00000	0.070234	0.00001
4	High_Kitchen_Quality	4	4	0.57537	0.00000	0.035920	0.00001
5	Total_Bsmt_SF	5	5	0.44553	0.00000	0.035561	0.00001
6	Vinyl_Siding	6	8	0.42397	0.00000	0.017192	0.00001
7	Lot_Area	7	6	0.42184	0.00000	0.031046	0.00001
8	Fireplace_1plus	8	7	0.41753	0.00000	0.018828	0.00001
9	AboveAverage_Condition	9	9	-0.32587	0.00000	0.011161	0.00001
10	Irreq_Lot_Shape	10	10	0.31056	0.00000	0.009685	0.00001
11	BelowAverage_Quality	11	14	-0.23791	0.00000	0.001141	0.01416
12	Has_Fence	12	11	-0.21988	0.00000	0.003197	0.00009
13	Paved_Driveway	13	15	0.20885	0.00000	0.000773	0.03705
14	C_Air	14	17	0.16156	0.00000	-0.000352	0.96679
15	BelowAverage_Condition	15	19	-0.13948	0.00000	-0.000593	1.00000
16	CuldeSac	16	18	0.13861	0.00000	-0.000371	0.98445
17	One_Floor	17	13	-0.13734	0.00000	0.001357	0.00817
18	Bsmt_Unf_SF	18	12	0.13506	0.00000	0.002738	0.00028
19	Normal_Prox_Cond	19	16	0.12976	0.00000	0.000041	0.31818
20	Total_Functionality	20	21	0.08453	0.00162	-0.000723	1.00000
21	High_Exterior_Cond	21	20	-0.07683	0.00417	-0.000610	1.00000
22	Land_Level	22	22	-0.05089	0.05792	-0.000836	1.00000
23	nbr_clus3	23	23	-0.03228	0.22922	-0.000970	1.00000

The question then becomes: What are the criteria for determining irrelevance? In general, if a variable has p-values for both Spearman's correlation coefficient and Hoeffding's D greater than .50, then that variable and all variables with higher ranks on both should be reviewed for possible exclusion from further analysis (SAS Institute, 2012; Canes, 2014). Keep in mind that the final decision to eliminate an input variable is subjective and should consider the business context.

For illustration purposes, we will use p> 0.20 as the criterion. An inspection of the correlation data reveals that the one variable, NBR_CLUS3, has a Spearman's p-value of 0.2292 which is the largest p-value with rank 23. When reviewing Hoeffding's D, note that eight variables have a p-value greater than .20; the lowest rank of those eight is 16.

A plot of the Spearman's and Hoeffding's ranks can be used to visualize the ranks and is generated using the SGPLOT in Part C of Program 8.5 Description of Input Variables Screened for Relevance for Ames Housing Data.

The SGPLOT procedure is applied to the FINAL data set, where the rank of Hoeffding's D represents the x-axis and the rank of the Spearman's correlation coefficient represents the y-axis. The DATALABEL option requests that the data points be represented by the variable name for ease of identification. A reference line for the x-axis is inserted at X=16 and one for the y-axis is inserted at Y=23, each identifying the rank where the p-value exceeds 0.20.

In Output 8.5d Rank of Spearman's Correlation by Rank of Hoeffding's D, it is easy to identify the eight variables that have Hoeffding p-values greater than 0.20 as those variables are listed either on or to the right of the reference line at X=16. Again, only one variable has Spearman's p-value greater than 0.20, namely NBR_CLUS3, as it either on or above the reference line at Y=23.

Output 8.5d Rank of Spearman's Correlation by Rank of Hoeffding's D

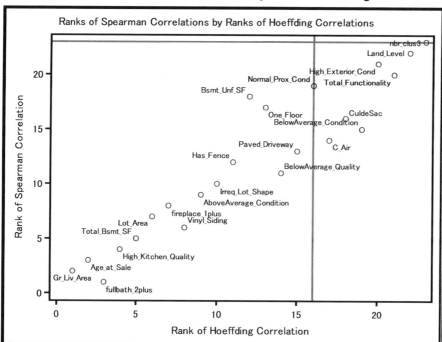

In general, any variable that is either in the top right region or on its borders should be eliminated from further analyses because of its irrelevance to the target. In our example, the variable, NBR_CLUS3, will be eliminated from subsequent analyses because it has no monotonic relationship with the target, as measured by Spearman's correlation coefficient, and at the same time, appears to have no relationship (monotonic, non-monotonic, nor linear) with the target as measured by Hoeffding's D.

If a variable has a point on the plot that tends to fall above the trend of the other points, indicating a relatively low rank for Hoeffding's D and a relatively high rank for Spearman, there may be a non-monotonic relationship between the input variable and the target. In other words, Hoeffding's D may detect a non-monotonic relationship that is not, as stated earlier, detected by the Spearman correlation coefficient.

In any event, the analyst should follow up with the empirical logit plot to determine if there are any input variables which may have a non-linear relationship with the target. From Output 8.5d Rank of Spearman's Correlation by Rank of Hoeffding's D, we see that the point for variable, BSMT_UNF_SF, falls slightly above the trend of the other points. Therefore, in the next section, we will investigate that variable for non-linear association with the target variable.

Using the Empirical Logit to Detect Non-Linear Associations

As illustrated in Chapter 9, "Linear Regression Analysis," residual plots are created to check the assumptions of linear regression. Because logistic regression is based upon a binary target variable, a plot using the target variable would be useless. However, recall that for logistic regression, it is assumed that the logit is a linear combination of predictors, defined as:

$$logit(p_i) = ln\left(\frac{p_i}{1-p_i}\right) = \beta_0 + \beta_1 X_{1i} + \beta_2 X_{2i} + \cdots + \beta_{pi} X_{pi}$$

where p_i is the probability of success. Therefore, the analyst can use the plot of the logit by the predictor to assess the nature of the relationship. Note that the logit is undefined when $p_i = 0$ or $p_i = 1$. Therefore the analyst must review, instead, the **empirical logit** for each quantile of the input variable under investigation. The empirical logit chosen for this book is defined as:

$$ln\left(\frac{m_i + \frac{\sqrt{M_i}}{2}}{M_i - m_i + \frac{\sqrt{M_i}}{2}}\right)$$

where M_i represents the total number of observations in bin i, m_i represents the number of observations in the event of interest for bin i, and $(M_i - m_i)$ represents the number of observations not in the event of interest for bin i (Santer and Duffy, 1989). Note that $p_i / (1-p_i)$ reduces to $m_i/(M_i - m_i)$ and $\sqrt{M_i}/2$ is included in the term to avoid an undefined logit when $p_i = 0$ or $p_i = 1$.

In order to produce an empirical logit plot, the analyst would use Program 8.6 Plot of Empirical Logit by Bsmt_Unf_SF.

Program 8.6 Plot of Empirical Logit by Bsmt_Unf_SF

```
libname sasba 'c:\sasba\ames';
data ames70;
   set sasba.ames70;
run;

proc rank data=ames70 groups=100 out=outrank;
  var Bsmt_Unf_SF;
  ranks bin;
run;

proc print data=outrank (obs=10);
  var Bsmt_Unf_SF bin;run;

proc means data=outrank noprint nway;
   class bin;
   var bonus Bsmt_Unf_SF;
   output out=bins sum(bonus)=bonus mean(Bsmt_Unf_SF)=Bsmt_Unf_SF;
run;

proc sort data=bins; by bin;
run;

proc print data=bins;
run;

data bins;
   set bins;
   elogit=log((bonus+(sqrt(_FREQ_)/2))/(_FREQ_ - bonus+(sqrt(_FREQ_)/2)));
 run;

proc sgplot data=bins;
   reg y=elogit x=Bsmt_Unf_SF/degree=2;
   series y=elogit x=Bsmt_Unf_SF;
   title 'Empirical Logit by Bsmt_Unf_SF';
run;
```

In order to create the bins, the RANK procedure is applied to the AMES70 data set so that all observations are ordered by the variable, BSMT_UNF_SF, as defined in the VAR statement. The GROUPS=100 option requests that the variable, BSMT_UNF_SF, be partitioned into 100 equal parts of equal size, which is equivalent to dividing the variable into percentiles. If the number of tied values exceeds the bin size, the bin size is increased so that all ties are in the same bin.

The values of the ranks are saved for each observation in the variable, called BIN, as requested in the RANKS statement; this variable is saved in the output data set, OUTRANK. In our case, the ranks range from 0 to 99, where the maximum of 99 is defined as the number of groups (GROUPS=100) minus 1.

The RANK procedure creates no output. However, you can see the ranks of BSMT_UNF_SF for the first eight houses of the Ames data using a PRINT procedure on the OUTRANK data set, as displayed in Output 8.6a Value of Bsmt_Unf_SF and Bin Variables for the First Eight Houses in Ames Housing. The output indicates, for example, that the first house has 270 square feet of unfinished basement area and is contained in the 30th bin (bin=29).

Output 8.6a Value of Bsmt_Unf_SF and Bin Variables for the First Eight Houses in Ames Housing

Obs	Bsmt_Unf_SF	bin
1	270	29
2	406	43
3	663	66
4	744	72
5	0	3
6	432	46
7	702	69
8	432	46
9	381	40
10	678	68

The MEANS procedure is applied to the variables BONUS and BSMT_UNF_SF in the OUTRANK data set for each bin as defined by the CLASS statement and the NWAY option. The new data set, called BINS, will contain the variable, BONUS, which is a count of the observations in that bin that have received a bonus (BONUS=1), and the variable, BSMT_UNF_SF, which is the mean of the unfinished basement square footage for that bin.

Note that the variable, BONUS, will be used as the value of m_i for that bin and the x-coordinate for the empirical logit plot will be the mean of the bin, BSMT_UNF_SF. The PRINT procedure is called to provide an excerpt of the listing of the data set, BINS, and is displayed in Output 8.6b Total Frequency, Number of Houses Earning a Bonus, and Average Bsmt_Unf_SF by Bin.

Output 8.6b Total Frequency, Number of Houses Earning a Bonus, and Average Bsmt_Unf_SF by Bin

Obs	bin	_TYPE_	_FREQ_	bonus	Bsmt_Unf_SF
1	3	1	99	20	0
2	7	1	12	3	28.25
3	8	1	13	6	54.461538462
4	9	1	12	6	74.5
5	10	1	16	12	85.5625
...	...	...	...	...	...
93	98	1	14	12	1649.2142857
94	99	1	13	13	1864.6153846

A review of Output 8.6b Total Frequency, Number of Houses Earning a Bonus, and Average Bsmt_Unf_SF by Bin shows, for example, that bin 9 has twelve houses with an average of 74.5 square feet of unfinished basement areas where half (BONUS=6) earned bonuses. The last bin contained 13 houses with an average of 1864.6 square feet of unfinished basement area where all (BONUS=13) earned bonuses. Note that all bins have essentially the same size, except bin 3, which has 99 houses. This occurred because there were 99 houses that had no unfinished basements (BSMT_UNF_SF=0); and because ties are assigned to the same bin, those houses were assigned to bin 3. Note also that because that bin is so large, bin 3 takes the place of all bins, 1 through 6.

Finally, the empirical logit, called ELOGIT, is calculated using the formula above, and the SGPLOT procedure is used to plot BSMT_UNF_SF, the mean of the unfinished basement square footage on the x-axis and the empirical logit on the y-axis. Initially, a straight line was fit to the data; however, after noting that the trend seemed to dip and then increase, we decided that a curvilinear trend fit the data best, as displayed in Output 8.6c Empirical Logit by the Variable Bsmt_Unf_SF.

Output 8.6c Empirical Logit by the Variable Bsmt_Unf_SF

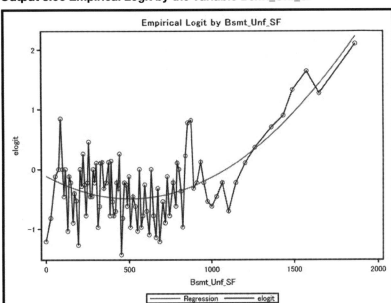

There are some things to consider before interpreting the plot. First, the binning of the input variable essentially splits the x-axis into 100 equal parts, where the average of BSMT_UNF_SF is used to represent the value of the bin. Given a specific bin (or average BSMT_UNF_SF), if the proportion of the event of interest is larger than the non-event ($p_1 > p_0$), then the empirical logit is positive; whereas if the proportion of the event of interest is smaller than the non-event ($p_1 < p_0$), then the empirical logit is negative. Finally, if $p_1 = p_0$, then the empirical logit is approximately zero.

Note the spike at the fifth point on the plot (bin=10); this occurs because $m_1 = 12$ and $(1-m_1) = 4$, or $p_1=.75$ and $p_0=.25$; in other words, there are a lot more houses where a bonus was earned. Note also the downward spike at bin=48; this drop occurs $m_1 = 2$ and $(1-m_1) = 15$, or $p_1=.12$ and $p_0=.88$; in other words, there are a lot more houses where a bonus was not earned.

In general, if the analyst expects the proportion of the event to increase as the input variable increases, then the empirical logit should increase. This is certainly not the case for our variable, BSMT_UNF_SF. In fact, a bivariate histogram of BSMT_UNF_SF by BONUS seems to indicate that the homes that receive a bonus are not discriminated from those not receiving a bonus until the unfinished basements reach much larger sizes. This seems to be the case, as seen in Output 8.6c Empirical Logit by the Variable Bsmt_Unf_SF, where there is a consistent increase in the empirical logit from bin 92 to 99.

In conclusion, the relationship is certainly not linear. The relationship does not seem to be monotonic either because it changes direction; in other words, the empirical logit is decreasing and then starts to increase as BSMT_UNF_SF increases. Remedies include transforming the input which may not be practical when there are a large number of inputs, and also impedes interpretation.

In this particular example, it could be a sign that interaction exists. It could be that there are other characteristics that play into the sale price (which determines bonus) for homes with smaller or no unfinished basements; however, once the unfinished basement becomes sizable, a larger sale price is commanded, thereby ensuring a bonus.

Finally, recall in the section on variable reduction, we opted to use TOTAL_BSMT_SF for Cluster 2 and drop the variable, BSMT_FIN_SF, the finished basement square footage. TOTAL_BSMT_SF includes the area of both finished and unfinished basements, so it makes sense to drop BSMT_UNF_SF as well.

As a result of screening for redundancy and irrelevancy, in addition to using some subjectivity, the initial list of inputs is reduced from 29 variables to 21. These variables certainly take into account all characteristics of a house that go into establishing a value, thereby determining BONUS. Those variables are:

Age_at_Sale, Total_Bsmt_SF, Gr_Liv_Area, Paved_Driveway, Irreq_Lot_Shape, Lot_Area, Fullbath_2plus, Total_Functionality, Normal_Prox_Cond, AboveAverage_Condition, High_Kitchen_Quality, Has_Fence,

Fireplace_1plus, Land_Level, BelowAverage_Quality, BelowAverage_Condition, High_Exterior_Cond, CuldeSac, C_Air, One_Floor, Vinyl_Siding.

We would like to add that a plot of the empirical logit by the input variable AGE_AT_SALE was created to assess other relationships. The plot shows a monotonic (curvilinear) decreasing relationship with BONUS which flattens as the age of the home increases. In short, as the age at sale increases, the proportion of houses where a bonus is earned decreases, resulting in a decrease in the logit; however, as the house gets older, the decrease slows.

Key Terms

bin	missing value indicator variable
complete-case analysis	monotonic
curse of dimensionality	not missing at random (NMAR)
data preparation	outliers
dendrogram	overfitting
eigenvalue	predictive modeling
empirical logit	principal component analysis
Greenacre's method	quasi-complete separation
high dimensionality	rare event
Hoeffding's D statistic	redundant
imputation	sparse
information leakage	Spearman's rank-order correlation coefficient
irrelevant	target variable
listwise deletion	training data set
missing completely at random (MCAR)	validation data set
missing data	

Chapter Quiz

1. Which of the following problems must be addressed when preparing data for predictive modeling?
    a. model validation
    b. quasi-complete-complete separation
    c. scoring new data
    d. delete all variables with missing data

2. Suppose an analyst is interested in using the categorical variable, HOUSE_STYLE (with the levels 1-Story, 1-1/2 Story with second level finished, 1-1/2 Story with second level unfinished, 2-Story, Split Foyer, Split Level), to predict the binary target variable, BONUS, but wants to first combine the levels using the Greenacre method. Which of the following procedures is used to generate the proportions of the target variable for each level of the variable, HOUSE_STYLE?
    a. proc freq; table Bonus*House_Style/chisq;
    b. proc varclus; var House_Style; by Bonus;
    c. proc means; class House_Style; var Bonus;
    d. proc corr; var House_Style; with Bonus;

3. As a result of the Greenacre method, suppose the analyst collapses the input variable, HOUSE_STYLE, into three new categories: one story, more than one story, and split floor plan. The analyst should create:
    a. one new variable representing house style now having three levels
    b. one indicator variable indicating that the Greenacre method has been applied
    c. three new variables for each of the three new levels
    d. two new variables representing two of the three levels

4. When levels of a categorical variable are collapsed so that no level has a 0 response nor 0 non-response, which of the following problems are remedied?

    a. curse of dimensionality

    ⓑ quasi-complete separation

    c. values not missing at random

    d. non-linearity

Suppose an analyst in interested in using demographic, aptitude, and extracurricular data in a testing instrument to predict whether or not students successfully complete their freshman year of college. The aptitude data consists of standardized test data in 10 areas (grammar, literature, writing, algebra, geometry, biology, chemistry, physics, history, and technology) each measured on a 100-point scale. Suppose the analyst uses the VARCLUS procedure to reduce the academic data. Use the information to answer questions 5 through 6:

```
proc varclus data=highschool maxeigen=1.0 hi short plots=dendrogram;
  var r1 -- r10;
run;
```

Cluster Summary for 3 Clusters					
Cluster	Members	Cluster Variation	Variation Explained	Proportion Explained	Second Eigenvalue
1	4	4	1.969186	0.4923	1.2893
2	4	4	1.922264	0.4806	0.9070
3	2	2	1.678999	0.8395	0.3210

Cluster Summary for 4 Clusters					
Cluster	Members	Cluster Variation	Variation Explained	Proportion Explained	Second Eigenvalue
1	2	2	1.79351	0.8968	0.2065
2	4	4	1.922264	0.4806	0.9070
3	2	2	1.678999	0.8395	0.3210
4	2	2	1.462309	0.7312	0.5377

Number of Clusters	Total Variation Explained by Clusters	Proportion of Variation Explained by Clusters	Minimum Proportion Explained by a Cluster	Maximum Second Eigenvalue in a Cluster	Minimum R-squared for a Variable	Maximum $1-R^{**}2$ Ratio for a Variable
1	2.373584		0.2374	1.811567	0.0269	
2	4.113747		0.3652	1.466969	0.1401	0.8803
3	5.570449		0.4806	1.289285	0.2190	0.7995
4	6.857083		0.4806	0.907041	0.2202	0.7812

5. Using the previous output, which of the following statements is true?

    ⓐ The algorithm stops at four clusters because the maximum second eigenvalue dropped below 1.0.

    b. Three clusters splits to form four clusters because the proportion of variance explained is less than 1.0.

    c. The algorithm will continue to form five clusters because the maximum eigenvalue for five clusters will be less than MAXEIGEN.

    d. The proportion of variance explained by four clusters is 0.4806.

6. Suppose the analyst modified the SAS code to get the following six-cluster solution. Which of the following statements is true?
   a. MAXEIGEN was increased from 1.0 in order to generate more clusters.
   b. Subsequent analyses would include only those variables with the largest R^2 with its own cluster.
   c. For each cluster, the analyst can select either of the two variables because the $1-R^2$ ratio values are close.
   d. The analyst should use all 10 variables because the clusters are still correlated.

6 Clusters		R-squared with		
Cluster	Variable	Own Cluster	Next Closest	1-R**2 Ratio
Cluster 1	R7	0.8968	0.0285	0.1063
	R8	0.8968	0.0342	0.1069
Cluster 2	R3	0.7536	0.1266	0.2821
	R4	0.7536	0.1120	0.2775
Cluster 3	R9	0.8395	0.0359	0.1665
	R10	0.8395	0.0151	0.1630
Cluster 4	R5	0.7312	0.0245	0.2756
	R6	0.7312	0.0345	0.2784
Cluster 5	R2	1.0000	0.0598	0.0000
Cluster 6	R1	1.0000	0.1582	0.0000

7. With the advent of sabermetrics, many statistics have been developed in an attempt to give a more comprehensive measure of value. In using these measures, or variables, to predict value, it is obvious that many of those variables have inherent redundant information. Suppose an analyst has 38 potential numeric input variables (number of At Bats through Walks Per Strikeout), all measuring variations of hitting opportunities and performance, and runs a VARCLUS procedure to reduce the set of inputs. Using the following partial output, which of the following input variables would be included in subsequent analyses based upon the 1-R square ratio?

   a. AtBat and BaseOnBalls
   b. RBI and SacFlies
   c. GroundBalls and NumPitches
   d. StolenBases and HomeRuns

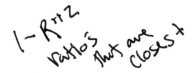

1-R††2
ratios that are closest

13 Clusters		R-squared with		
Cluster	Variable	Own Cluster	Next Closest	1-R**2 Ratio
Cluster 1	Triples	0.5281	0.1293	0.5420
	StolenBases	0.7630	0.1410	0.2759
	CaughtStealing	0.7694	0.1787	0.2808
Cluster 2	AtBat	0.8500	0.5971	0.3723
	GamesPlayed	0.8086	0.2190	0.2450
	TotalPlateAppear	0.9660	0.6065	0.0864
	NumPitches	0.7720	0.3308	0.3407
Cluster 3	HomeRuns	0.8538	0.3112	0.2122
	RBI	0.7379	0.2925	0.3704
Cluster 4	BaseOnBalls	0.9139	0.4707	0.1628
	PitchesPerPlateAppear	0.6461	0.2038	0.4445
	WalksPerPlateAppear	0.9435	0.4468	0.1021
Cluster 5	Runs	0.6117	0.4298	0.6810
	Avg	0.5547	0.3189	0.6538
	RunsCreated	0.9070	0.6760	0.2872
Cluster 6	GroundBalls	0.8764	0.2512	0.1650
	GroundtoFlyRatio	0.8764	0.1878	0.1521
Cluster 7	K_Strike_Outs	1.0000	0.1444	0.0000
...	...	...	...	...
Cluster 12	SacFlies	1.0000	0.0577	0.0000
Cluster 13	SacHits	1.0000	0.2024	0.0000

8. Suppose a national retailer wants to send emails to potential customers and is interested in using those variables related to the target, RESPOND, code 1 for Yes and 0 for No. Using the following plot, which of the following is true?

   a. All of the variables except USE_PAYPAL and NUMBER_OF_CARS have a linear relationship with the target variable.

   b. The input variables, USE_PAYPAL and NUMBER_OF_CARS, should be eliminated from further analyses because of irrelevance to the target.

   c. Experience has the strongest non-monotonic relationship with the target.

   d. SALARY, USE_PAYPAL, and NUMBER_OF_CARS should be eliminated because their Hoeffding ranks are at or beyond the reference line.

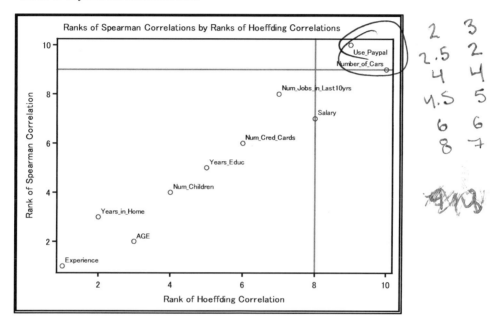

9. Suppose an analyst is screening a set of potential inputs using Spearman's correlation coefficient and Hoeffding's D. Which of the following situations is associated with a large Hoeffding's D and a near zero Spearman correlation coefficient?

   a. a nonmonotonic association between the variables

   b. linear association between the variables

   c. monotonic association between the variables

   d. no association between the variables

Suppose an analyst wants to predict academic major, CSC (code as 1 if the student will major in Computer Science or 0 otherwise), using several input variables and wants to explore the relationship between CSC and the input variable, TECH_LITERACY, measuring technical literacy. The relationship between TECH_LITERACY and CSC is _____ .

a. linear

b. monotonic, curvilinear

c. non-monotic

d. logarithmic

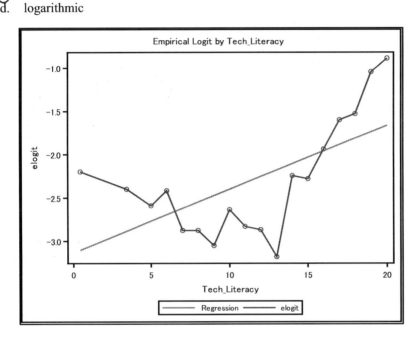

Chapter 9: Linear Regression Analysis

Introduction

In Chapter 7, "Analysis of Variance (ANOVA)," we discussed the general linear model for investigating the differences in a numeric continuous outcome across two or more populations (a factor), where the appropriate statistical test is an analysis of variance (ANOVA). We extended the general linear model to include additional factors (or variables) as a way to explain variation in the outcome variable of interest, using either a block design or two-factor ANOVA.

If our results are significant, we can say that the outcome is a function of one or more factors (or variables), where those variables are categorical. In this chapter, we extend the general linear model to include describing a numeric continuous outcome as a function of one or more numeric continuous and/or categorical variables (called predictors).

As discussed in Chapter 1, "Statistics and Making Sense of Our World," if the analyst is interested in investigating the relationship between a numeric continuous response variable and a set of predictors (whether categorical or numeric), then the appropriate statistical analysis is **linear regression analysis**.

In this chapter, we will introduce the idea of bivariate correlation and scatter plots as a way to assess the nature of the relationship between two numeric continuous variables. We will follow up with a discussion of simple linear regression where the goal is to predict a numeric continuous outcome from a numeric continuous predictor, and how that is related to correlational analysis.

We will provide the details of simple linear regression, including the concepts behind finding the slope and intercept of the line that best fits the data, how to measure the goodness of fit, inferences to the population, and using the results for purposes of explanation and prediction. Following, we extend those same concepts to the multiple regression situation where the analyst will consider two or more predictors.

With multiple predictors, we will discuss issues related to collinearity (redundancy), its diagnosis, and suggest remedies. Following we will discuss the variable selection (predictor relevancy) process using both the REG and GLMSELECT procedures in an attempt to find the best model based upon user-defined criteria.

This chapter ends with a statement of the assumptions and the application of regression diagnostics to assess those assumptions, including remedies to violations of the assumptions. Finally, we discuss deletion statistics for detecting outliers and influential observations and provide recommendations for handling influential observations.

In this chapter, you will learn how to:

- identify situations that require the use of linear regression analysis
- use the correlation coefficient and scatter plot to assess the relationship between two numeric continuous variables
- use the CORR and SGPLOT procedures to get correlation coefficients and scatter plots
- apply simple and multiple linear regression and understand the concept of fitting the best line (equation) using the OLS (ordinary least squares) criterion
- use the REG procedure to fit both simple and multiple linear regression
- use the GLM procedure to fit both simple and multiple linear regression, including a CLASS statement for categorical predictors
- convert the model from both PROC REG and PROC GLM to an algebraic expression
- interpret the slopes and intercept in the algebraic expression in order to describe the relationship between the outcome variable and its predictors
- conduct individual *t*-tests to assess the significance of one or more predictors
- identify the parts of the ANOVA table, including the sums of squares, degrees of freedom, mean square regression, mean square error, and the F-test statistic, and use the p-value for assessing the significance of the set of predictors
- identify the measures of fit (R^2, R^2_{adj}, and RMSE) for assessing the model adequacy
- identify R^2 as the proportion of variance in the outcome explained by the predictor (or predictors)
- identify the better model out of two models using the measures of fit
- use the STEPWISE, FORWARD, and BACKWARD selection methods using the SELECTION option in PROC REG
- use the STEPWISE, FORWARD, and BACKWARD selection methods using the SELECTION option in PROC GLMSELECT
- identify the best models using graphs of fit criteria in PROC REG, including R^2_{adj} and Mallows' C_p
- identify the best models using graphs of fit criteria in PROC GLMSELECT, including log p-value
- assign names to models using LABEL in the REG procedure to distinguish various output models
- describe the assumptions of linear regression and understand the consequences of violating those assumptions
- use PROC REG and the MODEL statement to generate residual plots to assess the assumptions
- use the residual plots to assess the assumptions
- understand how to fix the violations to assumptions
- use the PROC REG and the MODEL statement to produce deletion statistics to identify possible influential observations, including leverage, studentized residuals, Cook's D, DFFITS, and DFBETAS
- interpret the deletion statistics to identify possible influential observations
- describe remedies for handling influential observations
- use PROC REG and the MODEL statement to provide collinearity diagnostics, including variance inflation factors and condition number (VIF, COLLIN, COLLINOINT)
- identify collinearity using VIF, COLLIN, and COLLINOINT and give recommendations for resolving related issues

Exploring the Relationship between Two Continuous Variables

When ultimately using predictive modeling, the analyst should first conduct exploratory data analysis. Exploratory data analysis requires both data visualization and data summaries. In this section, we will explore the relationship between two (numeric) continuous variables using the scatter plot for visualizing the relationship and the correlation coefficient for numerical description.

Exploring the Relationship between Two Continuous Variables Using a Scatter Plot

Suppose the analyst is interested in examining the relationship between the sale price and the above ground living area of a particular group of houses. For each house, we can treat both continuous variables as an ordered pair (X,Y), where the dependent variable represents the y-coordinate and the independent variable represents the *x*-coordinate. A **scatter plot** can be constructed by plotting each point on an XY-coordinate plane. This visual display of the data provides the preliminary information we need to describe the type of relationship between the variables, whether positive, negative, linear, curvilinear, etc.

Consider the Ames Housing Case and the variables, sale price (SALEPRICE) and above ground living area (GR_LIV_AREA), where we take a random sample of 300 houses. The Program 9.1 Scatter Plot of Sale Price by Above Ground Living Area is used to generate the scatter plot:

Program 9.1 Scatter Plot of Sale Price by Above Ground Living Area

```
libname sasba 'c:\sasba\ames';
data amesreg300;
   set sasba.amesreg300;
   run;

proc sgplot data=amesreg300;
   reg x=Gr_Liv_Area Y=SalePrice;
run;
```

From Program 9.1 Scatter Plot of Sale Price by Above Ground Living Area, we can see that the SGPLOT procedure is applied to the Ames Housing data set, as defined by the DATA= option. The REG statement defines SALEPRICE as the dependent variable (Y) and the above ground living area, GR_LIV_AREA, as the independent variable (X). The output generated is illustrated in Output 9.1 Scatter Plot of Sale Price and Above Ground Living Area.

Output 9.1 Scatter Plot of Sale Price and Above Ground Living Area

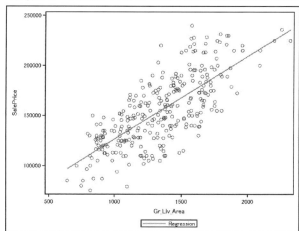

From the scatter plot we can see that there is a positive relationship between the two variables; namely, as above ground living area increases, the sale price increases as well. We also have some visual evidence from the plot that the relationship is linear. Finally, there do not seem to be any **outliers**--that is, observations that deviate from the general linear trend; however, we will discuss outlier detection later in this chapter.

Consider Program 9.2 Scatter Plot of Sale Price and Age at Time of Sale requesting a scatter plot of sale price by the age of the house at the time of the sale.

Program 9.2 Scatter Plot of Sale Price and Age at Time of Sale

```
libname sasba 'c:\sasba\ames';
data amesreg300;
   set sasba.amesreg300;
run;

proc sgplot data=amesreg300;
   reg x=Age_at_Sale Y=SalePrice;
run;
```

We can see from Output 9.2 Scatter Plot of Sale Price and Age at Time of Sale that the relationship between sale price and age at the time of the sale is negative, meaning that as the house gets older, the sale price decreases. Again, we can see that the relationship is linear.

Output 9.2 Scatter Plot of Sale Price and Age at Time of Sale

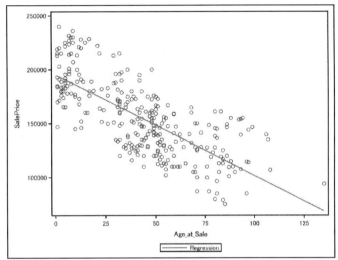

Finally, there may be situations, for example, where other amenities play into the sale price so that the sale price has less to do with square footage. Consider the following example as illustrated using Program 9.3 Scatter Plot of Sale Price and Square Footage.

Program 9.3 Scatter Plot of Sale Price and Square Footage

```
data housing;
    input SqFt SalePrice  @@;
    datalines;
    2135 95.27 850 43.03 800 213.82 865 93.98
    1515 75.15 1200 22.41 1200 216.13 1200 132.97
    1625 219 1595 238.19 2100 224.66 2000 23.1
    2000 195.56 1855 102.61 1700 130.27 1000 254.44
        ;
proc sgplot data=housing;
    reg x=SqFt Y=SalePrice;
run;
```

The relationship between sale price and square footage is flat, as illustrated Output 9.3 Scatter Plot of Sale Price and Square Footage. In other words, there does not seem to be a change in sale price associated with a change in the square footage; specifically, at each level of square footage (X), the average sale price seems to stay relatively constant, as indicated by the line with zero slope.

Output 9.3 Scatter Plot of Sale Price and Square Footage

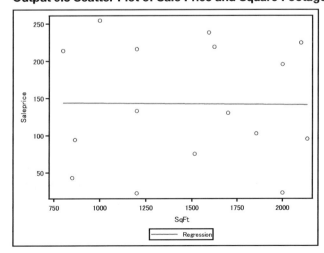

Quantifying the Degree of Association between Two Continuous Variables Using Correlation Statistics

Every data visualization should be coupled with descriptive statistics. For example, in Chapter 3, "Data Visualization," the histogram of numeric continuous data was accompanied by measures of center (mean, median, and mode), measures of dispersion (range, standard deviation, and variance), and measures of shape (skewness and kurtosis). Consequently, a scatter plot should be accompanied by the **correlation coefficient**.

Essentially, correlation describes how two variables change values in relation to one another. When describing the correlation between two continuous variables, where it is assumed the relationship is linear, the coefficient of interest is Karl Pearson's correlation coefficient (r). This correlation coefficient provides two bits of information about the relationship between X and Y: (1) the strength of the relationship and (2) its direction, whether positive or negative. The correlation between X and Y is calculated using:

$$r_{xy} = \frac{Cov_{xy}}{S_x S_y}$$

where r_{xy} is the sample correlation coefficient between X and Y, Cov_{xy} is the sample covariance of X and Y, S_x is the sample standard deviation of X, and S_y is the sample standard deviation of Y.

The range of r_{xy} is bounded between -1 to +1, inclusive. For a perfect positive linear relationship, $r_{xy} = +1$, as displayed in Figure 9.1 Scatter Plot of Perfect Positive, Perfect Negative, and No Relationship, Panel A. For a perfect negative linear relationship, $r_{xy} = -1$, as displayed in Figure 9.1 Scatter Plot of Perfect Positive, Perfect Negative, and No Relationship, Panel B. When there is no relationship, $r_{xy} = 0$, as displayed in Figure 9.1 Scatter Plot of Perfect Positive, Perfect Negative, and No Relationship, Panel C.

Figure 9.1 Scatter Plot of Perfect Positive, Perfect Negative, and No Relationship

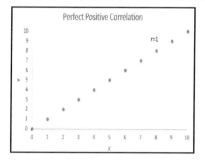

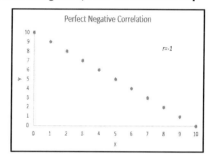

Panel A   *Panel B*

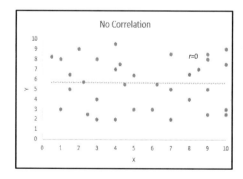

Panel C

Interpreting the strength of association using the correlation coefficient depends upon the particular situation. General rules can be followed: if the absolute value of a correlation coefficient is under .30, the relationship is considered weak; values between .30 and .50 are considered moderate; any value .50 and above is considered strong. These rules are general rules and business analysts have to consider the standards on the topic under investigation when interpreting the degree of association. Following this section will be a discussion on using hypothesis testing for confirming evidence of a significant relationship between X and Y in the population.

Producing Correlation Coefficients Using the CORR Procedure

PROC CORR is a procedure used to establish the relationship between two numeric continuous variables and has the general form:

PROC CORR DATA=SAS-data-set <options>;
    VAR variables;
    WITH variables;
    RUN;

Let's revisit the Ames Housing Case and explore potential predictors of sale price, using the following code in Program 9.4 Correlation Coefficient and Descriptive Statistics for Ames Housing.

Program 9.4 Correlation Coefficient and Descriptive Statistics for Ames Housing

```
libname sasba 'c:\sasba\ames';
data amesreg300;
    set sasba.amesreg300;
run;

proc corr data=amesreg300;
    var SalePrice Gr_Liv_Area Total_Bsmt_SF Lot_Area Age_at_Sale;
run;
```

From Program 9.4 Correlation Coefficient and Descriptive Statistics for Ames Housing, we can see that the CORR procedure is applied to the Ames Housing data set, as defined by the DATA= option. The VAR statement defines the five continuous variables for the correlational analysis. The results are displayed in Output 9.4 Correlation Coefficients and Descriptive Statistics for Ames Housing.

Output 9.4 Correlation Coefficients and Descriptive Statistics for Ames Housing

5 Variables:	SalePrice Gr_Liv_Area Total_Bsmt_ Lot_Area Age_at_Sale

Simple Statistics						
Variable	N	Mean	Std Dev	Sum	Minimum	Maximum
SalePrice	300	154910	34924	46473009	75200	240000
Gr_Liv_Area	300	1343	314.74797	402987	641.00000	2322
Total_Bsmt_SF	300	964.59667	297.74194	289379	0	1680
Lot_Area	300	10015	3799	3004352	2887	36500
Age_at_Sale	300	43.18333	27.45437	12955	1.00000	135.00000

Pearson Correlation Coefficients, N = 300 Prob > |r| under H0: Rho=0					
	SalePrice	Gr_Liv_Area	Total_Bsmt_SF	Lot_Area	Age_at_Sale
SalePrice	1.00000	0.74357 <.0001	0.45533 <.0001	0.31517 <.0001	-0.73675 <.0001
Gr_Liv_Area	0.74357 <.0001	1.00000	0.19077 0.0009	0.22958 <.0001	-0.38742 <.0001
Total_Bsmt_SF	0.45533 <.0001	0.19077 0.0009	1.00000	0.26236 <.0001	-0.32242 <.0001
Lot_Area	0.31517 <.0001	0.22958 <.0001	0.26236 <.0001	1.00000	-0.24354 <.0001
Age_at_Sale	-0.73675 <.0001	-0.38742 <.0001	-0.32242 <.0001	-0.24354 <.0001	1.00000

First, observe the table of Simple Statistics in Output 9.4 which summarizes information about the houses in the sample--namely, how many observations have complete data and descriptions of the center and spread. In short, the analyst can see that the sample of 300 houses has an average sale price of $154,910, average above ground living area of 1343 square feet, average basement area of 964.60 square feet, lot area of 10,015 square units, and an average age of 43.18

years. The minimum and maximum values, in addition to the standard deviation, are of interest as well in describing the variation.

Second, the table of Pearson Correlation Coefficients in Output 9.4 provides coefficients and p-values for every pair of variables listed in the VAR statement. Note that the diagonal entries each have correlation coefficients of 1, representing the fact that a variable is perfectly correlated with itself.

Note, in particular, the correlation coefficient in the second row of the first column having a value of 0.74357. The entry represents where the GR_LIV_AREA row intersects the SALEPRICE column, indicating that GR_LIV_AREA and SALEPRICE have a relatively large positive relationship (the p-value will be discussed in the next section). Note also that this same correlation coefficient is repeated in the first row of the second column. In fact, all entries above the diagonal are mirror images (repeats) of the entries below the diagonal; therefore, only the entries below the diagonal are of importance.

From the table, we can see that all potential predictors have a relatively strong correlation with SALEPRICE, ranging from a magnitude of 0.31517 (LOT_AREA) to 0.74357 (GR_LIV_AREA), including a strong negative correlation between AGE_AT_SALE and SALEPRICE (-0.73675). Keep in mind that while these bivariate correlations are relatively high, the analyst must consider multiple linear regression to see how these correlations may change in the presence of other predictors.

When conducting linear regression, the analyst will be concerned with minimizing the correlations among the potential predictors (Xs). The correlation matrix provides preliminary information about the relationship between the Xs and is displayed in the remaining entries. The correlations among the predictors range from 0.19077 (between GR_LIV_AREA and TOTAL_BSMT_SF) and -0.38742 (between GR_LIV_AREA and AGE_AT_SALE) which are somewhat smaller than the correlations with the outcome variable Y (SALEPRICE). Later in this chapter, you will see ways to determine if the correlations are large enough to deem that collinearity is a problem.

When using the CORR procedure, it is important to know that the default SAS setting utilizes **pairwise deletion**, whereas other procedures utilize **listwise deletion**. Pairwise deletion retains only those observations that have complete (non-missing) data on the two variables being analyzed or correlated. If the analyst wants to include only observations having complete data on all variables listed in the VAR statement, PROC CORR should include the NOMISS option.

If the analyst is interested only in the predictors associated with sale price, the WITH statement can be used; the PLOT=SCATTER option can be added to generate scatter plots illustrated in Program 9.5 Correlation Coefficients with Sale Price for Ames Housing.

Program 9.5 Correlation Coefficients with Sale Price for Ames Housing

```
libname sasba 'c:\sasba\ames';
data amesreg300;
    set sasba.amesreg300;
run;

proc corr data=amesreg300 plot=scatter;
    var Gr_Liv_Area Total_Bsmt_SF Lot_Area Age_at_Sale;
    with SalePrice;
run;
```

Output 9.5a Correlation Coefficients with Sale Price for Ames Housing

1 With Variables:				SalePrice
4 Variables:		Gr_Liv_Area Total_Bsmt_SF Lot_Area		Age_at_Sale

Pearson Correlation Coefficients, N = 300 Prob > |r| under H0: Rho=0				
	Gr_Liv_Area	**Total_Bsmt_SF**	**Lot_Area**	**Age_at_Sale**
SalePrice	0.74357 <.0001	0.45533 <.0001	0.31517 <.0001	-0.73675 <.0001

The information provided in Output 9.5a Correlation Coefficients with Sale Price for Ames Housing states that the variable SALEPRICE will be correlated with the 4 variables, GR_LIV_AREA, TOTAL_BSMT_SF, LOT_AREA, and AGE_AT_SALE. That information is followed with the associated four correlation coefficients. These correlation coefficients should be coupled with data visualizations, as displayed in Output 9.5b Scatter Plots for Sale Price with Potential Predictors.

The scatter plots of both SALEPRICE with GR_LIV_AREA and SALEPRICE with AGE_AT_SALE show a stronger relationship as indicated with the relatively small spread of points within the prediction ellipse. Note that the prediction ellipse represents the region for predicting the location of a new observation for each value of X, whereas, the confidence ellipse defines the confidence interval around the mean of the predicted values for each value of X.

These plots complement the information obtained using the correlations coefficients themselves. Note that there is a relatively larger spread in the linear trend for SALEPRICE by TOTAL_BSMT_SF, which is also represented by the relatively smaller correlation coefficient, indicating that while the relationship between SALEPRICE and TOTAL_BSMT_SF may be relatively strong, it is not as strong as the relationship of SALEPRICE with GR_LIV_AREA nor AGE_AT_SALE. Finally, the ellipse in the scatter plot of SALEPRICE by LOT_AREA is relatively tight: notice that several observations are relatively far from the ellipse, resulting in a reduction in the relationship as measured by the lowest correlation coefficient, 0.31517.

Output 9.5b Scatter Plots for Sale Price with Potential Predictors

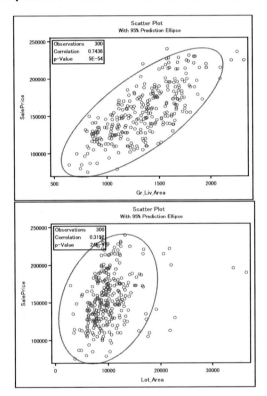
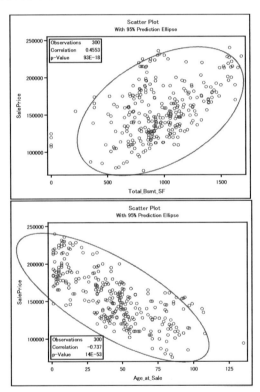

Testing the Hypothesis for a Bivariate Linear Relationship Using the CORR Procedure

In the last section, we used the correlation coefficient to describe the relationship between two continuous numeric variables. Suppose the analyst now wants to use the sample correlation coefficient (r_{xy}) to make inferences about the magnitude of the linear relationship between X and Y in the population. The question becomes: 'Is the sample correlation coefficient considered large enough to infer that the population correlation coefficient (ρ_{xy}) is large, that is, significantly different from zero. In this case, we are testing the following hypothesis set:

$$H_0: \rho_{xy} = 0$$

$$H_1: \rho_{xy} \neq 0$$

Suppose we consider the Ames Housing Case, where we want to make inferences about the population correlation coefficients using the sample coefficients in Output 9.4. In particular, consider the relationship between SALEPRICE and GR_LIV_AREA, with sample correlation coefficient equal to 0.74357.

The correlation coefficient has a sampling distribution shaped like a t-distribution, so the appropriate test is the *t*-test with n-2 degrees of freedom. The formula for the *t*-test statistics defined as:

$$t = \frac{r_{xy}\sqrt{n-2}}{\sqrt{1-r_{xy}^2}} = \frac{0.74357\sqrt{300}}{\sqrt{1-(0.74357)^2}} = 19.261$$

This t-value (19.261) is enormous and has a p-value < 0.0001 as found in the correlation table displayed in Output 9.4. In conclusion, the analyst would reject the null hypothesis and conclude that our sample provides evidence the correlation coefficient for SALEPRICE and GR_LIV_AREA in the population is different than zero. Note that the *t*-test statistic, in this case, is driven by the sample size; in other words, a large sample size in the numerator, holding all other terms constant, results in a large test statistic. Therefore, the analyst should interpret the results taking into account the sample size. (Note: It turns out that we would have arrived at the same conclusion with $r_{xy} = 0.74357$ for a sample size of 30).

Finally, let's consider testing the significance of all correlation coefficients provided in Output 9.4. In all, there are a total of 10 correlation coefficients, or (5)(5-1)/2 for 5 variables. When conducting many hypothesis tests as part of a single set of tests, the analyst expects to reject at least one of those tests by chance, even if there are no significant correlations. In other words, when conducting many tests at once, the chance of rejecting the null when we shouldn't increases (i.e., the probability of making a type I error increases). Therefore, when conducting hypothesis tests, the alpha-level used should be adjusted by dividing the alpha level by the number of tests. This is referred to as the **Bonferroni correction** (Dunn, O.J., 1961).

So when the analyst conducts the test of significance for 10 correlations, to have an effective alpha-level of, for example, 0.01, the analyst should divide that alpha by 10 (the number of tests) and use 0.001 as the significance level when deciding to reject the null. In our tests of the 10 correlations, we would reject the null and conclude that there are correlations among these five variables in the population.

In conclusion, correlational analyses with CORR and SGPLOT are good first steps in understanding bivariate data. These procedures give information about the characteristics of each variable and how two particular variables are related. In the remaining part of this chapter, we will discuss linear regression which is related to correlational analysis-- specifically, when looking at using a single X to predict Y. However, when using multiple Xs to predict Y, while correlations help in understanding the relationship between the pair of variables, linear regression with multiple predictors takes into account the relationship between an entire system of variables.

Understanding Potential Misuses of the Correlation Coefficient

There are limitations to the correlation coefficient. As with prior statistical techniques presented thus far, using the correlation coefficient to establish causal effects or direction of causal effects is not valid regardless of the size of the correlation coefficient. A significant correlation coefficient establishes only associations among continuous variables, not causality. Additional controls must be considered before causation can be established.

Secondly, the correlational analysis is appropriate when variables have a linear relationship. It is not valid to use the correlation coefficient to describe non-linear relationships between variables. Therefore, scatter plots are very important in assessing the nature of the relationship. In the sections on linear regression, there will be discussions on remedies when the relationship between X and Y is non-linear.

Caution must be used when using correlational analysis, in particular, when it comes to outliers. The correlation coefficient is calculated using all observations, so when any one observation deviates significantly from the linear trend of the remaining observations, the magnitude of the correlation is reduced (and biased). Again, a visual inspection of the scatter plot should always accompany the reporting of statistics to ensure an adequate assessment of influences. Outliers will be addressed in the following discussions of linear regression.

The correlation coefficient is useful when data values reflect the entire range of possible values in the population. If this is not the case, the correlation coefficient may be biased because of **restriction of range**. An example is as follows-- suppose you want to correlate the sale price of a house with the living area for a neighborhood of all large homes. When there is relatively little variation in X (here, square footage), there is probably very little variation in the sale price, resulting in a biased (reduced) correlation coefficient. As a result, the correlation between sale price and living area for that neighborhood would not be representative of the relationship among the population having larger ranges. As always, an inspection of the descriptive statistics, along with data visualizations, will aid in determining if restriction of range is an issue.

Finally, as illustrated earlier, correlation coefficients are often significant for large samples. The statistical significance is one component of the interpretation of the correlation coefficient; the analyst must always consider the magnitude of the correlation coefficient. If you have a correlation coefficient that is significant, but the strength of the association is less than 0.30, you should carefully consider the practical significance over the statistical significance.

Simple Linear Regression

The overall goal of simple linear regression is to develop a mathematical model, or equation, that linearly relates two numeric continuous variables. For purposes of regression analysis, we define Y to be the **dependent variable**, or outcome variable; X is defined as the **independent variable** or **predictor**. In **simple linear regression**, there is only one predictor, and the analysis has two main objectives:

1. to establish if there is a relationship between two variables-- similar to correlational analysis--and to describe that relationship
2. to predict the outcome (Y) of new observations based upon the values of their predictors (Xs)

Fitting a Simple Linear Regression Model Using the REG Procedure

When assessing the linear relationship between two variables, the assumption is that the form of the equation is linear; therefore, the simple linear regression model is defined as:

$$Y_i = \beta_0 + \beta_1 x_i + \varepsilon_i$$

where Y_i is the value of the dependent variable for observation i, X_i is the value of the predictor for observation i, β_0 is the intercept, β_1 is the slope, and ε_i is the error in prediction for observation i. The intercept, β_0, represents the value of Y_i when the independent variable X has a value of zero. The slope, β_1, represents the change in Y for every 1 unit change in X.

From the sample, the analyst will develop a **prediction equation** that best represents the relationship in the population. The prediction equation has the form:

$$\hat{Y}_i = b_o + b_1 X_i$$

where $\hat{Y}_i$ is the predicted value of Y for observation i, X_i is the value of the predictor for observation i, b_0 is the sample estimate of the population intercept β_0, and b_1 is the sample estimate of the population slope β_1.

When trying to find the 'best' linear equation that fits the points on a scatter plot, the formulae for calculating the slope and the intercept are based on the idea that the best line is the single line that is closest in proximity to all points. In other words, the desired line is the one that minimizes the **error in prediction (e)** for each observation, that is, the distance between the Y-coordinate of an observation and the point on the line, $\hat{Y}$, represented by , $Y - \hat{Y}$, as illustrated in Figure 9.2 Fitting the Line Closest to All Points.

It should be noted that the errors are negative for points below the line and positive for all points above the line. So if we attempt to minimize the sum of the errors, the positive errors and negative errors always cancel each other, and the sum of the errors will be zero for all lines. In short, the goal is to find the slope and intercept of the line that minimizes the 'squared' errors; therefore, the criterion for finding solutions is called the **Least-Squares Criterion**, and the method is referred to as **ordinary least squares (OLS)**.

Figure 9.2 Fitting the Line Closest to All Points

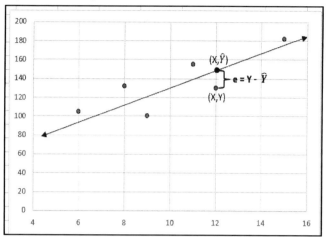

PROC REG is a procedure used to produce the linear equation and assessment information for establishing the relationship between a numeric continuous outcome variable and one or more numeric or dummy coded predictor variables and has the general form:

PROC REG DATA=SAS-data-set <options>;
    <label>: **MODEL** dependent(s)=regressor(s) </ options>;

RUN;

To illustrate, consider the Ames Housing data where the analyst is interested in relating the sale price of a house to its above ground living area. The necessary SAS code is displayed in Program 9.6 Linear Regression for Predicting Sale Price with Ground Living Area.

Program 9.6 Linear Regression for Predicting Sale Price with Ground Living Area

```
libname sasba 'c:\sasba\ames';
data amesreg300;
    set sasba.amesreg300;
run;

proc reg data=amesreg300;
    model SalePrice = Gr_Liv_Area;
run;
```

From Program 9.6 Linear Regression for Predicting Sale Price with Ground Living Area, we can see that the REG procedure is applied to the Ames Housing data set, as defined by the DATA= option. The MODEL statement is used to define the linear model; namely, SALEPRICE is equal to linear function of GR_LIV_AREA. The partial output, including all tables and one scatter plot, is illustrated in Output 9.6 Linear Regression Output for Predicting Saleprice with Ground Living Area.

Output 9.6 Linear Regression Output for Predicting Saleprice with Ground Living Area

Dependent Variable: SalePrice

Model: MODEL1

Number of Observations Read	300
Number of Observations Used	300

Analysis of Variance					
Source	DF	Sum of Squares	Mean Square	F Value	Pr > F
Model	1	2.016341E11	2.016341E11	368.51	<.0001
Error	298	1.63052E11	547154248		
Corrected Total	299	3.646861E11			

Root MSE	23391	R-Square	0.5529
Dependent Mean	154910	Adj R-Sq	0.5514
Coeff Var	15.09994		

Parameter Estimates					
Variable	DF	Parameter Estimate	Standard Error	t Value	Pr > |t|
Intercept	1	44081	5929.17772	7.43	<.0001
Gr_Liv_Area	1	82.50561	4.29790	19.20	<.0001

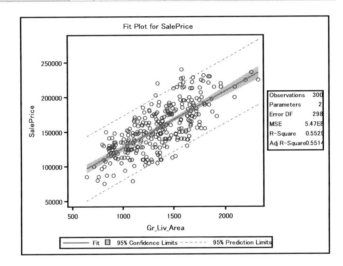

First, a preliminary inspection of the scatter plot of SALEPRICE by GR_LIV_AREA (referred to as the Fit Plot) seems to indicate no gross deviations from linearity. While this chapter will later cover ways to diagnose non-linearity problems and outliers, at this point, we will proceed with the interpretation of the output as if the model has been confirmed.

As displayed in Output 9.6 Linear Regression Output for Predicting Saleprice with Ground Living Area, the output begins with a statement of the dependent variable, namely, SALEPRICE, followed by the default model name (MODEL1), the number of observations read, and the number of observations used. Note that these are both 300, indicating that all 300 observations have complete data (no missing) and will be included in the regression analysis.

The table of Parameters Estimates provides information for defining the equation of the line that best fits the data; in particular, the intercept is defined to be 44,081 and the slope is defined to be 82.50561. From this, the analyst can provide the estimated regression equation for predicting Y, denoted by $(\hat{Y})$ as follows:

$$\hat{Y} = 44,081 + 82.51*Gr\_Liv\_Area$$

As far as interpretation, the analyst can use the slope to estimate the change in Y (SALEPRICE) per unit change in X (GR_LIV_AREA). In particular, the slope of 82.51 indicates that for every additional square foot of ground living area, the expected increase in the sale price is $82.51. (Note that the interpretation of slope uses the unit of measure of Y, specifically dollars in this example.) The intercept represents the value of Y (SALEPRICE) when X (GR_LIV_AREA) is zero; in other words, based upon this sample, the value of the home with no above ground living area is $44,081. This can be interpreted, possibly, as a base price, and the slope gives an indication of the additional price incurred for every additional square foot of above ground living area. (Note also that the intercept is interpreted in terms of dollars.)

In terms of prediction, let's assume we have a house on the market in the general area of the houses in the sample. Of course the house has not been sold, so we do not have a sale price, but we can estimate the sale price based upon our sample. Suppose this house has 2000 above ground living area (GR_LIV_AREA = 2000). The estimated sale price is:

$$\hat{Y} = 44,081 + 82.51*(2000) = \$209,101$$

In conclusion, based upon our sample of similar homes, we expect, or predict, the sale price to be approximately $209,101. Keep in mind that when conducting a linear regression, we should not predict Y until we have determined evidence that X is a good predictor for the population to which we want to infer. In the following sections, we will describe and interpret the remaining parts of the linear regression output, including a discussion of how well the regression line fits the data and how to assess the evidence that X and Y are related and that X would be a good predictor of Y.

Measures of Fit for the Linear Regression Model

Once the linear regression model is fit, the analyst may want to compare its performance to the model having no predictors. If the model with a single predictor is considered a good fit to the data, it is natural then to consider a second model with a different predictor to see which is better in terms of predictive accuracy. There are several fit indices that are used for comparison purposes, namely, (1) the **coefficient of determination (R^2)** and (2) the **standard error of the regression (S_e)**. In order to explain the rationale for R^2, you must first understand the meaning of three sums-of-squared-deviations: SST, SSE, and SSR.

Consider the first situation where the analyst has a set of observations where only Y is known (in other words, there is no predictor X). If the analyst wants to predict the Y values for future observations, the best estimate of Y is the average Y. How do you measure the overall error in predicting Y for all observations when the analyst uses $\bar{Y}$? The error in prediction for one observation is $(Y-\bar{Y})$, so the error for all observations can be represented by the **Total-Sum-of-Squares (SST)** as follows:

$$SST = \sum (Y - \bar{Y})^2$$

Note that the sum of the deviations is always zero because the positive deviations and negative deviations always cancel out; therefore, the deviations are squared to get the index. Note also that SST is the numerator when we calculate the variance in Y, and is a measure of how the Y values deviate from the mean of Y.

Consider now the situation where the analyst has a set of observations where both X and Y are known, and then builds an equation $(\hat{Y})$, to predict Y based upon X. The error in prediction for one observation is $(Y-\hat{Y})$, so the error for all observations when using X as a predictor can be represented by the **Error-Sum-of-Squares (SSE)** as follows:

$$SSE = \sum (Y - \hat{Y})^2$$

In fact, if X is 'good' at predicting Y, we expect SSE to be smaller than SST; in other words, we expect an improvement. That's where the **Regression-Sum-of-Squares (SSR)** comes into play. SSR represents the improvement in prediction by using X over the model which does not include X and is calculated as follows:

$$SSR = \sum (\hat{Y} - \bar{Y})^2$$

So in reviewing the linear regression output in Output 9.6 Linear Regression Output for Predicting Saleprice with Ground Living Area, we can see in the Sum of Squares column of the Analysis of Variance table that the total error without using X (SST) equals 3.646861×10^{11}, the error using X (SSE) is reduced at 1.63052×10^{11}, and the improvement in prediction (SSR) is 2.016341×10^{11}. (Note: The sums-of-squares are rounded to six decimal places, so calculations may have some rounding error.)

The Coefficient of Determination (R^2)

Keep in mind that our total improvement (SSR) in predicting Y with X can be no larger than SST. The proportion of improvement relative to the total possible improvement is defined to be **R-Square** and is calculated using:

$$R^2 = \frac{SSR}{SST}$$

In our example, as shown in Output 9.6 Linear Regression Output for Predicting Saleprice with Ground Living Area,

$$R^2 = \frac{2.016341 \times 10^{11}}{3.646861 \times 10^{11}} = 0.5529$$

In conclusion, 55.29% of the variation in SALEPRICE (Y) is explained by GR_LIV_AREA (X).

There are few notes to consider:

- The sums of squares are additive: SST = SSR + SSE.
- If we have perfect prediction using the prediction equation (i.e., using X), then SSE=0. In short, we would have total improvement where SSR=SST and R^2=1.0.
- If we have no predictive accuracy using the prediction equation, then our improvement (SSR) is 0, and our error in prediction using X (SSE) and error in predicting without using X (SST) are the same (SSE=SST), and R^2=0.
- R^2 ranges from 0 to 1, inclusive.

It should be noted that when the analyst uses just one predictor, the correlation coefficient can be directly calculated from R^2. The correlation coefficient (r_{xy}) is calculated as follows:

$$r_{xy} = (sign\ of\ the\ slope)\sqrt{R^2}$$

So, using the R^2 from the linear regression used to predict SALEPRICE (Y) using GR_LIV_AREA (X), we get

$$r_{xy} = (+)\sqrt{0.5529} = +0.74357$$

Which matches the correlation coefficient for SALEPRICE and GR_LIV_AREA, found in Output 9.4. Note that the R^2 for SALEPRICE and AGE_AT_SALE is positive, so when taking the square root to get r, you must also use the sign of the slope which would be negative.

The Standard Error of the Regression (S$_e$)

The second measure of fit measures the dispersion of the points around the prediction equation; basically, it is the standard deviation of the error, $(Y-\hat{Y})$. Let's consider first the variance of the points around the prediction line. Remember from Chapter 7 , "Analysis of Variance (ANOVA)" that variance is the sum of squared deviations divided by degrees of freedom, and is referred to as a **mean-square (MS)**. So in regression, the variance of the points around the line is the **mean-square-error (MSE)** and is defined as:

$$MSE = \frac{SSE}{df_{error}}$$

where the error degrees of freedom $df_{error} = n-k-1$, n = sample size, and k = the number of predictors used in the regression equation. In our Ames Housing example,

$$MSE = \frac{1.63052 \times 10^{11}}{298} = 547,154,248 \qquad where\ df_{error} = 300 - 1 - 1 = 298$$

Finally, the standard deviation of the error, referred to as the **standard error of the regression (S$_e$)**, is the square root of the variance, and is defined as:

$$S_e = \sqrt{MSE} = Root\ MSE = \sqrt{\frac{SSE}{df_{error}}}$$

In our Ames Housing example, $S_e = \sqrt{MSE} = \sqrt{547,154,248} = 23,391$, as displayed in Output 9.6 Linear Regression Output for Predicting Saleprice with Ground Living Area. The standard error gives us a measures of accuracy; in short, the standard error here tells us that on the average our predicted sale price will miss our actual sale price by $23,391. (Note that the standard error is in the same unit of measure as Y, in dollars).

At this point it is hard to tell if the standard error is large or small. You can use standard error to compare this model with the predictor X=GR_LIV_AREA to other models with other predictors. When we cover the material on how to determine if X is a good predictor, we will also discuss how this determines whether or not our standard error is considered small.

Just like R-squared, consider the following comments about the standard error of the regression:

- If the points all fall on the prediction line, S_e is 0; in other words, the points do not vary from the prediction line. This should make perfect sense--if the points fall on the line, we have perfect prediction, where SSE=0 and $S_e = \sqrt{\frac{0}{df_{error}}} = 0$.

- If the points are relatively close to the prediction line, S_e is relatively small; if the points are relatively 'far' from the prediction line, S_e is relatively large.

Using Measures of Fit to Compare Models

Suppose we wanted to know which model was best for predicting sale price: the model with above ground living area (GR_LIV_AREA) or the model using age of the house at the time of the sale (AGE_AT_SALE).

Table 9.1 Measures of Fit for Simple Linear Regression provides a summary of indices for the linear regression model just discussed, where the analyst is interest in predicting SALEPRICE using GR_LIV_AREA. The table also includes the same indices had the regression analysis been conducted for SALEPRICE and AGE_AT_SALE.

Table 9.1 Measures of Fit for Simple Linear Regression

Measures of Fit	Gr_Liv_Area (Model 1)	Age_at_Sale (Model 2)
R^2	0.5529	0.5428
S_e	23,391	23,654
SSR	2.016341×10^{11}	1.979537×10^{11}
SST	3.646861×10^{11}	3.646861×10^{11}

Note that the SST for both model 1 and model 2 are identical. This should make sense because this number measures how the sale price deviates from the average sale price and does not depend upon the predictor X. Note that the improvement, as measured by SSR, is slightly higher (better) when using model 1 compared to model 2. This is directly reflected in the value of the R^2 which measures the relative improvement. When using GR_LIV_AREA (model 1), 55.29% of the variation in SALEPRICE is explained; when using AGE_AT_SALE (model 2), 54.28% of the variation in SalePrice is explained.

Note also that the standard error for model 1 is slightly lower than that for model 2, meaning that there is less error in predicting SALEPRICE when using GR_LIV_AREA as compared to AGE_AT_SALE. In practical terms these models are basically equivalent. As we will soon see in multiple linear regression (where we have two or more predictors), it may make more sense to use both predictors at the same time.

Finally, in this section, we are using R^2 to compare models. In the section on multiple linear regression, the discussion will support the use of an adjustment to R^2 for comparing models. This index is referred to as the adjusted R^2, denoted by R^2_{adj}.

Hypothesis Testing for the Slope

In the last few sections, we discussed the interpretation of the slope and intercept as a way of describing how X and Y are related. We also discussed measures of fit as a way to describe the strength of the model. All of those discussions assume that X is a 'good' predictor of Y if applied to the population under consideration. In reality, that is not always the case – X may not be related to Y. In this section, we will discuss statistical tests for determining if we can use our sample data to make inferences about the 'goodness' or not of X as a predictor of Y. In fact, no interpretations should be made before confirming that the assumptions of linear regression are met and that X is considered, in general, a good predictor of Y.

It turns out that the hypothesis test for testing whether or not X is a statistically good predictor of Y is a hypothesis about the slope. Recall that the linear regression model has the form:

$$Y_i = \beta_0 + \beta_1 x_i + \varepsilon_i$$

From the linear equation, we can see that if the slope (β_1) is zero, then the X-term is zero no matter what. In that case, Y is a function of the intercept only, which is really the average value of Y. So the hypothesis set determining the goodness of X as a predictor is as follows:

$$H_0: \beta_1 = 0 \quad (\text{X and Y are not linearly related})$$

$$H_1: \beta_1 \neq 0 \quad (\text{X and Y are linearly related})$$

The null hypothesis, H_0, is that X is not a good predictor of Y; that is, there is no linear relationship between X and Y. The alternative hypothesis is that X is a good predictor of Y; there is a linear relationship between X and Y.

The *t*-Test for Slope

As discussed in Chapter 4, "The Normal Distribution and Introduction to Inferential Statistics," any statistical test requires using the sampling distribution to measure how far a sample statistic differs from its expected value if the null hypothesis is true. It turns out that if the analyst takes repeated random samples from the population and fits a slope for each sample, using X and Y values, then the sampling distribution of slopes is shaped like a t-distribution. The average of all possible slopes is equal to the population slope (β_1) and the standard deviation of the slope (S_{b_1}) is defined as:

$$S_{b_1} = \frac{S_e}{\sqrt{\Sigma(x_i - \bar{x})^2}}$$

where S_e is the standard error of the regression. Because the reference distribution is a t-distribution, the appropriate statistical test is the *t*-test of slope and the *t*-test statistic is defined as:

$$t = \frac{b_1 - \beta_1}{S_{b_1}}$$

with degrees of freedom $= \text{df}_{error} = n\text{-}k\text{-}1$, where b_1 is the sample slope, and β_1 is the hypothesized slope of 0.

Suppose we want to test to see if above ground living area (GR_LIV_AREA) is a significantly good predictor of SALEPRICE (Y). When inspecting the simple linear regression displayed in Output 9.6 Linear Regression Output for Predicting Saleprice with Ground Living Area, note that the sample slope is 82.50561 and the standard deviation of the slope (S_{b_1}) is 4.29790. So the *t*-test statistic is:

$$t = \frac{82.50561 - 0}{4.29790} = 19.197 \quad \text{with } \text{df}_{error} = 300\text{-}1\text{-}1 = 298$$

Notice also in Output 9.6 Linear Regression Output for Predicting Saleprice with Ground Living Area that the p-value for the two-tailed test of slope is less than 0.0001, and the null hypothesis is rejected (for any alpha .01, .05, or .10). In conclusion, we have evidence that β_1 is significantly different from zero. In other words, we have evidence, based upon the sample, that GR_LIV_AREA is a good predictor of SALEPRICE in the population. Note that the *t*-test statistic is identical (within rounding error) to the *t*-test statistic for correlation. This is no coincidence--testing the co-relationship between X and Y is equivalent to testing the significance of the slope in simple linear regression.

The F-Test for Slope

In simple linear regression, the analyst can also use an F-test to test hypotheses about the slope:

$$H_0: \beta_1 = 0 \quad (\text{ no linear relationship})$$

$$H_1: \beta_1 \neq 0 \quad (\text{linear relationship})$$

Recall from Chapter 7, "Analysis of Variance (ANOVA)" that an F-test statistic is the ratio of two variances. So consider the following two variances. First, the mean-square-error (MSE) measures the variance of the points around the estimated regression equation.

Consider the second variance, the **mean-square-regression (MSR).** Recall that a variance is a sum-of-squared deviations divided by its degrees of freedom. So MSR = SSR/df_{reg}, where the degrees freedom (df_{reg}) = k, and k = the number of predictors in the model (of course, in simple linear regression, k is always equal to 1).

We can then define the F-test statistic as follows:

$$F = \frac{MSR}{MSE} \quad \text{with } df_{reg} = k, \text{ and } df_{error} = n-k-1$$

So how do we use the F-ratio to test our hypothesis? It turns out that if the null hypothesis is true, then MSR is an unbiased estimate of the variance of the points around the line; consequently, in this case, MSE = MSR, and F=1.0. However, if the null hypothesis is false, MSR is an overestimate of the variance of the points around the line; as a result, MSR > MSE and F > 1.0.

The question then becomes--how much greater than 1 should the F-ratio be in order to reject the null hypothesis and control for a specific level of significance? The answer requires using the F-table to find the critical value. Or, the analyst can use the p-value for the F-test to make conclusions.

The results of the F-test can be found in the **analysis of variance (ANOVA)** table which has the general form as displayed in Table 9.2 Analysis of Variance (ANOVA) Table for Linear Regression.

Table 9.2 Analysis of Variance (ANOVA) Table for Linear Regression

Source of Variation	Sums-of-Squares (SS)	Degrees of Freedom	Mean Square	F-Ratio
Regression	SSR	k	MSR = SSR / k	F = MSR/MSE
Error	SSE	n-k-1	MSE = SSE / (n-k-1)	
Total	SST	n-1		

So, the decision rule is: if the F-test statistic is greater than the critical value, then reject the null hypothesis and conclude that the slope in the population is significantly different than zero.

Recall that in the previous section, the *t*-test was used to confirm evidence that above ground living areas (GR_LIV_AREA) is a good predictor of SALEPRICE. Let's consider the F-test for arriving at the decision.

Referring to the ANOVA table in Output 9.6 Linear Regression Output for Predicting Saleprice with Ground Living Area, we can see that the degrees of freedom regression = k = 1, the degrees of freedom error = n-k-1 = 300 – 1 – 1 = 298. The values of SSR, SSE, and SST were calculated in a previous section. Note that the two mean-squares, MSR and MSE, were calculated by taking the sums-of-squares and dividing by their respective degrees of freedom. Finally the F-test statistic is calculated using F=MSR/MSE and displayed as 368.51 with a p-value less than 0.0001. If we set the level of significance at 0.01 ($\alpha = 0.01$), the p-value is less than α, so the null hypothesis is rejected. In conclusion, above ground living area (GR_LIV_AREA) is a good predictor of SALEPRICE. Keep in mind that this also allows us to say that the standard error is considered statistically low and the R^2 is considered statistically large (i.e., different from zero).

In simple linear regression, the *t*-test and the F-test are different approaches to testing the same hypothesis, so the results are always identical. In fact, t^2 is equal to F; in our example, $(19.197^2) \approx 368.51$. We will see, in the later discussion of multiple linear regression, that the F-test will test the overall relationship between the outcome Y and the entire set of predictors (Xs).

Producing Confidence Intervals

The chance that our sample slope is identical to the population slope is zero. In fact, because there are many possible samples, every sample has its own slope and it's probable that none of them will be identical to the population slope. Therefore, the analyst should consider a **confidence interval** around the estimated slope. As illustrated in Chapter 4, "The Normal Distribution and Introduction to Inferential Statistics," a confidence interval takes into account the sampling variability and is calculated as follows:

$$CI_{100\%(1-\alpha)} = b_1 \pm t_{\alpha/2} S_{b_1} \quad \text{with (n-k-1) degrees of freedom}$$

Where $t_{\alpha/2} S_{b_1}$ is the margin of error. So for the Ames Housing Case, a 95% confidence interval for the slope is:

$$CI_{95\%} = 82.50561 \pm 1.967956(4.29790) = 82.50561 \pm 8.45808$$

$$= [74.04753, 90.96369]$$

where $t_{.05/2}$ with 300-1-2 = 298 degrees of freedom is approximately 1.96 (SAS uses a t-value of 1.967956). The 95% confidence interval means that the criteria for calculating the margin of error ensure that if you had taken 100 random samples to run the regression, approximately 95% of the confidence intervals of the slope would actually contain the true population slope. Here the confidence interval indicates that for a one-square-foot increase in above ground living area, the sale price will increase anywhere from $74.05 to $90.96.

In order to produce the confidence interval of the slope using SAS, the analyst would include the CLB option in the MODEL statement as illustrated in Program 9.7 Confidence Interval for Effect of Gr_Liv_Area on Sale.

Program 9.7 Confidence Interval for Effect of Gr_Liv_Area on Sale Price

```
libname sasba 'c:\sasba\ames';
data amesreg300;
    set sasba.amesreg300;
run;

proc reg data=amesreg300;
    model SalePrice = Gr_Liv_Area/clb;
run;
```

The 95% confidence interval is displayed in Output 9.7 Confidence Interval for Effect of Gr_Liv_Area on SalePrice. Note that the confidence interval does not contain zero. In other words, the sample slope is far enough from zero, that even the interval around the sample slope does not contain zero; therefore, we can infer that the population slope is significantly different than zero. This can be used for hypothesis testing. In short, if the interval contains zero, we do not reject the null; however, if the interval does not contain zero, we do reject the null.

When the confidence level is 95%, using the confidence interval is equivalent to conducting a two-tailed test at alpha of 0.05. The default confidence level in SAS is 95%. In order to change the level of confidence, the analyst can use the ALPHA= option in the MODEL statement.

Output 9.7 Confidence Interval for Effect of Gr_Liv_Area on SalePrice

		Parameter Estimates					
Variable	DF	Parameter Estimate	Standard Error	t Value	Pr > |t|	95% Confidence Limits	
Intercept	1	44081	5929.17772	7.43	<.0001	32413	55749
Gr_Liv_Area	1	82.50561	4.29790	19.20	<.0001	74.04753	90.96369

Multiple Linear Regression

Many real-world questions are too complex to be represented by only one explanatory variable as is the case in simple linear regression. To reflect the complex nature of business, the analyst should use **multiple linear regression**. In multiple regression, the analyst is able to assess the relationship between the outcome variable, Y, and an entire *set* of predictors simultaneously, while taking into account the interrelationships among the multiple predictors. As stated earlier, the goal of linear regression is both to describe relationships and to predict future outcomes.

In this section, we will apply the concepts discussed in simple linear regression to the multiple predictor case. Subsequently, we will discuss how to determine which variable has the largest relative impact on the model, in the presence of other predictors. A natural follow-up is to ask the question--should a predictor be included in the model when other predictors are already in the model? Related to that topic is the idea of variable selection; in other words, the analyst is interested in finding the best model for explaining the outcome variable taking into account model fit indices and **parsimony**.

Fitting a Multiple Linear Regression Model Using the REG Procedure

As with simple linear regression, the form of the multiple linear regression equation *with k* predictors is defined as:

$$Y_i = \beta_0 + \beta_1 X_{i1} + \beta_2 X_{i2} + \ldots \beta_k X_{ik} + \varepsilon_i$$

where Y_i is the dependent variable, k is the number of predictors, β_0 is the intercept, and each β_k is the coefficient for each respective predictor, X_{ik}, and ε_i is the error.

From the sample, the analyst will develop a prediction equation that best represents the relationship in the population. The prediction equation has the form:

$$\hat{Y}_i = b_o + b_1 X_{i1} + b_2 X_{i2} + \cdots + b_k X_{ik}$$

where $\hat{Y}_i$ is the predicted value of Y for observation i, X_i is the value of the predictor for observation i, b_0 is the sample estimate of the population intercept β_0, and b_k is the sample estimate of the population slope β_k.

Consider the following example using the Ames Housing Case. Suppose we want to predict sale price based upon above ground living area, having at least two full bath rooms or not, total basement square footage, age at sale, square footage of the open porch, and garage area. The analyst would use Program 9.8 Multiple Linear Regression for Predicting Sale Price with Six Predictors.

Program 9.8 Multiple Linear Regression for Predicting Sale Price with Six Predictors

```
libname sasba 'c:\sasba\ames';
data amesreg300;
    set sasba.amesreg300;
run;

proc reg data=amesreg300;
    model SalePrice= Gr_Liv_Area Fullbath_2plus Total_Bsmt_SF
                     Age_at_Sale Open_Porch_SF Garage_Area
    /clb alpha=.05;
run;
```

From Program 9.8 Multiple Linear Regression for Predicting Sale Price with Six Predictors, we can see that the REG procedure is applied to the Ames Housing data set, as defined by the DATA= option. The MODEL statement is used to define the linear model, namely SALEPRICE is equal to linear function of the predictors GR_LIV_AREA through GARAGE_AREA. The CLB option with ALPHA= requests that 95% confidence intervals be included as well. The partial output is illustrated in Output 9.8 Multiple Linear Regression for Predicting SalePrice with Six Predictors.

Output 9.8 Multiple Linear Regression for Predicting SalePrice with Six Predictors

Dependent Variable: SalePrice

Model: MODEL1

Number of Observations Read	300
Number of Observations Used	300

Analysis of Variance

Source	DF	Sum of Squares	Mean Square	F Value	Pr > F
Model	6	3.063744E11	51062396999	256.57	<.0001
Error	293	58311700187	199016042		
Corrected Total	299	3.646861E11			

Root MSE	14107	R-Square	0.8401
Dependent Mean	154910	Adj R-Sq	0.8368
Coeff Var	9.10677		

Parameter Estimates

Variable	DF	Parameter Estimate	Standard Error	t Value	Pr > |t|	95% Conf Limits	
Intercept	1	74697	5766.25317	12.95	<.0001	63349	86046
Gr_Liv_Area	1	51.43011	3.45007	14.91	<.0001	44.64006	58.22016
Fullbath_2plus	1	6005.85200	2500.87545	2.40	0.0170	1083.89541	10928
Total_Bsmt_SF	1	21.13561	2.96919	7.12	<.0001	15.29196	26.97925
Age_at_Sale	1	-513.50416	39.35261	-13.05	<.0001	-590.95378	-436.05455
Open_Porch_SF	1	-5.25951	15.13243	-0.35	0.7284	-35.04155	24.52253
Garage_Area	1	24.87604	6.08830	4.09	<.0001	12.89370	36.85839

Consider the following interpretation of the output based upon the discussion thus far. First, using the parameter estimates, the estimated regression equation is:

$$\hat{Y} = 74697 + 51.43*Gr\_Liv\_Area + 6005.85*Fullbath\_2plus + 21.14*Total\_Bsmt\_SF$$

$$- 513.50*Age\_at\_Sale - 5.26*Open\_Porch\_SF + 24.88*Garage\_Area.$$

The estimate of the slope for GR_LIV_AREA indicates that for each additional square foot of above ground living area, the sale price will increase by $51.43, holding all other variables constant (in other words when comparing houses that are equivalent on all other variables). In fact, the estimates of slopes are referred to as partial slopes, because they measure the effect of the variable on Y, controlling for the other predictors. Note also that the slope for GR_LIV_AREA changed significantly from the bivariate case (as shown in Output 9.6 Linear Regression Output for Predicting Saleprice with Ground Living Area); remember that slope ignores the presence of other variables.

The R^2 indicates that 84.01% of the variation in SALEPRICE is accounted for by using the predictors GR_LIV_AREA through GARAGE_AREA (in the next section, we will see that adjusted R^2 is a better measure of fit). The standard error of the regression indicates that, on average, the estimate of sale price will miss the actual price by $14,107.

The F-test statistic is used to test if the entire set of predictors is considered good when predicting sale price for the population. In other words, the appropriate set of hypotheses is:

$$H_o: \beta_1 = \beta_2 = ... = \beta_6 \quad \text{(none of the 6 predictors are good)}$$

$$H_1: \text{at least one } \beta_j \neq 0 \quad \text{(at least one predictor is good), for any } j = 1,...,k$$

From Output 9. 8 Multiple Linear Regression for Predicting SalePrice with Six Predictors, we can see that the p-value for the F-test is less than 0.0001; therefore, the null hypothesis is rejected, indicating evidence in the population, that at least one predictor is good when predicting sale price.

Referring now to the individual *t*-tests, we can see that OPEN_PORCH_SF (p=0.7284 > .01) is not a good predictor when considered together with the other predictors. Keep in mind that this test is not saying that OPEN_PORCH_SF is not a good predictor. Used alone there may actually be a relationship between SALEPRICE and OPEN_PORCH_SF. This test simply gives evidence that OPEN_PORCH_SF does not add to the accuracy in prediction in the presence of the other predictors.

This is further evidenced using the confidence interval as well. Note that the 95% confidence interval for the slope of OPEN_PORCH_SF, (-35.04155, 24.52253), contains zero, so the null hypothesis is not rejected.

Measures of Fit for the Multiple Linear Regression Model

As seen in the simple linear regression section, measures of fit were used to compare the performance of the simple linear regression model using either above ground living area (GR_LIV_AREA) or age at the time of sale (AGE_AT_SALE). In multiple linear regression, measures of fit can be used to compare various models, as well.

Consider the example just described where the analyst wants to predict sale price based upon above ground living area, having at least two full bath rooms or not, total basement square footage, age at sale, square footage of the open porch, and garage area. Referring to Output 9.8 Multiple Linear Regression for Predicting SalePrice with Six Predictors, the standard error of the regression is 14,107 and the R^2 is 0.8401. Again, this means that, on the average, the predicted value of sale price will miss the actual sale price by $14,107 when using those six variables. The R^2 indicates that 84.01% of the variance in SalePrice is explained by using those six variables to predict SalePrice.

Adjusted R-Square

Note that the R^2 produced by six predictors (0.8401) has increased over that R^2 value produced by using just GR_LIV_AREA (0.5529). It seems obvious that as more predictors are added to the model (at least those related to the outcome variable), the fit of the model improves and, as a result, the R^2 increases. It turns out that even when a variable not related to the outcome variable is included in the model, R^2 still increases.

The R^2 is basically inflated as the number of predictors increases and is an overestimate of the relationship between the outcome Y and the set of predictors; therefore, the more common measure of fit is the **adjusted R^2** and is calculated as follows:

$$R^2_{adj} = 1 - \left[(1 - R^2)\left(\frac{n-1}{n-k-1}\right)\right]$$

The adjusted R^2 (denoted by R^2_{adj}) includes a penalty for adding more predictors. The formula also takes into account that, as the sample size (n) increases, the penalty for using k predictors becomes smaller; in other words, as the sample size increases, the value of R^2_{adj} approaches R^2. It should be noted, also that R^2_{adj} is better estimate of the fit in the population, denoted by ρ^2.

As an illustration, consider comparing the performance of the linear regression model with six predictors, having R^2_{adj} of 0.8368, as found in Output 9.8 Multiple Linear Regression for Predicting SalePrice with Six Predictors, with the same model with five predictors excluding, OPEN_PORCH_SF. The R^2_{adj} with five predictors is 0.8373, as displayed in Output 9.9 Multiple Linear Regression for Predicting SalePrice with Five Predictors. It is, therefore, evident that there is essentially zero loss of accuracy when dropping the non-significant variable, OPEN_PORCH_SF.

Output 9.9 Multiple Linear Regression for Predicting SalePrice with Five Predictors

Dependent Variable: SalePrice

Model: MODEL1

Number of Observations Read	300
Number of Observations Used	300

Analysis of Variance

Source	DF	Sum of Squares	Mean Square	F Value	Pr > F
Model	5	3.063503E11	61270068111	308.79	<.0001
Error	294	58335741627	198420890		
Corrected Total	299	3.646861E11			

Root MSE	14086	R-Square	0.8400
Dependent Mean	154910	Adj R-Sq	0.8373
Coeff Var	9.09315		

Parameter Estimates

Variable	DF	Parameter Estimate	Standard Error	t Value	Pr > |t|
Intercept	1	74606	5751.64527	12.97	<.0001
Gr_Liv_Area	1	51.27981	3.41774	15.00	<.0001
Fullbath_2plus	1	5975.69610	2495.63000	2.39	0.0173
Total_Bsmt_SF	1	21.14003	2.96472	7.13	<.0001
Age_at_Sale	1	-511.85215	39.00605	-13.12	<.0001
Garage_Area	1	24.99176	6.07009	4.12	<.0001

Consider also the comparison of the standard error of the regression for the six-predictor model versus the five-predictor model, as illustrated in Table 9.3 Measures of Fit for Multiple Linear Regression. When dropping OPEN_PORCH_SF from the model, the standard error is $14,086, indicating that with five predictors, the predicted sale price will, on average, miss the actual sale price by $14,086.

Table 9.3 Measures of Fit for Multiple Linear Regression

	Gr_Liv_Area, Fullbath_2plus, Total_Bsmt_SF, Age_at_Sale, Garage_Area, Open_Porch_SF	Gr_Liv_Area, Fullbath_2plus, Total_Bsmt_SF, Age_at_Sale, Garage_Area
Number of Predictors	6	5
R^2	0.8401	0.8400
R^2_{adj}	0.8368	0.8373
S_e	14107	14086

Based upon the combination of the hypothesis tests and the measures of fit, the best model would be the five-predictor model. In practice, the analyst would consider that model for predicting sale price.

Quantifying the Relative Impact of a Predictor

Once the analyst fits a linear regression model, it is natural to follow up with the question--what is the relative impact of a predictor in the model; in other words, what is the unique contribution of a predictor to the model in the presence of other predictors?

The answer is the **squared semi-partial correlation** (sr_j^2), which represents the proportion of variance in Y explained by X alone, over and above the variance explained by the remaining predictors. This index also measures the reduction in the R^2 when that predictor is removed from the model, and can be calculated using the following formula:

$$sr_j^2 = R^2_{Y \cdot 12 \ldots j \ldots k} - R^2_{Y \cdot 12 \ldots (i) \ldots k}$$

where $R^2_{Y.123\ldots j\ldots k}$ is the R^2 that measures the association between Y with all predictors including predictor j and $R^2_{Y.123\ldots(j)\ldots k}$ is the R^2 that measures the association between Y with all other predictors except predictor j.

In order to get that index for the six-predictor case, the analyst would include the SCORR2 option in the MODEL statement as in Program 9.9 Measures of Relative Predictor Importance in Multiple Linear Regression.

Program 9.9 Measures of Relative Predictor Importance in Multiple Linear Regression

```
libname sasba 'c:\sasba\ames';
data amesreg300;
    set sasba.amesreg300;
run;

proc reg data=amesreg300;
    model SalePrice= Gr_Liv_Area Fullbath_2plus Total_Bsmt_SF
                     Age_at_Sale Open_Porch_SF Garage_Area
    /scorr2;
run;
```

The output is identical to those illustrated previously and now includes an additional column displaying the squared semi-partial correlations (Type II), as shown in Output 9.10 Measure of Relative Predictor Impact in Multiple Linear Regression. Using that information, we can see that GR_LIV_AREA is best in explaining the variation in SALEPRICE, with $sr_1^2 = 0.12127$. The predictor, OPEN_PORCH_SF, has the least impact, with $sr_5^2 = 0.00006592$; in fact, the magnitude of the squared semi-partial correlation illustrates the fact that the R^2 is basically unchanged when OPEN_PORCH_SF is removed.

Output 9.10 Measure of Relative Predictor Impact in Multiple Linear Regression

Variable	DF	Parameter Estimate	Standard Error	t Value	Pr > |t|	Squared Semi-partial Corr Type II
Intercept	1	74697	5766.25317	12.95	<.0001	.
Gr_Liv_Area	1	51.43011	3.45007	14.91	<.0001	0.12127
Fullbath_2plus	1	6005.85200	2500.87545	2.40	0.0170	0.00315
Total_Bsmt_SF	1	21.13561	2.96919	7.12	<.0001	0.02765
Age_at_Sale	1	-513.50416	39.35261	-13.05	<.0001	0.09292
Open_Porch_SF	1	-5.25951	15.13243	-0.35	0.7284	0.00006592
Garage_Area	1	24.87604	6.08830	4.09	<.0001	0.00911

Checking for Collinearity Using VIF, COLLIN, and COLLINOINT

As mentioned earlier, the analyst is sometimes faced with hundreds of potential input variables. Recall, specifically from Chapter 8, "Preparing the Input Variables for Production," that there are strategies for addressing the issue of **redundancy** where the predictor variables are highly correlated and have overlapping information.

In multiple linear regression, if the predictors under consideration are highly correlated, the analyst may encounter results that seem ambiguous. This condition is known as **collinearity** and should be remedied. When collinearity exists, for example, the output may show a negative slope for at least one of the predictors when it is common knowledge that X and Y are positively related.

Another example exists when the overall F-test shows that the set of predictors as a whole is significantly related to the outcome variable, while the *t*-tests for testing the significance of specific variables indicate that no predictors are significantly related to the outcome variable. This occurs because the estimates of the slopes are unstable and have inflated standard errors (Belsley, Kuh, and Welsch, 1980). Consequently, if a slope has an inflated standard error, its *t*-test statistic is deflated, resulting in an inflated p-value; here, the analyst would conclude that the predictor under consideration is non-significant, when in reality, the predictor would be significant in the absence of collinearity.

In this section, we will discuss a strategy for detecting if collinearity exists and provide recommendations for deleting the redundant predictor. Once one or more potential predictors are deleted because of collinearity, the analyst must next consider the idea of **relevancy** of the predictor to the outcome variable. Relevancy will be discussed in the next section in the context of variable selection.

The Variance Inflation Factor (VIF) for Detecting Collinearity

An index for detecting possible collinearity is referred to as the **Variance Inflation Factor (VIF)**. This index is calculated for each predictor using the following formula:

$$VIF_j = \frac{1}{Tolerance_j} = \frac{1}{1 - R^2_{j.12...(j)...k}}$$

where $R^2_{j.12...(j)...k}$ is the R^2 that measures the association between *predictor j* with all other predictors except *j*.

So, consider the case where the analyst is interested in detecting collinearity among three predictors. The variance inflation factor for X_1 (VIF_1) would be calculated as follows:

1. Conduct a linear regression to predict X_1 using the remaining predictors, X_2 and X_3.
2. Use the R^2 value from that model for $R^2_{1.23}$.
3. Calculate VIF_1 using $1/(1-R^2_{1.23})$.
4. Repeat steps 1 through 3 for X_2, where $VIF_2 = 1/(1-R^2_{2.13})$.
5. Repeat steps 1 through 3 for X_3, where $VIF_3 = 1/(1-R^2_{3.12})$.

If there is absolutely no relationship among all predictors, 1,2,…, k, then $R^2_{j.12...(j)...k}$ is 0, the tolerance is 1 and the VIF is 1. If all of the predictors are perfectly related and $R^2_{j.12...(j)...k}$ is 1, then the tolerance is 0 and the VIF is ∞. So the range of the VIF is $[1, \infty)$. As $R^2_{j.12...(j)...k}$ increases, tolerance decreases, and VIF increases.

The VIF_j measures the inflation in the variance of b_j when X_j is linearly related to the other predictors as compared to the variance of b_j when X_j is not linearly related to the other predictors. For example, if the VIF_j is 12, then the estimated variance of X_j is 12 times larger than if X_j has no correlation with the other predictors. The question then becomes what value must the VIF exceed for collinearity to be suspect? A common criterion is $VIF \geq 10$ (tolerance ≤ 0.10, $R^2_{j.12...(j)...k} \geq 0.90$).

The Condition Index (C) for Detecting Collinearity

Another approach to investigating collinearity involves principal component analysis, where each predictor can be represented as a linear combination of all predictors. The linear combination is referred to as a **principal component**. As described in Chapter 8 , "Preparing the Input Variables for Prediction," principal component analysis produces a set of k principal components which are weighted linear combinations of the standardized versions (Z_1 through Z_k) of the original variables (X_1 through X_k), and have the form:

$$PRIN_1 = a_{11}Z_1 + a_{12}Z_2 + \ldots + a_{1k}Z_k$$

$$PRIN_2 = a_{21}Z_1 + a_{22}Z_2 + \ldots + a_{2k}Z_k$$

$$PRIN_3 = a_{31}Z_1 + a_{32}Z_2 + \ldots + a_{3k}Z_k$$

. .

$$PRIN_q = a_{q1}Z_1 + a_{q2}Z_2 + \ldots + a_{qk}Z_k$$

…

$$PRIN_k = a_{k1}Z_1 + a_{k2}Z_2 + \ldots + a_{pk}Z_k$$

The values of the principal components ($PRIN_1$ through $PRIN_k$) are calculated for each observation using its standardized values of the X_1 through X_k. The **eigenvalue** (λ_j) for $j = 1, 2, \ldots, k$ represents the variance of $PRIN_j$, where the weights (**eigenvectors**) are derived so that λ_1 represents the maximum amount of the total variance in the original set of Xs, λ_2 represents the next largest proportion of variance, and so on.

If all λ's are equal to 1.0, the original variables have no linear relationship (i.e., the original variables are **orthogonal**), and collinearity does not exist. If any λ is 0, the original variables have a perfect linear relationship, and collinearity is extreme.

In practice, the analyst is interested in the case where one λ is small relative to the others, indicating the existence of collinearity. To aid in the diagnosis, the analyst is interested in how much smaller one λ is compared to the others and can use the following **condition number (C)**:

$$C = \sqrt{\frac{Largest\ Eigenvalue}{Smallest\ Eigenvalue}}$$

When C is large, there is evidence of collinearity. Based upon their experience, Chatterjee and Hadi (2006) suggest that collinearity affects regression coefficients when the condition number exceeds 15 and argues for necessary corrective action if it exceeds 30. Belsey, Kuh, and Welch (1980) suggest that weak collinearity will have effects for condition numbers as low as 10. In any situation, the analyst should proceed with caution and use subject matter expertise to guide in the final determination.

For simplicity, let's consider the four predictors considered in the correlation section, as displayed in Output 9.4, where the correlation coefficient with the largest magnitude is between GR_LIV_AREA and AGE_AT_SALE ($r = -0.38742$). Consider Program 9.10 VIF and Condition Numbers for Detecting Collinearity.

Program 9.10 VIF and Condition Numbers for Detecting Collinearity

```
libname sasba 'c:\sasba\ames';
data amesreg300;
    set sasba.amesreg300;
run;

proc reg data=amesreg300;
    model SalePrice = Gr_Liv_Area Total_Bsmt_SF Lot_Area
                Age_at_Sale/collinoint vif;
run;
```

The REG procedure and the MODEL statement are identical to those illustrated thus far. However, notice that the options COLLINOINT and VIF are added. The COLLINOINT option requests that principal component analysis be provided with the condition numbers and VIF requests variance inflation factors. (Note: using the COLLIN assumes that the intercept is an effect and can contribute to collinearity; this is used when the intercept has an interpretable meaning and is assumed not equal to zero.) The results are displayed in Output 9.11 VIF and Condition Numbers for Detecting Collinearity.

Output 9.11 VIF and Condition Numbers for Detecting Collinearity

Parameter Estimates						
Variable	DF	Parameter Estimate	Standard Error	t Value	Pr > |t|	Variance Inflation
Intercept	1	77779	5785.70319	13.44	<.0001	0
Gr_Liv_Area	1	57.55856	2.94407	19.55	<.0001	1.20677
Total_Bsmt_SF	1	23.29239	3.05811	7.62	<.0001	1.16517
Lot_Area	1	0.28425	0.23598	1.20	0.2293	1.12938
Age_at_Sale	1	-590.53302	34.89945	-16.92	<.0001	1.29021

Collinearity Diagnostics (intercept adjusted)						
			Proportion of Variation			
Number	Eigenvalue	Condition Index	Gr_Liv_Area	Total_Bsmt_SF	Lot_Area	Age_at_Sale
1	1.82419	1.00000	0.11374	0.10814	0.10129	0.13217
2	0.84073	1.47301	0.38476	0.27045	0.27026	0.08120
3	0.75940	1.54989	0.04891	0.41296	0.60782	0.06989
4	0.57568	1.78010	0.45258	0.20845	0.02063	0.71673

Notice that all VIF values are reasonably low, ranging from 1.12938 to 1.29021; therefore, there is no evidence that collinearity exists. A review of the condition indices also indicates that collinearity is not a problem.

In situations when collinearity is detected, the analyst can delete the redundant predictor or predictors, or combine the predictors if it makes good business sense. If the analyst chooses to delete the redundant predictor, a common approach is to run a regression with each predictor separately to see which contributes more to the fit of the model, therefore keeping that variable in the final predictor set. If the suspect predictor (or predictors) must be included for substantive reasons, the analyst can consider either ridge regression or principal component regression.

Note also that the existence of collinearity results in biased parameter estimates which hinders using regression analysis in 'explaining' relationships. If the purpose of linear regression is 'prediction' only, collinearity does inflate the variance of the predictions; therefore, reducing redundancy is important, as addressed in Chapter 8, "Preparing the Input Variables for Prediction."

Fitting a Simple Linear Regression Model Using the GLM Procedure

In previous sections, linear regression analyses have been conducted using the REG procedure. The analyst can also use the GLM procedure which is designed to estimate parameters for a **general linear model** (GLM). General linear models are a broad class of statistical models having the form (Rutherford, 2001):

$$Data = Model + Error$$

As seen in Chapter 7, "Analysis of Variance (ANOVA)," the analysis of variance (ANOVA) model falls under the umbrella of GLM which assumes that a continuous numeric outcome variable is a function of one or more categorical predictors (called factors, including interactions) and an error term. In that case, analyses are conducted using PROC GLM.

When conducting a linear regression analysis, both REG and GLM procedures produce the ordinary least squares solutions and under the same assumptions. While PROC GLM includes a CLASS statement to allow automatic dummy coding for categorical predictors and provides many of the statistics related to predicted and residual values as found in PROC REG, it does not provide scatter plots, collinearity diagnostics, nor outlier diagnostics. Also PROC GLM allows for only one MODEL statement and has no variable selection capabilities; PROC REG allows multiple MODEL statements for generating multiple model results for comparison purposes and also includes options for variable selection.

Recall from Chapter 7, "Analysis of Variance," (ANOVA)" the syntax for the GLM procedure:

PROC GLM DATA=*SAS-data-set* <**PLOTS**=*options*>;
CLASS *variables*;
MODEL *dependents*=*independents* </ *options*>;
OUTPUT OUT=*SAS-data-set* <keyword=variable…>;
RUN;

Let's first consider the GLM procedure for the specific case where one categorical predictor is used in a regression analysis. Revisiting the Ames Housing Case, suppose we want to predict sale price (SALEPRICE) based upon the overall quality of the house. Remember the variable, OVERALL_QUALITY, is categorical where below average quality, average, and above average are coded as 1, 2, and 3, respectively. Program 9.11 PROC GLM for Prediction Using One Categorical Variable would be used to define OVERALL_QUALITY as a CLASS variable.

Program 9.11 PROC GLM for Prediction Using One Categorical Variable

```
libname sasba 'c:\sasba\ames';
data amesreg300;
   set sasba.amesreg300;
run;

proc glm data=amesreg300;
   class Overall_Quality;
   model SalePrice = Overall_Quality/solution;
   means Overall_Quality/tukey;
run;
```

Notice that the code is equivalent to running an analysis of variance (ANOVA) where the analyst in interested in testing for mean differences in SALEPRICE across the three groups defined by OVERALL_QUALITY. The CLASS statement indicates that the variable, OVERALL_QUALITY, is a categorical predictor variable. The estimated regression equation will be provided only if the SOLUTION option is used. The output can be found in Output 9.12a PROC GLM for Prediction Using One Categorical Variable.

Output 9.12a PROC GLM for Prediction Using One Categorical Variable

Class Level Information		
Class	Levels	Values
Overall_Quality	3	1 2 3

Number of Observations Read	300
Number of Observations Used	300

Source	DF	Sum of Squares	Mean Square	F Value	Pr > F
Model	2	115956795154	57978397577	69.23	<.0001
Error	297	248729287029	837472346.9		
Corrected Total	299	364686082183			

R-Square	Coeff Var	Root MSE	SalePrice Mean
0.317963	18.68124	28939.11	154910.0

Parameter	Estimate		Standard Error	t Value	Pr > |t|
Intercept	173230.9057	B	2295.021063	75.48	<.0001
Overall_Quality 1	-47467.9427	B	6023.671306	-7.88	<.0001
Overall_Quality 2	-36970.4232	B	3551.530703	-10.41	<.0001
Overall_Quality 3	0.0000	B	.	.	.

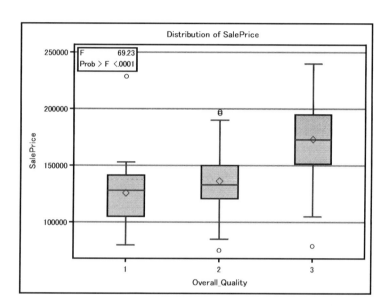

First, the CLASS statement requests that SAS automatically create dummy variables, called **design variables**, for the categorical variable, OVERALL_QUALITY. There are three levels (C=3) for OVERALL_QUALITY (having values 1, 2, and 3, respectively); therefore SAS creates design variables for each of the first (C-1) levels in alpha-numeric order; namely OVERALL_QUALITY 1 and OVERALL_QUALITY 2, as displayed in the table of parameter estimates in Output 9.12a PROC GLM for Prediction Using One Categorical Variable. (OVERALL_QUALITY 3 is created as a reference for comparison.)

Next, upon inspection of the ANOVA table, the analyst can see there are significant differences in the average SalePrice across the three levels of OVERALL_QUALITY, with F-test statistic = 69.23, p < 0.0001, $R^2 = 0.3180$, and RMSE = 28939.11. In other words, OVERALL_QUALITY is considered a good predictor of SALEPRICE. The estimated regression equation is

$$\hat{Y} = 173230.91 - 47467.94*\text{Overall\_Quality 1} - 36970.42*\text{Overall\_Quality 2}$$

So, if the house has above average quality (where the reference group is OVERALL_QUALITY 3 = 1; and OVERALL_QUALITY 1 = 0, OVERALL_QUALITY 2 = 0), then the predicted SalePrice is

$$\hat{Y} = 173230.91 - 47467.94(0) - 36970.42(0) = \$173,230.91 = \text{intercept}$$

If the house has below average quality (OVERALL_QUALITY 1 = 1, all else 0), then the predicted SalePrice is

$$\hat{Y} = 173230.91 - 47467.94(1) - 36970.42(0) = \$125,764.97.$$

Finally, if the house has average quality (OVERALL_QUALITY 2 = 1, all else 0), then the predicted SalePrice is

$$\hat{Y} = 173230.91 - 47467.94(0) - 36970.42(1) = \$136,260.49.$$

The three group means are displayed in the Distribution of SalePrice found in Output 9.12a PROC GLM for Prediction Using One Categorical Variable.

Note also that the slopes for below average quality (OVERALL_QUALITY=1) and average quality (OVERALL_QUALITY=2), respectively, represent how those group means differ from the mean of the reference group (OVERALL_QUALITY=3). So consider the p-value for OVERALL_QUALITY 1 (p<.0001, t = -7.88); in conclusion, the slope is significantly different from zero, indicating that the difference in the average SalePrice for below average quality houses (OVERALL_QUALITY=1) and above average quality houses (OVERALL_QUALITY=3) is significantly different from zero.

Next, consider the p-value for OVERALL_QUALITY 2 (t = -10.41); in conclusion, the slope is significantly different from zero, indicating that the difference in the average SalePrice for average quality houses (OVERALL_QUALITY=2) and above average quality homes (OVERALL_QUALITY=3) is significantly different from zero.

In short, the analyst can see that the average sale prices differ when comparing above average with both average and below average quality houses. However, there is no test provided for testing the difference in sale price when comparing houses with below average (OVERALL_QUALITY=1) and average quality (OVERALL_QUALITY=2).

Finally, notice in Output 9.12a, PROC GLM for Prediction Using One Categorical Variable, the terms whose estimates are followed by the letter B. This indicates that the parameter estimates are not uniquely estimable. This is known as **overparameterization**. Use of the CLASS statement always produces a linear dependency among the levels of the CLASS variables. Simply put--there are too many unknown variables to uniquely solve the set of equations, thereby resulting in infinitely many solutions.

To overcome the issue in SAS, the last level of the categorical variable is defined as the reference group and assigned a parameter estimate of 0. As a result, the parameter estimates of the other levels represent differences in effects between that level and the **reference group**, as illustrated in the predicted Sales Price for OVERALL_QUALITY = 1, 2, and 3, respectively.

The MEANS statement with the TUKEY option provides the results of the multiple comparisons, as shown in Output 9.12b Tukey Procedure for Detecting Differences in Mean Sale Price. As just seen with the *t*-tests, there are significant differences in means when comparing OVERALL_QUALITY 3 with both OVERALL_QUALITY 1 and 2 (indicated by ***); however, there are no differences in the mean saleprice when comparing OVERALL_QUALITY 1 and 2, as indicated by no asterisks.

Output 9.12b Tukey Procedure for Detecting Differences in Mean Sale Price

Overall_Quality Comparison	Difference Between Means	Simultaneous 95% Confidence Limits		
3 - 2	36970	28605	45336	***
3 - 1	47468	33279	61657	***
2 - 3	-36970	-45336	-28605	***
2 - 1	10498	-4092	25087	
1 - 3	-47468	-61657	-33279	***
1 - 2	-10498	-25087	4092	

Comparisons significant at the 0.05 level are indicated by ***.

Finally, the regression output illustrated in Output 9.12b Tukey Procedure for Detecting Differences in Mean Sale Price is equivalent to the output generated by Program 9.12 PROC REG for Prediction Using One Categorical Variable which uses the OVERALL_QUALITY dummy codes created beforehand, as illustrated in Output 9.13 PROC REG for Prediction Using One Categorical Variable.

Program 9.12 PROC REG for Prediction Using One Categorical Variable

```
libname sasba 'c:\sasba\ames';
data amesreg300;
   set sasba.amesreg300;
   Average_Quality=(Overall_Quality=2);
   BelowAverage_Quality=(Overall_Quality=1);
run;
```

```
proc reg;
    model saleprice=average_quality belowaverage_quality;
run;
```

Output 9.13 PROC REG for Prediction Using One Categorical Variable

Root MSE	28939	R-Square	0.3180
Dependent Mean	154910	Adj R-Sq	0.3134
Coeff Var	18.68124		

Parameter Estimates					
Variable	DF	Parameter Estimate	Standard Error	t Value	Pr > |t|
Intercept	1	173231	2295.02106	75.48	<.0001
Average_Quality	1	-36970	3551.53070	-10.41	<.0001
BelowAverage_Quality	1	-47468	6023.67131	-7.88	<.0001

While this example illustrates how to interpret the output when using only one categorical predictor, similar interpretations can be applied in the multiple regression case, as will be illustrated later.

Keep in mind that once a model is constructed using PROC GLM, the analyst can use PROC REG to follow up with diagnostics and residual analyses related to checking assumptions and outlier detection. Note also that GLM allows for defining interaction terms in the MODEL statement, whereas PROC REG does not and requires, instead, creating an interaction variable beforehand (interaction will be addressed in Chapter 10, "Logistic Regression Analysis," and applies here as well).

Variable Selection Using the REG and GLMSELECT Procedures

As mentioned earlier, the analyst is sometimes faced with hundreds of variables as potential inputs for predictive models. Recall that there are strategies for addressing the issue of **redundancy,** that is, where the predictor variables are highly correlated and have overlapping information. Specifically, we discussed using the VIFs (variance inflation values) and condition numbers to address the problem of collinearity. Once one or more potential predictors are deleted because of collinearity, the analyst must next consider the idea of **relevancy** of the predictor to the outcome variable.

In this section, we will discuss the process of variable selection where the analyst is interested in selecting a subset of *j* variables (*j* < *k*) related to the outcome variable, so that the reduced subset, or **reduced model**, provides the 'best' model fit to the data, according to a desired **selection criterion**.

When the number of predictors is small, eliminating one variable at a time is a manageable approach and allows for using knowledge of the subject to guide in selecting the best variable subset. However, when the number of variables is large, eliminating one variable at a time is unreasonable, time consuming, and sometimes impossible; therefore, the analyst must resort to automatic selection procedures.

The first question concerning variable selection is: What SAS procedure should the analyst use? Recall that both the REG and GLM procedures give output for analyzing the relationship between a numeric continuous outcome and a set of predictors, but each have their limitations. So the analyst has two choices for variable selection: (1) PROC REG when all predictors have numeric variable types; or (2) PROC GLMSELECT, an alternative to PROC GLM, for the analyst wanting to perform variable selection procedures and include one or more categorical variables as predictors.

For both procedures, the variable selection process can be conducted using the SELECTION= option within the MODEL statement. The default for the SELECTION option is to fit a **full model**, that is, with all predictors defined in the MODEL statement; the specific option is SELECTION=NONE. PROC REG provides an option to investigation of **all-possible subsets**. For less exhaustive approaches, both PROC REG and PROC GLMSELECT provide options that allow for **sequential searches**; these methods include backward, forward, and stepwise selection.

In this section, we will describe the selection approaches, first using PROC REG, followed by examples using PROC GLMSELECT.

The REG Procedure for Variable Selection

All Possible Subsets

An all possible subset approach provides the analyst with key selection criteria for all possible regression models. In general, if the full model contains k predictors, then there are 2^k-1 possible models from which to choose based upon specified criteria. As the number of predictors increases, the number of models to review becomes unmanageable; therefore, the analyst must resort to various criteria for narrowing the candidate models.

The common criteria for variable selection are the adjusted R^2, the standard error of the regression (S_e), and Mallows' C_p (Mallow, 1973). The first indices have been discussed previously; let's now consider Mallows' C_p which is calculated using:

$$C_p = p + \frac{(MSE_p - MSE_{full})(n - p)}{MSE_{full}}$$

where p is the number of parameters in the model under review (including the intercept), MSE_p is the mean-squared-error for the model containing p parameters, MSE_{full} is the mean-square-error for the full model representing an estimate of the variance of the residuals, and n is the sample size.

When the full model and the model with p parameters explain the same variance in the outcome variable, MSE_p and MSE_{full} are equal and $C_p = p$. In other words, when $C_p = p$, the full model adds no information that is not already provided by the model with p parameters. Therefore, the reduced model with p parameters is preferred. In conclusion, Mallow suggested the following rule:

Selection Criterion: Select the model having the least number of variables where $C_p \leq p$. In other words, select the most parsimonious model where C_p is closest to p.

Hocking (1976) suggested that the model selection criteria should take into account the purpose of the analysis, whether prediction or estimation. Hocking suggested the use of Mallows' C_p with the following selection criteria based upon the purpose:

For prediction, use $\quad C_p \leq p$

For estimation, use $\quad C_p \leq 2p - p_{full} + 1$

Consider the Ames Housing Case where the analyst is interested in relating the outcome variable, SALEPRICE, to the predictor set made up of twelve possible predictors.

From Program 9.13 Best Subsets Regression Models Ranked by Adjusted R-Square, we can see that the REG procedure is applied to the Ames Housing data set, as defined by the DATA= option. The MODEL statement is used to define the linear model and the SELECTION=ADJRSQ option requests that the models are ranked from best to worst according to the R^2_{adj} value. Including RSQUARE and CP in the selection option requests that those values are printed for each model as well. The BEST=200 option requests output for the top, or best, 200 models out of the 4095 total possible models. The PLOTS(ONLY)=(ADJRSQ) option requests that the R^2_{adj} values be plotted by each subset size for each of the 200 models.

Finally, note that the MODEL statement is prefaced with the label, ALL_MODELS. This is especially useful when there are multiple MODEL statements and allows for labeling, or describing, each model in the output, as opposed to each model being labeled with the default Model 1, Model 2, etc. The results of the code are displayed in Output 9.14 Best Subsets Regression Models Ranked by Adjusted R-Square.

Program 9.13 Best Subsets Regression Models Ranked by Adjusted R-Square

```
libname sasba 'c:\sasba\ames';
data amesreg300;
   set sasba.amesreg300;
run;

proc reg data=amesreg300
   plots(only)=(adjrsq);
   ALL_MODELS: model SalePrice = Gr_Liv_Area Total_Bsmt_SF
               Lot_Area Age_At_Sale High_Kitchen_Quality
               Fullbath_2Plus Fireplace_1Plus TwoPlusCar_Garage
```

```
            High_Exterior_Cond CuldeSac Has_Fence Land_Level
            /selection=adjrsq rsquare cp best=200;
run;
```

Output 9.14 Best Subsets Regression Models Ranked by Adjusted R-Square

Model: ALL_MODELS
Dependent Variable: SalePrice
Adjusted R-Square Selection Method

Model Index	Number in Model	Adjusted R-Square	R-Square	C(p)	Variables in Model
1	9	0.8565	0.8608	8.1014	Gr_Liv_Area Total_Bsmt_SF Lot_Area Age_at_Sale High_Kitchen_Quality Fullbath_2plus Fireplace_1plus TwoPlusCar_Garage Land_Level
2	10	0.8564	0.8612	9.2010	Gr_Liv_Area Total_Bsmt_SF Lot_Area Age_at_Sale High_Kitchen_Quality Fullbath_2plus Fireplace_1plus TwoPlusCar_Garage CuldeSac Land_Level
3	8	0.8561	0.8600	7.7557	Gr_Liv_Area Total_Bsmt_SF Lot_Area Age_at_Sale High_Kitchen_Quality Fullbath_2plus Fireplace_1plus TwoPlusCar_Garage
4	10	0.8561	0.8609	9.8807	Gr_Liv_Area Total_Bsmt_SF Lot_Area Age_at_Sale High_Kitchen_Quality Fullbath_2plus Fireplace_1plus TwoPlusCar_Garage High_Exterior_Cond Land_Level
5	9	0.8561	0.8604	8.8865	Gr_Liv_Area Total_Bsmt_SF Lot_Area Age_at_Sale High_Kitchen_Quality Fullbath_2plus Fireplace_1plus TwoPlusCar_Garage CuldeSac
6	9	0.8560	0.8604	8.9502	Gr_Liv_Area Total_Bsmt_SF Lot_Area Age_at_Sale High_Kitchen_Quality Fireplace_1plus TwoPlusCar_Garage CuldeSac Land_Level
7	8	0.8560	0.8599	7.9867	Gr_Liv_Area Total_Bsmt_SF Lot_Area Age_at_Sale High_Kitchen_Quality Fireplace_1plus TwoPlusCar_Garage Land_Level
8	11	0.8560	0.8613	11.0068	Gr_Liv_Area Total_Bsmt_SF Lot_Area Age_at_Sale High_Kitchen_Quality Fullbath_2plus Fireplace_1plus TwoPlusCar_Garage High_Exterior_Cond CuldeSac Land_Level
9	10	0.8560	0.8608	10.0999	Gr_Liv_Area Total_Bsmt_SF Lot_Area Age_at_Sale High_Kitchen_Quality Fullbath_2plus Fireplace_1plus TwoPlusCar_Garage Has_Fence Land_Level
10	9	0.8559	0.8603	9.1346	Gr_Liv_Area Total_Bsmt_SF Age_at_Sale High_Kitchen_Quality Fullbath_2plus Fireplace_1plus TwoPlusCar_Garage CuldeSac Land_Level
11	11	0.8559	0.8612	11.1964	Gr_Liv_Area Total_Bsmt_SF Lot_Area Age_at_Sale High_Kitchen_Quality Fullbath_2plus Fireplace_1plus TwoPlusCar_Garage CuldeSac Has_Fence Land_Level
12	8	0.8558	0.8597	8.3876	Gr_Liv_Area Total_Bsmt_SF Age_at_Sale High_Kitchen_Quality Fullbath_2plus Fireplace_1plus TwoPlusCar_Garage Land_Level

Model Index	Number in Model	Adjusted R-Square	R-Square	C(p)	Variables in Model
13	8	0.8557	0.8596	8.5371	Gr_Liv_Area Total_Bsmt_SF Age_at_Sale High_Kitchen_Quality Fullbath_2plus Fireplace_1plus TwoPlusCar_Garage CuldeSac
14	8	0.8557	0.8596	8.6028	Gr_Liv_Area Total_Bsmt_SF Lot_Area Age_at_Sale High_Kitchen_Quality Fireplace_1plus TwoPlusCar_Garage CuldeSac
15	7	0.8557	0.8591	7.6048	Gr_Liv_Area Total_Bsmt_SF Lot_Area Age_at_Sale High_Kitchen_Quality Fireplace_1plus TwoPlusCar_Garage
16	9	0.8557	0.8601	9.6123	Gr_Liv_Area Total_Bsmt_SF Lot_Area Age_at_Sale High_Kitchen_Quality Fullbath_2plus Fireplace_1plus TwoPlusCar_Garage High_Exterior_Cond
17	7	0.8556	0.8590	7.7305	Gr_Liv_Area Total_Bsmt_SF Age_at_Sale High_Kitchen_Quality Fullbath_2plus Fireplace_1plus TwoPlusCar_Garage
18	9	0.8556	0.8600	9.7550	Gr_Liv_Area Total_Bsmt_SF Lot_Area Age_at_Sale High_Kitchen_Quality Fullbath_2plus Fireplace_1plus TwoPlusCar_Garage Has_Fence
19	10	0.8556	0.8605	10.7644	Gr_Liv_Area Total_Bsmt_SF Lot_Area Age_at_Sale High_Kitchen_Quality Fullbath_2plus Fireplace_1plus TwoPlusCar_Garage High_Exterior_Cond CuldeSac
20	10	0.8556	0.8605	10.7712	Gr_Liv_Area Total_Bsmt_SF Age_at_Sale High_Kitchen_Quality Fullbath_2plus Fireplace_1plus TwoPlusCar_Garage High_Exterior_Cond CuldeSac Land_Level

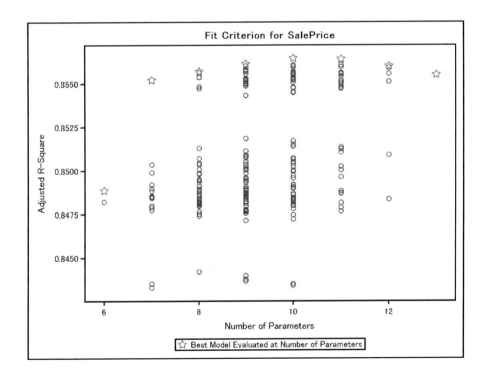

Notice at the top of the output, there is a label 'ALL_MODELS' which can be used to distinguish the output from the output of other models. Included in the heading is the dependent variable and the type of method used for sorting, namely, adjusted r-square.

The first item found in the output is an excerpt from the line listing of 200 models in order of their R^2_{adj} values, including the number of predictors (k) in each model, R^2_{adj}, R^2, Mallows' C_p, and the variables that make up the model. This information is voluminous. Therefore, the plot of R^2_{adj} by number of parameters (included in the figure also) can be used to aid in the selection process.

The plot shows the number of parameters on the X-axis and the R^2_{adj} on the Y-axis. There are several things to note. There is relatively little variation in the R^2_{adj} for the top 200 models, ranging in values from around 0.8525 to 0.8565; however, among those 200 models, there are three distinct groups--the top set with R^2_{adj} around 0.8550, the middle with R^2_{adj} from around 0.8475 to 0.8520, and the lower set with R^2_{adj} below 0.8450. Also, the 'best' models at each size, represented by the stars, have relatively little variation, specifically from seven to thirteen parameters (six to twelve predictors).

So if the criterion is to pick the single best model based upon R^2_{adj}, the decision is the model labeled as Model Index 1 (R^2_{adj} = 0.8565) with nine predictors in the model (k=9, p=10). If the analyst wants to consider the most parsimonious model, reviewing the difference in the top three models seems to indicate that they all have the first eight predictors in common and differ only by the inclusion or exclusion of LAND_LEVEL or CULDESAC.

So choosing as best the model of size eight seems reasonable, which is the model having predictors GR_LIV_AREA, TOTAL_BSMT_SF, LOT_AREA, AGE_AT_SALE, HIGH_KITCHEN_QUALITY, FULLBATH_2PLUS, FIREPLACE_1PLUS, and TWOPLUSCAR_GARAGE. In addition, of the top 200 models, all 200 models contain GR_LIV_AREA, TOTAL_BSMT_SF, AGE_AT_SALE, and HIGH_KITCHEN_QUALITY; 128 contain FIREPLACE_1PLUS, 128 contain TWOPLUSCAR_GARAGE, 104 contain FULLBATH_2PLUS, 103 contain LOT_AREA, 103 contain LAND_LEVEL; three variables show up in a little less than half of those--99 models contain HIGH_EXTERIOR_CONDITION, 98 contain CULDESAC, and 98 contain HAS_FENCE. In short, eight of the twelve possible predictors showing up most in the top 200 are included in the best subset of size eight.

Consider now using Mallows' C_p for the selection criterion. The SAS code would be identical to the previous code with two exceptions in the PLOT(ONLY)= and the SELECTION= options, as illustrated in Program 9.14 Best Subsets Regression Models Ranked by Mallows' C_p.

Program 9.14 Best Subsets Regression Models Ranked by Mallows' Cp

```
libname sasba 'c:\sasba\ames';
data amesreg300;
   set sasba.amesreg300;
run;

proc reg data=amesreg300
   plots(only)=(cp);
   ALL_MODELS: model SalePrice = Gr_Liv_Area Total_Bsmt_SF
               Lot_Area Age_At_Sale High_Kitchen_Quality
               Fullbath_2Plus Fireplace_1Plus TwoPlusCar_Garage
               High_Exterior_Cond CuldeSac Has_Fence Land_Level
               /selection=cp adjrsq rsquare best=200;
run;
```

The output is displayed in Output 9.15a Mallows' C_p Plot for Variable Selection and Output 9.15b Best Subsets Regression Models Ranked by Mallows' C_p.

Upon inspection of the Mallows' C_p, plot, first note the solid line representing Mallows' criterion, where $C_p = p$. Note that the points either on or slightly below match Mallows' criterion. Therefore, the analyst should select the one that has the least number of variables (remember parsimony). An inspection of the excerpt from the line listing will aid in identifying the top candidate models. Those are Model Index 2 (where C_p=7.6048 < p=k+1=8, for k=7, R^2_{adj} = 0.8557), Model Index 3 (where C_p=7.7305 < p=k+1=8, for k=7, R^2_{adj} = 0.8556), Model Index 12 (where C_p=8.8728 < p=k+1=9, for k=8, R^2_{adj} = 0.8556), and Model Index 29 (where C_p=9.9621 < p=k+1=10, for k=9, R^2_{adj} = 0.8555).

All of the candidate models have practically the same R^2_{adj} and follow Mallows' criterion; therefore, selecting the model with the least number of predictors seems reasonable. The two models having the least number of predictors (k=7) differ by the variables LOT_AREA and FULLBATH_2PLUS and match on all other variables. Practically speaking, it may be better to select the variable, FULLBATH_2PLUS, being that it is easier to measure or obtain in future samples than, say, LOT_AREA.

Output 9.15a Mallows' Cp Plot for Variable Selection

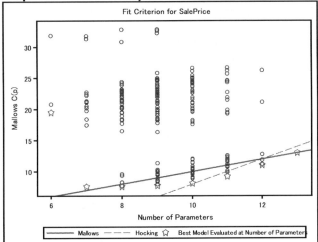

Output 9.15b Best Subsets Regression Models Ranked by Mallows' Cp

Model Index	Number in Model	C(p)	R-Square	Adjusted R-Square	Variables in Model
1	6	7.5948	0.8581	0.8552	Gr_Liv_Area Total_Bsmt_SF Age_at_Sale High_Kitchen_Quality Fireplace_1plus TwoPlusCar_Garage
2	7	7.6048	0.8591	0.8557	Gr_Liv_Area Total_Bsmt_SF Lot_Area Age_at_Sale High_Kitchen_Quality Fireplace_1plus TwoPlusCar_Garage
3	7	7.7305	0.8590	0.8556	Gr_Liv_Area Total_Bsmt_SF Age_at_Sale High_Kitchen_Quality Fullbath_2plus Fireplace_1plus TwoPlusCar_Garage
4	8	7.7557	0.8600	0.8561	Gr_Liv_Area Total_Bsmt_SF Lot_Area Age_at_Sale High_Kitchen_Quality Fullbath_2plus Fireplace_1plus TwoPlusCar_Garage
5	8	7.9867	0.8599	0.8560	Gr_Liv_Area Total_Bsmt_SF Lot_Area Age_at_Sale High_Kitchen_Quality Fireplace_1plus TwoPlusCar_Garage Land_Level
6	9	8.1014	0.8608	0.8565	Gr_Liv_Area Total_Bsmt_SF Lot_Area Age_at_Sale High_Kitchen_Quality Fullbath_2plus Fireplace_1plus TwoPlusCar_Garage Land_Level
7	7	8.2461	0.8588	0.8554	Gr_Liv_Area Total_Bsmt_SF Age_at_Sale High_Kitchen_Quality Fireplace_1plus TwoPlusCar_Garage CuldeSac
8	7	8.2856	0.8588	0.8554	Gr_Liv_Area Total_Bsmt_SF Age_at_Sale High_Kitchen_Quality Fireplace_1plus TwoPlusCar_Garage Land_Level
9	8	8.3876	0.8597	0.8558	Gr_Liv_Area Total_Bsmt_SF Age_at_Sale High_Kitchen_Quality Fullbath_2plus Fireplace_1plus TwoPlusCar_Garage Land_Level
10	8	8.5371	0.8596	0.8557	Gr_Liv_Area Total_Bsmt_SF Age_at_Sale High_Kitchen_Quality Fullbath_2plus Fireplace_1plus TwoPlusCar_Garage CuldeSac

Model Index	Number in Model	C(p)	R-Square	Adjusted R-Square	Variables in Model
11	8	8.6028	0.8596	0.8557	Gr_Liv_Area Total_Bsmt_SF Lot_Area Age_at_Sale High_Kitchen_Quality Fireplace_1plus TwoPlusCar_Garage CuldeSac
12	8	8.8728	0.8594	0.8556	Gr_Liv_Area Total_Bsmt_SF Age_at_Sale High_Kitchen_Quality Fireplace_1plus TwoPlusCar_Garage CuldeSac Land_Level
13	9	8.8865	0.8604	0.8561	Gr_Liv_Area Total_Bsmt_SF Lot_Area Age_at_Sale High_Kitchen_Quality Fullbath_2plus Fireplace_1plus TwoPlusCar_Garage CuldeSac
14	9	8.9502	0.8604	0.8560	Gr_Liv_Area Total_Bsmt_SF Lot_Area Age_at_Sale High_Kitchen_Quality Fireplace_1plus TwoPlusCar_Garage CuldeSac Land_Level
15	9	9.1346	0.8603	0.8559	Gr_Liv_Area Total_Bsmt_SF Age_at_Sale High_Kitchen_Quality Fullbath_2plus Fireplace_1plus TwoPlusCar_Garage CuldeSac Land_Level
16	10	9.2010	0.8612	0.8564	Gr_Liv_Area Total_Bsmt_SF Lot_Area Age_at_Sale High_Kitchen_Quality Fullbath_2plus Fireplace_1plus TwoPlusCar_Garage CuldeSac Land_Level
17	7	9.3591	0.8582	0.8548	Gr_Liv_Area Total_Bsmt_SF Age_at_Sale High_Kitchen_Quality Fireplace_1plus TwoPlusCar_Garage High_Exterior_Cond
18	8	9.4202	0.8592	0.8553	Gr_Liv_Area Total_Bsmt_SF Age_at_Sale High_Kitchen_Quality Fullbath_2plus Fireplace_1plus TwoPlusCar_Garage High_Exterior_Cond
19	8	9.5110	0.8591	0.8553	Gr_Liv_Area Total_Bsmt_SF Lot_Area Age_at_Sale High_Kitchen_Quality Fireplace_1plus TwoPlusCar_Garage High_Exterior_Cond
20	8	9.5865	0.8591	0.8552	Gr_Liv_Area Total_Bsmt_SF Lot_Area Age_at_Sale High_Kitchen_Quality Fireplace_1plus TwoPlusCar_Garage Has_Fence
21	7	9.5926	0.8581	0.8547	Gr_Liv_Area Total_Bsmt_SF Age_at_Sale High_Kitchen_Quality Fireplace_1plus TwoPlusCar_Garage Has_Fence
22	9	9.6123	0.8601	0.8557	Gr_Liv_Area Total_Bsmt_SF Lot_Area Age_at_Sale High_Kitchen_Quality Fullbath_2plus Fireplace_1plus TwoPlusCar_Garage High_Exterior_Cond
23	8	9.7174	0.8590	0.8552	Gr_Liv_Area Total_Bsmt_SF Age_at_Sale High_Kitchen_Quality Fullbath_2plus Fireplace_1plus TwoPlusCar_Garage Has_Fence
24	9	9.7550	0.8600	0.8556	Gr_Liv_Area Total_Bsmt_SF Lot_Area Age_at_Sale High_Kitchen_Quality Fullbath_2plus Fireplace_1plus TwoPlusCar_Garage Has_Fence
25	9	9.8304	0.8599	0.8556	Gr_Liv_Area Total_Bsmt_SF Lot_Area Age_at_Sale High_Kitchen_Quality Fireplace_1plus TwoPlusCar_Garage High_Exterior_Cond Land_Level

Model Index	Number in Model	C(p)	R-Square	Adjusted R-Square	Variables in Model
26	10	9.8807	0.8609	0.8561	Gr_Liv_Area Total_Bsmt_SF Lot_Area Age_at_Sale High_Kitchen_Quality Fullbath_2plus Fireplace_1plus TwoPlusCar_Garage High_Exterior_Cond Land_Level
27	9	9.9462	0.8599	0.8555	Gr_Liv_Area Total_Bsmt_SF Lot_Area Age_at_Sale High_Kitchen_Quality Fireplace_1plus TwoPlusCar_Garage Has_Fence Land_Level
28	8	9.9509	0.8589	0.8550	Gr_Liv_Area Total_Bsmt_SF Age_at_Sale High_Kitchen_Quality Fireplace_1plus TwoPlusCar_Garage High_Exterior_Cond Land_Level
29	9	9.9621	0.8599	0.8555	Gr_Liv_Area Total_Bsmt_SF Age_at_Sale High_Kitchen_Quality Fullbath_2plus Fireplace_1plus TwoPlusCar_Garage High_Exterior_Cond Land_Level
30	8	10.0567	0.8589	0.8550	Gr_Liv_Area Total_Bsmt_SF Age_at_Sale High_Kitchen_Quality Fireplace_1plus TwoPlusCar_Garage High_Exterior_Cond CuldeSac

Now let's consider Hocking's criteria for variable selection when the purpose of regression analysis is estimation. Upon inspection of Output 9.15a Mallows' Cp Plot for Variable Selection, notice that only models having eleven or more parameters (ten or more predictors) fit the criterion, where the Mallows' C_p falls below the dotted line. Therefore, the analyst could select the smallest predictor set (p=11, k=10) based upon parsimony. Here, for p=11,

$$C_p \leq 2p - p_{full} + 1 = 2(11) - 13 + 1 = 10$$

where p_{full} = 13 (12 predictors and an intercept). So for ten predictors (k=10), the model where $C_p \leq 10$ is best. This corresponds to Model Index 16 (where C_p=9.201 < 10, R^2_{adj} = 0.8564), and Model Index 26 (where C_p=9.8807 < 10, R^2_{adj} = 0.8561), differing only by the variables CULDESAC and HIGH_EXTERIOR_COND. These models are indistinguishable in performance; however, it may be practical to have a model with CULDESAC as opposed to HIGH_EXTERIOR_COND, as HIGH_EXTERIOR_COND may be harder to collect and may be subject to opinion.

Whether selecting a model for either explanation or prediction, it is easy to see that there are many equivalent models that perform equally well based upon the selection criterion; therefore, it is important to consider the subject matter, past research, and/or industry standards when selecting the model that makes most sense. In fact, the analyst may consider validation procedures to see which model performs best on an external data set, which will be discussed in Chapter 11 "Measure of Model Performance."

Also keep in mind, that while the best subset approach provides a relatively easy way to select from the top performing candidates, one drawback is that the model selection progresses blindly without regard to actual parameters estimates nor p-values. Investigating the details of each model can aid in selecting that final one.

Backward Elimination

Backward elimination starts with the model containing all variables specified in the MODEL statement, and then the variable deemed least important is removed when that variable fails to satisfy the criterion for staying in the model. Each subsequent predictor is evaluated for removal, and predictors are removed, one at time, until all remaining variables are considered important based upon their p-values. At this point, the variable selection process ends. Note that, for backward elimination, once a variable is dropped, it cannot be added.

So how is a variable deleted? A variable is deleted if its presence in the model results in the smallest reduction in the error sums-of-squares; in other words, if its presence does not significantly improve the fit of the model. This is equivalent to running a linear regression analysis with all predictors, reviewing the *t*-test statistics (equal to the partial F-test) of those predictors, and dropping the predictor having the largest p-value only if that p-value exceeds the criterion to stay.

To illustrate the backward elimination process, consider the Ames Housing Case. Suppose we used preliminary analyses to arrive at a candidate set of twelve possible predictor variables; note that the binary predictors are already dummy coded, so using the PROC REG is allowed. The goal is to eliminate those variables considered unimportant, using Program 9.15 Backward Elimination for the Ames Housing Case.

Program 9.15 Backward Elimination for the Ames Housing Case

```
libname sasba 'c:\sasba\ames';
data amesreg300;
   set sasba.amesreg300;
run;

proc reg data=amesreg300
   plots(only)=(adjrsq);
   BACKWARD: model SalePrice= Gr_Liv_Area Total_Bsmt_SF Lot_Area
               Age_At_Sale High_Kitchen_Quality Fullbath_2Plus
               Fireplace_1Plus TwoPlusCar_Garage
               High_Exterior_Cond CuldeSac Has_Fence Land_Level
               /selection=backward slstay=0.01 details;
run;
```

In Program 9.15 Backward Elimination for the Ames Housing Case, the MODEL statement is used to define the outcome variable, SALEPRICE, and the twelve variables to be included in the selection process. The PLOTS(ONLY)=(ADJRSQ) option requests the plot of the R^2_{adj} values at each step of the selection process.

The MODEL statement defines the linear model and has three options. First, the SELECTION=BACKWARD requests that the backward elimination method be used, where the *t*-test is used for determining the removal of a predictor from the model. Second, the SLSTAY specifies the significance level for the test; in other words, it defines the minimum p-value necessary for any predictor to stay in the model (in our case, that is 0.01). Finally, the DETAILS option requests a summary of each step in the elimination process.

Note also that the MODEL statement is prefaced with the label, BACKWARD. This requests that the analysis output have the label, BACKWARD, as opposed to using the default Model 1, Model 2, etc.; and can be used to distinguish the output here from, for example, the previous output, labeled ALL_MODELS, as found in Program 9.14. The results of the backward elimination method are displayed in Output 9.16a Backward Elimination Step 0 through Output 9.16f Plot of Adjusted R-Square by Backward Elimination Step.

In Output 9.16a Backward Elimination Step 0, first notice that the label, Model: BACKWARD, is provided to distinguish the model from any other regression models. Step 0 is displayed first and includes the R^2 value (0.8613) and Mallows' C_p (13.0000) for the full model containing all twelve predictors. Step 0 also includes the list of parameter estimates for the full model, along with the partial F-values and associated p-values.

Output 9.16a Backward Elimination Step 0

Model: BACKWARD

Backward Elimination: Step 0

All Variables Entered: R-Square = 0.8613 and C(p) = 13.0000

Variable	Parameter Estimate	Standard Error	Type II SS	F Value	Pr > F
Intercept	72826	6307.56022	23491999677	133.31	<.0001
Gr_Liv_Area	45.55652	3.47401	30304724751	171.96	<.0001
Total_Bsmt_SF	21.81672	2.81430	10590313390	60.09	<.0001
Lot_Area	0.29337	0.22044	312133280	1.77	0.1843
Age_at_Sale	-454.62039	39.36062	23509636603	133.41	<.0001
High_Kitchen_Quality	10443	1865.65794	5521121968	31.33	<.0001
Fullbath_2plus	3216.45903	2425.98935	309777810	1.76	0.1859
Fireplace_1plus	6711.36945	1718.54076	2687662044	15.25	0.0001
TwoPlusCar_Garage	6314.38162	1980.70645	1790991211	10.16	0.0016
High_Exterior_Cond	1062.45435	2397.25317	34615036	0.20	0.6580
CuldeSac	3572.79614	3813.64165	154670947	0.88	0.3496

Variable	Parameter Estimate	Standard Error	Type II SS	F Value	Pr > F
Has_Fence	-147.80588	1792.54270	1198164	0.01	0.9343
Land_Level	4354.28123	3278.14701	310919624	1.76	0.1851

Step 1 is displayed in Output 9.16b Backward Elimination Step 1 and contains the statistics for removal for all twelve predictors in the model. Note that the variable, HAS_FENCE, is the least related to SALEPRICE as indicated by the largest p-value (0.9343); therefore, HAS_FENCE is removed from the model. As a result, the model with eleven predictors, excluding HAS_FENCE, has an R^2 value (0.8613) and Mallows' C_p (11.0068).

Output 9.16b Backward Elimination Step 1

Model: BACKWARD

Backward Elimination: Step 1

Statistics for Removal DF = 1,287				
Variable	Partial R-Square	Model R-Square	F Value	Pr > F
Gr_Liv_Area	0.0831	0.7782	171.96	<.0001
Total_Bsmt_SF	0.0290	0.8323	60.09	<.0001
Lot_Area	0.0009	0.8605	1.77	0.1843
Age_at_Sale	0.0645	0.7968	133.41	<.0001
High_Kitchen_Quality	0.0151	0.8462	31.33	<.0001
Fullbath_2plus	0.0008	0.8605	1.76	0.1859
Fireplace_1plus	0.0074	0.8539	15.25	0.0001
TwoPlusCar_Garage	0.0049	0.8564	10.16	0.0016
High_Exterior_Cond	0.0001	0.8612	0.20	0.6580
CuldeSac	0.0004	0.8609	0.88	0.3496
Has_Fence	0.0000	0.8613	0.01	0.9343
Land_Level	0.0009	0.8605	1.76	0.1851

Variable Has_Fence Removed: R-Square = 0.8613 and C(p) = 11.0068

Step 2 of the backward elimination is displayed in Output 9.16c Backward Elimination Step 2, and contains the statistics for removal for the remaining eleven predictors in the model. Note that the variable, HIGH_EXTERIOR_COND, is the least related to SALEPRICE as indicated by the largest p-value (0.6592); therefore, HIGH_EXTERIOR_COND is removed from the model. As a result, the model with ten predictors, excluding now HAS_FENCE and HIGH_EXTERIOR_COND, has an R^2 value (0.8612) and Mallows' C_p (9.2010).

Output 9.16c Backward Elimination Step 2

Model: BACKWARD

Backward Elimination: Step 2

Variable	Partial R-Square	Model R-Square	F Value	Pr > F
Gr_Liv_Area	0.0836	0.7777	173.68	<.0001
Total_Bsmt_SF	0.0290	0.8323	60.32	<.0001
Lot_Area	0.0009	0.8605	1.77	0.1844
Age_at_Sale	0.0645	0.7968	133.90	<.0001
High_Kitchen_Quality	0.0152	0.8461	31.57	<.0001
Fullbath_2plus	0.0009	0.8604	1.82	0.1790
Fireplace_1plus	0.0074	0.8539	15.38	0.0001
TwoPlusCar_Garage	0.0050	0.8563	10.33	0.0015
High_Exterior_Cond	0.0001	0.8612	0.19	0.6592
CuldeSac	0.0004	0.8609	0.88	0.3498
Land_Level	0.0008	0.8605	1.76	0.1852

Statistics for Removal DF = 1,288

Variable High_Exterior_Cond Removed: R-Square = 0.8612 and C(p) = 9.2010

The process continues until no variables are removed; in other words, the removal stops when all remaining predictors have p-values less than 0.01 as defined in the SLSTAY=0.01 option, as displayed in Output 9.16d Backward Elimination Step 7. In Step 7, notice that all remaining six variables meet the 0.01 criterion to stay in the model; therefore, the backward elimination process stops.

Output 9.16d Backward Elimination Step 7

Model: BACKWARD

Backward Elimination: Step 7

Variable	Partial R-Square	Model R-Square	F Value	Pr > F
Gr_Liv_Area	0.1284	0.7298	265.09	<.0001
Total_Bsmt_SF	0.0325	0.8257	67.06	<.0001
Age_at_Sale	0.0831	0.7750	171.72	<.0001
High_Kitchen_Quality	0.0166	0.8415	34.28	<.0001
Fireplace_1plus	0.0074	0.8508	15.19	0.0001
TwoPlusCar_Garage	0.0067	0.8514	13.88	0.0002

Statistics for Removal DF = 1,293

All variables left in the model are significant at the 0.0100 level

Because the DETAILS option is included with the SELECTION= option, a summary of the steps is provided as displayed in Output 9.16e Summary of Backward Elimination. Here the analyst can see the six variables removed from the initial set of twelve possible predictors, retaining the other six variables, GR_LIV_AREA, TOTAL_BSMT_SF, AGE_AT_SALE, HIGH_KITCHEN_QUALITY, FIREPLACE_1PLUS, and TWOPLUSCAR_GARAGE for the final model.

Output 9.16e Summary of Backward Elimination

		Summary of Backward Elimination					
Step	Variable Removed	Number Vars In	Partial R-Square	Model R-Square	C(p)	F Value	Pr > F
1	Has_Fence	11	0.0000	0.8613	11.0068	0.01	0.9343
2	High_Exterior_Cond	10	0.0001	0.8612	9.2010	0.19	0.6592
3	CuldeSac	9	0.0004	0.8608	8.1014	0.91	0.3420
4	Land_Level	8	0.0008	0.8600	7.7557	1.67	0.1979
5	Fullbath_2plus	7	0.0009	0.8591	7.6048	1.86	0.1740
6	Lot_Area	6	0.0010	0.8581	7.5948	1.99	0.1591

Finally, the plot of R^2_{adj} is provided in Output 9.16f Plot of Adjusted R-Square by Backward Elimination Step, illustrating that the fit improved through the third step, after CULDESAC was removed, and then diminished for the remaining steps. While the drop seems drastic, notice that the range of the Y-axis is small so that a relatively small difference in R^2_{adj} seems large. In fact, the difference between the largest and smallest R^2_{adj} is about 0.0012; therefore, opting to delete six variables provides a much simpler model at very little expense to fit.

Output 9.16f Plot of Adjusted R-Square by Backward Elimination Step

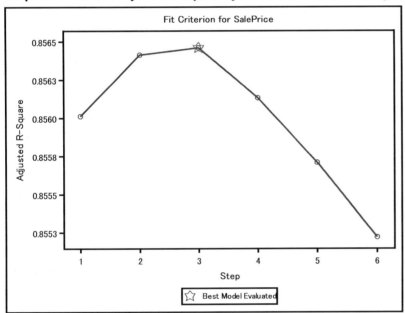

Forward Selection

Forward selection starts with the model containing only the intercept, and then adds variables one at a time as long as each satisfies the criterion for entry in the model. Once a model is fit such that no other remaining variables meet the criterion for entry, the variable selection process ends. Note, again, in forward selection, once a variable is added, it can never be removed.

So how is a variable selected for entry into the model? A variable is selected if it explains the most variation in the outcome variable of all variables considered for entry; this is equivalent to selecting the single predictor having the highest correlation with the outcome variable. This can be determined by conducting *k* simple linear regression models and selecting the single predictor with the smallest p-value (largest F-test statistic).

Once the first predictor is entered into the model, all *(k-1)* two-predictor models are run, where each model is made up of the first predictor paired with one of the remaining *(k-1)* predictors. The next (second) variable selected for entry is that variable having the largest correlation with the outcome variable, after adjusting for the presence of the first predictor. This is determined again by the smallest p-value (largest partial F-test statistic). The process of adding predictors continues until no variable meets the criterion for entry.

To illustrate the forward selection process, consider the Ames Housing Case, where the analyst is starting with a candidate set of twelve possible predictor variables. The goal is to add those variables considered important, using Program 9.16 Forward Selection for the Ames Housing Case:

Program 9.16 Forward Selection for the Ames Housing Case

```
libname sasba 'c:\sasba\ames';
data amesreg300;
   set sasba.amesreg300;
run;

proc reg data=amesreg300
   plots(only)=(adjrsq);
   FORWARD: model SalePrice= Gr_Liv_Area Total_Bsmt_SF Lot_Area
              Age_At_Sale High_Kitchen_Quality Fullbath_2Plus
               Fireplace_1Plus TwoPlusCar_Garage
                High_Exterior_Cond CuldeSac Has_Fence Land_Level
                /selection=forward slentry=0.01 details;
run;
```

In Program 9.16 Forward Selection for the Ames Housing Case, the MODEL statement is used to define the outcome variable, SALEPRICE, and the twelve variables to be included in the selection process. Like the backward elimination, here we are including the PLOTS(ONLY)=(ADJRSQ) option so that we can observe the R^2_{adj} values at each step of the selection process.

Note also that the MODEL statement is used to define the linear model, and three options are included. First, the SELECTION=FORWARD requests that the forward selection method be used, where the F-test is used for determining the entry of a predictor into the model. Second, the SLENTRY specifies the significance level for the test; in other words, it defines the minimum p-value necessary for any predictor to enter the model. Finally, the DETAILS option requests a summary of each step in the selection process.

The model statement is prefaced with the label, FORWARD, so that the output is labeled to distinguish it from the output of other regression analyses. The results of the code are displayed in Output 9.17a Forward Selection Step 1 through Output 9.17e Plot of Adjusted R-Square by Forward Selection Step.

In Output 9.17a Forward Selection Step 1, first notice that the label, Model: FORWARD, is provided to distinguish the model from any other regression models. Step 1 is displayed next and includes the list of parameter estimates for each model containing only the single predictor, along with their respective F-values, p-values, and R^2 values.

The smallest p-value is associated with both the largest F-value and R^2 value and is considered the best one-predictor model; therefore, the model with GR_LIV_AREA is selected first, having R^2 equal to 0.5529 and Mallows' C_p = 629.2392. Note that the tolerance equals 1.0 indicating that the addition of that variable results in no collinearity--which makes sense being that its addition results in a model with only one predictor.

Output 9.17a Forward Selection Step 1

Model: FORWARD

Forward Selection: Step 1

Statistics for Entry DF = 1,298				
Variable	Tolerance	Model R-Square	F Value	Pr > F
Gr_Liv_Area	1.000000	0.5529	368.51	<.0001
Total_Bsmt_SF	1.000000	0.2073	77.94	<.0001
Lot_Area	1.000000	0.0993	32.87	<.0001
Age_at_Sale	1.000000	0.5428	353.80	<.0001
High_Kitchen_Quality	1.000000	0.2464	97.45	<.0001
Fullbath_2plus	1.000000	0.5051	304.18	<.0001
Fireplace_1plus	1.000000	0.1363	47.03	<.0001
TwoPlusCar_Garage	1.000000	0.3430	155.61	<.0001
High_Exterior_Cond	1.000000	0.0035	1.05	0.3064
CuldeSac	1.000000	0.0421	13.09	0.0003
Has_Fence	1.000000	0.0285	8.74	0.0034
Land_Level	1.000000	0.0147	4.44	0.0358

Variable Gr_Liv_Area Entered: R-Square = 0.5529 and C(p) = 629.2392

Step 2 of the forward elimination is displayed in Output 9.17b Forward Selection Step 2, and contains the statistics for entry for the remaining eleven predictors in the model. Note that the variable, AGE_AT_SALE, is related to SALEPRICE, after controlling for the presence of the first predictor GR_LIV_AREA, as indicated by the smallest p-value (largest F-value = 334.62); therefore, AGE_AT_SALE is added to the model. As a result, the model with the two predictors has an R^2 value (0.78698) and Mallows' C_p (141.0667). Also, AGE_AT_SALE has tolerance equal to 0.849906, indicating that its addition to the model does not result in collinearity.

Output 9.17b Forward Selection Step 2

Model: FORWARD

Forward Selection: Step 2

Statistics for Entry DF = 1,297				
Variable	Tolerance	Model R-Square	F Value	Pr > F
Total_Bsmt_SF	0.963607	0.6549	87.76	<.0001
Lot_Area	0.947292	0.5749	15.39	0.0001
Age_at_Sale	0.849906	0.7898	334.62	<.0001
High_Kitchen_Quality	0.925716	0.6461	78.24	<.0001
Fullbath_2plus	0.583943	0.6444	76.38	<.0001
Fireplace_1plus	0.830426	0.5577	3.21	0.0742
TwoPlusCar_Garage	0.822817	0.6433	75.26	<.0001
High_Exterior_Cond	0.995966	0.5530	0.10	0.7564
CuldeSac	0.946641	0.5541	0.78	0.3773
Has_Fence	0.967962	0.5542	0.88	0.3493
Land_Level	0.994639	0.5574	3.01	0.0839

Variable Age_at_Sale Entered: R-Square = 0.7898 and C(p) = 141.0667

The process continues until variables are no longer added; in other words, the forward selection stops when all remaining predictors have p-values greater than 0.01 as defined in the SLSTAY=0.01 option, as displayed in Output 9.17c Forward Selection Step 7. In Step 7, notice that all remaining six variables fail the 0.01 criterion to enter into the model; therefore, the forward selection process stops.

Output 9.17c Forward Selection Step 7

Model: FORWARD

Forward Selection: Step 7

Variable	Tolerance	Model R-Square	F Value	Pr > F
Lot_Area	0.874069	0.8591	1.99	0.1591
Fullbath_2plus	0.419825	0.8590	1.87	0.1730
High_Exterior_Cond	0.970758	0.8582	0.23	0.6285
CuldeSac	0.925089	0.8588	1.35	0.2466
Has_Fence	0.941464	0.8581	0.00	0.9623
Land_Level	0.984457	0.8588	1.31	0.2537

Statistics for Entry DF = 1,292

No other variable met the 0.0100 significance level for entry into the model.

As illustrated previously, the DETAILS option requests a summary of the variable selection steps, as displayed in Output 9.17d Summary of Forward Selection. Here the analyst can see the six variables selected from the initial set of twelve possible predictors; in short, the final model contains the variables GR_LIV_AREA, AGE_AT_SALE, TOTAL_BSMT_SF, HIGH_KITCHEN_QUALITY, FIREPLACE_1PLUS, and TWOPLUSCAR_GARAGE. Note that this is the same model selected using backward elimination; this will not always be the case.

Output 9.17d Summary of Forward Selection

Step	Variable Entered	Number Vars In	Partial R-Square	Model R-Square	C(p)	F Value	Pr > F
1	Gr_Liv_Area	1	0.5529	0.5529	629.239	368.51	<.0001
2	Age_at_Sale	2	0.2369	0.7898	141.067	334.62	<.0001
3	Total_Bsmt_SF	3	0.0373	0.8271	65.8910	63.83	<.0001
4	High_Kitchen_Quality	4	0.0160	0.8431	34.7471	30.11	<.0001
5	Fireplace_1plus	5	0.0083	0.8514	19.5050	16.48	<.0001
6	TwoPlusCar_Garage	6	0.0067	0.8581	7.5948	13.88	0.0002

Summary of Forward Selection

Finally, the plot of R^2_{adj} is provided in Output 9.17e Plot of Adjusted R-Square by Forward Selection Step, illustrating that the fit improved through the last step where six variables are included.

Output 9.17e Plot of Adjusted R-Square by Forward Selection Step

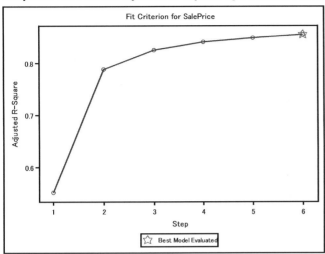

Stepwise Selection

Stepwise selection combines both the forward selection and backward elimination methods. Variables considered important are added one at a time based upon their p-values; however, at any point, a variable can be removed from the model when it is no longer significant in the context of the set of variables in the model at that time.

To illustrate the stepwise selection process, consider again the Ames Housing Case, using Program 9.17 Stepwise Selection for the Ames Housing Case.

Program 9.17 Stepwise Selection for the Ames Housing Case here is identical to that used for both the backward elimination and the forward selection methods, with the exception that SELECTION=STEPWISE. Note also that because a variable can be entered or eliminated at any point, the analyst can include both the SLENTRY= and SLSTAY= options. Finally, note that the label STEPWISE is used to distinguish this output from other models considered by the analyst.

Program 9.17 Stepwise Selection for the Ames Housing Case
```
libname sasba 'c:\sasba\ames';
data amesreg300;
   set sasba.amesreg300;
run;

proc reg data=amesreg300
   plots(only)=(adjrsq);
   STEPWISE: model SalePrice= Gr_Liv_Area Total_Bsmt_SF Lot_Area
             Age_At_Sale High_Kitchen_Quality Fullbath_2Plus
              Fireplace_1Plus TwoPlusCar_Garage
              High_Exterior_Cond CuldeSac Has_Fence Land_Level
             /selection=stepwise slentry=0.01 slstay=0.01
             details;
run;
```

When running the code, the analyst will see that the results of the stepwise analysis are identical to the results of the forward selection approach (this is not always the case). For this particular example, once a variable was added, it did not meet the threshold for elimination at any point; as a result, variables were added until no other variables met the threshold for entry.

Now that we have described the three sequential methods, consider the following. Because PROC REG allows multiple MODEL statements, the three sets of analyses illustrated previously could have been run in a single REG procedure as shown in Program 9.18 Three Variable Selection Methods for the Ames Housing Case.

Program 9.18 Three Variable Selection Methods for the Ames Housing Case

```
libname sasba 'c:\sasba\ames';
data amesreg300;
   set sasba.amesreg300;
run;

proc reg data=amesreg300
   plots(only)=(adjrsq);
   BACKWARD: model SalePrice= Gr_Liv_Area Total_Bsmt_SF Lot_Area
               Age_At_Sale High_Kitchen_Quality Fullbath_2Plus
                Fireplace_1Plus TwoPlusCar_Garage
                 High_Exterior_Cond CuldeSac Has_Fence Land_Level
                 /selection=backward slstay=0.01 details;
   FORWARD: model SalePrice= Gr_Liv_Area Total_Bsmt_SF Lot_Area
               Age_At_Sale High_Kitchen_Quality Fullbath_2Plus
                Fireplace_1Plus TwoPlusCar_Garage
                 High_Exterior_Cond CuldeSac Has_Fence Land_Level
                 /selection=forward slentry=0.01 details;
   STEPWISE: model SalePrice= Gr_Liv_Area Total_Bsmt_SF Lot_Area
               Age_At_Sale High_Kitchen_Quality Fullbath_2Plus
                Fireplace_1Plus TwoPlusCar_Garage
                 High_Exterior_Cond CuldeSac Has_Fence Land_Level
                 /selection=stepwise slentry=0.01 slstay=0.01
                 details;
run;
```

The GLMSELECT Procedure for Variable Selection

Now that you understand the basic concepts behind variable selection using the REG procedure, let's consider the GLMSELECT procedure which provides for variable selection when one or more predictors are categorical.

The syntax for the GLMSELECT procedure is as follows:

PROC GLMSELECT DATA=_SASdataset_ **<PLOTS=**_options_>;
CLASS _variables_;
MODEL _dependents=independents_ </ _options_>;
RUN;

Consider the Ames Housing Case where the analyst in interested in predicting the outcome variable, SALEPRICE. In the previous section on stepwise selection, twelve possible predictors were under investigation. Here we will add two categorical variables, OVERALL_QUALITY and LOT_SHAPE.

OVERALL_QUALITY has values 1, 2, and 3, corresponding to Below Average, Average, and Above Average, respectively. LOT_SHAPE has two values; namely, 'Reg' for regular shape and 'IRR' for irregular shape. The analysis will also include VINYL_SIDING (already dummy coded 1 for Yes and 0 for No), OPEN_PORCH_SF (porch area), GARAGE_AREA (garage area), and BEDROOM_ABVGR (number of bedrooms above ground) to see if including any other variables will improve the fit. In all, eighteen variables will be under consideration. The analysis will be conducted using the Program 9.19 PROC GLMSELECT with Stepwise Selection for the Ames Housing Case.

Program 9.19 PROC GLMSELECT with Stepwise Selection for the Ames Housing Case

```
libname sasba 'c:\sasba\ames';
data amesreg300;
   set sasba.amesreg300;
run;

proc glmselect data=amesreg300
   plots=candidates;
   class Overall_Quality Lot_Shape;
   model SalePrice= Gr_Liv_Area Total_Bsmt_SF Lot_Area
          Age_At_Sale Overall_Quality High_Kitchen_Quality
          Fullbath_2Plus Fireplace_1Plus TwoPlusCar_Garage
          Vinyl_Siding Lot_Shape High_Exterior_Cond CuldeSac
          Has_Fence Land_Level Open_Porch_SF Garage_Area
          Bedroom_AbvGr
        /selection=stepwise select=sl slentry=0.01 slstay=0.01
             details=all;
run;
```

From Program 9.19 PROC GLMSELECT with Stepwise Selection for the Ames Housing Case, we can see that the GLMSELECT procedure is applied to the Ames Housing data set, as defined by the DATA= option. The CLASS statement defines the two categorical variables (OVERALL_QUALITY and LOT_SHAPE) to be considered in the linear model.

The MODEL statement defines the outcome variable, SALEPRICE, and the eighteen variables to be considered for prediction. The SELECTION= option defines the selection procedure, namely, STEPWISE.

The SELECT= option defines the criterion used to determine the order in which variables are added or removed at each step of the selection method. SELECT=SL requests the traditional significance level as the selection criterion; the significance levels for entry and removal are defined as 0.01, using SLENTRY=0.01 and SLSTAY=0.01.

Note that SLENTRY and SLSTAY are invoked when SELECT=SL; if those are not explicitly stated, the default is 0.15.

The DETAILS=ALL option provides the following:

- statistics for entry (or removal) for the top ten candidate variables at each step in the variable selection process
- ANOVA tables, fit statistics, and parameters estimates after a variable is selected (or removed)
- a summary table of all steps in the variable selection process.

Finally, the PLOTS=CANDIDATES requests plots at each variable selection step. The plots are determined by the selection criterion, SELECT=SL; therefore, in this case, plots of p-values (or log p-values) are displayed to show the next variable to be added to the model.

The partial results of the SAS program are found in Output 9.18a PROC GLMSELECT for Stepwise Selection Step 1 through Output 9.18d The Selected Model from Stepwise Selection in PROC GLMSELECT. The first page of SAS output provides a summary of the analysis request, including the data set name, the variable name of the dependent variable, the selection method (Stepwise), the selection criterion (Significance Level), the stop criterion (Significance Level), entry significance level (0.01), and the stay significance level (0.01).

A Class Level Information table is displayed, indicating that OVERALL_QUALITY has three levels (1, 2, and 3) and LOT_SHAPE has two levels (IRR and Reg). Finally, a Dimensions table is displayed, indicating that there are 19 effects and 22 parameters under consideration.

The output then provides information for Step 0 where only the intercept is estimated. Following is Step 1, as displayed in Output 9.18a PROC GLMSELECT for Stepwise Selection Step 1, where the variable, GR_LIV_AREA is entered into the model. The output includes the ANOVA table for testing the significance of GR_LIV_AREA, along with the fit statistics (RMSE=23,391, $R^2_{adj} = 0.5514$, etc.), and the table of parameter estimates.

Step 1 also includes the table, Best 10 Entry Candidates, which ranks the variables in order of their worth in predicting SALEPRICE as measured by the smallest p-value (equivalent to the smallest log p-value), accompanied by the log p-value plot by variables as a visual for identifying the variable selected for entry, namely, GR_LIV_AREA.

Output 9.18a PROC GLMSELECT for Stepwise Selection Step 1

The GLMSELECT Procedure
Effect Entered: Gr_Liv_Area

Analysis of Variance				
Source	DF	Sum of Squares	Mean Square	F Value
Model	1	2.016341E11	2.016341E11	368.51
Error	298	1.63052E11	547154248	
Corrected Total	299	3.646861E11		

Root MSE	23391

Dependent Mean	154910
R-Square	0.5529
Adj R-Sq	0.5514
AIC	6340.06570
AICC	6340.14678
SBC	6045.47326

Parameter Estimates				
Parameter	DF	Estimate	Standard Error	t Value
Intercept	1	44081	5929.177724	7.43
Gr_Liv_Area	1	82.505608	4.297900	19.20

Best 10 Entry Candidates			
Rank	Effect	Log pValue	Pr > F
1	Gr_Liv_Area	-122.7218	<.0001
2	Age_at_Sale	-119.3869	<.0001
3	Fullbath_2plus	-107.5534	<.0001
4	TwoPlusCar_Garage	-65.1481	<.0001
5	Overall_Quality	-56.8268	<.0001
6	Garage_Area	-50.0664	<.0001
7	High_Kitchen_Quality	-44.5427	<.0001
8	Vinyl_Siding	-40.1855	<.0001
9	Total_Bsmt_SF	-36.9192	<.0001
10	Bedroom_AbvGr	-27.4951	<.0001

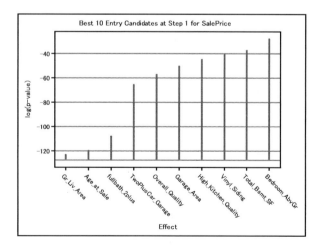

The results of Step 2 are displayed in Output 9.18b PROC GLMSELECT for Stepwise Selection Step 2, where the variable, AGE_AT_SALE is entered into the model. The output includes the ANOVA table for testing the significance of both GR_LIV_AREA and AGE_AT_SALE, along with the fit statistics (RMSE=16,607, R^2_{adj} = 0.7883, etc.), and the table of parameter estimates. Obviously the measures of fit indicate an improvement in fit, with an increase in R^2_{adj} and a reduction in RMSE. Finally, the table of Best 10 Entry Candidates and the plot of log p-values provide the evidence for selecting AGE_AT_SALE for entry into the model.

Output 9.18b PROC GLMSELECT for Stepwise Selection Step 2

The GLMSELECT Procedure

Effect Entered: Age_at_Sale

Analysis of Variance				
Source	DF	Sum of Squares	Mean Square	F Value
Model	2	2.880157E11	1.440078E11	557.85
Error	297	76670419313	258149560	
Corrected Total	299	3.646861E11		

Root MSE	16067
Dependent Mean	154910
R-Square	0.7898
Adj R-Sq	0.7883
AIC	6115.69980
AICC	6115.83539
SBC	5824.81115

Parameter Estimates				
Parameter	DF	Estimate	Standard Error	t Value
Intercept	1	103565	5211.590360	19.87
Gr_Liv_Area	1	59.811765	3.202224	18.68
Age_at_Sale	1	-671.549476	36.711592	-18.29

Best 10 Entry Candidates			
Rank	Effect	Log pValue	Pr > F
1	Age_at_Sale	-114.8099	<.0001
2	Total_Bsmt_SF	-40.7897	<.0001
3	High_Kitchen_Quality	-37.0246	<.0001
4	Fullbath_2plus	-36.2804	<.0001
5	TwoPlusCar_Garage	-35.8253	<.0001
6	Garage_Area	-33.9371	<.0001
7	Vinyl_Siding	-26.7316	<.0001
8	Overall_Quality	-20.0060	<.0001
9	Lot_Area	-9.1280	0.0001
10	Lot_Shape	-7.5678	0.0005

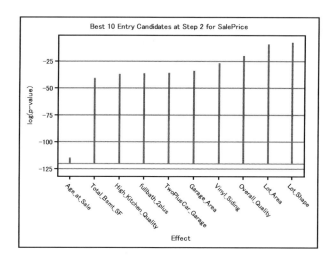

Recall that for stepwise analysis, once a variable is entered, the resulting model is tested to see if any variable in the model fails the criterion for staying. So, the process discussed in steps 1 and 2 continues until variables are no longer added (when all remaining predictors have p-values greater than 0.01 as defined in the SLSTAY=0.01) nor removed (when all predictors in the model have p-values greater than 0.01 as defined in the SLSTAY=0.01). In our example, the process continues for seven steps and is summarized in Output 9.18c Summary for Stepwise Selection in PROC GLMSELECT.

Output 9.18c Summary for Stepwise Selection in PROC GLMSELECT

		Stepwise Selection Summary				
Step	Effect Entered	Effect Removed	Number Effects In	Number Parms In	F Value	Pr > F
0	Intercept		1	1	0.00	1.0000
1	Gr_Liv_Area		2	2	368.51	<.0001
2	Age_at_Sale		3	3	334.62	<.0001
3	Total_Bsmt_SF		4	4	63.83	<.0001
4	High_Kitchen_Quality		5	5	30.11	<.0001
5	Overall_Quality		6	7	10.94	<.0001
6	Garage_Area		7	8	17.97	<.0001
7	Fireplace_1plus		8	9	13.64	0.0003

From the output displayed in Output 9.18c Summary for Stepwise Selection in PROC GLMSELECT, the analyst can see the order in which the variables were added, while no variables met the criterion for removal. Notice that there are eight effects in the model, namely, the intercept and seven predictors. The number of parameters estimated in the final linear regression model is nine; namely, the intercept, two levels of the categorical predictor OVERALL_QUALITY, and the remaining six predictors.

The last portion of the output contains information related to the final model and is displayed in Output 9.18d The Selected Model from Stepwise Selection in PROC GLMSELECT. First note that the nine effects are listed, including the intercept, followed by the ANOVA table, indicating a significantly good fit using the $k = 8$ predictors. The fit statistics show a considerable improvement in fit (RMSE=12,833, $R^2_{adj} = 0.8650$, etc.). Finally, using the parameter estimates, the final model has the following prediction equation:

$$\hat{Y} = 82{,}707 + 45.22(Gr\_Liv\_Area) + 20.29(Total\_Bsmt\_SF) - 475.78(Age\_at\_Sale)$$
$$- 11258(Overall\_Quality\ 1) - 7029.19(Overall\_Quality\ 2) + 8666.76(High\_Kitchen\_Quality)$$
$$+ 6097.74(Fireplace\_1plus) + 23.68(Garage\_Area)$$

Notice for a house with below average quality (Overall_Quality 1=1 and Overall_Quality 2=0), the intercept is 82,707 − 11,258 = 71,449; for a house with average quality (Overall_Quality 1=0 and Overall_Quality 2=1), the intercept is 82,707 − 7029.19 = 75,677.81; a house with above average quality has an intercept of 82,707.

Holding all other variables constant, the expected sale price will increase by $45.22 for every additional square foot of above ground living area. Each additional square foot of basement area is associated with a $20.29 increase; and each additional square foot of garage area is associated with a $23.68 increase. Having a high quality kitchen is associated with an increase in sale price of $8666.76, all other factors held constant; having at least one fireplace is associated with an additional $6097.74. For this population of houses, each additional year in age is associated with a $475.78 decrease in sale price, with all other factors held constant.

Output 9.18d The Selected Model from Stepwise Selection in PROC GLMSELECT

The selected model is the model at the last step (Step 7).

Effects:	Intercept Gr_Liv_Area Total_Bsmt_SF Age_at_Sale Overall_Quality High_Kitchen_Quality Fireplace_1plus Garage_Area

Analysis of Variance				
Source	DF	Sum of Squares	Mean Square	F Value
Model	8	3.16766E11	39595752470	240.45
Error	291	47920062420	164673754	
Corrected Total	299	3.646861E11		

Root MSE	12833
Dependent Mean	154910
R-Square	0.8686
Adj R-Sq	0.8650
AIC	5986.70529
AICC	5987.46653
SBC	5718.03933

Parameter Estimates				
Parameter	DF	Estimate	Standard Error	t Value
Intercept	1	82707	5729.095596	14.44
Gr_Liv_Area	1	45.219105	3.006767	15.04
Total_Bsmt_SF	1	20.287345	2.715321	7.47
Age_at_Sale	1	-475.782142	34.198190	-13.91
Overall_Quality 1	1	-11258	2922.041666	-3.85
Overall_Quality 2	1	-7029.186383	1828.576866	-3.84
Overall_Quality 3	0	0	.	.
High_Kitchen_Quality	1	8666.760442	1802.809359	4.81
Fireplace_1plus	1	6097.736909	1651.066636	3.69
Garage_Area	1	23.675454	5.571781	4.25

Other Features of the GLMSELECT Procedure

The GLMSELECT procedure allows for extensive capabilities in the variable selection process. In this section, we add comments to familiarize you with some of those capabilities.

The example just described utilized the SELECTION=STEPWISE in the MODEL. Other selection options include NONE, FORWARD, and BACKWARD. The GLMSELECT procedure also offers LAR (least angle regression), and LASSO (least absolute shrinkage and selection operator), neither of which are offered in PROC REG.

Similarly, the SELECT=SL option was used in the MODEL statement to illustrate the traditional approach where variables are either added or removed based upon the defined significance level. The SELECT=SBC (Schwarz Bayesian information criterion) is the default; other selection criteria include ADJRSQ, CP, RSQUARE, all discussed in this chapter, in addition to AIC (Akaike information criterion) , AICC (Corrected Akaike information criterion), BIC (Sawa Bayesian information criterion), PRESS (predicted residual sum of squares), and VALIDATE.

In the Ames Housing example just discussed, the default fit statistics were displayed and include RMSE (root mean square error), R^2, R^2_{adj}, AIC, AICC, and SBC. If the analyst adds the STATS=ALL option to the MODEL statement, additional statistics are supplied. These include BIC, CP (Mallows' C_p), PRESS, and ASE (the average square errors if training, test, and validation data are specified); these are not included as defaults because their inclusion has increased computational costs.

Notice also that the output for the GLMSELECT procedure is voluminous by using DETAILS=ALL in the MODEL. In order to reduce that volume, the analyst can use the default, DETAILS=SUMMARY, which produces only the selection summary table.

Finally, the GLMSELECT procedure provides a plethora of graphics capabilities by way of the PLOT= option. Our illustration provided the log p-value plot (PLOT=CANDIDATES) which provided a graphical representation of the selection criterion (defined by SELECT=SL) at each step. Other PLOT options include ASE, CRITERIA (which provides a panel of the requested fit criteria), and COEFFICIENTS (which shows how the estimates of slope stabilize as the variable selection steps progress), to name a few.

When conducting variable selection methods, keep in mind the default selection criteria, as displayed in Table 9.4 Default SLENTRY and SLSTAY Settings by Model Selection Method.

Table 9.4 Default SLENTRY and SLSTAY Settings by Model Selection Method.

	SLENTRY	SLSTAY
PROG REG, BACKWARD		0.10
PROC REG, FORWARD	0.50	
PROC REG, STEPWISE	0.15	0.15
PROC GLMSELECT, BACKWARD		0.10
PROC GLMSELECT, FORWARD	0.50	
PROC GLMSELECT, STEPWISE	0.15	0.15

Cautionary Note on Sequential Selection Methods

When using sequential selection methods, the analyst should exercise caution. First, when collinearity exists, the model selection process is very unstable. In other words, if conducted on repeated random samples, the model (or models) appearing as best does not show up in a consistent manner. In fact, it is very possible that important variables may be overlooked in the variable selection process.

As a result, it is important that the analyst resolve any collinearity (redundancy) issues before selecting variables (relevancy). In fact, when collinearity does not exist, the analyst will almost always arrive at the same model (or models) using each of the three sequential methods (Hosmer and Lemeshow, 2000).

Another problem with sequential methods is their reliance on p-values. In these methods, p-values are repeated and used to test the significance for adding or deleting variables. Of the many tests, just by chance, there are significant conclusions when in reality those conclusions are in error. In short, the probability of making a Type I error, in reality, is larger than the stated p-value. In other words, the inferences made using models selected in this way become less accurate as the number of tests increases (Chatfield, 1995). To overcome this problem, the analyst may try splitting the sample, and using one portion for variable selection, and the other portion for confirming hypotheses through inference (*t*- and F-tests).

In short, if the number of predictors is small, then specifying all possible subsets is the best route to take. Otherwise, when the number of variables is large so that an all possible subsets is time prohibitive, the analyst should use the sequential methods as a guide to reduce the candidate models, and use subject matter expertise to select a model that makes sense.

Assessing the Validity of Results Using Regression Diagnostics

The topics covered so far have concentrated on describing the linear relationship between the outcome variable (Y) and the predictors (Xs) and using those descriptions to make inferences about the population. The calculations discussed are derived using certain assumptions, and if those assumptions are violated, then any inferences about the relationship between X and Y are in error. In this section, we will list the assumptions of linear regression, discuss a set of tools for assessing those assumptions, and provide possible recommendations on how to alleviate the violations.

The Assumptions of Linear Regression

There are four key assumptions that must be verified before the analyst can conclude that the linear regression analysis results are valid. The assumptions are:

- The predictor terms enter the model equation linearly.
- The errors in prediction $(Y-\hat{Y})$ are normally distributed having a mean of zero.
- The variance of the errors in prediction $(Y-\hat{Y})$ are constant for each value of X. In other words, the observations have the same variance around the estimated regression line for each X, across the range of X. The condition of equal variances is also referred to as **homoscedasticity**.
- The errors in prediction $(Y-\hat{Y})$ are independent of each other.

The first assumption implies that the form of the predictor itself can also be nonlinear, either a higher order term or the result of a transformation.

When the linearity assumption is violated, the model fit is obviously reduced indicating that accurate predictions break down, specifically at different ranges of the predictor in question. When the equal variance assumption is violated, while the parameter estimates of the slope are unbiased, their standard errors are overestimated, resulting in non-significant slopes (errors in hypothesis tests) and inflated confidence intervals. When the errors are dependent, the standard errors are underestimated and, similarly, non-significant relationships may show up as significant. Finally, non-normal errors may indicate that either the form of the model is misspecified or an important variable is left out of the model.

There are other conditions that compromise the validity of the linear regression results. These are:

- collinearity, where the predictor variables are 'highly' correlated, which was addressed earlier in this chapter, and
- the existence of outliers, or observations that have 'extreme' Y values and large errors, which will be covered later in this chapter.

Residual Analysis for Checking Assumptions

In regression analysis, the analyst should always begin with an exploration of the data using bivariate scatter plots in order to make some preliminary observations about the reasonableness of the assumptions. However, departures from the assumptions sometimes go undetected using the ordinary scatter plot of Y by X; therefore, additional data visualizations should follow in order to specifically assess the violations of assumptions and ensure linear regression is the appropriate model. Because the assumptions address requirements for the errors, a **residual analysis** is the appropriate tool for detecting any violations.

A residual analysis requires first that the regression model be fit to the data and the errors, or **residuals**, are computed for all observations. The residuals are used to create various **residual plots** for testing the assumptions and include:

- a scatter plot of the residuals by the predictor variable (X) for each X
- a scatter plot of the residuals by the predicted values $(\hat{Y})$
- the normal probability plot of the standardized residuals

Let's now consider examples of regression analysis with one predictor, accompanied by the scatter plot of X and Y and the resulting plot of residual by the predictor. In Figure 9.3 Fit Plot and Residual Plot for Illustrating a Linear Trend with Constant Variance the left panel displays a scatter of Y by X where there appears to be a linear trend and the points are somewhat evenly spread around the estimated regression line, indicating that the equal variance assumption is reasonably met.

The residual for each point is computed and the resulting plot of the residual by the predictor variable is produced, as seen on the right panel. Note also that the residual plot seems to indicate a linear trend around the expected line of zero and has an even spread indicating that both the linearity and equal variance assumptions are reasonable.

In general, any analyses having a residual plot which resembles that in Figure 9.3 Fit Plot and Residual Plot for Illustrating a Linear Trend with Constant Variance indicates that those assumptions are reasonably met, and the analyst can proceed with the analysis. Of course, in practice, there will be slight deviations from this standard; however, knowledge of the subject matter should aid in the interpretation.

Figure 9.3 Fit Plot and Residual Plot for Illustrating a Linear Trend with Constant Variance

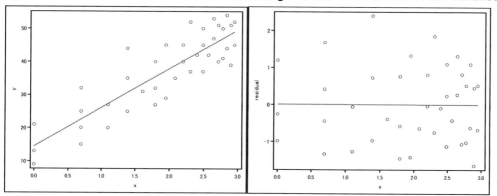

An inspection of the residual plot in Figure 9.4 Residual Plot Illustrating a Curvilinear Trend indicates that the linearity assumption is in question. When a curvilinear trend exists, the analyst can transform the predictor variables using either log, square root, quadratic, or inverse, to name a few. An example when the analyst uses a natural log transformation will be provided later in this section.

Figure 9.4 Residual Plot Illustrating a Curvilinear Trend

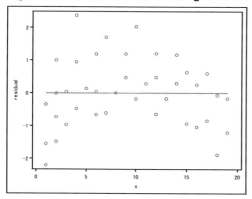

In the Figure 9.5 Residual Plot Illustrating Unequal Variance, we can see from the residual plot that the unequal variance assumption is violated. Again the analyst can transform the predictor variable. In fact, many transformations used to fix nonlinearity problems are also effective in stabilizing the variances. Other solutions include using a weighted least squares analysis or the GLIMMIX or GENMOD procedures to fit a generalized linear model that accounts for non-constant variance.

Figure 9.5 Residual Plot Illustrating Unequal Variance

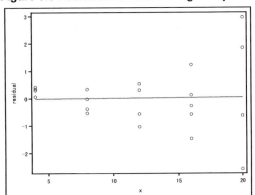

Finally, there are times where the residual plot may resemble that in Figure 9.6 Residual Plot Illustrating Autocorrelation. Note that the residuals here are not randomly scattered around the expected line of zero; in fact, points with positive residuals tend to be next to points with positive residuals and points with negative residuals tend to be next to points with negative residuals. This sometimes occurs when observations are collected over time and the residuals are characterized as **autocorrelated**. In this case, the analyst should model the data using a time series analysis.

Figure 9.6 Residual Plot Illustrating Autocorrelation

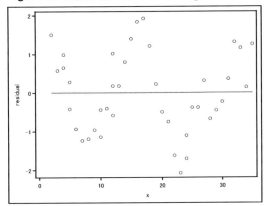

In the next example, we will illustrate how to generate the plot of the residual by the predictor, in addition to the plot of the residual by the predicted value and the normal probability plot of the standardized residuals.

Consider the following example where a sample of companies are purchasing advertising to generate sales. Suppose the marketing analyst wants to determine if the ads are effective and wants to quantify the impact of sales on revenue. Specifically, the analyst conducts a linear regression to predict revenue from advertising expenses using Program 9.20 Linear Regression Analysis Diagnostics Panel.

Program 9.20 Linear Regression Analysis Diagnostics Panel

```
libname sasba 'c:\sasba\data';
data Revenue;
    set sasba.revenue;
run;

proc reg data=Revenue;
   model Revenue = AdExpense;
   output out=diagnostics predicted=yhat residual=residual;
run;

data res;
  set diagnostics;
proc print data=res (obs=5);
  var AdExpense Revenue yhat residual;
run;
```

From Program 9.20 Linear Regression Analysis Diagnostics Panel, we can see that the REG procedure is applied to the Revenue data set, as defined by the DATA= option. The MODEL statement is used to define the linear model, namely REVENUE is equal to linear function of ADEXPENSE. The output, including all tables and scatter plots, is illustrated in Output 9.19a Linear Regression on Revenue with Diagnostics Panel.

Output 9.19a Linear Regression on Revenue with Diagnostics Panel

Root MSE	7.13262	R-Square	0.6548
Dependent Mean	37.05000	Adj R-Sq	0.6457
Coeff Var	19.25134		

		Parameter Estimates			
Variable	DF	Parameter Estimate	Standard Error	t Value	Pr > |t|
Intercept	1	21.76874	2.12411	10.25	<.0001
AdExpense	1	1.65203	0.19459	8.49	<.0001

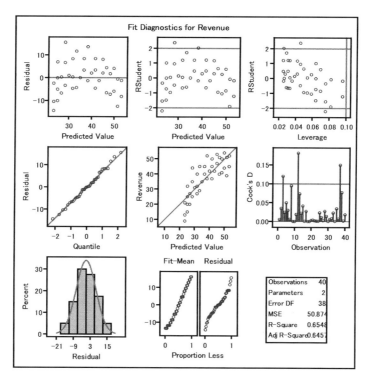

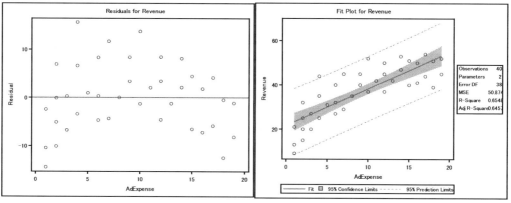

Note first that the plot of residuals by AdExpense shows a clear curvilinear relationship between ADEXPENSE and REVENUE. It does make perfect business sense that revenue increases as advertising expenses increase, but at some point, the revenue may increase at a lesser rate indicating that the additional money spent on advertising has a lesser effect on revenue. Notice that the curvilinear relationship is more obvious in the residual plot compared to the scatter plot of the original data.

The output also includes the panel of Fit Diagnostics for Revenue. In the upper left corner is the plot of the residual by predicted value--when there is only one predictor, this plot is identical in shape to the residual by ADEXPENSE plot because the predicted value is a linear function of ADEXPENSE. This plot shows the same nonlinear relationship between REVENUE and ADEXPENSE. It should be noted that when the analyst conducts a multiple linear regression, the plot of the residual by predicted value detects violations across all predictors because the predicted value is a function of all Xs. If violations are detected, the analyst must look at each predictor separately in order to detect from which predictor the violation originates.

The panel of Fit Diagnostics also includes the quantile plot of residuals for assessing the normality of error assumption. As described in Chapter 6, "Two-Sample t-Test," if data is normal, the points on the quantile plot follow a straight line and have a 45-degree angle. Here the points seem to follow fairly closely to the line; therefore, the normal errors assumption seems reasonable. The analyst could apply the UNIVARIATE procedure to the residuals to test the normality assumption using the Kolmogorov–Smirnov.

Finally, on the Fit Diagnostics panel, note the REVENUE by predicted revenue plot displays a curvilinear relationship, further indicating that the linearity assumption is suspect.

In order to illustrate how the data in the residual plot is created, we illustrate the use of the OUTPUT statement to create a temporary data set called DIAGNOSTICS. This new data set includes the original data and additional information for each observation as defined by the keywords. Note that the analyst creates a new variable called YHAT as defined by the PREDICTED= option and RESIDUAL as defined by the RESIDUAL= option.

For example, in observation 1, after plugging in the amount spent on advertising ($1 thousand), the predicted revenue is $23.421 ($1000), resulting in an error of -2.4208. This observation has the ordered pair (1, -2.4208) on the residual by ADEXPENSE plot, displayed in Output 9.19a Linear Regression on Revenue with Diagnostics Panel and listed in Output 9.19b Predicted Revenue and Residuals Using the Predictor AdExpense.

Output 9.19b Predicted Revenue and Residuals Using the Predictor AdExpense

Obs	AdExpense	Revenue	yhat	residual
1	1	21	23.4208	-2.4208
2	1	13	23.4208	-10.4208
3	7	45	33.3329	11.6671
4	14	47	44.8971	2.1029
5	17	54	49.8532	4.1468

When looking at the p-value for ADEXPENSE and the adjusted R^2, it appears that ADEXPENSE is a good predictor, having a relatively good fit. However, because the linearity assumption is violated, the strength of that relationship is stunted. Once the form of the correct relationship is used, the analyst expects the measures of fit and the test statistic to increase.

So, when the linearity assumption is violated, the analyst should consider transforming the predictor variable in an attempt to fit a curve to the data. For this specific example, we tried several transformations of X (X-square, natural log of X, square root of X, and the inverse of X); the natural log seemed to be the best transformation. Higher order terms can also be used when dealing with nonlinear relationships.

To see if the transformation was effective in correcting the violation of the linearity assumption, the analyst would use Program 9.21 Linear Regression Analysis Using Transformed Ad Expense (LnAdExp).

Program 9.21 Linear Regression Analysis Using Transformed Ad Expense (LnAdExp)

```
libname sasba 'c:\sasba\data';
data Revenue;
    set sasba.revenue;
    LnAdExp = log(AdExpense);
run;
```

```
proc reg data=Revenue
plots(only)=(QQ residuals residualbypredicted fitplot);
   model Revenue = LnAdExp;
run;
```

Program 9.21 Linear Regression Analysis Using Transformed Ad Expense (LnAdExp) is identical to the code used previously for predicting REVENUE, with two exceptions. First, notice that the analyst created a new transformed predictor, named LNADEXP. Second, the PLOT(ONLY)= option was added to PROC REG to specifically request the QQ (quantile-quantile) plot, the residual by predictor plot, the residual by the predicted plot and the scatter plot of Y by X, as defined by QQ, RESIDUAL, RESIDUALBYPREDICTED, and FITPLOT.

From Output 9.20 Linear Regression on Revenue Using Transformed Ad Expense (LnAdExp), notice that both residual plots give identical information and seem to show a linear trend of residuals evenly spread around the expected value of zero, indicating that the natural-log transformation is effective in modeling the curvilinear trend. This is further evidenced by the scatter plot of the original data. Note also that the adjusted R^2 increased to 0.7518 (compared to $R^2_{adj} = 0.6457$ before the transformation) and the standard error decreased to 5.96960 (compared to 7.13262).

Output 9.20 Linear Regression on Revenue Using Transformed Ad Expense (LnAdExp)

Root MSE	5.96960	R-Square	0.7582
Dependent Mean	37.05000	Adj R-Sq	0.7518
Coeff Var	16.11227		

Parameter Estimates					
Variable	DF	Parameter Estimate	Standard Error	t Value	Pr > |t|
Intercept	1	14.45638	2.27497	6.35	<.0001
LnAdExp	1	11.72517	1.07421	10.92	<.0001

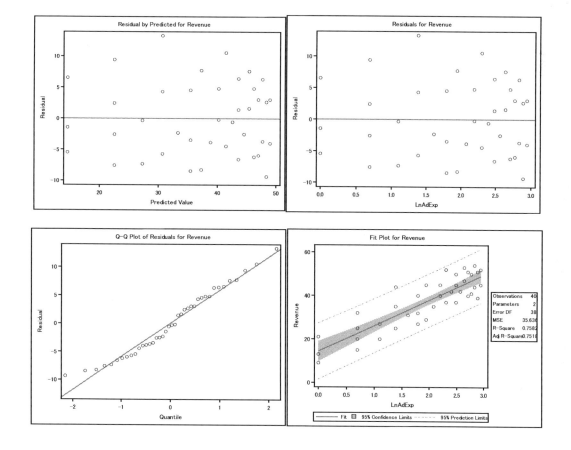

The p-value for slope indicates that the natural log of AdExpense is a good predictor of Revenue. Using the parameter estimates, the prediction equation is:

$$\hat{Y}_i = 14.45638 + 11.72517 * LnAdExpense$$

While the slope has the same interpretation (change in Y per unit change in X), how do you interpret the fact that as the natural log of ADEXPENSE increases by one unit, revenue increases by 11.72517 ($1000s). Suffice it to say that the analyst can simply explain that as ADEXPENSE increases, REVENUE increases; however, REVENUE increases at a smaller rate as for larger amounts spent on advertising.

Now that we have discussed diagnostics when using one predictor, how does that translate to the case of multiple predictors? Consider again the Ames Housing Case, with fit measures summarized earlier in Table 9.3 Measures of Fit for Multiple Linear Regression, where we want to predict SALEPRICE using the five predictors, GR_LIV_AREA, FULLBATH_2PLUS, TOTAL_BSMT_SF, AGE_AT_SALE, and GARAGE_AREA. In order to assess the linear regression assumptions, the analyst would use Program 9.22 Diagnostics for Multiple Linear Regression.

Program 9.22 Diagnostics for Multiple Linear Regression

```
libname sasba 'c:\sasba\ames';
data amesreg300;
    set sasba.amesreg300;
run;

proc reg data=amesreg300
    plots(only)=(QQ residuals residualbypredicted);
    model SalePrice= Gr_Liv_Area Fullbath_2plus Total_Bsmt_SF
                    Age_at_Sale Garage_Area;
run;
```

Program 9.22 Diagnostics for Multiple Linear Regression is identical to the previous code used for one predictor, with one exception; the bivariate fitplot is not requested for each of the predictors. The output is found in Output 9.21a Multiple Linear Regression for Predicting SalePrice through Output 9.21c Panel of Residual by Regressors for SalePrice.

Output 9.21a Multiple Linear Regression for Predicting SalePrice

Number of Observations Read	300
Number of Observations Used	300

Analysis of Variance					
Source	DF	Sum of Squares	Mean Square	F Value	Pr > F
Model	5	3.063503E11	61270068111	308.79	<.0001
Error	294	58335741627	198420890		
Corrected Total	299	3.646861E11			

Root MSE	14086	R-Square	0.8400
Dependent Mean	154910	Adj R-Sq	0.8373
Coeff Var	9.09315		

Parameter Estimates					
Variable	DF	Parameter Estimate	Standard Error	t Value	Pr > |t|
Intercept	1	74606	5751.64527	12.97	<.0001
Gr_Liv_Area	1	51.27981	3.41774	15.00	<.0001
Fullbath_2plus	1	5975.69610	2495.63000	2.39	0.0173
Total_Bsmt_SF	1	21.14003	2.96472	7.13	<.0001
Age_at_Sale	1	-511.85215	39.00605	-13.12	<.0001
Garage_Area	1	24.99176	6.07009	4.12	<.0001

Before interpreting the regression model in Output 9.21a Multiple Linear Regression for Predicting SalePrice, there must be an assessment of the assumptions. First, note the residual by predicted plot--specifically the x-axis, representing by the predicted value, as displayed in Output 9.21b Residual by Predicted Plot and Q-Q Plot of Residuals for SalePrice. The predicted value is a function of all predictors; therefore, if any deviation from linearity or equal variance exists, the analyst must investigate further what specific assumption is violated and for *which* predictor (or predictors). An inspection of the plot seems to suggest that the assumptions of linearity and equal variance are reasonably met. Note also that the Q-Q plot suggests that the residuals are normally distributed.

If the residual by predicted plot indicated issues concerning assumptions, the analyst would review the panel of residual by regressors for each of the five predictors, as displayed in Output 9.21c Panel of Residual by Regressors for SalePrice, in order to diagnose where the problem (or problems) exist. Once the problem is diagnosed, the analyst can proceed to the remedy. An inspection of the panel of residuals shows that there are no violations, which concurs with the conclusions made previously based upon Output 9.21b Residual by Predicted Plot and Q-Q Plot of Residuals for SalePrice.

Output 9.21b Residual by Predicted Plot and Q-Q Plot of Residuals for SalePrice

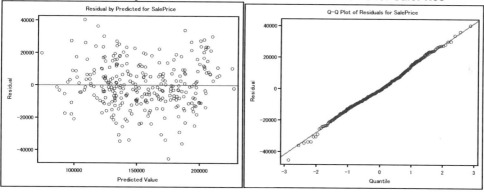

Output 9.21c Panel of Residual by Regressors for SalePrice

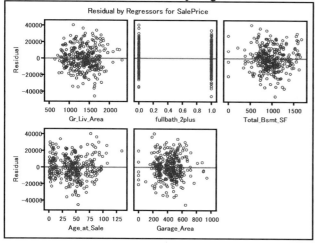

Studentized Residuals

Many regression books illustrate the use of standardized residual when assessing the assumptions of linear regression (Chatterjee and Hadi, 2006). The **studentized residual**, also known as the **standardized residual**, is calculated using the following formula:

$$studentized\ residual_i = \frac{e_i}{standand\ error\ of\ e_i}$$

The patterns found in a standardized residual plot are identical to those found in a residual plot; however, the scale is obviously different. If the residuals are normal, then 95% of the time the standardized residuals are expected to be within -1.96 and +1.96; therefore, the rule of thumb is that the standardized residuals are expected to fall between -2 and +2. Using this fact with standardized residual plots makes interpretation somewhat easier.

Let's revisit the example where the marketing analyst wants to determine if the advertising expense is related to revenue. Consider Program 9.23 Residuals and Studentized Residuals by AdExpense for Saleprice.

Program 9.23 Residuals and Studentized Residuals by AdExpense for Saleprice

```
libname sasba 'c:\sasba\data';
data Revenue;
    set sasba.revenue;
run;

proc reg data=Revenue;
   model Revenue = AdExpense;
   output out=diagnostics predicted=yhat residual=residual
             stdr=stderr_residual student=student ;
plot residual.*adexpense modelht=3 statht=3;
plot student.*adexpense modelht=3 statht=3;
run;

data res;
   set diagnostics;
run;
proc print data=res (obs=5);
   var adexpense revenue yhat residual stderr_residual student;
run;
```

Program 9.23 Residuals and Studentized Residuals by AdExpense for Saleprice is identical to the code used previously for predicting revenue, with several additions. First, notice that the OUT= option in the OUTPUT statement is used to create a temporary SAS data‚set called DIAGNOSTICS, containing original variables in the REVENUE data set, in addition to the new variables created using PREDICTED=, RESIDUAL=, STDR=, and STUDENT=, to represent the predicted revenue, the residual, the **standard error of the residual**, and the studentized residual, respectively, to name a few.

The first PLOT statement requests the residual by predictor plot, as displayed in the left plot of Output 9.22a Residual and Studentized Residuals by AdExpense for SalePrice, and is identical to that displayed in Output 9.19a Linear Regression on Revenue with Diagnostics Panel. The second PLOT statement requests the studentized residual by predictor plot, as displayed in the right plot of Output 9.22a Residual and Studentized Residuals by AdExpense for SalePrice. The MODELHT= and STATHT= plot options were added so that the prediction equation and statistics included on the plots are readable; otherwise the print size is too small. Note, specifically, that the Y-axis of the studentized residual usually ranges from -2 to +2.

Output 9.22a Residual and Studentized Residuals by AdExpense for SalePrice

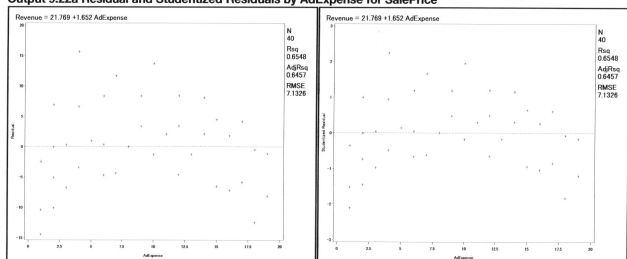

Finally, the PRINT procedure is supplied to provide the output, as displayed in Output 9.22b Residuals and Studentized Residuals by AdExpense for SalePrice, so that you can apply the formula. Consider observation 1 as follows:

Observation 1 spent $1000 in advertising (AdExpense=1) and experienced $21,000 in revenues (Y=21). Based upon the estimated regression equation, the predicted revenue for observation 1 is $23,420.80 ($\hat{Y} = 23.4208$), resulting in a residual of -2.4208. The standard error of that residual is 6.85749, resulting in a studentized residual = -2.4208 / 6.85749 = -0.35301.

Output 9.22b Residuals and Studentized Residuals by AdExpense for Saleprice

Obs	AdExpense	Revenue	yhat	residual	stderr_residual	student
1	1	21	23.4208	-2.4208	6.85749	-0.35301
2	1	13	23.4208	-10.4208	6.85749	-1.51962
3	7	45	33.3329	11.6671	7.02928	1.65978
4	14	47	44.8971	2.1029	6.98198	0.30118
5	17	54	49.8532	4.1468	6.87954	0.60277

Using Statistics to Identify Potential Influential Observations

Every regression analysis should be accompanied by an inspection of the data for outliers. An **outlier** is an observation that has a large residual (Chatterjee and Hadi, 1986); in other words, the observation has a Y value that is relatively far from the predicted Y. So why is outlier detection important? In short, an outlier can be **influential** in the sense that its removal produces significantly different linear regression results, and consequently, inferences to the population can be in error.

So how does the analyst detect outliers? As with any regression analysis, the inspection of data should, first, be accompanied by bivariate scatter plots to see if any unusual trends occur in the data, including the existence of outliers. However, there are many situations where outliers and/or influential observations exist but are not easily identified, especially when multiple predictors are involved. So the analyst must supplement visual displays with **regression diagnostics**.

Consider the following generic housing data where the analyst is interested in predicting sale price using living area of the house, as illustrated in Output 9.23 Comparing Regression Lines Based on Influence of Obs 15, and generated by Program 9.24 Comparing Regression Lines Based on Influence of Obs 15.

Program 9.24 Comparing Regression Lines Based on Influence of Obs 15

```
data housing;
    input Example SqFt SalePrice  @@;
    datalines;
  1 1050 175 1 2100 120 1 1050 80  1 2800 170
  1 3150 155 1 3000 275 1 6500 370 1 3500 280
```

```
      1 700   90  1 1750 218 1 3800 325 1 2100 210
      1 2450 120 1 3850 270 1 4300 275
      2 1050 175 2 2100 120 2 1050 80  2 2800 170
      2 3150 155 2 3000 275 2 6500 50  2 3500 280
      2 700   90  2 1750 218 2 3800 325 2 2100 210
      2 2450 120 2 3850 270 2 4300 275
         ;
run;

proc sgplot data=housing;
    reg x=SqFt Y=SalePrice/group=example;
run;
```

The DATA step creates a temporary data set called HOUSING and reads in data for the variables EXAMPLE, SQFT, and SALEPRICE. Note that the first fifteen observations have a value of '1' for the variable EXAMPLE and the second fifteen observations have a value of '2' for the variable EXAMPLE. PROC SGPLOT requests a scatter plot of SALEPRICE by SQFT and a fitted regression line for each group, EXAMPLE=1 and EXAMPLE=2, as illustrated in Output 9.23 Comparing Regression Lines Based on Influence of Obs 15.

Output 9.23 Comparing Regression Lines Based on Influence of Obs 15

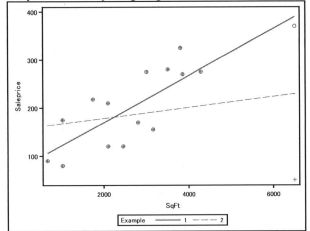

The solid line represents the prediction equation fitted to the 15 observations represented by 'o.' The dotted line represents the prediction equation fitted to the 15 observations represented by '+.' Note that 14 observations are identical as indicated by the 'o' and '+' so that the two data sets differ only on their fifteenth observation. The fifteenth observation in the lower right corner has a sale price of 50 ($1000) with 6500 square feet; this observation is considered influential in that its inclusion results in a prediction line (the dotted line) that is much different than that prediction line (solid line) which has its fifteenth observation in the upper right corner.

Notice that the fifteenth observation (for both data sets) is far, on the X-axis, from the X-values of the remaining fourteen points; as a result, both observations are said to have high **leverage**. It turns out that, in general, an observation with high leverage has a larger influence on the prediction line if it is also an outlier, that is, when its Y-value is far from the Y-values of the remaining points. The deviation on the Y-axis is referred to as **discrepancy**.

In order to identify 'problem' observations in a data set, the analyst will review various statistics for each observation to determine if an observation has any of the following three characteristics (Chatterjee and Hadi, 2006):

1. High Leverage--when an observation has an extreme X-value that deviates from the X-values of the other points as represented by the $\bar{X}$.

2. High Discrepancy (distance squared)--when an observation has an extreme Y-value that deviates from the Y-values of the other points, where its residual is large; this observation is considered an outlier.

3. Influence--the extent to which regression estimates change once the outlier is removed. This measure reflects the combination of leverage and discrepancy.

There are statistics that represent each of the three characteristics (leverage, discrepancy, and influence), and when generating the regression diagnostics, these statistics are provided for every observation. Consequently, these statistics are referred to as **case statistics**, or **deletion statistics**. So, for example, if you have 50 observations, or cases, in your regression analysis, you will have 50 sets of statistics. Following we will discuss each set of statistics.

Leverage (h$_{ii}$)

Leverage indicates how far an observation's X value is from the mean of the Xs calculated from all observations, and is basically used to determine if an observation is considered an outlier on the X-axis. The formula is

$$Leverage = h_{ii} = \frac{1}{n} + \frac{(X_i - \bar{X})^2}{\sum_{i=1}^{n}(X_i - \bar{X})^2}$$

where h_{ii} is the leverage for observation i, n is the sample size, X_i is the value of X for observation i, $\sum_{i=1}^{n}(X_i - \bar{X})^2$ is a number that measures the variation across all Xs. Note that leverage is based upon the difference between an observation's vector of X's and the centroid of X's.

If an X_i has the same value as $\bar{X}$, then its leverage is $1/n$; in this case, leverage is a function of only sample size. In fact, as sample size gets larger, 1/n approaches zero, and the leverage approaches zero as well. In other words, if an observation has an X-value close to the mean ($\bar{X}$), then an observation has low leverage; and, for large sample sizes, the leverage is reduced further.

As X gets further from the mean ($\bar{X}$), the leverage increases. The range of the leverage value is [0, 1]; in short, the maximum value of leverage is 1.0, when $n=1$ and $X_i = \bar{X}$, and the minimum value of leverage is 0 as $n \to \infty$. (as sample size gets larger).

Observations with higher leverage (X values further from $\bar{X}$) potentially have large influence on the regression results; however, leverage alone does not tell the whole picture. Just because an observation has a 'large' leverage does not mean it is problematic, but should be flagged for further review.

The rule of thumb for identifying observations with high leverage (Belsley, Kuh, and Welsch, 1980) is as follows:

$$\text{if} \quad h_{ii} > \frac{2(k+1)}{n}, \quad \text{then the observation has high leverage,}$$

where k = number of predictors and n=sample size

Discrepancy (RSTUDENT$_i$)

Now consider a measure that indicates how far an observation's Y value is from the prediction line ($\hat{Y}$). As displayed in Output 9.23 Comparing Regression Lines Based on Influence of Obs 15, the influential observation 'pulls' the estimated regression equation closer to it so that the residual, Y_i-$\hat{Y}$, is deflated. So this deflated value of the residual may mask the true effect of the influential observation.

Therefore, when diagnosing potential influential observations, an 'external' method is applied. This requires using the **studentized deleted residual** for each observation, sometimes referred to as the **externally studentized residuals** (Belsley, Kuh, and Welsch, 1980). The n studentized deleted residuals for a data set are calculated as follows:

1. Delete observation 1 and conduct the regression analysis using the remaining (n-1) observations, to get the equation for $\hat{Y}_{(1)}$ and value of MSE$_{(1)}$.
2. For observation 1, plug its X value into the equation fitted in #1 to get the value of $\hat{Y}_{(1)}$, which is the predicted value for observation 1 using the equation with observation 1 deleted.
3. For observation 1, calculate the **deleted residual**, $e_{1(1)}$, using $Y_1 - \hat{Y}_{(1)}$, where Y_1 is the actual Y value for observation 1. In general, $e_{i(i)}$ is the residual of observation i using the equation with i deleted.
4. Repeat steps 1 through 3 for observation 2 to get the deleted residual, $Y_2 - \hat{Y}_{(2)}$.
5. Continue the steps through observation n to get the deleted residual, $Y_n - \hat{Y}_{(n)}$.
6. For each observation, calculate the studentized deleted residual, by dividing its deleted residual by the standard error of the deleted residual. The formula is as follows:

$$t_i = \frac{e_{i(i)}}{\sqrt{MSE_{(i)}(1-h_{ii})}}$$

where $MSE_{(i)}$ is the mean-square-error with observation i deleted.

This externally studentized residual (t_i), referred to in SAS as **RSTUDENT**, is a deletion statistic. The criterion for identifying observations with high discrepancy is based upon the idea that approximately 95% of t-values fall between -2.0 and +2.0.; therefore, the rule of thumb for identifying highly discrepant observations is as follows:

$$\text{if } |t_i| > 2.0 \text{, then the observation has high discrepancy}$$

Now that we have established the criteria for both high leverage and high discrepancy, let's consider how both of those are used to identify observations that are influential.

Influence

Measures of influence use both leverage and discrepancy to provide information about how the regression equation will change if observation i were removed from the data set, and are, therefore, referred to as deletion statistics. There are global measures of influence (which include Cook's D and DFFITS) and local measures of influence (DFBETAS).

The first global measure of influence is **Cook's D** (Cook, 1977) and is defined as follows:

$$Cook's\ D_i = \frac{\sum_{i=1}^{n}(\hat{Y}_i - \hat{Y}_{i(i)})^2}{(k)MSE}$$

where $\hat{Y}_i - \hat{Y}_{i(i)}$ is the difference in the predicted Y based upon the model with all observations and the model with observation i deleted, k is the number of predictors, MSE is the mean-square-error for the model with all observations, and n is the sample size.

If observation i is influential, where inclusion of the observation results in a regression line that is relatively far from the other points and minimizes the fit, then the numerator of Cook's D will be relatively large, resulting in a relatively large Cook's D value. If observation i has no influence, the numerator corresponds to the least squares criterion for fitting the line and has the minimum possible value; therefore, Cook's D is at a minimum. Note that the smallest possible value of Cook's D is zero being that it can never be negative.

There are several rules of thumb for identifying potential influential observations using Cook's D:

$$Cook's\ D_i > 1.0 \qquad \text{(Cook and Weisberg 1982)}$$

$$Cook's\ D_i > \frac{4}{n} \qquad \text{(Bollen and Jackman, 1990)}$$

Chatterjee and Hadi (2006) make several suggestions with respect to cutoff values. First, they suggested using a critical F value, using .50 level of significance with k and (n-k) degrees of freedom for a sample size of n with k predictors. Secondly, for ease of use, they concur with Cook and Weisberg's suggested cutoff of 1.0.

Finally, they suggest an approach that departs from the more rigid cutoff by taking into account the size of an observation's Cook's D relative to the Cook's D of all other observations. This approach requires either a ranking or plotting of the Cook's D for comparison purposes. In general, if the values are all the same, then the analyst can conclude that no observations are influential. If there are values that deviate significantly from the other values, then those should be flagged for further inspection. Of course, this approach relies heavily on experience and subject-matter expertise in determining what values constitute a large deviation.

A second measure of global influence is the **DFFITS** (Welsch and Kuh, 1977) and is calculated for each observation i as follows:

$$DFFITS_i = \frac{\hat{Y}_i - \hat{Y}_{i(i)}}{\sqrt{MSE_{(i)}h_{ii}}} = t_i\sqrt{\frac{h_{ii}}{(1-h_{ii})}}$$

Notice, from the latter formula, that as discrepancy (t_i) increases, with leverage (h_{ii}) constant, DFFITS increases indicating that observation i is influential; for a fixed discrepancy (as measured by t_i), as leverage increases, the term $\sqrt{h_{ii}/(1-h_{ii})}$ inceases, resulting in an increase in DFFITS, or influence. Finally, the largest impact is when both discrepancy (t_i) and leverage are large.

The rule of thumb for identifying potential influential observations using DFFITS (Belsley, Kuh, and Welsch, 1980) is:

$$|DFFITS_i| > 2\sqrt{\frac{k+1}{n}}$$

Where k = the number of predictors and n = sample size. As stated previously, the analyst should also consider looking at the values of DFFITS to see if any values deviate significantly from the others, as opposed to relying on a hard rule.

Let's revisit the generic housing case from Output 9.23 Comparing Regression Lines Based on Influence of Obs 15 which includes the one observation that seems to be influential. Consider Program 9.25 Identifying Suspicious Observations Using Measures of Influence for generating measures of leverage, discrepancy, and influence for identifying suspicious observations:

Program 9.25 Identifying Suspicious Observations Using Measures of Influence

```
data housing;
   input ID SqFt SalePrice  @@;
   datalines;
 1   1050 175 2  2100 120 3   1050 80   4   2800 170   4 3150 155
   6   3000 275 7  6500 50   8   3500 280 9  700   90   10 1750 218
   11 3800 325 12 2100 210 13 2450 120 14 3850 270 15 4300 275
      ;
run;

proc reg data=housing
   plots (only)=(rstudentbyleverage cooksd dffits);
   model SalePrice = SqFt;
   output out=diagnostics
        h=leverage rstudent=rstudent cookd=cooksd dffits=dffits;
run;

data review;
   set diagnostics;
   flag=0; n=15; k=1; cooksd_cut = 4/n; h_cut=2*(k+1)/n; dffits_cut=2*sqrt((k+1)/n);
   if cooksd > cooksd_cut then flag+1;
   if abs(dffits) > dffits_cut then flag+1;
   if abs(rstudent)> 2 then flag+1;
   if leverage >  h_cut then flag+1;
run;

proc print data=review;
   var ID SalePrice SqFt leverage rstudent cooksd dffits flag;
run;
```

The DATA step creates a temporary data set called HOUSING and reads in data for the variables ID, SQFT, and SALEPRICE. PROC REG with the MODEL statement requests a linear regression for predicting SALEPRICE by SQFT. The PLOTS(ONLY)= option requests visual displays for RSTUDENT by LEVERAGE, COOKSD, and DFFITS. The OUTPUT statement with the OUT=option requests that the listed deletion statistics are saved to a temporary SAS data set called DIAGNOSTICS for further review.

The second DATA step creates a temporary data set called REVIEW where the cutoffs for each deletion statistic are computed and a counter variable called FLAG is incremented by 1 every time an observation is flagged for exceeding the cutoff for the deletion statistic. Finally, the PRINT procedure is included so that the deletion statistics can be reviewed. The output can be found in Output 9.24a Linear Regression Output for SalePrice with Influential Observation through Output 9.24d Deletion Statistics for Detecting Influence.

Before reviewing the output, let's first determine the cutoff values for each of the deletion statistics:

Leverage cutoff: $\quad h_{ii} > \frac{2(k+1)}{n} = \frac{2(1+1)}{15} = 0.2667$

Rstudent: $\quad |t_i| > 2.0$

Cook's D: $\quad D_i > \frac{4}{15} = 0.2667$

DFFITS: $\quad |DFFITS_i| > 2\sqrt{\frac{k+1}{n}} = 2\sqrt{\frac{1+1}{15}} = 0.7303$

First, note that the output seems to indicate that square footage is not a good predictor (p-value = 0.4775) and the fit is very poor with R^2_{adj} = -0.0344. However, we know that this is because observation 15 is influential. Knowing that, let's review the remaining output to see how the deletion diagnostics will aid in identifying observation 15 as influential.

Output 9.24a Linear Regression Output for SalePrice with Influential Observation

Root MSE	86.64727	R-Square	0.0395
Dependent Mean	187.53333	Adj R-Sq	-0.0344
Coeff Var	46.20366		

Parameter Estimates					
Variable	DF	Parameter Estimate	Standard Error	t Value	Pr > |t|
Intercept	1	155.80562	48.80515	3.19	0.0071
SqFt	1	0.01130	0.01545	0.73	0.4775

Consider first Output 9.24b Leverage by RStudent Plot for detecting leverage and discrepancy. The X-axis represents leverage and has the vertical reference line at 0.2667; therefore, any observation to the right of that line has high leverage. One observation, indicated by the triangle, has high leverage.

The Y-axis represents the RStudent values which measure discrepancy and have two horizontal reference lines at -2 and +2 indicating that any observation falling outside of those values has high discrepancy. Again, one observation, indicated by the triangle, has its RStudent value below -2. This observation is a great candidate to review for possible influence on the regression results.

Output 9.24b Leverage by RStudent Plot

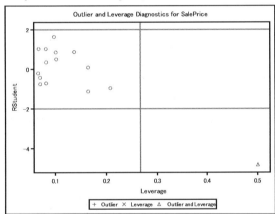

To further identify influence, the analyst can inspect the plots provided in Output 9.24c Cook's D and DFFITS Plots for Detecting Influence. Consider first the plot of Cook's D. The cutoff for Cook's D is 0.2667 as shown by the horizontal reference line. The X-axis identifies the observation number. Observation 7 is determined to have influence because its Cook's D exceeds the cutoff. Similarly, Observation 7 is shown to have influence because its DFFITS falls outside of the range of ± 0.7303.

Output 9.24c Cook's D and DFFITS Plots for Detecting Influence

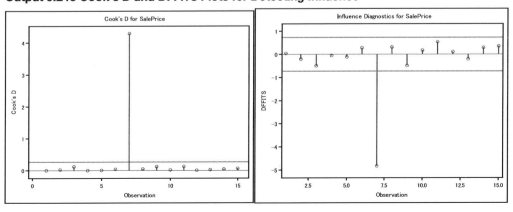

The specific values of the deletion statistics for Observation 7 can be found in Output 9.24d Deletion Statistics for Detecting Influence. In particular, Observation 7 has exceeded four of the displayed deletion statistics (flag=4) with leverage = 0.50061 > 0.2667, Rstudent = -4.82064 < -2.0, Cook's D = 4.29699 > 0.2667, and DFFITS = -4.82652 < -0.7303. Also note that while the cutoffs were used here to diagnose influence, the fact that all of the deletion statistics for Observation 7 deviated from the deletion statistics of the other observations, is evidence enough that Observation 7 is influential.

Output 9.24d Deletion Statistics for Detecting Influence

Obs	ID	SalePrice	SqFt	leverage	Rstudent	cooksd	dffits	flag
1	1	175	1050	0.16484	0.08890	0.00084	0.03950	0
2	2	120	2100	0.08255	-0.70338	0.02316	-0.21099	0
3	3	80	1050	0.16484	-1.11780	0.12098	-0.49660	0
4	4	170	2800	0.06667	-0.20071	0.00155	-0.05364	0
5	4	155	3150	0.07042	-0.42188	0.00720	-0.11611	0
6	6	275	3000	0.06786	1.02110	0.03783	0.27550	0
7	7	50	6500	0.50061	-4.82064	4.29699	-4.82652	4
8	8	280	3500	0.08196	1.02104	0.04638	0.30508	0
9	9	90	700	0.20785	-0.95250	0.11988	-0.48791	0
10	10	218	1750	0.10219	0.50149	0.01519	0.16919	0
11	11	325	3800	0.09806	1.62865	0.12792	0.53700	0
12	12	210	2100	0.08255	0.35440	0.00606	0.10631	0
13	13	120	2450	0.07071	-0.74722	0.02199	-0.20612	0
14	14	270	3850	0.10130	0.85121	0.04172	0.28577	0
15	15	275	4300	0.13761	0.86891	0.06139	0.34710	0

If the analyst does not want to create a temporary data set with diagnostic information, but instead wants a simple table, the INFLUENCE option can be used in MODEL statement which requests the deletion statistics suggested by Belsley, Kuh, and Welsch (1980). The option is used as follows:

```
model SalePrice = SqFt/influence;
```

The resulting output is displayed in Output 9.25 Influence Statistics Using the INFLUENCE Option which gives identical information for flagging possible influential observations. Keep in mind that the Hat Diag H column in the output corresponds to the leverage. Using the previously defined cutoffs, the analyst can see that Observation 7 should be investigated further for possible influence. (Note: DFBETAS will be discussed in the next section).

Output 9.25 Influence Statistics Using the INFLUENCE Option

Output Statistics							
						DFBETAS	
Obs	Residual	RStudent	Hat Diag H	Cov Ratio	DFFITS	Intercept	SqFt
1	7.3248	0.0889	0.1648	1.4034	0.0395	0.0386	-0.0305
2	-59.5449	-0.7034	0.0826	1.1799	-0.2110	-0.1692	0.0926
3	-87.6752	-1.1178	0.1648	1.1527	-0.4966	-0.4854	0.3832
4	-17.4580	-0.2007	0.0667	1.2490	-0.0536	-0.0248	0.0002
5	-36.4145	-0.4219	0.0704	1.2259	-0.1161	-0.0280	-0.0268
6	85.2811	1.0211	0.0679	1.0658	0.2755	0.0928	0.0365
7	-179.2843	-4.8206	0.5006	0.2725	-4.8265	3.1863	-4.4937
8	84.6289	1.0210	0.0820	1.0822	0.3051	0.0090	0.1318
9	-73.7187	-0.9525	0.2079	1.2806	-0.4879	-0.4840	0.4021
10	42.4117	0.5015	0.1022	1.2541	0.1692	0.1513	-0.0997
11	126.2376	1.6287	0.0981	0.8727	0.5370	-0.0671	0.3038
12	30.4551	0.3544	0.0826	1.2529	0.1063	0.0852	-0.0466
13	-63.5014	-0.7472	0.0707	1.1531	-0.2061	-0.1356	0.0493
14	70.6724	0.8512	0.1013	1.1614	0.2858	-0.0422	0.1671
15	70.5854	0.8689	0.1376	1.2045	0.3471	-0.1107	0.2492

The deletion statistics discussed so far are used to diagnose influence, in general, and are referred to as global measures. In the previous example, where we determined that Observation 7 was influential, it was obvious from the scatter plot that the observation had an influence on both the slope of that one predictor and its intercept.

When multiple predictors are involved, the 'location' of the influence is usually not obvious. It could be that an observation is influential on b_1 because of its value on X_1, but has no influence on the other parameter estimates with respect to its values on X_2 nor X_3 nor … nor X_k. The analyst must dig deeper to find exactly where the influence occurs and must use local measures of influence, referred to as **DFBETAS**.

DFBETAS are computed for each observation *i* and each (*k+1*) parameter, including the intercept to see if the deletion statistic exceeds the cutoff. The formula for the $DFBETAS_{ij}$, which measures the influence of observation *i* on parameter *j*, is defined as:

$$DFBETAS_{ij} = \frac{b_j - b_{j(i)}}{SE_{b_{j(i)}}}$$

where b_j is the slope for parameter *j* using all observations, $b_{j(i)}$ is the slope for parameter *j* with observations *i* deleted, and $SE_{bj(i)}$ is the standard error of the *jth* parameter estimate with observation *i* deleted.

The cutoff value for DFBETAS is: $|DFBETAS_{ij}| > 2\sqrt{\frac{1}{n}}$

For the hypothetical housing example, the cutoff is: $|DFBETAS_{ij}| > 2\sqrt{\frac{1}{15}} = 0.5164$. To get a visual display, the analyst will add DFBETAS to the PLOTS statement. The INFLUENCE option is used to get a listing of the deletion statistics, including the DFBETAS for the slope and the intercept, as illustrated in Program 9.26 DFBETA Plots for Assessing Local Influence.

Program 9.26 DFBETA Plots for Assessing Local Influence

```
data housing;
   input ID SqFt SalePrice  @@;
   datalines;
1  1050 175 2  2100 120 3  1050 80   4  2800 170   4 3150 155
6  3000 275 7  6500 50  8  3500 280 9  700  90   10 1750 218
```

```
     11 3800 325 12 2100 210 13 2450 120 14 3850 270 15 4300 275
       ;
run;
```

```
proc reg data=housing
    plots (only)=(rstudentbyleverage cooksd dffits dfbetas);
    model SalePrice = SqFt/influence;
run;
```

The output is displayed in Output 9.26 DFBETA Plots for Assessing Local Influence and shows the value of the DFBETAS for each of the 15 observations for both the intercept (left panel) and the slope for SQFT (right panel). Note for both panels the reference lines show the cutoffs of ±0.5614.

A large positive DFBETA on the intercept panel shows that the inclusion of Observation 7 has a large positive influence on the intercept (pushes the intercept up); a large negative DFBETA on the right panel shows that the inclusion of Observation 7 has a large negative influence on the slope (pushes the slope downward). See also in Output 9.25 Influence Statistics using the INFLUENCE Option that the DFBETAS for Observation 7 are +3.1863 and -4.4937 for the intercept and slope, respectively.

Output 9.26 DFBETA Plots for Assessing Local Influence

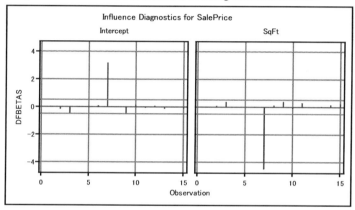

Consider now the Ames Housing Case where we are interested in predicting SALEPRICE using GR_LIV_AREA and AGE_AT_SALE. The cutoffs for two predictors (k=2) and 300 houses (n=300) are defined as follows:

Leverage cutoff: $h_{ii} > \frac{2(k+1)}{n} = \frac{2(2+1)}{300} = 0.0200$

Rstudent: $|t_i| > 2.0$

Cook's D: $D_i > \frac{4}{300} = 0.0133$

DFFITS: $|DFFITS_i| > 2\sqrt{\frac{k+1}{n}} = 2\sqrt{\frac{2+1}{300}} = 0.2000$

Program 9.27 Regression Diagnostics for the Ames Housing Case is identical to the previous program with two exceptions. The flag is incremented only if the observation exceeds either the Cook's D or DFFITS; the observation is printed if it exceeds at least one of the cutoffs (where flag > 0), as shown in Output 9.27b Observations Flagged as Influential for Ames Housing.

Program 9.27 Regression Diagnostics for the Ames Housing Case

```
libname sasba 'c:\sasba\ames';
data amesreg300;
    set sasba.amesreg300;
run;
```

```
proc reg data=amesreg300
    plots (only)=(rstudentbyleverage cooksd dffits dfbetas);
    model SalePrice= Gr_Liv_Area Age_at_Sale/influence;
    output out=diagnostics
        h=leverage rstudent=rstudent cookd=cooksd dffits=dffits;
run;
```

```
data review;
   set diagnostics;
   flag=0; n=300; k=2; cooksd_cut = 4/n; h_cut=2*(k+1)/n; dffits_cut=2*sqrt((k+1)/n);
   if cooksd > cooksd_cut then flag+1;
   if abs(dffits) > dffits_cut then flag+1;
   if flag>0;
run;

proc sort data=review;
   by cooksd;
run;

proc print data=review;
   var SalePrice Gr_Liv_Area Age_at_Sale
   leverage rstudent cooksd dffits flag;
run;
```

A review of the leverage by Rstudent plot, Output 9.27a Influence Panels and Influential Observations for Ames Housing shows one observation (indicated by the triangle) that has both high leverage and high discrepancy. The line listing shows that Observation 15 exceeds both cutoffs.

Of course because the sample size is much larger than our hypothetical example, the cutoffs are much smaller. As a result, we have 15 observations that are flagged for potential influence using the Cook's D as shown in Output 9.27a Influence Panels and Influential Observations for Ames Housing.

Output 9.27a Influence Panels and Influential Observations for Ames Housing

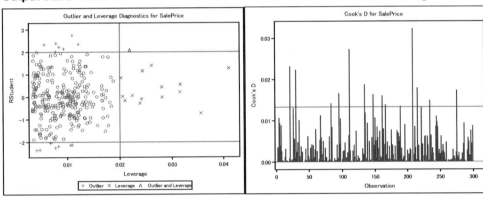

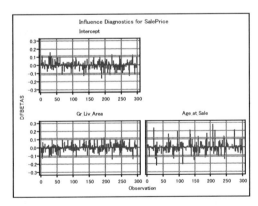

Output 9.27b Observations Flagged as Influential for Ames Housing

Obs	SalePrice	Gr_Liv_Area	Age_at_Sale	leverage	rstudent	cooksd	dffits	flag
1	130000	1630	54	0.008304	-2.18847	0.013199	-0.20026	1
2	147000	1143	1	0.017198	-1.52639	0.013530	-0.20192	2
3	228500	1689	17	0.008466	2.22282	0.013878	0.20539	2
4	227000	1573	7	0.009332	2.14214	0.014236	0.20790	2
5	228000	1592	13	0.007898	2.38975	0.014918	0.21322	2
6	165400	1656	5	0.010616	-2.13102	0.016051	-0.22074	2
7	79000	1096	84	0.010899	-2.12194	0.016345	-0.22274	2
8	154900	1343	88	0.013815	1.89493	0.016622	0.22428	2
9	139900	1428	106	0.026097	1.39652	0.017364	0.22860	2
10	153575	1396	92	0.016793	1.78254	0.017959	0.23296	2
11	153900	1416	93	0.017778	1.77072	0.018782	0.23822	2
12	220000	1346	2	0.012149	2.35169	0.022331	0.26080	2
13	94000	1020	135	0.041024	1.27795	0.023239	0.26432	2
14	240000	1578	2	0.010966	2.74553	0.027258	0.28909	2
15	135000	1174	107	0.021922	2.09310	0.032362	0.31336	2

Recommendations for Handling Influential Observations

First, all observations that exceed any of the deletion statistics should be flagged for further inspection. Once those are flagged, the first step is to verify that the variables values are valid and not the result of recording errors. Once all errors are resolved, special care should be taken to further resolve the problem.

One strategy involves digging deeper to see if the outliers have any similarities. For example, it could be that most of the flagged houses come from a specific neighborhood where the linear regression equation does not account for the fact that location drives up the sale price. In that case, the analyst could consider including a dummy variable code as 1 if the house is in the neighborhood or 0 otherwise, to see if that variable is significant and resolves the existence of influential observations.

It could be that the observation is unusual. For example, everyone knows of a neighborhood with a huge house having extraordinary amenities that costs several times more than the other houses. Obviously this observation should be removed.

The analyst could try running the regression analysis with and without the observation to see the extent of the influence (never delete multiple observations at the same time as the source of the impact will be confounded). If a low cutoff value is used and most observations have no obvious impact on the regression coefficients after their removals, then you should use a higher cutoff value (Bollen & Jackman, 1990).

As a last resort, the analyst may exclude an observation (or observations); in that case, the reason for deletion and the impact should be reported to ensure maximized transparency.

As a final note, consider the fact that outliers can influence the assumptions. For example, if you fit a straight line to curved data, observation on either ends of the X axis are further from the line, therefore showing up as highly discrepant. Fitting a curved line will eliminate discrepancy in that case. Also, outliers can contribute to violation of the equal variance assumption. Therefore, outliers should be investigated in conjunction with the assessment of assumptions.

Concluding Remarks

Many topics have been covered to ensure the analyst has the necessary tools to conduct a regression analysis for both explanation and prediction purposes. The tools include how to construct the models and ways to ensure their validity. After a thorough review, the analyst may ask the question: in which order should these tools be applied?

Should the analyst fit the model, and then look for collinearity, outliers, and violations of assumptions? Or does the existence of collinearity, outliers, and/or violations to assumptions affect the modeling process--in other words, should the assessment of the various issues be done first, before model building?

Remember our initial example of an outlier showed where its influence deflated the slope so that the inferences showed no significant relationship between X and Y. Also, in the case of collinearity, the significance of one potential predictor may be masked by the existence of another, ultimately affecting the model building process.

Keeping these considerations in mind, we suggest the following steps for carrying out a linear regression project:

1. Always conduct exploratory analyses to produce univariate and bivariate descriptive statistics and data visualizations as a way to familiarize yourself with the data and to warn of any data problems that may jeopardize the validity of your project.

2. As a preliminary analysis, consider data reduction methods, mentioned earlier in this book, to eliminate predictors that may be highly correlated as a way to mitigate redundancy and collinearity.

3. Review bivariate analyses, including simple linear regression, to assess any violations to the linearity or equal variance assumption so that predictors can be transformed if necessary. If any transformations are needed, care should be taken in selecting the correct form (natural log, square root, quadratic, etc.).

4. Once the data is in an adequate form (after completing steps 2 and 3 above), the analyst is ready for the model building process. Once candidate models are considered, the analyst should once more consider verifying the assumptions and checking for outliers and collinearity.

In the age of big data, the analyst should consider carrying out steps 1 through 4 above on a training data set, and then apply the resulting candidate models on an external data set to validate an assess which model performs best. For more information on the validation process for building classifiers, refer to Chapter 11, "Measure of Model Performance."

Finally, when the purpose of linear regression is prediction, many times the analyst prefers to develop a model and save it for future use. In this case, the analyst can use the STORE statement within the REG procedure to save the model in a binary file format, followed presumably later by the RESTORE option and SCORE statement within the PLM procedure when new data needs to be scored.

The purpose of the PLM procedure is to recall **stored models** from various statistical procedures and apply those models to new data. While we will not cover PLM in the context of linear regression, you are referred to Chapter 10 , "Logistic Regression Analysis," for a discussion of the PLM procedure and how it is used for model production.

Key Terms

adjusted R^2

all-possible subsets

analysis of variance (ANOVA)

autocorrelated

backward elimination

Bonferroni correction

case statistics

coefficient of determination (R^2)

collinearity

condition number (C)

confidence interval for the slope

Cook's D

correlation coefficient.

deleted residual

deletion statistic

dependent variable

discrepancy

design variables

DFBETAS

DFFITS

eigenvalue (λj)

eigenvector

error in prediction (e)

error-sum-of-squares (SSE)

externally studentized residuals

forward selection

full model

general linear model (GLM)

homoscedasticity

independent variable

influential

least squares criterion

leverage

listwise deletion

Mallows' Cp

mean-square (MS)

mean-square-error (MSE)

mean-square-error (MSE)

mean-square-regression (MSR)

multiple linear regression

ordinary least squares (OLS)

orthogonal

outlier

outliers

overparameterization
pairwise deletion
parsimony
prediction equation
predictor
principal component
reduced model
redundancy
reference group
regression diagnostics.
regression-sum-of-squares (SSR)
relevancy
residual analysis
residual plots
residuals
restriction of range
r-square

scatter plot
selection criterion
sequential searches
simple linear regression
squared semi-partial correlation
standard error of the regression (Se)
standard error of the residual
standardized residual
stepwise selection
stored model
studentized deleted residual
studentized residual
tolerance
total-sum-of-squares (SST)
t-test of slope
variance inflation factor (VIF)

Chapter Quiz

1. Which of the following is an assumption of linear regression?
   a. The parameters enter the model equation linearly.
   b. The residuals have a normal distribution.
   c. The variance of the outcome is equal across all values of the predictor.
   d. All of the above.
   e. None of the above.

2. Suppose you have a model r-square=.84 and adjusted r-square=.75. Which statement below best explains which value you should report?
   a. Report either r-square or adjusted r-square as both values are valid.
   b. Report only r-square because it is most often reported in prior research.
   c. Report only adjusted r-square because it is less influenced by the number of predictors in the model.
   d. Report none of the values as long as the slope is considered zero.
   e. None of the above statements is true.

3. Which of the following MODEL statements will provide Mallows' Cp for model selection?
   a. model SalePrice = Gr_Liv_Area Total_Bsmt_SF
      Lot_Area Age_At_Sale High_Kitchen_Quality
      /selection=cp;
   b. model SalePrice = Gr_Liv_Area Total_Bsmt_SF
      Lot_Area Age_At_Sale High_Kitchen_Quality
      /best=cp;
   c. model SalePrice = Gr_Liv_Area Total_Bsmt_SF
      Lot_Area Age_At_Sale High_Kitchen_Quality
      /plot=cp;
   d. model SalePrice = Gr_Liv_Area Total_Bsmt_SF
      Lot_Area Age_At_Sale High_Kitchen_Quality
      /cp;
   e. None of the above.

4. Which of the following statements is true about PROC REG and PROC GLMSELECT?
    a. PROC GLMSELECT can be used to select variables, whereas PROC REG does not provide options for variable selection.
    b. PROC REG and PROC GLMSELECT both provide options in the MODEL statement for outlier detection.
    c. PROC REG and PROC GLMSELECT provide options in the MODEL statement for best subsets analysis.
    d. PROC GLM uses a CLASS statement to allow for categorical predictors, whereas PROC REG does not.
    e. None of the above.

Refer to the following SAS output for questions 5 through 7.

Number of Observations Read	990
Number of Observations Used	990

Analysis of Variance					
Source	DF	Sum of Squares	Mean Square	F Value	Pr > F
Model	5	1.022351E12	2.044702E11	1027.14	<.0001
Error	984	1.958829E11	199068030		
Corrected Total	989	1.218234E12			

Root MSE	14109	R-Square	0.8392
Dependent Mean	154845	Adj R-Sq	0.8384
Coeff Var	9.11179		

Parameter Estimates							
Variable	DF	Parameter Estimate	Standard Error	t Value	Pr > |t|	95% Confidence Limits	
Intercept	1	74063	3188.57981	23.23	<.0001	67806	80321
Gr_Liv_Area	1	53.45849	1.51279	35.34	<.0001	50.48982	56.42716
Total_Bsmt_SF	1	19.94240	1.65322	12.06	<.0001	16.69815	23.18664
Lot_Area	1	0.32838	0.14583	2.25	0.0246	0.04220	0.61456
Age_at_Sale	1	-554.57738	19.74839	-28.08	<.0001	-593.33118	-515.82359
Garage_Area	1	25.83541	3.11126	8.30	<.0001	19.72994	31.94088

5. Which of the following statements is true?
    a. Age_at_Sale is most important because it has the largest slope in magnitude.
    b. Lot_Area is non-significant because its slope is close to zero.
    c. It is expected that adding a garage adds $25,835 to the sale price of the house.
    d. This model is the best model because the r-square is significant.
    e. None of the above.

6. Which statement was used to generate the output?
    a. The MODEL statement with the VIF option
    b. The MODEL statement with the clb option
    c. The cli and vif options within the MODEL statement
    d. The MODEL statement with the SCORR2 option

7. What value do you report to explain how well your model fits the data?
   a. 1027.14
   b. <.0001
   c. 0.8384
   d. None of the above.

Refer the following SAS output to answer questions 8, 9, and 10.

Analysis of Variance					
Source	DF	Sum of Squares	Mean Square	F Value	Pr > F
Model	5	1.022351E12	2.044702E11	1027.14	<.0001
Error	984	1.958829E11	199068030		
Corrected Total	989	1.218234E12			

Root MSE	14109	R-Square	0.8392
Dependent Mean	154845	Adj R-Sq	0.8384
Coeff Var	9.11179		

Parameter Estimates							
Variable	DF	Parameter Estimate	Standard Error	t Value	Pr > |t|	Squared Semi-partial Corr Type II	Variance Inflation
Intercept	1	74063	3188.57981	23.23	<.0001	.	0
Gr_Liv_Area	1	53.45849	1.51279	35.34	<.0001	0.20405	1.22562
Total_Bsmt_SF	1	19.94240	1.65322	12.06	<.0001	0.02378	1.21184
Lot_Area	1	0.32838	0.14583	2.25	0.0246	0.00082855	1.13940
Age_at_Sale	1	-554.57738	19.74839	-28.08	<.0001	0.12886	1.42589
Garage_Area	1	25.83541	3.11126	8.30	<.0001	0.01127	1.29628

8. What variable contributes most to the explanation of saleprice?
   a. Gr__Liv_Area
   b. Total_Bsmt_SF
   c. Lot_Area
   d. Age_at_Sale

9. What do you report when determining if there is collinearity in your model?
   a. Squared semi-partial correlation type II
   b. Variance inflation
   c. F-value
   d. Adjusted r-square

10. Which model statement would generate the output?
    a. model saleprice= Gr_Liv_Area Total_Bsmt_SF Lot_Area Garage_Area/ scorr2 vif;
    b. model saleprice= Gr_Liv_Area Total_Bsmt_SF Lot_Area Age_at_Sale Garage_Area/ scorr2 vif;
    c. model saleprice= Gr_Liv_Area Total_Bsmt_SF Lot_Area Age_at_Sale Garage_Area/ scorr2;
    d. model saleprice= Gr_Liv_Area Total_Bsmt_SF Lot_Area Age_at_Sale Garage_Area;

Chapter 10: Logistic Regression Analysis

Introduction

In this chapter, we continue to explore statistical models aimed at answering various business questions. As seen in Chapter 1, "Statistics and Making Sense of Our World," if the analyst is interested in determining whether or not a categorical response variable is related to a set of predictors (whether categorical or numeric), then the appropriate statistical analysis is **logistic regression analysis**. Now, we will provide the basis for the logistic regression model by defining the logit and a model for developing a linear relationship between the logit and a set of input variables, or predictors. This chapter will provide the syntax for using the LOGISTIC procedure, describe the output of the logistic regression analysis, and explain how the parameters estimates are obtained, how to test their significance, and how they are used for both prediction and explanation via the odds ratio. This chapter will describe the design, or dummy, variables needed when categorical predictors are used and how to interpret the output depending on how the design variables are created. Once the basic model is introduced, this chapter will continue with multiple logistic regression analysis, the interpretation of output, followed by a description of the code needed for the variable selection methods, including forward, backward, and stepwise methods. The multiple logistic regression analysis is extended to the case where interaction effects exist, with a description of the code needed to produce the output, and how to interpret using conditional odds ratios and data visualization. Finally, this chapter will describe the various ways to score new observations once the final model is selected for deployment.

In this chapter, you will learn how to:

- identify situations that require the use of logistic regression analysis

- identify the assumptions of logistic regression

- understand concepts related to logistic regression, such as log-odds, logit transformation, and sigmoidal relationship between the probability of success and a predictor

- use the LOGISTIC procedure with the MODEL and CLASS statements to fit a binary logistic regression

- use the LOGISTIC procedure to fit a multiple logistic regression model

- interpret the output from the LOGISTIC procedure, including the Model Convergence section, the Testing Global Null Hypothesis table, the Type 3 Analysis of Effects table, the Analysis of Maximum Likelihood Estimates table, and the Association of Predicted Probabilities and Observed Responses table

- perform model selection using stepwise, forward selection, and backward elimination

- use the SELECTION=SCORE option to run a best subset analysis

- understand the concept of scoring

- use the SCORE statement within the LOGISTIC procedure for scoring new cases

- use the SCORE statement within the PLM procedure for scoring new cases
- use the CODE statement within the LOGISTIC procedure for scoring new cases
- use the OUTMODEL and INMODEL options within the LOGISTIC procedure to score new cases
- describe the fundamental differences between the methods for coding new cases

The Logistic Regression Model

There are many applications of logistic regression where the goal is to predict a binary outcome. For example, in retail, the analyst may be interested in determining factors associated with whether or not a customer churns; or a manager may be interested in the characteristics of salespeople associated with meeting or falling short of monthly sales goals. Similarly, human resource managers are interested in determining the factors associated with employee turnover, that is, if the employee will have resigned or not in a specified period of time. In education, administrators are interested in finding factors associated with whether or not a student graduates; or in healthcare, caregivers are interested in what conditions lead to a patient being discharged from a hospital in a standard length of time or not. In each of these situations, if the event of interest exists (defined as success), the observation under investigation has a value of 1 assigned to its outcome variable; otherwise its outcome is defined as a failure and assigned a value of 0.

Development of the Logistic Regression Model

As described in Chapter 9, "Linear Regression Analysis," when developing a model to predict a numeric continuous outcome, analysts use ordinary least squares estimation. However, this approach is not reasonable when the goal is to predict a binary outcome. A linear combination of predictors can assume any real-numbered values and would fail at predicting, specifically, ones and zeros. In addition, modeling a binary outcome in this way would violate the assumptions of linear regression, namely, the normality of the error term and homoscedasticity.

As an illustration, consider the Ames Housing Case introduced in Chapter 1, "Statistics and Making Sense of Our World." Suppose we were to predict BONUS (1=Yes or 0=No) using the predictor above ground living area (GR_LIV_AREA) and applied the ordinary least squares regression to the data set AMES300. Consider the output as depicted in Figure 10.1 Scatter Plot of Gr_Liv_Area by Bonus.

Figure 10.1 Scatter Plot of Gr_Liv_Area by Bonus

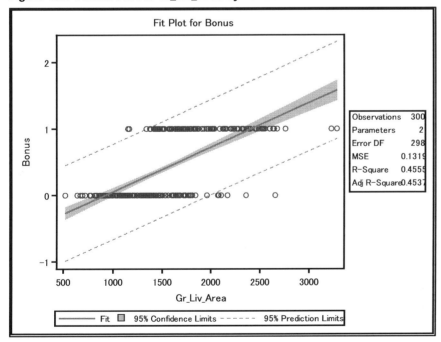

Note that, while it seems that larger values of living area are associated with a bonus (BONUS=1) and smaller values of living area are associated with not receiving a bonus (BONUS=0), the relationship is certainly not linear, and accordingly, the errors are not normal. From the range of the prediction line, it is also evident that predicted values have no real meaning, in addition to falling outside of the range of 0 and 1.

As an alternative, because probabilities have numeric continuous values, modeling the probability of a binary outcome, say, the probability a success may seem reasonable; however, that approach has the same inherent problem in that a linear combination of predictors is not constrained to values between 0 and 1. Again, the assumptions of linear regression are violated. In addition, the relationship between the probability of success and a predictor variable is non-linear, similar to an S-shaped, or **sigmoid**, curve, as illustrated in Output 10.1 Scatter Plot of Binned Living Area by Proportion of Successes using Program 10.1 Scatter Plot of Binned Living Area by Proportion of Successes.

Program 10.1 Scatter Plot of Binned Living Area by Proportion of Successes

```
libname sasba 'c:\sasba\ames';
data ames300;
   set sasba.ames300;
   If Gr_Liv_Area le 500 then Living_Area=1;
   If Gr_Liv_Area gt 500 and Gr_Liv_Area le 1000 then Living_Area=2;
   If Gr_Liv_Area gt 1000 and Gr_Liv_Area le 1500 then Living_Area=3;
   If Gr_Liv_Area gt 1500 and Gr_Liv_Area le 2000 then Living_Area=4;
   If Gr_Liv_Area gt 2000 and Gr_Liv_Area le 2500 then Living_Area=5;
   If Gr_Liv_Area gt 2500 and Gr_Liv_Area le 3000 then Living_Area=6;
   If Gr_Liv_Area gt 3000 and Gr_Liv_Area le 3500 then Living_Area=7;
run;

 proc format;
   value LA 1='<500' 2='500-<1000' 3='1000-<1500'
            4='1500-<2000' 5='2000-<2500' 6='2500-<3000'
            7='3000-<3500';
run;

proc means data=ames300 noprint;
   class Living_Area;
   var bonus;
   output out=propbonus mean=ProportionOfSuccesses;
run;

proc sgplot data=propbonus;
      reg x=Living_Area y=ProportionOfSuccesses / degree=1;
      format Living_Area LA.;
run;
```

Output 10.1 Scatter Plot of Binned Living Area by Proportion of Successes

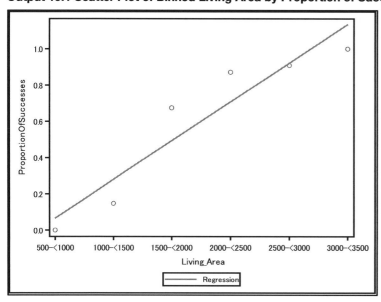

The Logit Transformation

There are several functions that serve as linear transformations for probabilities. One such function is the **logit transformation** and is defined as follows:

$$logit(p_i) = ln\left(\frac{p_i}{1-p_i}\right)$$

where p_i is the probability of success and $p_i/(1-p_i)$ is the **odds** of success for observation *i*, respectively. The logit function transforms the range of probabilities [0,1] to the set of real numbers ranging from $-\infty$ to $+\infty$. In fact, if the odds for an observation are greater than 1.0, then the logit will be positive; if the odds are less than 1.0, the logit will be negative; an odds of 1.0 results in a logit of 0. Consequently, the logistic regression model makes the assumption that the logit can be represented as a linear combination of predictors, or inputs, and can be written as follows:

$$logit(p_i) = \beta_0 + \beta_1 X_1 + \beta_2 X_2 + \cdots + \beta_k X_k$$

where the parameters, β_1 through β_k are estimated from the data. This logistic regression model addresses the aforementioned issues and provides a functional means of arriving at probability values ranging from 0 to 1. Algebraically solving for p_i results in the following:

$$p_i = \frac{e^{\beta_0 + \beta_1 x_1 + \cdots + \beta_k x_k}}{1 + e^{\beta_0 + \beta_1 x_1 + \cdots + \beta_k x_k}}$$

where p_i is now referred to as the **posterior probability** of success for observation *i* given the set of predictor values, X_1, X_2, ..., X_k for observation *i*, and can be represented by the term $P(Y=1|X_1, X_2,..., X_k)$.

Estimating the Logistic Regression Parameters

When estimating the unknown parameters, $\beta_0, \beta_1,..., \beta_k$, we want values that will result in the largest possible probability of success, p_i, for all of those observations where Y=1 (success) and the largest possible probability of failure, $1-p_i$, for all observations where Y=0 (failure). For each observation *i*, this probability can also be written as follows:

$$(p_i)^{Y_i}(1 - p_i)^{1-Y_i} \text{ for Yi} = 0 \text{ or } 1; \text{ for observation i} = 1,..., n$$

We want this probability to be maximized for all *n* observations. Because each observation's outcome is independent of the other, the probability that Y_1 occurs for observation 1 and Y_2 occurs for observation 2, ... and Y_n occurs for observation *n* is equal to the product of the individual probabilities and can be written as:

$$L = \prod_{i=1}^{n}(p_i)^{Y_i}(1 - p_i)^{1-Y_i}$$

This probability over all observations is called the likelihood (L), so the estimates that result in the maximum value of the likelihood are called Maximum Likelihood Estimates (MLEs). In reality, it is mathematically more expedient to solve for values that maximize the log of the likelihood. The methods used to arrive at the solutions are iterative; that is, the methods involve plugging in various values until arriving at the maximum value of the log-likelihood. **Fisher scoring** is one of the most popular methods for estimating logistic regression parameters and is the default method used in SAS. The details of this approach, along with other computational methods that are used in the LOGISTIC procedure, can be found in Hirji, Mehta, and Patel (1987), Hirji (1992), and Mehta, Patel, and Senchaudhuri (1992).

Syntax for the Logistic Regression Procedure

PROC LOGISTIC is a procedure used to establish the relationship between a categorical response variable and categorical and/or numeric predictors and has the general form:

PROC LOGISTIC DATA=*SAS-data-set* *<options>*;
CLASS *variables* *</ options>*;
MODEL *response=predictors* *</ options>*;
ODDSRATIO *<'label'> variable </ options>*;
SCORE *<options>*;
STORE *<options></***LABEL**=*'label'>*
CODE *<options>*;
UNITS predictor1=list1 ... *</ options>*;
RUN;

Before discussing logistic regression analysis, it should be noted that all analyses in this chapter will be conducted on training data, the SAS data set called AMES70, created from the Ames Housing data and that validation procedures using the AMES30 data set will be discussed in Chapter 11, "Measure of Model Performance."

To illustrate the LOGISTIC procedure, consider the Ames Housing Case where the analyst wants to predict whether or not a real estate agent earns a bonus in the sale of a house (target=BONUS) based upon its above ground living area (GR_LIV_AREA). Program 10.2 Simple Logistic Regression would be used to carry out the analysis.

Program 10.2 Simple Logistic Regression

```
libname sasba 'c:\sasba\ames';
run;

proc logistic data=sasba.ames70;
   model Bonus (Event = '1')= Gr_Liv_Area
   /link=logit;
run;
```

From Program 10.2 Simple Logistic Regression, we can see that the LOGISTIC procedure is applied to the Ames Housing data set, as defined by the DATA= option. The MODEL statement defines BONUS as the dependent variable and the above ground living area, GR_LIV_AREA, as the independent variable. Note that the (EVENT=) option is included in the MODEL statement to ensure that the event of interest to be modeled is BONUS=1, or those houses where a bonus is earned; if the (EVENT=) option had been omitted, the default response would be to model the first ordered category, which is '0' as opposed to '1.' Finally, there are several functions that 'link' probabilities to a linear combination of predictors. While the default link function is logit, we have included the LINK= option to illustrate that there are other options as well.

The output generated is voluminous and is illustrated in Output 10.2a Model Information and Response Profile for Simple Logistic Regression through Output 10.2e Association of Predicted Probabilities and Observed Responses. First, Output 10.2a Model Information and Response Profile for Simple Logistic Regression provides preliminary information about the analysis. The Model Information table gives the data set name and indicates that there are two levels of the binary response variable, BONUS. The output verifies that the model transformation utilizes the logit transformation (which is the default model when there are only two response levels); and defines the estimation technique for maximizing the log-odds, namely, Fisher's scoring method.

The second table reports the number of observations read and will match the number of records contained in the data set. The number of observations used reflects the number of observations that have complete data, or nonmissing values, on all variables listed in the MODEL statement. Here we can see that the Ames Housing data set (AMES70) has 1389 observations and that all 1389 observations have complete data on the variables, BONUS and GR_LIV_AREA. If the number used is less than the number read, that is an indication that some observations are missing on at least one variable listed in the MODEL statement.

The third table reports the profile of the response variable, BONUS, where the values are listed by their ordered values, 0 and 1, respectively, including the number of houses in each group. Here we can see that 826 (59.47%) are houses where the agent did not earn a bonus, and 563 (40.53%) are houses where the agent did earn a bonus. Under the response profile table is the model response intended, namely, BONUS=1, as defined in the (EVENT=) option.

Output 10.2a Model Information and Response Profile for Simple Logistic Regression

Model Information	
Data Set	SASBA.AMES70
Response Variable	Bonus
Number of Response Levels	2
Model	binary logit
Optimization Technique	Fisher's scoring

Number of Observations Read	1389
Number of Observations Used	1389

Response Profile		
Ordered Value	Bonus	Total Frequency
1	0	826
2	1	563

Probability modeled is Bonus=1.

There are times when the nature of the data structure prevents the logistic regression algorithm from converging on a maximum likelihood solution, specifically when either complete or quasi-complete separation occurs, as described in Chapter 8, "Preparing the Input Variables for Prediction." If the convergence criterion is not satisfied, the results of the logistic regression are erroneous and should not be used. As illustrated in Output 10.2b Model Convergence, Fit Statistics, and Testing Global Null, in the Model Convergence Status table, we can see that the estimation algorithm does converge. Therefore, we can continue with interpreting the remaining output. For situations where the model does not converge, see Allison (2008) for an explanation on why estimation algorithms for logistic regression fail to converge and how SAS procedures can be used to resolve the problem.

The next table provides the Model Fit Statistics, namely, the **Akaike Information Criterion** (AIC), the **Schwarz Criterion** (SC), and -2LogL, as shown in Output 10.2b Model Convergence, Fit Statistics, and Testing Global Null. These measures have no real meaning and are used for model comparison purposes only, where the model with the smaller values has the better fit. However, note that -2LogL should be used only when comparing models having the same number of predictors, as its value can be reduced by adding more variables, regardless of their contribution to the fit. AIC is an adjusted version of the -2LogL value and penalizes for the number of predictors. The formula for AIC is:

$$AIC = -2LogL + 2(k+1)$$

where $k+1$ is the number of parameters to be estimated, including the intercept. SC adjusts for both the sample size and number of predictors and is calculated using:

$$SC = -2LogL + (k+1)Log(n)$$

where n is the sample size. It is obvious from the formula that, as the number of predictors and/or sample size increases, the values of these indices increase as well. For the Ames Housing Case, where we are estimating one slope and the intercept, $(k+1=2)$, we have:

$$AIC = 1099.405 + 2(2) = 1103.405$$

$$SC = 1099.405 + (2)Log(1389) = 1113.878$$

Finally, the table used for Testing the Global Null Hypothesis is displayed. This is the most important table of all in that it provides a statistical test for determining if any predictors are significant. It tests the hypothesis:

H_o: $\beta_1 = \beta_2 = \ldots \beta_k = 0$ (none of the predictors are good) for predictors, 1, 2, ..., k

H_1: at least one $\beta_j \neq 0$ (at least one predictor is good), for any j = 1,...,k

The null hypothesis represents the case where no predictors are related to the categorical response variable; the alternative hypothesis represents the case where at least one of the predictors is related to the response variable. This test is analogous to the global F-test used in multiple linear regression analysis.

The first test statistic is the Likelihood Ratio statistic and compares the goodness of fit between two models; specifically here, we are comparing the model with k-predictors and the model with no predictors, having just an intercept. The difference (D) in fit can be rewritten in terms of a ratio:

$$D = -2LogL(baseline) - (-2LogL(model \text{ with k predictors}))$$

$$= -2[LogL(baseline)-LogL(model \text{ with k predictors})]$$

$$= -2Log\left[\frac{Likelihood(baseline)}{Likelihood(model \text{ with k predictors})}\right]$$

where the likelihood ratio has a chi-square distribution with degrees of freedom equal to the difference between the number of predictors in the baseline and k in the proposed model. So in our Ames Housing Case, if we are testing the significance of our model (with the intercept and one predictor, GR_LIV_AREA) against the model with no predictors (intercept only), the difference in fit is

$$D = 1875.463 - 1099.405 = 776.058$$

with p-value <.0001 (degrees of freedom=1), as shown in Output 10.2b Model Convergence, Fit Statistics, and Testing Global Null. Because our p-value is less than, say, 0.05, we reject the null hypothesis; therefore, we have evidence that above ground living area is related to whether or not a bonus is earned.

The output also includes the **score chi-square** test statistic and the **Wald** test statistic. Based upon the p-values found in Output 10.2b Model Convergence, Fit Statistics, and Testing Global Null, we can see that both tests support the evidence that above ground living area is related to bonus. Using these tests is asymptotically equivalent; in other words, as the sample size increases, the distributional properties of the estimators are identical (Hosmer and Lemeshow, 2000).

Output 10.2b Model Convergence, Fit Statistics, and Testing Global Null

Model Convergence Status
Convergence criterion (GCONV=1E-8) satisfied.

Model Fit Statistics		
Criterion	Intercept Only	Intercept and Covariates
AIC	1877.463	1103.405
SC	1882.700	1113.878
-2 Log L	1875.463	1099.405

Testing Global Null Hypothesis: BETA=0			
Test	Chi-Square	DF	Pr > ChiSq
Likelihood Ratio	776.0584	1	<.0001
Score	584.5319	1	<.0001
Wald	333.8138	1	<.0001

The next table, found in Output 10.2c Analysis of Maximum Likelihood Estimates, provides the Analysis of Maximum Likelihood Estimates. From the column of estimates, we can see that the logistic regression equation is:

$$\text{Logit}(p_i) = -8.0903 + 0.00513(\text{Gr\_Liv\_Area})$$

The slope indicates that we expect the logit, or log-odds, to increase by 0.00513 for every additional square foot in the above ground living area. (Note: In the next section, we will relate the slope to the odds ratio.) The table also includes the standard error of the parameter estimate, 0.000281, and is used to test the hypothesis that the slope is significantly different from zero:

$$H_0: \beta_j = 0 \quad \text{for predictor } j=1, 2, ..., \text{ or, } ..., k$$

$$H_1: \beta_j \neq 0$$

Recall, from Chapter 4, "The Normal Distribution and Introduction to Inferential Statistics," that a test statistic is a parameter estimate divided by its standard error. Here the Wald Chi-Square test statistic is that ratio squared and defined by:

$$\chi_j{}^2 = \left[\frac{b_j}{StdError(b_j)}\right]^2$$

where b_j is the parameter estimate for predictor j, with degrees of freedom equal to 1. For the Ames Housing Case, the Wald test statistic is 333.8138, with p-value <.0001, so we reject the null hypothesis, and conclude we have evidence that β_1 is significantly different from zero. In other words, there is evidence that above ground living area is related to bonus. Note that when the number of predictors equals 1, the results of the global hypothesis, found in Output 10.2b Model Convergence, Fit Statistics, and Testing Global Null, are identical to the Wald Chi- Square test of β_1.

Output 10.2c Analysis of Maximum Likelihood Estimates

Analysis of Maximum Likelihood Estimates					
Parameter	**DF**	**Estimate**	**Standard Error**	**Wald Chi-Square**	**Pr > ChiSq**
Intercept	1	-8.0903	0.4313	351.8515	<.0001
Gr_Liv_Area	1	0.00513	0.000281	333.8138	<.0001

Estimating the Odds Ratio from the Parameter Estimates

As seen in linear regression, the slope gives an estimated change in Y per unit change in X. In logistic regression, the slope gives an estimated change in the logit per unit change in X. Because the change in probability is not constant for a unit change in X, a common approach in logistic regression is to transform the logit to odds and describe the change in **odds ratio** per unit change in X. Consider the logistic regression equation:

$$ln\left(\frac{p_i}{1 - p_i}\right) = ln(Odds) = \beta_0 + \beta_1X_1 + \beta_2X_2 + \cdots + \beta_kX_k$$

Solving for odds, we get:

$$Odds = e^{\beta_0+\beta_1X_1+\beta_2X_2+\cdots+\beta_kX_k}$$

Now consider comparing the Odds$_i$ of success when a value of X is incremented by 1 to the base Odds at X in the form of an odds ratio:

$$\frac{e^{\beta_0+\beta_1(X_1+1)+\beta_2X_2+\cdots+\beta_kX_k}}{e^{\beta_0+\beta_1X_1+\beta_2X_2+\cdots+\beta_kX_k}} = \frac{e^{\beta_0+\beta_1X_1+\beta_1+\beta_2X_2+\cdots+\beta_kX_k}}{e^{\beta_0+\beta_1X_1+\beta_2X_2+\cdots+\beta_kX_k}}$$

To simplify, remember that dividing like bases with exponents is equivalent to subtracting the exponents. Therefore, the odds ratio reduces to:

$$e^{\beta_1}$$

In other words, the odds ratio for β_1 tells us that for every one-unit increase in X, the odds that the event of interest occurs increases by e^{β_1}. So, in the Ames Housing Case, the odds ratio, as provided in Output 10.2d Odds Ratio Estimate for GR_LIV_AREA based upon Default UNITS=1, is:

$$Odds\ Ratio = e^{0.00513} = 1.005143$$

Output 10.2d Odds Ratio Estimate for Gr_Liv_Area Based upon Default UNITS=1

Odds Ratio Estimates			
Effect	**Point Estimate**	**95% Wald Confidence Limits**	
Gr_Liv_Area	1.005	1.005	1.006

This means for every 1-square foot increase in above ground living area, the agent is 1.005 times more likely to receive a bonus. This odds ratio is obviously small (remember an odds ratio of 1.0 means that the two events under consideration are equally likely to occur); however, we are talking about the change in likelihood when comparing one house and another house with one additional square foot. In order to make a more reasonable statement about the association, the analyst could add the UNITS statement to the LOGISTIC procedure as follows:

```
units Gr_Liv_Area=100;
```

Here, the analyst is requesting that the odds ratio be reported in terms of a 100-square foot change in the above ground living area, as indicated in Output 10.3 Odds Ratio Estimate for Gr_Liv_Area Based upon UNITS=100, under the heading Unit. The odds ratio now indicates that the agent is 1.670 times more likely to earn a bonus for every 100-unit increase in above ground living area. Another interpretation is that the odds of earning a bonus increases by 67% for a 100-unit increase in square footage.

Output 10.3 Odds Ratio Estimate for Gr_Liv_Area Based upon UNITS=100

Odds Ratios		
Effect	Unit	Estimate
Gr_Liv_Area	100.0	1.670

Changing the unit is common when the predictor variable is numeric continuous. You may want to know the odds ratio when the predictor is incremented by a constant C. In this case, the odds ratio has the form:

$$\frac{e^{\beta_0+\beta_1(X_{1i}+C)+\beta_2X_{2i}+\cdots+\beta_{pi}X_{pi}}}{e^{\beta_0+\beta_1X_{1i}+\beta_2X_{2i}+\cdots+\beta_{pi}X_{pi}}} = e^{\beta_1 C} = (e^{\beta_1})^C$$

So, in our example, the odds ratio when comparing one house to another house with an additional 100 square feet (C=100) is the odds ratio provided in Output 10.3 Odds Ratio Estimate for Gr_Liv_Area Based upon UNITS=100, and can be obtained by

$$(e^{\beta_1})^C = (e^{.00513})^{100} = (1.005143)^{100} = 1.670$$

It should be noted that the confidence interval for the odds ratio can be used for testing the significance of the predictor's relationship with the outcome. Remember that an odds ratio of 1.0 means that both outcomes (BONUS=0 or BONUS=1) are equally likely. So if the confidence interval does not contain 1.0, we can basically say that the estimate of the odds ratio is far enough from 1.0 that the interval does not contain 1.0. In essence, using that rule with a 90%, 95%, or 99% confidence interval is equivalent to using the Wald Chi-Square statistic to test the null hypothesis H₀: $\beta_i \neq 0$ at 0.10, 0.05, or 0.01 level of significance, respectively.

As far as the Ames Housing Case, we can see that the 95% confidence interval (1.580, 1.764) does not contain 1.0; therefore we would reject the null concluding that there is evidence that $\beta_1 \neq 0$ and that above ground living area (GR_LIV_AREA) is significantly related to bonus.

Additional Measures of Fit

Another way to assess the model performance has more to do with how well the logistic regression model predicts the event (either BONUS=1 or BONUS=0). These are provided in Output 10.2e Association of Predicted Probabilities and Observed Responses (and was generated using Program 10.2 Simple Logistic Regression). The first three measure the degree to which pairs of observations are either concordant, discordant, or tied. But first consider how the pairs are created.

The data set is split into two groups, namely, those 563 houses receiving a bonus (BONUS=1) and those 826 not receiving a bonus (BONUS=0). Every observation in the bonus group (BONUS=1) is paired with every observation in the no bonus group (BONUS=0), resulting in 465,038 pairs of observations with different outcomes, as indicated in Output 10.2e Association of Predicted Probabilities and Observed Responses. For each pair, if the observation having a value of 1 for bonus has the highest predicted probability of being a 1, then that pair is considered **concordant**; if the observation having a value of 1 for bonus has the lowest predicted probability of being a 1, then that pair is considered **discordant**. If both observations have the same predicted probability of being a 1, then that pair is considered a tie.

For the Ames Housing Case, we can see that 90.3% of the 465,038 pairs are concordant, whereas 9.6% are discordant; none of the pairs are tied. The goal is to get a high percent concordant and low percent discordant; so for our example, there is some evidence that the logistic regression model fits the actual data.

Finally, in the last four measures in Output 10.2e Association of Predicted Probabilities and Observed Responses, **Somer's D**, **Gamma**, **Tau-a**, and the **concordance statistic (c),** are rank correlations indices. When the analyst uses these indices to compare models, the model with the highest values is better at predicting the event of interest than those models with lower values.

The **concordance statistic** (c), in particular, measures the probability that a randomly selected observation with the outcome of interest (BONUS=1) has a higher predicted probability than a randomly selected observation without the outcome of interest (BONUS=0). The value of c is equivalent to the area under the ROC (Receiver Operating Curve) and is covered in detail in Chapter 11, "Measure of Model Performance." The value ranges from .50, indicating no predictive power, to 1.0, indicating perfect prediction (Hosmer and Lemeshow, 2000). For our example, where c = 0.904, we can see that our model has relatively strong predictive power.

Output 10.2e Association of Predicted Probabilities and Observed Responses

Association of Predicted Probabilities and Observed Responses			
Percent Concordant	90.3	Somers' D	0.807
Percent Discordant	9.6	Gamma	0.807
Percent Tied	0.0	Tau-a	0.389
Pairs	465038	C	0.904

Assumptions of Logistic Regression

The assumptions of logistic regression are somewhat similar to those of linear regression. While the logistic regression model does not require that the dependent variable and predictor variables be linearly related, it does, however, require that the logit, or log-odds, is linearly related to the predictor variables, as assessed in Chapter 11, "Measure of Model Performance."

Logistic regression does require that observations are independent of each other and that there is little correlation, or collinearity, among the predictor variables. In fact, the same diagnostic procedures for detecting collinearity, as described in Chapter 9, "Linear Regression Analysis," can also be used for logistic regression because those procedures deal only with the predictor variables, not the response variable. Like linear regression analysis, the analyst should pay close attention to outliers, as well. Unlike linear regression analysis, there is no normality assumption nor constant variance assumption when conducting a logistic regression analysis.

Plots for Probabilities of an Event and for the Odds Ratios

Recall that the analyst can use the parameter estimates to arrive at a formula for calculating the posterior probabilities of the event of interest for any observation. Consider the Ames Housing Case where we are interested in predicting whether the agent earns a bonus or not from the sale of a house based upon the above ground living area (GR_LIV_AREA). Using the parameter estimates from Output 10.2c Analysis of Maximum Likelihood Estimates, we get the probability of the event (Y=1) as follows:

$$P(Y = 1|X_1) = \frac{e^{-8.0903 + 0.00513x_1}}{1 + e^{-8.0903 + 0.00513x_1}}$$

where Y=1 corresponds to getting a bonus (BONUS=1) and X_1=GR_LIV_AREA. Suppose you want to know the probability that the agent will earn a bonus for a house with 2000 square feet of above ground living area. You would simply plug in X_1=2000 to get:

$$P(Y = 1|X_1 = 2000) = \frac{e^{-8.0903 + 0.00513(2000)}}{1 + e^{-8.0903 + 0.00513(2000)}} = 0.8975$$

Ordinarily, the analyst uses a cutoff of 0.50, so because the posterior probability of earning a bonus (BONUS=1) for a house with 2000 square feet of above ground living area is greater than 0.50, you would classify that observation as a Yes (BONUS=1).

In order to get the plot of the posterior probability function for all possible values of X_1, the analyst could include the PLOTS option below within the logistic procedure as indicated in the syntax, and as shown in Figure 10.2 Plot of Gr_Living Area by Probability for Bonus=1.

```
proc logistic data=sasba.ames70 plots(only)=effect;
```

Figure 10.2 Plot of Gr_Living Area by Probability for Bonus=1

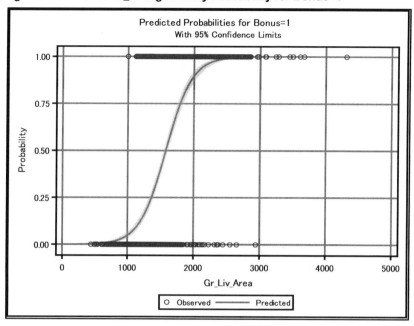

From the plot, it is evident that as above ground living area increases, the probability of BONUS=1 increases as well. In fact, there is a point on the S-curve where the value of X_1 (GR_LIV_AREA) has probability exactly equal to 0.50. Solving the following equation for X_1:

$$0.50 = \frac{e^{-8.0903+0.00513x_1}}{1+e^{-8.0903+0.00513x_1}} \quad \text{reduces to} \quad e^{-8.0903+0.00513x_1} = 1$$

and finally to $X_1 = \frac{8.0903}{0.00513} = 1577.06$ square feet. So for any house having above ground living area greater than 1577.06 square feet, the posterior probability of BONUS=1 is greater than 0.50 and will be classified as BONUS=1. For any house having above ground living area less than 1577.06 square feet, the posterior probability of BONUS=1 is less than 0.50 and will be classified as BONUS=0.

Another useful plot represents the confidence interval for the odds ratio. There are several ways to generate that plot. First, the analyst can include the PLOTS= option within the logistic procedure as displayed in Program 10.3 Odds Ratio with 95% Confidence Interval for Gr_Liv_Area (UNITS=100).

Program 10.3 Odds Ratio with 95% Confidence Interval for Gr_Liv_Area (UNITS=100)

```
libname sasba 'c:\sasba\ames';
run;

proc logistic data=sasba.ames70 plots(only)=oddsratio;
  model Bonus (Event='1')=Gr_Liv_Area
     /selection=none link=logit alpha=0.05;
  units Gr_Liv_Area=100;
run;
```

The PLOTS= option with the ONLY option requests that only the odds ratios be displayed, suppressing all default plots, as seen in Output 10.4 Plot of Odds Ratio with 95% Confidence Interval for Gr_Liv_Area (UNIT=1). Note that, while the UNITS statement requests the odds ratio be reported for a 100 square foot change in above ground living area, namely 1.670 as displayed in Output 10.3 Odds Ratio Estimate for Gr_Liv_Area Based upon UNITS=100, the plot of the odds ratio here is for a single square foot change.

Output 10.4 Plot of Odds Ratio with 95% Confidence Interval for Gr_Liv_Area (UNIT=1)

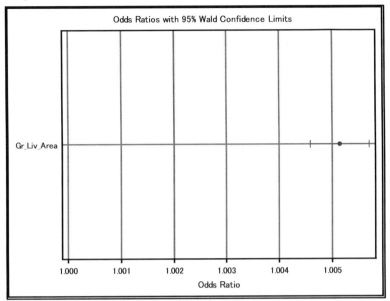

Secondly, if the analyst, instead, prefers that the odds ratio plot matches that provided in the UNITS statement, then the CLODDS= should be included in the MODEL statement options, as illustrated in the Program 10.4 Odds Ratio with 95% Confidence Interval for Gr_Liv_Area (UNIT=100). For small sample sizes, the analyst is advised to use CLODDS=PL which is based upon the profile likelihood. Here we use the CLODDS=WALD which provides the Wald confidence limits based upon the defined ALPHA (default = 0.05), as illustrated in Output 10.5 Plot of Odds Ratio with 95% Confidence Interval for Gr_Liv_Area (UNITS=100).

Program 10.4 Odds Ratio with 95% Confidence Interval for Gr_Liv_Area (UNITS=100)

```
libname sasba 'c:\sasba\ames';
run;

proc logistic data=sasba.ames70;
   model Bonus (Event = '1')=Gr_Liv_Area
       /selection=none link=logit clodds=wald alpha=0.05;
   units Gr_Liv_Area=100;
run;
```

Output 10.5 Plot of Odds Ratio with 95% Confidence Interval for Gr_Liv_Area (UNITS=100)

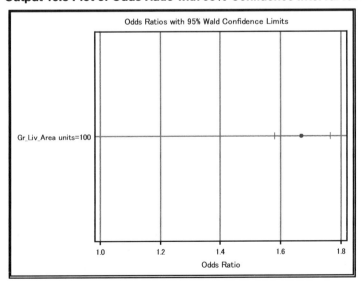

Finally, the analyst could simply use the ODDSRATIO statement with a list of predictor variables (here, GR_LIV_AREA) in order to get the plot of odds ratios. If the UNITS statement is included with the ODDSRATIO statement, then the odds ratio plots are displayed for both UNITS=1 and the unit defined in the UNITS statement, as illustrated in Program 10.5 UNITS Statement and ODDSRATIO Statement.

Program 10.5 UNITS Statement and ODDSRATIO Statement

```
libname sasba 'c:\sasba\ames';
run;

proc logistic data=sasba.ames70;
   model Bonus (Event = '1')=Gr_Liv_Area
        /selection=none link=logit alpha=0.05;
   oddsratio Gr_Liv_Area;
   units Gr_Liv_Area=100;
run;
```

Logistic Regression with a Categorical Predictor

Many times in logistic regression, we will have categorical predictor variables. Sometimes the values of those variables are in the form of text and cannot be used in the modeling process. For example, the variable HOME_TYPE may have values '1-story,' '2-story,' or 'split-level.' Sometimes categorical variables are represented by numbers serving as identifiers. For example, HOME_TYPE may have values 1, 2, and 3, representing 1-story, 2-story, and split-level houses, respectively. In this case, the values have no real quantitative meaning; therefore, it would be inappropriate to include that variable in the model. For these variable types, the analyst must create **dummy variables** if those variables are to be used in the modeling purposes.

Generally, in the case of a dichotomous categorical variable, a dummy variable is created for each observation, so that a value of 1 is assigned if the attribute represented by the variable exists, or 0 if the attribute does not exist.

For cases where the categorical variable has more than two levels ($C > 2$), the number of dummy variables used to represent that single categorical variable is *(C-1)*, the number of levels of that variable minus one. So, for example, if a categorical variable has three levels—say, high, medium, and low, the analysis requires the creation of *two* dummy variables (three levels minus one).

If the analyst does not create dummy variables for categorical predictor variables, many logistic regression programs will automatically create the dummy variables. There are several ways to define the dummy variables, also referred to as **design variables**, and the analyst must know what method is used by SAS in order to correctly interpret the results of the logistic regression.

Effect Coding Parameterization

Consider the Ames Housing Case, where the analyst is interested in the relationship between BONUS and the overall quality of the house, where the variable, OVERALL_QUALITY, has values 1, 2, and 3, corresponding to Below Average, Average, and Above Average, respectively. To conduct a logistic regression analysis, consider Program 10.6 Logistic Regression for One Categorical Predictor Using Effect Coding.

Program 10.6 Logistic Regression for One Categorical Predictor Using Effect Coding

```
libname sasba 'c:\sasba\ames';
data ames;
   set sasba.ames70;
   run;
proc logistic data=ames;
   class Overall_Quality; * default is (param=effect);
   model Bonus (Event = '1')=Overall_Quality
        /selection=none link=logit;
run;
```

As illustrated previously, Program 10.6 Logistic Regression for One Categorical Predictor Using Effect Coding provides a simple logistic regression model with BONUS as the dependent variable, where the event to be modeled is BONUS=1, and OVERALL_QUALITY as the independent variable. Note also that the CLASS statement is used to indicate that the variable, OVERALL_QUALITY, is a categorical input variable. The initial output generated will be identical to that provided in Output 10.2a Model Information and Response Profile for Simple Logistic Regression, in addition to the excerpts provided in Output 10.6 Logistic Regression for One Categorical Predictor Using Effect Coding.

First, notice that for *C*=3 levels of the categorical variable, two design variables (*C-1*) are created and displayed in the Class Level Information. If a house has OVERALL_QUALITY=1, then design variable 1 is coded as 1, or 0 otherwise; if a house has OVERALL_QUALITY=2, then design variable 2 is coded as 1, or 0 otherwise; finally, if a house has OVERALL_QUALITY=3, then the two design variables are coded as -1 and -1, respectively.

This method of parameterization is referred to as **effect coding** and is used as the SAS default for the CLASS statement. Basically, SAS sorts the OVERALL_QUALITY in order (1, 2, and 3), creates two design variables corresponding to the first two values, OVERALL_QUALITY equal to 1 and 2, and then assigns the value of -1 to each of the two design variables for the last value of OVERALL_QUALITY (equal to 3). Note that when effect coding is used, the design variables for the last level are all equal to -1.

This method of coding is also referred to as **deviation from the mean coding**, where each parameter estimate measures the difference between the effect at that level and the average effect of all levels combined. So, from the Analysis of Maximum Likelihood Estimates, found in Output 10.6 Logistic Regression for One Categorical Predictor Using Effect Coding, we see that the estimate of the intercept, -1.8547, is the average value of the logit for all categories (just like the intercept in linear regression is equal to the average Y). The estimate of β_1, -1.5465, is the difference between the logit for OVERALL_QUALITY=1 (below average) and the average logit. Finally, the estimate of β_2, -0.9203, is the difference between the logit for OVERALL_QUALITY=2 (average) and the average logit. Note also that, with this method of coding, there are slopes only for *C-1* levels of the categorical variable, OVERALL_QUALITY.

Output 10.6 Logistic Regression for One Categorical Predictor Using Effect Coding

Class Level Information		
Class	**Value**	**Design Variables**
Overall_Quality	1	1 0
	2	0 1
	3	-1 -1

Analysis of Maximum Likelihood Estimates						
Parameter		**DF**	**Estimate**	**Standard Error**	**Wald Chi-Square**	**Pr > ChiSq**
Intercept		1	-1.8547	0.1839	101.6639	<.0001
Overall_Quality	1	1	-1.5465	0.3463	19.9392	<.0001
Overall_Quality	2	1	-0.9203	0.2178	17.8475	<.0001

Odds Ratio Estimates			
Effect	**Point Estimate**	**95% Wald Confidence Limits**	
Overall_Quality 1 vs 3	0.018	0.007	0.049
Overall_Quality 2 vs 3	0.034	0.022	0.052

One drawback to using effect coding is that the parameter estimates of the dummy variables are not easily interpretable; in fact, notice that the odds ratios cannot be calculated directly from the parameter estimates as we saw earlier. So, what do you do?

Suppose you want to look at the odds of a bonus when comparing houses that have below average quality (OVERALL_QUALITY=1) and above average quality (OVERALL_QUALITY=3). Consider the difference in the logit for the two groups, based upon the design variables:

For OVERALL_QUALITY=1, $logit(p_i) = \beta_0 + \beta_1(1) + \beta_2(0) = \beta_0 + \beta_1$

For OVERALL_QUALITY=3, $logit(p_i) = \beta_0 + \beta_1(-1) + \beta_2(-1) = \beta_0 - \beta_1 - \beta_2$

so the difference $= \beta_0 + \beta_1 - (\beta_0 - \beta_1 - \beta_2) = 2\beta_1 + \beta_2 = 2(-1.5465) + (-0.9203) = -4.0133$

Remember the odds ratio can be obtained by:

$$e^{-4.0133} = 0.01807 \sim 0.018 \quad \text{(as seen in Output 10.6)}$$

You can see that, when the parameter estimate is negative, the odds ratio is less than 1.0, meaning that the event modeled (BONUS=1) is less likely than BONUS=0. The odds ratio indicates that the odds of getting a bonus decrease by 98.20% (1-0.018 times 100%) when comparing houses with below average quality (OVERALL_QUALITY=1) to those with above average quality (OVERALL_QUALITY=3), as noted by the 1 vs 3 in the output.

The analyst could use the same derivation to arrive at the odds ratio when comparing houses with average and above average overall quality (OVERALL_QUALITY = 2 and 3), which is 0.034, as found in Output 10.6 Logistic Regression for One Categorical Predictor Using Effect Coding.

Keep in mind that odds ratios can be converted to values greater than 1.0 by inverting and changing the order of the group comparison. Consider the odds ratio for comparing groups 1 versus 3. Inverting that, or taking the reciprocal, gives 55.3, which is now interpreted as follows: An agent is 55.3 times more likely to earn a bonus when selling a house with above average quality (OVERALL_QUALITY=3) when compared to a house with below average quality (OVERALL_QUALITY=1); designated as 3 versus 1.

Reference Cell Coding Parameterization

The aforementioned method of parameterization takes much thought. For ease of interpretation, the analyst may, instead, want to use **reference cell coding**, where a reference group, or a baseline level, is defined, and the other levels of the categorical variable are compared to the baseline. Consider the same Ames Housing example, with the same code used previously, but with the addition of the PARAM option within the CLASS statement as in Program 10.7 Logistic Regression for One Categorical Predictor Using Reference Coding.

Program 10.7 Logistic Regression for One Categorical Predictor Using Reference Coding

```
libname sasba 'c:\sasba\ames';
data ames;
   set sasba.ames70;
run;

proc logistic data=ames plots(only)=effect;
   class Overall_Quality (param=ref ref='1');
   model Bonus (Event = '1')=Overall_Quality
        /selection=none link=logit;
run;
```

The PARAM=REF option requests that SAS use reference cell coding and the REF=1 defines the first value of 1 for OVERALL_QUALITY (below average) to be the reference group for comparison purposes. Notice the class level information as illustrated in Output 10.7 Logistic Regression for One Categorical Predictor Using Reference Coding. Again, SAS sorts the OVERALL_QUALITY in order (1, 2, and 3), and assigns a value of zero for the two design variables for the reference group (OVERALL_QUALITY=1). For the first 'non-reference' group (OVERALL_QUALITY=2), the design variable 1 is coded as 1 if the house is average quality, or 0 otherwise; followed by the next group (OVERALL_QUALITY=3), where design variable 2 is coded as 1 if the house is above average quality, or 0 otherwise.

Now the parameter estimates measure the differences in logits between OVERALL_QUALITY=1 (the reference group) and each of the logits for Overall_Quality equal to 2 and 3, respectively. For example, consider the difference in the log-odds of a bonus when comparing houses that have above average quality (OVERALL_QUALITY=3) and below average quality OVERALL_QUALITY=1). Using the design variables, consider the following logits:

For OVERALL_QUALITY=3, $\quad logit(p_i) = \beta_0 + \beta_1(0) + \beta_2(1) = \beta_0 + \beta_2$

For OVERALL_QUALITY=1, $\quad logit(p_i) = \beta_0$

so the difference $= (\beta_0 + \beta_2) - \beta_0 = \beta_2 = 4.0133$

as seen in the Analysis of Maximum Likelihood Estimates in Output 10.7 Logistic Regression for One Categorical Predictor Using Reference Coding. When we exponentiate the estimate, 4.0133, we get the odds ratio of 55.33, which means that those agents selling houses with above average quality (OVERALL_QUALITY=3) are 55.33 times more likely to receive a bonus than those with below average quality (OVERALL_QUALITY=1). (Remember: we obtained an odds ratio to 55.3 when we inverted the odds ratio from the output generated from the effect coding parameterization).

A similar calculation can be done when comparing houses that have average quality (OVERALL_QUALITY=2) and below average quality (OVERALL_QUALITY=1). Using the design variables, consider the following logit:

For Overall_Quality=2, $\quad logit(p_i) = \beta_0 + \beta_1(1) + \beta_2(0) = \beta_0 + \beta_1$

So the difference $= (\beta_0 + \beta_1) - \beta_0 = \beta_1 = 0.6262$

As seen in the Analysis of Maximum Likelihood Estimates in Output 10.7 Logistic Regression for One Categorical Predictor Using Reference Coding, when we exponentiate the estimate, 0.6262, we get the odds ratio of 1.870, which means that those agents selling houses with average quality (OVERALL_QUALITY=2) are 1.870 times more likely to receive a bonus than those with below average quality (OVERALL_QUALITY=1), also seen in Output 10.7 Logistic Regression for One Categorical Predictor Using Reference Coding. Note also that the odds ratios are identical regardless of the parameterization method used.

Output 10.7 Logistic Regression for One Categorical Predictor Using Reference Coding

Class Level Information			
Class	Value	Design Variables	
Overall_Quality	1	0	0
	2	1	0
	3	0	1

Model Convergence Status
Convergence criterion (GCONV=1E-8) satisfied.

Model Fit Statistics		
Criterion	Intercept Only	Intercept and Covariates
AIC	1877.463	1305.232
SC	1882.700	1320.941
-2 Log L	1875.463	1299.232

Testing Global Null Hypothesis: BETA=0			
Test	Chi-Square	DF	Pr > ChiSq
Likelihood Ratio	576.2312	2	<.0001
Score	493.9597	2	<.0001
Wald	298.2137	2	<.0001

Type 3 Analysis of Effects			
Effect	DF	Wald Chi-Square	Pr > ChiSq
Overall_Quality	2	298.2137	<.0001

Analysis of Maximum Likelihood Estimates						
Parameter		DF	Estimate	Standard Error	Wald Chi-Square	Pr > ChiSq
Intercept		1	−3.4012	0.5083	44.7805	<.0001
Overall_Quality	2	1	0.6262	0.5470	1.3105	0.2523
Overall_Quality	3	1	4.0133	0.5135	61.0870	<.0001

Odds Ratio Estimates		
Effect	Point Estimate	95% Wald Confidence Limits
Overall_Quality 2 vs 1	1.870	0.640 5.464
Overall_Quality 3 vs 1	55.327	20.224 151.359

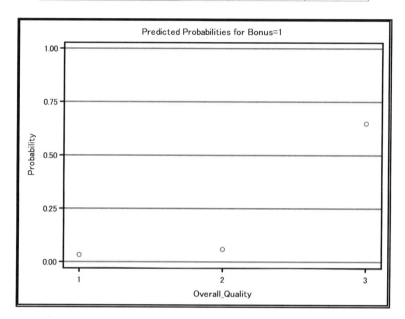

As far as statistical tests, when the CLASS statement is used, the output always includes the Type 3 Analysis of Effects to show effects of all predictors, specifically the significance of the categorical predictor. From Output 10.7 Logistic Regression for One Categorical Predictor Using Reference Coding, the chi-square test statistic is 298.2137 (p<.0001), with two degrees of freedom for the 2 design variables. In conclusion, there is evidence that the variable, OVERALL_QUALITY, is related to BONUS. Further inspection of significance tests in the Analysis of Maximum Likelihood Estimates table shows that there are different effects ($\chi^2 = 61.0870$, degrees of freedom=1, p<.0001) on BONUS when comparing above average quality houses to below average quality houses (3 vs 1); however when comparing average to below average (2 vs 1), there are no differences ($\chi^2 = 1.3105$, degrees of freedom=1, p=0.2523) in the probability of getting a bonus. These effects are also displayed in the effects plot in Output 10.7 Logistic Regression for One Categorical Predictor Using Reference Coding, where it is evident that the probability of getting a bonus is significantly higher for above average quality (OVERALL_QUALITY=3).

Finally, it is worth mentioning that when a variable is already dummy coded, the CLASS statement is not necessary. For example, in the Ames Housing data, the variable, HIGH_KITCHEN_QUALITY, is coded as 1 if the kitchen quality is good or excellent, or 0 otherwise. So Program 10.8 CLASS Statement with Dummy Coded Variable with or without the CLASS statement would give identical results.

Program 10.8 CLASS Statement with Dummy Coded Variable

```
libname sasba 'c:\sasba\ames';
data ames;
   set sasba.ames70;
run;

proc logistic data=ames;
   class High_Kitchen_Quality (param=ref ref=first);
   model Bonus (Event = '1')=High_Kitchen_Quality
        /selection=none link=logit;
run;

proc logistic data=ames;
   model Bonus (Event = '1')=High_Kitchen_Quality
        /selection=none link=logit;
run;
```

The Multiple Logistic Regression Model

Ordinarily, an outcome can be predicted with more than one variable. This section will apply topics covered previously to the multivariate case. Consider the Ames Housing Case. In reality, we all know that the value of house is directly related to the amount of living area. Previously, we saw that BONUS (defined by selling price) is significantly related to above ground living area (GR_LIV_AREA). It also seems reasonable to assume that the selling price is related the total area of the basement (TOTAL_BSMT_SF) which plays into the total size of the house. Also related to size is the lot size on which the house is built; it seems that the same house would sell for more if it is on a large lot versus small lot. Consequently, lot area (LOT_AREA) should be considered as well. Similarly, it seems that both age and overall quality matter when a buyer is considering price, when the aforementioned factors are considered.

Multiple Logistic Regression by Example

Now that we have considered the obvious factors, let's consider additional factors. Note that in Chapter 8, "Preparing the Input Variables for Prediction," we started with 29 input variables, in addition to the three neighborhood cluster/dummy variables created after applying the Greenacre method, ending with 23 potential input variables after the variable clustering. For ease of illustration here, we will limit the initial set of inputs to thirteen variables.

As mentioned in Chapter 5, "Analysis of Categorical Variables, architects agree that the kitchen and baths are the most expensive areas of the house with respect to construction costs, not to mention those are the rooms where people spend the most time. So here, we will consider also kitchen quality (HIGH_KITCHEN_QUALITY) and whether the house has at least two full bathrooms (FULLBATH_2PLUS). Many real estate agents argue that houses located on a cul-de-sac can command a higher sales price for reasons related to curb appeal and privacy. Finally, we will consider other amenities such as having a fireplace, size of the garage, exterior condition, condition of the lot (level or not), and a fenced-in yard to see how those are related to bonus when all characteristics are considered together.

Consider Program 10.9 Multiple Logistic Regression for Ames Housing Using Reference Coding.

Program 10.9 Multiple Logistic Regression for Ames Housing Using Reference Coding

```
libname sasba 'c:\sasba\ames';
data ames;
   set sasba.ames70;
run;

proc logistic data=ames;
  class Overall_Quality (param=ref ref=first);
  model Bonus (Event = '1')= Gr_Liv_Area Total_Bsmt_SF Lot_Area
      Age_At_Sale Overall_Quality High_Kitchen_Quality Fullbath_2Plus
      Fireplace_1Plus TwoPlusCar_Garage High_Exterior_Cond CuldeSac Has_Fence
      Land_Level  /selection=none link=logit;
    units Gr_Liv_Area=100 Total_Bsmt_SF=100
        Lot_Area=10000 Age_At_Sale=10;
run;
```

First, the EVENT='1' in the MODEL statement defines the event to be modeled, namely, BONUS=1, as a function of the thirteen variables listed. The CLASS statement specifics that OVERALL_QUALITY is categorical, and the REF=FIRST defines the first ordered category (1=below average) as the reference group, as displayed in Output 10.8a Class Level Information Using Reference Coding. It should be noted that there are eight other categorical variables (HIGH_KITCHEN_QUALITY through LAND_LEVEL); these are all pre-defined dichotomous dummy variables, as defined by the data dictionary. Specifically, each is coded as '1' if the attribute represented by the variable exists, or '0' otherwise. Therefore, parameterization is not necessary and those variables do not appear in the CLASS statement.

Output 10.8a Class Level Information Using Reference Coding

Class Level Information			
Class	Value	Design Variables	
Overall_Quality	1	0	0
	2	1	0
	3	0	1

Note that the MODEL statement defines NONE as the method of selection (default) and the LINK function as the logit (default). The UNITS statement requests different units for reporting the odds ratios for the numeric continuous variables, GR_LIV_AREA, TOTAL_BSMT_SF, LOT_AREA, AGE_AT_SALE. The output indicates that the model does meet the convergence criterion, so the remaining output will be described below.

The Model Information and Response Profile tables are identical to those found in Output 10.2a Model Information and Response Profile for Simple Logistic Regression. Next, the Model Fit Statistics and Testing Global Null Hypotheses, as displayed in Output 10.8b Fit Statistics and Global Null Test for Multiple Logistic Regression, are provided to test the following hypothesis that none of the predictors are significantly related to BONUS:

$$H_o: \beta_1 = \beta_2 = \beta_3 = \ldots = \beta_{14} \qquad \text{(none of the predictors are good)}$$

$$H_1: \text{at least one } \beta_j \neq 0 \qquad \text{(at least one predictor is good, for any predictor j)}$$

We can see that the p-value for the likelihood ratio test is less than 0.0001; therefore, the null hypothesis is rejected. In short, there is evidence from the data that at least one predictor is good. Notice that there are fourteen degrees of freedom-- remember there are thirteen variables; however, one of those (OVERALL_QUALITY) is represented by two design variables, adding a degree of freedom for the additional variable. From the fit statistics, we can see a significant reduction in the AIC, SC, and -2LogL, respectively, indicating that the model fits the data better than the model with the intercept only.

Output 10.8b Fit Statistics and Global Null Test for Multiple Logistic Regression

Model Fit Statistics		
Criterion	Intercept Only	Intercept and Covariates
AIC	1877.463	549.338
SC	1882.700	627.883
-2 Log L	1875.463	519.338

Testing Global Null Hypothesis: BETA=0			
Test	Chi-Square	DF	Pr > ChiSq
Likelihood Ratio	1356.1251	14	<.0001
Score	948.8095	14	<.0001
Wald	267.4416	14	<.0001

Because a CLASS statement was used to create design variables, the Type 3 Analysis of Effects is provided as illustrated in Output 10.8c Test 3 Analysis of Effects for Multiple Logistic Regression. This table lists all of the input variables, along with their unique contribution to the model fit controlling for all other input variables. Using 0.01 level of significance, we can see, for example, that above ground living area (GR_LIV_AREA) is significantly related to BONUS, in the presence of all other input variables. In fact, we can see that variables TOTAL_BSMT_SF through FIREPLACE_1PLUS all have multivariate significance. In other words, those variables are uniquely related to BONUS in the presence of the others.

However, because the p-values for the remaining variables (TWOPLUSCAR_GARAGE, HIGH_EXTERIOR_COND, CULDESAC, HAS_FENCE, and LAND_LEVEL) are all greater than 0.01, there is no evidence that those variables, separately, are related to BONUS in the presence of all predictors. In other words, once you take into account variables related to size (GR_LIV_AREA, TOTAL_BSMT_SF, LOT_AREA), the age of the house (AGE_AT_SALE), quality and condition (OVERALL_QUALITY, OVERALL_CONDITION), variables related to kitchen and number of bathrooms (HIGH_KITCHEN_QUALITY and FULLBATH_2PLUS), and having at least one fireplace (FIREPLACE_1PLUS), the other variables add no more to the model fit.

In the Type 3 Analysis of Effects, keep in mind that the degrees of freedom for each quantitative variable is one. The degrees of freedom for the categorical variables are *C-1* (equivalent to the number of design variables, where *C*=number of levels for the categorical variable). So for OVERALL_QUALITY, having 3 levels (below average, average, and above average), the degrees of freedom are 3-1 or 2.

Output 10.8c Test 3 Analysis of Effects for Multiple Logistic Regression

Type 3 Analysis of Effects			
Effect	DF	Wald Chi-Square	Pr > ChiSq
Gr_Liv_Area	1	75.3062	<.0001
Total_Bsmt_SF	1	34.6892	<.0001
Lot_Area	1	7.4191	0.0065
Age_at_Sale	1	30.3284	<.0001
Overall_Quality	2	36.3609	<.0001
High_Kitchen_Quality	1	45.4299	<.0001
Fullbath_2plus	1	12.8562	0.0003
Fireplace_1plus	1	13.4279	0.0002
TwoPlusCar_Garage	1	0.5337	0.4651
High_Exterior_Cond	1	2.9088	0.0881
CuldeSac	1	0.7639	0.3821
Has_Fence	1	0.0393	0.8429
Land_Level	1	6.4113	0.0113

The parameter estimates and odds ratios for the multiple logistic regression, including the design variables, are found in Output 10.8d Maximum Likelihood Estimates and Odds Ratios for Multiple Logistic Regression. Note that when the parameter estimates are negative, then the odds ratios are less than 1.0; when the parameters estimates are positive, the odds ratios are greater than 1.0.

Note that for the significant predictors, those with odds ratios greater than 1.0 are more likely to be houses where the agent earned a bonus, whereas predictors with odds ratios less than 1.0 are more less likely to be houses where the agent earned a bonus. For example, the parameter estimate for AGE_AT_SALE is negative with an odds ratio of 0.723 (for UNITS=10). This means that the odds of getting a bonus decrease by 27.7% (1-0.723 times 100%) when comparing one house to another that is ten years older, holding all other factors constant.

Finally, the analyst should consider omitting the insignificant predictors from the final model. In the next section, method of variable selection will be discussed to illustrate strategies for selecting the final model.

Output 10.8d Maximum Likelihood Estimates and Odds Ratios for Multiple Logistic Regression

Analysis of Maximum Likelihood Estimates						
Parameter		DF	Estimate	Standard Error	Wald Chi-Square	Pr > ChiSq
Intercept		1	-11.4203	1.3082	76.2149	<.0001
Gr_Liv_Area		1	0.00399	0.000460	75.3062	<.0001
Total_Bsmt_SF		1	0.00218	0.000371	34.6892	<.0001
Lot_Area		1	0.000067	0.000024	7.4191	0.0065
Age_at_Sale		1	-0.0325	0.00590	30.3284	<.0001
Overall_Quality	2	1	0.3410	0.8543	0.1593	0.6898
Overall_Quality	3	1	2.2262	0.8223	7.3298	0.0068
High_Kitchen_Quality		1	1.6887	0.2505	45.4299	<.0001
Fullbath_2plus		1	1.0395	0.2899	12.8562	0.0003
Fireplace_1plus		1	0.9377	0.2559	13.4279	0.0002
TwoPlusCar_Garage		1	0.2549	0.3489	0.5337	0.4651
High_Exterior_Cond		1	0.6540	0.3835	2.9088	0.0881
CuldeSac		1	0.3973	0.4546	0.7639	0.3821
Has_Fence		1	-0.0563	0.2838	0.0393	0.8429
Land_Level		1	-1.0182	0.4021	6.4113	0.0113

Odds Ratio Estimates			
Effect	Point Estimate	95% Wald Confidence Limits	
Gr_Liv_Area	1.004	1.003	1.005
Total_Bsmt_SF	1.002	1.001	1.003
Lot_Area	1.000	1.000	1.000
Age_at_Sale	0.968	0.957	0.979
Overall_Quality 2 vs 1	1.406	0.264	7.504
Overall_Quality 3 vs 1	9.264	1.849	46.424
High_Kitchen_Quality	5.413	3.312	8.845
Fullbath_2plus	2.828	1.602	4.991
Fireplace_1plus	2.554	1.547	4.218
TwoPlusCar_Garage	1.290	0.651	2.557
High_Exterior_Cond	1.923	0.907	4.078
CuldeSac	1.488	0.610	3.627
Has_Fence	0.945	0.542	1.649
Land_Level	0.361	0.164	0.794

Association of Predicted Probabilities and Observed Responses			
Percent Concordant	97.9	Somers' D	0.957
Percent Discordant	2.1	Gamma	0.957
Percent Tied	0.0	Tau-a	0.462
Pairs	465038	c	0.979

Odds Ratios		
Effect	Unit	Estimate
Gr_Liv_Area	100.0	1.490
Total_Bsmt_SF	100.0	1.244
Lot_Area	10000.0	1.945
Age_at_Sale	10.0000	0.723

Variable Selection

As mentioned earlier, the analyst is sometimes faced with hundreds, even thousands, of input variables. In Chapter 8, "Preparing the Input Variables for Prediction," we discussed strategies for tackling the issue of **redundancy**. Recall, that is the situation where input variables have overlapping information and the inclusion of one or the other provides no additional information to the set of input variables. Once the analyst reduces the initial set of input variables by eliminating those that are redundant, the next step is to consider the **relevancy** of the input variables with respect to the dependent variable.

In this section, we will discuss variable selection methods aimed at selecting a subset of q variables ($q <$ k) related to the outcome variable, so that the reduced subset provides the 'best' model fit to the data. These methods can be carried out by using the SELECTION= option within the MODEL statement.

The default selection option for the logistic regression procedure is the SELECTION=NONE where the full model is estimated using all variables defined in the MODEL statement. So using the SAS code below, for example, the logistic regression model would be estimated using all three input variables, above ground living area, total basement square footage, and lot area.

```
proc logistic data=ames;
   model Bonus (Event = '1')= Gr_Liv_Area Total_Bsmt_SF Lot_Area
   /selection=none;
run;
```

Sequential searches include backward, forward, and stepwise selection methods. The following sections will describe these methods, with a short commentary about the best subset selection method, as well.

Backward Elimination

Backward selection starts with the model containing all of the specified variables, and then each variable deemed least important is removed one at a time when that variable fails to satisfy the criterion for staying in the model. Once a model is fit such that no other variables fail the criterion for staying (in other words, when all remaining variables are considered important), the variable selection process ends. Note that, for backward selection, once a variable is dropped, it cannot be added.

To illustrate the backward elimination process, consider the Ames Housing Case. Suppose we used preliminary analyses to arrive at a candidate set of thirteen possible input variables; we want to start with those thirteen variables and eliminate those that are considered unimportant. We would use Program 10.10 Backward Elimination for Ames Housing.

In Program 10.10 Backward Elimination for Ames Housing, we see the CLASS statement which defines the categorical input variable, along with the PARAM=REF option requesting that SAS use the reference cell coding. The MODEL statement defines the outcome variable, BONUS, and the thirteen variables to be included in the selection process. Note also that the MODEL statement has three options. First, SELECTION=BACKWARD requests that the backward elimination method be used, where the Wald Chi-Square test is used for determining the removal of a predictor from the model under investigation. Second, SLSTAY specifies the significance level for the test; in other words, it defines the minimum p-value necessary for staying in the model. Finally, the DETAILS option requests a summary of each step in the elimination process.

Program 10.10 Backward Elimination for Ames Housing

```
libname sasba 'c:\sasba\ames';
data ames;
   set sasba.ames70;
run;
```

```
proc logistic data=ames;
   class Overall_Quality (param=ref ref=first);
   model Bonus (Event = '1')= Gr_Liv_Area Total_Bsmt_SF Lot_Area
        Age_At_Sale Overall_Quality High_Kitchen_Quality Fullbath_2Plus
        Fireplace_1Plus TwoPlusCar_Garage High_Exterior_Cond CuldeSac
        Has_Fence Land_Level/selection=backward slstay=0.01 details;
run;
```

The first few tables generated from Program 10.10 Backward Elimination for Ames Housing are identical to the tables generated when running a single logistic regression model; namely, the Model Information, the Number of Observations Read and Used, the Response Profile, and Class Level Information tables. The output then displays Step 0 of the backward elimination method indicating that all thirteen effects were entered into the model.

Included under Step 0 are the typical tables for the full model-- Convergence Status, the Model Fit Statistics, Testing Global Null Hypothesis: BETA=0, Type 3 Analysis of Effects, Analysis of Maximum Likelihood Estimates, Odds Ratios Estimates, and Association of Predicted Probabilities and Observed Responses.

The next table provided is unique to the backward selection process, namely the Analysis of Effects Eligible for Removal and is the first table, as displayed in Output 10.9a Effects Eligible for Removal for Step 1 of Backward Elimination. This table displays information identical to the Type 3 Analysis of Effects table and provides the p-values for the Wald Chi-Square test statistic for each predictor. Remember each Wald Chi-Square test measures whether or not the slope for that predictor is significantly different from zero in the presence of the other predictors. Using 0.01 level of significance, as defined by SLSTAY=0.01, we can see that the last five variables fail the test for staying in the model. Because the p-value for the variable, HAS_FENCE, is largest at 0.8429, that variable is removed from the candidate of variables, as indicated by the 'Step 1. Effect Has_Fence is removed' message.

Output 10.9a   Effects Eligible for Removal for Step 1 of Backward Elimination

Analysis of Effects Eligible for Removal			
Effect	DF	Wald Chi-Square	Pr > ChiSq
Gr_Liv_Area	1	75.3062	<.0001
Total_Bsmt_SF	1	34.6892	<.0001
Lot_Area	1	7.4191	0.0065
Age_at_Sale	1	30.3284	<.0001
Overall_Quality	2	36.3609	<.0001
High_Kitchen_Quality	1	45.4299	<.0001
Fullbath_2plus	1	12.8562	0.0003
Fireplace_1plus	1	13.4279	0.0002
TwoPlusCar_Garage	1	0.5337	0.4651
High_Exterior_Cond	1	2.9088	0.0881
CuldeSac	1	0.7639	0.3821
Has_Fence	1	0.0393	0.8429
Land_Level	1	6.4113	0.0113

Step 1. Effect Has_Fence is removed:

The backward elimination process continues with fitting the model for the remaining twelve predictors, providing all of the typical output, ending with the Analysis of Effects Eligible for Removal used for Step 2, as illustrated in Output 10.9b Effects Eligible for Removal for Step 2 of Backward Elimination. Using 0.01 level of significance, we can see that the last four variables fail the test for staying in the model. Because the p-value for the variable, TWOPLUSCAR_GARAGE, is largest at 0.4586, that variable is removed from the candidate of variables, as indicated by the 'Step 2. Effect TwoPlusCar_Garage is removed' message.

Output 10.9b Effects Eligible for Removal for Step 2 of Backward Elimination

Analysis of Effects Eligible for Removal			
Effect	DF	Wald Chi-Square	Pr > ChiSq
Gr_Liv_Area	1	75.8107	<.0001
Total_Bsmt_SF	1	34.6671	<.0001
Lot_Area	1	7.5509	0.0060
Age_at_Sale	1	31.5647	<.0001
Overall_Quality	2	36.8515	<.0001
High_Kitchen_Quality	1	45.6473	<.0001
Fullbath_2plus	1	12.8136	0.0003
Fireplace_1plus	1	13.3911	0.0003
TwoPlusCar_Garage	1	0.5493	0.4586
High_Exterior_Cond	1	2.9017	0.0885
CuldeSac	1	0.7716	0.3797
Land_Level	1	6.5480	0.0105

Step 2. Effect TwoPlusCar_Garage is removed:

The backward elimination process continues with fitting the model for the remaining eleven predictors, providing the Analysis of Effects Eligible for Removal used for Step 3, as illustrated in Output 10.9c Effects Eligible for Removal for Steps 3 through 5 of Backward Elimination. Using 0.01 level of significance, we can see that the last three variables fail the test for staying in the model. Here, the variable, CULDESAC, is removed, with the largest p-value of 0.3737.

Note that this process continues through Step 5 where a total of five variables have been eliminated. When the model for the remaining eight variables is fitted, it is evident from the p-values displayed in the Analysis of Effects Eligible for Removal table (not displayed here), that none of the remaining variables meet the criterion for removal and the backward elimination process is stopped. This is indicated by the 'Note' after Step 5, as indicated in Output 10.9c Effects Eligible for Removal for Step 3 through 5 of Backward Elimination.

Output 10.9c Effects Eligible for Removal for Steps 3 through 5 of Backward Elimination

Analysis of Effects Eligible for Removal			
Effect	DF	Wald Chi-Square	Pr > ChiSq
Gr_Liv_Area	1	77.9877	<.0001
Total_Bsmt_SF	1	35.1362	<.0001
Lot_Area	1	8.5826	0.0034
Age_at_Sale	1	37.6108	<.0001
Overall_Quality	2	38.7543	<.0001
High_Kitchen_Quality	1	45.3149	<.0001
Fullbath_2plus	1	14.4793	0.0001
Fireplace_1plus	1	13.4759	0.0002
High_Exterior_Cond	1	2.8856	0.0894
CuldeSac	1	0.7914	0.3737
Land_Level	1	6.5462	0.0105

Step 3. Effect CuldeSac is removed:

Analysis of Effects Eligible for Removal			
Effect	DF	Wald Chi-Square	Pr > ChiSq
Gr_Liv_Area	1	78.6921	<.0001
Total_Bsmt_SF	1	35.2652	<.0001
Lot_Area	1	9.6417	0.0019
Age_at_Sale	1	39.1726	<.0001
Overall_Quality	2	39.2477	<.0001
High_Kitchen_Quality	1	44.8324	<.0001
Fullbath_2plus	1	14.4208	0.0001
Fireplace_1plus	1	13.3569	0.0003
High_Exterior_Cond	1	3.0582	0.0803
Land_Level	1	6.5291	0.0106

Step 4. Effect High_Exterior_Cond is removed:

Analysis of Effects Eligible for Removal			
Effect	DF	Wald Chi-Square	Pr > ChiSq
Gr_Liv_Area	1	78.2193	<.0001
Total_Bsmt_SF	1	34.3788	<.0001
Lot_Area	1	9.7845	0.0018
Age_at_Sale	1	36.7145	<.0001
Overall_Quality	2	38.4213	<.0001
High_Kitchen_Quality	1	47.5371	<.0001
Fullbath_2plus	1	16.4911	<.0001
Fireplace_1plus	1	12.4484	0.0004
Land_Level	1	6.1019	0.0135

Step 5. Effect Land_Level is removed:

Note: No (additional) effects met the 0.01 significance level for removal from the model.

Once the backward elimination process is stopped, a summary of the removal is provided as specified by the DETAILS option in the MODEL statement. That summary is displayed in Output 10.9d Summary of Effects Removed in Backward Elimination.

Output 10.9d Summary of Effects Removed in Backward Elimination

Summary of Backward Elimination					
Step	Effect Removed	DF	Number In	Wald Chi-Square	Pr > ChiSq
1	Has_Fence	1	12	0.0393	0.8429
2	TwoPlusCar_Garage	1	11	0.5493	0.4586
3	CuldeSac	1	10	0.7914	0.3737
4	High_Exterior_Cond	1	9	3.0582	0.0803
5	Land_Level	1	8	6.1019	0.0135

In conclusion, we can see that the model selected by the backward elimination method contains eight predictors. Recall, in the last section, that these eight predictors are the same found to be significant in the full model. This is not always the case, but the models should be similar.

Forward Selection

Forward selection starts with the model containing only the intercept, and then adds variables one at a time as long as each satisfies the criterion for entry in the model. Once a model is fit such that no other remaining variables meet the criteria for entry, the variable selection process ends. Note that, for forward selection, once a variable is added, it cannot be removed.

In the forward selection process, the Score Chi-Square Score test statistic is used for entry (see the LOGISTIC Procedure in the SAS/STAT User's Guide for the formulation of the Score statistic). This tests the null hypothesis that the current estimated model is adequate, with no need for additional predictors.

To illustrate the forward selection process, consider again the Ames Housing Case, where the analyst has used preliminary analyses to arrive at a candidate set of thirteen possible input variables. Basically, we want to start with the intercept (no predictors), and then add variables one at a time that are considered important according to the score chi-square. We would use Program 10.11 Forward Selection for Ames Housing.

Program 10.11 Forward Selection for Ames Housing

```
libname sasba 'c:\sasba\ames';
data ames;
   set sasba.ames70;
run;

proc logistic data=ames;
  class Overall_Quality (param=ref ref=first);
  model Bonus (Event = '1')= Gr_Liv_Area Total_Bsmt_SF Lot_Area
      Age_At_Sale Overall_Quality High_Kitchen_Quality Fullbath_2Plus
      Fireplace_1Plus TwoPlusCar_Garage High_Exterior_Cond CuldeSac Has_Fence
    Land_Level/selection=forward slentry=0.01 details;
run;
```

Program 10.11 Forward Selection for Ames Housing provided here is identical to that used for the backward elimination with a couple of exceptions. First, the SELECTION=FORWARD option is used instead. Because the forward selection starts with no predictors with the goal of adding potential predictors, the appropriation selection option is SLENTRY, which specifies the significance level needed for entry.

Beginning with Step 1, after the intercept-only model is estimated, SAS calculates the Score Chi-Square Score test statistic for every variable not yet in the model, along with their p-values; the variable with the largest test statistic (lowest p-value) is selected for entry only if the p-value is below that value specified in the SLENTRY option. At Step 2, the same process is implemented; after the model with the intercept and the first selected predictor is estimated, the p-value for the Score test is calculated for every other variable not yet in the model. The variable with the lowest p-value is selected next as long as it meets the SLENTRY criteria. This process continues until no additional variables meet the criterion for entry. Remember that once a variable is entered into the model, it is never eliminated.

As illustrated in the backward elimination, the output provided first includes the information typically found in a logistic regression analysis, followed by the first Analysis of Effects Eligible for Entry table, as displayed in Output 10.10a Effects Eligible for Entry for Step 1 of Forward Selection. Here, we can see the Score Chi-Square statistic and p-value for all thirteen variables not yet entered into the model. Note that while SAS rounds the p-value, resulting in many variables having $p<.0001$, the smallest p-value is that associated with the largest chi-square statistic. As a result, the variable, FULLBATH_2PLUS, is selected for entry, with the largest chi-square statistic of 667.2729, as illustrated in Step 1.

Output 10.10a Effects Eligible for Entry for Step 1 of Forward Selection

Analysis of Effects Eligible for Entry			
Effect	DF	Score Chi-Square	Pr > ChiSq
Gr_Liv_Area	1	584.5319	<.0001
Total_Bsmt_SF	1	314.2380	<.0001
Lot_Area	1	69.3485	<.0001
Age_at_Sale	1	460.2132	<.0001
Overall_Quality	2	493.9597	<.0001
High_Kitchen_Quality	1	459.8347	<.0001
Fullbath_2plus	1	667.2729	<.0001
Fireplace_1plus	1	242.1424	<.0001
TwoPlusCar_Garage	1	375.2390	<.0001
High_Exterior_Cond	1	8.1981	0.0042
CuldeSac	1	26.6874	<.0001
Has_Fence	1	67.1557	<.0001
Land_Level	1	3.5978	0.0579

Step 1. Effect Fullbath_2plus entered:

The forward selection process continues with fitting the model for the one predictor selected, providing all of the typical output, followed by the Analysis of Effects Eligible for Entry table for Step 2, resulting in the variable, HIGH_KITCHEN_QUALITY, selected for entry.

Once it is determined that no additional variables contribute to the fit, the forward selection process ends and a summary of the forward selection is provided as specified by the DETAILS option in the MODEL statement. That summary is displayed in Output 10.10b Summary of Effects Entered in Forward Selection. Note that the variable subset selected using forward selection is identical to that selected using backward elimination. Again, that is not always the case.

Output 10.10b Summary of Effects Entered in Forward Selection

	Summary of Forward Selection				
Step	Effect Entered	DF	Number In	Score Chi-Square	Pr > ChiSq
1	Fullbath_2plus	1	1	667.2729	<.0001
2	High_Kitchen_Quality	1	2	205.2677	<.0001
3	Gr_Liv_Area	1	3	134.2660	<.0001
4	Age_at_Sale	1	4	115.8901	<.0001
5	Total_Bsmt_SF	1	5	46.7676	<.0001
6	Overall_Quality	2	6	43.8657	<.0001
7	Fireplace_1plus	1	7	16.9617	<.0001
8	Lot_Area	1	8	13.5743	0.0002

Stepwise Selection

Stepwise selection combines both the forward selection and backward elimination methods. Variables considered important are added one at a time; however, at any point, a variable can be removed from the model when it is no longer significant in the context of the set of variables in the model at that time.

For illustration, consider the Ames Housing Case and the thirteen possible input variables. In order to conduct a stepwise method of selection, we would use the previous SAS code with the following MODEL statement and the SELECTION=STEPWISE option as in the partial program, Program 10.12 Stepwise Selection for Ames Housing.

Program 10.12 Stepwise Selection for Ames Housing

```
libname sasba 'c:\sasba\ames';
data ames;
   set sasba.ames70;
run;

proc logistic data=ames;
  class Overall_Quality (param=ref ref=first);
  model Bonus (Event = '1')= Gr_Liv_Area Total_Bsmt_SF Lot_Area
          Age_At_Sale Overall_Quality High_Kitchen_Quality Fullbath_2Plus
          Fireplace_1Plus TwoPlusCar_Garage High_Exterior_Cond CuldeSac
          Has_Fence Land_Level/selection=stepwise slentry=0.01 slstay=0.01
          details;
run;
```

Here, note that because the stepwise procedure involves adding and removing variables, the analyst must define both the SLENTRY and SLSTAY options as well. Again, see that the DETAILS option is included so that a summary of the selection steps is provided.

The output provided first includes the information typically found in a logistic regression analysis, followed by the first Analysis of Effects Eligible for Entry table, Output 10.11a Effects Eligible for Entry for Step 1 of Stepwise Selection. This step is identical to the first step of the forward selection method. The criterion for entry is the Score Chi-Square statistic and, based upon SLENTRY=0.01, we can see that the variable, FULLBATH_2PLUS, is selected for entry, with the largest chi-square statistic of 667.2729.

Output 10.11a Effects Eligible for Entry for Step 1 of Stepwise Selection

Analysis of Effects Eligible for Entry			
Effect	DF	Score Chi-Square	Pr > ChiSq
Gr_Liv_Area	1	584.5319	<.0001
Total_Bsmt_SF	1	314.2380	<.0001
Lot_Area	1	69.3485	<.0001
Age_at_Sale	1	460.2132	<.0001
Overall_Quality	2	493.9597	<.0001
High_Kitchen_Quality	1	459.8347	<.0001
Fullbath_2plus	1	667.2729	<.0001
Fireplace_1plus	1	242.1424	<.0001
TwoPlusCar_Garage	1	375.2390	<.0001
High_Exterior_Cond	1	8.1981	0.0042
CuldeSac	1	26.6874	<.0001
Has_Fence	1	67.1557	<.0001
Land_Level	1	3.5978	0.0579

Step 1. Effect Fullbath_2plus entered:

After the variable, FULLBATH_2PLUS, is entered, all logistic regression output is provided, followed by the test for removal. As illustrated in Output 10.11b Effects Eligible for Removal After Step 1 of Stepwise Selection, the Wald Chi-Square test is used for removal; based upon the p-value and the SLSTAY=0.01 option, FULLBATH_2PLUS is retained in the current model.

Output 10.11b Effects Eligible for Removal After Step 1 of Stepwise Selection

Analysis of Effects Eligible for Removal			
Effect	DF	Wald Chi-Square	Pr > ChiSq
Fullbath_2plus	1	471.3694	<.0001

Note: No effects for the model in Step 1 are removed.

The process continues with the second Analysis of Effects Eligible for Entry table, followed by the Analysis of Effects Eligible for Removal table as illustrated in Output 10.11c Effects Eligible for Entry for Step 2 of Stepwise Selection. The second variable selected using the Score Chi-Square test is HIGH_KITCHEN_QUALITY (note that while OVERALL_QUALITY has the highest chi-square value, one of its levels is nonsignificant; so when levels are considered alone, HIGH_KITCHEN_QUALITY has the highest value). Once HIGH_KITCHEN_QUALITY is added, we can see from the Wald Chi-Square test that it meets the criterion for staying.

Output 10.11c Effects Eligible for Entry for Step 2 of Stepwise Selection

Analysis of Effects Eligible for Entry			
Effect	DF	Score Chi-Square	Pr > ChiSq
Gr_Liv_Area	1	169.2967	<.0001
Total_Bsmt_SF	1	131.9973	<.0001
Lot_Area	1	30.5306	<.0001
Age_at_Sale	1	144.8863	<.0001
Overall_Quality	2	207.8815	<.0001
High_Kitchen_Quality	1	205.2677	<.0001
Fireplace_1plus	1	91.6061	<.0001
TwoPlusCar_Garage	1	110.7687	<.0001
High_Exterior_Cond	1	4.2946	0.0382
CuldeSac	1	11.9763	0.0005
Has_Fence	1	21.1929	<.0001
Land_Level	1	21.1507	<.0001

Step 2. Effect High_Kitchen_Quality entered:

Analysis of Effects Eligible for Removal			
Effect	DF	Wald Chi-Square	Pr > ChiSq
High_Kitchen_Quality	1	170.2730	<.0001
Fullbath_2plus	1	328.2947	<.0001

Note: No effects for the model in Step 2 are removed.

The process of testing for inclusion using the Score Chi-Square test and for removal using the Wald Chi-Square continues until no further predictors are added nor removed. The DETAILS option provides for the summary of steps as illustrated in Output 10.11d Summary of Effects Entered or Removed in Stepwise Selection.

Output 10.11d Summary of Effects Entered or Removed in Stepwise Selection

	Effect						
				Number	Score	Wald	
Step	Entered	Removed	DF	In	Chi-Square	Chi-Square	Pr > ChiSq
1	fullbath_2plus		1	1	667.2729		<.0001
2	High_Kitchen_Quality		1	2	205.2677		<.0001
3	Gr_Liv_Area		1	3	134.2660		<.0001
4	Age_at_Sale		1	4	115.8901		<.0001
5	Total_Bsmt_SF		1	5	46.7676		<.0001
6	Overall_Quality		2	6	43.8657		<.0001
7	fireplace_1plus		1	7	16.9617		<.0001
8	Lot_Area		1	8	13.5743		0.0002

This illustrates the rare event when the same model is selected using all three selection methods. Finally, when conducting the sequential methods, keep in mind the default selection criteria, as displayed in Table 10.1 Summary of Effects Entered or Removed in Stepwise Selection.

Table 10.1 Summary of Effects Entered or Removed in Stepwise Selection

	SLENTRY	SLSTAY
BACKWARD		0.05
FORWARD	0.05	
STEPWISE	0.05	0.05

Customized Options within the Sequential Methods

The three sequential methods described so far--backward, forward, and stepwise--illustrate the basic ideas behind those various strategies. However, these can be very rigid at times when the analyst wants to use a different rationale, such as always including a specific set of predictors in the final model or limiting the size of the final model, for example. In these cases, there are additional options that can be included in the SELECTION= option. These options are START, STOP, and INCLUDE.

START=n can be used in all methods of selection (FORWARD, BACKWARD, and STEPWISE) and requests that the first n variables listed in the MODEL statement be included when the procedure starts; however, any of those variables can be deleted at any point after if the variable fails the criterion to stay. For the START option, note the following:

- n ranges from 0 to (k) the number of variables in the model list.
- The default value of n is k for BACKWARD and 0 for FORWARD and STEPWISE.
- The START option has no effect for SELECTION=NONE.

STOP=n can be used for FORWARD and BACKWARD selection. For FORWARD selection, n defines the maximum number of predictors to be included in the model; for BACKWARD selection, n defines the minimum. The selection process ends when n predictors are selected. For the STOP option, note the following:

- n ranges from 0 to (k) the number of variables in the model list.
- The default value of n is 0 for BACKWARD and k for FORWARD.
- The STOP= option has no effect for SELECTION=NONE or STEPWISE.

INCLUDE=*n* requests that the first *n* predictors listed in the MODEL statement be included in every model, including the final model. This option can be used for any method of selection. For the INCLUDE option, note the following:

- The default value of *n* is 0 for all methods of selection.

- The INCLUDE= option has no effect for SELECTION=NONE.

- The INCLUDE= differs from START= in that it requires that the first *n* predictors stay in the model.

Consider the following examples of MODEL statements using the Ames Housing Case:

Example 1:

```
model Bonus (Event = '1')= Gr_Liv_Area Total_Bsmt_SF Lot_Area
   Age_At_Sale Overall_Quality High_Kitchen_Quality Fullbath_2Plus
   Fireplace_1Plus TwoPlusCar_Garage High_Exterior_Cond
   CuldeSac Has_Fence Land_Level
   /selection=backward stop=10 slstay=0.01 details;
```

The MODEL statement defines thirteen predictors and the BACKWARD selection starts with all of them. Remember previously in this example, that the model selection process continued until five predictors were removed, leaving eight in the model. Because STOP=10, variables are removed one at a time based upon contribution to the fit until the model contains ten predictors, thereby ignoring the SLSTAY=0.01 option.

The resulting summary is displayed in Output 10.12 Summary of Effects Removed in Backward Elimination Using the STOP= Option.

Output 10.12 Summary of Effects Removed in Backward Elimination Using the STOP= Option

Note: The number of effects in the model has reached STOP=10.

	Summary of Backward Elimination				
Step	**Effect Removed**	**DF**	**Number In**	**Wald Chi-Square**	**Pr > ChiSq**
1	Has_Fence	1	12	0.0393	0.8429
2	TwoPlusCar_Garage	1	11	0.5493	0.4586
3	CuldeSac	1	10	0.7914	0.3737

Example 2:

```
model Bonus (Event = '1')= Gr_Liv_Area Total_Bsmt_SF Lot_Area
   Age_At_Sale Overall_Quality Overall_Condition High_Kitchen_Quality
   Fullbath_2Plus Fireplace_1Plus TwoPlusCar_Garage High_Exterior_Cond
   CuldeSac Has_Fence Land_Level
   /selection=forward start=5 slstay=0.01 details;
```

Again, the MODEL statement defines thirteen predictors and the FORWARD selection starts with the first five as seen in Step 0 of Output 10.13 Summary of Effects Entered in Forward Selection Using START= Option, ignoring the SLSTAY=0.01. Once the variables are added and the SLSTAY=0.01 is ignored, the default value of 0.05 is used. As a result, four additional predictors are added to the five initially entered, resulting in a total of nine. This is in contrast to the eight predictors selected using forward selection where SLSTAY=0.01 without the START=5 option, as displayed in Output 10.10b Summary of Effects Entered in Forward Selection. Note also that because the first 5 variables are strongly related to BONUS, the results of using START=5 are identical to those results using INCLUDE=5.

3 Summary of Effects Entered in Forward Selection Using START= Option

Step 0. The following effects were entered:

Intercept Gr_Liv_Area Total_Bsmt_SF Lot_Area Age_at_Sale Overall_Quality

.ote: No (additional) effects met the 0.05 significance level for entry into the model.

	Summary of Forward Selection				
Step	**Effect Entered**	**DF**	**Number In**	**Score Chi-Square**	**Pr > ChiSq**
1	High_Kitchen_Quality	1	6	47.0710	<.0001
2	Fullbath_2plus	1	7	14.8199	0.0001
3	Fireplace_1plus	1	8	13.6898	0.0002
4	Land_Level	1	9	6.1591	0.0131

Best Subset Selection

Best subset selection provides a way for the analyst to look at all possible subsets and select the best model based upon some selection criterion. This approach is exhaustive in that, for k predictors, it provides results for 2^k-1 possible subsets. For the best subset method to perform more efficiently, the criterion for selection is the highest score chi-square which does not require the same rigor involved in finding the maximum likelihood estimates (Furnival and Wilson, 1974). The results provide the best models for each subset size. The code for conducting a best subset analysis uses the SELECTION=SCORE and it is in Program 10.13 Score Chi-Square Statistics for the Best Subsets of Size 1 through 8.

Program 10.13 Score Chi-Square Statistics for the Best Subsets of Size 1 through 8

```
libname sasba 'c:\sasba\ames';
data ames;
   set sasba.ames70;
   AboveAverage_Quality=(Overall_Quality=3);
   BelowAverage_Quality=(Overall_Quality=1);
run;

proc logistic data=ames;
    model Bonus (Event = '1')= Gr_Liv_Area Total_Bsmt_SF Lot_Area
        Age_At_Sale AboveAverage_Quality BelowAverage_Quality
        High_Kitchen_Quality Fullbath_2Plus Fireplace_1Plus TwoPlusCar_Garage
        High_Exterior_Cond CuldeSac Has_Fence Land_Level
        /selection=score best=1 stop=8;
run;
```

First notice that the SCORE option does not allow for class variables, so the DATA step includes statements to create dummy codes for OVERALL_QUALITY. The BEST=1 option requests the *one* subset be selected for each subset size and STOP=8 requests that the selection process stop once eight predictors have been provided as displayed in Output 10.14 Score Chi-Square Statistics for the Best Subsets of Size 1 through 8.

Output 10.14 Score Chi-Square Statistics for the Best Subsets of Size 1 through 8

	Regression Models Selected by Score Criterion	
Number of Variables	Score Chi-Square	Variables Included in Model
1	667.2729	Fullbath_2plus
2	805.5378	Gr_Liv_Area Age_at_Sale
3	862.5226	Gr_Liv_Area Age_at_Sale Fullbath_2plus
4	899.3914	Gr_Liv_Area Age_at_Sale High_Kitchen_Quality Fullbath_2plus
5	921.0078	Gr_Liv_Area Age_at_Sale AboveAverage_Quality High_Kitchen_Quality Fullbath_2plus
6	930.8868	Gr_Liv_Area Total_Bsmt_SF Age_at_Sale AboveAverage_Quality High_Kitchen_Quality Fullbath_2plus
7	936.1503	Gr_Liv_Area Total_Bsmt_SF Age_at_Sale AboveAverage_Quality High_Kitchen_Quality Fullbath_2plus Land_Level
8	940.1635	Gr_Liv_Area Total_Bsmt_SF Age_at_Sale AboveAverage_Quality High_Kitchen_Quality Fullbath_2plus fireplace_1plus Land_Level

The START= option can be used when the analyst wants output starting at a specific size. So, for example, START=2 STOP=5 BEST=3 provides the best three models of sizes, 2, 3, 4, and 5.

From the output, the analyst can see that as the model size increases, the score chi-square statistic increases as well; therefore, the Bayesian Information Criterion (BIC) should be used instead.

Modeling Interaction

When modeling, the analyst should always take into account **interaction**. Interaction occurs when the relationship between the outcome (Y) and a predictor (X_1) varies depending upon the values of a second predictor (X_2). Consider the following example, displayed in Figure 10.3, where we are interested in the relationship between the outcome salary and the two grouping variables, level of degree and occupational area. The analyst would have several questions: First, is salary related to level of degree; second, is salary related to occupational area; or more, importantly, does it depend? In other words, do differences in salary depend upon the combinations of degree and occupational area? This third question answers the question concerning interaction.

From the first plot, it is hard to make a blanket statement with respect to salary and occupational area alone. It is not necessarily true to say that the highest salaries go to IT, followed by Financial, then Education. At the high school level, it seems that the salaries are pretty much the same; for those with a BS degree, IT and Financial are about the same, but both seem to be slightly more than employees in the Education area. For those with an MS degree, there seems to be a difference in salaries across all levels, and for those with a PhD, that difference is even greater.

The fact that mean differences must be explained by both variables, occupational area and degree, at the same time is an indication that interaction exists. In fact, interaction can be detected by mean plots, called **interaction plots**, as displayed in first plot of Figure 10.3 Mean Plots by Degree and Occupational Area, and is evidenced by the non-parallel lines for occupational area. When interaction does not exist, the interaction plots will display parallel lines as shown in the second plot of Figure 10.3 Mean Plots by Degree and Occupational Area .

Figure 10.3 Mean Plots by Degree and Occupational Area

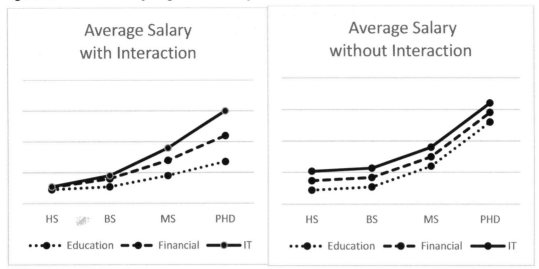

Interaction can also occur if the outcome variable is categorical, as is the case for logistic regression. In the case of two predictors, X_1 and X_2, if interaction between the predictors exists, the logistic regression model has the form:

$$logit(p_i) = \beta_0 + \beta_1 X_1 + \beta_2 X_2 + \beta_3 X_1 X_2$$

where the test for β_3 is testing for interaction, in the presence of the **main effects** of X_1 and X_2. If the interaction term is significant, then the analyst can say that the relationship between the probability of success (p_i) and X_1 depends upon X_2.

So how would the analyst incorporate interaction into the logistic regression model using SAS? Consider the Ames House Case, and for simplicity's purposes, let's investigate the relationship between BONUS and the variables overall quality (OVERALL_QUALITY) and kitchen quality (HIGH_KITCHEN_QUALITY), as well as whether or not the house has at least two full bathrooms or not (FULLBATH_2PLUS). We'll include their interactions. Note here that, in general, with three predictors, there are three main effects (A, B, C), three double interactions (A*B, A*C, B*C), and one triple interaction (A*B*C). To test our model, we would use Program 10.14 Testing Main Effects and Interactions for Ames Housing.

Program 10.14 Testing Main Effects and Interactions for Ames Housing

```
libname sasba 'c:\sasba\ames';
data ames;
   set sasba.ames70;
run;

proc logistic data=ames;
   class Overall_Quality (param=ref ref=first);
   model Bonus (Event = '1')=
      Overall_Quality|High_Kitchen_Quality|Fullbath_2Plus @2;
run;
```

The LOGISTIC procedure and CLASS statement are identical to past examples. In the MODEL statement, when interaction effects are requested, the predictors (or main effects) must be separated by a bar '|' followed by @n, where n represents the highest order interaction. If the @n is omitted, all interaction terms are provided. Here, the example code uses @2 requesting that main effects and all two-way interactions be estimated, omitting or ignoring three-way interactions, as displayed in Output 10.15 Testing Main Effects and Interactions for Ames Housing.

Model Purchase×Gender Age Region
Purchase×Gender|Age|Region @1

Output 10.15 Testing Main Effects and Interactions for Ames Housing

Model Fit Statistics		
Criterion	Intercept Only	Intercept and Covariates
AIC	1877.463	841.896
SC	1882.700	894.260
-2 Log L	1875.463	821.896

Testing Global Null Hypothesis: BETA=0			
Test	Chi-Square	DF	Pr > ChiSq
Likelihood Ratio	1053.5671	9	<.0001
Score	876.4384	9	<.0001
Wald	424.4395	9	<.0001

Joint Tests			
Effect	DF	Wald Chi-Square	Pr > ChiSq
Overall_Quality	2	27.9485	<.0001
High_Kitchen_Quality	1	4.2715	0.0388
High_Kitchen_Quality*Overall_Quality	2	1.3344	0.5132
Fullbath_2plus	1	0.2336	0.6288
Fullbath_*Overall_Quality	2	2.1327	0.3443
High_Kitchen_Quality*Fullbath_2plus	1	6.1696	0.0130

Note: Under full-rank parameterizations, Type 3 effect tests are replaced by joint tests. The joint test for an effect is a test that all the parameters associated with that effect are zero. Such joint tests might not be equivalent to Type 3 effect tests under GLM parameterization.

Analysis of Maximum Likelihood Estimates						
Parameter		DF	Estimate	Standard Error	Wald Chi-Square	Pr > ChiSq
Intercept		1	-4.7587	1.0298	21.3554	<.0001
Overall_Quality	2	1	0.6522	1.1042	0.3488	0.5548
Overall_Quality	3	1	2.7975	1.0489	7.1128	0.0077
High_Kitchen_Quality		1	2.6435	1.2790	4.2715	0.0388
High_Kitchen_Quality*Overall_Quality	2	1	-1.5821	1.3697	1.3344	0.2480
High_Kitchen_Quality*Overall_Quality	3	1	-1.3897	1.3005	1.1419	0.2853
Fullbath_2plus		1	0.5961	1.2332	0.2336	0.6288
Fullbath_*Overall_Quality	2	1	1.8848	1.2944	2.1204	0.1453
Fullbath_*Overall_Quality	3	1	1.6845	1.2202	1.9058	0.1674
High_Kitchen_Quality*Fullbath_2plus		1	0.9577	0.3856	6.1696	0.0130

From the Model Fit Statistics found in Output 10.15 Testing Main Effects and Interactions for Ames Housing, we can see that the model is a dramatic improvement over the intercept-only model. This is specifically verified by the p-value included for testing the global null hypothesis. When interaction terms are included in the model, the Joint Tests table is provided which summarizes the individual effects under consideration.

For illustration purposes, let's set our alpha to 0.05 for testing effects. Also note that interaction effects must be tested first because the very existence of interaction has implications for interpreting main effects. We see that only one interaction term, HIGH_KITCHEN_QUALITY*FULLBATH_2PLUS, is significant with a p-value of 0.0130. Because interaction exists, we cannot attempt to interpret each of the main effects for HIGH_KITCHEN_QUALITY nor FULLBATH_2PLUS.

The tests also indicate that OVERALL_QUALITY is related to Bonus (p<.0001). So in conclusion, BONUS is related to both OVERALL_QUALITY and the interaction of HIGH_KITCHEN_QUALITY by FULLBATH_2PLUS.

If the analyst had wanted to include the three-way interactions in the analysis, the MODEL statement would have excluded the @n notation as seen below and all two-way and three-way interactions would have been displayed. The output would have been identical to using the @3 option as well.

```
model Bonus (Event = '1')=
        Overall_Quality|High_Kitchen_Quality|Fullbath_2Plus
```

Keep in mind that three-way interaction is hard to interpret. In fact, for the Ames Housing Case, running the code would have resulted in the warning messages as found in Output 10.16 Example of Failed Model Convergence. Remember quasi-complete separation occurs when there is sparse data. In the Ames Housing data set, there are no houses where the agent earned a bonus (BONUS=1) and the house had below average quality (OVERALL_QUALITY=1), low kitchen quality (HIGH_KITCHEN_QUALITY=0), with only one full bathroom (FULLBATH_2PLUS=0). This is not surprising. In fact, there are 5 combinations of these predictors out of 24 (2 levels of BONUS X 3 levels of OVERALL_QUALITY X 2 levels of HIGH_KITCHEN_QUALITY X 2 levels of FULLBATH_2PLUS) where there exist only one or two houses. In this case, the validity of the results is suspect.

Output 10.16 Example of Failed Model Convergence

Model Convergence Status
Quasi-complete separation of data points detected.

Warning: **The maximum likelihood estimate may not exist.**

Warning: **The LOGISTIC procedure continues in spite of the above warning. Results shown are based on the last maximum likelihood iteration. Validity of the model fit is questionable.**

Now let's consider the same model above and apply a backward selection approach for getting a reduced model. In this situation, all terms are entered into the model as a Step 0: specifically, the three main effects and the three two-way interactions, as illustrated in Output 10.17a Step 0 of Backward Elimination for Main and Interactions Effects. As before, each term is tested for removal using the Wald Chi-Square test. However, the terms considered for removal must follow the **model hierarchy** rule.

Model hierarchy is the rule that requires a main effect to remain in a model as long as that effect exists in any interaction term. For example, as long as the interaction term, OVERALL_QUALITY*HIGH_KITCHEN_QUALITY, is in the model, the main effects, OVERALL_QUALITY and HIGH_KITCHEN_QUALITY, must also remain in the model. Let's look at the previous example with interaction from the Ames Housing Case where now we perform a backward model selection as illustrated in Program 10.15 Backward Model Selection for Ames Housing.

Program 10.15 Backward Model Selection for Ames Housing

```
libname sasba 'c:\sasba\ames';
data ames;
   set sasba.ames70;
run;

proc logistic data=ames;
   class Overall_Quality (param=ref ref=first);
   model Bonus (Event = '1')=
      Overall_Quality|High_Kitchen_Quality|Fullbath_2Plus @2
      /selection=backward slstay=0.05 hierarchy=single details;
run;
```

From the MODEL statement, we see that the logistic regression model is to be fit for only main effects and the two-way interactions. The backward selection is requested using the SELECTION=BACKWARD option, the alpha level for a term to stay in the model is 0.05 (SLSTAY=0.05), and DETAILS are requested for providing a summary of steps. Note that for illustrative purposes, we have set the alpha to 0.05; however, the analyst may prefer to be a bit more conservative by setting the level to 0.01. HIERARCHY=SINGLE is the default option, indicating that only one effect can leave the model at one time, subject to the model hierarchy rule; see SAS documentation for defining other rules for entry or exit. Excerpts from the output can be found in Output 10.17a Step 0 of Backward Elimination for Main and Interactions Effects through Output 10.17e Final Model Selected Using Backward Elimination.

Output 10.17a Step 0 of Backward Elimination for Main and Interactions Effects

Step 0. The following effects were entered:

**Intercept Overall_Quality High_Kitchen_Quality High_Kitchen_Quality*Overall_Quality
Fullbath_2plus Fullbath_2plus*Overall_Quality High_Kitchen_Quality*Fullbath_2plus**

Model Convergence Status
Convergence criterion (GCONV=1E-8) satisfied.

From Output 10.17a Step 0 of Backward Elimination for Main and Interactions Effects, we can see that all six effects, three main and three two-way interactions, are entered into the model. The model converges and the output includes Model Fit Statistics, which match the fit statistics found in Output 10.15.

In this example, because of model hierarchy, none of the main effects will be considered for removal; therefore, the Analysis of Effects for Removal table contains only the three two-way interactions, as illustrated in Output 10.17b Interaction Effects Eligible for Removal for Step 1 of Backward Elimination.

Output 10.17b Interaction Effects Eligible for Removal for Step 1 of Backward Elimination

Analysis of Effects Eligible for Removal			
Effect	DF	Wald Chi-Square	Pr > ChiSq
High_Kitchen_Quality*Overall_Quality	2	1.3344	0.5132
Fullbath_2plus*Overall_Quality	2	2.1327	0.3443
High_Kitchen_Quality*Fullbath_2plus	1	6.1696	0.0130

Step 1. Effect High_Kitchen_Quality*Overall_Quality is removed:

Model Convergence Status
Convergence criterion (GCONV=1E-8) satisfied.

Model Fit Statistics		
Criterion	Intercept Only	Intercept and Covariates
AIC	1877.463	839.356
SC	1882.700	881.247
-2 Log L	1875.463	823.356

From Output 10.17b Interaction Effects Eligible for Removal for Step 1 of Backward Elimination, we can see that the p-value for the interaction, HIGH_KITCHEN_QUALITY*OVERALL_QUALITY, is greater than the 0.05 level required for staying and is largest at 0.5132. Therefore, that interaction term is removed in Step 1. The model with the remaining terms has AIC, SC, and -2LogL values of 839.356, 881.247, and 823.356, respectively. When these are compared to the full model, the analyst can see that there is relatively little fit lost by removing the interaction term.

Because the remaining two interaction terms include all three main effects, no main effects can be removed, so the next removal step must consider only the two interaction terms, as found in Output 10.17c Interaction Effects Eligible for Removal for Step 2 of Backward Elimination. Based upon the p-value of 0.4962, the interaction term, FULLBATH_2PLUS*OVERALL_QUALITY, is removed in Step 2. Note also in the figure that the resulting model with the three main effects and the one remaining interaction term have a relatively small reduction in AIC, SC, and -2LogL, when compared to the fit in Step 1, indicating an insignificant reduction in fit.

Output 10.17c Interaction Effects Eligible for Removal for Step 2 of Backward Elimination

Analysis of Effects Eligible for Removal			
Effect	DF	Wald Chi-Square	Pr > ChiSq
Fullbath_2plus*Overall_Quality	2	1.4016	0.4962
High_Kitchen_Quality*Fullbath_2plus	1	5.8860	0.0153

Step 2. Effect Fullbath_2plus*Overall_Quality is removed:

Model Convergence Status
Convergence criterion (GCONV=1E-8) satisfied.

Model Fit Statistics		
Criterion	Intercept Only	Intercept and Covariates
AIC	1877.463	836.718
SC	1882.700	868.136
-2 Log L	1875.463	824.718

It should be noted, at this point, that the only interaction term remaining is HIGH_KITCHEN_QUALITY*FULLBATH_2PLUS; therefore, the main effect, OVERALL_QUALITY, does not exist in any interaction terms and is now eligible for removal as well, as displayed in Output 10.17d Effects Eligible for Removal for Step 3 of Backward Elimination.

Output 10.17d Effects Eligible for Removal for Step 3 of Backward Elimination

Analysis of Effects Eligible for Removal			
Effect	DF	Wald Chi-Square	Pr > ChiSq
Overall_Quality	2	89.3491	<.0001
High_Kitc*Fullbath_2	1	5.9083	0.0151

Note: No (additional) effects met the 0.05 significance level for removal from the model.

Summary of Backward Elimination					
Step	Effect Removed	DF	Number In	Wald Chi-Square	Pr > ChiSq
1	High_Kitchen_Quality*Overall_Quality	2	5	1.3344	0.5132
2	Fullbath_2plus*Overall_Quality	2	4	1.4016	0.4962

Finally, because no terms have p-values greater than 0.05, none are removed, and the backward selection process is terminated. From the summary, we can see that two of the three interactions were removed, thereby leaving the three main effects and one two-way interaction effect, as found in Output 10.17e Final Model Selected Using Backward Elimination. Note also that had the alpha been set to 0.01, the last interaction term would have been removed and the final model would have contained the three main effects alone with no interaction.

Output 10.17e Final Model Selected Using Backward Elimination

Analysis of Maximum Likelihood Estimates					
Parameter	DF	Estimate	Standard Error	Wald Chi-Square	Pr > ChiSq
Intercept	1	-4.8369	0.5976	65.5182	<.0001
Overall_Quality 2	1	0.7672	0.6166	1.5480	0.2134
Overall_Quality 3	1	2.8689	0.5803	24.4387	<.0001
High_Kitchen_Quality	1	1.2667	0.3053	17.2177	<.0001
Fullbath_2plus	1	2.2971	0.2551	81.1129	<.0001
High_Kitchen_Quality*Fullbath_2plus	1	0.9237	0.3800	5.9083	0.0151

Odds Ratio Estimates		
Effect	Point Estimate	95% Wald Confidence Limits
Overall_Quality 2 vs 1	2.154	0.643 7.212
Overall_Quality 3 vs 1	17.617	5.649 54.942

Once the final model is determined, the analyst should note that the odds ratios are not reported for any terms related to the interaction. In fact, the effects of HIGH_KITCHEN_QUALITY on the probability of BONUS are different when comparing at the two levels of FULLBATH_2PLUS; similarly, the effects of FULLBATH_2PLUS on the probability of BONUS are different when comparing at the two levels of HIGH_KITCHEN_QUALITY.

To get the desired conditional odds ratios, the analyst could use the AT option in the ODDSRATIO statement in Program 10.16 Odds Ratios with Plots for Main Effects and Conditional Effects. Keep in mind that the ODDSRATIO statements require that HIGH_KITCHEN_QUALITY and FULLBATH_2PLUS be added to the CLASS statement because their variable type is numeric even though those variables have been dummy coded anyway. The PLOTS(ONLY)=EFFECTS option will provide the probability of success plot which will aid in interpreting the interaction effects.

Program 10.16 Odds Ratios with Plots for Main Effects and Conditional Effects

```
libname sasba 'c:\sasba\ames';
data ames;
   set sasba.ames70;
run;

proc logistic data=ames;
   class High_Kitchen_Quality (param=ref ref=first)
         Fullbath_2plus (param=ref ref=first)
         Overall_Quality (param=ref ref=first);
   model Bonus (Event = '1')=
      Overall_Quality High_Kitchen_Quality Fullbath_2Plus
      High_Kitchen_Quality*Fullbath_2plus;
      oddsratio High_Kitchen_Quality / at (Fullbath_2plus=all);
      oddsratio Fullbath_2plus / at (High_Kitchen_Quality=all);
      oddsratio Overall_Quality;
run;
```

The results of the odds ratios for main effect and conditional effects are displayed in Output 10.18a Odds Ratios with Plots for Main Effects and Conditional Effects. For example, an agent is 17.617 times more likely to earn a bonus for a house with above average overall quality compared to a house with below average overall quality.

For interactions, first consider those houses with high quality kitchens (HIGH_KITCHEN_QUALITY=1). An agent is 25.048 times more likely to get a bonus for a house having two or more full bathrooms (FULLBATH_2PLUS=1) compared to a house with just one full bathroom (FULLBATH_2PLUS=0).

For houses with low quality kitchens (HIGH_KITCHEN_QUALITY=0), an agent is 9.945 times more likely to get a bonus for a house having two or more full bathrooms (FULLBATH_2PLUS=1) compared to a house with just one full bathroom (FULLBATH_2PLUS=0). These interaction effects are also illustrated in Output 10.18b Probabilities for

HIGH_KITCHEN_QUALITY by FULLBATH_2PLUS for OVERALL_QUALITY=1. This plot is obtained by adding PLOTS(ONLY)=EFFECTS as an option in the LOGISTIC procedure.

Output 10.18a Odds Ratios with Plots for Main Effects and Conditional Effects

Odds Ratio Estimates and Wald Confidence Intervals		
Odds Ratio	**Estimate**	**95% Confidence Limits**
High_Kitchen_Quality 1 vs 0 at Fullbath_2plus=0	3.549	1.951	6.456
High_Kitchen_Quality 1 vs 0 at Fullbath_2plus=1	8.939	5.736	13.930
Fullbath_2plus 1 vs 0 at High_Kitchen_Quality=0	9.945	6.033	16.395
Fullbath_2plus 1 vs 0 at High_Kitchen_Quality=1	25.048	14.398	43.575
Overall_Quality 2 vs 1	2.154	0.643	7.212
Overall_Quality 3 vs 1	17.617	5.649	54.942
Overall_Quality 2 vs 3	0.122	0.075	0.200

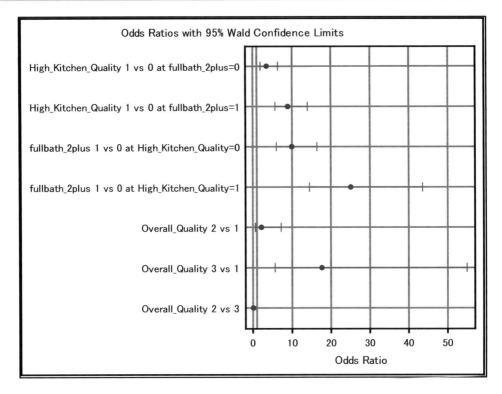

Output 10.18b Probabilities for High_Kitchen_Quality by Fullbath_2plus for Overall_Quality=1

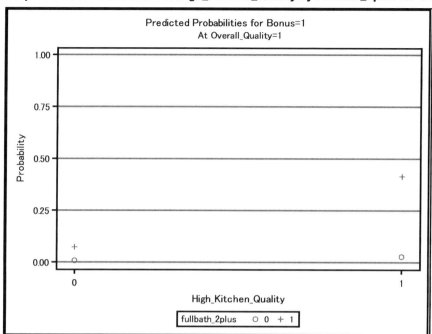

Scoring New Data

The discussions in this chapter have so far covered the methods used for relating a categorical outcome variable with numeric and categorical predictors for purposes of explanation. It is natural to take the 'best' model and predict outcomes for new observations; this is the purpose in **predictive modeling**.

Predicting, or **scoring**, is the process of applying the parameter estimates of the fitted model to new observations to arrive at their posterior probability of occurrence for each level of the outcome variable for purposes of classifying an observation as a 1 or 0 (success or failure). In this section, we will discuss four ways for saving the selected model and how to score new observations. The first approach requires that the model development and the scoring of new observations occur in the same procedure at the same time. The remaining three approaches involve creating and saving a permanent score model (or file) for future use in scoring new observations.

The SCORE Statement with PROC LOGISTIC

The SCORE statement is used within the logistic procedure to apply the model results to a new data set and to save the results of the scoring to an external data set. To illustrate, let's return to the Ames Housing Case. For simplicity's purposes, suppose the analyst wishes to fit a model with four predictors. Program 10.17 Predicted Class for New Observations Using the SCORE Statement in PROC LOGISTIC would be used to score a new data set called AMESNEW:

Program 10.17 Predicted Class for New Observations Using the SCORE Statement in PROC LOGISTIC

```
libname sasba 'c:\sasba\ames';
data ames;
   set sasba.ames70;
run;

proc logistic data=ames;
  model Bonus (Event = '1')= Gr_Liv_Area Total_Bsmt_SF Lot_Area
        Fullbath_2Plus;
  score data=sasba.amesnew out=amesnew_scored;
run;

proc print data=amesnew_scored;
   var F_Bonus I_Bonus P_0 P_1 Gr_Liv_Area Total_Bsmt_SF Lot_Area
        Fullbath_2Plus;
run;
```

First, the AMES70 data is read into the temporary data set AMES. The LOGISTIC procedure is called to create a model using the AMES data set based upon the specifications defined in both the MODEL and CLASS statements. The SCORE statement defines the data set on which the model is applied, namely, AMESNEW, and the results of the scoring are saved in the temporary data set, AMESNEW_SCORED. An excerpt from the PRINT procedure is found in Output 10.19 Predicted Class for New Observations Using the SCORE Statement in PROC LOGISTIC.

Consider the house labeled as observation 592, where the above ground living area is 988 square feet (GR_LIV_AREA=988), the total basement area is 938 square feet (TOTAL_BSMT_SF=938), the lot area is 21453 (LOT_AREA=21453), and the house has only one full bathroom (FULLBATH_2PLUS=0). Based upon the derived model, the estimated posterior probability of getting a bonus (P_1) is 0.03867; the estimated posterior probability of not getting a bonus (P_0) is 0.96133. Because the posterior probability of not getting a bonus is greater than 0.50 (the default cutoff value), that house is classified into the 0 group (i.e., classified as not getting a bonus). Therefore I_BONUS (Into Bonus) is assigned a value of 0. Note that the output includes all of the typical tables found in logistic regression; Model Information, Response Profile, Convergence Status, Model Fit Statistics, Testing Global Null Hypothesis, etc., unless the NOPRINT option is used.

Ordinarily the actual outcome is unknown for 'new' data; however, for the data set AMESNEW, the outcome is known, so the analyst can see the extent to which the observations are correctly classified, by comparing the F_BONUS (From Bonus) variable to see if it matches I_BONUS. For example, observations 592 and 593 were incorrectly classified as 0 (I_BONUS=0) when they actually originated from 1 (F_BONUS=1).

Output 10.19 Predicted Class for New Observations Using the SCORE Statement in PROC LOGISTIC

Obs	F_Bonus	I_Bonus	P_0	P_1	Gr_Liv_Area	Total_Bsmt_SF	Lot_Area	Fullbath_2plus
1	0	0	0.97659	0.02341	1004	1004	11241	0
2	0	0	0.96063	0.03937	1078	1078	12537	0
3	0	0	0.97398	0.02602	1056	1056	8450	0
4	0	0	0.98996	0.01004	894	894	8450	0
...	...	...	...	...	...	...	...	...
590	1	1	0.42931	0.57069	1855	528	9600	1
591	1	1	0.31103	0.68897	1875	675	10530	1
592	1	0	0.96133	0.03867	988	938	21453	0
593	1	0	0.73055	0.26945	1922	0	7301	1
594	1	1	0.25020	0.74980	1478	1418	7380	1
595	1	1	0.00067	0.99933	2687	2062	13108	1

Using the PLM Procedure to Call Score Code Created by PROC LOGISTIC

In the last section, we saw that the SCORE statement requires the logistic regression model be derived and the data scored in the same procedure (i.e., at the same time). Suppose, instead, that the analyst prefers to develop a model and save it for future use. In this case, the analyst can use the STORE statement within the LOGISTIC procedure to save the model in a binary file format, followed presumably later by the RESTORE option and SCORE statement within the PLM procedure when new data needs to be scored.

The purpose of the PLM procedure is to recall stored models from various statistical procedures and apply those models to new data. Using the same logistic model defined in the previous example, Program 10.18 Predicted Class for New Observations Using PROC PLM with the SCORE Statement illustrates the use of the PLM procedure.

Program 10.18 Predicted Class for New Observations Using PROC PLM with the SCORE Statement

```
libname sasba 'c:\sasba\ames';
data ames;
   set sasba.ames70;
run;

proc logistic data=ames;
  model Bonus (Event = '1')= Gr_Liv_Area Total_Bsmt_SF Lot_Area
         Fullbath_2Plus;
  store sasba.ames_score_code;
run;

proc plm restore=sasba.ames_score_code;
  score data=sasba.amesnew out=amesnew_scored;
run;

data predbonus1;
  set amesnew_scored;
  P_1 = exp(Predicted)/(1+exp(Predicted));
proc print data=predbonus1 (obs=4);
  var P_1 Predicted Gr_Liv_Area Total_Bsmt_SF Lot_Area
        Fullbath_2Plus;
run;
```

As found in Program 10.18 Predicted Class for New Observations Using PROC PLM with the SCORE Statement, the logistic regression procedure is applied to the AMES data (AMES70) and the model is saved in the permanent file called AMES_SCORE_CODE in the SASBA library. The PLM procedure calls the AMES_SCORE_CODE using the RESTORE statement and the code is used to score AMESNEW as defined in the SCORE statement. As a result, each newly scored observation now has a new variable, PREDICTED, representing the predicted logit, and all observations are saved in the file AMESNEW_SCORED as defined by the OUT= option.

In order to compare to previous output, the DATA step was used to calculate P_1, the posterior probability of success (BONUS=1), and is displayed in Output 10.20 Predicted Class for New Observations Using PROC PLM with the SCORE Statement, along with the Store Information table.

Output 10.20 Predicted Class for New Observations Using PROC PLM with the SCORE Statement

Store Information	
Item Store	SASBA.AMES_SCORE_CODE
Data Set Created From	WORK.AMES
Created By	PROC LOGISTIC
Date Created	02FEB18:14:05:14
Response Variable	Bonus
Link Function	Logit
Distribution	Binary
Class Variables	Overall_Quality Bonus
Model Effects	Intercept Gr_Liv_Area Total_Bsmt_SF Lot_Area Fullbath_2plus

Obs	P_1	Predicted	Gr_Liv_Area	Total_Bsmt_SF	Lot_Area	fullbath_2plus
1	0.023405	-3.73110	1004	1004	11241	0
2	0.039368	-3.19464	1078	1078	12537	0
3	0.026016	-3.62267	1056	1056	8450	0
4	0.010038	-4.59127	894	894	8450	0

The Store Information table is printed when the PLM procedure is applied. It provides detailed information pertinent to how the model was created. From the first four observations, it is evident that the posterior probabilities of success match those found in Output 10.19 Predicted Class for New Observations Using the SCORE Statement in PROC LOGISTIC.

The CODE Statement within PROC LOGISTIC

An alternative for saving score code for future use is the CODE statement used within the LOGISTIC procedure. This approach specifically allows for creating a SAS program for scoring new observations.

As found in Program 10.19 Predicted Class for New Observations Using PROC PLM with the SCORE Statement, the logistic regression procedure is applied to the AMES data (AMES70) and the model is saved in the permanent SAS file called AMES_SCORE_CODE on the C: drive. The new cases from AMESNEW are read into the temporary data file called SCORE. In the same DATA step, the %INCLUDE statement calls the saved SAS code and applies the code to the SCORE data set.

Program 10.19 Predicted Class for New Observations Using PROC PLM with the SCORE Statement
```
libname sasba 'c:\sasba\ames';
data ames;
    set sasba.ames70;
run;

proc logistic data=ames;
    model Bonus (Event = '1')= Gr_Liv_Area Total_Bsmt_SF Lot_Area
          Fullbath_2Plus;
    code file="C:\sasba\ames\ames_score_code.sas";
run;

data Score;
    set sasba.amesnew;
    %include "c:\sasba\ames\ames_score_code.sas";
run;

proc print data=score (obs=4);
    var I_Bonus U_Bonus P_Bonus1 P_Bonus0 Gr_Liv_Area Total_Bsmt_SF
        Lot_Area Fullbath_2Plus;
run;
```

The partial output from the PROC PRINT is displayed in Output 10.21 Predicted Class for New Observations Using PROC PLM with the SCORE Statement and provides for comparing posterior probabilities in Output 10.19 and Output 10.20. The code created by the CODE statement is found in Program 10.20 SAS Scoring Code Created by the PLM Procedure. It should be noted that the scoring code must be dropped into a data step and applied to any new data.

Output 10.21 Predicted Class for New Observations Using PROC PLM with the SCORE Statement

Obs	I_Bonus	U_Bonus	P_Bonus1	P_Bonus0	Gr_Liv_Area	Total_Bsmt_SF	Lot_Area	Fullbath_2plus
1	0	0	0.023405	0.97659	1004	1004	11241	0
2	0	0	0.039368	0.96063	1078	1078	12537	0
3	0	0	0.026016	0.97398	1056	1056	8450	0
4	0	0	0.010038	0.98996	894	894	8450	0

Program 10.20 SAS Scoring Code Created by the PLM Procedure
```
*******************************************;
** SAS Scoring Code for PROC Logistic;
*******************************************;
length I_Bonus $ 12;
label I_Bonus = 'Into: Bonus' ;
label U_Bonus = 'Unnormalized Into: Bonus' ;
label P_Bonus1 = 'Predicted: Bonus=1' ;
label P_Bonus0 = 'Predicted: Bonus=0' ;
drop _LMR_BAD;
_LMR_BAD=0;
*** Check interval variables for missing values;
if nmiss(Gr_Liv_Area,Total_Bsmt_SF,Lot_Area,fullbath_2plus)
    then do;   _LMR_BAD=1; goto _SKIP_000;
end;
```

```
*** Compute Linear Predictors;
drop _LP0;_LP0 = 0;
*** Effect: Gr_Liv_Area, Total_Bsmt_SF, Lot_Area, Fullbath_2plus;
_LP0 = _LP0 + (0.00343130327968) * Gr_Liv_Area;
_LP0 = _LP0 + (0.00254775621396) * Total_Bsmt_SF;
_LP0 = _LP0 + (0.00007254452013) * Lot_Area;
_LP0 = _LP0 + (2.42751762568077) * fullbath_2plus;
*** Predicted values;
drop _MAXP _IY _P0 _P1;
_TEMP = -10.5495532923216  + _LP0;
if (_TEMP < 0) then do; _TEMP = exp(_TEMP); _P0=_TEMP/(1+_TEMP);
                   end;
   else _P0 = 1 / (1 + exp(-_TEMP)); _P1 = 1.0 - _P0;
        P_Bonus1 = _P0; _MAXP = _P0; _IY = 1; P_Bonus0 = _P1;
if (_P1 >  _MAXP + 1E-8) then do; _MAXP = _P1;_IY = 2;
     end;
select( _IY ); when (1) do;I_Bonus = '1'; U_Bonus = 1; end;
               when (2) do;I_Bonus = '0'; U_Bonus = 0; end;
   otherwise do; I_Bonus = ''; U_Bonus = .; end;
end;
_SKIP_000:
if _LMR_BAD = 1 then do;
   I_Bonus = ''; U_Bonus = .; P_Bonus1 = .; P_Bonus0 = .;
end;
drop _TEMP;
```

The OUTMODEL and INMODEL Options with PROC LOGISTIC

A third alternative for saving score code involves using the OUTMODEL= option within the LOGISTIC procedure. Once the estimated model is saved, it can be called and applied to new observations by using the INMODEL option and the SCORE statement within the LOGISTIC procedure. Program 10.21 Model Saved as SAS Data Set Created by the OUTMODEL Option in PROC LOGISTIC will reproduce the same results as those discussed previously.

Program 10.21 Model Saved as SAS Data Set Created by the OUTMODEL Option in PROC LOGISTIC

```
libname sasba 'c:\sasba\ames';
data ames;
   set sasba.ames70;
run;

proc logistic data=ames outmodel=sasba.amescorecode;
   model Bonus (Event = '1')= Gr_Liv_Area Total_Bsmt_SF Lot_Area
        Fullbath_2Plus;
run;

proc logistic inmodel=sasba.amescorecode;
   score data=sasba.amesnew out=newames_scored;
run;

proc print data=newames_scored (obs=4);
   var F_Bonus I_Bonus P_0 P_1 Gr_Liv_Area Total_Bsmt_SF Lot_Area
        Fullbath_2Plus;
run;

proc print data=sasba.amescorecode;
run;
```

The initial SAS code is identical to all past examples. Note that in the first logistic regression, the OUTMODEL= option requests that the model be saved to a permanent SAS data set named AMESCORECODE. This code is solely created for use by a subsequent INMODEL= option. The typical logistic regression output is provided as well.

The INMODEL= option in the second logistic regression calls the code in the permanent data set, AMESCORECODE. The SCORE statement then requests that the model be applied to the permanent data set AMESNEW as defined in the DATA= option and that all scored observations be saved in the data set named AMES_SCORED. It should be noted that the model is not refitted when the second LOGISTIC procedure is run.

The results of the PRINT procedure match those found in Output 10.19, 10.20, and 10.21. The last PRINT procedure is used to display the SAS data set, AMESCORECODE, which is created by the OUTMODEL option and can be found in Output 10.22 Model Saved as SAS Data Set Created by the OUTMODEL Option in PROC LOGISTIC.

Before concluding this section on scoring, we must make one final comment. In the case where the event of interest is considered a **rare event** (i.e., occurs a relatively small proportion of the time), the data set, by definition, has a small number of 1s. In this case, there is insufficient information to model the event. Where possible, the analyst may want to **oversample** the event of interest; that is, take all of the observations having the event, and sample an equal number of observations that do not have the event. In this case, the logistic regression intercept is biased and must be adjusted before scoring new cases.

In Chapter 11, "Measure of Model Performance," we will discuss how to adjust the logistic regression model for purposes of scoring new cases, and specifically for validating predictive models.

Output 10.22 Model Saved as SAS Data Set Created by the OUTMODEL Option in PROC LOGISTIC

Obs	_TYPE_	_NAME_	_CATEGORY_	_NAMEIDX_	_CATIDX_	_MISC_
1	L			.	.	0.00
2	M	NYYNYNNN		.	.	5.00
3	G	Bonus	0	0	0	-11.00
4	G	Bonus	1	0	1	11.00
5	G	Bonus		-1	0	826.00
6	G	Bonus		-1	1	563.00
7	G	Bonus		-1	-2	-12.00
8	Z	Gr_Liv_Area		0	.	1.00
9	Z	Total_Bsmt_SF		1	.	1.00
10	Z	Lot_Area		2	.	1.00
11	Z	fullbath_2plus		3	.	1.00
12	E	Intercept	E	0	0	-10.55
13	E	EFFECT	Z	0	0	0.00
14	E	EFFECT	E	0	0	0.00
15	E	EFFECT	Z	1	0	1.00
16	E	EFFECT	E	1	0	0.00
17	E	EFFECT	Z	2	0	2.00
18	E	EFFECT	E	2	0	0.00
19	E	EFFECT	Z	3	0	3.00
20	E	EFFECT	E	3	0	2.43
21	E	EFFECT	V	.	0	0.41
22	E	EFFECT	V	.	1	-0.00
23	E	EFFECT	V	.	2	0.00
24	E	EFFECT	V	.	3	-0.00
25	E	EFFECT	V	.	4	0.00
26	E	EFFECT	V	.	5	0.00
27	E	EFFECT	V	.	6	-0.00
28	E	EFFECT	V	.	7	-0.00
29	E	EFFECT	V	.	8	-0.00

Obs	_TYPE_	_NAME_	_CATEGORY_	_NAMEIDX_	_CATIDX_	_MISC_
30	E	EFFECT	V	.	9	0.00
31	E	EFFECT	V	.	10	-0.02
32	E	EFFECT	V	.	11	-0.00
33	E	EFFECT	V	.	12	0.00
34	E	EFFECT	V	.	13	0.00
35	E	EFFECT	V	.	14	0.04
36	X	36		21	109	1451.46

Key Terms

Akaike Information Criterion (AIC)
backward selection
best subset selection
concordance statistic
design variables
deviation from the mean coding
dummy variables
effect coding
Fisher scoring
forward selection
Gamma
interaction
interaction plots
logistic regression analysis
logit transformation

main effects
model hierarchy
odds ratio
posterior probability
predictive modeling
redundancy
reference cell coding
relevancy
Schwarz Criterion (SC)
score chi-square statistic
scoring
Somer's D
stepwise selection
Tau-a
Wald test statistic

Chapter Quiz

1. Suppose the odds ratio for a 100-square-foot-increase in total basement area (TOTAL_BSMT_SF) is 1.284. This means that the
   a. probability of the event increases by 28.4%
   b. the odds of the event increases by 28.4%
   c. the logit increases by 128.4%
   d. the log-odds of the event increases by 71.6%

2. An assumption of logistic regression is:
   a. the outcome variable is linearly related to the predictors
   b. the residuals have a normal distribution
   c. the variance of the outcome is equal across all values of the predictor
   d. the logit is linear related to the predictors

3. What is the range of the logit function?
   a. $(-\infty, +\infty)$
   b. $[0, +\infty)$
   c. $[0,1]$
   d. $[1, +\infty)$

4. Suppose the predictor variable, FULLBATH_2PLUS, is a character variable coded as '1' if the house has two or more full bathrooms, or '0' if the house has only one full bathroom. You run a logistic regression to predict whether or not the agent earns a bonus (BONUS=0 for No; BONUS=1 for Yes). You get the following output. Which set of SAS statements would result in the following output?

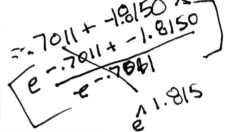

Class Level Information		
Class	Value	Design Variables
fullbath_2plus	0	1
	1	-1

Analysis of Maximum Likelihood Estimates					
Parameter		DF	Estimate	Standard Error	Wald Chi-Square	Pr > ChiSq
Intercept		1	-0.7011	0.0703	99.4285	<.0001
fullbath_2plus	0	1	-1.8150	0.0703	666.2498	<.0001

a. libname sasba 'c:\sasba\ames';
   data ames;
   set sasba.ameshousing;
   proc logistic data=ames;
   class Fullbath_2plus (param=ref);
   model Bonus (Event = '1')=Fullbath_2plus;
   run;

b. libname sasba 'c:\sasba\ames';
   data ames;
   set sasba.ameshousing;
   proc logistic data=ames;
   model Bonus (Event = '1')=Fullbath_2plus;
   run;

c. libname sasba 'c:\sasba\ames';
   data ames;
   set sasba.ameshousing;
   proc logistic data=ames;
   class Fullbath_2plus (param=effect ref=last);
   model Bonus (Event = '1')=Fullbath_2plus;
   run;

d. libname sasba 'c:\sasba\ames';
   data ames;
   set sasba.ameshousing;
   proc logistic data=ames;
   model Bonus (Event = '1')=Fullbath_2plus;
   run;

5. Consider the output provided in #4. What is the odds ratio when comparing houses with FULLBATH_2PLUS=1 versus FULLBATH_2PLUS=0?

   a. 0.027
   b. 37.713
   c. 0.163
   d. 6.141

6. Which of the following combinations of procedures, statements, and/or options for scoring new cases requires that the new cases must be scored at the same time the model is estimated?
    a. The SCORE statement within the PLM procedure
     b. The CODE statement within the LOGISTIC procedure
    c. The OUTMODEL and INMODEL options within the LOGISTIC procedure
    d. The SCORE statement within the PROC LOGISTIC procedure

7. Which of the following combination of procedures, statements, and/or options creates a SAS program for scoring new cases?
    a. The SCORE statement within the PLM procedure
    b. The CODE statement within the LOGISTIC procedure
    c. The OUTMODEL and INMODEL options within the LOGISTIC procedure
    d. The SCORE statement within LOGISTIC procedure

8. Suppose you want to find the best logistic regression model to predict an outcome, using main effects (A, B, C) and two-way interactions only. Which of the following sets of effects is possible when running a forward 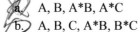 selection, backward elimination, or stepwise method of selection?
    a. A, B, A*B, A*C
    b. A, B, C, A*B, B*C
    c. B, C, A*B, B*C
    d. A*B, A*C, B*C

9. Suppose you conducted a logistic regression to assess the relationship between BONUS and the three predictors found in the following Analysis of Maximum Likelihood Estimates table. Which of the following effects would be removed from the model using a backward elimination with SLSTAY=0.01?
    a. High_Kitchen_Quality
    b. Overall_Condition
    c. Fullbath_2plus*Overall_Condition
    d. Overall_Condition*High_Kitchen_Quality

Analysis of Maximum Likelihood Estimates					
Parameter	DF	Estimate	Standard Error	Wald Chi-Square	Pr > ChiSq
Intercept	1	-3.6163	0.8082	20.0229	<.0001
Fullbath_2plus	1	2.8101	0.8858	10.0638	0.0015
Overall_Condition	1	0.2267	0.3001	0.5707	0.4500
Fullbath_2plus *Overall_Condition	1	0.0219	0.3352	0.0042	0.9480
High_Kitchen_Quality	1	3.7459	0.9669	15.0086	0.0001
Fullbath_2plus *High_Kitchen_Quality	1	0.5927	0.3888	2.3239	0.1274
Overall_Condition *High_Kitchen_Quality	1	-0.8036	0.3416	5.5334	0.0187

10. Suppose you conducted a logistic regression to assess the relationship between BONUS and the three predictors. Based upon the Testing Global Null Hypothesis table, which of the following is true?

    a. There is a significant reduction in the measures of fit for the model when compared to the intercept-only model.

    b. There is evidence that all three predictors are significantly related to Bonus.

    c. All odds ratio estimates are significantly different from 1.0.

    d. No effects would be eliminated in backward selection using SLSTAY=0.01.

Testing Global Null Hypothesis: BETA=0			
Test	Chi-Square	DF	Pr > ChiSq
Likelihood Ratio	933.2455	3	<.0001
Score	781.7884	3	<.0001
Wald	438.7907	3	<.0001

Chapter 11: Measure of Model Performance

Introduction

In Chapter 10, "Logistic Regression Analysis," the worth of a logistic regression model was based upon goodness of fit measures for assessing the extent to which the model fit the data at hand. When a logistic regression model is, instead, used for prediction, as is the case for **predictive modeling**, the emphasis shifts to measuring how well the model predicts outcomes, or classes, for future observations. In this sense, logistic regression falls under the general topic of classifier. A **classifier** is a derived rule that maps a set of inputs or predictors into one of two or more mutually exclusive classes. In the case of logistic regression, a prediction equation is derived using the set of inputs, and based upon the predicted posterior probability of being a success, the observation is classified into either the success class or the failure class. Other examples of classifiers are linear discriminant analysis, decision tree, nearest neighbor, and neural networks, to name a few. While this chapter specifically addresses topics related to logistic regression as a classifier, many of these topics apply to the assessment of other classifiers as well.

In this chapter, we first discuss partitioning the data in order to ensure an honest assessment of the classifier performance. We then introduce the confusion matrix and define performance measures for both the training and validation data, and discuss the naïve rule and the idea of validation as a way to determine the worth of a classifier. Next, we discuss how the classification matrix changes as the analyst changes the cutoff value and the development of the Receiver-Operating-Characteristic (ROC) Curve as a measure of performance for model selection. When the purpose of predictive modeling is targeting customers, we describe the use of gains and lift charts for determining how many customers to target to ensure a certain level of performance over the chance model. In practice, there are many situations where the event of interest is considered a rare event; therefore, a section is included which describes how to adjust the classification matrix, posterior probabilities, and performance measures when the analyst oversamples the rare event. Finally, this chapter describes a decision theory approach to determining the cutoff value needed to maximize the average expected profit when applying a classifier.

In this chapter, you will learn how to:

- explain supervised learning methods

- use techniques for honestly assessing classifier performance

- create a training and validation data set using PROC SURVEYSLECT

- explain the difference between validation data and test data

- explain the importance of performing data preparation before the data is split

- generate the confusion matrix using the CTABLE option and be able to explain the terms true negative (TN), true positive (TP), false negative (FN), and false positive (FP)

- define and calculate assessment measures using the confusion matrix, including accuracy, error rate, sensitivity, specificity, positive predicted value (PV+), negative predicted value (PV-), false positive rate (P_{F+}), and false negative rate (P_{F-})
- assess classifier performance using the confusion matrix
- explain the maximum-chance criterion, also known as the naïve rule
- validate a classifier by applying the SCORE statement to validation data
- explain the effects of cutoff value on both sensitivity and specificity
- explain the Receiver-Operating-Characteristic (ROC) curve and understand that it is an assessment measure independent of cutoff values
- create an ROC curve using the OUTROC option in the SCORE statement
- use the ROC statements to create a ROC curve for each model and an overlay plot of ROC curves for two or more models, including ROC statistics for each model
- use the ROCCONTRAST statement to provide the statistical test for comparing ROC curves to a reference curve
- explain the concept of depth and how it relates to cutoff and predicted values
- use depth to produce gains and lift charts and be able to interpret them
- develop a decision rule that maximizes expected profit
- define the profit matrix and how to use profit information to estimate the average profit per observation, or customer
- calculate decision cutoffs, given a profit matrix and using Bayes' rule
- create an average profit plot using PROC SGPLOT and to determine optimum cutoff values
- determine the model with the highest average profit, given a profit matrix and estimated model

Preparation for the Modeling Phase

Before the modeling process begins, the analyst must ensure the integrity and reliability of the results. The main objective of the analyst is to select a classifier that performs well when applied to future observations. In this section, we discuss the standard process for assessing classifier performance and provide some preliminary recommendations.

Honest Assessment of a Classifier

When a classifier is constructed and its performance is then assessed using the same data on which the classifier was constructed, there is an inherent overestimate in its performance. In other words, the classifier is built taking into account both legitimate patterns in the data and its random idiosyncrasies, and performs better on that data set as opposed to external observations. This issue is referred to as **overfitting** the model (Hand, 1983; McLachlan, 1977). When overfitting exists, it is unlikely that the model will generalize well to the population of interest.

In order to avoid overfitting and ensure an **honest assessment** of the classifier, an 'external' prediction error must be calculated by applying the classifier to new data--or scoring new data that was not used during the training process (Wujek, Hall, and Günes, 2016). In particular, the common practice is to split the available data into two parts before the modeling process begins. These two data sets are referred to as the training data and the validation data, respectively.

The **training data** set is the data set used to fit the classification model and is called such because it is 'trained' to represent the relationship between the outcome and the set of predictors. The **validation data** set has the same structure as the training data set with the known outcome variable and the set of predictors, but has no role in determining the model. In fact, the validation data set is handled as if it were a new data set. In practice, the classifier based upon the training data is applied to the validation data and performance measures are calculated to assess the extent to which the predicted outcomes 'match' the known outcomes for this 'external' data set. The proportion of mismatches in the validation data set provides an unbiased estimate of the error rate of the classifier when applied to future observations with unknown outcomes (Michie, et al., 1994). Note that any modeling process used to predict outcomes where the outcomes are known in advance is referred to as **supervised learning methods**.

In practice, assessment measures calculated on the validation data are used to select the final model from among many candidate models. The candidate models may be the result of testing various distributional assumptions, variable selection, or changing model parameters (such as the number of neighbors in *k*-nearest-neighbor classification, number of hidden layers or nodes for neural networks, etc.). Finally, it should be noted that the process of comparing candidate models using validation data also has inherent bias; therefore, the fully defined final model should be assessed using a third hold-out data set, referred to as the **test data** (Ripley, 1996).

PROC SURVEYSELECT for Creating Training and Validation Data Sets

In order to conduct predictive modeling, the analyst must first partition the data using **stratified random sampling**. In stratified random sampling, a data set is divided into groups, or **strata**, and observations are randomly selected from each of the strata.

In predictive modeling, the levels of the target variable make up the strata. So, consider a binary target variable. If the analyst is interested in creating a 70%-30% split of the data, corresponding to the training and the validation data sets, the analyst will randomly select 70% from the strata corresponding to target=0 and 70% of the strata corresponding to target=1 and place those observations into the training data set; the remaining 30% of the data from each strata will be placed into the validation data set.

The SURVEYSELECT procedure can be used to create various types of random samples. For purposes of data partitioning, we will describe how to perform stratified random sampling using the general form:

PROC SURVEYSELECT *<options>*;
STRATA *variables*;
RUN;

To illustrate the SURVEYSELECT procedure, consider the Ames Housing Case introduced in Chapter 1, "Statistics and Making Sense of Our World," where the analyst wants to predict whether or not a real estate agent earns a bonus in the sale of a house (target=BONUS). Here, the target variable, BONUS, has two levels (BONUS=0 and BONUS=1), with proportions 0.595 and 0.405, respectively. So, to create a 70%-30% data partition, 70% of the observations with BONUS=0 and 70% of the observations with BONUS=1 will be randomly selected and placed into the training data set; the remaining 30% will be placed in the validation data set. Program 11.1 Partitioning Ames Housing into Training and Validation Data Sets illustrates the data partition.

Program 11.1 Partitioning Ames Housing Data into Training and Validation Data Sets

```
libname sasba 'c:\sasba\ames';
data ames;
   set sasba.ameshousing;
run;

proc freq data=ames;
   tables bonus;
run;

proc sort data=ames out=amesort;
   by bonus;
run;

proc surveyselect data=amesort
   method=srs samprate=0.70 out=sampleames seed=12345 outall;
   strata bonus;
run;

data sasba.ames70;
   set sampleames;
   if selected=1;
   drop selected SamplingWeight SelectionProb;
run;

proc freq data=sasba.ames70; tables bonus;
    title '70 percent Sample of Ames Total - FileName = ames70';
run;

data sasba.ames30;
   set sampleames;
   if selected=0;
   drop selected SamplingWeight SelectionProb;
run;
```

```
proc freq data=sasba.ames30; tables bonus;
   title '30 percent Sample of Ames Total - Filename=ames30';
run;
```

The **sampling frame** is the list of houses, as found in the AMESHOUSING SAS data set, and is the data set to be partitioned. Before proceeding with the data partition, note that the SAS code requests a frequency distribution for the variable, BONUS, as illustrated in Output 11.1a PROC FREQ on Bonus for Ames Housing Data. Output 11.1a PROC FREQ on Bonus for Ames Housing Data shows a total of 1984 houses, where 59.48% did not result in a bonus and 40.52% resulted in a bonus.

Before the SURVEYSELECT procedure can be called, the data must be sorted by the strata, as shown in the SORT procedure. The new data, sorted by BONUS, is saved in the AMESORT temporary data set using the OUT= option.

Following the sort, the SURVEYSELECT procedure is applied to the AMESORT data set, where 70% of the data from each strata (BONUS=0 and BONUS=1) are sampled, as defined by the SAMPRATE=0.70 option and the STRATA statement. The METHOD=SRS option is the default method and requests that observations have an equal probability of being selected, without replacement. The SEED= option defines the starting point for the random number generator, and ensures that you generate the same random sample for a given set of procedural parameters each time that seed is used. Finally, the OUTALL option requests that all observations from the input data set (DATA=AMESORT) be saved in the temporary data set, SAMPLEAMES, as defined by the OUT= option; this data set contains all variables from the input data set, in addition to a variable called SELECTED, which is defined as 1 if the observation was selected for the sample, or 0 otherwise. If the OUTALL option had been omitted, only those observations selected would be retained for the training data set, and the remaining observations would not have been retained for the validation data set.

Once the SURVEYSELECT procedure is completed, the analyst is now interested in the SAMPLEAMES data set which contains all 1984 houses from the original data. The next two DATA steps now involve the actual partitioning of the original data set using the variable, SELECTED. In the first DATA step, 70% of the observations selected (by strata) for the training data set are placed into the permanent data set (AMES70) using the SET SAMPLEAMES statement and SELECT=1. In the second DATA step, 30% of the observations not selected will be placed into the permanent data set (AMES30), using the SET SAMPLEAMES statement and SELECT=0. As a result, the training data set (AMES70) has 1389 observations and the validation data set (AMES30) has 595 observations as displayed in Log 11.1 Partial Log for PROC SURVEYSELECT Using Ames Housing Data. The specific parameters of the SURVEYSELECT procedure are displayed in Output 11.1b PROC SURVEYSELECT Using Ames Housing Data.

Finally, note that the FREQ procedure is applied to each of the data sets (AMES70 and AMES30) to illustrate the percentages for each level of BONUS for both the training and validation data sets. In Output 11.1c PROC FREQ on Bonus for Ames Training and Validation Data, note that for all three data sets--the original, training, and validation data sets--approximately 59.5% did not result in a bonus and 40.5% resulted in a bonus. In short, we expect the population proportion of homes where the agent receives a bonus to be approximately 0.4050 and the population proportion of homes where the agent does not receive a bonus to be approximately 0.5950. These proportions are obviously reflected in the training and validation data sets. (Note: later in this chapter, we will discuss the need for oversampling of rare events, where the sample proportions do not reflect those in the population, followed by a discussion on how to make the necessary adjustments.)

Output 11.1a PROC FREQ on Bonus for Ames Housing Data

All Ames Housing Data
The FREQ Procedure

Bonus	Frequency	Percent	Cumulative Frequency	Cumulative Percent
0	1180	59.48	1180	59.48
1	804	40.52	1984	100.00

Output 11.1b PROC SURVEYSELECT Using Ames Housing Data

The SURVEYSELECT Procedure

Selection Method	Simple Random Sampling
Strata Variable	Bonus

Input Data Set	AMESORT
Random Number Seed	12345
Stratum Sampling Rate	0.7
Number of Strata	2
Total Sample Size	1389
Output Data Set	SAMPLEAMES

Output 11.1c PROC FREQ on Bonus for Ames Training and Validation Data

70 percent Sample of Ames Total - FileName = ames70

The FREQ Procedure

Bonus	Frequency	Percent	Cumulative Frequency	Cumulative Percent
0	826	59.47	826	59.47
1	563	40.53	1389	100.00

30 percent Sample of Ames Total - filename=ames30

The FREQ Procedure

Bonus	Frequency	Percent	Cumulative Frequency	Cumulative Percent
0	354	59.50	354	59.50
1	241	40.50	595	100.00

Log 11.1 Partial Log for PROC SURVEYSELECT Using Ames Housing Data

NOTE: There were 1984 observations read from the data set
    WORK.SAMPLEAMES.
NOTE: The data set SASBA.AMES70 has 1389 observations and
    103 variables.
...
NOTE: There were 1984 observations read from the data set
    WORK.SAMPLEAMES.
NOTE: The data set SASBA.AMES30 has 595 observations
    and 103 variables.

Recommendations for the Model Preparation Stage

There are some things to consider when preparing for the modeling stage. The first is the impact on overfitting due to both sample size and flexibility of the classifier. If the analyst fits a model using a relatively small data set, there is instability in the model selection process. In other words, over repeated random samples, the model selected very rarely replicates. As a result, we expect the performance of any model selected using a small sample to exhibit a breakdown in performance when applied to larger external data. In short, overfitting is the problem.

Consider now model flexibility. The more flexible the model, the higher the tendency to fit the specific peculiarities of the data and, as a result, a more flexible model is less likely to validate on external data. Overfitting becomes a real consideration when the analyst fits a more flexible model using less data. Therefore, the data analyst may require much larger data sets when using decision trees and other machine learning algorithms, as opposed to the less flexible logistic regression classifier, for example.

The number of inputs is also a source of overfitting. Specifically, an analyst can attempt to use many predictors and to pick the 'best' subset as a way to improve the performance of a model. In other words, extra information can be used to 'fit' specific details of the training data, so that the model performs poorly on the validation data. In fact, variable selection methods are very susceptible to overfitting and validation is imperative.

Note also that sample size becomes more of an issue when the data is partitioned and the smaller training data set is used for the modeling process. In this case, the analyst may opt for a 70-30 training-validation split, as opposed to a 50-50 split.

Another consideration is referred to as **information leakage**. This occurs when any information from a holdout data set 'leaks' into the training data set (Wujek, Hall, and Günes, 2016). As mentioned earlier in this section, the validation data set should be treated as if it were truly a new data set. Therefore, any methods used for data preparation should be done only on the training data set, after the split, so that the validation data set has no 'knowledge' of or influence on the patterns that exist in the training data set. After the data preparation process has been completed on the training data, those same rules should then be applied to the validation data set; otherwise, any model assessment using the validation data will have some inherent bias in the performance results.

For example, when applying the Greenacre method for collapsing levels of a categorical input variable, as discussed in Chapter 8, "Preparing the Input Variables for Prediction," the resulting cluster levels are determined based upon the relationship between the categorical input and the target variable of interest. So the cluster levels should be determined using the training data set only; otherwise if all of the data were included in the Greenacre analysis, the resulting cluster levels are based also upon the validation data and, consequently, more favorable performance measures would be obtained in the validation process.

While all data preparation methods involving the target variable should be applied only to the training data, there are some suggestions that data preparation which does not involve the target can be used on the entire data set. However, we argue here for a more conservative approach and make all data preparation decisions using training data only. In fact, the validation process itself can be a way of testing the value of decisions made in the data preparation stage as it applies to the training data.

Assessing Classifier Performance

When conducting statistical analyses and, specifically, fitting predictive models, it is natural to use statistical indices to measure model performance. These measures are used to both describe the worth of a model and provide a basis for model comparisons. In this section, we discuss the classification table, the receiver-operator-characteristic (ROC) curve, along with the gains and lift charts, as measures of classifier performance.

Measures of Performance Using the Classification Table

At a very basic level, the proportion of correct classification is a good measure of classifier **accuracy**. We refer to this proportion as the **hit rate**. There are two hit rates of interest. First, the **actual hit rate** is the proportion of observations correctly classified when applying a classifier rule based upon a specific sample to the population. This hit rate is usually unknown because population data is usually not available. As an alternative, the analyst relies on an estimate of hit rate, known as the **apparent hit rate**. The apparent hit rate is the proportion of sample observations correctly classified using the sample-specific classifier.

The apparent hit rate, referred hereafter as hit rate, is calculated using the **classification table**, sometimes referred to as the **confusion matrix**. The classification table, for a binary outcome variable, is a two-by-two frequency table of the actual class by the predicted class and has the general form, as displayed in Table 11.1 General Form of the Classification Table.

Table 11.1 General Form of the Classification Table

Actual CLASS	Predicted CLASS		
	0=NO (predicted negative)	1=YES (predicted positive)	
0=NO (actual negative)	Number of negatives correctly classified as negative (**TN**)	Number of negatives incorrectly classified as positive (**FP**)	Number of actual negatives in the data set (**TN+FP**)
1=YES (actual positive)	Number of positives incorrectly classified as negatives (**FN**)	Number of positives correctly classified as positives (**TP**)	Number of actual positives in the data set (**FN+TP**)
	Number of observations classified as negative = (**TN+FN**)	Number of observations classified as positive = (**FP+TP**)	Total number of cases in the data set (**TN+FN+FP+TP**)

In order to understand the various measures of performance, consider the entries in the classification table. The number of negatives correctly classified as negative is referred to as the number of **true negatives (TN)**; the number of positives correctly classified as positive is referred to as the number of **true positives (TP)**. The number of positives incorrectly classified as negative is referred to as the number of **false negatives (FN)**; the number of negatives incorrectly classified as positive is referred to as the number of **false positives (FP)**.

The two numbers, TP and TN (on the diagonal from upper-left to lower-right), represent the total number of correct classifications. These two numbers added together and divided by the total number of cases is a measure of accuracy and is referred to as the **hit rate.** It is represented by the formula:

$$\text{Hit rate} = \frac{TP+TN}{TN+FN+FP+TP} = Accuracy$$

The **error rate** is defined as:

$$\text{Error Rate} = 1 - \text{Hit rate} = \frac{FP+FN}{TN+FN+FP+TP}$$

Other measures of classifier performance involve the proportion of correct classifications for specific conditional events, which requires looking at either a single column or a single row. Consider, first, the success class, where the class outcome equals 1. Suppose, for example, you are interested in the performance of a classifier in terms of how well it correctly identifies the actual positive events. In this case, you would be interested only in the row representing the total number of positives (FN+TP). Therefore, the **sensitivity,** also referred to as **recall** or true positive rate, is the proportion of true positives out of the total number of actual positives. This proportion of positive cases correctly predicted to be positive is defined as:

$$\text{Sensitivity} = \frac{TP}{FN+TP}$$

Suppose, now, that the analyst is interested in looking at the observations predicted as positive (the column) to determine the proportion of true positives. That measure is called the **positive predicted value (PV+),** also referred to as **precision,** and is defined as:

$$PV+ = \frac{TP}{FP+TP}$$

While the analyst would like both of these measures (sensitivity and PV+) to be large, the existence of one does not guarantee the other. As the chapter unfolds, you will see that the purpose of the analysis drives the measure on which to place emphasis.

For example, if the analyst is interested in the actual positive event (the row), he or she would be more interested in sensitivity, which is the ability to correctly classify the 'actual' positive event. An example of this is in disease diagnosis, where the analyst is more interested in the accuracy associated with diagnosing the disease (the actual positive case) as opposed to the accuracy in diagnosing that no disease exists. The sensitivity would measure, of those positive patients who actually have the disease, the probability that the disease is detected.

Suppose, instead, that the analyst is more interested in the predicted positives (the column); consequently, he or she would be more interested in the positive predicted value (PV+). A good example is target marketing. Suppose an analyst is reviewing potential customers that were predicted to respond to an email solicitation to buy the company's product (a column, classified as a yes). He or she is interested to see, when those predicted positive customers are solicited, what proportion will respond (PV+).

Consider, now, the failure class, where the class outcome equals 0. Suppose you are interested in how well a classifier correctly identifies the actual negative events. You would be interested only in the row representing total number of negatives (TN+FP). So the **specificity**, also known as true negative rate, is the proportion of true negatives out of the total number of actual negatives. This proportion of negative cases correctly predicted as negative is defined as:

$$\text{Specificity} = \frac{TN}{TN+FP} \quad \text{True negative}$$

Suppose, instead, that the analyst is interested in looking at the observations predicted as negative (column) to determine the proportion of true negatives. That measure is called the **negative predicted value (PV-)** and is defined as:

$$\text{PV-} = \frac{TN}{TN+FN}$$

The CTABLE Option for Producing Classification Results

Consider the Ames Housing Case and the logistic regression model using just four predictors, for example. Program 11.2 Classification Tables for Ames Training and Validation Data Sets can be used to generate the classification table for both the training data set and the validation data set:

Program 11.2 Classification Tables for Ames Training and Validation Data Sets

```
libname sasba 'c:\sasba\ames';
data ames;
   set sasba.ames70;
run;

proc format;
   value $yesno '0'='NO' '1'='YES';
run;

proc logistic data=ames;
   model Bonus (Event = '1')= Gr_Liv_Area Total_Bsmt_SF Lot_Area
         Fullbath_2Plus / ctable pprob=.50;
   score data=sasba.ames30 out=pred_amesvalidation;
run;

proc freq data=pred_amesvalidation;
   tables f_bonus*i_bonus;
   format f_bonus i_bonus $yesno.;
   title 'Classification Table for Ames Validation Data';
run;
```

In the DATA step, the training data set, AMES70, is saved to the temporary data set AMES, and the LOGISTIC procedure is applied to that data using the MODEL statement; BONUS is defined as the response variable and the four predictors are GR_LIV_AREA, TOTAL_BSMT_SF, LOT_AREA, and FULLBATH_2PLUS. Note that the logistic regression model is not displayed here, although it will be produced by the LOGISTIC procedure.

The CTABLE option requests that observations are classified into the event of interest (BONUS=1) if the estimated posterior probability of the event exceeds a particular cutoff value; the cutoff is specified using the PPROB= option. Here we explicitly define a cutoff value of 0.50, which is the default, and the resulting classification table for the training data is shown in Output 11.2a Classification Table for Ames Training Data, and restructured in Table 11.2 Classification Table for Ames Training Data.

Note that the PPROB option can include either a single cutoff value or a list of cutoff values as long as the values are between 0 and 1. If the CTABLE option is not used the PPROB option will be ignored and no classification table will be displayed. If the CTABLE option is used with no PPROB option, classification tables will be displayed for a range of cutoff values, from the 0.00 to 1.00 in increments of 0.02, as we will see in the next section.

Finally, the classifier is applied to the validation data set, AMES30, using the SCORE statement and the predicted values are saved in a temporary file, PRED_AMESVALIDATION, as defined in the OUT= option. In the file of predicted values, F_BONUS represents the actual class (or the From BONUS group) and I_BONUS represents the predicted class (or the Into BONUS group). Note that an observation is classified into the class having the largest posterior probability as determined by the classifier. The FREQ procedure requests a classification table for the validation data, as displayed in Output 11.2b Classification Table for Ames Validation Data.

Output 11.2a Classification Table for Ames Training Data

	Classification Table								
	Correct		Incorrect		Percentages				
Prob Level	Event	Non-Event	Event	Non-Event	Correct	Sensi-tivity	Speci-ficity	False POS	False NEG
0.500	484	734	92	79	87.7	86.0	88.9	16.0	9.7

In both Output 11.2a Classification Table for Ames Training Data and Table 11.2 Classification Table for Ames Training Data, we can see that the number of true positives (TP) is 484, the number of true negatives (TN) is 734, the number of false positives (FP) is 92, and the number of false negatives (FP) is 79. Also the number of actual positives is 563 (484+79), the number of actual negatives is 826 (734+92), the number of predicted positives is 576 (484+92), and the number of predicted negatives is 813 (734+79). The row totals and column totals each add up to the total number of houses, 1389, as displayed in Table 11.2 Classification Table for Ames Training Data.

Table 11.2 Classification Table for Ames Training Data

	Predicted CLASS		
Actual CLASS	0=NO	1=YES	
0=NO	734 (TN)	92 (FP)	826
1=YES	79 (FN)	484 (TP)	563
	813	576	1389

Upon inspection of the classification table for the Ames Housing training data, we can see that the overall accuracy as measured by the hit rate is

$$\text{Hit rate} = \frac{734+484}{1389} = 0.8769 \quad \text{with Error Rate} = 1 - 0.8769 = 0.1231$$

Other training measures found in Output 11.2a Classification Table for Ames Training are:

$$\text{Sensitivity} = \frac{484}{563} = 0.8597 \quad \text{and} \quad \text{Specificity} = \frac{734}{826} = 0.8886.$$

Among the predicted classes (columns), the positive predicted value and negative predicted value are:

$$\text{PV+} = \frac{484}{576} = 0.8403 \quad \text{and} \quad \text{PV-} = \frac{734}{813} = 0.9028$$

Note also that among the predicted classes (column), the analyst can also calculate the proportion of incorrect decisions. Specifically, the false positive rate (P_{F+}) and the false negative rate (P_{F-}), as displayed in Output 11.2a Classification Table for Ames Training, are calculated as follows:

$$P_{F+} = \frac{92}{576} = 1 - \text{PV+} = 0.1597 \quad \text{and} \quad P_{F-} = \frac{79}{813} = 1 - \text{PV-} = 0.0972.$$

As always, classification performance should be assessed using the classification results of the validation data set, as displayed in Output 11.2b Classification Table for Ames Validation Data. Upon inspection, we can see that the overall accuracy as measured by the hit rate is

$$\text{Hit rate} = \frac{206+319}{595} = 0.8824 \quad \text{with Error Rate} = 1 - 0.8824 = 0.1176$$

Other validation measures are: $\text{Sensitivity} = \dfrac{206}{241} = 0.8548, \quad \text{Specificity} = \dfrac{319}{354} = 0.9011,$

and are listed as row percents in Output 11.2b Classification Table for Ames Validation Data. The performance measures listed as column percents are:

$$PV+ = \dfrac{206}{241} = 0.8548, \qquad PV\text{-} = \dfrac{319}{354} = 0.9011$$

$$P_{F+} = 1 - PV+ = 1 - 0.8548 = 0.1452 \qquad \text{and} \qquad P_{F-} = 1 - PV\text{-} = 1 - 0.9011 = 0.0989.$$

Output 11.2b Classification Table for Ames Validation Data

F_Bonus	I_Bonus		
Frequency Percent Row Pct Col Pct	NO	YES	Total
NO	319 53.61 90.11(Specificity) 90.11 (PV-)	35 5.88 9.89 14.52 (P_{F+})	354 59.50
YES	35 5.88 14.52 9.89 (P_{F-})	206 34.62 85.48 (Sensitivity) 85.48 (PV+)	241 40.50
Total	354 59.50	241 40.50 (depth)	595 100.00

It should be noted that it is a coincidence that both sensitivity and PV+ are identical and specificity and PV- are identical. This occurs because the number of actual positive cases (241) and the number of predicted positive cases (241) are the same; this, by default, means the number of actual negative cases (354) is identical to the number of predicted negative cases (354). This in practice will, more than likely, not happen.

Assessing the Performance and Generalizability of a Classifier

In order to assess the worth of a classifier, we must first establish a criterion for performance. To do this, we must ask the question: 'How well can we do in classifying observations if we know nothing about those observations?' In other words, how well can we classify observations if we have no predictors (i.e., no model)? With no information, we could simply classify all observations into the largest class and be correct a majority of the time. This criterion for performance is referred to as the **naïve rule**, or the **maximum chance criterion**.

Consider the Ames Housing Case, where the largest class of the target variable, BONUS, is the failure class. The proportion of the failure class (BONUS=0) is 0.5950; therefore, if we classify all houses as having no bonus earned, our proportion correct is 0.5950. Consequently, any predictive model worth using has to 'beat' the 0.5950 accuracy rate.

While the goal of the analyst is to ensure that the model beats the naïve rule, special attention should be paid to the issue of overfitting. As mentioned earlier, the analyst expects the training hit rate to be slightly larger than the validation hit rate. When the training and validation hit rates are relatively close, the model is said to validate, and is, therefore, expected to perform well when deployed for predicting future observations.

However, as the analyst continues to 'tweak' the model by fitting to the unique characteristics of the training data, thereby increasing the training hit rate, there will be a breakdown in the performance of the classifier when applied to the validation data, resulting in a decrease in the validation hit rate. Consequently, as the difference between the training and validation hit rates becomes larger, there is an increased chance that the model is overfit, and will, therefore, not generalize to future data. In this case, the model should be eliminated for consideration.

In conclusion, an acceptable model is one that validates and beats the naïve rule. When deciding among competing models, the models under consideration must first be acceptable--that is, validates and beats the naïve rule. Then the model that has the highest validation hit rate can be selected because it is expected to outperform the other models when deployed on future data.

It should be noted that all of the above calculations assume that the samples are randomly selected from the population and, as a result, the sample prior probabilities (p_0 and p_1) are unbiased estimates of the population prior probabilities (π_0 and π_1). Later, in this chapter, we will discuss the need for oversampling when the event of interest is considered rare. This requires stratified random sampling where the sample priors are not good estimates of population priors, and consequently, adjustments to some performance measures must be made.

The Effect of Cutoff Values on Sensitivity and Specificity Estimates

The previous discussion on accuracy measures assumes that the **cutoff** value for classifying an observation is 0.50. In other words, if the posterior probability of belonging to the success class is greater than 0.50, then the observation is classified into the success class; otherwise the observation is classified into the failure class. This rule assumes that overall accuracy is most important and ignores the fact that the analyst may be more interested in the accuracy in predicting one class over the other.

Once the model is specified, the analyst may be more interested in the accuracy of a specific class over the other. In this case, the analyst can define an alternative cutoff value. Consider the following example in banking, where the loan officer is interested in predicting whether or not a customer will default on a loan (class = 1 or 0, respectively) based upon customer characteristics (or predictors).

Suppose the loan officer wants to minimize risk. He or she would award a loan to a select few where there is relatively high confidence that the loan will be repaid. In other words, the loan officer would assume that most customers will default, and decides, therefore, to reduce the cutoff value. The loan officer could, for example, set the cutoff to 0.30, and as a result, the classification rule is:

If $P(1|X_1, X_2,\ldots X_k) > 0.30$, classified the observation into group 1 (default); otherwise group 0

Consequently, the threshold for determining risk is low, and as a result, the classifier will classify more observations into group 1 (i.e., the number of positive predicted will increase and the number of negative predicted will decrease); also all performance measures discussed previously will change.

Suppose, instead, the loan officer wants to give a loan to high risk customers. In other words, he or she wants to target a market on which no one else wants to take a chance. The loan officer could, for example, set the cutoff to 0.70, and use the classification rule:

If $P(1|X_1, X_2,\ldots X_k) > 0.70$, classified the observation into group 1 (default); otherwise group 0

In this case, the threshold for determining risk is high, and as a result, the classifier will classify more observations into group 0 (i.e., the number of negative predicted will increase and the number of positive predicted will decrease); again, all performance measures discussed previously will change.

Consider the Ames Housing Case and the same logistic regression model previously run using just four predictors. To obtain classification results for various cutoff values, the analyst can use the PPROB= option as displayed:

```
/ ctable pprob= 0.0 to 1.0 by 0.10;
```

As illustrated in Output 11.3 Classification Table for Multiple Cutoff Values for Ames Training Data, the numbers that make up the classification table are provided for cutoff values, 0.0 to 1.0 in increments of 0.10, respectively, along with the percentages of correct observations overall, sensitivity, specificity, false positives, and false negatives.

From the classification table, it is evident that as the cutoff increases, a smaller number of observations are classified into the success class (i.e., the positive predicted values decrease); consequently, both sensitivity and false positives decrease, while specificity and false negatives increase.

On the other hand, as the cutoff decreases, a larger number of observations are classified into the success class (i.e., the positive predicted values increase); consequently, sensitivity and false positives increase, while specificity and false negatives decrease.

Finally, note that when the goal is to increase either sensitivity or specificity, there is an associated loss of overall accuracy as measured by the hit rate. For example, as the cutoff decreases from 0.50 to 0.0, sensitivity increases to 100%, while accuracy drops to 40.5%; as the cutoff increases from 0.50 to 1.0, specificity increases to 100%, while accuracy drops to 59.5%.

Output 11.3 Classification Table for Multiple Cutoff Values for Ames Training Data

Prob Level	Correct		Incorrect		Percentages				
	Event	Non-Event	Event	Non-Event	Correct	Sensi-tivity	Speci-ficity	False POS	False NEG
0.000	563	0	826	0	40.5	100.0	0.0	59.5	.
0.100	549	580	246	14	81.3	97.5	70.2	30.9	2.4
0.200	539	649	177	24	85.5	95.7	78.6	24.7	3.6
0.300	525	679	147	38	86.7	93.3	82.2	21.9	5.3
0.400	511	713	113	52	88.1	90.8	86.3	18.1	6.8
0.500	484	734	92	79	87.7	86.0	88.9	16.0	9.7
0.600	458	754	72	105	87.3	81.3	91.3	13.6	12.2
0.700	412	779	47	151	85.7	73.2	94.3	10.2	16.2
0.800	353	796	30	210	82.7	62.7	96.4	7.8	20.9
0.900	262	815	11	301	77.5	46.5	98.7	4.0	27.0
1.000	0	826	0	563	59.5	0.0	100.0	.	40.5

Using this table, the analyst can then select the cutoff value that best fits the goal, while at the same time taking into account overall accuracy. To facilitate selection of the cutoff value, the analyst could plot the performance measures (overall accuracy, sensitivity, and specificity) by cutoff values as a way to select the cutoff value that meets the specific goal while at the same time taking into account overall accuracy, as displayed in Figure 11.1 Performance Measures by Cutoff Values for Ames Training Data.

Figure 11.1 Performance Measures by Cutoff Values for Ames Training Data

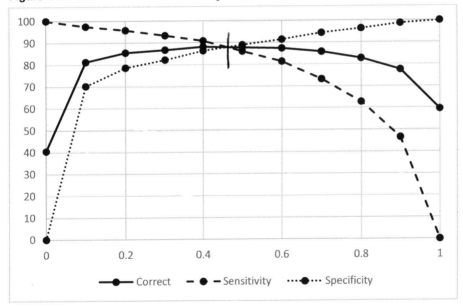

Suppose the goal of the analyst is to maximize sensitivity, and after reviewing the plot of performance measures, the analyst decides on a cutoff value of 0.20. Suppose then that the analyst is interested in validating the classification results for that cutoff. The analyst can request estimated posterior probabilities for each observation of the validation data using the SCORE statement, the observation can be assigned to a particular class based upon the cutoff value, and the resulting validation classification matrix can be produced. Consider, for example, a cutoff value of 0.20. Observations in the validation set can be classified using Program 11.3 Classification Table Using Cutoff=0.20 for Ames Validation Data.

Program 11.3 Classification Table Using Cutoff=0.20 for Ames Validation Data

```
libname sasba 'c:\sasba\ames';
data ames;
   set sasba.ames70;
run;

proc format;
  value $yesno '0'='NO' '1'='YES';
run;

proc logistic data=ames;
  model Bonus (Event = '1')= Gr_Liv_Area Total_Bsmt_SF Lot_Area
         Fullbath_2Plus / ctable pprob=.50;
  score data=sasba.ames30 out=pred_amesvalidation;
run;

data cutoff;
  set pred_amesvalidation;
  I_Bonus='0';
  if p_1 > 0.20 then I_Bonus='1';
run;

proc freq data=cutoff;
  tables f_bonus*i_bonus;
  format f_bonus i_bonus $yesno.;
run;
```

First, recall from Program 11.2 Classification Tables for Ames Training and Validation Data Sets, that the SCORE statement was used to score the validation data and the predicted values were saved in the temporary SAS data set called PRED_AMESVALIDATION. That same SAS code is included here. Those predicted values for each observation are read into the temporary SAS data set called CUTOFF, where the variable P_1 represents the posterior probability of being in CLASS=1, F_BONUS represents the actual class, and the predicted class (with variable name I_BONUS) is initialized at '0.'

To apply a cutoff of 0.20, the IF statement assigns the predicted class of 1 (I_BONUS='1') if the posterior probability is greater than 0.20, and the resulting classification table is produced using the FREQ procedure, as displayed in Output 11.4 Classification Table for Cutoff = 0.20 for Ames Validation Data.

Output 11.4 Classification Table for Cutoff = 0.20 for Ames Validation Data

Table of F_Bonus by I_Bonus			
F_Bonus	**I_Bonus**		
Frequency Percent Row Pct Col Pct	**NO**	**YES**	**Total**
NO	278 46.72 78.53 96.19	76 12.77 21.47 24.84	354 59.50
YES	11 1.85 4.56 3.81	230 38.66 95.44 75.16	241 40.50
Total	289 48.57	306 51.43	595 100.00

Using the classification matrix in Output 11.4 Classification Table for Cutoff = 0.20 for Ames Validation Data, the values for the performance measures can be calculated. For example, note that the validation sensitivity value is 230/241, or 95.4%, as compared to the training sensitivity value of 95.7%.

Note that the predicted class for the scored validation data is not influenced by the PPROB= option. Recall that the scored data is classified using the default cutoff of 0.50; therefore, Program 11.3 Classification Table Using Cutoff=0.20 for Ames Validation Data can be modified to use other cutoff values.

Measure of Performance Using the Receiver-Operator-Characteristic (ROC) Curve

As discussed in the previous section, the ability to detect the success or the failure (as measured by sensitivity and specificity, respectively) depends upon the cutoff value. The choice of a single cutoff--resulting is a single pair of values for sensitivity and specificity--may be insufficient to assess the overall performance of a classifier. In fact, in many situations, the value of the cutoff value may not be obvious and even difficult or impractical to choose. Consequently, the analyst may want to compare classifier performance using an index that takes into account many cutoff values simultaneously and is, therefore, independent of the cutoff value.

In order to interpret both sensitivity and specificity values for many cutoff values, it is common to represent the pairs of numbers graphically using a **Receiver-Operating-Characteristic (ROC) curve**. Here the y-axis is represented by the sensitivity and the x-axis is represented by 1 – specificity. The ROC curve is a tool that enables the analyst to select the model that simultaneously maximizes both sensitivity and specificity (which is equivalent to maximizing sensitivity and minimizing 1-specificity).

Consider for example, the previous model run for the Ames Housing Case using training data, where the cutoff is defined as 0.0 to 1.0 in .00 increments, with performance measures as displayed in Output 11.3 Classification Table for Multiple Cutoff Values for Ames Training Data. The values for sensitivity and (1-specificity) across the various cutoffs are displayed in the following ROC curve (Figure 11.2 ROC Curve for Ames Training Data).

Figure 11.2 ROC Curve for Ames Training Data

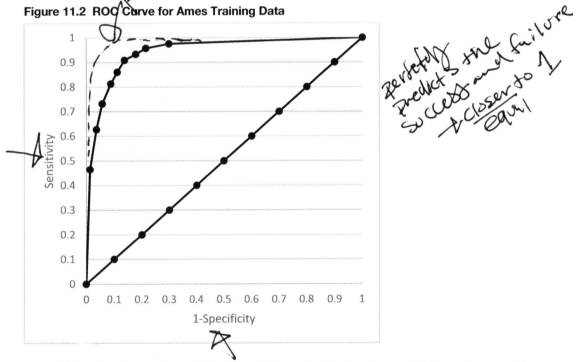

A model that simultaneously maximizes sensitivity and minimizes 1 – specificity produces points on a curve that are closer to (0,1). In other words, the model that performs well over all possible cutoff values has a curve that hovers closest to the upper left area, resulting in the largest area under the curve. So, if a model achieves higher sensitivity (as the cutoff increases), while the false positive percent (1-specificity) does not diminish rapidly, the curve will have a sharp increase, and an area approaching 1.0. In fact, the performance measure is referred to as **AUC**, or **area under the ROC curve**.

Note that a classifier which perfectly predicts the success and failure classes will have both sensitivity and specificity equal to 1. That is, all of the 1's are correctly classified as 1's and all of the 0's are correctly classified as 0's; as a result, the points (0,0), (0,1), and (1,1) make up the ROC curve having AUC equal to 1.0. On the other hand, a classifier that does not discriminate between the two classes, having no predictive power, has a diagonal line from the point (0,0) to the point (1,1), with AUC = 0.50, as displayed in Figure 11.2 ROC Curve for Ames Training Data. It should be noted that if, in reality, the AUC=1, then information leakage is probable.

Producing an ROC Curve Using the SCORE Statement with the OUTROC Option

It should be noted that there is bias in the estimates when using the training data set. Therefore, an ROC curve for the validation data should be produced, as well, for assessing the performance of the model. Furthermore, the area under the curve for both the training and validation data should be compared to assess the degree to which the model is overfitted.

The necessary information can be produced using Program 11.4 ROC Curves for Ames Housing Training and Validation Data.

Program 11.4 ROC Curves for Ames Housing Training and Validation Data

```
libname sasba 'c:\sasba\ames';
data ames;
   set sasba.ames70;
proc logistic data=ames;
  model Bonus (Event = '1')= Gr_Liv_Area Total_Bsmt_SF Lot_Area
        Fullbath_2Plus;
  score data=sasba.ames70 outroc=roctrain;
  score data=sasba.ames30 outroc=rocvalidation;
proc print data=rocvalidation (obs=10);
  var _prob_ _pos_ _neg_ _falpos_ _falneg_ _sensit_ _1mspec_;
run;
```

In Program 11.4 ROC Curves for Ames Housing Training and Validation Data, as before, the logistic regression model is fit to the training data and the first SCORE statement is used to score the training data set (AMES70). The OUTROC= option requests that all data pertinent to the ROC curve is produced and saved in a temporary SAS data set (ROCTRAIN); a training ROC curve is also produced, as displayed in Output 11.5a Training and Validation ROC Curves for Ames Housing Data. The second SCORE statement with the OUTROC= option requests the same for the validation data (AMES30), including a validation ROC curve, also displayed in Output 11.5a Training and Validation ROC Curves for Ames Housing Data.

Output 11.5a: Training and Validation ROC Curves for Ames Housing Data

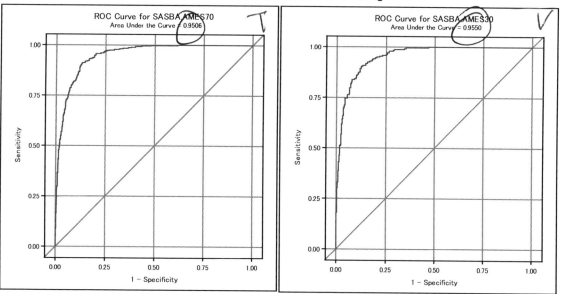

An inspection of the validation ROC curve and the AUC (0.9550) indicates that the model performs very well. Also, because the validation AUC (0.9550) is relatively close to the training AUC (0.9506), there seems to be no overfitting. In short, the model for predicting BONUS using the four predictors is a good model.

Finally, the PRINT procedure requests that ROC information be printed for the first ten observations from the temporary data set, ROCVALIDATION, by cutoff (_PROB_), as displayed in Output 11.5b ROC Information for Ames Validation Data:

Output 11.5b: ROC Information for Ames Validation Data

Obs	_PROB_	_POS_	_NEG_	_FALPOS_	_FALNEG_	_SENSIT_	_1MSPEC_
1	1.00000	1	354	0	240	0.004149	0
2	0.99999	2	354	0	239	0.008299	0
3	0.99999	3	354	0	238	0.012448	0
4	0.99987	4	354	0	237	0.016598	0
5	0.99984	5	354	0	236	0.020747	0
6	0.99977	6	354	0	235	0.024896	0
7	0.99969	7	354	0	234	0.029046	0
8	0.99959	8	354	0	233	0.033195	0
9	0.99944	9	354	0	232	0.037344	0
10	0.99933	10	354	0	231	0.041494	0

Model Comparison Using the ROC and ROCCONTRAST Statements

So far we have seen performance measures for determining if both a model validates and performs better than having no model as measured by the naïve rule. In the next section, we discuss the comparison of competing models. Specifically, the goal is to select the model that performs best as measured by the performance measures on the validation data, while at the same time balancing model simplicity (**parsimony**).

To illustrate the use of the ROC curve for model comparison, consider the Ames Housing Case. Recall in Chapter 10, "Logistic Regression Analysis," the results of both the forward and backward selection resulted in the model consisting of eight predictors. Let's now compare a model with nine predictors (the eight predictors selected in Chapter 10, in addition to the variable, Overall_Condition) to the reduced model consisting of four predictors, as referenced previously in this chapter. Consider Program 11.5 Comparing Two Models Using Validation ROC Curves for Ames Housing.

Program 11.5 Comparing Two Models Using Validation ROC Curves for Ames Housing

```
libname sasba 'c:\sasba\ames';
data ames;
   set sasba.ames70;
run;

proc logistic data=ames noprint;
   model Bonus (Event = '1')= Gr_Liv_Area Total_Bsmt_SF Lot_Area
        Fullbath_2Plus;
   score data=sasba.ames30 out=score_validation (rename=(p_1=p_4preds));
run;

proc logistic data=ames noprint;
    class Overall_Quality Overall_Condition /param=ref ref=first;
   model Bonus (Event = '1')= Gr_Liv_Area Total_Bsmt_SF Lot_Area
        Age_At_Sale High_Kitchen_Quality Overall_Quality
        Overall_Condition Fullbath_2Plus Fireplace_1Plus;
   score data=score_validation out=score_validation
        (rename=(p_1=p_9preds));
run;

proc logistic data=score_validation;
   model Bonus (Event = '1') = p_9preds p_4preds / nofit;
   roc "Nine Preds" p_9preds;
   roc "Four Preds" p_4preds;
   roccontrast "Comparing TWO Models";
run;
```

First, notice that the logistic regression model is run for the first model with four predictors, and then that model is applied to the validation data set using the SCORE statement. The scoring results are saved in the SCORE_VALIDATION temporary SAS data set, where the predicted posterior probability variable (P_1) is renamed

P_4PREDS. This data set has all information from the original validation data set (AMES30), in addition to the scoring information.

The second logistic regression model with nine predictors is run, and then that model is applied to the validation data set (now named SCORE_VALIDATION). Finally, the predicted posterior probability variable (P_1) is renamed P_9PREDS). In short, the validation data set now has the original information, along with scoring information for two models--the four-predictor model and nine-predictor model.

Finally, the last logistic regression is run on the validation data; the NOFIT option requests that no model is fitted. The ROC statements request ROC curves and define which models are to be compared using the ROCCONTRAST statement. The ROCCONTRAST statement requests the statistical tests for comparing the two models. The partial output generated is displayed in Output 11.6a ROC Curves for Two Models Applied to Ames Validation Data and Output 11.6b ROC Contrast Results for Two Models Applied to Ames Validation Data.

Output 11.6a: ROC Curves for Two Models Applied to Ames Validation Data

From the area under the validation ROC curve for both models, it is evident that both models perform very well in terms of predicting the bonus status of a house. It also appears that the model with nine predictors, (AUC=0.9800), performs better than the model with four predictors (AUC=0.9550). However, the contrasts results, as displayed in Output 11.6b ROC Contrast Results for Two Models Applied to Ames Validation Data, can be used to test for statistically significant differences. The areas under the curve, referred to as the c-statistic, for both models are provided, along with their standard errors and confidence intervals. The chi-squared test, with p-value less than 0.0001, suggests evidence that the curves are significantly different if applied to the population. Note also that the confidence intervals do not overlap, also indicating evidence of significant differences. In short, the data supports the conclusion that the model with nine predictors is better than that with four predictors.

Output 11.6b: ROC Contrast Results for Two Models Applied to Ames Validation Data

ROC Association Statistics							
	Mann-Whitney						
ROC Model	Area	Standard Error	95% Wald Confidence Limits		Somers' D	Gamma	Tau-a
Nine Preds	0.9800	0.00441	0.9714	0.9887	0.9601	0.9601	0.4635
Four Preds	0.9550	0.00747	0.9404	0.9697	0.9101	0.9101	0.4394

ROC Contrast Test Results			
Contrast	DF	Chi-Square	Pr > ChiSq
Comparing TWO Models	1	18.1348	<.0001

Measures of Performance Using the Gains and Lift Charts

The measures of model performance illustrated so far include overall accuracy, sensitivity, specificity, and the area under the ROC curve (AUC). These measures are used for either overall accuracy or the accuracy in predicting either actual positives (sensitivity) or actual negatives (specificity), where the actual classes are displayed as rows in the classification matrix.

Suppose, instead, that the analyst is more interested in targeting those observations that are most likely to have the outcome of interest (Y=1), that is, those observations with the highest posterior probability of being in the class of interest. Specifically, the analyst is more interested in the predicted positive observations, as displayed as a column in the classification matrix. When the goal is **targeting** observations, the appropriate measures of performance, related to the predicted positive cases, include the **lift chart** and **gains charts**.

In this discussion of lift and gains, we refer to the observations belonging to the event of interest as responders. The analyst will use a model to rank observations by their **propensity**, or posterior probability, of being a responder and select the top proportion of that list for targeting (thereby defining a cutoff). If the classifier performs well, then the analyst would expect a larger number of true responders than obtained had a random sample been selected instead.

The Gains Chart

A **gains chart** is a data visualization tool that compares the ability of the classifier to capture the true responders (Y=1) when selecting the top proportion of the data sorted by propensity to the ability to capture true responders obtained by random chance (referred to as the baseline).

The gains chart is simply a plot of the proportion of positive predicted values (PV$^+$) by depth across all cutoff values. Consider the following facts that go into constructing the gains chart.

1. The **depth** of a classifier is the proportion of observations classified as responders; in short, it is the proportion of predicted positive observations out of the entire data set. The depth is equal to the number of false positives plus the number of true positives divided by the total sample size. (depth = (TP+FP)/n; see Table 11.1 for TP and FP in the classification matrix.) Note that the depth is determined by the cutoff value.

2. Recall from the previous section, that as cutoff decreases, the number of observations classified as responders increases; in other words, as cutoff decreases, depth increases until it reaches the actual response rate (π_1). Specifically, if the cutoff is 0.0, then all observations are classified as responders (TP+FP = n), depth = 1.0, and the proportion of positive predicted values is equal to actual response rate (π_1).

3. The analyst obviously wants the biggest bang for the buck when targeting. In other words, as the depth decreases (i.e., as fewer observations are selected), the analyst hopes for an increase in the response rate as measured by the proportion of positive predicted values.

Consider now, for example, the Ames Housing Case where the logistic regression model is used to predict BONUS as a function of four predictors. Program 11.6 Gains Information for Ames Validation Data can be used to generate the gains chart for the validation data set:

Program 11.6 Gains Information for Ames Validation Data

```
libname sasba 'c:\sasba\ames';
proc format;
  value $yesno '0'='NO' '1'='YES';
run;

data ames70;
   set sasba.ames70;
data ames30;
   set sasba.ames30;
run;

proc logistic data=ames70 noprint;
   model Bonus (Event = '1')= Gr_Liv_Area Total_Bsmt_SF Lot_Area
          Fullbath_2Plus;
```

```
   score data=ames30 out=pred_amesvalidation outroc=roc;
run;

data gains;
   set roc;
   cutoff=_prob_; pi1=0.4053;
   tp_prop = pi1*_sensit_;  fp_prop = (1-pi1)*_1mspec_;
   depth = tp_prop + fp_prop;
   pv_plus = tp_prop / depth;
   lift = pv_plus / pi1;
run;

proc print data=gains;
   var cutoff pi1 _sensit_ _1mspec_ tp_prop fp_prop depth pv_plus lift;
run;

proc sgplot data=gains;
   where 0.000 < depth < 1.00;
   series y = pv_plus x = depth;
   refline pi1 /axis=y;
   refline 0.10 /axis=x;
   xaxis values=(0 to 1.0 by 0.10);
run;
```

As seen in Program 11.6 Gains Information for Ames Validation Data, the logistic regression model is fit using the training data set, AMES70, and that model is used to score the validation data set (AMES30) as requested in the SCORE statement; the ROC information for each cutoff (_PROB_) value is saved in a temporary SAS data set (called ROC) as requested using the OUTROC= option.

The ROC data set is then placed into the temporary SAS data set (called GAINS) using the SET statement and the appropriate statistics are calculated for generating the lift curve. A partial printout of the information is displayed in Output 11.7a Gains Information for Ames Validation Data. The SGPLOT procedure is applied to the GAINS data to produce the gains chart, which shows the relationship between depth and the positive predicted values (PV+), as displayed in Output 11.7b Gains Chart for Ames Validation Data.

Output 11.7a Gains Information for Ames Validation Data

Obs	cutoff	pi1	_SENSIT_	_1MSPEC_	tp_prop	fp_prop	depth	pv_plus	Lift
1	1.00000	0.4053	0.00415	0.00000	0.00168	0.00000	0.00168	1.00000	2.46731
...									
59	0.96893	0.4053	0.24066	0.00282	0.09754	0.00168	0.09922	0.98307	2.42553
...									
119	0.87671	0.4053	0.46888	0.01695	0.19004	0.01008	0.20012	0.94963	2.34303
...									
179	0.73656	0.4053	0.69295	0.03390	0.28085	0.02016	0.30101	0.93303	2.30207
...									
238	0.51441	0.4053	0.84647	0.09605	0.34308	0.05712	0.40019	0.85727	2.11516
...									
297	0.26080	0.4053	0.94606	0.19492	0.38344	0.11592	0.49935	0.76787	1.89904
...									
592	0.00012	0.4053	1.00000	1.00000	0.40530	0.59470	1.00000	0.40530	1.00000

From Program 11.6 Gains Information for Ames Housing Data and Output 11.7a Gains Information for Ames Validation Data, we can see that the proportion of true positives (TP_PROP) and the proportion of false positives (FP_PROP) is calculated using the proportion of actual positives ($p_1 = 0.4053$) along with sensitivity and (1-specificity), respectively. The depth, which is the proportion of predicted positives out of the total data set is just the sum of the proportions of true positives and false positives. Finally, the proportion of responders out of the total number of predicted positive observations (PV+) is defined to be PV_PLUS.

From the gains chart in Output 11.7b Gains Chart for Ames Validation Data, we can see that PV+ (the proportion of responders out of the total predicted) is in the 0.90 range through a depth of 0.30. Specifically, in line 59, if a cutoff value (0.96893) is set so that the analyst targets the top 10% based upon propensity (depth ~ 0.10), it is expected that approximately 98% of those targeted will result in a bonus (PV_PLUS = 0.98307). Note that at a depth of about 0.10, the proportion of responders (.98307) is found where the vertical reference line crosses the gains line.

Also, note, that if every house is targeted (cutoff ~ 0, depth=1.0), we expect 40.53% to result in a bonus (which corresponds to the proportion of bonuses earned in the entire data set), as indicated by the horizontal reference line in Output 11.7b Gains Chart for Ames Validation Data and the last line of the listing in Output 11.7a Gains Information for Ames Validation Data.

Output 11.7b Gains Chart for Ames Validation Data

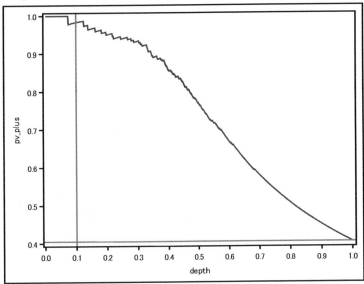

The Lift Chart

Another tool for measuring performance of a classifier for purposes of targeting observations is the **lift chart**. **Lift** is the ratio of the performance of the classifier to the performance obtained by chance and is calculated over all values of depth (or cutoff). Lift is defined as follows:

$$\text{Lift} = PV+ / \pi_1$$

and can be found in Output 11.7a as a function of cutoff (and depth). So, for a particular depth, if lift has a value of 2.0, by algebra, we get: proportion of PV+ = 2 π_1. In other words, at that depth, the classifier will obtain 2 times as many responders as that obtained by random sampling (chance).

Note that the lift chart is the result of adjusting the gains chart by a constant ($1/\pi_1$), and as result, the lift and gains charts have the same general shape. The following lines of SAS code can be appended to the Program 11.6 Gains Information for Ames Validation Data, where the SGPLOT procedure is called to produce the lift chart, as displayed in Output 11.8 Lift Chart for Ames Validation Data.

```
proc sgplot data=gains;
  where 0.000 < depth < 1.00;
  series y = lift x = depth;
  refline 1.0 /axis=y;
  refline 0.10 /axis=x;
  xaxis values=(0 to 1.0 by 0.10);
run;
```

Output 11.8 Lift Chart for Ames Validation Data

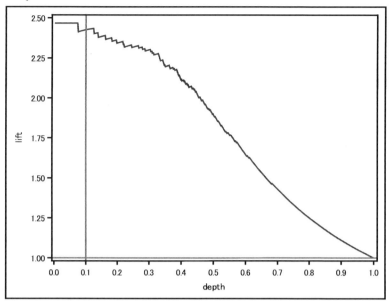

As before, if the analyst sets a cutoff value (0.96893) so that the top 10% of houses is targeted (depth ~ 0.10 as shown by the vertical reference line), the lift is approximately 2.4 (see 2.42553 in Output 11.7a Gains Information for Ames Validation Data). In short, at that depth, the classifier will obtain 2.43 times as many bonuses (98.307%) as that obtained by random sampling (40.53%).

Adjustment to Performance Estimates When Oversampling Rare Events

In general, the hit rate is an acceptable measure of accuracy when the classes have similar sample sizes (Chawla, N.V., 2010). In many classification problems, however, this is not the case. When data is imbalanced--that is, when the sample size for one class is significantly larger than that of the other class--classification methods tend to have a higher degree of accuracy for the larger class and a smaller degree of accuracy for the smaller class (He and Garcia, 2009).

Consider the situation where the negative cases (Y=0) represent the larger class. The overall accuracy is driven by the larger class (the non-event) and reflects little information about the smaller class (Y=1) which is usually the class of interest. For example, if 95% of a data set consists of the larger class, a classifier would have 95% accuracy if all observations were assigned to the larger class, but would ignore the fact that all observations in the smaller class are incorrectly classified (specificity=1.0 and sensitivity=0).

It turns out that the problem of 'rare events' is related to the bias in the maximum likelihood estimates, specifically, because the sample size of the rarer event is small (Allison, 2012; King and Zeng, 2001). Many sampling approaches have been proposed to combat the problem of imbalanced data (Chawla, N.V., 2010). Here we will discuss and illustrate the use of the oversampling of rare events.

Oversampling basically requires that the analyst take a stratified sample where more cases are selected from the strata representing the rare event (Y=1) and fewer cases are selected from the strata representing the common event (Y=0) so that the two respective samples sizes are somewhat balanced.

When conducting classification analyses, it is assumed that the sample is selected randomly, and consequently, for sufficiently large sample sizes, the sample prior probabilities for events 0 and 1, p_0 and p_1, are unbiased estimates of the population priors, π_0 and π_1, respectively.

In the case of oversampling, or stratified sampling, however, the sample prior probabilities are not random and are not adequate estimates of the population prior probabilities. Because estimated prior probabilities are used to calculate the intercept of the logit, the intercept is also biased. As a result the estimated intercept must be adjusted, or shifted by a constant, referred to as the **offset**. The offset is defined as follows:

$$offset = ln\left(\frac{p_1 \pi_0}{p_0 \pi_1}\right)$$

and the unadjusted logit (Scott and Wild, 1991) is:

$$Logit(p_i^*) = \beta_0^* + \beta_1 X_1 + \cdots + \beta_k X_k$$

where the unbiased intercept, β_0 is equal to $(\beta_0^* - offset)$, p_i^* is the posterior probability of the biased sample, p_0 and p_1 are the sample priors for classes 0 and 1, respectively, for the biased sample, and π_0 and π_1 are the population priors for classes 0 and 1, respectively. In fact, in the case of oversampling where $p_1 > \pi_1$ and $p_0 < \pi_0$, the natural log (offset) is positive. As a result, the intercept is overestimated and the logit is too large.

If the analyst chooses to ignore the offset in the modeling stage, the **adjusted estimated posterior probabilities**, $\hat{p}_i$, can be calculated directly from the unadjusted—biased--estimate of the posterior probabilities, $\hat{p}_i^*$, using the following:

$$\hat{p}_i = \frac{\hat{p}_i^* p_0 \pi_1}{(1 - \hat{p}_i^*) p_1 \pi_0 + \hat{p}_i^* p_0 \pi_1}$$

The PEVENT Option for Defining Prior Probabilities

Because the sample prior probabilities do not reflect the population prior probabilities, the analyst can define the population prior probabilities using the PEVENT option. Consider the Ames Housing Case as illustrated earlier where the analyst is interested in developing a logistic regression model using just four predictors. Suppose also, for example, that the sample is selected from a population where only 2% of agents receive a bonus and 98% do not receive a bonus when selling a house. Finally, suppose, for illustration purposes only, that the AMES70 training data was created as a result of oversampling, where 59.47% of the homes sampled result in no bonus upon the sale ($p_0 = 0.5947$) and 40.53% of the homes sampled do result in a bonus ($p_1 = 0.4053$). As a result, the sample priors do not reflect the population priors. Therefore, Program 11.7 Use of PEVENT Option to Define Prior Probabilities can be used to set the population priors and automatically adjust the performance measures:

Program 11.7 Use of PEVENT Option to Define Prior Probabilities

```
libname sasba 'c:\sasba\ames';
data ames70;
   set sasba.ames70;
run;

data ames30;
   set sasba.ames30;
run;

proc logistic data=ames70
   model Bonus (Event = '1')= Gr_Liv_Area Total_Bsmt_SF Lot_Area
         Fullbath_2Plus / ctable pprob=0.50 pevent= 0.02 0.4053;
   score data=ames30 out=pred_adj_validation priorevent=0.02;
run;
```

Notice in Program 11.7 Use of PEVENT Option to Define Prior Probabilities that the CTABLE option is included and requests that a classification table be provided. The PPROB=0.50 option requests classification results for a cutoff value of 0.50; note that this is the default setting. The PEVENT option defines two population posterior probabilities, namely, 0.02 and 0.4053, for creating two different classification tables. The value 0.02 assumes that the true population prior probability of the event of interest (Y=1) is 0.02, and differs from the sample prior because of oversampling; here, the sample prior (p_1) is not a good estimate of π_1, and the analyst must define $\pi_1 = 0.02$. The use of 0.4053 is equivalent to the default which assumes that the population prior probability of the event of interest (Y=1) is identical to the sample proportion--which is the case for random sampling (note that we are using pevent=0.4053 illustrating the default setting where PEVENT is not used).

The SCORE statement is used to score and save adjusted posterior probabilities (in the temporary SAS data set, PRED_ADJ_VALIDATION) and will be described later in this section. The results are found in Output 11.9a The Logistic Regression Model for Ames Training Data and Output 11.9b Classification Table for PEVENT = 0.02 and PEVENT = 0.4053.

Output 11.9a The Logistic Regression Model for Ames Training Data

			Analysis of Maximum Likelihood Estimates		
Parameter	DF	Estimate	Standard Error	Wald Chi-Square	Pr > ChiSq
Intercept	1	-10.5496	0.6389	272.6451	<.0001
Gr_Liv_Area	1	0.00343	0.000325	111.4009	<.0001
Total_Bsmt_SF	1	0.00255	0.000290	77.1269	<.0001
Lot_Area	1	0.000073	0.000020	12.8995	0.0003
Fullbath_2plus	1	2.4275	0.2085	135.4892	<.0001

In Output 11.9a The Logistic Regression Model for Ames Training Data, we illustrate the fact that the model is not affected by the PEVENT option. While the intercept is biased, the parameters estimates for the predictors remain unchanged, as do the odds-ratios, and are representative of the relationship between the predictors and the target variable (BONUS). (Note that this model is identical to the four-predictor model used for scoring previously.)

Output 11.9b Classification Table for PEVENT = 0.02 and PEVENT = 0.4053

		Classification Table								
		Correct		Incorrect		Percentages				
Prob Event	Prob Level	Event	Non-Event	Event	Non-Event	Correct	Sensi-tivity	Speci-ficity	False POS	False NEG
0.020	0.500	484	734	92	79	88.8	86.0	88.9	86.4	0.3
0.405	0.500	484	734	92	79	87.7	86.0	88.9	16.0	9.7

In Output 11.9b Classification Table for PEVENT=0.02 and PEVENT=0.4053, notice that there are classification numbers for both PEVENT equal to 0.02 and 0.4053, respectively, as indicated by the Prob Event Column. Each of those are provided for the Prob Level of 0.50 as requested by the PPROB. Note also that the second row (PEVENT = 0.4053) corresponds to the default and has numbers identical to those found in Output 11.2a Classification Table for Ames Training.

The first line, with PEVENT = 0.02, corresponds to the scenario where we know that the actual probability of the event of interest, π_1, is 0.02 and not represented by p_1, having a value of 0.4053, because of oversampling. Notice that sensitivity and specificity are the same for both values of PEVENT, 0.02 and 0.4053, because these numbers are calculated for each group separately and do not take into account the prior probabilities. Furthermore, because the sensitivity and specificity values remain unchanged, the ROC curve needs no adjustment. Finally, the frequencies that make up the classification table remain unchanged and correspond to the default results where PEVENT is not used.

However, when oversampling is used, the probabilities for both false positives and false negatives must be computed using Bayes' theorem which takes into account the true prior probabilities (Fleiss, 1981). First consider a version of Table 11.2 Classification Table for Ames Housing Data as represented in Table 11.3 Classification Table for Ames Housing Training Data Labeled for Bayes' Theorem.

Table 11.3 Classification Table for Ames Housing Training Data Labeled for Bayes' Theorem

	Predicted CLASS		
Actual CLASS	0=NO (A^C)	1=YES (A)	
0=NO (B^C)	734	92	826
1=YES (B)	79	484	563
	813	576	1389

In the table, the events A and A^C correspond to the predicted class equal to YES and NO, respectively; the events B and B^C correspond to the actual class equal to YES and NO, respectively. It turns out that the false positive (P_{F+}) and false negative (P_{F-}) rates must be calculated using the true prior probabilities and Bayes' theorem (Fleiss, 1981) as follows:

$$P_{F+} = P(B^c|A) = \frac{P(A|B^C)[1-P(B)]}{P(A|B^C)+P(B)[P(A|B)-P(A|B^C)]} = \frac{\left(\frac{92}{826}\right)(1-0.02)}{\left(\frac{92}{826}\right)+0.02\left[\left(\frac{484}{563}\right)-\left(\frac{92}{826}\right)\right]} = 0.8639 \sim 86.4\%$$

$$P_{F-} = P(B|A^C) = \frac{[1-P(A|B)]P(B)}{1-P(A|B^C)-P(B)[P(A|B)-P(A|B^C)]} = \frac{\left(1-\frac{484}{563}\right)(0.02)}{1-\left(\frac{92}{826}\right)-0.02\left[\left(\frac{484}{563}\right)-\left(\frac{92}{826}\right)\right]} = 0.0032 \sim 0.3\%$$

where the true prior probabilities are $\pi_1 = P(B) = 0.02$ and $\pi_0 = P(B^C) = 0.98$, respectively. Also, PV+ = 1 - P_{F+} and PV- = 1 - P_{F-}. When oversampling is used, the proportion of correct classifications, or hit rate, must also be calculated taking into account the true prior probabilities as follows:

hit rate = π_1(sensitivity) + π_0(specificity) = (0.02)(0.8597) + (0.98)(0.8886) = 0.8880 $\sim$ 88.8%

These adjusted values are all found in Output 11.9b Classification Table for PEVENT=0.02 and PEVENT=0.4053.

Manual Adjustment of the Classification Matrix

Finally, in order to report a classification table that reflects the true population prior probabilities, the classification table obtained with oversampling must be adjusted. Using the sensitivity, specificity, and population prior probabilities, the entries of the adjusted classification table are calculated using the formulae displayed in Table 11.4 General Classification Table Adjusted for Oversampling as follows:

Table 11.4 General Classification Table Adjusted for Oversampling

Actual CLASS	Predicted CLASS		
	0=NO	1=YES	
0=NO	$n \cdot \pi_0$(specificity)	$n \cdot \pi_0$(1-specificity)	$n \cdot \pi_0$
1=YES	$n \cdot \pi_1$(1-sensitivity)	$n \cdot \pi_1$(sensitivity)	$n \cdot \pi_1$
			N

where $n \cdot \pi_0$(specificity)   = 1389(0.98)(0.8886)   = 1209.6
$n \cdot \pi_0$(1-specificity) = 1389(0.98)(1-0.8886) = 151.6
$n \cdot \pi_1$(1-sensitivity) = 1389(0.02)(1-0.8597) = 3.9
$n \cdot \pi_1$(sensitivity)   = 1389(0.02)(0.8597)   = 23.9

The following classification table is obtained for Ames Training data when the adjustments are applied, as displayed in Table 11.5 Classification Table for Ames Housing Training Data Adjusted for Oversampling.

Table 11.5 Classification Table for Ames Housing Training Data Adjusted for Oversampling

Actual CLASS	Predicted CLASS		
	0=NO	1=YES	
0=NO	1210	151	1361 (0.98)
1=YES	4	24	28 (0.02)
	1214	175	1389

Note that table entries have been rounded so that all numbers add to 1389.

When the classification matrix has been adjusted, the values of the adjusted performance measures can be obtained directly from the matrix, without having to apply the complicated Bayes' formula. For example,

Hit rate = (1209.6 + 23.9)/1389 = 0.8880

$$P_{F+} = \frac{151.6}{(151.6+23.9)} = 0.8638 \qquad \text{and} \qquad P_{F-} = \frac{3.9}{(1209.6+3.9)} = 0.0032$$

Note that decimal values for frequencies were used to eliminate rounding differences. Finally, it is important to point out that in the case where PEVENT=0.4053 (i.e., where the analyst defines the population priors so that they are identical to the sample priors), the formula using Bayes' theorem with $P(B) = 0.4053 = \pi_1$ reduces to using counts as illustrated in Output 11.2a Classification Table for Ames Housing Training Data. This is also equivalent to the default where PEVENT is not used.

Scoring the Validation Data Using Adjusted Posterior Probabilities

When the analyst oversamples for rare events, there are several ways to obtain the adjusted posterior probabilities in order to score new data. Here we will illustrate, with the Ames Housing Case, three equivalent ways to score our validation data set using: (1) the formula to manually adjust the posterior probabilities, (2) the offset to obtain the unbiased intercept, and (3) the PEVENT option to automatically adjust for oversampling. The model to be used is the same logistic regression model using four predictors applied to the training data set (AMES70), and the goal is to score the validation data (AMES30).

Manually Adjusting Posterior Probabilities to Account for Oversampling

Recall, previously, that if the analyst chooses to ignore the offset in the modeling stage and instead fits a logistic regression model without taking into account oversampling, then adjusted posterior probabilities can be calculated directly for purposes of classification. This approach requires that the analyst know in advance the population priors, π_0 and π_1; the values of the sample priors, p_0 and p_1, are calculated from the data. Consider Program 11.8 Posterior Probabilities Manually Adjusted for Oversampling:

Program 11.8 Posterior Probabilities Manually Adjusted for Oversampling

```
libname sasba 'c:\sasba\ames';
data ames70;
   set sasba.ames70;
run;

data ames30;
   set sasba.ames30;
run;

proc format;
   value $yesno '0'='NO' '1'='YES';
run;

proc logistic data=ames70;
   model Bonus (Event = '1')= Gr_Liv_Area Total_Bsmt_SF Lot_Area
         Fullbath_2Plus;
   score data=ames30 out=pred_amesvalidation;
run;

data adjust;
   set pred_amesvalidation;
   pi1=.02; pi0=0.98; p1=0.4053; p0=0.5947;
   man_adj_p_1 = (p_1*(p0*pi1))/((1-p_1)*p1*pi0+p_1*p0*pi1);
   if man_adj_p_1 > .50 then i_bonus='1';
   if man_adj_p_1 <= .50 then i_bonus='0';
run;

proc freq data=adjust;
   tables f_bonus*i_bonus;
   format f_bonus i_bonus $yesno.;
run;
```

Again, the logistic regression model is fit using the training data set and the SCORE statement with the OUT=PRED_AMESVALIDATION option is used to save the validation data. This temporary SAS data set is saved to a data set called ADJUST using the SET statement. This data set contains the saved, unadjusted, posterior probabilities (P_1) for each observation, the actual class (F_BONUS), and the predicted class using unadjusted posterior probabilities (I_INTO).

In the DATA step, the analyst must define the values of the population prior probabilities, defined as pi0 and pi1, respectively; from the data, we know that p0=0.5947 and p1=0.4053. The next statement in the DATA step defines the adjusted posterior probability (MAN_ADJ_P_1) using the unadjusted posterior probability (P_1). Finally the DATA step reassigns the predicted class (I_BONUS) using the adjusted posterior probabilities (MAN_ADJ_P_1) and applying the

0.50 cutoff value. The results are summarized using the FREQ procedure, as displayed in Output 11.10 Classification Table for Ames Housing Validation Data Adjusted for Oversampling.

Output 11.10 Classification Table for Ames Housing Validation Data Adjusted for Oversampling

Table of F_Bonus by I_Bonus			
F_Bonus	**I_Bonus**		
Frequency **Percent** **Row Pct** **Col Pct**	**NO**	**YES**	**Total**
NO	353 59.33 99.72 65.74	1 0.17 0.28 1.72	354 59.50
YES	184 30.92 76.35 34.26	57 9.58 23.65 98.28	241 40.50
Total	537 90.25	58 9.75	595 100.00

Manually Adjusted Intercept Using the Offset

As stated earlier, the sample prior probabilities are ordinarily used to estimate the population prior probabilities; so when the analyst oversamples the rare event, the estimates of the population priors are biased and, as a result, the intercept of the logistic regression model is biased as well. To remedy this situation, the analyst can adjust the biased intercept by an offset value in order to obtain the unbiased intercept. Program 11.9 Posterior Probabilities Using Manually Adjusted Intercept illustrates how to calculate the posterior probabilities directly for the validation data set once the intercept has been adjusted:

Program 11.9 Posterior Probabilities Using Manually Adjusted Intercept

```
libname sasba 'c:\sasba\ames';
data ames30;
   set sasba.ames30;

proc format;
  value $yesno 0='NO' 1='YES';
run;

data offsetadj;
set ames30;
   pi1=.02; pi0=0.98; p1=0.4053; p0=0.5947;
   offset = log((p1*pi0)/(p0*pi1));
   logit_offset = (-10.5496-offset)+0.00343*Gr_Liv_Area
       +0.00255*Total_Bsmt_SF+0.000073*Lot_Area+2.4275*fullbath_2plus;
   offset_adj_p_1 = exp(logit_offset)/(1+exp(logit_offset));
   if offset_adj_p_1 > .50 then i_bonus='1';
   if offset_adj_p_1 <= .50 then i_bonus='0';
   f_bonus = put(bonus, $1.);
run;

proc freq data=offsetadj;
   tables f_bonus*i_bonus;
   format f_bonus  i_bonus $yesno.;
run;
```

First, the Ames Validation data set is saved in the temporary SAS data set, called OFFSETADJ. The offset for the intercept is then calculated using the values of the population prior probabilities, defined as pi0=0.98 and pi1=0.02, respectively, and the prior probabilities calculated from the data, p0=0.5947 and p1=0.4053.

The unadjusted intercept (-10.5496) obtained from logistic regression applied to the training data set is adjusted by subtracting the offset, and the adjusted logit (LOGIT_OFFSET) is calculated using the adjusted intercept and the parameter estimates for the predictors obtained from Output 11.9a The Logistic Regression Model for Ames Training

Data. Finally, the adjusted posterior probability (OFFSET_ADJ_P_1) is calculated using the general form (as seen in the logistic regression chapter):

$$p_i = \frac{e^{\beta_0 + \beta_1 x_1 + \cdots + \beta_k x_k}}{1 + e^{\beta_0 + \beta_1 x_1 + \cdots + \beta_k x_k}}$$

Finally the DATA step reassigns the predicted class (I_BONUS) using the adjusted posterior probabilities (OFFSET_ADJ_P1) and applying the 0.50 cutoff value. The actual class (BONUS) is used to create a character version (F_BONUS), and the results are summarized using the FREQ procedure. The results, of course, are identical to those found in Output 11.10 Classification Table for Ames Housing Validation Data Adjusted for Oversampling.

It should be noted that the analyst can generate the model with the adjusted, unbiased, intercept using the OFFSET= option, as in Program 11.10 Adjusting the Model Intercept Using the OFFSET Option.

Program 11.10 Adjusting the Model Intercept Using the OFFSET Option

```
libname sasba 'c:\sasba\ames';
data ames70;
   set sasba.ames70;
   pi1=.02; pi0=0.98; p1=0.4053; p0=0.5947;
   offset = log((p1*pi0)/(p0*pi1));proc logistic data=ames70;
   model Bonus (Event = '1')= Gr_Liv_Area Total_Bsmt_SF Lot_Area
           Fullbath_2Plus / offset=offset;
run;
```

The offset is calculated using:

$$offset = ln\left(\frac{p_1 \pi_0}{p_0 \pi_1}\right) = ln\left(\frac{0.4053 x 0.98}{0.5947 x 0.02}\right) = 3.5084$$

and the unbiased intercept, β_0, is $\beta_0^* - offset$ = - 10.5496 – 3.5084 = -14.058, which matches the adjusted intercept in Output 11.11 Logistic Regression Model for Ames Training with Intercept Adjusted for Oversampling. Notice that the estimated coefficients for the predictors remain unchanged.

Output 11.11 Logistic Regression Model for Ames Training with Intercept Adjusted for Oversampling

Analysis of Maximum Likelihood Estimates					
Parameter	DF	Estimate	Standard Error	Wald Chi-Square	Pr > ChiSq
Intercept	1	-14.0591	0.6390	484.1061	<.0001
Gr_Liv_Area	1	0.00343	0.000325	111.4093	<.0001
Total_Bsmt_SF	1	0.00255	0.000290	77.1319	<.0001
Lot_Area	1	0.000073	0.000020	12.9010	0.0003
Fullbath_2plus	1	2.4277	0.2086	135.4945	<.0001
Offset	0	1.0000	0	.	.

Automatically Adjusted Posterior Probabilities to Account for Oversampling

Previously, we illustrated the use of the PEVENT option for displaying performance measures adjusted for oversampling rare events. In this section, we will illustration how the two approaches for manually adjusting posterior probabilities (saved in ADJUST and OFFSETADJ, respectively) match those automatically generated using the PEVENT option. Consider Program 11.11 Comparison of the Three Approaches to Adjusting for Oversampling where all approaches are used and results are merged into a single data set for comparisons:

Program 11.11 Comparison of the Three Approaches to Adjusting for Oversampling

```
libname sasba 'c:\sasba\ames';
data ames70;
   set sasba.ames70;
data ames30;
   set sasba.ames30;
run;
```

```
*****************************************************************;
proc logistic data=ames70 noprint;
   model Bonus (Event = '1')= Gr_Liv_Area Total_Bsmt_SF Lot_Area
        Fullbath_2Plus / ctable pprob=0.50 pevent= 0.02 0.4053;
   score data=ames30 out=pred_adj_validation priorevent=0.02;
run;

*****************************************************************;
proc logistic data=ames70 noprint;
   model Bonus (Event = '1')= Gr_Liv_Area Total_Bsmt_SF Lot_Area
        Fullbath_2Plus;
   score data=ames30 out=pred_amesvalidation;
run;

*****************************************************************;
data offsetadj;
set ames30;
   pi1=.02;  pi0=0.98;  p1=0.4053; p0=0.5947;
   offset = log((p1*pi0)/(p0*pi1));
   logit_offset = (-10.5496-offset)+0.00343*Gr_Liv_Area
      +0.00255*Total_Bsmt_SF+0.000073*Lot_Area+2.4275*fullbath_2plus;
   offset_adj_p_1 = exp(logit_offset)/(1+exp(logit_offset));
   if offset_adj_p_1 > .50 then i_bonus='1';
   if offset_adj_p_1 <= .50 then i_bonus='0';
run;

*****************************************************************;
data adjust;
   set pred_amesvalidation;
   pi1=.02;  pi0=0.98; p1=0.4053; p0=0.5947;
   man_adj_p_1 = (p_1*(p0*pi1))/((1-p_1)*p1*pi0+p_1*p0*pi1);
run;

*****************************************************************;
data pred_adj_validation;
   set pred_adj_validation;
   auto_adj_p_1 = p_1;
   drop p_1;
run;

*****************************************************************;
proc sort data=pred_adj_validation; by pid;
proc sort data=adjust; by pid;
proc sort data=offsetadj; by pid;
data final;
   merge pred_adj_validation adjust offsetadj;
   by pid;
run;

proc print data=final (obs=10); var pid auto_adj_p_1 man_adj_p_1 offset_adj_p_1;
run;
```

From Program 11.11 Comparison of the Three Approaches to Adjusting for Oversampling, you should recognize that the first logistic regression model is fit using the training data set (AMES70) and scored using the validation data set (AMES30). The results of the SCORE statement are saved in the temporary data set (PRED_ADJ_VALIDATION) using the OUT=option; note that including the PRIOREVENT=0.02 requests that the posterior probabilities (P_1) are automatically adjusted using pi1=.02, along with the values of p_0 and p_1, which are calculated directly from the data.

The second logistic regression is conducted in the same way. However, no adjustments are made because the PEVENT option is not used. The SCORE statement is applied to the validation data set and the unadjusted posterior probabilities are saved in the temporary data set PRED_AMESVALIDATION.

The next two DATA steps, described in the previous sections, contain the adjusted posterior probabilities. The data set, OFFSETADJ, contains the posterior probabilities for each house in the validation data set, adjusted using the offset to the logistic regression intercept. The data set, ADJUST, contains the posterior probabilities for each house in the validation data set, adjusted using the formula for posterior probabilities.

The next DATA step is used simply to rename the adjusted posterior probabilities, from P_1 to AUTO_ADJ_P_1, in the data set PRED_ADJ_VALIDATION so that the variable name is more descriptive.

To create a final data set, all three versions of the validation data set are sorted by PID which is the unique identifier for each house. Finally, the three data sets are merged by PID, saved in the temporary SAS data set called FINAL, and the first ten observations are printed for comparison purposes, as displayed in Output 11.12 Posterior Probabilities for Ames Validation Data Using Three Approaches.

Output 11.12 Posterior Probabilities for Ames Validation Data Using Three Approaches

Obs	PID	auto_adj_p_1	man_adj_p_1	offset_adj_p_1
1	0526302040	0.00074	0.00074	0.00074
2	0526352090	0.00350	0.00350	0.00352
3	0526353030	0.85752	0.85754	0.85839
4	0526353050	0.41125	0.41128	0.41268
5	0527105050	0.04164	0.04164	0.04180
6	0527105060	0.02346	0.02346	0.02354
7	0527105070	0.04894	0.04895	0.04916
8	0527106150	0.04966	0.04967	0.04986
9	0527107020	0.04922	0.04923	0.04948
10	0527110020	0.00686	0.00686	0.00688

It is important for the analyst to understand the effects of oversampling, so we summarize those points here. If any calculations depend upon the intercept, then the appropriate adjustments should be made. If any analyses depend upon false positive (P_{F+}) and/or false negative (P_{F-}) values, adjustments are a necessity.

There are situations where no adjustments are needed. For example, if the analyst wishes to make any conclusions about the relationship between the target and the predictors, then no adjustments are needed; in short, there is no bias in the odds-ratios. In fact, because the sensitivity and specificity values remain unchanged, no adjustments are needed for the ROC curve. Finally, if observations are to be ranked by their posterior probabilities, then oversampling has no effect on the ranks because the adjusted posterior probabilities are simply the result of a linear transformation of the biased posterior probability.

The Use of Decision Theory for Model Selection

Consider, again, the situation where the goal of the analyst is to target those most likely to be in the class of interest (Y=1), or a responder. Obviously, different cutoff values result in different decisions, thereby influencing the number of observations classified as a responders--the total number of predicted positives, TP + FP. Previously, we illustrated how the gains and lift charts could be used to establish the desired cutoff value.

In this section, we will illustrate an alternative approach which assumes that there are profits associated with targeting a true positive (TP) and costs associated with targeting a false positive (FP). As a result, the goal of the analyst is to determine the optimal cutoff value that maximizes the total expected profit. Essentially, the analyst is asking the question--how many observations, or customers, should I target so that the expected profit is greater than zero?

Decision Cutoffs and Expected Profits for Model Selection

To arrive at a rule, we will use both expected values and decision theory (McLachlan, 1992). For any discrete random variable, with k possible outcomes, $X_1, X_2, ..., X_k$, each having probabilities, $P(X_1), P(X_2), ... P(X_k)$, respectively, the mean, or **expected value**, is defined as follows:

$$E(X) = \sum_{i=1}^{k} X_k P(X_k)$$

To calculate the expected profit, we must define both our outcomes and the profits for each of those outcomes. In classification analysis, when we make decisions, the possible outcomes are true negatives, false negatives, false positives, and true positives, each having their associated profits (represented by δ). That information can be summarized in a **profit matrix** as seen in Table 11.6 Profit Matrix for Classification Decisions.

Table 11.6 Profit Matrix for Classification Decisions

Actual CLASS	Decision to Target	
	0=NO	1=YES
0=NO	δ_{TN}	δ_{FP}
1=YES	δ_{FN}	δ_{TP}

If the analyst targets an observation, or customer i, (Decision=YES), then the expected profit for that customer is defined as:

$$E(\text{profit}_i|\text{Decision=YES}) = p_i(\delta_{TP}) + (1-p_i)(\delta_{FP})$$

where p_i is the posterior probability for customer i. Similarly, if the analyst does not target customer i, (Decision=NO), the expected profit for that customer is defined as:

$$E(\text{profit}_i|\text{Decision=NO}) = p_i(\delta_{FN}) + (1-p_i)(\delta_{TN})$$

Consequently, the analyst will target an observation (classify an observation into Class=1) if the expected profit of targeting exceeds the expected profit of not targeting. In other words, target an observation if

$$p_i(\delta_{TP}) + (1-p_i)(\delta_{FP}) > p_i(\delta_{FN}) + (1-p_i)(\delta_{TN})$$

Solving for p_i, the decision rule becomes: Target an observation (Decision = YES) if their posterior probability (p_i) is:

$$p_i > \frac{1}{1+\left(\frac{\delta_{TP}-\delta_{FN}}{\delta_{TN}-\delta_{FP}}\right)}$$

This rule is an extension of **Bayes' rule** (Wielenga, 2007). Consider now the Ames Housing Case where we assume the cost incurred by an agent soliciting a homeowner to list the house with his or her real estate agency is $100 and the bonus earned (profit) is $1000 (ignoring commission) if the home is in fact sold for more than $175,000, as illustrated in the profit matrix in Table 11.7 Profit Matrix for Ames Housing.

Table 11.7 Profit Matrix for Ames Housing

Actual CLASS	Decision to Target	
	0=NO	1=YES
0=NO	0	-100
1=YES	0	+900

Note first, that if a homeowner is not targeted for business (Decision=NO), the cost incurred is $0; therefore, the total profit/cost for true negatives and false negatives is $0. The true positives (TP) are those that were targeted (cost=$100) and the event resulted in earning a bonus ($1000), so the total profit is $900.

In this case, the analyst would set the optimal cutoff probability as:

$$p_i > \frac{1}{1+\left(\frac{900-0}{0-(-100)}\right)} = 0.10$$

Now, given profit information, the analyst can build a classifier and use the optimal cutoff for classifying observations. Once an observation is classified, its profit can be calculated. Then, profit can be added across all observations to get a total profit for the model (note that this can be done for both the training and validation data sets). In short, total profit can be used as an assessment criterion for model performance and provides a good approach for model selection.

In the event that profit information is not available, the analyst can use the population prior (π_1) as the cutoff. Using this cutoff results in a fixed number for both sensitivity and specificity, where the mean of those two numbers is maximized compared to other cutoff values. Recall that it is impossible to control both sensitivity and specificity at the same time. Therefore, using π_1 as a cutoff is a way to equalize both.

Consider, again, the Ames Housing Case where we will assess classifier performance based upon total and average profits. Suppose the analyst uses the profit matrix as defined in Table 11.7 Profit Matrix for Ames Housing, thereby implementing a cutoff value of 0.10. Program 11.12 Classification Results and Profit Information for Ames Validation Data can be used to provide profit information:

Program 11.12 Classification Results and Profit Information for Ames Validation Data

```
libname sasba 'c:\sasba\ames';
proc format;
  value yesno 0='NO' 1='YES';
run;

data ames70;
   set sasba.ames70;
data ames30;
   set sasba.ames30;
run;

proc logistic data=ames70 noprint;
   model Bonus (Event = '1')= Gr_Liv_Area Total_Bsmt_SF Lot_Area
          Fullbath_2Plus;
   score data=ames30 out=pred_amesvalidation;
run;

data profit;
   set pred_amesvalidation;
   target=0; profit=0;
   if p_1 > .10 then do;
      target=1; profit=bonus*900 - (1-bonus)*100;
      end;
run;

proc freq data=profit;
   tables bonus*target;
   format bonus target yesno.;
run;

proc means data=profit;
   var profit;
run;

proc print data=profit;
   var p_1 bonus target profit;
run;
```

Just as in the previous example, the logistic regression model is fit using the training data set (AMES70) and scored using the validation data set (AMES30), and the resulting posterior probabilities (P_1) are saved for all observations in the validation data PROFIT data set using the DATA step.

For the PROFIT data set, all observations are initially defined as not targeted (TARGET=0) and earning no profit (PROFIT=0) until the posterior probability is used for targeting that observation. If the posterior probability exceeds 0.10, the decision criterion, then that observation is targeted (TARGET=1) and the profit is defined as follows:

If the agent was not awarded a bonus on the sale of the house (BONUS=0), then the profit is:

$$\text{Profit} = (0)(\$900) - (1-0)(\$100) = -\$100$$

which is the case for the house (observation 10) displayed in Output 11.13c Line Listing for Several Houses in the Ames Validation Data Set. If the agent was awarded a bonus on the sale of the house (BONUS=1), then the profit is:

$$\text{Profit} = (1)(\$900) - (1-1)*100 = \$900$$

which is the case for the house (observation 355) displayed in Output 11.13c Line Listing for Several Houses in the Ames Validation Data Set. Furthermore, if the posterior probability was less than 0.10, then the observation is not targeted (TARGET=0) and there is no chance to make a profit (PROFIT=0), which is the case for both houses (observations 1 and 580).

The classification results are displayed in Output 11.13a Classification Matrix for Ames Validation Data Based upon 0.10 Cutoff, using the FREQ procedure. There the analyst can see that of the 595 houses, 346 are targeted (TARGET=1) because their posterior probabilities exceed 0.10. Of those, 238 are houses where a bonus is earned (BONUS=1), whereas 108 houses resulted in no bonus earned (BONUS=0). As a result, $900 is earned for each of the 238 houses, whereas $100 cost is incurred for soliciting the 108 houses where no bonus is earned. In short, the total expected profit for the houses in the validation data set is:

$$\text{Total Expected Profit} = 238(\$900) + 108(-\$100) = \$203,400,$$

resulting in an average profit per house of $341.84 (=$203,400/595), as produced in Output 11.13b Average Expected Profit for Ames Validation Data Based upon 0.10 Cutoff, using the MEANS procedure. Finally, a line listing is created using the PRINT procedure, with excerpts provided in Output 11.13c Line Listing for Several Houses in the Ames Validation Data Set .

Output 11.13a Classification Matrix for Ames Validation Data Based upon 0.10 Cutoff

Table of Bonus by target			
Bonus	**target**		
Frequency Percent Row Pct Col Pct	**NO**	**YES**	**Total**
NO	246 41.34 69.49 98.80	108 18.15 30.51 31.21	354 59.50
YES	3 0.50 1.24 1.20	238 40.00 98.76 68.79	241 40.50
Total	249 41.85	346 58.15	595 100.00

Output 11.13b Average Expected Profit for Ames Validation Data Based upon 0.10 Cutoff

Analysis Variable : profit				
N	**Mean**	**Std Dev**	**Minimum**	**Maximum**
595	341.8487395	457.5000991	-100.0000000	900.0000000

Output 11.13c Line Listing for Several Houses in the Ames Validation Data Set

Obs	P_1	Bonus	target	profit
1	0.02341	0	0	0
...				
10	0.22602	0	1	-100
...				
355	0.99505	1	1	900
...				
580	0.07608	1	0	0
...				

Keep in mind, that if the analyst targeted every observation (595 houses), where 241 agents earned a bonus and 354 did not, the total expected profit is:

$$\text{Total Expected Profit} = 241(\$900) + 354(-\$100) = \$181,500,$$

which is clearly less profit than that when the analyst targeted 346 houses. It should be noted that the average expected profit can be used to compare this model to other candidate models. Also, in the case of oversampling, a weight can be used for each observation before calculating the average profit.

Using Estimated Posterior Probabilities to Determine Cutoffs

In the previous section, we discussed an extension of Bayes' rule for determining the optimal cutoff value for maximizing the profit. Because the posterior probabilities are estimated from a model, the average expected profit may not be optimal if the posterior probabilities are poorly estimated. Consequently, the analyst can explore various cutoff values (or depth) for a given model to see how average profit varies across cutoff values. Here the analyst is answering the question--how many observations should be targeted--or what is the depth--to ensure maximal profits. To illustrate this concept, consider Program 11.13 Average Profit for Ames Validation Data by Depth and Cutoff applied to the Ames Housing Case.

Program 11.13 Average Profit for Ames Validation Data by Depth and Cutoff

```
libname sasba 'c:\sasba\ames';
proc format;
   value yesno 0='NO' 1='YES';
data ames70;
    set sasba.ames70;
run;

data ames30;
    set sasba.ames30;
run;

proc logistic data=ames70 noprint;
   model Bonus (Event = '1')= Gr_Liv_Area Total_Bsmt_SF Lot_Area
          Fullbath_2Plus;
   score data=ames30 out=pred_amesvalidation outroc=roc;
run;

data cutoff;
   set roc;
   cutoff=_prob_;  pi1=0.4053; specificity = 1 - _1mspec_;
   tp_prop = pi1*_sensit_;  fp_prop = (1-pi1)* _1mspec_;
   depth = tp_prop + fp_prop;
   aveprof = 900*tp_prop - 100*fp_prop;
run;

proc sgplot data=cutoff;
   where 0.000 < depth < 1.00;
   series y = aveprof x = depth;
   refline 0.5733 /axis=x;
   xaxis values=(0 to 1.0 by 0.10);
   yaxis label = 'Average Profit';
run;

proc sgplot data=cutoff;
   where 0.000 < cutoff < 1.00;
   series y = aveprof x = cutoff;
   refline 0.11505 / axis=x;
   xaxis values=(0 to 1.0 by 0.10);
   yaxis label='Average Profit';
run;

proc sort data=cutoff; by descending aveprof;
data maxprofit;
   set cutoff; by descending aveprof;
run;

proc print data=maxprofit (obs=1);
   var depth cutoff aveprof;
run;
```

As illustrated previously, the logistic regression model is fit using the training data set, AMES70, and that model is used to score the validation data set (AMES30) as requested in the SCORE statement. ROC information for each cutoff (_PROB_) value is saved in a temporary SAS data set (called ROC) as requested using the OUTROC= option. For each cutoff value, both the depth and average profit (AVEPROF) are calculated. The two SGPLOT procedures are used to create the average profit by depth and cutoff, respectively, as displayed in Output 11.14a Average Profit for Ames Validation Data by Depth and Cutoff.

Output 11.14a Average Profit for Ames Validation Data by Depth and Cutoff

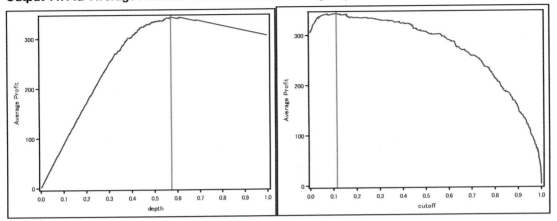

The SORT procedure, DATA step, and PRINT procedure are used to determine the highest average profit, along with its depth and cutoff value, as displayed in Output 11.14b Maximum Average Profit for Ames Validation Data. Using the reference lines, the plots show that the highest average profit of $342.93 occurs at a depth of 0.573 obtained by using a cutoff value of 0.115.

Output 11.14b Maximum Average Profit for Ames Validation Data

Obs	depth	cutoff	aveprof
1	0.57329	0.11505	342.926

Key Terms

accuracy

actual hit rate

adjusted estimated posterior probabilities

apparent hit rate

area under the ROC curve (AUC)

Bayes' rule

classification table

classifier

confusion matrix

depth

error rate

expected value

false negatives (FN)

false positives (FP).

gains chart

hit rate

honest assessment

information leakage

lift

lift chart

maximum chance criterion

naïve rule

negative predicted value (PV-)

offset

overfitting

oversampling

parsimony

positive predicted value (PV+)

precision

predictive modeling

profit matrix

propensity

recall

receiver-operating-characteristic (ROC) curve

sensitivity

specificity

strata

stratified random sampling

supervised learning methods

targeting

training data

true negatives (TN)

true positives (TP)

validation data

Chapter Quiz

1. When data is partitioned, what data is best for model assessment?
   a. training data
   b. validation data
   c. all of the data
   d. complete data

2. Suppose you have a customer database where you want to build a predictive model to predict whether or not your customer purchased your new product, where the variable PURCHASE is coded as 0 for 'No' or 1 for "Yes.' Which of the following SAS statements will divide the original data set into 70% training and 30% validation data sets, stratified by PURCHASE?
   a. proc sort data=customerdata out=one; by purchase;
      proc surveyselect data=one samprate=0.70 out=sample outall;
      by purchase;
      run;
   b. proc sort data=customerdata out=one; by purchase;
      proc surveyselect data=one samprate=0.70 out=sample outall;
      strata purchase;
      run;
   c. proc sort data=customerdata out=one; strata purchase;
      proc surveyselect data=one samprate=0.70 out=sample;
      strata purchase;
      run;
   d. proc surveyselect data=one samprate=0.70 out=sample;
      strata purchase;
      run;

3. A logistic regression model is fit and the classification matrix is adjusted for oversampling due to rare events. Which of the following is not affected by oversampling?
   a. Sensitivity and Positive Predictive Value (PV+)
   b. Specificity and Negative Predicted Value (PV-)
   c. Accuracy
   d. The ROC curve

4. Using the lift chart below, interpret the chart at a depth of 0.2 where Lift = 2.34

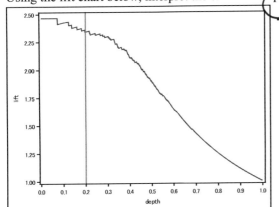

a) Selecting the top 20% of the population scored by the model should result in 2.34 times more responders than a random draw of 20%.

b. Selecting the observations with a response probability of at least 20% should result in 2.34 times more responders than a random draw of 20%.

c. Selecting the top 20% of the population scored by the model should result in 2.34 times greater accuracy than a random draw of 20%.

d. Selecting the observations with a response probability of at least 20% should result in 2.34 times greater accuracy than a random draw of 20%.

5. Suppose the following classification matrix is obtained when a logistic regression model is fit using four predictors and applied to the Ames Housing validation data set with a cutoff value of 0.20. Which of the following statements is true?

From _Bonus	Into_Bonus		
	NO	YES	Total
NO	291	63	354
YES	16	225	241
Total	307	288	595

a. accuracy = 0.1328

b. depth = 0.5160

c.) sensitivity = 0.9336

d. PV+ = 0.9479

6. Suppose you have a customer database where you want to build a predictive model to predict whether or not your customer purchased your new product, where the variable PURCHASE is coded as 0 for 'No' or 1 for "Yes,' using three predictors X1, X2, and X3. Suppose only 10% of customers ordinarily respond and you oversample to account for rare events, so that 50% of your sample is responders. Which of the following MODEL statements will give you an accuracy rate adjusted for oversampling?

a. model Purchase (Event = '1')= X1 X2 X3
   / ctable pprob=0.10 pevent= 0.50;

b. model Purchase (Event = '1')= X1 X2 X3
   / ctable pprob=0.10;

c.) model Purchase (Event = '1')= X1 X2 X3
   / ctable pprob=0.50 pevent= 0.10;

d. model Purchase (Event = '1')= X1 X2 X3
   / ctable pevent= 0.10 0.50;

7. Using the following profit matrix, what is the optimal cutoff value if the goal of the model is to maximize the average expected profit?

Actual CLASS	Decision to Target	
	0=NO	1=YES
0=NO	0	-100
1=YES	0	+400

a. 0.20
b. 0.25
c. 0.04
d. 0.01

8. Suppose three logistic regression models are estimated and applied to the Ames Housing validation data and the following information is provided for model selection. Which of the following statements is true?

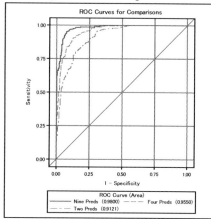

ROC Association Statistics							
			Mann-Whitney				
ROC Model	Area	Standard Error	95% Wald Confidence Limits		Somers' D	Gamma	Tau-a
Nine Preds	0.9800	0.00441	0.9714	0.9887	0.9601	0.9601	0.4635
Four Preds	0.9550	0.00747	0.9404	0.9697	0.9101	0.9101	0.4394
Two Preds	0.9121	0.0112	0.8902	0.9340	0.8242	0.8242	0.3979

ROC Contrast Test Results			
Contrast	DF	Chi-Square	Pr > ChiSq
Comparing THREE Models	2	44.2375	<.0001

a. There is a difference in performance between at least two models because the p-value < 0.0001.
b. The nine variable model and the four variable model are significantly different in performance because the p-value < 0.0001.
c. The model with nine predictors is best because it is the only model that performs better than chance.
d. All of the above statements are true.

9. Suppose the analyst is trying to determine how many customers to select in order to maximize the average expected profit. Using the plots below, which of the following statements is true?

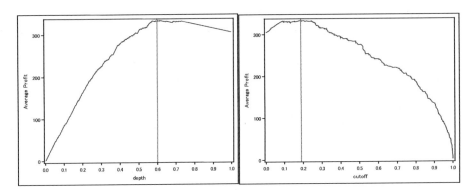

a. The average expected profit is maximized if 19% of the customer base is targeted, resulting in a 60% response rate.

b. The average expected profit is maximized if 60% of the customer base is targeted, resulting in a 19% response rate.

c. The average expected profit is 60% higher than chance is the analyst uses a cutoff value of 0.19.

d. The average expected profit is maximized if the analyst uses a cutoff value of 0.19, resulting in targeting 60% of the customer base.

10. Suppose you have a customer database where you want to build a predictive model to predict whether or not your customer purchased your new product, where the variable PURCHASE is coded as 0 for 'No' or 1 for "Yes,' using three predictors X1, X2, and X3. When using the LOGISTIC procedure is applied to validation data (called CUST_VAL), which of the following is required in order to generate the sensitivity and specificity values for various cutoff values?

a. model purchase (event= '1') = x1 x2 x3 / outroc=roc;

b. model purchase (event"1") = x1 x2 x3 / out=roc;

c. score data=cust_val outroc=roc;

d. score data=cust_val out=roc;

References

Agresti, Alan. 1992. "A Survey of Exact Inference for Contingency Tables." *Statistical Science* 7(1):131–153.

Allison, Paul D. 2008. "Convergence Failures in Logistic Regression." In *Proceedings of the SAS Global Forum 2008 Conference*. Cary, NC: SAS Institute, Inc.

Allison, Paul D. 2012. Logistic Regression for Rare Events. http://www.statisticalhorizons.com/logistic-regression-for-rare-events.

Anderson, David R., Sweeney, Dennis J., Williams, Thomas A., Camm, Jeffrey D., and James J. Cochran. 2014. *Statistics for Business and Economics*, 12th Edition. Stanford, CT: Cengage Learning.

Bellman, Richard. E. 1957. *Dynamic Programming*. Princeton. NJ: Princeton University Press.

Belsley, David. A., Kuh, Edwin, and Roy E. Welsch. 1980. *Regression Diagnostics: Identifying Influential Data and Sources of Collinearity*. New York: John Wiley & Sons.

Bollen, Kenneth. A. and Robert W. Jackman. 1990. "Regression Diagnostics: An Expository Treatment of Outliers and Influential Cases." In *Modern Methods of Data Analysis*. Edited by John Fox and Scott J. Long, 257–91. Newbury Park, CA: Sage.

Canes, Aran. 2014. *Identifying Superutilizers in the Medicaid Population—A Simple and Powerful Technique*. SESUG 2014, Paper PH-26, Cary, NC: SAS Institute, Inc.

Centers for Disease Control and Prevention. 2017. About Adult BMI. https://www.cdc.gov/healthyweight/assessing/bmi/adult_bmi/.

Chatfield, Chris. 1995. *Problem Solving A statistician's Guide*, Second Edition. University of Bath, UK: Chapman & Hall.

Chatterjee, Samprit and Ali S. Hadi. 1986. "Influential Observations, High Leverage Points, and Outliers in Linear Regression." *Statistical Science* 1:379-393.

Chatterjee, Samprit and Ali S. Hadi. 2006. *Regression Analysis by Example*, 4th Edition. New Jersey: John Wiley & Sons.

Chawla, Nitesh V. 2010. "Data Mining for Imbalanced Datasets: An Overview." In *Data Mining and Knowledge Discovery Handbook*, eds. Oded Maimon and Lior Rokach. Boston MA: Springer.

Cody, Ron. 2017. *Cody's Data Cleaning Techniques Using SAS®*, Third Edition. Cary, North Carolina: SAS Institute.

Cohen, Jacob. 1988. *Statistical Power and Analysis for the Behavioral Sciences* (2nd ed.). Hillsdale, N.J.: Lawrence Erlbaum Associates, Inc.

Church, Russel. 1979. "How to Look at Data: A Review of John W. Tukey's Exploratory Data Analysis." *Journal of the Experimental Analysis of Behavior* 31(3):433–440.

Cook, R. Dennis. 1977. "Detection of Influential Observation in Linear Regression." *Technometrics* 19(1):15-18.

Cook, R. Dennis and Sanford Weisberg. 1982. *Residuals and Influence in Regression*. New York, NY: Chapman & Hall.

deCock, Dean. 2011. "Ames, Iowa: Alternative to the Boston Housing Data." *Journal of Statistics Education* 19(3):1-14. http://ww2.amstat.org/publications/jse/v19n3/decock.pdf.

Dunn, Olive Jean. 1961. "Multiple Comparisons among Means." *Journal of the American Statistical Association* 56(293):52–64.

Ferdman, Roberto A. 2015. "Where People Around the World Eat the Most Sugar and Fat." *Washington Post*. https://www.washingtonpost.com/.

Fernandez, George. 2010. *Statistical Data Mining using SAS® Applications*, 2nd Edition. Boca Raton, FL: CRC Press.

Fleiss, Joseph L. 1981. *Statistical Methods for Rates and Proportions*, Second Edition. New York: John Wiley & Sons.

Furnival, George M. and Robert W. Wilson. 1974. "Regression by Leaps and Bounds." *Technometrics* 16:499–511.

Greenacre, Michael J. 1988. "Clustering the rows and columns of a contingency table." *Journal of Classification* 5(1):39-15.

Groves, Robert M., Fowler, Jr., Floyd J., Couper, Mick P., Lepkowski, James M., Singer, Eleanor, and Roger Tourangeau. 2009. *Survey Methodology*, 2nd Edition. New Jersey: John Wiley & Sons.

Hand, David J. 1983. "Common Errors in Data Analysis: The Apparent Error Rate of Classification Rules." *Psychological Medicine* 13:201-203.

Harris, Chester W. and Henry F. Kaiser. 1964. "Oblique factor analytic solutions by orthogonal transformations." *Psychometrika* 29:347–362.

He, Haibo and Edwardo A. Garcia. 2009. "Learning from imbalanced data." *IEEE Transactions on Knowledge and Data Engineering* 21(9):1263-1284.

Heath, Dan. 2007. *New SAS/GRAPH ® Procedures for Creating Statistical Graphics in Data Analysis*. Cary, NC: SAS Institute, Inc.

Hirji, Karim F. 1992. "Computing Exact Distributions for Polytomous Response Data." *Journal of the American Statistical Association* 87:487-492.

Hirji, Karim F., Mehta, Cyrus R. and Nitin R. Patel. 1987. "Computing Distributions for Exact Logistic Regression." *Journal of the American Statistical Association* 82:1110 - 1117.

Hoeffding, Wassily. 1948. "A Class of Statistics with Asymptotically Normal Distribution." *Annals of Mathematical Statistics* 19(3):293-325.

Hocking, Ronald R. 1976. "A Biometrics Invited Paper: The Analysis and Selection of Variables in Linear Regression." *Biometrics* 32(1):1-49.

Hosmer, David W. and Stanley Lemeshow. 2000. *Applied Logistic Regression*, 2nd edition. New York: John Wiley & Sons, Inc.

Jackson, J. Edward. 1991. *A User's Guide to Principal Components*. New York, NY: John Wiley and Sons.

King, Gary and Langche Zeng. 2001. "Logistic Regression in Rare Events Data." *Political Analysis* 9: 137–163. https://gking.harvard.edu/files/0s.pdf.

Little, Roderick J.A. and Donald B. Rubin. 2002. *Statistical Analysis with Missing Data*, 2nd Edition. New Jersey: John Wiley & Sons.

Mallows, Colin L. 1973. "Some Comments on C_P." *Technometrics* 15(4):661–675.

McLachlan, Geoffrey J. 1977. "The Bias of Sample-based Posterior Probabilities." *Biomedical Journal* 19:421-426.

McLachlan, Geoffrey J. 1992. *Discriminant Analysis and Statistical Pattern Recognition*. New York: John Wiley & Sons.

Mehta, Cyrus. R., Patel, Nitin, and Pralay Senchaudhuri. 1992. "Exact Stratified Linear Rank Tests for Ordered Categorical and Binary Data." *Journal of Computational and Graphical Statistics* 1:21-40.

Michie, Donald, Spiegelhalter, David J., and Charles Taylor, editors. (1994). *Machine Learning, Neural and Statistical Classification.* New York: Ellis Horwood.

National Center for Health Statistics. 2009. *Health, United States, 2009: With Special Feature on Medical Technology.* Hyattsville, MD. https://www.cdc.gov/nchs/data/hus/hus09.pdf.

National Center for Health Statistics. 2016. *Health, United States, 2015: With Special Feature on Racial and Ethnic Health Disparities.* Hyattsville, MD.

Ripley, Brian D. 1996. *Pattern Recognition and Neural Networks.* New York: Cambridge University Press.

Rubin, Donald. B. 1976. "Inference and missing data." *Biometrika* 63(3):581-592.

Rutherford, Andrew. 2001. *Introducing ANOVA and ANCOVA: A GLM Approach.* Thousand Oaks, CA: Sage.

Santer, Thomas. J. and Diane E. Duffy. 1989. *The Statistical Analysis of Discret Data.* New York: Springer-Verlag.

Sarma, Kattamuri.S. 2013. *Predictive Modeling with SAS® Enterprise Miner: Practical Solutions for Business Applications*, 2nd Edition. Cary, NC: SAS Institute, Inc.

SAS Institute, Inc. 1995. *Logistic Regression Examples Using the SAS® System.* Cary. NC: SAS Institute, Inc.

SAS Institute, Inc. 2004. SAS/STAT 13.1 User's Guide. Cary, NC: SAS Institute, Inc.

SAS Institute, Inc. 2011. *SAS® Certification Prep Guide: Base Programming for SAS® 9*, Third Edition. Cary, NC: SAS Institute, Inc.

SAS Institute, Inc. 2012. *Predictive Modeling Using Logistic Regression: Course Notes.* Cary, NC: SAS Institute, Inc.

SAS Institute, Inc. 2014. *Predictive Modeling Using Logistic Regression: Course Notes.* Cary, NC: SAS Institute, Inc.

SAS Institute, Inc. 2018. Data Mining: What It Is and Why It Matters. https://www.sas.com/en_us/insights/analytics/data-mining.html.

SAS Institute Inc. 2018. SAS OnlineDoc® 9.4. Procedures Guide: Statistical Procedures, Third Edition/Product Documentation. http://support.sas.com/documentation/cdl/en/procstat/67528/HTML/default/viewer.htm#procstat_univariate_details03.htm.

Satterthwaite, Franklin E. 1946. "An Approximate Distribution of Estimates of Variance Components." *Biometrics Bulletin* 2(6):110–114.

Schlomer, Gabriel L., Sheri Bauman and Noel A. Card. 2010. "Best Practices for Missing Data Management in Counseling Psychology." *Journal of Counseling Psychology* 57(1):1–10.

Schwartz, Theresa and Rachel Zeig-Owens. 2012. *Knowledge (of your missing data) is Power: Handling Missing Values in Your SAS® Dataset.* Orlando, FL: SAS Global Forum Paper 319-2012.

Scott, Alistair J. and C. J. Wild. 1991. "Fitting Logistic Regression Models in Stratified Case-Control Studies." *Biometrics* 47(2):497-510.

Tukey, John W. 1977. *Exploratory Data Analysis.* Reading, MA: Addison-Wesley Publishing Company.

U.S. Bureau of Labor Statistics and U.S. Census Bureau. 2015. American Time Use Survey. https://www.bls.gov/tus/charts/sleep.htm.

U.S. Census Bureau, Current Population Survey. 2007. "US Census Bureau, income quintile and top 5% household income distribution and demographic characteristics, 2006". In *Annual Social and Economic Supplement.* https://www2.census.gov/programs-surveys/cps/tables/hinc-05/2007/new05_000.txt.

Warren, Anne W. 2007. "Adding One Value to All Observations." In *Proceedings of the NESUG 2007, Coder's Corner.* Cary, NC: SAS Institute, Inc. https://lexjansen.com/nesug/nesug07/cc/cc45.pdf.

WHO. 2015. Sugar intake for Adults and Children Guideline. http://www.who.int/nutrition/publications/guidelines/sugars_intake/en/.

Wielenga, Doug. 2007. "Identifying and Overcoming Common Data Mining Mistakes." In *Proceedings of the SWSUG 2007.* Cary, NC: SAS Institute, Inc. https://www.mwsug.org/proceedings/2007/saspres/MWSUG-2007-SAS01.pdf.

Wujek, Brett, Patrick Hall, and Funda Günes. 2016. "Best Practices for Machine Learning Applications." In Proceedings of the Analytics Experience 2016 Conference. Cary, NC: SAS Institute, Inc. https://support.sas.com/resources/papers/proceedings16/SAS2360-2016.pdf.